Arms Control and Disarmament,
Defense and Military,
International Security,
and Peace

Arms Control and Disarmament, Defense and Military, International Security, and Peace

An Annotated Guide to Sources
1980–1987

Stephen E. Atkins

ABC-CLIO

Santa Barbara, California
Oxford, England

Library of Congress Cataloging-in-Publication Data

Atkins, Stephen E.
    Arms control and disarmament, defense and military, international security, and peace : an annotated guide to sources, 1980–1987 / Stephen E. Atkins.

    Includes index.
    1. Arms control—Bibliography. 2. Disarmament—Bibliography. 3. Security, International—Bibliography. 4. Peace—Bibliography. I. Title.
Z6464.D6A85   1988   [JX1974]   016.3271'74—dc19   88-21822

ISBN 0-87436-488-4 (alk. paper)

10   9   8   7   6   5   4   3   2   1

ABC-Clio, Inc.
Riviera Campus
2040 Alameda Padre Serra, Box 4397
Santa Barbara, California 93140–4397

Clio Press Ltd.
55 St. Thomas' Street
Oxford, OX1 1JG, England

This book is printed on acid-free paper ∞ .
Manufactured in the United States of America

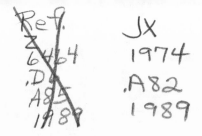
Contents

Acknowledgments

Sincere appreciation is given to those who have helped in the accumulation of materials for this volume. This book would have never been possible without the support of the Research Council of the University of Illinois Library. They provided the funds for a research assistant. Release time from job responsibilities has also been appreciated. Help on computer application questions from ACDIS office staff has been another source of assistance. But most of all I want to thank my wife for allowing me to acquire my MacPlus Computer system, and the time to work with my materials.

Introduction

The issues of arms control and disarmament, defense and military, international security, and peace are all subjects of worldwide concern. International tensions during the last decade have stimulated an explosion of publications on the topics of the arms race and international security. A myriad of research centers and think tanks specializing in these types of publications have appeared in response to the collapse of superpower détente and the intensifying of the arms race. But the output of these centers and of the academic and commercial presses has been unable to match the insatiable demand for more information on these issues by scholars, researchers, students, and the general public. While part of this demand is fueled by daily newspaper headlines and television programs, the issues of peace and war command the attention of all intelligent observers. The inability of even the most knowledgeable specialists in these fields to master the flow of information makes it necessary to obtain bibliographic control in these subjects.

Bibliographic control over such a wide range of issues has been sporadic in the past. While there have been bibliographies published on specific topics, the interdisciplinary nature of arms control, disarmament, defense, international security, military, and peace has made bibliographic control difficult. Fortunately, some bibliographic control over journal articles has been improved in the last few years by a series of bibliographies published in book and serial formats. But there has been no corresponding effort for monographs. This book is an attempt to balance the ledger by providing bibliographic control for monographs, hearings, papers, serials, and miscellaneous other materials. Included are materials published between 1980 and midyear 1987, because this period witnessed an ongoing demand for bibliographic information. Moreover, this period covers the transition between the Carter and Reagan administrations, and the Reagan

administration's changes in defense and security policies during the
early and mid-1980s. Because of the shift in U.S. policies and the
subsequent Soviet reactions, this period has now become and will
continue to be an era of intense research interest for U.S. and foreign
scholars.

The stimulus for this book comes from my role as arms control
bibliographer for the arms control collection at the University of
Illinois Library. This collection was started in 1981 to serve as
research support for the Arms Control, Disarmament and International Security Office (ACDIS) of the University of Illinois at Urbana-
Champaign. ACDIS is an interdisciplinary research organization
founded in 1978 whose purpose is to provide a forum for research
and teaching on arms control, disarmament, and international security topics. Other related issues—defense, military, and peace—
have also developed research constituencies in ACDIS. Because this
organization supports the activities of nearly 150 University of Illinois faculty members and a large number of undergraduate and graduate students, ACDIS has actively supported the building of the arms
control collection. The arms control collection now consists of 180
reference sources, 75 serials, 3 microfilm collections, and nearly
25,000 monographs. It has been my close affiliation with this collection that convinced me of the need for bibliographic control of these
subjects. In addition, faculty members expressed a need for annotated bibliographies in their areas of research. After working on a
number of these bibliographies, I decided to combine them and
expand their scope: the result is this book.

Some explanation is necessary regarding the method, organization, and scope of the entries. While the bulk of the citations are
English language materials, selective citations are also taken from
French, German, and Spanish language materials. Foreign language
materials are restricted to the most significant works in the field. The
result has been the inclusion of 1,596 books, hearings, papers, and
reports. My original intent was for this bibliography to be comprehensive, but several months into the project the mass of material
convinced me that comprehensiveness was an illusionary goal.
While this book intends to be as complete as possible, there are gaps,
especially in recent European and Asian materials. These gaps
resulted from the inability to acquire these materials in a timely
fashion. Instead of a comprehensive bibliography, this work will
provide the scholar, student, and general public with as complete a
bibliography as possible for their respective research needs.

Each citation consists of publishing information and a three-
to four-sentence abstract. Since government, institute, and some
private publishers in the Soviet bloc and the Third World, and in

Western Europe, Canada, and the United States do not include ISBN data, certain works will have no ISBN number. Price information is included, if available, for those items published on an ongoing basis.

Each abstract consists of the subject, thesis, and the importance of the item to the literature in the field. The importance of a work to the field is, of course, a subjective evaluation. My intent is to make a qualitative assessment of the value of the volume for researchers in the field. Works for general readers and students are also noted. Since only a small portion of the works cited here are ever reviewed in journals, this assessment assumes some importance.

The material best falls into four subject categories: (1) arms control and disarmament; (2) defense and military; (3) international security; and (4) peace. Scope notes at the beginning of each section will explain the philosophy behind the inclusion of a topic. A combination author and subject index provides citation access. In addition, a list of publishers will facilitate acquisition of a particular item or other materials on a similar topic from the publishing houses.

Seventeen types of materials are included. A brief description of each follows to distinguish the various types of reference sources from the monographs.

1. **Annuals and yearbooks** have proved to be invaluable tools for research on arms control, defense, disarmament, international security, the military, and peace subjects. These sources appear on an annual basis and contain a summary of developments that occurred during the course of the year. Although much of the data in these works are no longer up-to-date at the time of publication, researchers can use the materials to study trends. Institutions, think tanks, and government agencies produce the majority of these studies, as they have access to the necessary statistical sources. These sources can also help novice researchers to become familiar with differing viewpoints.

2. **Bibliographies** have a place in research on these subjects because of the need to consult retrospective materials. There is, however, an ongoing problem with bibliographies since there exists no single bibliographic source that deals with works on all facets of the issues. Instead, there exists a number of single-subject bibliographies, most of which age quickly because of the length of time required for publication. The result is that most bibliographies prove more useful for retrospective studies rather than for current research.

3. **Databooks, handbooks, and sourcebooks** provide researchers with an abundance of data. They are filled with a mass of statistical data presented in a way to facilitate research. While these materials also age quickly, they have the added virtue of including statistical

data difficult to locate elsewhere. Special effort must be made, however, to acquire the most current versions of these works.

4. **Dictionaries** have a limited but necessary place in research.
They are most useful for students beginning research in the field, but
technical dictionaries can also be valuable for the advanced scholar.

5. **Digests** have a brief span of usefulness to researchers. They have
reproductions of magazine articles, radio and TV broadcasts, newspaper editorials, and technical reports, all of which are difficult to
find otherwise. In addition to providing random facts, digests are
considered important because of the differing viewpoints expressed
in broadcasts and periodicals.

6. **Directories** are most useful as primary sources for gathering
more information. They contain the names of prominent businesses,
organizations, and individuals whose roles are important in that discipline. They are a major source of information for further research.

7. **Encyclopedias** have only a marginal value for research, because
only a few encyclopedias provide sufficient depth of analysis to be
useful.

8. **Guidebooks** serve as sources of new materials for scholars and
the general public. The guidebooks included have a background
function for the average reader, but can direct the advanced research
scholar toward more specialized data.

9. **Hearings** are a unique source of information because they combine the testimony of witnesses with supporting documents. Both
the commentaries and the documents serve as a forum where a variety of viewpoints are exchanged. Some documents appear here and
nowhere else.

10. **Journals** provide a forum for the most current research on
these subjects. The quality of research and the authors' expertise
make journals a prime source for viewpoints and ideas for further
study. Academic scholars prefer to publish in journals because of
the speed of publication and the space to work out specialized topics.

11. **Microfilms** are the most recent development in providing formerly unavailable or expensive materials to researchers. Several
microfilm companies market these collections. Researchers find
these collections difficult to use but nevertheless invaluable.

12. **Newsletters** are of little use to scholars in most disciplines, but
for research on certain subjects they are most necessary. They
provide scholars with a vehicle for communicating with colleagues
about articles, books, and developments in the field. Direct-action
groups use these publications to spread information about their organizational efforts.

13. **Papers** are larger and more specialized than journal articles.
They appear at regular intervals and the subject matter is restricted to

a single topic. Most originate from institutions—strategic institutes and think tanks—that specialize in international studies.

14. **Slide programs** constitute a different kind of educational source. Most are programs for direct action to influence national politics toward peace.

15. **Strategic atlases** are materials that use pictorial representation to show strategic relationships. Most of these atlases also include interpretative texts. This source can be useful for comprehending geopolitical realities.

16. **Textbooks** can be used for either high school or college courses. While many of these books deal with technical questions, all are designed for use in the classroom.

17. **Monographs** are single-issue books, booklets, and reports. The length of these materials can vary from about twenty-five pages to several volumes. They intend to be self-contained works with in-depth analyses. Monographs are the forum whereby scholars present the final versions of their research.

CHAPTER ONE:
Arms Control
and Disarmament

Although arms control and disarmament subjects differ in orientation, there is enough in common for them to fit into a single subject category. Therefore, all arms control and disarmament subject materials have been grouped together. Researchers, however, make a rigid separation between the two concepts. Arms control proponents insist that limits be placed on current weapons systems inventories, with the goal of a gradual reduction of such systems. Disarmament supporters insist on the abolition of nuclear weapons and/or a reduction of other weapons systems on a fixed timetable basis. A total of 267 sources make up this subject category.

Annuals and Yearbooks

1 Spector, Leonard S. *The Spread of Nuclear Weapons.* New York: Vintage, 1984– . $5.95 (pbk.). ISBN 0–39472–901–3. ISBN 0–39474–189–7. ISBN 0–88730–145–2.

This volume initiates a series of annual reports sponsored by the Carnegie Endowment for International Peace on the spread of nuclear weapons. It provides a detailed analysis of the nuclear programs of all countries that have the potential to develop nuclear weapons. Each volume appears under a separate title: *Nuclear Proliferation Today* (1984), *The New Nuclear States* (1985), and *Going Nuclear* (1987). This source is invaluable in determining trends in nuclear proliferation.

2 *The United Nations Disarmament Yearbook.* New York: United Nations, 1976– . $22.

The main developments in the disarmament field are reviewed in this yearbook. Although all disarmament activities are noted, the bulk of the publication deals with the UN's role in disarmament. A listing of the General Assembly's disarmament resolutions along with key votes makes this source a valuable reference tool for researchers. A drawback of this publication is the slowness of issue appearance.

3 *World Armaments and Disarmament: SIPRI Yearbook*. London: Taylor and Francis, 1967– . ISSN 0347–2205. $31.

The Stockholm International Peace Research Institute (SIPRI) produces this excellent series of yearbooks on world armaments and disarmament. SIPRI is an independent institute founded to conduct research on problems of peace and conflict. Although all information in these yearbooks has been obtained from international sources on the open market, the experts attracted by the prestige of this yearbook make it one of the most valuable sources of its type on the market. Each issue's appearance is eagerly awaited by both arms control and disarmament scholars.

4 *World Military Expenditures and Arms Transfers*. Washington, DC: U.S. Arms Control and Disarmament Agency, 1974– . $5.50.

This invaluable source for arms control researchers is a compilation of data on world military expenditures and arms transfers for 145 countries over a ten-year period. A floating point is established ten years in the past as the base point for the statistical data. This information has been gathered by the Arms Control and Disarmament Agency from U.S. and official non-U.S. sources and from international organizations. Data from this source are most useful for comparisons over time.

Bibliographies

5 Burns, Grant. *The Atomic Papers: A Citizens' Guide to Selected Books and Articles on the Bomb, the Arms Race, Nuclear Power, the Peace Movement, and Related Issues*. Metuchen, NJ: Scarecrow Press, 1984. 309pp. ISBN 0–8108–1692–X.

Most of the significant books and articles on the nuclear question since 1945 have been collected in this bibliography. While periodical literature since 1980 has also been highlighted, the author confesses his selection of periodicals is nowhere near as complete as is his coverage of books. Nevertheless, this work is a good starting place for researching nuclear issues.

6 Caldwell, Dan. *Bibliography on Contemporary Arms Control and Disarmament*. Providence, RI: Center for Foreign Policy Development, 1983. 47pp.

This bibliography contains book and article citations on arms control and disarmament issues. A total of 609 citations have been gathered from a variety of English language sources. An index of authors and a subject division make this source easy to use for the general reader. While this work is stronger on journal and newspaper articles than on books and monographs, it is a solid short bibliography of use to all researchers in the field.

7 Chand, Attar. *Disarmament, Detente and World Peace: A Bibliography with Selected Abstracts, 1916–1981*. New Delhi: Sterling, 1982. 167pp.

The author presents in his view the most significant books and periodical articles to appear on disarmament and world peace during the period from 1916 to 1981. Although the author has a militant procommunist viewpoint, his work still has value since it lists Soviet and East European works on disarmament and peace research. Less useful is the limited scope of the abstracts. This bibliography is of limited use except for its access to communist sources.

8 Kohler, Gernot, Antnie Hakim, and Rosina Bisci. *Arms Control and Disarmament: A Bibliography of Canadian Research, 1965–1980.* Ottawa, Canada: Operational Research and Analysis Establishment, Department of National Defence, 1981. 168pp.

All Canadian research on arms control and disarmament published between 1965 and 1980 has been brought together in this bibliography. An official government publication, its purpose is to assist the Canadian government in formulating policies on arms control and disarmament. Besides disarmament issues, this bibliography also contains references to Canadian peace-keeping activities and peace research. While this bibliography refers to materials not available in any other source, its limited scope makes it a necessary reference work only for those scholars interested in Canadian materials.

9 *Repertory of Disarmament Research.* Geneva, Switzerland: Palais des Nations, 1982. 449pp. ISBN 92–9045–002–9.

In 1980 the UN Institute for Disarmament Research (UNIDIR) launched an automated system for the collection, processing, and dissemination of information on the arms race and disarmament. This bibliography is a part of that effort. UNIDIR has attempted to make this a comprehensive bibliography dealing with international disarmament issues, but at present Western European sources predominate. This publication contains material unavailable in other sources, but most researchers will find other bibliographies more useful.

10 *Strategic Nuclear Arms Control Verification: An Annotated Bibliography, 1977–1984.* Edited by Richard A. Scribner and Robert Travis Scott. Washington, DC: American Association for the Advancement of Science, 1985. 90pp. ISBN 0–87168–276–1.

The editors have produced an annotated bibliography of strategic nuclear arms control verification materials. A total of 333 articles, books, and reports are covered. Each entry has one- to two-sentence annotations on the thesis of each work. This work is a useful source for arms control researchers, but its limited size will make it necessary to consult other bibliographies.

Databooks, Handbooks, and Sourcebooks

11 *Arms Control and Disarmament Agreements: Texts and Histories of Negotiations.* Washington, DC: U.S. Arms Control and Disarmament Agency, 1982. 290pp.

Now in its fifth edition, this sourcebook contains the complete texts of the major arms control and disarmament agreements in force in 1982. It includes all agreements concluded after 1945 in which the United States has been a participant. A significant feature of this work is a list of signatories and parties to each agreement. This sourcebook is one of the more authoritative sources on arms control and disarmament agreements available.

12   *Arms Control Handbook: A Guide to the History, Arsenals and Issues of U.S.-Soviet Negotiations.* Edited by W. Bruce Weinrod. Washington, DC: Heritage Foundation, 1987. 175pp. ISBN 0–89195–221–7.

The Heritage Foundation, a conservative think tank, produced this handbook to provide its assessment of the arms control process. While most of the information included is intended to prove that past arms control treaties have led to a Soviet military advantage, the up-to-date material makes this book valuable for both its data and its orientation. Particularly useful are the sections on negotiating chronologies and the information on the military strategic balance between the United States and the Soviet Union. Despite its hardline conservative viewpoint, this handbook can be recommended for both the general reader and the specialist.

13   *The Arms Race and Arms Control.* Edited by Frank Blackaby. London: Taylor and Francis, 1982. 242pp. ISBN 0–85066–232–X.

Facts and figures on the arms race and arms control efforts have been gathered by the Stockholm International Peace Research Institute (SIPRI) in this book. Most of the material is drawn from the 1982 SIPRI yearbook of *World Armaments and Disarmament,* but it has been repackaged and augmented for this publication. The combination of statistical data and charts make this book a good basic source on arms control issues from its 1982 perspective.

14   Crawford, A., et al. *Compendium of Arms Control Verification Proposals,* 2d ed. Ottawa, Canada: Operational Research and Analysis Establishment, Department of National Defence, 1982. 485pp.

A total of 296 arms control verification proposals in arms control literature are abstracted and classified in this study. Material is divided according to two types of criteria: (1) arms control objectives, and (2) types of verification. A reference matrix, a subject index, and an author index are also provided. Although this work is published under the auspices of the Canadian government, the report is an independent analysis of arms control proposals.

15   *The Disarmament Catalogue.* Edited by Murray Polner. New York: Pilgrim Press, 1982. 209pp. ISBN 0–8298–0627–X.

This direct-action handbook is in opposition to the prevailing official U.S. government's attitude toward the feasibility of nuclear war. It lists a variety of resources for peace studies, including audiovisual materials, checklists of books, and disarmament organizations. It also has numerous short essays on antiwar themes. This handbook is one of the better examples of its type.

16   *Documents on Disarmament, 1984.* Washington, DC: U.S. Arms Control and Disarmament Agency, 1986. 964pp.

Basic documents on arms control and disarmament developments in 1984 have been accumulated by the U.S. Arms Control and Disarmament Agency. The coverage is almost encyclopedic, with every imaginable document, report, and statement appearing here. Although most of the emphasis is on U.S. disarmament positions, there is a considerable amount of material from foreign sources. This book is the best source on arms control and disarmament material for the year 1984 on the market.

17   Goldblat, Jozef. *Agreements for Arms Control: A Critical Survey.* 2 vols. London: Taylor and Francis, 1982. ISBN 0–85066–229–X.

This two-volume set contains all bilateral and multilateral arms control agreements in force since World War II. The author has broadened the definition of arms control to include arms limitation and disarmament issues. Although the introductions to the agreements are informative, it is the text on each agreement that makes this reference source so useful. This book is another of the excellent publications published under the auspices of the Stockholm International Peace Research Institute (SIPRI).

18 Goldblat, Jozef. *Arms Control Agreements: A Handbook.* New York: Praeger, 1983. 328pp. ISBN 0–03–063709–0.

Bilateral and multilateral arms control agreements in existence since 1945 are analyzed in this handbook. The author has limited the scope to include only those agreements arrived at in time of peace among sovereign states. Strong points of the book, besides a lengthy selection of arms control agreements, include a country-by-country chart of the status of the implementation of the major multilateral arms control agreements and an index to the SALT II agreements. This handbook is best used in conjunction with the author's earlier two-volume text of agreements.

19 Menos, Dennis. *Arms Control Fact Book.* Jefferson, NC: McFarland, 1985. 140pp. ISBN 0–89950–180–X.

This handbook is a basic reference source for researchers and students in the arms control field. It has three sections: (1) a treatment of the international arms control system; (2) an analysis of U.S. and world organizations active in arms control and disarmament; and (3) general data on arms control. It also includes an informative bibliography on arms control materials. This fact book is the best source of its type available.

20 *Nuclear Arms Control: Background and Issues.* Washington, DC: National Academy Press, 1985. 378pp. ISBN 0–30903–491–4.

The Committee on International Security and Arms Control, a subcommittee of the National Academy of Sciences, produced this overview of the historical development of the Soviet and U.S. positions on arms control proposals. Rather than attempt to reach conclusions or make recommendations, the committee chose to present opposing points of view without taking extreme arguments that would distort the issues. Inclusion of the texts of agreements between the two superpowers is the most useful feature of this book.

21 *Nuclear Disarmament: Key Statements of Popes, Bishops, Councils and Churches.* Edited by Robert Heyer. New York: Paulist Press, 1982. 278pp. ISBN 0–8091–2456–4.

Statements by religious leaders on nuclear disarmament issues of the 1970s and 1980s are contained in this book. There are three parts: (1) conciliar documents and papal statements; (2) North American Catholic bishops' statements; and (3) ecumenical statements. These positions by both Catholic and Protestant religious leaders reflect a growing concern over the direction of the arms race and the need for disarmament. This book provides a good sourcebook for the positions of the Catholic and Protestant thinkers on nuclear disarmament.

22 *Nuclear Proliferation Factbook*, 3d ed. Washington, DC: U.S. Government Printing Office, 1980. 531pp.

The Congressional Research Service, Library of Congress, prepared this sourcebook on the state of nuclear proliferations as of 1980. Basic documents and national and international statistical data on the spread of nuclear weapons are included in this third edition. Monitoring of the effectiveness of the Non-Proliferation Treaty (NPT) is also a significant part of this work. This book and its earlier editions provide a way to study proliferation topics over time.

23 *Status of Multilateral Arms Regulation and Disarmament Agreements,* 2d ed. New York: United Nations, 1983. 176pp. ISBN 92–1–142047–4.

This reference document contains complete information on the status of all disarmament agreements as of 31 December 1982. Information was supplied by the Office of Legal Affairs of the United Nations Secretariat and by the United Nations Department for Disarmament Affairs. Subsequent agreements after December 1982 will be reported in each year's volume of *The United Nations Disarmament Yearbook.*

24 Wilson, Andrew. *The Disarmer's Handbook of Military Technology and Organization.* Harmondsworth, England: Penguin, 1983. 318pp. ISBN 0–1400–6805–8.

This is a fact book for those involved in fighting the arms race. The author decided to use his military knowledge to produce a compendium of facts to be used in argument against military professionals by anyone engaged in disarmament work. Wilson does not claim that it is the definitive source, only useful. The short bibliographical essays at the end of each section are the most valuable part of this handbook.

Dictionaries

25 *Disarmament Terminology.* Berlin, West Germany: Walter de Gruyter, 1982. 645pp. ISBN 3–11–008858–4.

This dictionary covers terms and phrases relating to disarmament as well as the official designations of relevant organizations, authorities, conferences, and bilateral and multilateral agreements. Five languages are presented in the following order: English, German, French, Spanish, and Russian. This dictionary is the most up-to-date on the market.

26 *Strategic Nuclear Arms Control Verification: Terms and Concepts.* By Richard A. Scribner and Kenneth N. Luongo. Washington, DC: American Association for the Advancement of Science, 1985. 42pp. ISBN 0–871682–73–7.

Two specialists on arms control produced this glossary of strategic nuclear arms control verification terms and concepts. Each citation provides a lengthy treatment of its subject with a definition and brief history. It is also cross-referenced for ease of usage. This glossary is the best reference source of its type on the market.

Guidebooks

27 Goldblat, Jozef. *Nuclear Non-Proliferation: A Guide to the Debate.* London: Taylor and Francis, 1985. 95pp. ISBN 0–85066–310–5.

This guidebook is a study of the nonproliferation policies of the fifteen leading candidate states for the acquisition of nuclear weapons. It was prepared as part of the third Review Conference of the Treaty on the Non-Proliferation of Nuclear Weapons (NPT), September 1985. The author concludes that in the foreseeable future there is little danger of an open expansion of the nuclear club, but the incentives are there for an expansion in the long run. This guidebook serves as an excellent introduction to future trends in nuclear nonproliferation.

28 Florini, Ann. *Nuclear Proliferation: A Citizen's Guide to Policy Choices.* New York: United Nations Association of the United States of America, 1983. 48pp. ISBN 0–934654–48–4.

The United Nations Association of the USA (UNA-USA) produced this guidebook to inform the general public of the dangers of nuclear proliferation. It is intended to serve as a resource for the formation of direct-action groups to lobby on nonproliferation issues. The result is an illustrated and readable booklet of moderate length, which is full of reference material. This guide is valuable both for the information it contains and the evidence of the activities of UNA-USA.

29 Lester, Robert C. *A Guide to Nuclear Weapons, Arms Control, and the Threat of Thermonuclear War.* Frederick, MD: University Publications of America, 1981. 38pp.

This booklet serves as a guide to the special studies microfilm collection set dealing with the issues of nuclear weapons, arms control, and thermonuclear war. Most of these studies are previously unpublished products of governmental and private think tanks. There are two sets available: (1) a set of publications from the 1969–1981 era, and (2) a supplementary set of those from 1981–1983.

30 Mayers, Teena. *Understanding Nuclear Weapons and Arms Control: A Guide to the Issues,* 3d ed. Washington, DC: Pergamon-Brassey's, 1986. 121pp. ISBN 0–08–034483–6.

Teena Mayers, formerly with the U.S. Arms Control and Disarmament Agency, presents a guide to understanding arms control issues. While the facts and information contained in this guidebook have been assembled from documents published by the U.S. government and other materials in the public domain, it gives a good overview of nuclear arms control efforts since 1945. This book's chief virtue is the balanced presentation of the issues. It is a quality work from a respected authority in the field.

Hearings

31 U.S. Congress. Congressional Budget Office. *An Analysis of Administration Strategic Arms Reduction and Modernization Proposals.* Washington, DC: U.S. Congress, 1984. 75pp.

This study of the Reagan administration's strategic modernization program was commissioned by the House Budget Committee to examine the consistency of the administration's Strategic Arms Reduction Talks (START) proposal with its plan for upgrading U.S. strategic forces. While Congress has little control over arms control negotiations, it does have a budgetary say on weapons systems. The most cost-effective plan would be a START/Builddown concept, which would allow modernization while at the same time retiring many existing forces. These types of studies are invaluable because they allow arms control and security researchers access to thinking in congressional circles.

32 U.S. Congress. House. Committee on Armed Services. *The MX Missile and the Strategic Defense Initiative: Their Implications on Arms Control Negotiations.* Washington, DC: U.S. Government Printing Office, 1985. 285pp.

Six hearings were conducted by the Defense Policy Panel in 1985 on the arms control implications of the MX missile and the Strategic Defense Initiative (SDI) systems. Reagan administration spokesmen insisted that both the MX and SDI systems have arms control purposes and research up to deployment is acceptable within an elastic interpretation of the ABM Treaty. The testimony of Arkady N. Shevchenko on Soviet perceptions of MX and SDI is particularly enlightening. These hearings present testimony on these two defense systems, which will prove useful to any researcher in the field.

33 U.S. Congress. House. Committee on Foreign Affairs. *Arms Control in Outer Space.* Washington, DC: U.S. Government Printing Office, 1984. 480pp.

Four hearings were held in November 1983 and the spring and summer of 1984 to study the impact of the Strategic Defense Initiative (SDI) on arms control in space. Various experts debated the merits of the SDI and its impact on arms control in space without settling the issue. Most of the interesting material resides in the forty appendices. This source is more valuable for the continuing debate over the SDI than the arms control debate.

34 U.S. Congress. House. Committee on Foreign Affairs. *Calling for a Mutual and Verifiable Freeze On and Reductions in Nuclear Weapons.* Washington, DC: U.S. Government Printing Office, 1983. 403pp.

Administration and private witnesses gave testimony in a series of hearings held during the winter of 1983 on the subject of nuclear arms control. Both the testimony and supporting documents indicate the divisions within U.S. public opinion over a mutual freeze on nuclear weapons. Disagreements also surfaced on possible reductions of nuclear arsenals. Each side had an opportunity to present its view, but the committee passed a resolution supporting arms control agreements in this area.

35 U.S. Congress. House. Committee on Foreign Affairs. *Foreign Policy and Arms Control Implications of Chemical Weapons.* Washington, DC: U.S. Government Printing Office, 1982. 249pp.

Two hearings were held in the middle of 1982 to receive testimony on the evidence of illegal chemical warfare in Southeast Asia and Afghanistan. The intent was to have such evidence buttress attempts to expand arms control on chemical weapons. Most of the witnesses and supporting documents indicate that chemical weapons have been used in these regions. These hearings produced most of the evidence available on current use of chemical weapons in warfare, but doubts remain over usage in both regions.

36 U.S. Congress. House. Committee on Foreign Affairs. *Overview of Nuclear Arms Control and Defense Strategy in NATO.* Washington, DC: U.S. Government Printing Office, 1982. 225pp.

A series of hearings were held in the late winter of 1982 to study possible nuclear arms control initiatives in an attempt to enhance U.S. and Western security interests. Critics charge that the Reagan administration's policy is to pursue military buildup at the expense of arms control, and government officials deny any such policy. Both sides present statements supporting their side of the issue. These hearings give experts on both sides of the debate a forum for presentation of their views.

37 U.S. Congress. House. Committee on Foreign Affairs. *Proposals to Ban Nuclear Testing*. Washington, DC: U.S. Government Printing Office, 1985. 410pp.

These hearings on proposals to ban nuclear testing were held between February and May 1985. The hearings were notable for the testimony of witnesses, but the value was increased by the addition of seventy-two appendices of supporting documents and statements. While the bulk of the testimony is in favor of a ban on nuclear testing, there are several significant dissenting opinions. This volume offers a wealth of useful information.

38 U.S. Congress. House. Committee on Foreign Affairs. *Review of Arms Control Implications of the Report of the President's Commission on Strategic Forces*. Washington, DC: U.S. Government Printing Office, 1983. 225pp.

Three hearings were held in the spring of 1983 on the arms control implications of the Scowcroft report. Most attention has been directed toward the MX and small single-warhead missiles parts of this report, but the committee wanted to study the arms control part of the document. The witnesses were much more concerned about the deployment of the weapons systems rather than arms control issues, but they always tied the issues together. These hearings give considerable detail on the weapons systems, but little on the arms control possibilities.

39 U.S. Congress. House. Committee on Foreign Affairs. *The Role of Arms Control in U.S. Defense Policy*. Washington, DC: U.S. Government Printing Office, 1984. 430pp.

Four hearings were conducted in the summer of 1984 on the role of arms control in U.S. defense policy. Representatives from arms control agencies and lobbying groups presented testimony on the need for arms control to become a part of U.S. defense strategy. Other witnesses downplayed arms control issues. This testimony and the supporting documentation make these hearings a good introductory source on the arms control-defense debate.

40 U.S. Congress. Senate. Committee on Appropriations. *Salt II Violations*. Washington, DC: U.S. Government Printing Office, 1984. 109pp.

The military implications of the Soviet SALT II violations are examined in this special hearing of the Senate in March 1984. Defense witnesses testified on Soviet violations of SALT II and other treaties. This testimony included a step by step rebuttal of Soviet charges of U.S. noncompliance with arms control agreements. This hearing allows the researcher access to U.S. government charges and Soviet countercharges about treaty violations, and this exchange is most useful for any study on differing perspectives on arms control.

41   U.S. Congress. Senate. Committee on Foreign Relations. *Arms Control and the Militarization of Space*. Washington, DC: U.S. Government Printing Office, 1982. 69pp.

Statements on the possible return to the Soviet-U.S. Antisatellite (ASAT) Weapons Talks were compiled at a hearing in September 1982. These talks had been interrupted by the Soviet invasion of Afghanistan. The consensus among government and other arms control witnesses is that there is a need for such negotiations. The hearing was low-key, and most witnesses made positive statements in favor of the resumption of ASAT talks.

42   U.S. Congress. Senate. Committee on Foreign Relations. *Controlling Space Weapons*. Washington, DC: U.S. Government Printing Office, 1983. 173pp.

These Senate hearings on the direction of Soviet and U.S. space weapons programs and their arms control implications were conducted in April and May of 1983. Both statements and insertions of other printed materials into the record are used to debate the pros and cons of space weapons. Most of the testimony is directed toward warning of the dangers of carrying the arms race into space. These types of hearings always provide a mass of data useful for arms control researchers.

43   U.S. Congress. Senate. Committee on Foreign Relations. *Nuclear Arms Reduction Proposals*. Washington, DC: U.S. Government Printing Office, 1982. 402pp.

Five sessions of the Senate's Committee on Foreign Relations were held to study ways to reduce U.S. and Soviet nuclear inventories. Most witnesses were interested in the possibility of beginning new strategic arms reduction talks (START). Considerable attention was also paid to SALT I and SALT II. This hearing is a solid source for viewpoints from a variety of perspectives on nuclear arms reduction proposals.

44   U.S. Congress. Senate. Committee on Foreign Relations. *Nuclear Risk Reduction*. Washington, DC: U.S. Government Printing Office, 1984. 71pp.

A Senate hearing was held in early 1984 on a resolution for support of confidence-building measures between the United States and the Soviet Union. This resolution called for the establishment of nuclear risk reduction centers in Washington and Moscow. Most of the testimony was in favor of these measures, and supporting documentation also backed this resolution. This hearing provides some suggestions on ways to reduce chances for an unintentional war.

Journals

45   *Arms Control: The Journal of Arms Control and Disarmament*. London: Frank Cass, 1980– . ISSN 0144–0381. $69.

Arms control is interpreted broadly in this journal to include any serious proposal to curb or reduce the probability or severity of war, or to bring down international levels of peacetime expenditure and preparation for warlike activity. While this journal is published only three times a year, its articles make it one of the most influential journals in the arms control field. It specializes in moderate-length articles of a substantive nature.

46 *The Arms Control Reporter.* Brookline, MA: Institute for Defense and Disarmament Studies, 1982– . $297.

This monthly looseleaf publication provides ready reference information on arms control and weapons systems developments. Over thirty-five control treaties, negotiations, and proposals are covered. The Institute for Defense and Disarmament Studies is a private, nonprofit research center that devotes its efforts to studying arms control and disarmament issues. This source is a major contributor to the distribution of arms control information.

47 *Disarmament: A Periodic Review by the United Nations.* New York: UN Department for Disarmament Affairs, 1978– . $18.

This periodical is published by the UN Department for Disarmament Affairs to serve as a source of information and a forum for ideas on the United Nations and the international community's activities on disarmament. It features substantive articles on arms limitation and disarmament from a variety of international contributors. There is also a section on documents relating to disarmament. Both the articles and the documents combine to make this journal a solid source on disarmament issues.

48 *End: Journal of European Nuclear Disarmament.* London: European Nuclear Disarmament, 1983– . ISSN 0267–0224. $24.

Nuclear disarmament and other peace issues are the subjects presented in this journal. This publication appears five times a year and includes in-depth articles on arms control and disarmament issues. Despite its attempt to provide a balanced viewpoint, the United States receives the majority of the attention and most of the blame for the failure of arms control initiatives. This journal serves as a valuable source for British disarmament and peace movement opinion.

49 *Survival.* London: International Institute for Strategic Studies, 1959– . ISSN 0039–6338. $20.

The International Institute for Strategic Studies, London, publishes this bimonthly journal, which deals with a variety of strategic questions. While this journal has an excellent international reputation for its articles on arms control, disarmament, and peace issues, its strength lies in its documentation section and its list of newly arrived titles. This journal has a high reputation in arms control circles and is considered the top journal in the field.

Microfilm Collections

50 *Nuclear Weapons, Arms Control, and the Threat of Thermonuclear War.* Frederick, MD: University Publications of America, 1982.

The University Publications of America has published an invaluable microfilm collection on literature dealing with arms control, nuclear weapons, and nuclear war. These reels of 35-mm positive silver halide film conform to archive standards for film permanence. A title/subject guide is provided for the convenience of the user of this collection. This source allows researchers access to information otherwise unavailable.

Newsletters

51 *ACDA News Today.* Washington, DC: Office of Public Affairs, 1975– . Free.

The Arms Control and Disarmament Agency (ACDA) prepares this newsletter to inform key government personnel about arms control issues. Each week a select number of newspaper articles with arms control subjects are reproduced. This newsletter has wide distribution throughout the U.S. government. Despite its limited format, it is one of the better sources for easy access to arms control news.

52 *ACDIS Bulletin.* Champaign, IL: Office of Arms Control, Disarmament, and International Security, 1979–1986. Free.

This newsletter is a monthly compilation of excerpted and new articles, bibliographies, news items, summaries, and general announcements produced by the University of Illinois's Office of Arms Control, Disarmament, and International Security (ACDIS). On occasion, special features are also highlighted for the benefit of researchers on these topics. It is an excellent source for news from one of the more active research centers in the United States.

53 *ADIU Report: Armament and Disarmament Information Unit.* Brighton, England: University of Sussex, 1978– . ISSN 0264–0643. $15.

News relating to defense, disarmament, and arms control are provided in this newsletter from the Armament and Disarmament Information Unit (ADIU) of the Science Policy Unit at Sussex University. Although much of the information is gathered from the United Kingdom, the publishers make an effort to include information from elsewhere. Besides substantive articles, this newsletter features short bibliographies of recent publications. These bibliographies make this newsletter a desirable commodity.

54 *Arms Control Today.* Washington, DC: Arms Control Association, 1971– . ISSN 0196–125X. $30.

The Arms Control Association produces this monthly newsletter to promote public understanding of effective policies and programs in arms control and disarmament. While the newsletter has short articles on arms control activities, its major contribution is a bibliography of books and articles appearing in print since the last issue. These bibliographies alone make this newsletter worthy of acquisition.

55 *Arms Control Update.* Washington, DC: U.S. Arms Control and Disarmament Agency, 1987– . Free.

The U.S. Arms Control and Disarmament Agency publishes this newsletter as part of its legislatively mandated obligation to inform the U.S. public on arms control and disarmament issues. Key government officials use this publication as a forum to state the government's negotiating position on arms control talks in progress and future negotiations. Other useful features are chronologies on negotiations and a roundup and calendar of forthcoming talks. This newsletter is a good source on official U.S. government negotiating strategy on arms control issues.

56 *Disarmament Forum.* Helsinki, Finland: World Peace Council, 1981– . $10.

This newsletter chronicles worldwide disarmament activities from a European perspective, featuring short articles and news briefs on European disarmament topics. The World Peace Council, Helsinki, Finland, publishes this newsletter as a service to all organizations working for disarmament. It is the neutral viewpoint expressed in this newsletter that makes it a valuable source for disarmament researchers.

57 *Disarmament Newsletter*. New York: UN Department for Disarmament Affairs, 1983– . Free.
The World Disarmament Campaign Unit for the United Nations publishes this newsletter on disarmament affairs. It has short features on disarmament topics and summaries of reports from disarmament organizations. While the newsletter's scope includes all international disarmament activities, most of its emphasis is upon the participation of the United Nations. This concentration on UN activities makes this newsletter of only passing interest.

58 *Disarmament Times*. New York: NGO Disarmament Committee, 1977– . $15.
This publication is more a newspaper than a newsletter, but it fulfills the same function as a newsletter by providing news about disarmament issues. It is published under the auspices of the NGO (Non-Government Organizations) Committee on Disarmament at the UN headquarters to report on disarmament developments in the UN system. By fulfilling the function of providing UN disarmament news, this publication has a place in most disarmament collections.

59 *National Network for Direct Action: Nonviolent Struggle for Disarmament*. Nyack, NY: Disarmament Program Fellowship of Reconciliation, n.d. $10.
Short articles, news briefs, and a chronology of upcoming direct-action events characterize this newsletter. The sponsoring agency, the National Network for Direct Action, uses this newsletter to organize disarmament activities in various parts of the country. This type of newsletter provides valuable information on grassroots disarmament activities in the United States.

60 *Northwest Nuclear Xchange: Disarmament Calendar and News for Puget Sound*. Seattle, WA: Northwest Nuclear Xchange, 1982– . Free.
This newsletter is another new regional newsletter on the nuclear race and disarmament. Disarmament events and news of the Puget Sound region are covered in depth. Short informative articles and news briefs characterize this newsletter. These regional newsletters contain a variety of information valuable for arms control and disarmament researchers.

61 *The Nuclear Free Press*. Peterborough, Ontario: The Nuclear Free Press, 1980– . ISSN 0709–082X. $7.50.
Formerly *The Birch Bark Alliance*, this quarterly newsletter-newspaper is filled with information on nuclear affairs. It consists of newspaper-length articles on Canadian, international, and U.S. nuclear news. In addition, it contains a variety of Canadian antinuclear information. The primary value of this publication is in its information on grassroots activities for disarmament.

62 *Nukewatch: A Public Education Project of the Progressive Foundation*. Madison, WI: Nukewatch, n.d. Free.

This newsletter is a product of an activist group involved in monitoring the movements of nuclear materials and weapons. This group has branches all over the United States, and this publication helps to coordinate its activities. Short antinuclear articles also appear in this work. This organization is one of the more active antinuclear groups in the country, and this newsletter reflects its activities.

63 *Swords and Ploughshares.* Urbana, IL: Arms Control, Disarmament and International Security Office, 1986– . Free.

The Office of Arms Control, Disarmament, and International Security (ACDIS) at the University of Illinois at Urbana-Champaign publishes this newsletter as a replacement for the *ACDIS Bulletin*. A change in title is also matched by a different format. News of ACDIS activities still appears, but now more articles are also featured. The publication's change in format does not reflect any change in ACDIS activities in the arms control, disarmament, and international security fields.

Papers

64 *Adelphi Papers.* London: International Institute for Strategic Studies, 1964– . ISSN 0567–932X. $6.50.

This series of papers is acknowledged to be one of the leading research sources in the arms control field. These papers appear at frequent intervals, averaging eight to ten papers a year. The International Institute for Strategic Studies, London, sponsors the series, whose prestige attracts some of the top names in the field as contributors.

Textbooks

65 *Armaments, Arms Control and Disarmament: A Unesco Reader for Disarmament Education.* Edited by Marek Thee. Paris: Unesco, 1981. 445pp. ISBN 92–3–101920–1.

This reader has been designed to promote disarmament education at the university level. While most of the material is published elsewhere, the editor sorted and rearranged the material to be used as background reading for undergraduate or postgraduate courses on disarmament-related issues. A glossary and select bibliography are solid features of this book. This reader is an excellent source for introductory level courses.

66 Stanford Arms Control Group. *International Arms Control: Issues and Agreements,* 2d ed. Edited by Coit D. Blacker and Gloria Duffy. Stanford, CA: Stanford University Press, 1984. 502pp. ISBN 0–8047–1211–5.

A revision of an earlier text designed for classroom use, this book presents a variety of information on arms control subjects. There has been a change from the optimistic appraisal for arms control of the first edition to the more realistic tone of this edition. A useful feature is the complete texts of the major arms control agreements now in force. This book is a balanced textbook that can be recommended for a course on arms control.

67 *Toward Nuclear Disarmament and Global Security: A Search for Alternatives.* Edited by Burns H. Weston. Boulder, CO: Westview Press, 1984. 746pp. ISBN 0–86531–642–2.

This book is a combination of a textbook of readings and a source to provide students and others with a theoretical and factual base for understanding the issues of the arms race and disarmament. The editor intends this book to be used for world order studies, peace studies, national security studies, and courses on international law and relations. While most of the readings are short, they are written by top specialists in the field.

Monographs

68 Abarenkov, V., L. Semeiko, and R. Timerbaev. *Problems of Nuclear Disarmament.* Moscow: Scientific Research Council on Peace and Disarmament, 1983. 83pp.

This book is the Soviet response to the U.S. and NATO's position on nuclear disarmament. The authors blame the United States for the nuclear arms race and the Reagan administration for its acceleration in the 1980s, claiming that Soviet efforts to promote nuclear disarmament have been rebuffed at every opportunity. As the official Soviet position on nuclear disarmament in the early 1980s, this work is a good source of the current Soviet viewpoint on disarmament.

69 *The ABM Treaty: To Defend or Not to Defend?* Edited by Walther Stutzle, Bhupendra Jasani and Regina Cowen. Oxford, England: Oxford University Press, 1987. 219pp. ISBN 0–19–829123–X.

These essays on the Anti-Ballistic Missile (ABM) Treaty are published under the auspices of the Stockholm International Peace Research Institute (SIPRI). The authors studied the 1972 treaty in response to challenges to the treaty from the perspective of the United States and the Strategic Defense Initiative (SDI). Despite arguments from the U.S. government, they are adamant that there are no technological loopholes for the development of new antiballistic systems. This book continues the debate over the provisions of the ABM treaty, but, unlike many other studies, the analysis is first-rate.

70 Aizenstat, A. J. *Survival for All: The Alternative to Nuclear War with a Practical Plan for Total Denuclearization.* New York: Billner and Rouse, 1985. 216pp. ISBN 0–932755–14–3.

Rather than disarmament, the author proposes a policy of worldwide, unilateral denuclearization, involving the total removal of nuclear weapons from the arsenal of any state. Conventional forces will be left out of the plan, and any deficiencies between NATO and the Warsaw Pact can be easily made up in short order. This book is a creative approach to the problem of the nuclear arms race, but has weaknesses in the author's plans for implementation.

71 *Alternative Methods for International Security.* Edited by Carolyn M. Stephenson. Lanham, MD: University Press of America, 1982. 246pp. ISBN 0–8191–2472–9.

The authors of these essays intend to find the linkage between disarmament and international security and to create alternatives to a reliance on arms. These papers are a product of the 1979 Conference on Alternative International Security Systems, held at Colgate University in Hamilton, New York. This book attempts to synthesize research on conflict resolution and conflict management with an emphasis toward peace. Activists, educators, and peace researchers will find this work an excellent source for approaches in disarmament and peace research.

72 *Anti-Satellite Weapons: Arms Control or Arms Race?* Cambridge, MA: Union of Concerned Scientists, 1983. 44pp.

The Union of Concerned Scientists published this short work to outline its opposition to antisatellite weapons (ASAT), claiming that it is in the long-term interests of both the Soviet Union and the United States to minimize the likelihood of war in space. The United States should respond in the affirmative to a draft treaty submitted by the Soviet Union to the United Nations prohibiting space weapons. This position paper is the official position on ASATs of one of the main U.S. lobbying groups for arms control.

73 *Anti-Satellite Weapons, Countermeasures, and Arms Control.* Washington, DC: U.S. Government Printing Office, 1985. 146pp.

The Office of Technology Assessment, U.S. Congress, undertook this assessment of antisatellite weapons (ASAT) and arms control at the request of Congress. While both the United States and the Soviet Union have been active in developing ASATs, the Soviet threat to U.S. satellites is greater because the United States is more dependent on satellites for important military functions. An arms control agreement would limit U.S. development of ASATs, a fact that must be considered in deciding on such agreements. This report is a major piece of analysis on a complicated subject.

74 Archer, Clive. *Deterrence and Reassurance in Northern Europe.* Aberdeen, Scotland: Centre for Defence Studies, 1983. 69pp.

Nordic security and the possibility of a Nordic Nuclear-Free Zone (NNFZ) are the subjects of this short monograph. The author doubts that a Nordic Nuclear-Free Zone would provide enough security for the region, but the Scandinavian people are concerned about the arms race. Nordic states need to put pressure on their larger NATO partners to encourage them toward arms control agreements, the author maintains. Although this monograph is restricted to a narrow topic, the depth of the analysis makes it valuable for understanding Nordic security concerns.

75 *Armed Peace: The Search for World Security.* Edited by Josephine O'Connor Howe. London: Macmillan, 1984. 191pp. ISBN 0–333–37171–2.

The Council for Arms Control commissioned this book to promote its mission to study arms control and disarmament issues. Much of the analysis revolves around commentaries and critiques of the report of the Palme Commission for a battlefield nuclear-free zone. The consensus is that this approach works better than NATO's step-by-step negotiating stance. This book is a valuable companion piece to the Palme Commission's *Common Security* (New York: Simon and Schuster, 1982).

76 *Arms and Disarmament: SIPRI Findings.* Edited by Marek Thee. Oxford, England: Oxford University Press, 1986. 491pp. ISBN 0–19–829111–6.

This book celebrates twenty years of peace research by the Stockholm International Peace Research Institute (SIPRI) by publishing selected studies on the arms race and disarmament subjects. These papers are abridged versions of more substantial works published by SIPRI in recent years. The need for arms control and disarmament is behind each paper presented in this volume. Together these articles give a good selection of the type of research coming out of SIPRI in recent years.

77 *Arms and Survival.* Edited by Radhakrishna Mahendra Agrawal. New Delhi: Satvahan, 1982. 312pp.

These essays from Indian disarmament scholars are oriented toward a "survival perspective" of disarmament. Most disarmament negotiations in this century have had the goal of security, but today there is a need for the wide application of the principle of international distributive justice, which will replace security as a goal. This holistic approach seeks to understand the modern nation-state and replace it as the focus for disarmament. While these writings attempt to alter the approach to disarmament, their recommendations appear simplistic in comparison to the problem.

78 *Arms Control: The Multilateral Alternative.* Edited by Edward C. Luck. New York: New York University Press, 1983. 258pp. ISBN 0–8147–5005–2.

In this book of essays, U.S. scholars comment on the successes and failures of the multilateral approach to arms control negotiations. Each author addresses an aspect of the multilateral approach, and the resulting papers are well worth consideration. However, the general conclusion is that chances of a multilateral arms control agreement have lessened in recent years because of increased international tension and division among the nonaligned countries. The authors recommend that the United States take a more positive role in advocating the multilateral approach.

79 *Arms Control: Myth Versus Reality.* Edited by Richard F. Staar. Stanford, CA: Hoover Institution Press, 1984. 211pp. ISBN 0–8179–8041–5.

Sixty experts on arms control and international security gathered at Stanford University in 1983 to discuss papers, nine of which are published in this book. Most of the participants believe that the Soviet Union is superior in virtually all indices of strategic nuclear capability, and that there is also a need to change Western military strategy from deterrence to one of protective defense utilizing new military technology. Arms control is not considered a realistic possibility by these writers, and this hardline viewpoint makes this book a source worth reading.

80 *Arms Control and Defense Postures in the 1980s.* Edited by Richard Burt. Boulder, CO: Westview Press, 1982. 230pp. ISBN 0–86531–162–5.

These papers study the utility of arms control as an instrument of Western national security. Arms control has fallen into disrepute because it suffers from inherent political and technical difficulties involved in controlling the arms race by mutual agreement. Most of the authors conclude that too much has been expected from past arms control agreements, and that arms control needs to be correlated with national defense policy. This book is a solid contribution to arms control literature because it advocates arms control as an instrument of defense policy.

81 *Arms Control and European Security.* Edited by Jonathan Alford. Aldershot, England: Gower, 1984. 147pp. ISBN 0–566–00675–8.

These essays address Western European efforts to resolve its security problems through arms control. Since détente has been a popular cause in Western Europe, its collapse in the early 1980s has been difficult for Europeans to accept. This book maintains that European efforts toward arms control have benefited the Soviet Union and hurt European security. While all of the essays are of a high quality, their hardline attitude toward the Soviet Union colors the account.

82 *Arms Control and International Security.* Edited by Roman Kolkowicz and Neil Joeck. Boulder, CO: Westview Press, 1984. 157pp. ISBN 0–86531–662–7.

This book contains a series of papers from a 1982 conference on international security and arms control at UCLA. A growing sense of skepticism over the prospects of arms control reflects the mood of these papers. An increase in tensions between the superpowers has made arms control negotiations almost impossible. Most of the essays are too short to cover substantive issues, but the galaxy of big names makes this book important as a sounding board for opinion on arms control in 1983.

83 *Arms Control and Military Force.* Edited by Christoph Bertram. Westmead, England: Gower, 1980. 258pp. ISBN 0–566–00344–9.

The International Institute for Strategic Studies, London, sponsored this book of essays on the threat of growing militarization and its impact on arms control efforts. Each author takes a substantive issue and devotes considerable space dealing with that topic. Many of the issues have changed since the late 1970s, but the juxtaposition of the rising tide of militarization in both the industrial and developing countries with the likelihood of arms control is still valid. This book makes a solid contribution to arms control literature.

84 *Arms Control and Strategic Stability: Challenges for the Future.* Edited by William T. Parsons. Lanham, MD: University Press of America, 1986. 175pp. ISBN 0–8191–5474–1.

These papers are the result of a 1984 seminar on arms control and strategic stability, held in Charlottesville, Virginia. Two representatives from the Reagan administration furnished keynote speeches, and the remainder of the seminar was devoted to responding to the issues presented in these statements. The administration's arms control policy and the Strategic Defense Initiative (SDI) were both supported and criticized in these papers. This book gives a good sample of the issues in arms control during the mid-1980s.

85 *Arms Control, East-West Relations and the Atlantic Alliance: Closing the Gaps.* By George M. Seignious et al. Washington, DC: Atlantic Council of the United States, 1983. 70pp.

The Atlantic Council's Working Group on Arms Control produced this study on the relationship of arms control and economic policy to the cohesion and security of the NATO alliance. Despite some dissent among working group members, the consensus is that security and arms control considerations should be combined in a total package. There is also a need for improvement in the alliance's policy-making machinery to include more European input. This report demonstrates the difficulty that alliance leaders have in formulating a common policy.

86 *Arms Control in Asia.* Edited by Gerald Segal. Houndmills, England: Macmillan, 1987. 187pp. ISBN 0–333–42400–X.

These papers are the product of a 1985 conference on Asian arms control subjects held in Bristol, England, and published under the auspices of the British International Association (BIA). Most of the British participants are concerned with the current status of arms control negotiations on the major Asian conflict regions. They believe that arms control efforts in Asia differ considerably from those in Europe, because the Asian negotiators are more interested in limiting conventional weapons and in establishing demilitarized zones than in controlling nuclear weapons. Because these essays deal with arms control in a strategic but neglected region, the material here provides insights unavailable elsewhere.

87 *Arms Control in Space: Workshop Proceedings.* Washington, DC: U.S. Government Printing Office, 1984. 64pp.

The Office of Technology Assessment, U.S. Congress, sponsored a workshop in 1984 on antisatellite weapons (ASAT) as one aspect of space arms control. Senator Pressler (R-S.D.) had requested this workshop, and twenty-four politicians, scientists, and scholars debated the merits and demerits of ASAT and space arms control. These proceedings were not intended to resolve issues, but to raise questions and to clarify issues. This source shows the mixed response among defense experts on prospects for arms control in space.

88 *Arms Control II: A New Approach to International Security.* Edited by John H. Barton and Ryukichi Imai. Cambridge, MA: Oelgeschlager, Gunn and Hain, 1981. 328pp. ISBN 0–89946–069–0.

A joint U.S.-Japanese working group produced this book on rethinking the role of arms control on international security. The Japanese contributors maintain that arms control is only acceptable as a part of broader security agreements. *Arms Control II* is a means of discouraging nations' desire for arms rather than prohibiting them from acquiring arms. While this book makes an important contribution by shifting the arms control discussion, the practicality of its approach is open to debate.

89 *Arms Limitation and the United Nations.* Edited by R. B. Byers and Stanley C. M. Ing. Toronto, Canada: Canadian Institute of Strategic Studies, 1982. 128pp. ISBN 0–919769–10–1.

In these papers representatives of the Canadian Institute of Strategic Studies, Toronto, study the role of the United Nations in arms control and disarmament. A pessimistic tone pervades this work as it becomes apparent that no meaningful progress has been made on arms limitations at the second United Nations Special Session on Disarmament (UNSSOD II) during the summer of 1982. Failure of UNSSOD II was forecasted by the chilly relations between the Soviet Union and the United States. This book is an excellent introduction to the difficulties that the United Nations has had in dealing with disarmament.

90 *The Arms Race in the 1980s.* Edited by David Carlton and Carlo Schaerf. London: Macmillan, 1982. 338pp. ISBN 0–333–32669–5.

These essays are an outgrowth of the eighth course of the International School on Disarmament and Research on Conflicts (ISODARCO) held in Venice, Italy, in 1980. An international cast of authors present papers on current and future trends in the arms race. The participants developed a consensus that only some sort of arms control will end the seeming endless arms race. This book's value is in the quality of the papers and the variety of viewpoints expressed by the authors.

91 *Australia and Disarmament: Steps in the Right Direction.* Canberra, Australia: Australian Government Publishing Service, 1986. 32pp. ISBN 0–644–05171–X.

Australian efforts for arms control and disarmament are enumerated in this publication by the Australian Department of Foreign Affairs. The focus of this booklet is that the Australian government is unwilling to leave the field of nuclear disarmament and arms control to the superpowers. Special emphasis is given to Australian efforts on nuclear nonproliferation and proposals of a South Pacific nuclear-free zone. While this publication reflects the views of the current Australian government, it still provides a useful record of Australian efforts in this field.

92   Babin, Ronald. *The Nuclear Power Game.* Montreal, Canada: Black Rose Books, 1985. 235pp. ISBN 0–920057–30–6.

The author outlines the history of Canada's nuclear industry. Canada is the world's largest exporter of uranium, and has supplied uranium for nuclear weapons for Great Britain, the United States, and other countries with ambitions to develop nuclear arsenals. Efforts by Canadians to protest Canada's nuclear role have become a political force in Canadian politics. Any researcher interested in Canadian nuclear policies will find this book informative.

93   Barton, John H. *The Politics of Peace: An Evaluation of Arms Control.* Stanford, CA: Stanford University Press, 1981. 257pp. ISBN 0–8047–1081–3.

The author analyzes the benefits and dangers of past and present arms control efforts. Self-interest arms control agreements are never successful, and these are the types of agreements negotiated in the past between the United States and the Soviet Union. Only by introducing popular attitudes toward arms restraint among all nations, including the United States and the Soviet Union, will arms control have a chance of succeeding. The author's realistic perspectives make this book valuable.

94   Beckman, Robert L. *Nuclear Non-Proliferation: Congress and the Control of Peaceful Nuclear Activities.* Boulder, CO: Westview Press, 1985. 446pp. ISBN 0–8133–7040–X.

The tensions created by U.S. promotion of peaceful uses of nuclear energy while simultaneously attempting to restrict the spread of nuclear weapons are the subject of this monograph. In particular, the changing political role of Congress in the policy-making aspects of this debate is emphasized. Mixed signals from the executive branch have made Congress indecisive in establishing controls over nuclear proliferation. This book is an outstanding example of a comprehensive study of the congressional role in the control of nuclear affairs.

95   Beker, Avi. *Disarmament without Order: The Politics of Disarmament at the United Nations.* Westport, CT: Greenwood Press, 1985. 212pp. ISBN 0–313–24362–X.

The connection between disarmament and politics in the United Nations is the subject of this book. At the beginning of the United Nations, the disarmament debate revolved around an East-West confrontation, but by the second decade there developed a shift to a North-South axis of Third World countries. Again in the 1980s the East-West confrontation has reappeared, but this time the Soviet Union has the advantage with more allies in the United Nations. This book is a solid addition to the study of disarmament problems.

96   *Belgrade and Beyond: The CSCE Process in Perspective.* Edited by Nils Andren and Karl E. Birnbaum. Alphen aan den Rijn, the Netherlands: Sijthoff and Noordhoff, 1980. 179pp. ISBN 90–286–0250–X.

This book examines the role of the Conference on Security and Cooperation in Europe (CSCE) in the negotiating process. The CSCE represents thirty-five states, and it has been active in negotiations in Helsinki, Geneva, and Belgrade. These papers, statements, and documents provide a picture of the role of the CSCE in these negotiations. Both the documents and papers make this book a good source for understanding CSCE's status in the negotiations during the 1970s.

97 Bentley, Judith. *The Nuclear Freeze Movement*. New York: Franklin Watts, 1984. 122pp. ISBN 0–531–04772–5.

The author, a Seattle psychiatrist, has written this brief history of the nuclear freeze movement to educate young readers about the dangers of nuclear war. Although most of the material is presented for educational purposes, the author appeals to readers to become active in antinuclear affairs. Good illustrations and a readable text make this book a good source for young readers, but some readers may object to the author's activist tone.

98 *Beyond Survival: New Directions for the Disarmament Movement.* Edited by Michael Albert, David Dellinger. Boston, MA: South End Press, 1983. 365pp. ISBN 0–89608–175–3.

These papers from U.S. disarmament activists detail the need for the disarmament movement to reach out to the American public for support. All of the contributors have their roots in the antiwar movement of the 1960s and want to turn this type of energy toward disarmament. They consider the Reagan administration's policies disastrous, and encourage the antinuclear and disarmament movements to coalesce into a large mass movement. This book espouses the ideological position of the left wing of the disarmament movement.

99 Bhandari, B. K. *Control of Nuclear Arms Race from Hiroshima to SALT II: Success or Failure?* New Delhi: ABC Publishing House, 1984. 230pp.

Failure to control the nuclear arms race is the story of this book by a senior Indian Army officer, who maintains that developing countries have been caught up in the arms race instigated by the Soviet Union and the United States. A workable, verifiable, and mutually accepted arms control agreement can only work under the supervision of the United Nations. While this book is a positive approach to arms control, almost none of the author's requirements for arms control are attainable at the present time.

100 Bilder, Richard B. *Managing the Risks of International Agreement*. Madison, WI: University of Wisconsin Press, 1981. 302pp. ISBN 0–299–08360–8.

Managing the risks of international agreements is the subject of this book. The author uses risk-management techniques to establish a basis of trust for negotiators. While he claims there are risks in using these techniques, the benefits of these methods allow agreements to be concluded that might otherwise never be negotiated. This book is most useful in listing the pros and cons of risk-management in international negotiations.

101 Blomley, Peter. *The Arms Trade and Arms Conversion*. London: The Council for Arms Control, 1983. 19pp.

The conversion of industries producing military weapons to other uses is the subject of this study by a British author affiliated with the Council for

Arms Control. Blomley concludes that such a conversion would be difficult unless there was a commitment from a variety of government and private sources, as well as international cooperation. This working paper explores a topic necessary for disarmament to succeed.

102 Bowman, William R. *Limiting Conventional Forces in Europe: An Alternative to the Mutual and Balanced Force Reduction Negotiations.* Washington, DC: National Defense University Press, 1985. 84pp.

This book is a critique of the Mutual and Balanced Force Reduction (MBFR) negotiations by a senior officer in the U.S. Air Force. Bowman contends that the United States is at such a disadvantage in conventional forces that any MBFR treaty will leave NATO at a marked disadvantage. By turning to the ongoing Conference on Disarmament in Europe (CDE), many of the objections against the MBFR can be alleviated by the obligatory measures in the CDE. This argument of shifting negotiations from a deadlock to another forum is a novel approach, and it deserves consideration.

103 Brenner, Michael J. *Nuclear Power and Non-Proliferation: The Remaking of U.S. Policy.* Cambridge, England: Cambridge University Press, 1981. 324pp. ISBN 0–521–23517–0.

The subject of this book is U.S. policies toward nuclear proliferation in the late 1970s. Inadequacy and poor timing rather than outright mistakes have been the chief failings of U.S. policies. But the author's major criticism has been the "failure to provide clear and continuous political guidance to its international program for supporting the civilian use of nuclear power." This book is a major contribution to understanding the politics of decision making on nuclear power issues in the 1970s.

104 Brito, Dagobert L., Michael D. Intriligator, and Adele E. Wick. *Strategies for Managing Nuclear Proliferation: Economic and Political Issues.* Lexington, MA: Lexington Books, 1983. 311pp. ISBN 0–669–06442–4.

This book contains the proceedings of a 1982 conference on nuclear proliferation, held at Tulane University. Most of the authors were more interested in managing the spread of nuclear weapons than the prevention of proliferation. The emphasis that political and economic factors determine proliferation make this book a different approach to proliferation issues. The arguments and the debate on proliferation issues combine to make this book a valuable source on the future directions of nuclear proliferation.

105 Brown, Harold and Lynn E. Davis. *Nuclear Arms Control Choices.* Boulder, CO: Westview Press, 1984. 55pp. ISBN 0–86531–888–3.

Two arms control experts with extensive government service survey possible arms control options in the 1980s. This analysis is based upon projections of U.S. and Soviet nuclear forces in 1990. After studying various proposals, the authors conclude that the best arms control agreement will have an overall equivalence of nuclear arsenals but at reduced levels. This study is based upon a series of statistical surveys of nuclear forces in 1983 and a projection for 1990, and both the surveys and the conclusions combine to make this book a good source for further research in the arms control field.

106 Burrows, William E. *Deep Black: Space Espionage and National Security.* New York: Random House, 1986. 401pp. ISBN 0–394–54124–3.

This book is the story of space reconnaissance and surveillance capabilities of the United States. These systems have three benefits: (1) technical collection systems on Soviet weapons; (2) an early warning system to prevent a surprise attack; and (3) a monitor for arms control. The caliber of U.S. technical information collection from space reconnaissance is extremely high, so much so that it could be used for verification of any arms control agreement. This book challenges most of the arguments advanced by the Reagan administration on the verification of arms control agreements.

107 Chand, Attar. *Nonaligned Nations, Arms Race and Disarmament.* Delhi, India: UDH, 1983. 373pp.

The role of the nonaligned states in the arms race is the subject of this book by a Marxist Indian scholar. He places most of the blame for the failure of arms control and disarmament on the policies of the United States and its allies, maintaining that by using the United Nations as a forum, the nonaligned states can apply pressure toward disarmament. Little effort is made by the author to hide his pro-Soviet bias, and there is little to recommend this book except for the author's viewpoint.

108 *Chemical Weapon Free Zones?* Edited by Ralf Trapp. Oxford, England: Oxford University Press, 1987. 211pp. ISBN 0–19–829113–2.

These papers on the possibility of chemical weapon-free zones in Europe have been published under the auspices of the Stockholm International Peace Research Institute (SIPRI). Contributors of papers come from both NATO and Warsaw Pact countries. The ramifications of European chemical weapon-free zones are examined with both pro and con papers. This book maintains the high standards of SIPRI publications.

109 Chirouf, Lamri. *From Giscard to Mitterand: French Disarmament Policy between the First and Second United Nations Special Sessions.* Falmer, England: Armament and Disarmament Information Unit, 1982. 54 leaves.

This paper is an assessment of the change of French policy on disarmament between the administrations of Valéry Giscard d'Estaing and François Mitterrand. Mitterrand adopted much of his predecessor's program by moving toward multilateral disarmament negotiations and changing little on nuclear nonproliferation and arms sales. In fact, Mitterrand has initiated closer ties with the United States without ending French commitment to disarmament. This paper is a balanced assessment of changes and continuity in French disarmament policy.

110 Chopra, Ashwani Kumar. *India's Policy on Disarmament.* New Delhi: ABC Publishing, 1984. 356pp.

This book examines India's policy on nuclear disarmament. India had a record of opposition toward nuclear weapons until the explosion of a nuclear device in 1964 by the People's Republic of China. Opposition to the Non-Proliferation Treaty (NPT) is based on the belief that this treaty protects the monopoly of the nuclear powers and ensures a widening of the economic and technological gap between the developing and developed countries. This book is an articulate defense of present obstructionist Indian policy on disarmament issues.

111 Coffey, Joseph I. *Deterrence and Arms Control: American and West German Perspectives on INF.* Denver, CO: Graduate School of International Studies, University of Denver, 1985. 116pp. ISBN 0–87940–079–X.

This study focuses on differing U.S. and West German perspectives on intermediate range nuclear forces and arms control. Political and media elites of both the United States and West Germany have been surveyed to establish informed public opinion on the deployment of intermediate-range missiles and arms negotiations. While there has been considerably more opposition to deployment in West Germany than in the United States, European deployment has proceeded at a slow pace. This book set itself an ambitious goal, and the fact that it is only partially successful in reaching that goal does not detract from its worth.

112   *Conflict and Arms Control: An Uncertain Agenda.* Edited by Paul R. Viotti. Boulder, CO: Westview Press, 1986. 320pp. ISBN 0–8133–7081–7.

Arms control and security are the twin problems covered in this book of essays. Each essay deals with an aspect of the search for security through arms control agreements. A variety of options are explored with no consensus developing except the belief that arms control agreements will advance international security. Both the scholarship and the arguments in this work make it one of the more valuable resources on arms control on the market.

113   Dahlitz, Julie. *Nuclear Arms Control with Effective International Agreements.* Boston: Allen and Unwin, 1983. 238pp. ISBN 0–04341–023–5.

The author, an Australian lawyer, presents the issues of nuclear arms control and the role of international law in any effective agreement. She emphasizes the feasibility of nuclear arms control from the legal point of view. At present, technological advances on nuclear weapons and skepticism over international organizations monitoring agreements have made the five major nuclear states (United States, Soviet Union, Great Britain, France, and China) reluctant to accept international agreements to control nuclear weapons. The legal orientation gives this work another perspective useful for arms control researchers.

114   David, Peter. *"Star Wars" and Arms Control.* London: Council for Arms Control, 1985. 19pp. ISBN 0–947844–03–1.

The technology correspondent for the British journal *The Economist*, the author gives a sharp technical critique of the Reagan administration's Strategic Defense Initiative (SDI). He notes the disagreements by U.S. physicists over the technical feasibility of the SDI, but he believes the real impact has been introducing new tensions among NATO members and stimulating the Soviet Union to increase its missile forces. This short study is recommended for its succinct critique of the SDI program on arms control.

115   *Decisionmaking for Arms Limitation: Assessments and Prospects.* Edited by Hans Guenter Brauch and Duncan L. Clarke. Cambridge, MA: Ballinger, 1983. 332pp. ISBN 0–88410–864–3.

Experts on arms control from Western Europe and the United States have written these essays on governmental decision making and arms control. Case studies of the Soviet Union, the United States, and Western Europe provide the data. General conclusions are that arms limitation proposals must be accorded greater prominence in government and in public opinion, and arms control considerations need to be integrated into the national defense and foreign policies of every state. This book is recommended for the high quality of its essays.

116   *Defended to Death: A Study of the Nuclear Arms Race from the Cambridge University Disarmament Seminar.* Edited by Gwyn Prins. Harmondsworth, England: Penguin Books, 1983. 387pp. ISBN 0–14–022471–8.

This book is a collective statement by a group of Cambridge dons on the need for a reexamination of the nuclear arms race. They believe that nuclear war is not inevitable and that chances for nuclear disarmament are improved by rejecting the standard interpretation of aggressive Soviet expansionism. The authors' proposals include that all nuclear facilities and weapons be removed from Great Britain, that NATO be converted into a nonnuclear force, and that a comprehensive disarmament treaty be negotiated with the Warsaw Pact. This book presents a program that is more practical than it might seem on the surface in its attempt to end the deadlock of Cold War mentality.

117 *Defense Planning and Arms Control.* Washington, DC: The National Security Affairs Institute, 1980. 170pp.

This book contains the proceedings of a 1980 conference of the National Security Affairs Institute. Prominent defense analysts were invited to deliberate with arms control specialists over the problem of the integration of defense planning and arms control. Both the problem of combining defense planning and arms control and the future of arms control were questioned by the two panels. This publication reinforces the belief among many that arms control is in disfavor among security specialists.

118 Delf, George. *Humanizing Hell! The Law v. Nuclear Weapons.* London: Hamish Hamilton, 1985. 367pp. ISBN 0–241–11593–0.

This book is an indictment of the present nuclear environment and the policies of the nuclear powers. The nuclear powers are pursuing policies that threaten nuclear annihilation with the compliance of the power establishment. Law is the approach that has the potential to control the dangerous policies of the present. This author uses various professions as examples to make his thesis, but the excess of polemics weakens the effect.

119 *The Denuclearisation of the Oceans.* Edited by R. B. Byers. London: Croom Helm, 1986. 270pp. ISBN 0–7099–3936–1.

These papers were presented at a 1984 conference on denuclearization of the oceans in Norrtalje, Sweden. Scholars and government officials from fourteen countries gathered to study the issue of ridding the ocean waterways of nuclear weapons. While there is little current movement toward denuclearization of the oceans, and the 1982 Law of the Sea ignores the question, a change in political climate might alter this attitude. This book contains a variety of essays on ending the arms race on the oceans, and it is a worthwhile study of a neglected subject.

120 *Disarmament: The Human Factor.* Edited by Ervin Laszlo and Donald Keys. Oxford, England: Pergamon Press, 1981. 164pp. ISBN 0–08–024703–2.

These papers are a product of a series of symposiums organized jointly by the Planetary Citizens, a nongovernmental organization affiliated with the United Nations, and UNITAR, the United Nations Institute for Training and Research. The thesis of these papers is that progress toward disarmament must come not from generals and politicians but from people from all walks of life. This means that the increase of armaments must be separated from the issue of national security. The book is divided between papers and discussion; the value of both makes this work worthwhile.

121 *Disarmament: Who's Against?* Moscow: Military Publishing House, 1983. 62pp.

This booklet compares the policies on nuclear and conventional arms limitation between the Soviet bloc and NATO. It has a pro-Soviet viewpoint; so much so that the authors claim that the United States wants the USSR to disarm unilaterally. Peace from "positions of strength" in the U.S. negotiating stance means to them a dictated peace on U.S. terms. While this treatise has several bias flaws, the statistical tables on Warsaw and NATO troop strengths as of 1980 are most illuminating.

122 *Disarmament and Development: A Global Perspective.* Edited by Pradip K. Ghosh. Westport, CT: Greenwood Press, 1984. 444pp. ISBN 0–313–24153–8.

The interaction between disarmament and economic and social developments in the Third World countries is the focus of this book by the president of the World Academy of Development and Cooperation, Washington, DC. By reversing the arms race, resources can be reallocated to speed up socioeconomic development in less developed regions. Economic development is a necessity for Third World countries because of population pressure. Most of the articles are reprints from other sources, but combining them into a single source makes this book valuable.

123 *Disarming Europe.* Edited by Mary Kaldor and Dan Smith. London: Merlin Press, 1982. 196pp. ISBN 0–85036–277–6.

This book is the product of a conference sponsored by an organization called The Appeal for European Nuclear Disarmament. A peace group formed in 1980, the organization's goal is to educate the general public about the dangers of nuclear war. This series of essays is part of this effort, and neither the Soviet Union nor the United States is immune from attack. The quality of the essays ranges from only fair to excellent.

124 Drell, Sidney D. *Facing the Threat of Nuclear Weapons.* Seattle, WA: University of Washington Press, 1983. 120pp. ISBN 0–295–96082–5.

The author combines his background as a theoretical physicist and a founding member of Stanford University's Arms Control and Disarmament Program to critique past and present nuclear deterrence policies. These criticisms originate from a series of lectures given by the author at the University of Washington, Seattle, in 1983. An added feature is the publication of a letter from Andrei Sakharov commenting on an earlier lecture by the author. Both the lectures and the letter make this book a worthwhile addition to arms control literature.

125 Dunn, Lewis A. *Controlling the Bomb: Nuclear Proliferation in the 1980s.* New Haven, CT: Yale University Press, 1982. 209pp. ISBN 0–300–02820–2.

The author examines current nuclear proliferation trends and U.S. policy. His analysis suggests that the United States is powerless to stop nuclear proliferation, but U.S. policies can curtail the rate of acquisition of nuclear weapons by Third World powers. U.S. policy should concentrate on tightening export controls over nuclear technology, supporting nuclear-free zones, and initiating regional security agreements. This book is a major effort to change U.S. policies toward nuclear proliferation.

126 *The Dynamics of European Nuclear Disarmament.* Rudolf Bahro et al. Nottingham, England: Spokesman, 1981. 306pp. ISBN 0–85124–320–7.

This is a book of essays by prominent members of the European nuclear disarmament movement. The authors maintain that the bankruptcy of the doctrine of deterrence and the danger of nuclear proliferation make nuclear disarmament a necessity. Disarmament movements are growing in Europe to counter U.S. and Soviet warlike strategies. These essays are of mixed quality; several of them are substantial efforts, but others are of a lesser quality.

127 *The Economic Consequences of a Nuclear Freeze.* William D. Hartung et al. New York: Council on Economic Priorities, 1984. 120pp. ISBN 0–87871–023–X.

This book analyzes the economic impact of a nuclear weapons freeze on the United States. While the author and other contributors believe that the fate of a nuclear freeze should rise or fall on its merits as a means of reducing the risks of nuclear war, they recognize that the economic consequence question must be answered. They conclude that the "economic opportunities offered by a nuclear freeze far outweigh its costs," but careful planning and a national approach to economic conversion are necessary to minimize transition problems. Anyone concerned about the economic consequences of a weapons freeze or disarmament should read this book.

128 *The Effects of Nuclear War.* Detroit, MI: Gale Research Company, 1984. 283pp. ISBN 0–8103–0999–8.

This publication is an augmented edition of a work originally published by the Office of Technology Assessment in 1979 on the effects of nuclear war on the populations and economies of the United States and the Soviet Union. This report is the result of the efforts of the Nuclear War Effects Advisory Panel and provides background material for a debate on strategic weapons and foreign policy. The original report has been augmented by two reports projected for a second volume.

129 *Effects of Nuclear War on Health and Health Services.* International Committee of Experts in Medical Sciences and Public Health. Geneva, Switzerland: World Health Organization, 1984. 176pp. ISBN 92–415–6080–0.

The International Committee of Experts in Medical Sciences and Public Health prepared this report on the impact of nuclear war on health and health services for the World Health Organization (WHO). Its conclusion is that no health service is capable of dealing adequately with the effects of a nuclear blast. Projections of deaths, injuries, and health problems of the survivors are examined to understand the complexities of the problem. This report gives a good picture of the medical consequences of a nuclear war.

130 Einhorn, Robert J. *Negotiating from Strength: Leverage in U.S.-Soviet Arms Control Negotiations.* New York: Praeger, 1985. 120pp. ISBN 0–03–004769–2.

The author is a prominent member of the U.S. delegation to the Strategic Arms Reduction Talks with the Soviet Union. In this work he outlines the negotiating strategy of using U.S. weapons systems as bargaining leverage. Leverage theory claims that by introducing new weapons systems into the negotiating process the U.S. negotiating team can modify Soviet negotiating behavior. But the author is cautious about this strategy because he believes that weapons systems should be considered on their merits rather than as bargaining chips. This book gives valuable insights into U.S.-Soviet negotiating tactics.

131   *Ethics and Nuclear Deterrence.* Edited by Geoffrey Goodwin. London: Croom Helm, 1982. 199pp. ISBN 0–7099–1129–7.

This collection of essays deals with the ethical issues raised by deterrence policies and proposals for disarmament and arms control. The Council on Christian Approaches to Defence and Disarmament (CCADD) commissioned these essays in response to a request by the British Council of Churches. A lack of agreement on the role that Christian ethics should play in confronting war reveals the difficulty that philosophers have in dealing with conventional and nuclear war in the modern world.

132   *A European Non-Proliferation Policy: Prospects and Problems.* Edited by Harald Muller. Oxford, England: Clarendon Press, 1987. 416pp. ISBN 0–190829702–5.

The prospects of a European nuclear nonproliferation policy are analyzed in a series of papers published under the auspices of the Centre for European Policy Studies (CEPS). The authors agreed that Europe has the responsibility to be a leader in the nuclear nonproliferation movement. Western European influences on the nuclear threshold countries (Argentina, Brazil, India, Iran, Israel, Libya, Pakistan, and South Africa) are examined for policy options. This book is a major undertaking, and the results are a credit to the authors.

133   *Explosive Remnants of War: Mitigating the Environmental Effects.* Edited by Arthur H. Westing. London: Taylor and Francis, 1985. 141pp. ISBN 0–85066–303–2.

The aftermath of war is explored in this book of essays on the technical aspects of removing explosive remnants. Both case studies and legal arguments are combined to show the need for the adoption of munitions that become automatically deactivated after use in combat. An international standing mechanism is necessary to solve this problem. This book is an excellent introduction to the issue of postwar explosives.

134   Feld, Werner J. *Arms Control and the Atlantic Community.* New York: Praeger, 1987. 144pp. ISBN 0–275–92457–2.

The positions of the various members of the Western alliance on arms control issues in the 1980s are examined in this book. There have been changes of attitude toward arms control during the second Reagan administration, but the U.S. position still remains behind the Western Europeans in the desire for arms control. The author surveys possible arms control agreements with the best prospect in the intermediate-range nuclear weapons category. This book combines a good retrospective overview with first-rate analysis.

135   Fischer, David, and Paul Szasz. *Safeguarding the Atom: A Critical Appraisal.* London: Taylor and Francis, 1985. 243pp. ISBN 0–85066–306–7.

This book is a reappraisal of the safeguards system of the International Atomic Energy Agency from the perspective of an earlier work on the subject a decade before. This earlier work, *Safeguards against Nuclear Proliferation* (1975), and the present version contain critical appraisals and recommendations for ways of improving procedures and for confronting political realities. The safeguards system is of most interest to researchers of arms control and nonproliferation issues. Both the text and appendices on documents make this book an excellent source on proliferation issues.

136 Fischer, Dietrich. *Preventing War in the Nuclear Age.* Totowa, NJ: Rowman and Allanheld, 1984. 236pp. ISBN 0–8476–7342–1.

The intention of this book is to provide solutions to the danger of nuclear war. Emphasis is placed on the adoption of the theory of *transarmament*, or the shift from offensive to defensive arms. The author maintains that by refusing to play the game of aggression the threat of nuclear war can be neutralized, because it takes two states to conduct a war. This approach to arms control is novel, but the conclusions are much too simplistic to solve the arms race.

137 Ford, Daniel, Henry Kendall, and Steven Nadis. *Beyond the Freeze: The Road to Nuclear Sanity.* Boston, MA: Beacon Press, 1982. 132pp. ISBN 0–8070–0484–7.

The authors, three members of the Union of Concerned Scientists, have produced a step-by-step primer on ways to curb the arms race. They advocate a freeze on nuclear weapons because neither technological advances nor large nuclear arsenals will ensure survival. Moreover, the economic benefits of the transfer from military to civilian industrial production will relieve the economy of a drag on its capacity to produce. While this book is an articulate statement of the benefits of a freeze on nuclear weapons, it is not effective as a primer for implementation.

138 Freedman, Lawrence. *Arms Control in Europe.* London: The Royal Institute of International Affairs, 1981. 59pp. ISBN 0–905031–23–7.

The state of arms control negotiations in the early 1980s is the subject of this paper. Despite pressure from European governments for further arms control negotiations, the Reagan administration's policies in Europe have proven counterproductive. NATO's relative military weakness, however, has resulted in negotiations to achieve military parity with the Warsaw Pact forces, but parity is too obscure an issue for conclusion of an arms control agreement. This pessimistic look at arms control in the early 1980s is a solid assessment of the chances of an arms control agreement for Europe.

139 Frei, Daniel. *Assumptions and Perceptions in Disarmament.* New York: United Nations, 1984. 321pp. ISBN 92–904–5006–1.

The author studies the psychological assumptions and perceptions of the major participants in the arms race to understand the failure to disarm. Particular emphasis is placed on the interaction between the Soviet Union and the United States. A survey of the contrasting perceptions indicates that the views of each superpower show striking similarities and a few contrasts. While the conclusions of the author tend on the pessimistic side, this book is, nevertheless, a sincere effort to show the extent to which disarmament is hampered by psychological realities.

140 Frei, Daniel. *Perceived Images: U.S. and Soviet Assumptions and Perceptions in Disarmament.* Totowa, NJ: Rowman and Allanheld, 1986. 323pp. ISBN 0–8476–7443–6.

A Swiss disarmament specialist compares and contrasts U.S. and Soviet perceptions of disarmament issues, concluding that U.S. and Soviet views exhibit striking similarities in thought patterns and language, but differences in worldview. This analysis concludes that the general climate for disarmament and arms control is not favorable because of U.S. and Soviet mindsets. An analysis by a neutral observer, this book is an important contribution for any arms control and disarmament researcher.

141 *From Distrust to Confidence: Concepts, Experiences and Dimensions of Confidence-Building Measures.* Edited by Wolf Graf von Baudissin. Baden-Baden, West Germany: Nomos Verlagsgesellschaft, 1983. 124pp. ISBN 3–798008–40–0.

These papers are the product of a joint 1981 workshop on confidence-building measures (CBM) for arms control and peace negotiations by the Pugwash Symposium and the Institüt für Friedensforschung und Sicherheitspolitik an der Universitat Hamburg. The role of CBM theory in the promotion of SALT and the Helsinki Accords is examined for lessons. These authors are convinced that few settlements are possible without utilization of confidence-building measures. This book is a good indication of the interest among Europeans in CBM.

142 Fry, Greg. *A Nuclear-Free Zone for the Southwest Pacific: Prospects and Significance.* Canberra, Australia: The Strategic and Defence Studies Centre, 1983. 44pp. ISBN 0–86784–354–3.

The Australian government's effort to promote the concept of a nuclear-free zone for the southwestern Pacific is the subject of this paper. A nuclear-free zone for this region has been proposed before by Labor governments, but each time a Conservative government has shelved the issue. The author believes that this time the proposal has a chance for success, and it should be adopted as a first step toward worldwide arms control. This paper is a suggestive treatment of a topic still under debate among southwestern Pacific governments.

143 *The Future of Arms Control.* Edited by Desmond Ball and Andrew Mack. Sydney, Australia: Australian National University Press, 1987. 342pp. ISBN 0–08–033040–1.

A stocktaking of the status of arms control on the international scene is the theme of these essays from a 1985 conference held at the Australian National University, Canberra, Australia, under the auspices of the Strategic and Defence Studies Centre. Arms control efforts have achieved little of significance since the ABM and SALT I treaties, and these authors expect few dramatic policy changes in the late 1980s. They maintain that the future of arms control is tied to the fate of the Strategic Defense Initiative (SDI) and the interaction between the leaders of the two superpowers. These essays are suggestive and argumentative, making this book a major addition to arms control literature.

144 *A Game for High Stakes: Lessons Learned in Negotiating with the Soviet Union.* Edited by Leon Sloss and M. Scott Davis. Cambridge, MA: Ballinger, 1986. 184pp. ISBN 0–88730–072–3.

These papers are a product of a series of seminars on negotiating with the Soviets held under the auspices of the Roosevelt Center for American Policy Studies in 1984. All the participants were veterans of arms control and/or business negotiations with the Soviets. These negotiators believe that agreements are difficult to obtain, but not impossible. This volume has an impressive list of findings, and the papers combine with these findings to form a source not easily rivaled.

145 Garfinkle, Adam M. *The Politics of the Nuclear Freeze.* Philadelphia, PA: Foreign Policy Research Institute, 1984. 254pp. ISBN 0–910191–08–5.

The range of political opinion in U.S. politics on a nuclear freeze is the subject of this book. Five schools of thought on the freeze—the Professional Left, the Far Right, the Left-Liberal Establishment, the Pragmatic Center, and the Conservative Mainstream—are examined. The author maintains that the freeze movement has been so buffeted by conflicting agendas and goals that it has sharpened national disagreements over strategic issues, and in this sense has been counterproductive to arms control agreements. This book's strength is that it shows the political spectrum that any arms control idea must pass through.

146 Garrison, Jim. *The Plutonium Culture: From Hiroshima to Harrisburg.* New York: Continuum, 1980. 275pp. ISBN 0–8264–0029–9.

This book is a history of the development of nuclear weapons and nuclear energy from 1939 to 1979. The author stresses the human dimension rather than the economic, political, and/or scientific parts of the subject. While he is concerned about public safety aspects, nuclear weapons developments and nuclear proliferation are emphasized. This book is intended for the general reader, and it is recommended for this audience.

147 Garthoff, Raymond L. *Policy versus the Law: The Reinterpretation of the ABM Treaty.* Washington, DC: Brookings Institution, 1987. 117pp. ISBN 0–8157–3049–7.

The author, one of the principal negotiators of the Anti-Ballistic Missile Treaty (ABM), utilizes this book to refute the Reagan administration's effort to reinterpret the ABM Treaty to permit work on the Strategic Defense Initiative (SDI). He reviews the treaty point by point to demonstrate that the ABM Treaty bans the development, testing, and deployment of the SDI. His arguments also reinforce the view that the broad interpretation of the ABM Treaty shows weaknesses in the decision-making processes of the U.S. government. Despite its short length, this book is a masterpiece of argument and presentation.

148 Gasteyger, Curt. *Searching for World Security: Understanding Global Armament and Disarmament.* London: Frances Pinter, 1985. 216pp. ISBN 0–86187–562–1.

The author seeks to find the middle ground between the global growth of armaments and disarmament. Studying worldwide arms trends and the expansion of domestic arms production, he emphasizes the dangers of weapon developments and technology. Gasteyger believes that total disarmament is unrealistic at this time, but that arms control is possible if, rather than stabilizing nuclear terror, it is part of a process toward disarmament. This book is a sophisticated analysis of the arms race and disarmament problem and deserves a serious reading.

149 Generals for Peace and Disarmament. *The Arms Race to Armageddon: A Challenge to US/NATO Strategy.* Leamington Spa, England: Berg Publishers, 1984. 151pp. ISBN 0–907582–26–5.

A critical analysis of the introduction of more nuclear weapons into Europe is presented in this book by the Generals for Peace and Disarmament.

These military men, mostly former NATO generals and admirals, are critical of present NATO policies and propose that the European allies regain control of their defense policies. They maintain that the Reagan administration's disregard for positive arms negotiations and U.S. control over NATO have increased the chances of nuclear war. This critique of NATO by retired senior officers serves to balance the debate over NATO.

150 *Gerard Piel on Arms Control: Science and Economics.* Edited by Kenneth W. Thompson. Lanham, MD: University Press of America, 1987. 84pp. ISBN 0–8191–6385–6.

These essays on science policy and arms control by the chairman of the board of *Scientific American* are the culmination of nearly four decades of writings on these topics. Although most of the contributions are reprints of earlier essays, the issue of the nuclear arms race remains the central theme. The author is most concerned with the contributions science can make toward arms control and disarmament, and the economics of disarmament. Despite the age of many of the essays, the author's views still have relevance for scholars in the field of arms control and disarmament.

151 *Gerard Smith on Arms Control.* Edited by Kenneth W. Thompson. Lanham, MD: University Press of America, 1987. 270pp. ISBN 0–8191–6450–X.

The author, the chief U.S. delegate to the Strategic Arms Limitations Talks (SALT) held in Helsinki and Vienna and now the chairman of the board of the Arms Control Association in Washington, DC, has compiled a collection of thirty-six articles and speeches expressing his views on arms control issues. He demonstrates in this material that arms control agreements are possible, even in the post-SALT environment. His views are less optimistic on the impact of the Strategic Defense Initiative (SDI) on arms control talks. It is the combination of the author's negotiating experience and the quality of his contributions that makes this collection of writings important.

152 *Global Perspectives on Arms Control.* Edited by Adam M. Garfinkle. New York: Praeger, 1984. 172pp. ISBN 0–03–069658–5.

These papers originate from the Seventh International Arms Control Symposium (SIACS), sponsored by the Foreign Policy Research Institute (FPRI), in Philadelphia in 1982. An international cast of scholars assembled to discuss papers on differing perspectives on arms control. While no consensus developed during this symposium, the variety of viewpoints from contributors made the gathering worthwhile. This book presents a number of solid papers, but the most intriguing contribution is an objective piece of scholarship by the Soviet participant.

153 Goetze, Bernd A. *Security in Europe: A Crisis of Confidence.* New York: Praeger, 1984. 225pp. ISBN 0–03–001089–6.

The East-West rivalry in Europe and the efforts to ease these tensions are examined in this book authored by a Canadian specialist in security affairs. Goetze maintains that arms control is necessary to prevent further escalation of the arms race in Europe. He proposes a five-phase process using the Conference on Security and Cooperation in Europe (CSCE) framework. This book is a positive but realistic assessment of the necessity for arms control in Europe.

154 Gray, Colin S., and Keith B. Payne. *SALT: Deep Force Level Reductions: Final Report.* Croton-on-Hudson, NY: Hudson Institute, 1981. 141pp.

Two critics of the SALT agreements prepared this report for the SALT/ Arms Control Support Group, Secretary of Defense (Atomic Energy). They indicate that the deep reductions in strategic force level in SALT II and envisaged in SALT III are not feasible. There is a need for a U.S. denial of victory strategy that will cause the Soviet Union to pause in its expansionist policies. This report argues against SALT III, and the authors were gratified over the SALT II defeat.

155 *Hedley Bull on Arms Control.* Selected by Robert O'Neill and David N. Schwartz. Houndmills, England: Macmillan, 1987. 302pp. ISBN 0–333–43592–3.

This volume is a collection of essays from the writings of one of Great Britain's foremost authorities on arms control. The author's death in 1985 and his preeminence in the field led two British scholars to produce this book of his most significant work on arms control. Bull was both a critic and an advocate of arms control, and his writings reveal the intellectual depth of his scholarship. This book is a lasting legacy from an outstanding scholar in the field of arms control.

156 Holst, Johan J. *Arms Control as Defense Policy.* Oslo, Norway: Norsk Utenrikspolitisk Institutt, 1981. 20pp.

The integration of arms control into defense policy is the subject of this paper. "A prudent defense policy should incorporate and contribute to arms control" is the viewpoint of the author. But arms control cannot be instituted in a political vacuum, and this is the reason that linkage between specific negotiations on arms control and international behavior is a faulty policy. This paper's argument for arms control negotiations as part of NATO defense strategy is worth noting.

157 Holst, Johan J. *Arms Control for the 1980's: A European Perspective.* Oslo, Norway: Norsk Utenrikspolitisk Institutt, 1983. 12pp.

Arms control as an integral element of a prudent international security policy is the theme of this paper. While arms control cannot substitute for a defense policy, it can be a necessary complement of such a policy. By its rigid stance on arms control, the U.S. is alienating European public opinion, but the author is in favor of reducing weapons systems as advocated by Reagan administration proposals. This paper is a quality product by Norway's foremost security analyst.

158 Hussain, Farooq. *The Future of Arms Control: Part IV: The Impact of Weapons Test Restrictions.* London: International Institute for Strategic Studies, 1981. 55pp. ISBN 0–86079–039–8.

Consideration of restricting the testing of strategic weapons as an arms control measure is studied in this paper. By examining general technological processes underlying nuclear weapons and ballistic missile developments, the author seeks to gauge the influence of testing weapons development. The author concludes that restrictions on testing slow the rate of progress, but the more serious political problem remains verification. This paper looks at a specific problem, but it does so in a superior manner.

159 *In Quest of Nuclear Disarmament: Proceedings of the Asahi International Symposium.* Tokyo: Asahi Evening News, 1983. 144pp.

A Tokyo newspaper, the *Asahi Evening News*, sponsored this symposium on the present state of disarmament. Eleven representatives from Japan and Western nations participated. While all participants agreed that the arms race has increased and the disarmament movement has weakened, they also concluded that the necessity for disarmament is more imperative than ever. Little new information is contained in this publication, but the viewpoints are informative.

160 The Independent Commission on Disarmament and Security Issues. *Common Security: A Blueprint for Survival*. New York: Simon and Schuster, 1982. 202pp. ISBN 0–671–45880–9.

The Independent Commission on Disarmament and Security Issues, or the Palme Commission, is an organization founded in 1980 whose members are present and former government officials from a variety of countries. Because of differing viewpoints, there are only a few issues that most members can agree upon, but one such issue is the need for progress in U.S.-Soviet negotiations on nuclear weapons. The blueprint for this organization is a strategy of common security based upon general disarmament. This book is valuable not only for the information contained within it, but also because of the issuing organization.

161 *The International Nuclear Non-Proliferation System: Challenges and Choices*. Edited by John Simpson and Anthony G. McGrew. New York: St. Martin's Press, 1984. 209pp. ISBN 0–312–42296–2.

These papers are the product of a 1982 seminar on the fate of the Non-Proliferation Treaty (NPT) held in London. The NPT comes up for renewal in 1995, and there are fears that Third World dissatisfaction with the implementation will lead to its demise. This dissatisfaction is noted in these papers, and, unless there is more of a commitment to nonproliferation by the superpowers and the system works more efficiently, the NPT will lapse. These papers make a solid contribution to an understanding of nonproliferation issues and the future of the NPT.

162 Issraelyan, Victor L., and Charles C. Flowerree. *Radiological Weapons Control: A Soviet and US Perspective*. Muscatine, IA: Stanley Foundation, 1982. 30pp. ISSN 0145–8841.

Control of radiological weapons is the subject of these two essays from U.S. and Soviet representatives of the arms control negotiating teams. Use of radiological material weapons has been considered as a potential weapon by both superpowers, but these representatives from the two major powers argue against their deployment and use. Both authors agree that there is a need for an arms control agreement to cover radiological weapons. While neither essay breaks new ground, it is interesting to note that both representatives use the same type of language and similar logic.

163 Jabber, Paul. *Not by War Alone: Security and Arms Control in the Middle East*. Berkeley, CA: University of California Press, 1981. 212pp. ISBN 0–520–04050–3.

This book critically examines the possibility of arms control in the Middle East. Despite some arms control efforts by the United States in the late 1970s, arms transfers to the Middle East have continued at a steady rate. Only multinational action by agreement among all the major arms exporters offers realistic chances for lasting reductions in the international arms trade to this region. This book is a solid assessment of the failure to control arms transfers into one of the most politically volatile regions in the world.

164 Jasani, Bhupendra, and Frank Barnaby. *Verification Technologies: The Case for Surveillance by Consent.* Leamington Spa, England: Berg Publishers, 1984. 130pp. ISBN 0–907582–28–1.

The authors give an overview of the mechanisms for effective weapon verification. Such techniques of verification as on-site, satellite, seismic monitoring, and nonseismic detection are analyzed for effectiveness. Other useful features are the summary of multilateral arms control agreements from 1925 to the present, and the U.S. and United Kingdom's proposals on chemical weapons. This source provides valuable background information on current verification technologies.

165 Johansen, Robert C. *Toward an Alternative Security System: Moving beyond the Balance of Power in the Search for World Security.* New York: World Policy Institute, 1983. 57pp. ISBN 0–911646–12–5.

The author analyzes various international relations policy models in an effort to reexamine international security. Johansen claims that a balance of power system no longer works because technological changes and their military consequences have altered the power structure. Arms control, a freeze on testing, international agreements, and nuclear-free zones will ensure an alternative security system. This short paper is a positive approach to an old problem, and the conclusions require some serious thinking.

166 Jones, Rodney W. *Small Nuclear Forces.* New York: Praeger, 1984. 128pp. ISBN 0–03–063418–0.

This study is an analysis of nuclear proliferation to the smaller states of the Middle East and South Asia and the extent to which the possession of nuclear weapons by these states will destabilize the international situation. Acquisition of nuclear weapons by developing countries will have serious implications for both the Soviet Union and the United States. The author recommends a blend of preventive policies and crisis management to minimize potential damage from small nuclear forces. While this book is a major contribution to the understanding of nuclear proliferation, Jones's remedies fall far short of dealing with the problem.

167 Joyce, James Avery. *The War Machine: The Case against the Arms Race.* London: Quartet Books, 1980. 210pp. ISBN 0–7043–2254–4.

This work chronicles the rivalry between the Soviet Union and the United States for military supremacy. Disarmament is the only way to end this rivalry, and the utilization of the United Nations for disarmament is the best chance for success. Smaller countries can take the lead in pressuring the superpowers toward disarmament. This book is more a plea for disarmament than an analysis of the arms race, but it has valuable suggestions for both ending the arms race and beginning disarmament.

168 Katz, Milton S. *Ban the Bomb: A History of SANE, the Committee for a Sane Nuclear Policy, 1957–1985.* New York: Greenwood Press, 1986. 215pp. ISBN 0–313–24167–8.

This book is a history of the largest and most influential nuclear disarmament organization in the United States. From its beginning in 1957, SANE has used direct-action methods to persuade and to protest in an effort to change government policy. While this organization has never accomplished its goal of reducing nuclear arms, it is still active in nuclear arms control educational efforts. This book is a solid history of SANE, and the author has done a service for other researchers in the field.

169   Kaul, B. N. *Disarmament Dilemma.* New Delhi: Pulse Publishers, 1984. 288pp.
The author analyzes the causes of the international arms race and attributes the main responsibility for it and the failure of disarmament to the ruling classes of the West. He places most of the blame on past and present U.S. political leaders. In contrast, Kaul claims that the Soviet Union has made positive arms control and disarmament proposals, most of which are worthy of serious consideration. While this book is neither objective nor scholarly, its pro-Soviet orientation makes it a source noteworthy for its viewpoint.

170   Keliher, John G. *The Negotiations on Mutual and Balanced Force Reductions: The Search for Arms Control in Central Europe.* New York: Pergamon Press, 1980. 204pp. ISBN 0–08–025764–2.
This book is an assessment of the negotiations on Mutual and Balanced Force Reductions (MBFR) by a former member of the U.S. MBFR delegation. The author maintains that unacceptable proposals have been made by both sides, resulting in stalemated negotiations. U.S. efforts to prevent the threat of a surprise attack by the Warsaw Pact forces have hindered agreement. The difficulties of reaching an arms reduction treaty are highlighted in this study.

171   Kennedy, Robert. *START: Problems and Prospects.* Carlisle Barracks, PA: Strategic Studies Institute, 1983. 38pp.
The author, a professor at the U.S. Army War College, surveys the history of SALT negotiations for clues for the possible renewal of arms limitation talks. Kennedy believes that despite a chill in the relationship between the Soviet Union and the United States in the late 1970s and early 1980s, most of the reasons for negotiating arms control pacts remain. He concludes that there is reason for guarded optimism on reopening arms control negotiations. This short analysis is a solid interpretation of the superpowers' underlying principles and their negotiating stances.

172   Kenny, Anthony. *The Logic of Deterrence.* London: Firethorn Press, 1985. 103pp. ISBN 0–947752–07–2.
This book is advertized as a philosopher's look at the pro and con arguments on nuclear disarmament, but the key issue for the author is the effectiveness of the doctrine of deterrence. His objection to deterrence is that it is based on an uncertain calculation of risk, and he argues instead for a prudent and gradual program for disarmament. This book is a different approach toward the goal of disarmament and deserves a serious reading.

173   Krass, Allan S. *Verification: How Much Is Enough?* London: Taylor and Francis, 1985. 271pp. ISBN 0–85066–305–9.
Both the technological and the political issues of arms control verification, which has become the crucial issue in arms control negotiations between the United States and the Soviet Union, are dealt with in this book. Krass maintains that, while the technology has been developed for arms control verification, it is the political climate that needs to be altered before any

verification system can work. This book makes a positive contribution by outlining the benefits and the problems of verification.

174 Krepon, Michael. *Strategic Stalemate: Nuclear Weapons and Arms Control in American Politics.* New York: St. Martin's Press, 1984. 191pp. ISBN 0–312–76434–0.

The difficulty of achieving a consensus in U.S. politics over nuclear weapons and arms control is the subject of this book. U.S. arms control experts and the general public are so divided over the nuclear arms control debate that a stalemate has developed. This stalemate can only be broken by the formation of a broad coalition in favor of an arms control agreement with phased reductions, overall parity, and greater survivability in nuclear forces. This book is a solid effort to trace the difficulty of achieving arms control in the present U.S. political climate.

175 Lehman, John F., and Seymour Weiss. *Beyond the SALT II Failure.* New York: Praeger, 1981. 195pp. ISBN 0–03–059448–0.

Two experts on the SALT II Treaty have collected their essays on the treaty and published them in this book. Both authors argue that the SALT II Treaty was seriously flawed and that the United States needs to rebuild its military forces to regain strategic superiority. They criticize the Carter administration for reducing the military budget, and, instead, propose an increase of $30 billion in additional funding. Most of the criticism in these essays has been adopted as fact by the Reagan administration, and this book should be read as the harbinger of the Reagan administration's arms control and defense strategy.

176 Leitenberg, Milton. *The Neutron Bomb and European Arms Control.* Los Angeles, CA: Center for the Study of Armament and Disarmament, 1983. 55pp.

This study is a reprint of an article in the *Journal of Strategic Studies* (1982) with an expanded bibliography by Leon Wazak. The author believes that the neutron bomb, or enhanced radiation warheads (ERW), are counterproductive and dangerous for Western Europe and totally useless in the United States. Further, he believes that the introduction of these weapons in a European crisis would escalate any crisis in this theater to total war. The quality of this essay is so high it is not surprising it has been republished in this format.

177 *Lessons before Midnight: Educating for Reason in Nuclear Matters.* By John Austin Baker, Bishop of Salisbury et al. London: Institute of Education, University of London, 1984. 72pp. ISBN 0–85473–187–X.

These essays on educating the British public about the dangers of nuclear war are a supplement to the Bishop of Salisbury's lecture, "The Future and the Bomb." The bishop's lecture called for a campaign of public education on the dangers of nuclear weapons and nuclear warfare. Complementary articles embellish this theme. This book should be considered as a political statement by the British disarmament movement in support of nuclear disarmament.

178 *Limiting Nuclear Proliferation.* Edited by Jed C. Snyder and Samuel F. Wells. Cambridge, MA: Ballinger, 1985. 363pp. ISBN 0–88730–042–1.

A number of experts on nuclear proliferation have produced this series of essays on the present and future growth of the nuclear club. Nonsuperpower proliferation remains a growing danger, and the number of threshold states will increase by the turn of the century. There is an ongoing need for East-West cooperation to retard the growth of the nuclear community. This book provides a serious look at a problem that is, at present, not in favor with the Reagan administration.

179 Longstreth, Thomas K., and John B. Rhinelander. *The Impact of U.S. and Soviet Ballistic Missile Defense Programs on the ABM Treaty*, 3d ed. Washington, DC: National Campaign to Save the ABM Treaty, 1985. 99pp.

This report assesses the impact of Soviet and U.S. antimissile programs on the Anti-Ballistic Missile (ABM) Treaty. It concludes that the present and future U.S. and Soviet antimissile systems threaten the ABM Treaty. Particular emphasis is placed on the destabilizing influence of the Reagan administration's Strategic Defense Initiative (SDI). This defense of the ABM Treaty and the charges against both the Soviet Union and the United States make this report worth reading.

180 *Maintaining Outer Space for Peaceful Uses*. Edited by Nandasiri Jasentuliyana. Tokyo: The United Nations University, 1984. 332pp. ISBN 92-8080-53-71.

These papers originate from a 1984 symposium entitled "Conditions Essential for Maintaining Outer Space for Peaceful Uses" at The Hague, the Netherlands. The participants shared a fear of the extension of the arms race into outer space and the resulting potential for future conflict there. International agreements and laws were proposed to safeguard outer space for peaceful uses. An international cast of scholars produced these papers, and most of their contributions have substantial merit.

181 Malcomson, Robert W. *Nuclear Fallacies: How We Have Been Misguided since Hiroshima*. Kingston, Canada: McGill-Queen's University Press, 1985. 152pp. ISBN 0-7735-0585-7.

This book is a historical analysis of the nuclear arms race since 1945. The author is most concerned about the way the political culture has adapted to this new nuclear technology. He maintains that the nuclear powers have lost control of their nuclear technology. While interpretation and synthesis was the intent of the author, the analysis is not sufficiently sophisticated to be of much use other than for background purposes or introductory college-level coursework.

182 Maresca, John J. *To Helsinki: The Conference on Security and Cooperation in Europe, 1973–1975*. Durham, NC: Duke University Press, 1985. 292pp. ISBN 0-8223-0652-2.

The author is a career Foreign Service officer, and he writes about the Conference on Security and Cooperation in Europe (CSCE) negotiations leading up to the Helsinki Accords. As part of the U.S. delegation in the CSCE negotiations, he witnessed the compromises necessary for the success of Helsinki. Helsinki marked the high point of détente, and from 1975 onwards the U.S. government's attitude toward Helsinki matched its deteriorating regard for détente. This book is an important source on the history of the Helsinki Accords and NATO negotiating tactics.

183 Markey, Edward J., and Douglas C. Waller. *Nuclear Peril: The Politics of Proliferation*. Cambridge, MA: Ballinger, 1982. 183pp. ISBN 0-88410-892-9.

The authors, a congressman from Massachusetts and his senior legislative assistant for arms control and nuclear proliferation, have written this book to warn of the dangers of present U.S. nonproliferation policies. The authors examine causes of nuclear proliferation and its relationship to the arms race in the context of current U.S. policies, maintaining that nuclear power must be phased out by the United States before meaningful nonproliferation policies can work on the international scene. This book is more a critique of present U.S. nonproliferation policies than a scholarly assessment.

184 May, Brian. *Russia, America, the Bomb and the Fall of Western Europe.* London: Routledge and Kegan Paul, 1984. 248pp. ISBN 0–7100–9757–3.

The author foresees a moral crisis overwhelming both the East and the West unless positive steps are undertaken toward disarmament. Atomic annihilation and environmental pollution are the twin dangers facing both the Soviet Union and the Western states. The antinuclear movement is a step in the right direction toward reform. This book follows the Toynbee thesis of a moral decline of the West, but with a modern twist.

185 McNamara, Robert S., and Hans A. Bethe. *Reducing the Risk of Nuclear War: Geneva Can Be a Giant Step toward a More Secure Twenty-first Century.* Washington, DC: McNamara, 1985. 14pp.

This policy statement by a former secretary of defense and a prominent physicist is an adaptation of an article in the *Atlantic Monthly*. Both agree that arms control negotiations at Geneva are an opportunity for positive achievement, but that the Strategic Defense Initiative (SDI) will end this initiative. The authors believe that the Reagan administration is pursuing "the right problem with the wrong solution." This study is an articulate critique of present arms control negotiating strategy.

186 Menos, Dennis. *World at Risk: The Debate over Arms Control.* Jefferson, NC: McFarland, 1986. 133pp. ISBN 0–89950–237–7.

This book is a treatment of the basic issues of nuclear arms control by an arms control specialist. The author intended for this work to help laypersons understand the status of arms control today and the chances of progress for the future. While there have been some advances toward arms control in the past, the future of arms control depends on the superpowers and their future negotiating stances. This book is the best general work on the present status of arms control on the market.

187 Meyer, Stephen M. *The Dynamics of Nuclear Proliferation.* Chicago: University of Chicago Press, 1984. 229pp. ISBN 0–226–52148–6.

The author uses this book to study the capabilities and incentives for states to develop nuclear weapons. He is particularly concerned whether there is a technological imperative in proliferation, or whether politico-military forces are more important. He concludes that there is no technological imperative; instead, there is a complex series of motivational profiles that produce nuclear proliferation. This book shows the difficulty of preventing proliferation without understanding the political process.

188 *Militarization and Arms Production.* Edited by Helena Tuomi and Raimo Vayrynen. New York: St. Martin's Press, 1983. 310pp. ISBN 0–312–53255–5.

This book of essays, from a 1981 international seminar sponsored by the Tampere Peace Research Institute (TAPRT) at Tampere, Finland, studies militarization and disarmament as options in worldwide economic development. A consensus developed that militarization by means of building armament industries or purchasing foreign military weapons is counterproductive to economic development. Disarmament and conversion of economic resources to the domestic and/or international markets promote economic development. This book provides a wealth of useful information on the relationship of militarization to economic development.

189 Molander, Roger, and Robbie Nichols. *Who Will Stop the Bomb: A Primer on Nuclear Proliferation.* New York: Facts on File, 1985. 150pp. ISBN 0–8160–1283–0.

The Roosevelt Center for American Policy Studies sponsored this book on the dangers of nuclear proliferation. Both authors envisage a world where maverick states and terrorists will have access to nuclear weapons and the prospect terrifies them. They maintain that more vigorous enforcement of nonproliferation policies by the U.S. government will help control proliferation, as will more public involvement. This work is more a warning than a scholarly treatise, but it contains some interesting charts and maps.

190 Murphy, Sean, Alastair Hay, and Steven Rose. *No Fire, No Thunder: The Threat of Chemical and Biological Weapons.* London: Pluto Press, 1984. 145pp. ISBN 0–86104–738–9.

The authors study the status of chemical and biological weapons (CBW) in the arms race. Both superpowers are in the middle of building their CBW arsenals. The authors seek a ban on CBW in Europe as the first step in a global banning. This book posits a reasoned argument against chemical and biological weapons, and it is both a timely and important reference.

191 Myrdal, Alva. *The Game of Disarmament: How the United States and Russia Run the Arms Race,* rev. ed. New York: Pantheon Books, 1982. 433pp. ISBN 0–394–70649–8.

The author advances the thesis that neither the Soviet Union nor the United States has made a serious effort to negotiate disarmament. Arms control is a myth since it does so little to lessen the chances of nuclear war, but it is better than nothing. The growing antagonism between the superpowers has increased since the Reagan administration took office, but the responsibility for increased tensions should be shared by both powers. This book by one of Sweden's most respected authors is an indictment of the policies of both superpowers.

192 *Navies and Arms Control.* Edited by George H. Quester. New York: Praeger, 1980. 212pp. ISBN 0–03–056847–1.

The possibility of including naval forces into arms control agreements is the subject of this book of essays by naval authorities. Since the rapid increase in Soviet naval forces, naval arms control has become a serious issue. Strategic and tactical considerations are making the Western naval leaders consider the possibility of smaller and more mobile ships and larger fleets in the future. Arms control for naval forces has not been discussed in recent arms control talks, but this book makes a case that these types of talks should be considered in the future.

193 Neild, Robert. *How to Make Up Your Mind about the Bomb*. London: Andre Deutsch, 1981. 144pp. ISBN 0–233–97382–6.

A British economics professor addresses whether nuclear weapons are appropriate for Great Britain. He assesses the risks and benefits of nuclear weapons and concludes that nuclear disarmament is in Great Britain's best interests. Unilateral disarmament is proposed in stages, with Great Britain using itself as an example to take a leading role in international disarmament. This book is oriented toward the British general reader and therefore has limited interest for U.S. readers.

194 *New Directions in Disarmament*. Edited by William Epstein and Bernard T. Feld. New York: Praeger, 1981. 222pp. ISBN 0–03–059366–2.

Twenty scientists from eight countries participated in the 1980 Pugwash International Symposium on Disarmament in Racine, Wisconsin. These papers are a product of this symposium, and they cover the spectrum of subjects on disarmament. All participants agree that stopping the arms race is imperative, because weapons technology is expanding at a dangerous rate. Both the variety of the disarmament topics and the quality of the papers make this book an excellent source for disarmament studies.

195 *Nonproliferation: 1980s*. Muscatine, IA: Stanley Foundation, 1980. 56pp.

This booklet is a report from the Stanley Foundation from a 1980 conference on nonproliferation held in Vienna, Austria, where twenty-four participants from sixteen countries discussed the problems of nuclear proliferation. The need to strengthen the international nonproliferation regime was agreed upon, but there was considerable uncertainty over the best way to accomplish this. This report shows the diversity of opinion and the difficulty of implementing measures to control nuclear proliferation.

196 *The Nonproliferation Predicament*. Edited by Joseph F. Pilat. New Brunswick, NJ: Transaction Books, 1985. 137pp. ISBN 0–88738–047–6.

This book of essays highlights the successes and the future of the international policy of nonproliferation of nuclear weapons. Nonproliferation has worked because the nonnuclear weapon states have had political, economic, and/or technological limitations preventing them from joining the nuclear club. All of the authors are supportive of nonproliferation efforts, but most of them believe that changes will have to occur in the international arena to prevent proliferation. These essays are of a high quality, making for a solid book.

197 *Nuclear Armament and Disarmament*. Edited by Marvin E. Wolfgang and Robert H. Kupperman. Beverly Hills, CA: Sage, 1983. 213pp. ISBN 0–803–2115–2.

These essays on nuclear weapons and arms control are a product of the American Academy of Political and Social Science and its bimonthly publication, *The Annals* (vol. 469). A variety of viewpoints on nuclear disarmament were solicited by the editors, and the results indicate that this effort was successful. Nearly all of the articles deal with some aspect of arms control and/or disarmament, either pro or con. These articles are all high caliber and worth serious study.

198 *Nuclear Arms Control: Options for the 1980s*. By Philip J. Farley et al. Washington, DC: Arms Control Association, 1983. 58pp.

These short articles on arms control issues by arms control experts comprise an effort to influence the Strategic Arms Reduction Talks (START) negotiations. The Arms Control Association commissioned these articles, and the pro–arms control message of the contributions is apparent. Charts and tables on weapons systems are the strength of this book. This work is a lobbying effort for arms control, and, as such, is effective.

199 *The Nuclear Debate: Issues and Politics.* Edited by Phil Williams. London: Routledge and Kegan Paul, 1984. 81pp. ISBN 0–7102–0313–6.

Four British scholars assess the status of arms control after the breakdown of the Intermediate Nuclear Forces (INF) disarmament talks in Geneva in November 1983. Each paper addresses an aspect of the issue, from the introduction of U.S. missiles to the growth of the European peace movement. All of the authors are uncertain over the long-range implications of the breakdown of the talks on renewal of negotiations or growth of the peace movement. While these essays deal with substantive issues, they also show the dangers of assessing the situation so close to the events.

200 *Nuclear Exports and World Politics: Policy and Regime.* Edited by Robert Boardman and James F. Keeley. New York: St. Martin's Press, 1983. 256pp. ISBN 0–312–57976–4.

Canadian and Western European specialists on nuclear proliferation produced these essays on the effectiveness of nuclear nonproliferation. The nuclear exporting countries examined for policy decision making are Australia, Canada, France, Great Britain, the United States, and West Germany. A central characteristic of each of these countries is that they have responded to international nuclear issues on the basis of foreign policy considerations. The benefit of this book is that it traces nonproliferation issues from the perspective of the exporting state.

201 *Nuclear-Free Zones.* Edited by David Pitt and Gordon Thompson. London: Croom Helm, 1987. 145pp. ISBN 0–7099–4076–9.

These papers on nuclear-free zones (NFZ) are the product of the Geneva International Peace Research Institute's (GIPRI) research program. The idea of nuclear weapon–free zones has become popular because of strong public opinion in favor of such zones. Most of the contributors to this book come from small countries where nuclear-free zones have the most vocal adherents. While this pro-zones viewpoint is challenged by the editors, it is the pro and con aspect of this work that makes it worth reading.

202 *The Nuclear Freeze Controversy.* Edited by Keith B. Payne and Colin S. Gray. Lanham, MD: Abt Books, 1984. 179pp. ISBN 0–8191–4364–2.

The goal of this book is to present the viewpoints of partisans and opponents of a mutual U.S.-Soviet freeze on the testing, production, and deployment of nuclear weapons. However, both editors believe that a nuclear freeze is an unacceptable option, and most of the papers reflect this viewpoint. Considerable space is devoted to defending the defense and budgetary requests of the Reagan administration against the arguments of the nuclear freeze proponents. While this book makes only a pretense at presenting both sides of the issue, this does not detract from the scholarship in the papers presented.

203 *Nuclear Negotiations: Reassessing Arms Control Goals in U.S.-Soviet Relations.* Edited by Alan F. Neidle. Austin, TX: Lyndon B. Johnson School of Public Affairs, 1982. 166pp. ISBN 0–89940–004–3.

These essays originate out of a 1982 symposium on arms control and disarmament at the University of Texas in Austin, where fourteen of the nation's leading arms control authorities presented papers and discussed arms control topics. While most of the participants were pessimistic over present and future arms control negotiations, they were favorable toward the process of negotiations between the superpowers. This book's strong point is the variety of opinions expressed by the members of the symposium, but many of the contributions were on the weak side.

204 *Nuclear Non-Proliferation and Global Security.* Edited by David B. Dewitt. London: Croom Helm, 1987. 283pp. ISBN 0–7099–0896–2.

These papers on nuclear proliferation security problems are the product of a 1985 conference at York University, Toronto. Most of the papers are concerned with the third review of the Non-Proliferation of Nuclear Weapons (NPT) Treaty and the lack of progress in controlling nuclear proliferation. These authors maintain that the acquisition of nuclear weapons is a destabilizing factor in the relations between Third World countries. This book contains a number of excellent papers on proliferation topics, and the enumeration of specific nuclear proliferation security problems makes it a good source of proliferation issues.

205 *The Nuclear Non-Proliferation Treaty.* Edited by Ian Bellany, Coit D. Blacker, and Joseph Gallacher. London: Frank Cass, 1985. 134pp. ISBN 0–7146–3250–3.

This book of essays by British academics deals with the state of opinion on the Nuclear Non-Proliferation Treaty (NPT) after nearly twenty years of this treaty in force. The authors agree that, with minor exceptions, the treaty has held up well under considerable stress, but the future course is not so favorable. Noncompliance and hostility by Third World countries endanger the renewal of the NPT. All the essays are valuable contributions to understanding the functioning of the treaty.

206 *Nuclear Proliferation in the 1980s: Perspectives and Proposals.* Edited by William H. Kincade and Christoph Bertram. New York: St. Martin's Press, 1982. 272pp. ISBN 0–312–57975–6.

The effectiveness of the Nuclear Non-Proliferation Treaty (NPT) is critiqued in these essays by young scholars from Western and Third World countries. Despite the apparent success of the NPT in limiting the number of new nuclear weapon states in the 1970s, there is growing evidence that several states will acquire nuclear weapon capability in the 1980s. Factors include advances in nuclear technology, increases in fuel costs, shifts in U.S. nonproliferation policy, limitations of preventive measures, delays in superpower arms control, and an increase in regional tensions. These scholars express their skepticism about the success of nonproliferation policies of the NPT.

207 *Nuclear War and Nuclear Peace.* By Gerald Segal et al. London: Macmillan, 1983. 162pp. ISBN 0–333–34087–6.

Four young academics authored this book in an effort to find the middle ground on the nuclear warfare issue. All agree that control and reduction rather than elimination of nuclear weapons has the best chance for success, claiming that deep cuts in nuclear inventories are necessary to reduce the totals below those necessary for a secure second strike. This book is a balanced assessment of the problem of nuclear weapons, and it deserves a reading.

208 *The Nuclear Weapons Freeze and Arms Control.* Edited by Steven E. Miller. Cambridge, MA: Ballinger, 1984. 204pp. ISBN 0–88730–010–3.

This book is a product of a conference held in early 1983, the purpose of which was to study the divergence of opinion between the supporters of arms control and backers of the nuclear freeze movement. By bringing together arms control and nuclear freeze proponents, this conference hoped to bridge the differences between the two sides. The papers show, however, that there are such substantial differences between the positions that little compromise is possible. This book reveals the breadth of the arms control and freeze debate, and, for this reason, is a valuable addition to arms control literature.

209 *Nuclear Weapons Proliferation and Nuclear Risk.* Edited by James A. Schear. Aldershot, England: Gower, 1984. 185pp. ISBN 0–566–00677–4.

These essays by prominent specialists on nuclear weapons survey the future of nuclear deterrence and stability. Three themes are examined: (1) the dilemmas posed by the potential use of nuclear weapons; (2) proliferation of nuclear systems; and (3) control of nuclear weapons. There are at least two essays on each of these themes. While no consensus is developed, each essay is useful for further research.

210 *Obstacles to Disarmament and Ways of Overcoming Them.* Edited by Swadesh Rana. Paris: Unesco Press, 1981. 233pp. ISBN 92–3–101879–5.

This book was prepared in response to a request by the 1978 disarmament session of the United Nations to provide disarmament education. An international cast of experts assembled in Paris in April 1978 to discuss obstacles to international disarmament. The result is a series of essays on ways to demilitarize education and promote the educational goals of disarmament. The authors have difficulty isolating the obstacles to disarmament, and even more trouble with solutions.

211 O'Heffernan, Patrick, Amory B. Lovins, and L. Hunter Lovins. *The First Nuclear World War: A Strategy for Preventing Nuclear Wars and the Spread of Nuclear Weapons.* New York: William Morrow, 1983. 444pp. ISBN 0–688–01589–1.

The dangers of nuclear proliferation in building momentum for a nuclear war are examined in this book by three U.S. authors. Their thesis is that proliferation of nuclear weapons to Third World countries is likely to cause the first nuclear war in one of the following regions: the Middle East, South Asia, or Latin America. Various scenarios are considered for the start of a nuclear war, and the results are used by the authors to argue for increasing nonproliferation measures. This book is a popularized version of studies in the academic world, and it is best recommended as a source for use by the general public.

212 O'Keefe, Bernard J. *Nuclear Hostages.* Boston, MA: Houghton Mifflin, 1983. 252pp. ISBN 0–395–34072–1.

The author, a U.S. businessman in the nuclear arms industry, surveys the history of nuclear energy for the development of nuclear weapons. His thesis is that the development of nuclear weapons has made hostages of the populations of the two superpower blocs. The strategic doctrine of deterrence has worked, but it cannot be expected to work indefinitely; therefore, some form of disarmament must be devised. This book offers little new information for the specialist, but it has value for the general reader.

213 Payne, Samuel B. *The Soviet Union and SALT.* Cambridge, MA: MIT Press, 1980. 155pp. ISBN 0–262–16077–3.

A U.S. scholar studies the arms control policies of the Soviet Union and its record on the initial SALT agreements. While there were serious differences of opinion within the Soviet ruling elite on the SALT agreements, the doctrinal differences between arms controllers and militarists narrowed by the end of SALT II negotiations. The Soviets fear negotiating from weakness, and the SALT agreements avoided this problem. The author's viewpoint is pro-SALT, but his belief that no agreement will prevent the Soviet Union from seeking more influence on the international scene makes this book a realistic assessment of a difficult topic.

214 *The Political Economy of Arms Reduction: Reversing Economic Decay.* Edited by Lloyd J. Dumas. Boulder, CO: Westview Press, 1982. 162pp. ISBN 0–86531–405–5.

The drain on the U.S. economy by the war industry is documented in these essays by economists and industrial engineers. These authors challenge the thesis that military spending stimulates the economy. In fact, they maintain that defense production has weakened the U.S. economy by turning resources to unproductive services, weakening productivity, and hurting technological advancement. This book makes a persuasive case for the economic advantages of arms reductions.

215 Potter, William C. *Nuclear Power and Nonproliferation.* Cambridge, MA: Oelgeschlager, Gunn and Hain, 1982. 281pp. ISBN 0–89946–019–4.

The author intended this book to provide a broad, interdisciplinary perspective on nuclear power and proliferation. There is a prevailing false dichotomy made between peaceful and military nuclear development, because once there is a capacity by a state for nuclear energy then the temptation to expand the system and make nuclear weapons is almost inescapable. The author claims that the best method discouraging proliferation is to combine security assurances with the strengthening of disincentives, but no methods including arms control are workable unless the nuclear powers discourage proliferation. This book is one of the better sources on the problem of nuclear proliferation.

216 Poulose, T. T. *Nuclear Proliferation and the Third World.* New Delhi: ABC Publishing House, 1982. 208pp.

The purpose of this study is to place into context the nuclear proliferation problem and the need of economic development in the Third World. By discouraging the development of nuclear weapons, the nuclear "haves" have made nonproliferation the cornerstone of their policy toward the Third World. But the Third World countries have an obligation to acquire nuclear power to fulfill the energy needs of their underdeveloped economies. This book is a mixture of solid data on Third World nuclear power requirements and polemics against the policies of the industrialized West.

217 Purver, Ronald G. *Arms Control in the North.* Kinston, Canada: Centre for International Relations, Queen's University, 1981. 159pp.

The author pursues the theme of arms control in the Arctic regions. Arms control in a remote area where there are at present no weapons systems makes sense, because once weapons are deployed there they tend to remain. There is doubt, however, that arms control can be achieved even in the

Arctic, and the best hope is to limit military competition in this region. The author's hopes for arms control in the Arctic clash with political realities, making this book an object lesson in wishful thinking.

218 *Quantitative Assessment in Arms Control: Mathematical Modeling and Simulation in the Analysis of Arms Control Problems.* Edited by Rudolf Avenhaus and Reiner K. Huber. New York: Plenum Press, 1984. 480pp. ISBN 0–306–41818–5.

This book is the proceedings of a 1983 seminar on quantitative approaches to arms control held at the Hochschule der Bundeswehr in Munich, West Germany. These seminars were intended to review the present state-of-the-art of systems analysis and to investigate arms control methodologies. The result is a series of papers dealing with the problems of arms control from a rigorous mathematic approach. This volume breaks new ground that researchers and students can continue to study for the foreseeable future.

219 *The Race for Security: Arms and Arms Control in the Reagan Years.* Edited by Robert Travis Scott. Lexington, MA: Lexington Books, 1987. 297pp. ISBN 0–669–09552–4.

Articles published from 1981 to 1986 in *Arms Control Today* make up the bulk of this book. This journal is the organ of the Arms Control Association, which has been active in lobbying for arms control for the last two decades. Forty-three articles by top names in the arms control field appear here. This book gives a representative sampling of the pro–arms control research in the early and mid-1980s.

220 *Reassessing Arms Control.* Edited by David Carlton and Carlo Schaerf. London: Macmillan, 1985. 211pp. ISBN 0–333–36202–0.

An international cast of scholars met in 1982 at the International School on Disarmament and Research on Conflicts (ISODARCO) in Verona, Italy, and presented the papers published here. There was general agreement that arms control is no longer viable because of current political realities and the difficulties of verification. While there remains considerable interest in new directions in arms control, the earlier promise for arms control has turned to realism. Differing opinions on the future of arms control make this book of essays valuable for the viewpoints it contains.

221 Record, Jeffrey. *Force Reductions in Europe: Starting Over.* Cambridge, MA: Institute for Foreign Policy Analysis, 1980. 92pp. ISBN 0–89549–027–7.

This study is a critique of the premises behind the Mutual and Balanced Force Reductions (MBFR) negotiations. MBFR talks began in 1973 with the purpose of stabilizing the military balance in Europe by reducing the size of conventional forces. The author claims that by 1980 the situation behind the talks had changed so that the talks needed to be expanded. Combining both a positive and a negative analysis, this book presents an excellent introduction to the reasons behind the MBFR negotiations.

222 Robinson, Julian Perry. *Chemical Warfare Arms Control: A Framework for Considering Policy Alternatives.* London: Taylor and Francis, 1985. 116pp. ISBN 0–85066–308–3.

This monograph examines the chemical weapons arms control negotiations in Geneva for past and future negotiating positions. These negotiations are presented in a way to better understand national policy making of the negotiating parties. Major effort is made to consider verification techniques for a chemical weapons arms control pact. This book is another of the excellent monographs issued under the auspices of SIPRI.

223 Rosenberg, Daniel. *The Unbroken Record: Soviet Treaty Compliance.* New York: International Publishers, 1985. 111pp. ISBN 0–7178–0636–7.

An American academic scholar challenges the common assertion that the Soviet Union violates its treaty commitments. Despite evidence showing that the Soviet Union has honored its treaty obligations in the past, the Reagan administration has used the theme of Soviet treaty violations to justify any program or weapon system. While the author makes an effective case for Soviet treaty compliance, the truth appears to fall somewhere between his treatment and those of conservative critics.

224 Rowell, William F. *Arms Control Verification: A Guide to Policy Issues for the 1980s.* Cambridge, MA: Ballinger, 1986. 167pp. ISBN 0–88730–093–6.

Verification as an arms control policy is the subject of this book. All Soviet-U.S. arms control negotiations have floundered over guarantees of verification, and the Reagan administration's policy has been to emphasize the problems. While new technology has modified the need for some types of verification, it is still a roadblock to arms control negotiations between the Soviet Union and the United States. This book is an excellent introduction to the arms control verification problem.

225 Russett, Bruce. *The Prisoners of Insecurity: Nuclear Deterrence, the Arms Race, and Arms Control.* San Francisco, CA: Freeman, 1983. 204pp. ISBN 0–7167–1472–8.

The thesis of this book is that most of the fundamental questions about national security and arms control are political ones. This means that the U.S. public needs information on these issues rather than leaving the decisions in the hands of experts. All aspects of the U.S. side of the arms race and arms control are examined, with the author opting for renewed emphasis on arms control. This book is an incisive analysis of the U.S. scene and deserves a look by both students and scholars.

226 *SALT II and American Security.* By Gordon J. Humphrey et al. Cambridge, MA: Institute for Foreign Policy Analysis, 1980. 65pp. ISBN 0–89549–024–2.

These papers were presented at a 1979 conference on SALT II held under the joint sponsorship of the Institute for Foreign Policy Analysis and the U.S. Army's Ballistic Missile Defense Advanced Technology Center. Five authors present their assessments of SALT II, and each finds this treaty deficient in protecting U.S. security interests because it gives too many military advantages to the Soviet Union. They conclude that, combined with verification problems, these advantages make SALT II a bad treaty for U.S. purposes. This critique of SALT II by many of the future leaders of the Reagan administration's foreign policy makes this work important for its viewpoints.

227 *Satellites for Arms Control and Crisis Monitoring.* Edited by Bhuprendra Jasani and Toshibomi Sakata. Oxford, England: Oxford University Press, 1987. 176pp. ISBN 0–19–829191–9.

The use of reconnaissance satellites to monitor arms control agreements and crisis situations is assessed by fourteen experts from seven countries at a 1984 symposium held in Stockholm, Sweden. Both the technology and the politics of satellite monitoring are studied, the resulting consensus being that it is possible to detect treaty violations from satellites. The problem, however, is that the United States and the Soviet Union are not willing to part with their monopoly on verification satellites. This book shows that satellite monitoring is a viable method of verification, and that politics rather than technology is the limiting factor.

228 Schaefer, Henry W. *Nuclear Arms Control: The Process of Developing Positions.* Washington, DC: National Defense University Press, 1986. 103pp.
    This book is a mathematical approach for quantifying the net worth of nuclear arms control measures by addressing "the interrelationships among weapons, yields, strategies and force levels." The author has had extensive experience in the U.S. Arms Control and Disarmament Agency, and this book is an outgrowth of his dissatisfaction about vague methodologies in use in U.S. arms control negotiations. His conclusion is that unless the United States develops a conceptual framework, arms control negotiations will continue to be inconclusive. This book is must reading for arms control researchers, if only to stimulate further research.

229 *Scientists, the Arms Race and Disarmament: A UNESCO/Pugwash Symposium.* Edited by Joseph Rotblat. London: Taylor and Francis, 1982. 322pp. ISBN 92–3–102021–8.
    The role of scientists in the arms race and disarmament is analyzed in the papers from this UNESCO/Pugwash-sponsored 1982 symposium held in Ajaccio, Corsica. An international cast of scientists from the West and the Soviet Union contributed essays on this problem. Certain views were held in common, i.e., that scientists must play a more active role in determining policy on the fruits of their research and that they should be more active in disarmament activities. Both the problems and the solutions presented make this book an important source for ideas on disarmament.

230 *Search for Sanity: The Politics of Nuclear Weapons and Disarmament.* Edited by Paul Joseph and Simon Rosenblum. Boston: South End Press, 1984. 604pp. ISBN 0–89608–204–0.
    The arms race and the means to control it are examined in this collection of essays by prominent critics of present U.S. policies. These critics survey U.S. nuclear weapons policy and nuclear strategy and find the arms race almost uncontrollable. The section on arms control and disarmament surveys the range of proposals to end the arms race. This book serves as a basic reference source for sampling viewpoints of critics of past and present policies on the arms race.

231 *Security and Arms Control: The Search for a More Stable Peace,* rev. ed. Washington, DC: U.S. Department of State, 1984. 76pp.
    This booklet gives the official position of the U.S. government on the relationship between national security and arms control. It claims that the United States has had a long record of seeking verifiable arms control agreements, but that the Soviet Union has not lived up to previous agreements. While there is still a commitment on the part of the United States for arms control, collective security will remain U.S. policy until the Soviet Union

restrains its adventurism. This booklet gives the status of arms control in the middle 1980s.

232 Sederberg, Peter C. *Nuclear Winter, Deterrence and the Prevention of Nuclear War.* New York: Praeger, 1986. 200pp. ISBN 0–275–92160–3.

This volume contains versions of papers originally presented at a 1984 conference on nuclear winter and the prevention of nuclear war held at the University of South Carolina. The theoretical consequences of a nuclear war, including the possibility of nuclear winter, are analyzed, as is deterrence as an operating mode of prevention of a nuclear war. Together these papers envisage a frightening specter on the eventuality of a nuclear war.

233 *Seeds of Promise: The First Real Hearings on the Nuclear Arms Freeze.* Andover, MA: Brick House, 1983. 213pp. ISBN 0–931790–55–7.

In 1982, at a hearing sponsored by the Federation of American Scientists (FAS), four arms control experts presented their views on a nuclear arms freeze and then were questioned on their positions. One government and three nongovernment witnesses delivered the expert testimony. The result is a number of opinions on the merits and demerits of a nuclear arms freeze. This book is a good source of a variety of informed views on the prospects for a nuclear weapons freeze in the early 1980s.

234 Shearer, Richard L. *On-Site Inspection for Arms Control: Breaking the Verification Barrier.* Washington, DC: National Defense University, 1984. 69pp.

A senior officer in the U.S. Air Force proposes a renewed effort at on-site inspection as a means of verification of an arms control agreement. Verification remains central to any meaningful arms control agreement, and the author claims that on-site inspection is the best method to ensure compliance. He believes that Soviet leaders may be more receptive to on-site verification now than in the past. This book reexamines an old controversy, but the solution still depends on a political decision by Soviet leadership.

235 Sheehan, Michael. *The Arms Race.* Oxford, England: Martin Robertson, 1983. 242pp. ISBN 0–85520–630–6.

The book describes and explains the contemporary arms race, emphasizing prospects for arms control and/or disarmament. Each chapter describes aspects of the arms race from the author's prodisarmament perspective. This book is most useful as an introduction to the study of arms control.

236 Sherr, Alan B. *The European Nuclear Negotiations: Paths to War or Peace?* Boston, MA: Lawyers Alliance for Nuclear Arms Control, 1983. 50pp.

The author surveys the state of nuclear arms negotiations in Europe in this booklet. His thesis is that the nuclear arms race in Europe is accelerating, and arms control negotiations have not advanced much beyond public posturing. Nevertheless, there is enough self-interest in an arms control agreement for both sides to promote an effective and lasting agreement. This essay combines both realism and optimism, and its points are worth serious consideration.

237 Sherr, Alan B. *Legal Issues of the "Star Wars" Defense Program.* Boston, MA: The Lawyers Alliance for Nuclear Arms Control, 1984. 38pp.

Legal questions about the Strategic Defense Initiative (SDI) compliance with the Anti-Ballistic Missile (ABM) Treaty of 1972 are studied in this book.

The author contends that the ABM Treaty prohibits not only the development but the testing of these weapons. Moreover, the adoption of SDI would hurt further attempts at arms control. This assessment of the legal side of SDI by a lawyer is an important source in the debate over the Star Wars defense program.

238 Sloan, Stanley R., and Robert C. Gray. *Nuclear Strategy and Arms Control: Challenges for U.S. Policy.* New York: Foreign Policy Association, 1982. 80pp. ISBN 0–87124–079–3.

This assessment of the Reagan administration's arms control policies was written by two U.S. foreign policy experts. They maintain that Reagan administration officials are so suspicious of Soviet intentions that there are doubts about whether these officials would sign any arms control agreements. The Soviets, however, are unlikely to make what the United States considers to be the necessary compromises, thereby making an arms control agreement almost impossible. This tract is a realistic assessment of arms control agreements in the early 1980s that still has value for readers today.

239 Sonntag, Philipp. *European Hopes and Fears for Arms Control: A Message about Nervous Partners.* Berlin, West Germany: International Institute for Comparative Social Research, 1980. 30pp.

The concern of Europeans, especially West Germans, about the impact of fighting a tactical nuclear war in Europe is the subject of this paper. Physical and environmental damage of nuclear weapons would destroy most of West Germany. The fear of a war fought on European soil makes the West Germans nervous about decision making on both sides and possible arms control proposals. While this paper is limited in scope, the section on potential battle damage in West Germany is a valuable contribution.

240 *Space Weapons: The Arms Control Dilemma.* Edited by Bhupendra Jasani. London: Taylor and Francis, 1984. 255pp. ISBN 0–85066–262–1.

These papers are the product of a 1983 symposium on the militarization of outer space sponsored by the Stockholm International Peace Research Institute (SIPRI) at Stockholm, Sweden. All the authors subscribe to the view the further refinement of antisatellite (ASAT) weapons makes arms control for outer space desirable, and they marshal considerable data to reinforce their viewpoint. Besides high-quality articles, this book contains all the treaties and treaty proposals for any form of arms control in space, and a list of satellite launches in 1982 and 1983.

241 Stanley, C. Maxwell. *Multilateral Disarmament: Conspiracy for Common Sense.* Muscatine, IA: Stanley Foundation, 1982. 36pp.

The case for multilateral disarmament is presented in this essay by a prominent U.S. businessman. Discouraged by the lack of progress on bilateral negotiations between the U.S. and the Soviet Union, the author opts for a discussion on the potential for multilateral disarmament. He believes that there is sufficient disarmament machinery available in the United Nations to carry out such a program. While this proposal seems a trifle naive, the author makes an intelligent effort to end the bilateral negotiations stalemate.

242 Steinberg, Gerald M. *Satellite Reconnaissance: The Role of Informal Bargaining.* New York: Praeger, 1983. 200pp. ISBN 0–03–063186–6.

This book details the role of satellite reconnaissance in national security and arms control agreements between the United States and the Soviet

Union. The benefits of satellite reconnaissance have been so great that both sides have been reluctant to create weapons to destroy the satellites. This has been an example of successful arms control between the superpowers. The appearance of this book preceded the attempts by the United States to introduce antisatellite weapons in the Strategic Defense Initiative (SDI), but this book still is worth study for the author's analysis.

243 Stockholm International Peace Research Institute. *Internationalization to Prevent the Spread of Nuclear Weapons*. London: Taylor and Francis, 1980. 224pp. ISBN 0–8448–1378–8.

Internationalizing the nuclear fuel cycle as a way to prevent the spread of nuclear weapons is the subject of this book. Twenty authors analyze the political, economic, technical, and legal issues involved in this internationalization. While acknowledging the benefits, most of the papers stress the difficulties of implementing this program. These papers add much useful information on approaches and methods to promote nonproliferation, but the approach proposed by SIPRI seems doomed by political and legal difficulties.

244 Storella, Mark C. *Poisoning Arms Control: The Soviet Union and Chemical/Biological Weapons*. Cambridge, MA: Institute for Foreign Policy Analysis, 1984. 102pp. ISBN 0–89549–063–3.

The Soviet Union's record of noncompliance with chemical and biological weapons (CBW) arms control agreements is the subject of this book. Violations of the 1925 Geneva Protocol and the 1972 Biological and Toxin Weapons Convention by the Soviet Union and its proxies since 1975 make future arms control agreements difficult. The United States will have to develop a chemical weapons retaliatory capability and to insist upon stricter verification systems before acceptance of any new CBW arms control proposals. This book is more an indictment than a scholarly treatise, but it still has useful information on chemical and biological weapons.

245 Sullivan, David S. *The Bitter Fruit of SALT: A Record of Soviet Duplicity*. Houston: Texas Policy Institute, 1982. 105pp.

The author, a former CIA official and staff worker on the U.S. Senate Armed Services Committee during the SALT II debate, documents his contentions that the SALT treaties were a mistake because the Soviets never had any intention to abide by them. He further claims that U.S. security is better achieved by acceleration of unilateral strategic programs to achieve military parity with the Soviet Union than arms control agreements. This short book is strong on polemics and shows the depth of distrust of the Soviets in U.S. right-wing circles.

246 Talbott, Strobe. *Deadly Gambits: The Reagan Administration and the Stalemate in Nuclear Arms Control*. New York: Knopf, 1984. 380pp. ISBN 0–394–53637–1.

This book studies the first term record of the Reagan administration on arms control. Neither the president nor most of his advisors have faith in arms control negotiations, and this is partially the reason for the lack of progress of negotiations with the Soviets. But toward the end of Reagan's first term the impetus for arms control negotiations has reasserted itself. The strength of this book lies in its analysis of the individuals concerned with decision making in the Reagan administration.

247   Tatchell, Peter. *Democratic Defence: A Non-Nuclear Alternative.* London: GMP Publishers, 1985. 223pp. ISBN 0–946097–16–X.

A return to the amateur British defense forces of pre–World War I is envisaged as a way to promote nuclear disarmament. It is a proposal for a socialist solution to the debate within the Labor and peace movement for an alternative nonnuclear defense strategy. Reducing the British armed forces and creating a community-based citizen's army has little possibility of happening as long as Great Britain belongs to NATO. This book is significant only as an indication of the type of thinking present in certain British left-wing circles.

248   *Technology, Strategy, and Arms Control.* Edited by Wolfram F. Hanrieder. Boulder, CO: Westview Press, 1986. 162pp. ISBN 0–8133–0177–7.

These essays are the result of a 1984–1985 series of lectures from the Program on Global Peace and Security at the University of California, Santa Barbara. Most of the essays deal with arms control, East-West military balance, and technological issues. The variety of subjects and the difference in viewpoints means that the only common theme is a concern to understand the political, ethical, and technological context of the arms race. It is the overall quality of the essays that makes this book worthwhile.

249   Towle, Philip. *Arms Control and East-West Relations.* London: Croom Helm, 1983. 187pp. ISBN 0–7099–2416–X.

Arms control as a part of the ongoing relations between the Soviet Union and the United States is the subject of this book, in which the author maintains that because of the hostility between the superpowers too much has been expected of the arms control agreements in the 1960s and 1970s. He posits that political and military détente must be achieved by the two superpowers before there can be meaningful arms control. By placing arms control within a political context, the author makes a solid contribution to arms control literature.

250   *The United Nations and Disarmament, 1945–1985.* By the United Nations Department for Disarmament Affairs. New York: United Nations, 1985. 166pp.

The role of the United Nations in disarmament activities since 1945 is the subject of this booklet. It updates and revises two earlier publications, *The United Nations versus the Arms Race* (1980) and *The United Nations and Disarmament, 1945–1970* (1970). All United Nations disarmament activities are surveyed with special emphasis on the World Disarmament Campaign. This booklet gives an overview of United Nations contributions to disarmament, and it provides a good starting point for further research.

251   *Uranium Enrichment and Nuclear Weapon Proliferation.* By Allan S. Krass. New York: Taylor and Francis, 1983. 296pp. ISBN 0–8002–3079–5.

Four specialists on nuclear proliferation maintain that it has been the acceleration of technological advances in enrichment technology that has advanced the danger of nuclear proliferation. They devote most of the book to the scientific technology of uranium enrichment to reinforce their thesis. They then provide a status of nuclear and enrichment programs of all countries involved in enrichment activities. This book is the best source on uranium enrichment available.

252 U.S. Department of State. *National Negotiating Styles.* Edited by Hans Binnendijk. Washington, DC: Foreign Service Institute, 1987. 147pp.

The negotiating styles of six countries are examined for national characteristics and their importance to the United States. China, Egypt, France, Japan, Mexico, and the Soviet Union make up the group under study. Differences in negotiating style range from the confrontational style of the Soviets to the subtle maneuvering of the Chinese. While these papers are intended for U.S. negotiators, arms control scholars will find them valuable in understanding the negotiation process.

253 Van Cleave, William R., and S. T. Cohen. *Nuclear Weapons, Policies, and the Test Ban Issue.* New York: Praeger, 1987. 104pp. ISBN 0–275–92312–6.

The authors argue that the United States should continue to develop and test nuclear weapons. This is in part a response to past Soviet violations of arms control agreements, but also because it is in the best interests of the United States to develop new nuclear weapons. The authors maintain that the benefits to national security from arms control have been negligible, and the record of arms control has been one of failure. This attack on arms control by two advocates of nuclear testing is flawed by its insistence on accepting data from U.S. agencies with a vested interest in a renewed U.S. arms buildup.

254 *Verification and Arms Control.* Edited by William C. Potter. Lexington, MA: Lexington Books, 1985. 266pp. ISBN 0–669–09554–0.

Verification of arms control proposals has been the most controversial of arms control issues during the 1980s. The effectiveness of different types of verification methods are analyzed in this book, which posits that the chief stumbling block to verification has become the politics of verification rather than the technology. This book is essential in understanding the political side of the verification process.

255 *The Verification of Arms Control Agreements.* Edited by Ian Bellany and Coit D. Blacker. London: Frank Cass, 1983. 95pp. ISBN 0–7146–3228–7.

This book is a reprint of a 1982 special issue of *Arms Control* (Vol. 3, No. 3), but the caliber of the papers is such that they deserve reappraisal. A verification system of any arms control agreement is the key to determining whether such an agreement is working. Any system of verification must ensure that breaches can be detected and that the technology is available to guarantee verification. These papers discuss these and other issues, making this book a good source for arms control researchers.

256 *Verification of Arms Control Agreements: The Role of Third Countries.* Edited by Rene Haug. Geneva, Switzerland: Programme for Strategic and International Security Studies, 1985. 95pp.

These papers are the product of a 1984 international meeting in Geneva on the feasibility of neutral countries participating in the verification of existing and future arms control agreements. The authors agreed that third, or neutral, countries should have a role in the verification process of multinational arms control agreements. But there is also a need for future verification schemes to avoid politically ambiguous situations, which threaten any verification plan. This publication considers another option in the verification debate, and this approach makes a solid contribution.

257 *Verifying a Nuclear Freeze.* By Roger Harrison et al. Leamington Spa, England: Berg, 1986. 207pp. ISBN 0–907582–75–3.

Verification of nuclear freeze proposals is the subject of this book. The authors maintain that without an adequate verification system, no arms control or nuclear freeze agreement will work. They outline the requirements necessary for any verification system to succeed, concluding that such a system can be implemented and work. This book contains a wealth of useful information, and it should be a good source for the next several years.

258 Vigor, P. H. *The Soviet View of Disarmament.* Houndmills, England: Macmillan, 1986. 189pp. ISBN 0–333–37929–2.

Soviet views on arms control and disarmament since 1917 are detailed in this book. It is the author's thesis that Soviet attitudes toward disarmament always originate from members of the Politburo of the Communist Party of the Soviet Union, and that the Soviet leadership's views are conditioned by Marxist-Leninist concepts of militarism as a stage of capitalism. The Soviets desire disarmament, but they believe the best negotiating comes from a position of military superiority. This book is a major contribution to disarmament literature.

259 Waller, Douglas C. *Congress and the Nuclear Freeze: An Inside Look at the Politics of a Mass Movement.* Amherst, MA: University of Massachusetts Press, 1987. 346pp. ISBN 0–87023–559–1.

The successful legislative struggle to enact the Nuclear Freeze Resolution in Congress in 1983 is chronicled in this book. Beginning in early 1982, the author served as the legislative assistant to the sponsor of this legislation, and he steered the resolution through its nearly two year lifespan in Congress. The book deals more with the politics of the freeze rather than the merits of this type of arms control. This book does show, however, the sort of political battle any type of arms control measure will face to pass Congress.

260 *We Can Avert a Nuclear War.* Edited by William Epstein and Lucy Webster. Cambridge, MA: Oelgeschlager, Gunn and Hain, 1983. 181pp. ISBN 0–89946–202–2.

This book is the product of a 1982 commemorative meeting of the Canadian Pugwash Group at Pugwash, Nova Scotia, Canada. This meeting was held to assess progress of the Pugwash movement, and the presentations addressed this issue. The disarmament message of this movement has been spread among the initiated and the general public, but additional effort needs to be made to influence governments and leaders. Most of this book consists of personal statements by people long active in the Pugwash movement, and it is a good source for these views.

261 *The Western Panacea: Constraining Soviet Power through Negotiation.* Edited by Uwe Nerlich. Cambridge, MA: Ballinger, 1983. 464pp. ISBN 0–88410–921–6.

In this work nineteen arms control specialists from NATO countries present papers on the effectiveness of arms control agreements in constraining Soviet military power. Most of the authors are pessimistic about the influence of arms control agreements in limiting Soviet military power, and they believe that arms negotiation policies ought to be designed to meet strategic requirements. This book is one of the better works on the limitations of arms control agreements on the market.

262 Wiehmiller, Gordon R. *U.S.-Soviet Summits: An Account of East-West Diplomacy at the Top, 1955–1985,* Lanham, MD: University Press of America, 1986. 211pp. ISBN 0–8191–5442–3.

Eleven U.S.-Soviet summit meetings have been examined in order to understand the preparation and the results of these meetings. Preparation, timing, and goals appear to be the key ingredients of a summit. A special feature is an appendix on the chronology, synopses, and final documents of U.S.-Soviet summit meetings from 1955 to 1985. This book is far from definitive, but it is a good starting point for further research on superpower summits.

263 Wilke, Peter, and Herbert Wulf. *Manpower Conversion in Defence Related Industry.* Hamburg, West Germany: Institüt für Friedensforschung und Sicherheitspolitik, 1986. 62pp.

Manpower conversion in defense-related industries as part of disarmament or reduction of military expenditures is examined in this report for the International Labour Office. Relying on case studies from several countries, the authors insist that a conversion can only succeed with advance planning. This means that there must be state intervention, because market forces will not be able to cure unemployment and stagnation problems of conversion. This report is another valuable contribution to the debate on the economic consequences of arms control and disarmament.

264 Wong-Fraser, Agatha S. Y. *The Political Utility of Nuclear Weapons: Expectations and Experience.* Washington, DC: University Press of America, 1980. 343pp. ISBN 0–8191–1234–8.

The value of having nuclear weapons for a state is analyzed in this book by a U.S. scholar who maintains that nuclear weapons bestow political benefits on the holding state in terms of prestige and power. These benefits are such that proliferation of nuclear weapons to near-nuclear states will continue. This book gives the political reasons why nonproliferation policies are unlikely to deter nuclear proliferation.

265 *World Disarmament: An Idea Whose Time Has Come.* Nottingham, England: Spokesman, 1985. 238pp. ISBN 0–85124–412–2.

This book is an outgrowth of earlier UN efforts to promote disarmament. The authors of these papers are British peace activists and representatives from the United Nations. Besides essays on disarmament issues, the book includes the 1982 and 1983 voting records of the UN General Assembly on disarmament issues, and a list of organizations in the Disarmament and Development Network. While this book is a mixed bag, the ideas of the authors are worth noting.

266 *World Military Expenditures and Arms Transfers, 1985.* Washington, DC: U.S. Government Printing Office, 1985. 145pp.

The U.S. Arms Control and Disarmament Agency produces this assessment of world military expenditures and arms transfers on a frequent basis. It serves as a ready reference on statistical data for 145 countries. The decade from 1973 to 1983 is covered in depth, as well as projections for 1984 and 1985. This book is the most authoritative source on arms transfers available on the market.

267   Zartman, I. William, and Maureen R. Berman. *The Practical Negotiator.*
New Haven, CT: Yale University Press, 1982. 250pp. ISBN 0–300–2523–8.

This book is the culmination of nearly twenty years of research on the
problem of dispute resolution by the Communication and Conflict Program,
which was formed in 1968 by a group of independent scholars to study
conflict management problems. Interviews of negotiators have been conducted since 1971, and conferences of scholars and practitioners were held
in 1971 and 1973 to improve the program's resources. The result is a manual
of both the theoretical and practical sides of any type of international negotiations. No study of arms control and disarmament negotiations should be
undertaken without consulting this work.

CHAPTER TWO:
Defense and Military

Defense and military are natural companion subjects, because so often the issues are tied closely together. Defense involves any topic on national security, civil defense, or formulation of defense policy. Military includes any topic relating to the conduct of military operations and/or military tactics. These materials included in this chapter give a good overview of defense and military research worldwide. These subjects also comprise the largest block of any of the categories with 625 entries.

Annuals and Yearbooks

268 *Air Forces of the World*. Edited by D. H. Chopping. Geneva, Switzerland: Interavia, 1985– . $500.

Military aircraft in the air force inventories of 142 countries throughout the world is the speciality of this annual. Interavia has a computerized data bank on these air forces, which was used in preparing this book. The first part of the work contains information on the air forces of each country, and the second part groups tabular information on each military aircraft type. This book is one of the better sources on military aircraft on the market but is expensive.

269 *American Defense Annual*. Edited by Joseph Kruzel. Lexington, MA: Lexington Books, 1985– . ISSN 0882–1038. $20.

This annual is part of a new series published under the auspices of the Mershon Center for Education in National Security at Ohio State University explaining the operations of the U.S. defense establishment. Its chapters address all aspects of the U.S. military including defense strategy. It also includes appendices containing a defense chronology and a summary of U.S. defense commitments, and an annotated bibliography of defense literature. It is the best annual of its type on the market.

270 *Defense and Foreign Affairs Handbook*. Washington, DC: Defense and Foreign Affairs, 1976– . ISSN 0160–5836. $82.

Nearly two hundred countries' defense policies and foreign affairs are handled in this annual handbook. General statistical information is provided on each country, but the major feature is the data on the defense structure including army and navy orders of battle. Defense production figures and tables on missiles, arms transfers, and military power relationships are other useful features. This publication has long been a standard reference source in the defense field.

271 International Institute for Strategic Studies. *The Military Balance.* London: International Institute for Strategic Studies, 1967– . ISSN 0459–7222. $24.95.

The military power and defense expenditures of each country worldwide are covered in this annual quantitative assessment. All regions are studied, and each country's military establishment is examined in depth. It is published by the International Institute for Strategic Studies, London, as part of its ongoing research mission. This reference is another excellent source for studying worldwide military trends.

272 Jaffee Center for Strategic Studies. *The Middle East Military Balance.* Tel Aviv: Jaffee Center for Strategic Studies, 1984– . ISSN 0334–5041. $36.50.

This yearbook is a quantitative assessment of the military balance of armed forces in the Middle East. The book is divided into three parts: part one reviews the major strategic developments in the Middle East during the current year; part two presents a database of regional military forces; and part three analyzes the most important subregional military balances of forces. It is produced by the Israeli think tank the Jaffee Center for Strategic Studies, Tel Aviv. This book is the best source on Middle East military affairs available.

273 *Jane's Aviation Review.* Edited by Michael J. W. Taylor. London: Jane's Publishing, 1981– . ISBN 0–7106–0368–1. $16.95.

Commercial and military aviation news from around the world is the specialty of this annual. Short informative and interpretive articles from aviation experts are featured in each issue. A special section lists new aircraft that appeared during the previous year. This annual is a good source for recent developments in aviation.

274 *Jane's Fighting Ships.* Edited by John Moore. London: Jane's Publishing, 1898– . ISBN 0–7106–0814–4. $112.50.

This annual is an encyclopedic treatment of the inventory of fighting ships in every navy of the world. Illustrations and the most up-to-date information on every warship that has a role in any modern navy is provided. Particularly valuable is the pennant list of major surface ships. Every attempt is made to keep information current, with addenda for late-breaking naval news.

275 *Jane's Infantry Weapons.* Edited by Ian V. Hogg. London: Jane's Publishing, 1973– . ISBN 0–7106–0843–8. $112.50.

All the information on military small arms and more is presented in this encyclopedia of infantry weapons. It is another product of the Jane's Publishing Company, which specializes in these types of publications. Revolvers, pistols, submachine guns, rifles, shotguns, machine guns, cannons, grenades, flamethrowers, mortars, support rocket launchers, antiaircraft weapons, antitank weapons, and electronics and optics are covered in depth. This annual on infantry weapons is the most up-to-date source on the market.

276 *Jane's Merchant Shipping Review*. Edited by A. J. Ambrose. London: Jane's Publishing, 1983– . ISBN 0–7106–0332–0. $16.95.

Trends in the world's merchant marine fleets are traced in this annual. A noteworthy feature is the maritime chronology of events for the year under coverage. While most of the information in this publication involves commercial shipping, military and strategic considerations are also noted. Little information on maritime affairs escapes the preparers of this annual.

277 *Jane's Military Communications*. Edited by R. J. Raggett. London: Jane's Publishing, 1980– . ISBN 0–7106–0824–1. $140.

Jane's Publishing produces this annual to survey trends in military communications systems. Besides inventories of each country's equipment, particular emphasis is placed on gauging technological progress in communication systems. The editor concludes that Soviet communication systems are considerably behind those in operation with Western armed forces. By combining an inventory and an analysis function, this annual is unrivaled as a source in the defense field.

278 *Jane's Military Review*. Edited by Ian V. Hogg. London: Jane's Publishing, 1981– . ISBN 0–7106–0269–X. $16.95.

This annual serves as a forum for opinions on military development for the year under consideration. While considerable attention is given to new military equipment, most of the articles interpret tactical applications of weapons systems. A special feature is the listing of new military equipment introduced by armed forces during the current year. This annual makes its contribution as a forum for the introduction of new military equipment.

279 *Jane's Military Vehicles and Ground Support Equipment*. Edited by Christopher F. Foss and Terry J. Gander. London: Jane's Publishing, 1980– . ISBN 0–7106–0825–X. $137.50.

Each year this publication grows in size, as more information about military vehicles and ground support equipment becomes available. The transportation and combat vehicle inventories of each military establishment in the world are covered along with assault crafts, chemical equipment, demolition equipment, and mines. No study of logistical problems of military forces is complete without examining this source.

280 *Jane's Naval Review*. Edited by John Moore. London: Jane's Publishing, 1981– . ISBN 0–7106–0335–5. $16.95.

Naval developments during the current year are highlighted in this annual. It specializes in short feature articles about the principal naval forces in the world. The articles on the Soviet Navy are especially valuable. This source is one of the best reviews on the market.

281 *Jane's Weapons Systems*. Edited by Ronald T. Pretty. London: Jane's Publishing, 1969– . ISBN 0–7106–0819–5. $125.

This annual is the definitive authority on weapons systems in operational use among the world's military forces for the current year. The book is divided into three sections: systems, equipment, and analysis. No effort is spared to describe each weapon system in depth. Defense scholars will find this annual a valuable asset to their research.

282 Laffin, John. *War Annual*. London: Brassey's Defence Publishers, 1986– . ISBN 0–08–031211–X.

The author started this annual to describe all the wars in progress during a particular year. Each war's background, course, conduct and possible conclusion are analyzed and supported by the most up-to-date information available. Maps and illustrations help the reader understand the conduct of these wars. This annual is one of the most up-to-date sources of interstate and civil wars on the market.

283 *Military Yearbook*. Compiled and edited by Sukhdeo Prasad Baranwal. New Delhi: Guide Publications, 1967– . $42.

Military information about the Indian military forces and articles on international defense topics are contained in this yearbook. It has complete organization, structure, and functions data on the current state of India's armed forces. An added feature is a biographical section on the leaders of India's defense community. This yearbook gives a succinct treatment of current readiness and equipment of the Indian defense forces.

284 NATO. *NATO and the Warsaw Pact: Force Comparisons*. Brussels, Belgium: NATO Information Service, 1982– . Free.

Each year since 1982 NATO has published an official comparison of the military forces that make up NATO and the Warsaw Treaty Organization (WTO). The avowed purpose is to provide an authoritative, factual, and objective source of information. Illustrations and maps help the reader understand the statistical data. Despite its pro-NATO bias, this booklet is a good introduction to the study of the military balance between NATO and WTO.

285 *RUSI and Brassey Defence Yearbook*. Oxford, England: Brassey's Defence Publishers, 1886– . ISBN 0–08–030552–0. $45.

Among the most authoritative sources in the defense field, this yearbook provides up-to-date information about international defense trends. It has able editorial support from the Royal United Services Institute for Defence Studies (RUSI), London. Although this publication started out as an exclusively naval annual, over the years it expanded its scope to include the entire range of international defense issues.

286 Senger und Etterlin, F. M. von. *Tanks of the World*. Annapolis, MD: Nautical and Aviation, 1983– . ISSN 0264–8784. $54.95.

An English translation of the *Taschenbuch der Panzer*, this annual publication is by the foremost German expert on armored land vehicles. It is an encyclopedia of information on tanks of all nations. An inventory of each country's armored forces is provided along with numerous illustrations and drawings of types of tanks. This annual is the best source about tanks on the market.

287 Sivard, Ruth Leger. *World Military and Social Expenditures*. Leesburg, VA: World Priorities, 1975– . ISSN 0363–4795. $5.

This annual has an accounting of the use of world resources for social and military purposes. Its approach is statistical, with numerous graphs and charts. The author is the director of World Priorities, a nonprofit research organization devoted to educating the public on the hazards of the international weapons race. The appearance of this annual is always eagerly awaited by scholars because of the authoritative nature of its statistics.

288 *Soviet Armed Forces Review Annual.* Edited by David R. Jones. Gulf Breeze, FL: Academic International Press, 1976– . ISBN 0–87569–078–5. $64.50.

This annual on the Soviet armed forces is sponsored by the Russian Research Center of Nova Scotia and Dalhousie University. A team of U.S., British, and Canadian military specialists produces evaluations on the Soviet air force, army, navy, and strategic rocket forces. Especially valuable are the statistics and the chronology of Soviet military events it provides. This publication combines excellent analyses with a mass of statistical data useful for any type of research on Soviet armed forces.

289 *Soviet Military Power.* Washington, DC: U.S. Department of Defense, 1981– . $5.

Each year since the appearance of the second version in 1983, the U.S. government has presented its official assessment of Soviet military strength. While important to the defense community for its arguments for increasing the defense budget, each version presents current statistical information on the Soviet armed forces. Despite some overblown rhetoric, this annual presents useful statistical information and many excellent illustrations of the newest Soviet weapons.

290 *United States Military Posture.* Organization of the Joint Chiefs of Staff. Washington, DC: U.S. Government Printing Office, 1982– . $5.

The Joint Chiefs of Staff's (JCS) support staff prepares this annual on U.S. military forces to supplement testimony of the JCS at congressional hearings for increases in the defense budget. The publication presents the current state of the U.S. military forces with projections of Soviet and U.S. strengths and equipment. Any indication of Soviet superiority is highlighted as a weakness to be corrected by increased appropriations. While this publication's avowed purpose is for lobbying, it also serves as a good source of the current state of U.S. armed forces.

Bibliographies

291 *Aerospace/Defense Markets & Technology.* Cleveland, OH: Predicasts, 1983– . ISSN 0738–0461. $850.

This monthly publication contains abstracts from nearly a hundred aerospace- and defense-related periodicals. Each citation has a three- or four-sentence abstract of the article. An excellent source for finding information on the development and testing of new military technology, its biggest drawback is its high cost.

292 *Bibliography on Espionage and Intelligence Operations.* Compiled by Laird M. Wilcox. Kansas City, MO: Editorial Research Service, 1980. 12pp. ISBN 0–933152–03–5. $10.

This short bibliography gives 401 entries of books published since 1945 on espionage and intelligence operations. Many of the citations have one- or two-sentence annotations. The compiler makes no pretense about his right-wing orientation, and the annotations reflect his viewpoint. This bibliography is highly suspect and should be used with caution.

293   Champion, Brian. *Advanced Weapons Systems: An Annotated Bibliography of the Cruise Missiles, Laser and Space Weapons and Stealth Technology*. New York: Garland, 1985. 206pp. ISBN 0–8240–8793–3. $35.

This annotated bibliography of weapons systems has been compiled by a Canadian librarian from the University of Alberta. It consists of citations from a variety of influential military and scientific journals. Although this type of publication becomes dated quickly, nevertheless this bibliography will prove useful for scholars interested in these topics.

294   *Current Military Literature: Comment and Abstracts and Citations of Important Articles from International Military and Defence Periodicals.* Edited by J. I. H. Owen. Oxford, England: Military Press, 1983– . ISSN 0264–1674. $135.

An impressive list of military journals is scanned for this British bibliography on land warfare. While it is intended as a research aid for persons interested in military warfare, an editorial decision was made to exclude naval and aerospace materials. For those articles whose titles are not self-explanatory, an abstract or digest of the text is provided. The work is divided into fourteen subject sections and also includes three indexes for ease of usage: a source journal index, an author index, and a geographical index.

295   *Information-Dokumentation.* Vienna: Landesverleidigungsakakademie, Institüt für strategische Grundlagenforschung, Zentraldokumentation, n.d. $23.

One of Austria's premier institutes, Institüt für strategische Grundlagenforschung, publishes this review of writings on arms control, defense, and military subjects. Around three hundred journals are surveyed for articles for inclusion. Coverage is comprehensive, with contributions from both NATO and the Warsaw Pact blocs. There is no comparable source in English to match this Austrian publication.

296   *Naval Abstracts.* Alexandria, VA: Center for Naval Analyses, 1977– . ISSN 0192–320X. $150.

This work surveys over two hundred journals for articles on naval matters. Each article has a paragraph-size abstract, which is written from the point of view of the author of the article. A product of the Center for Naval Analyses, Alexandria, Virginia, this abstract service is one of the best around, although there is evidence that it may be discontinued.

297   *Scholar's Guide to Intelligence Literature: Bibliography of the Russell J. Bowen Collection.* Edited by Marjorie W. Cline, Carla E. Christiansen, and Judith M. Fontaine. Frederick, MD: University Publications of America, 1983. 236pp. ISBN 0–89093–540–8.

The National Intelligence Study Center in Washington, DC, published this bibliography on the intelligence literature contained in the Russell J. Bowen Collection at Georgetown University. It contains more than six thousand volumes on all aspects of intelligence gathering from the sixteenth century to the present. Author and title indexes make this bibliography easy to use. This source is one of the most complete collections on intelligence literature in existence, and is especially complete on materials from 1945 to 1980.

298   Smith, Myron J. *The Soviet Army, 1939–1980: A Guide to Sources in English.* Santa Barbara, CA: ABC-Clio, 1982. 551pp. ISBN 0–87436–307–1.

This publication is a working bibliography of English language sources dealing with all aspects of the Soviet Army. While the author does not claim this work to be definitive, it does cover the major sources in the subject area. Much of the material is more of historical than contemporary interest, but the author has tried to provide more current information by including a section on reference works. It is another solid contribution from the Center for the Study of Armament and Disarmament at California State University, Los Angeles.

Databooks, Handbooks, and Sourcebooks

299 *Australia's Defence Resources: A Compendium of Data*, 3d ed. By Ernest McNamara et al. Rushcutters, Bay, Australia: Pergamon Press (Australia), 1986. 186pp. ISBN 0–08–029881–8.

This book is a compendium of the most current information on Australia's defense resources. It includes a breakdown of all Australian defense forces and military obligations. Other features are information on the organization, order of battle, and equipment of the Australian Defence Force. Anyone concerned with Australian defense issues will find this work invaluable.

300 *Battlefield Europe: War Today: East versus West.* Edited by Nigel Flynn. New York: Arco, 1985. 66pp. ISBN 0–668–06517–6.

The military arsenals of NATO and the Warsaw Pact are detailed in this sourcebook, which compares the military organization and land armies of the two alliances. Sections on ground-to-ground missiles, antitank missiles, ground-to-air missiles, and helicopters are the book's strong points. The illustrations are excellent, although this sourcebook has too little material to compare favorably with other works of this type.

301 *Brassey's Artillery of the World: Guns, Howitzers, Mortars, Guided Weapons, Rockets and Ancillary Equipment in Service with the Regular and Reserve Forces of All Nations*, 2d ed. Oxford, England: Brassey's Publishers, 1981. 246pp. ISBN 0–08–027035–2.

All forms of artillery are featured in this systematic treatment of the subject. Besides an exhaustive analysis of each weapon and/or system, there is a valuable directory of manufacturers of artillery equipment. A glossary of artillery terms and an index make this book easy to consult. This work is an invaluable source of information, because many of these weapons are often ignored in other sourcebooks.

302 Campbell, Christy. *War Facts Now.* Glasgow: Fontana Paperbacks, 1982. 304pp. ISBN 0–00–636492–6.

Facts and figures about all aspects of modern warfare have been placed together in this handbook by the managing editor of Jane's Publishing. While there is a mass of technical data, the author concentrates most of his attention on an analysis of modern warfare. The section on future weapons systems is also useful. Although this sourcebook is becoming dated, it still has enough information to be a valuable asset to any collection.

303 Chant, Christopher. *Naval Forces of the World.* London: Winchmore Publishing Services, 1984. 192pp. ISBN 0–00218–113–4.

This illustrated account of the world's navies is among the more valuable of the reference works on naval developments. The book is divided into three sections corresponding to three naval types: naval forces, warships, and ship-launched missiles. Along with the factual material, this organization makes this source easy to use as well as informative.

304 *The Civil Defence of the USSR: This Everybody Must Know and Understand: A Handbook for the Population.* Canberra: Australian National University, 1984. 69pp.

Handbooks on civil defense can provide valuable information on attitudes of authorities toward the possibility of nuclear war. This translation of the Soviet Union's manual gives a good look at Soviet attitudes toward civil defense and survival in the eventuality of a nuclear war. The most noticeable feature is the feeling that the Soviets envisage the possibility of a nuclear war.

305 Collins, John M. *U.S.-Soviet Military Balance, 1980–1985.* Washington, DC: Pergamon-Brassey's, 1985. 360pp. ISBN 0–08033–130–0.

The author, a senior analyst on national security and military affairs for the Congressional Research Service, intends this publication to provide Congress and the general public with an account of the changes in the U.S.-Soviet military balance of forces since 1980. He documents the growing military strength of the Soviet Union over a five-year period. While his prodefense viewpoint is apparent, the data contained in this book make it a worthwhile source.

306 Constant, James N. *Fundamentals of Strategic Weapons: Offense and Defense Systems.* 2 vols. The Hague: Martinus Nijhoff, 1981. ISBN 9–024725–45–3.

The technology, evolution, functions, costs, societal impacts, and limitations of modern strategic weapons systems provide the subjects for this sourcebook. Although the purpose of the publication is to inform the general reader about these weapons, considerable expertise is required to understand the scientific principles involved in the analysis. It remains the best source available for textbook information on strategic weapons.

307 *DMS 1987 Defense Budget Handbook.* Greenwich, CT: Defense Marketing Services, 1986. 310pp.

The Defense Marketing Services produces this handbook on the Research, Development, Test and Evaluation (RDT & E) portion of the U.S. Department of Defense budget. It presents data from 1985 through 1988. Each defense line budget item is presented, along with the sums appropriated. Anyone interested in either the defense budget or research and development will find this volume a necessity.

308 *Documents on the Laws of War.* Edited by Adam Roberts. Oxford, England: Clarendon Press, 1982. 498pp. ISBN 0–19–876118–X.

The texts of twenty-five formal international agreements on the laws of war are contained in this sourcebook. It begins with the 1856 Paris Declaration and includes the 1981 United National Weapons Convention. A bibliography for future study and an index make this sourcebook easy to use. It can be recommended to any researcher interested in the laws of war.

309 Dupuy, Trevor N., Grace P. Hayes, and John A. C. Andrews. *The Almanac of World Military Power*, 4th ed. San Rafael, CA: Presidio Press, 1980. 418pp. ISBN 0–89141–070–8.

Three defense analysts have produced this sourcebook on the military forces of all the countries of the world with any organized military structure. Each citation covers power potential statistics, defense structure, politico-military policy, strategic problems, alliances, and military forces. Maps help the reader understand both external and internal defense problems. This book is an excellent background source for defense and international security specialists.

310 English, Adrian. *Armed Forces of Latin America: Their Histories, Development, Present Strength and Military Potential*. London: Jane's Publishing, 1984. 490pp. ISBN 0–7106–0321–5.

Latin America is a region of growing strategic importance, and this sourcebook of the armed forces of Latin American countries reflects this fact. Each country's military forces are examined in detail, from organizational structure to weapons arsenals. Military rivalries among Latin American countries are examined along with prospects for ending such rivalries. Any understanding of the Latin American military will be increased by use of this work.

311 Forster, Thomas M. *The East German Army: The Second Power in the Warsaw Pact*, 5th ed. London: Allen and Unwin, 1980. 310pp. ISBN 0–04–355012–6.

This book is a translation of the fifth edition of a standard reference work on the National People's Army (NVA) of the German Democratic Republic (GDR). The NVA is the second largest army in the Warsaw Pact, and is closely tied in doctrine and organization to the Soviet Army. Each chapter covers an aspect of the doctrine, organization, training, and weaponry of the NVA. Despite its publication date, this book is the best source on the East German army available.

312 Foss, Christopher F. *Artillery of the World*, 3d ed. New York: Scribner's, 1981. 176pp. ISBN 0–684–16722–0.

Now in its third edition, this sourcebook contains a complete inventory of current ground and antiaircraft artillery, multiple rocket systems, and their associated fire control systems, although several new artillery systems have been introduced in the seven years since the last edition. Each entry provides a description of a particular weapon and a list of countries using that particular weapon. This work is another in a series of excellent reference sources compiled by the author, which are invaluable for both the expert and novice researcher.

313 Foss, Christopher F. *Jane's Armoured Personnel Carriers*. London: Jane's Publishing, 1985. 216pp. ISBN 0–7106–0354–1.

Every variety of armored personnel carrier (APC) since 1945 is surveyed in this sourcebook. Each entry provides the development history, full specifications, and manufacturer of the various APCs. This book is a good companion work to other armored vehicle publications.

314 Gander, Terry. *Encyclopaedia of the Modern British Army*, 2d ed. Annapolis, MD: Nautical and Aviation Publishing, 1982. 280pp. ISBN 0–93–3852–33–9.

Now in its second edition, this databook covers the organization, equipment, and uniforms of the British army in the early 1980s. Information about these subjects is dealt with in detail. It serves as a handy reference guide for those scholars interested in research on the modern British army.

315 *Guided Weapons: Including Light, Unguided Anti-tank Weapons*. By R. G. Lee et al. Oxford, England: Brassey's Defence Publishers, 1983. 223pp. ISBN 0–08–028336–5.

Part of a series on battlefield weapons systems and technology, this book explains the technology involved in the design of guided weapons. An effective use of illustrations and statistical data shows how these weapons are used on the battlefield against armored vehicles, ground targets, and aircraft. The authors maintain that guided weapons have developed faster than any other type of weapon system, and that these weapons have had an enormous strategic and tactical impact on warfare. This sourcebook provides information unavailable in any other publication.

316 Heitman, Helmoed-Romer. *South African War Machine*. Novato, CA: Presidio Press, 1985. 192pp. ISBN 0–89141–240–9.

This book is an illustrated study of the armed forces of the Republic of South Africa by a veteran of the South African army. It covers all aspects of the military state of South African forces, including an inventory of military equipment. Although this work has security clearance from the South African government, it still provides a good picture of the military forces at the disposal of that government. The material in this sourcebook has been designed more for propaganda than information, but any material on the South African military forces is welcome.

317 Hilmes, Rolf. *Main Battle Tanks: Developments in Design since 1945*. London: Brassey's Defence Publishers, 1987. 130pp. ISBN 0–08–034756–8.

West Germany's foremost tank technology expert presents his analysis of developments in main battle tanks (MBT) since World War II. He concludes that improvements in tank design have been modest and that antitank weaponry has advanced to a state threatening tank supremacy in land warfare. Modern tanks have improved in firepower, mobility, and survivability, but the best prospects for future tank development reside in the external gun concept. This work is the best technical treatment on tank design on the market.

318 Hobbs, David. *Cruise Missiles: Facts and Issues*. Aberdeen, Scotland: Centre for Defence Studies, 1982. 62pp.

Cruise missiles were a controversial topic in both Europe and the United States during the early 1980s. A product of the Centre for Defence Studies, this sourcebook contains information on the technology of the Cruise missile and arguments pro and con on deployment. Although the technology on Cruise missiles has advanced beyond the stage indicated in this book, the publication presents both facts and issues that any researcher or student will find useful.

319 *The International Countermeasures Handbook*, 11th ed. Palo Alto, CA: EW Communications, 1986. 444pp. ISBN 0–918994–12–8.

This handbook examines all aspects of electronic warfare, including electronic warfare budgets, technological developments, and Soviet weapons and electronics. Electronic weapons systems and countermeasure systems are analyzed for specifications and manufacturers. This publication is the best source on electronic warfare on the market.

320 *International Weapons Developments: A Survey of Current Developments in Weapons Systems.* Oxford, England: Brassey's Publishers, 1980. 203pp. ISBN 0–0802–7028–X.
This sourcebook is an updated guide by the Royal United Services Institute for Defence Studies, London, of trends in international weapons development and technology. Although much of the material can be gathered in the *RUSI and Brassey Defence Yearbook*, each edition adds special features not available in that publication. This sourcebook is most useful for its authoritative analysis of different weapons systems.

321 Isby, David C., and Charles Kamps. *Armies of NATO's Central Front.* London: Jane's Publishing, 1985. 479pp. ISBN 0–7106–0341–X.
Capabilities, deployments, and tactics of NATO forces in Central Europe are featured in this sourcebook. Each NATO defense force is analyzed for its possible contributions toward warfare in Europe. Excellent illustrations and good charts characterize this publication. No study of NATO strategy and tactics can ignore the material in this book.

322 Ismael, Tareq Y. *Iraq and Iran: Roots of Conflict.* Syracuse, NY: Syracuse University Press, 1982. 226pp. ISBN 0–8156–2280–5.
This sourcebook contains documents on the origin and background of the Iran-Iraq War. The rivalry over the Shatt al-Arab has had a long history, and this rivalry is chronicled from documents gathered from 1847 to the present. A lengthy introduction places these documents in their historical perspective. This book is indispensable to an understanding of the legal and political arguments from both sides in this lengthy war.

323 Jordan, John. *Soviet Warships: The Soviet Surface Fleet, 1960 to the Present.* Annapolis, MD: Naval Institute Press, 1983. 128pp. ISBN 0–87021–878–6.
After a preliminary warning that most information about the Soviet warship fleet comes from "at best" educated guesswork, the author gives a ship-by-ship analysis of the Soviet Navy in the early 1980s. This analysis is accompanied by the author's interpretation of the strategic role of the Soviet Navy in Soviet military strategy. The stated purpose of this publication is to investigate and to compare, but its strong point remains the author's interpretations.

324 Krivinyi, Nikolaus. *Warplanes of the World, 1983/84.* Annapolis, MD: Nautical and Aviation Publishing Company of America, 1983. 559pp. ISBN 0–933852–37–1.
Each country's air force is analyzed in depth in this databook. Different types of aircraft and weaponry are studied for performance and reliability, with special attention accorded to performance characteristics of fighter aircraft. This book is an invaluable source for those scholars interested in the comparison of national warplane development.

325 Lyon, Hugh. *An Illustrated Guide to Modern Warships.* New York: Arco, 1980. 159pp. ISBN 0–668–04966–9.

Technological innovations make a slower impact on the world's navies than they do in other military forces. Consequently, the time lag between planning and implementation of a naval program takes from five to ten years. This is the reason that this dated guidebook remains a valuable source for modern warships. Good illustrations and coverage of the warships of minor naval powers contribute to making this reference work serviceable.

326   Marchant Smith, C. J., and P. R. Haslam. *Small Arms and Cannons.* Oxford, England: Brassey's Publishers, 1982. 202pp. ISBN 0–08–028330–6.

Rather than a descriptive catalogue of small arms types, this sourcebook deals with the military requirements of small arms and cannons. Weapons are studied with relationship to desirable characteristics, and types of weapons are compared and contrasted with these characteristics. Such studies are significant in comparing the potential effectiveness of combatants during hostilities.

327   McAllister, Chris. *Military Aircraft Today.* London: Batsford, 1985. 168pp. ISBN 0–71–343874–6.

This publication explains the function not only of the planes and engines of military aircraft but also the weapons systems, avionics, training, and tactics. Diagrams and illustrations are also included. This book is a solid reference for both background and future trends in military aircraft.

328   *Military Helicopters.* By P. G. Harrison et al. Oxford, England: Brassey's Publishers, 1985. 155pp. ISBN 0–08–029958–X.

The principles of wing flight and the characteristics and limitations of military helicopters are highlighted in this publication. Technological advances in aviation have been rapid, and the helicopter is sharing in these advancements. Besides outlining the general and tactical uses of the helicopter, the most significant part of this book is the section on future trends in military helicopter development.

329   Miller, D. M. O., et al. *The Balance of Military Power: An Illustrated Assessment Comparing the Weapons and Capabilities of NATO and the Warsaw Pact.* New York: Salamander Books, 1981. 208pp. ISBN 0–31–206587–6.

Facts, figures, and details on the military balance of power between NATO and the Warsaw Pact are presented in this book. Each military component (air force, army, navy, and nuclear forces) is compared by prominent military analysts. Although dated, this sourcebook provides a well-illustrated comparative study of NATO and the Warsaw Pact.

330   *The Nuclear War File.* Compiled by Christopher Chant and Ian Hogg. London: Ebury Press, 1983. 160pp. ISBN 0–85223–385–X.

Two prominent British defense specialists produced this sourcebook on nuclear weapons and delivery systems. The authors used official figures as much as possible to authenticate the data. An effective use of illustrations and drawings makes the material more understandable. This book is designed for the general reader, but even the advanced reader will find information of value.

331   *Nuclear Weapons and Nuclear War: A Source Book for Health Professionals.* Edited by Christine Cassel, Michael McCally, and Henry Abraham. New York: Praeger, 1984. 553pp. ISBN 0–03–063872–0.

Three medical doctors have prepared a sourcebook of thirty-one readings on the medical and human biological aspects of nuclear weapons and nuclear war. This book is a response to a demand for teaching material for courses in medical schools on medical problems of nuclear injuries. Although intended for health professionals, the editors hope that others will also use the work. This sourcebook contains articles of value to any researcher or person interested in gauging the effects of nuclear war.

332 *Nuclear Weapons Databook. Vol. 1: U.S. Nuclear Forces and Capabilities.* By Thomas B. Cochran, William M. Arkin, and Milton M. Hoenig. Cambridge, MA: Ballinger, 1984– . ISBN 0–88410–173–8.
Volume 1 is part of a projected eight-volume study on all aspects of the production and the deployment of nuclear weapons worldwide. This sourcebook provides an in-depth look at nuclear weaponry, beginning with a reference work on U.S. nuclear forces and their tactical capabilities. This series is published under the auspices of the Natural Resources Defense Council and is one of the best reference works on this subject on the market.

333 *Review of U.S. Military Research and Development, 1984.* Edited by Kosta Tsipis and Penny Janeway. Washington, DC: Pergamon-Brassey's, 1984. 229pp. ISBN 0–080316–22–0.
This product of the Program in Science and Technology for International Security (PSTIS) at the Massachusetts Institute of Technology reviews U.S. research efforts on military technology. It is intended to share technical information on military research and development with the general public, maintaining that only in this way can the U.S. public make more intelligent policy decisions on defense. This book makes its contribution by providing a solid overview of military research and development.

334 Scherer, John L. *Handbook on Soviet Military Deficiencies.* Minneapolis, MN: Scherer, 1983. 130pp. ISBN 0–960725–81–4.
The author identifies Soviet military deficiencies in an effort to balance Western perceptions of the Soviet armed forces. Any sources that indicate a real or potential Soviet weakness are chronicled in detail, with an effort to identify the source. While this work serves as a useful antidote to sources warning of Soviet military supremacy, the author falls into the same conceptual pitfall that he accuses others of doing by overemphasizing statistical data.

335 *Ships, Aircraft and Weapons of the United States Navy.* Washington, DC: U.S. Government Printing Office, 1984. 67pp.
The Department of the Navy has produced this series of fact sheets on the major navy weapons systems. It gives the mission, description, characteristics, and comments on ships, fixed wing aircraft, helicopters, missiles, and other weapons. Pictures or artists' conceptions are provided for each example. This sourcebook presents the official data on navy ships and equipment, and it is most valuable as a general reference source.

336 *Small Arms Today: Latest Reports on the World's Weapons and Ammunition.* Harrisburg, PA: Stackpole Books, 1984. 256pp. ISBN 0–8117–2197–3.
This databook catalogues the small caliber weapons in use and ammunition available for the world's armies. Each country's arsenal of handguns,

rifles, machine guns, and automatic cannons is listed, along with military requirements for ammunition. This publication is a good source for tracing information about types of arms transfers of small caliber weapons.

337 *Soviet Naval Developments*, 3d ed. Department of the Navy. Annapolis, MD: Nautical and Aviation Publishing, 1984. 139pp. ISBN 0–933852–44–4.

Now in its third edition, this reference source on the Soviet Navy is published under the auspices of the director of naval intelligence, U.S. Navy. The purpose is to provide up-to-date information on the current and future status of the Soviet Navy. It also serves as a justification for lobbying by the U.S. Navy for an increase in appropriations. Regardless of the intent, this book provides detailed information on each class of naval vessel in the Soviet Navy.

338 Streetly, Martin. *World Electronic Warfare Aircraft*. London: Jane's Publishing, 1983. 127pp. ISBN 0–7106–0665–9.

Current developments in airborne electronic warfare are featured in this sourcebook, which includes all electronic warfare aircraft produced by any air force since 1945. Some seventy types of electronic aircraft are described, with drawings noting the type of electronic equipment. While any treatment of electronic warfare aircraft runs into security requirements, this book makes its contribution in the lists of U.S. and Soviet electronic equipment.

339 *Surveillance and Target Acquisition Systems*. By A. L. Rodgers et al. Oxford, England: Brassey's Defence Publishers, 1983. 217pp. ISBN 0–08–028334–9.

The scientific techniques used to carry out surveillance and to find targets in limited visibility areas are the subjects of this publication. It covers optics, image intensification, thermal imaging, radar, and lasers and the military applications of these techniques. This sourcebook provides an excellent introduction for researchers and students interested in these technical subjects.

340 *Understanding Soviet Naval Developments*, 5th ed. Washington, DC: Office of the Chief of Naval Operations, 1985. 152pp.

The Office of the Chief of Naval Operations prepares this assessment of Soviet naval capabilities at regular four-year intervals. This assessment covers Soviet naval doctrine, naval personnel, organization, order of battle, aircraft, and warship descriptions. Such a survey gives the general public a good look at the chief adversary of the U.S. Navy. This sourcebook provides a mass of data and analysis, which is useful background material for any researcher on the Soviet Navy.

341 *Vehicles and Bridging*. By I. F. B. Tytler et al. London: Brassey's Defence Publishers, 1985. 239pp. ISBN 0–08–028322–5.

The title of this book is deceiving because most of the subject emphasis is on tanks rather than military vehicles and bridging techniques. All aspects of the origin, development, design, and operation of tanks are covered here. Other military vehicles are dealt with but not in nearly as much detail as with tanks. There is also a fine chapter on military bridging. The authors are affiliated with the Royal Military College of Science, Shrivenham, England, and have produced a solid treatment of the subjects.

342 Ward, J. W. D., and G. N. Turner. *Military Data Processing and Micro-computers.* Oxford, England: Brassey's Defence Publishers, 1982. 221pp. ISBN 0–08–028338–1.

This sourcebook is an introduction to the application of computer technology to the military environment. Although this work is oriented more toward the professional soldier than the scholar, the information on computer applications provides a good background for researchers interested in the tactical use of computers. The technical aspects make this book difficult for anyone but a specialist in military computing.

343 *Weapons Systems.* Washington, DC: U.S. Government Printing Office, 1985. 205pp.

Nearly every year the U.S. Army produces a handbook on weapons systems and equipment in the army inventory. This book lists each weapon system and equipment developed by the Army Research, Development and Acquisition (RDA) program. In addition, each weapon or piece of equipment is compared with its Soviet counterpart, and a listing of U.S. contractors is provided. This handbook is a good background source for any study of U.S. weapons systems.

344 *Weyers Warships of the World,* 57th ed. Edited by Gerhard Albrecht. Annapolis, MD: Nautical and Aviation Publishing, 1983. 730pp. ISBN 0–933852–43–6.

Now in its fifty-seventh edition, this handbook is produced in West Germany by the Monch Publishing Group and is one of the world's most authoritative sources on naval warships. It is filled with illustrations and in-depth statistical data on each country's naval forces. Since it is published in both English and German, there is some difficulty in using this handbook.

345 *What Should Be the Level of U.S. Commitments for National Defense?* Washington, DC: U.S. Government Printing Office, 1982. 883pp.

The Congressional Research Service, Library of Congress, prepared these documents for the National Debate competition in 1982–1983. But anyone interested in materials on U.S. national defense will find these documents and reprinted articles most useful. A selected bibliography of books and articles is also included for the convenience of the reader. This sourcebook can be recommended for both high school and undergraduate-level coursework.

346 *World Defense Forces: A Compendium of Current Military Information for All Countries of the World.* Santa Barbara, CA: ABC-Clio, 1987. 137pp. ISBN 0–87436–486–8.

This book is a collection of data on the current military forces and equipment inventories of every military power in the world. The data have been taken from ABC-Clio's *Kaleidoscope: Current World Data* database. Current information on military personnel, defense expenditures, and combat inventories of army, navy, and air force are provided for each country. This work provides a source for quick reference on defense forces worldwide, but there is no attempt at evaluation.

347 *World Weapon Database.* Edited by Randall Forsberg. Lexington, MA: Lexington Books, 1986–1987. 2 vols. ISBN 0–669–11798–6. ISBN 0–669–14887–3.

These two volumes are part of a projected dozen volumes published by the Institute for Defense and Disarmament Studies, Brookline, Massachusetts. The first volume on Soviet missiles and the second volume on Soviet military aircraft contain the most up-to-date data on these subjects. Every missile and military aircraft is inventoried from specification to deployment with individual sources identified. This work is the most detailed reference source on these subjects available.

Dictionaries

348 *Aviation-Space Dictionary*, 6th ed. Edited by Ernest J. Gentile. Fallbrook, CA: Aero, 1980. 272pp. ISBN 0–8168–3002–9.

Now in its sixth edition, this dictionary has been updated to incorporate the changes in terminology caused by the advancements in aeronautical technology. It is an excellent source of technical terms used in aviation and/or space research. This dictionary can be recommended for any type of collection.

349 *Brassey's Multilingual Military Dictionary*. London: Brassey's Defence Publishers, 1987. 815pp. ISBN 0–08–027032–8.

A team of British military specialists edited and translated the six languages in this military dictionary after the terms had been selected by Henry Stanhope, diplomatic correspondent at *The Times*. The six languages are English, French, Spanish, German, Russian, and Arabic in this order. This dictionary was compiled for the use of military personnel, but it has value for other researchers also. Such dictionaries are an invaluable addition to any research collection.

350 *Department of Defense Dictionary of Military and Associated Terms*. Washington, DC: Joint Chiefs of Staff, 1986. 399pp.

The purpose of this dictionary is to supplement English language dictionaries with a source of standard terminology for military use. It incorporates and identifies Department of Defense (DOD), NATO, and member countries of the Inter-American Defense Board (IADB) usage. DOD components are required to use the terminology in this dictionary. Anyone studying U.S. defense subjects will find this dictionary useful for understanding defense terminology.

351 Dobson, Christopher, and Ronald Payne. *The Dictionary of Espionage*. London: Harrap, 1984. 234pp. ISBN 0–345–54201–9.

This dictionary chronicles the most famous and significant agents and spies in espionage and intelligence since 1945. Each citation gives a brief biographical sketch of the agent or spy along with his or her significance. Another section gives a breakdown on the intelligence communities in all the major countries of the world. This dictionary is a useful source for background information on intelligence and counterintelligence activities since World War II.

352 Sheehan, Michael, and James H. Wyllie. *The Economist Pocket Guide to Defence*. Oxford, England: Blackwell, 1986. 269pp. ISBN 0–631–14725–X.

The authors have produced a dictionary of defense and security alliances, concepts, events, theories, and weapons. Each citation has a two- to three-paragraph explanation, and most of the key concepts and terms have been included. This reference work is oriented toward the general public, journalists, and students, and will prove a useful source for this audience.

353 Stephenson, Michael, and John Weal. *Nuclear Dictionary*. Harlow, England: Longman, 1985. 188pp. ISBN 0–582–89212–0.
A variety of sources were consulted in compiling this excellent dictionary of nuclear terms. *Nuclear* is defined to include any weapons system with a nuclear capability. A short but useful bibliography is provided at the end of the work. The coverage in this dictionary makes it a reference source recommended for anyone interested in nuclear terms.

Digests

354 *The Soviet Army Digest from the Soviet Press*. Jerusalem: International Research Center on Contemporary Society, 1985– .
This digest is a monthly compilation of materials gathered from the Soviet military press by the Israeli think tank, the International Research Center on Contemporary Society, Jerusalem. The contents of this digest are selected to be of value for scholars and students interested in the role of the Soviet armed forces in the Soviet Union and abroad. The translations are excellent. This source is invaluable for research on Soviet military topics.

Directories

355 *Interavia ABC Aerospace Directory*, 33d ed. Edited by J. Didelot. Geneva, Switzerland: Interavia, 1936– . ISSN 0074–1116. $222.
Now in its thirty-third edition, this directory covers every aspect of the international aerospace industry. It has information on the aerospace industries in each country along with addresses and telephone numbers. Several indexes are provided for the benefit of the users. Researchers will find this an outstanding source of information.

356 *International Defense Directory*. Geneva, Switzerland: Interavia, 1984– . $180.
The Interavia Company, a major source of international defense information for the past fifty years, publishes this defense directory, which lists suppliers of military equipment and services worldwide. A special feature is its list of procurement organizations within each defense company. This publication is the major directory for the international defense industry.

357 *Jane's Spaceflight Directory*. Edited by Reginald Turnill. London: Jane's Publishing, 1986. 453pp. ISBN 0–7106–0367–3. $120.
This directory is a compilation of information on space programs in operation in 1986. While the bulk of the information concerns Soviet space programs, there are data on the space programs from every country involved in space exploration. Other useful features are sections on military space projects, international space contractors, and satellite launch tables. Each of the Jane's publications provides a mass of material, and this book is no exception.

Encyclopedias

358 Chesneau, Roger. *Aircraft Carriers of the World, 1914 to Present: An Illustrated Encyclopedia.* Annapolis, MD: Naval Institute Press, 1984. 288pp. ISBN 0–87021–902–2.

The author catalogs all the aircraft carriers that have served in any of the world's navies since 1914. Besides specifications on each aircraft carrier, the author gives his interpretation of carrier design and tactics. While the United States continues to build "super carriers," the remainder of the world is more interested in smaller carriers with multimission V/STOL aircraft. This work is encyclopedic in coverage, and anyone interested in aircraft carriers will find the information valuable.

359 Gunston, Bill. *Aircraft of the Soviet Union: The Encyclopaedia of Soviet Aircraft since 1917.* London: Osprey, 1983. 414pp. ISBN 0–85045–445–X.

A noted expert on air forces of the world, the author produced this encyclopedia of every known aircraft developed in the Soviet Union since 1917. Entries are organized around the aircraft designers, and each model follows the developmental cycle. Excellent photographs and schematic drawings augment the author's analysis of each aircraft. This is the best source of its type on the market.

360 *The Illustrated Encyclopedia of the Strategy, Tactics and Weapons of Russian Military Power.* Edited by Ray Bonds. London: Salamander, 1980. 249pp. ISBN 0–312–40783–1.

This encyclopedia contains a mass of information on all aspects of the Soviet armed forces. Although organized more like a guidebook than an encyclopedia, the work covers all branches of the Soviet military organization. The illustrations serve as an excellent reinforcement for the statistical data. This encyclopedia is a useful first step for scholars, students, and the general public to consult before conducting further research.

Guidebooks

361 Bertsch, Kenneth A., and Linda S. Shaw. *The Nuclear Weapons Industry.* Washington, DC: Investor Responsibility Research Center, 1984. 405pp.

Corporate participation in the production of nuclear weapons and support equipment for the U.S. government is the subject of this guidebook. After a look at the nuclear weapons industry and its strategic implications, the authors profiled twenty-six leading companies in the nuclear field. Each company's involvement in nuclear transactions is studied in depth. This guidebook is a good introduction to further research on the nuclear weapons industry.

362 *Defense Dollars and Sense: A Common Cause Guide to the Defense Budget Process.* Washington, DC: Common Cause, 1983. 90pp. ISBN 0–914389–00–9.

The processes of the U.S. defense budget are scrutinized in this book, published under the auspices of Common Cause. Each step of the defense budget process is examined for cost benefits to the U.S. government. Inadequacies of the present system call for a series of reforms, i.e., more realistic defense goals, rethinking of roles and missions, reform of the Joint Chiefs of Staff, cancellation of unnecessary weapons systems, improvement in cost estimating, and ending of lobbying by defense contractors. This book is a major assessment and critique of the defense budget process.

363 Dunnigan, James F., and Austin Bay. *A Quick and Dirty Guide to War: Briefings on Present and Potential Wars*. New York: Morrow, 1985. 415pp. ISBN 0–688–04199–X.

Current and potential wars and violent political conflicts are the focus of this guidebook. By surveying the political, ethnic, and economic makeups of military hot spots, the authors believe that the reader can have a better comprehension of the possibility of the outbreak of hostilities in these localities. They place their reliability on the line by posting odds on the likelihood of hostilities breaking out in any region. This guidebook is a stimulating look at present and potential crises.

364 Green, William C. *Soviet Nuclear Weapons Policy: A Research and Bibliographic Guide*. Boulder, CO: Westview Press, 1987. 399pp. ISBN 0–86531–817–4.

This book is a research guide to Western and Soviet literature on Soviet nuclear weapons policy, which can also serve as a bibliography on the subject. More than a recitation of the information in each article or monograph, each annotation is a lengthy paragraph size to enable the reader to understand the source's relevance to the issue of Soviet nuclear weapons policy. This book is the best research guide of its type on the market.

365 Gunston, Bill. *An Illustrated Guide to Future Fighters and Combat Aircraft*. London: Salamander, 1984. 159pp. ISBN 0–668–06065–4.

The author, the former technical editor of *Flight International* and the assistant compiler of *Jane's All the World's Aircraft*, uses this guidebook to concentrate upon the technologies of military aircraft now in the process of development for the period after 1990. Many of the aircraft mentioned in this reference source will never be developed, but the author gives a look at trends in fighter design. This guidebook contributes to the study of international military aircraft trends for the next two decades.

366 Gunston, Bill. *An Illustrated Guide to Military Helicopters*. New York: Salamander, 1986. 159pp. ISBN 0–668–05345–3.

All types of military helicopters are surveyed and analyzed for performance and mission characteristics in this guidebook. Each helicopter type has a section with pictures and performance capacities. The contents of this guidebook show the importance that the major powers ascribe to the military utility of the helicopter. Data in this guidebook make it the best source on military helicopters on the market.

367 Gunston, Bill. *An Illustrated Guide to Modern Airborne Missiles*. New York: Salamander, 1983. 159pp. ISBN 0–668–05822–6.

Among the more valuable of the illustrated guidebooks is this guide to all the air-launched missiles in service with and under development for the world's armed forces. The treatment of semiactive radar homing (SARHO) and infrared homing (IR) missile systems makes this book useful for background data in arms control research. Illustrations and photographs help the reader understand the analysis. This guidebook serves as a good introduction to the study of modern airborne missiles.

368 Gunston, Bill. *An Illustrated Guide to NATO Fighters and Attack Aircraft.* New York: Salamander, 1986. 156pp. ISBN 0–668–05824–4.

This guidebook combines information on NATO fighter and attack aircraft and deployment patterns. Every combat aircraft in the NATO arsenal is examined for performance characteristics and deployment. Also useful is the breakdown of NATO air forces and a look at future fighter development. This book is another in a series of excellent handy reference works for both the specialist and the general reader.

369 Gunston, Bill. *An Illustrated Guide to Spy Planes and Electronic Warfare Aircraft.* New York: Salamander, 1983. 159pp. ISBN 0–668–05825–0.

Intelligence-gathering aircraft from the inventories of all the major air forces are surveyed in this guidebook. Reconnaissance, electronic warfare (EW), and airborne early warning (AEW) aircraft are examined for types of planes and equipment and intelligence capabilities. Use of colored illustrations makes this guidebook an excellent source for both the beginner and the scholar in the defense field.

370 Gunston, Bill. *An Illustrated Guide to the Israeli Air Force.* New York: Salamander, 1982. 159pp. ISBN 0–668–05506–5.

This guidebook is a complete catalog of every type of aircraft to have served in the Israeli Air Force from 1949 to 1982. This survey includes helicopters and light observation planes, as well as air-superiority aircraft. Because of its wide scope, this guidebook is more useful to trace the historical development of the Israeli Air Force than examine its current status.

371 Gunston, Bill. *An Illustrated Guide to the Modern Soviet Air Force.* New York: Salamander, 1982. 159pp. ISBN 0–668–05496–4.

The inventory of military aircraft in the Soviet Air Force is surveyed in this guidebook. Each type of aircraft is studied for origin, type, engine, performance, and specifications. While Soviet planes are outstanding, their rate of development has been relatively slow since 1967. This book is another excellent example of guidebooks serving as a source of study of aircraft development.

372 Gunston, Bill. *An Illustrated Guide to USAF: The Modern US Air Force.* New York: Salamander, 1982. 159pp. ISBN 0–668–05497–2.

Every fixed-wing aircraft of the U.S. Air Force as of 1982 is dealt with in this critical appraisal of the capabilities of the design and performance of each aircraft. The United States has produced a series of high-quality air-superiority aircraft in the last two decades, but the cost per aircraft and the low numbers are disturbing trends. This work covers every aircraft in the U.S. inventory in detail with a series of excellent illustrations. This guidebook is most valuable for the general reader.

373 Hoover, Robert A. *The MX Controversy: A Guide to Issues and References.* Claremont, CA: Regina Books, 1982. 116pp. ISBN 0–941690–00–8.

The controversy over the MX missile system during the six years of debate within three administrations is summarized in this guidebook. By the early

1980s no alternative for basing the MX providing for missile invulnerability, response time, and command and control had been decided upon during two presidential administrations. Besides analysis of the MX controversy, this book has a bibliography of 360 documents, pamphlets, books, and articles on the subject. This work is an excellent reference source for the controversy over the MX in the late 1970s and early 1980s.

374 *An Illustrated Anatomy of the World's Fighters: The Inside Story of 100 Classics in the Evolution of Fighter Aircraft.* Compiled by William Green and Gordon Swanborough. London: Salamander, 1981. 240pp. ISBN 0–86101–105–8.

The evolution of modern fighter aircraft is traced in this study of the one hundred most famous fighters. Each aircraft is studied for its contribution to the development of the modern fighter. The only problem is that materials on several of the most recent Soviet air-superiority fighters are missing. This guidebook gives basic technical data on each aircraft without frills, and it is recommended for either the general reader or the advanced student.

375 *An Illustrated Examination of Advanced Technology Warfare: A Detailed Study of the Latest Weapons and Techniques for Warfare Today and into the 21st Century.* By Richard S. Friedman et al. Sydney: Hodder and Stoughton, 1985. 208pp. ISBN 0–340–37311–3.

Six NATO defense analysts survey the impact of military technology on modern warfare in the next couple of decades. Each specialist gives his assessment of technological advances in his speciality. The result is an up-to-date analysis of the current state of military technology. This book contains a mass of technical data that both the novice and expert scholar can use.

376 *An Illustrated Guide to Modern Tanks and Fighting Vehicles.* Edited by Ray Bonds. New York: Salamander, 1980. 159pp. ISBN 0–668–04965–0.

The scope of this guidebook is the world's arsenal of tanks and other armored fighting vehicles. Armaments, dimensions, weights, engines, and battlefield performance are all analyzed for military potential. It also notes the potential export market for each type of armored vehicle. This guidebook is intended for the general public, but researchers will find the information handy as well.

377 *An Illustrated Guide to the Weapons of the Modern Soviet Ground Forces.* Edited by Ray Bonds. New York: Salamander, 1981. 158pp. ISBN 0–668–05344–5.

This guidebook is a basic reference source for information on the organization, equipment, and weapons of the Soviet Army. It lists every weapon in use in the Soviet ground forces, placing special emphasis on tanks. Excellent illustrations accompany the statistical data and assessments of the organization and equipment. Guidebooks of this caliber serve as good sources for basic information.

378 Miller, David. *An Illustrated Guide to Modern Submarines: The Undersea Weapons That Rule the Oceans Today.* New York: Salamander, 1982. 159pp. ISBN 0–668–05495–6.

All the principal types of submarines in service or projected to be developed in the world's navies are studied in this illustrated guidebook. It includes sections on strategic missile submarines, nuclear-powered attack submarines, and conventional submarines. Also valuable is a section on types of submarine-launched strategic missiles. This book is a good introduction to modern submarines.

379 Polmar, Norman. *Guide to the Soviet Navy*, 3d ed. Annapolis, MD: Naval Institute Press, 1983. 465pp. ISBN 0–87021–239–7.

This guidebook gathers information on the operational capacity, personnel requirements, and ships of the Soviet Navy from a variety of official Western sources and other published materials. While this publication resembles other guides on Soviet naval data, its strength is in its evaluation of the strategic uses of the Soviet naval forces. The author is a recognized authority on naval affairs, and this guidebook serves as one of the standard reference sources on the Soviet Navy.

380 Richardson, Doug. *An Illustrated Guide to the Techniques and Equipment of Electronic Warfare*. Sydney: Hodler and Stoughton, 1985. 151pp. ISBN 0–340–37307–5.

This guidebook focuses on trends in the development of electronic warfare equipment. Each type of electronic system is analyzed for performance effectiveness. Data have been gleaned from unclassified sources such as defense exhibitions, defense journals, and defense textbooks. This sourcebook is an excellent introduction to the field of electronic warfare.

381 Richardson, Doug. *An Illustrated Survey of the West's Modern Fighters: Technical Details of Today's Most Advanced Fighting Aircraft*. London: Salamander, 1984. 207pp. ISBN 0–668–1153–5.

Attack aircraft, tactical fighters, and air-superiority interceptors of the Western alliance are compared in detail in this guidebook. Each aircraft is examined with regard to development, structure, propulsion, avionics, armament, and performance. While the illustrations are excellent, it is in the commentary on the capabilities of each aircraft that this guidebook excels.

382 Rodgers, Paul. *Guide to Nuclear Weapons, 1984–85*. Bradford, England: School of Peace Studies, 1984. 124pp. ISBN 0–901945–54–4.

This guidebook is a survey of nuclear weapons in the world's military arsenals. The nuclear inventories of eight countries are explored, and the possibilities of proliferation are highlighted. In addition to each country's nuclear capability, delivery systems are analyzed in detail. This publication from Bradford University's School of Peace Studies is an excellent source for further study on nuclear weapons.

383 Shaw, Linda. *Stocking the Arsenal: A Guide to the Nation's Top Military Contractors*. Washington, DC: Investor Responsibility Research Center, 1985. 207pp. ISBN 0–93103–501–5.

The eighty-four leading U.S. military contractors are featured in this guidebook. Each contractor's defense and nuclear weapons–related contracts are listed by the author. It was prepared under the auspices of the Investor Responsibility Research Center (IRRC), an independent, nonprofit corporation founded in 1972. This source is an excellent introduction to the study of the U.S. military-industrial connection.

Hearings

384 U.S. Congress. Chemical Warfare Review Commission. *Report of the Chemical Warfare Review Commission.* Washington, DC: U.S. Government Printing Office, 1985. 104pp.

This report from the Chemical Warfare Review Commission on chemical warfare contains the final conclusions of a committee established by Congress and appointed by the president. The commission traveled extensively both in the United States and Europe to familiarize the members with the problems of chemical warfare. Conclusions are that the United States should modernize its chemical stockpile to promote chemical weapons negotiations with the Soviet Union and/or to serve as a deterrence. The conclusions of this commission are of no surprise, since the members are mostly military men and conservative spokespersons.

385 U.S. Congress. Congressional Budget Office. *Tactical Combat Forces of the United States Air Force: Issues and Alternatives.* Washington, DC: Congressional Budget Office, 1985. 79pp.

This report by the Congressional Budget Office (CBO) is an analysis of the effects of the Reagan administration's current tactical aircraft plans on cost and modernization. The Department of Defense plans in the next five years to include four new wings and to replace F-4 aircraft with newer F-15 and F-16 aircraft. Various estimates on the cost of this upgrading are considered along with different planning scenarios. This report reveals the complex decision making required in aircraft procurement.

386 U.S. Congress. House. Committee on Armed Services. *Implications of the President's Strategic Defense Initiative and Antisatellite Weapons Policy.* Washington, DC: U.S. Government Printing Office, 1985. 245pp.

Two hearings were held in the spring of 1985 by the Subcommittee on Arms Control, International Security and Science on the arms control and budgetary implications of the Strategic Defense Initiative (SDI). Various politicians and defense experts testified on the merits and demerits of SDI and whether research on it would be in violation of the ABM Treaty. Other testimony dealt with the funds necessary to build an SDI system. Both the hearing testimony and supporting documents make this record an important source for SDI research.

387 U.S. Congress. House. Committee on Foreign Affairs. *Implications of the President's Strategic Defense Initiative and Antisatellite Weapons Policy.* Washington, DC: U.S. Government Printing Office, 1985. 245pp.

Two hearings were held in the spring of 1985 on the strategic and budgetary implications of the Strategic Defense Initiative (SDI). Politicians and representatives from various private research institutes made their views known to the committee. Several supporting documents on aspects of the SDI are included with the testimony. These hearings are another good source of opinions on the feasibility and costs of SDI.

388 U.S. Congress. House. Committee on Foreign Affairs. *NATO's Future Role.* Washington, DC: U.S. Government Printing Office, 1982. 130pp.

This booklet is the record of hearings before the Subcommittee on Europe and the Middle East in May and June 1982 on NATO's capacity to fulfill its military obligations in Europe. A series of prepared statements is followed by personal statements of participants and a question and answer session. Most of the participants agreed that NATO's military forces needed strengthening and that more resources should come from our European allies. Hearings are often a mixed bag, but these hearings produced valuable viewpoints.

389 U.S. Congress. House. Committee on Foreign Affairs. *U.S. Support for the Contras.* Washington, DC: U.S. Government Printing Office, 1985. 374pp.

Three hearings were conducted in April 1985 on U.S. military operations in support of the Contras in their war against Nicaragua. Witnesses both pro and con provided testimony on support for the Contras. The intensity of feelings on this issue produced some interesting exchanges between members of the committee and the witnesses. These hearings are a vital source for viewpoints on Contra aid in 1985.

390 U.S. Congress. House. Select Committee on Intelligence. *CIA Estimates of Soviet Defense Spending.* Washington, DC: U.S. Government Printing Office, 1980. 95pp.

CIA estimates of Soviet defense spending are examined in this hearing held in the fall of 1980. Statements and witnesses from the CIA were presented, and a panel of four experts was formed to question the evidence, who were critical of both the methodology and the statistics. This source is important because numerous books and articles have been written attacking and defending the CIA estimates.

391 U.S. Congress. Senate. Committee on Appropriations. *MX Missile Basing Mode.* Washington, DC: U.S. Government Printing Office, 1980. 269pp.

One of the biggest controversies over the MX missile was the decision on its basing mode. These special hearings in the spring of 1980 indicate the nature of this controversy. Witnesses and supporting documents presented differing views on the basing modes. These hearings give a good indication of the type of arguments used over the problem of the MX missile.

392 U.S. Congress. Senate. Committee on Appropriations. *MX Peacekeeper Missile Program.* Washington, DC: U.S. Government Printing Office, 1985. 138pp.

Two hearings were held in March 1985 on approving funding for the MX missile system. These occasions were used by the Reagan administration officials to argue the merits of the MX missile program advocated by the administration. Both the statements and the supporting documents give the Reagan administration's position on the MX missile system. This source suffers from a lack of testimony from those opposing the system.

393 U.S. Congress. Senate. Committee on Armed Services. *Modernization of the U.S. Strategic Deterrent.* Washington, DC: U.S. Government Printing Office, 1982. 76pp.

Two hearings were conducted in the autumn of 1981 where representatives of the Reagan administration made proposals for the modernization of the U.S. strategic deterrence systems. The primary spokesman was Secretary of Defense Caspar Weinberger, who defended the MX deployment system and the acquisition of the B-1 bomber. Other defense officials also supported the Reagan administration's priorities on these issues. This source gives the official position on these controversial issues.

394 U.S. Congress. Senate. Committee on Foreign Relations. *Report of the Special Committee on Nuclear Weapons in the Atlantic Alliance.* Washington, DC: U.S. Government Printing Office, 1985. 152pp.

The Special Committee on Nuclear Weapons in the Atlantic made this report on NATO's dual-track decision of December 1979 to modernize its intermediate-range nuclear forces (INF). Parliamentarians from NATO's member nations formed this committee and conducted a series of interviews of officials from current and past governments involved in the original decision. The results show that NATO governments still support the 1979 decision, but this issue has destroyed the traditional postwar consensus on defense issues in several NATO countries. This report contains a wealth of useful data for defense and security specialists.

Journals

395 *Afghanistan Report.* Islamabad, Pakistan: Crisis and Conflict Analysis Team, 1984– . $60.

This publication covers all aspects of the military activities of the Afghanistan war. The Crisis and Conflict Analysis Team monitors broadcasting and publishing from a variety of sources in the region, and the information is as accurate and up-to-date as possible from a war zone. Special features are estimates of casualties from both Mujahideen and Soviet sources, and excellent maps of combat zones. This is the best source available on the war in Afghanistan.

396 *Armed Forces and Society: An Interdisciplinary Journal on Military Institutions, Civil-Military Relations, Arms Control and Peacekeeping, and Conflict Management.* Cabin John, MD: Seven Locks Press, 1974– . ISSN 0095–327X. $50.

This journal publishes a number of excellent articles on a range of significant defense and military issues. It is international in scope, while concentrating on historical, comparative, and interdisciplinary writings on the relationship of the military with society. It serves as the official journal of the Inter-University Seminar on Armed Forces and Society. Both the subject material and the quality of the articles make this journal worthwhile to consult.

397 *Combat Journal.* Mhow, India: College of Combat, 1974– . $20.

This journal is the professional forum for the exchange of ideas and research for the Indian Army. It is published by the College of Combat, Mhow, India. Articles range from leadership topics to technical reports on military computer applications. Since the Indian Army is the dominant military force in the south Asian region, this journal constitutes a valuable source for military thinking in the Indian Army.

398 *Defence Science Journal.* New Delhi: Defence Scientific Information and Documentation Centre, 1950– . ISSN 0011–748X. $15.

Science and technology are the topics covered by this Indian defense journal. All branches of science and technology are represented as long as there are defense implications. It is a good source for engineers and scientists interested in technical papers on defense subjects.

399 *Defensa Latino Americana.* Maidenhead, England: Whitton Press, 1977– . ISSN 9261–233X. $70.

All information on Latin American military affairs is covered in this bimonthly British journal. It combines current defense information with substantive articles by defense specialists interested in Latin America. There is also a synopsis in English and Portuguese for the non–Spanish-speaking reader. Anyone interested in Latin American defense issues will find this journal a necessity to consult.

400 *Defense Analysis.* London: Brassey's Defence Publishers, 1985– . ISSN 0743–0175. $84.

During its brief existence, this quarterly British journal on defense theory and analysis has become one of the top journals in the defense field. It is designed to be a forum for the exchange of ideas, and the scholarly articles are effective in accomplishing this goal. An added feature is the section on professional notes where contributors provide short notices about new developments in the defense field. This journal has the potential to become a significant force in the defense field in the next decade.

401 *Defense & Foreign Affairs.* Washington, DC: Defense & Foreign Affairs, 1973– . ISSN 0277–4933. $82.

This journal specializes in information about international defense trends. Each issue has a number of articles on defense issues, but the most valuable feature is the inclusion of tables on arms transfers, missile strengths, and political changes. Other notable features include a conflict index and a rumor mill.

402 *Défense et armement heracles international.* Paris: Editions Larivière, 1981– . $55.

Formerly published under the title *Heracles,* this journal fills the role of provider of defense and military information for the French market. While this publication has correspondents in the major defense markets in the Western countries, the viewpoint is predominantly French. Excellent articles and up-to-date information characterize its contents. This publication compares well with its U.S., Swiss, and West German counterparts.

403 *Défense nationale: problèmes politiques, economiques, scientifiques militaires.* Paris: Défense nationale, 1939– . ISSN 0035–1075. $7.50.

This publication is the most influential French journal in the field of military strategy. It publishes solid articles on both French and international security subjects. The most useful aspect of this publication for U.S. researchers is its articulation of the French viewpoint on defense issues.

404 *Defense Science and Electronics.* Campbell, CA: Rush Franklin Publishing, 1982– . ISSN 0744–6241. $36.

This journal is among the most important of the new publications on defense science on research and design of military computer and electronic systems. It emphasizes electronic technology development and its impact on defense policy. Each January issue also features a directory of U.S. electronic firms and their products. Specialists in defense science find this journal a good forum for the exchange of information.

405 *Defense Week.* Washington, DC: Llewellyn King Publishers, 1980– . ISSN 0273–3188. $595.

News and information about the U.S. defense industry are the speciality of this weekly publication, in which a team of defense analysts writes articles about defense industry trends and the international security situation. This publication is strong on both the technology and the politics of the U.S. defense industry scene. By providing weekly defense information, this newsletter serves a useful function in keeping researchers abreast of current trends in the defense industry.

406 *IDF Journal: Israel Defense Forces Spokesman.* Military Post, Israel: Israel Defense Forces, 1982– . ISSN 0333–8428. $16.

The Israel Defense Forces Spokesman's Unit publishes this quarterly journal to chronicle the achievements, doctrines, and tactics of Israel's armed forces. Most of the articles are by members of the Israeli military establishment, but outside military specialists are also invited to make contributions. Articles are of moderate length and on topics of interest to Middle East military specialists. This publication will be of value to anyone interested in Israeli military subjects.

407 *Indian Defence Review.* New Delhi: Lancer International, 1986– . $15.

This journal reflects the military concerns of the Indian armed forces. Published twice yearly, it provides a forum for research on Indian military topics. Each issue consists of approximately a dozen articles on a variety of military subjects, primarily on aspects of the military rivalry between India and Pakistan.

408 *International Defense Review.* Geneva, Switzerland: Interavia, 1968– . ISSN 0020–6512. $80.

This monthly defense journal traces international scientific and technological advances within the defense industry and provides information about major defense contracts. Heavily utilized by the international defense industry to announce new weapons systems and sell their products, this publication provides a forum for the exchange of research and business information. This is the top international defense journal on the market.

409 *Jane's Defence Weekly.* London: Jane's Publishing, 1982– . ISSN 0265–3818. $75.

Among the more current of the defense publications, this weekly product provides the latest information on trends in the defense industry. Special features include sections on military electronics, military contracts, and senior-level military and defense industry promotions. This journal makes a good companion source of current defense information with the *International Defense Review.*

410 *Journal of Political and Military Sociology.* DeKalb, IL: Office of Social Science Research, 1973– . ISSN 0047–2697. $18.50.

Defined as the study of the relationship of the military to society, approximately half of each issue of this journal consists of articles and book reviews on military sociology. Many of the articles on political sociology also deal with subjects useful for military research. Most of the articles will be of only marginal interest to defense and military specialists, but this publication still has an occasional article of value.

411 *Military Technology.* Koblenz, West Germany: Verlag Wehr und Wissen, 1977– . ISSN 0722–3226. $50.

This monthly product of the West German Monch Publishing Group is among the more informative journals on developments in military technology. It features short articles on all aspects of the application of technology to military affairs. This journal serves as an excellent companion piece to the *International Defense Review.*

412 *National Defense: Journal of the American Defense Preparedness Association.* Arlington, VA: National Defense, 1920– . ISSN 0092–1491. $25.

The prodefense American Defense Preparedness Association produces this monthly journal, which serves both as a sounding board for the U.S. defense community and as a place for defense contractors to advertise weapons systems. It also provides a good forum for military security analysts to study varieties of opinion within the U.S. prodefense lobby.

413 *NATO Review.* Brussels: NATO Information Service, 1953– . Free.

This journal is the bimonthly official organ of NATO. Its purpose is to contribute to a constructive discussion of Atlantic alliance problems. Most of the writing deals with organizational problems existing within the NATO alliance. This publication's objectivity is marred by its close association with NATO, but it still presents many of the issues important to its members.

414 *NATO's Sixteen Nations: Independent Review of Economic, Political and Military Power.* Amstelveen, the Netherlands: Jules Perel's Publishing, 1961– . $38.

This journal devotes most of its space to articles concerning the defense postures of the NATO alliance. Although it covers scientific and technological matters, the major emphasis is on NATO's military strategy and weaponry. This publication is a glossy journal containing a mass of information on NATO, and its major contribution is the information on NATO weapons systems.

415 *Soldat und Technik: Zeitschrift für technische Ausbildung, Fortbildung und Information in der Bundeswehr.* Frankfurt/Main, West Germany: Umschau Verlag Breidenstein, 1958– . ISSN 0038–0989. $98.

The subject of this monthly West German periodical is the relationship between technology and the military. It contains current military news and at least a dozen substantive articles. The emphasis is not restricted to any specific subject but includes writings on army, navy, and air force developments. This publication offers the military specialist a variety of opinion on military technology from the West German perspective.

416 *Soviet Military Review.* Moscow: Krasnaya Zwezda, 1965– . ISSN 0038–5220. $8.

This journal is the monthly foreign language organ of the Soviet military establishment. It is published for international distribution in Arabic, English, French, and Spanish. Although most of the articles are published for propaganda purposes, the viewpoints of the writers and the variety of military subjects make this source useful for defense and military research.

Newsletters

417 *Civilian-Based Defense: News and Opinion.* Omaha, NE: Association for Transarmament Studies, 1984– . $10.

The Association for Transarmament Studies publishes this quarterly newsletter as a vehicle of communication for individuals and groups who believe in the concept of civilian-based defense. Each issue features short scholarly articles followed by international news and announcements. Short book reviews are sometimes included on relevant subjects. Only researchers interested in this topic will find this newsletter of value.

418 *Current News.* Washington, DC: U.S. Air Force, ca. 1975– . Free.

This newsletter is a weekly compilation of newspaper articles from a wide variety of newspapers on defense issues. Published by the air force for the Department of Defense, its intent is to bring defense concerns to the attention of key Department of Defense personnel. Besides the weekly edition there is also a special edition of articles on selected defense issues. This publication is not for sale to nongovernment personnel, but it can be obtained from official sources.

419 *Defense and Disarmament News.* Brookline, MA: Institute for Defense and Disarmament Studies, 1985– . ISSN 0886–5590. $25.

The Institute for Defense and Disarmament Studies, Brookline, Massachusetts, publishes this newsletter to inform activists, teachers, analysts, and the general public of major aspects of military affairs. Each issue includes a section on military policy, arms control policy, and peace movement strategy. It features at least one special article in each issue on a topic of current interest.

420 *Defense and Economy.* Washington, DC: Government Business Worldwide Reports, 1969– . ISSN 0364–9008. $280.

Government Business Worldwide Reports has published this newsletter on defense issues and the U.S. economy since 1969. It consists of short statistical reports, directories of key personnel, and/or short surveys of facilities. Features such as NATO defense expenditures since 1949 and U.S. weapon/equipment acquisition costs make this a valuable reference for defense researchers.

421 *The Defense Monitor.* Washington, DC: Center for Defense Information, 1972– . ISSN 0195–6450. $25.

Short articles and informational factsheets on defense issues characterize this newsletter. It attempts to influence government policy and public opinion by featuring a selected topic on a defense subject of current and national interest in each issue. This newsletter provides as much defense information as any source in the field.

422 *Foreign Military Markets: NATO Weapons 1984.* Greenwich, CT: DMS Market Intelligence Reports, 1984– . $500.

This newsletter specializes in up-to-date detailed information on prospective arms purchasing deals involving NATO equipment. DMS Market Intelligence Company produces this newsletter, and the information is directed toward use by the defense community. This publication provides a wealth of information, but its cost is prohibitively high.

423 *International Defense Intelligence: Newsletter.* Greenwich, CT: DMS Market Intelligence Reports, 1984– . $250.

This weekly newsletter chronicles international defense news, specializing in information on military contracts and arms transfers between countries. Defense Marketing Services (DMS) produces this newsletter, but it is compiled by the DMS Foreign Military Markets Group with contributions from the DMS European Staff. It is another useful but expensive publication from a defense publisher.

424 *National Security Report.* Washington, DC: American Security Press, 1987– . $15.

The American Security Council and the American Security Council Foundation cosponsor this newsletter to disseminate their views on national security issues. Short articles and editorials make up the bulk of its contents. All of the writers advance hardline conservative positions on national security and defense issues. This publication is a good source for determining the conservative viewpoint on these issues.

425 *Nucleus: A Quarterly Report from the Union of Concerned Scientists.* Cambridge, MA: Union of Concerned Scientists, 1979– . ISSN 0888–5729. $10.

This combination journal-newsletter features substantive articles on defense and military issues and news of activities of the Union of Concerned Scientists (UCS). Published quarterly in a large-page format, the editors use illustrations to reinforce the points made by the authors in their articles. This is one of the best newsletters of its type in existence.

Slide Programs

426 *Nuclear War Graphics Package Slide Descriptions.* Cambridge, MA: Nuclear War Graphics Project, 1981. $10.

These slides contain statistical and visual data, compiled during the summer of 1981, on the characteristics and delivery of nuclear weapons. These 130 slides provide visual representation of the effect of nuclear armaments and information for steps to take in case of a nuclear war.

Strategic Atlases

427 Kidron, Michael, and Dan Smith. *The War Atlas: Armed Conflict— Armed Peace.* New York: Simon and Schuster, 1983. 124pp. ISBN 0–671–47249–6.

This atlas depicts the changing international military order since 1945. The author has identified nearly three hundred wars since World War II and analyzed them by means of forty maps. A special feature includes a study of the international military order by listing sixteen variables. This book is a unique source and a welcome addition to the field.

Textbooks

428 Dixon, James H., et al. *National Security Policy Formulation: Institutions, Processes, and Issues.* Lanham, MD: University Press of America, 1984. 237pp. ISBN 0–8191–4935–7.

This book serves as a textbook on the formulation of U.S. defense policy. It was written in part for the use of the National Defense University's resident and extension educational programs. Because it presumes little background on the U.S. government, this book is best used in undergraduate courses. Despite its elementary approach, the analysis is high quality, especially in placing present defense policies within their historical context.

429 *The Star Wars Controversy.* Edited by Steven E. Miller and Stephen Van Evera. Princeton, NJ: Princeton University Press, 1986. 327pp. ISBN 0–691–07713–4.

Various perspectives on the controversy over the Strategic Defense Initiative (SDI) are presented in this book of readings. Representatives of both sides of the SDI debate have prepared papers and/or statements on their views. The work also includes a section on the principal official documents of the controversy. This book is recommended for introductory college-level coursework and the general public.

430 *U.S. National Security: A Framework for Analysis.* Edited by Daniel J. Kaufman, Jeffrey S. McKitrick, and Thomas J. Leney. Lexington, MA: Lexington Books, 1985. 584pp. ISBN 0–669–09812–4.

The need for a textbook on U.S. national security for coursework at the U.S. Military Academy at West Point resulted in this book of readings. A representative sampling of articles since the 1950s has been selected for inclusion, most of which were taken from the mainstream of U.S. thinking on national security issues. This textbook can be recommended for introductory courses in U.S. international relations.

431 *War, Morality, and the Military Profession,* 2d ed. Edited by Malham M. Wakin. Boulder, CO: Westview Press, 1986. 521pp. ISBN 0–8133–0359–1.

This anthology is an update of an earlier work of writings on the military profession and morality and war. New contributions include excerpts from the U.S. Catholic bishops' pastoral letter, "The Challenge of Peace," and coverage on the Strategic Defense Initiative (SDI). Both the coverage and selections make this anthology useful for college coursework.

432 *What Kinds of Guns Are They Buying for Your Butter? A Beginner's Guide to Defense, Weaponry, and Military Spending.* By Sheila Tobias et al. New York: Morrow, 1982. 428pp. ISBN 0–688–01374–0.

Four authors have produced this book to provide the general public an overview of defense issues, including defense policy, equipment, weapons systems, and military strategy. Special effort was made to avoid editorializing. This book can be recommended as a textbook for introductory-level college courses.

Monographs

433 Abdulghani, J. M. *Iraq and Iran: The Years of Crisis.* Baltimore, MD: Johns Hopkins University Press, 1984. 270pp. ISBN 0–8018–2519–9.

Written by a Middle East specialist, the subject of this book is relations between Iran and Iraq since 1968. While Iran and Iraq have long been rivals because of the differences between Arab and Persian nationalism and Sunni-Shi'i divisions, the key reason for their rivalry has been Iran's historical quest to assume a paramount role in the Persian Gulf region. The Khomeini revolution triggered the Iran-Iraq War, and only a political change in either or both regimes will end the war. While this book is an excellent assessment of the causes and probable outcome of the Iran-Iraq War, the author's viewpoint leans more to the Iraqi side.

434 Adams, Gordon, Paul Murphy, and William Grey Rosenau. *Controlling Weapon Costs: Can the Pentagon Reforms Work?* New York: Council on Economic Priorities, 1983. 61pp. ISBN 0–87871–018–1.

Three defense specialists associated with the Council on Economic Priorities critique the Pentagon's reforms on defense procurement. The so-called Carlucci Initiative, these reforms promised realistic cost estimates, decentralization of weapons program management, more stringent cost controls, and less paperwork. The authors assert that these reforms failed to correct the problem of the lack of competition in contract awards, and many of the new requirements will cost more for arms procurement. This book is a solid assessment of the major problems of U.S. weapons procurement.

435 Adelman, Jonathan R. *The Revolutionary Armies: The Historical Development of the Soviet and the Chinese People's Liberation Armies.* Westport, CT: Greenwood Press, 1980. 230pp. ISBN 0–313–22026–3.

This book is a study of the comparative differences between the Soviet Red Army and the Chinese People's Liberation Army (PLA) in the decades following their respective civil wars. The Chinese military has played a far greater role in both the party and society than their Soviet counterparts. Part of this has been because the Soviets have always depended upon the secret police rather than the army to maintain order in contrast to the Chinese, who have trusted the army. Although this book is a historical study, the conclusions have relevance to modern conditions today both in the Soviet Union and China.

436 *African Armies: Evolution and Capabilities.* Edited by Bruce E. Arlinghaus and Pauline H. Baker. Boulder, CO: Westview Press, 1986. 202pp. ISBN 0–86531–757–7.

These essays survey sub-Saharan African military forces, evaluating the extent to which these armies can perform their defense functions. While the authors disagree over the capabilities and the future direction of African military forces, there is a consensus that the involvement of the military in politics has hurt military professionalism. The lack of verifiable data on African military forces hurts an otherwise solid book, but African governments have been reluctant to provide the necessary information.

437 Agursky, Mikhail. *The Soviet Military-Industrial Complex.* Jerusalem: Magnes Press, 1980. 32pp.

This paper deals with the set of Soviet military-industrial ministries whose function is to determine policy for Soviet military industries. Although the Soviet military industry responds to market mechanisms, it is weak on production methods and development. Much of its technical progress is drawn from Western sources and from the Soviet civilian sector. While this short study makes a number of useful points, the author's contentions are weakened by his bias against the Soviet system of weapons procurement.

438 Aldridge, Robert C. *First Strike! The Pentagon's Strategy for Nuclear War.* Boston, MA: South End Press, 1983. 325pp. ISBN 0–89608–154–0.

A former aeronautical engineer at Lockheed charges that the United States has built a first-strike nuclear weapons capability. He uses his expertise in the missile industry to outline the steps taken to develop this first-strike capability. Each weapons system is examined, and its role in a nuclear strike scenario is analyzed. This book combines a good analysis of weapons systems with a propeace viewpoint.

439 Alger, John I. *The Quest for Victory: The History of the Principles of War.* Westport, CT: Greenwood Press, 1982. 318pp. ISBN 0–313–23322–5.

The author surveys past military thought on the origins of the principles of war. Both the U.S. and British armies have codified the "principles of war" into official military doctrine. Several generations of modern officers have been trained by these principles. While this book traces a single theme in the history of military thought, the theme remains an integral part of the intellectual arsenal of Western military thinking.

440 Allen, Thomas B. *War Games: The Secret World of the Creators, Players, and Policy Makers Rehearsing World War III Today.* New York: McGraw-Hill, 1987. 402pp. ISBN 0–07–00195–8.

The significance of war-gaming in developing U.S. diplomatic, military, and strategic planning is analyzed in this book by a U.S. freelance writer for the journal *Sea Power.* The author participated in the Persian Gulf game at the U.S. Naval War College and observed the interactions among the participants, concluding that there are problems in this type of training because of misperceptions and biases of the participants. This book depends on interviews and knowledge of other war games for its analysis. Defense specialists should become aware of this source.

441 *Alternative Military Strategies for the Future.* Edited by Keith A. Dunn and William O. Staudenmaier. Boulder, CO: Westview Press, 1985. ISBN 0–8133–0065–7.

Participants from the academic world and government gathered at a 1983 conference at the U.S. Army War College to discuss U.S. military strategy. The essays in this work, taken from this meeting, are concerned that the present U.S. military strategy and force structure need reform. Despite differences of approach and viewpoint, there is a consensus that military parity between the two superpowers exists and that conventional rather than nuclear warfare is the main military concern. These essays should be read for their variety of opinions and substantive arguments.

442 *American Defense Policy,* 5th ed. Edited by John F. Reichart and Steven R. Sturm. Baltimore, MD: Johns Hopkins University Press, 1982. 860pp. ISBN 0–8018–2757–4.

This book of essays by the leading scholars on U.S. defense issues traces the present course of U.S. national security policy. While no single theme dominates, the viewpoints of sixty-seven authors provide a range of perspectives on defense subjects. Both in size and quality of the contributions, this book is a major asset for anyone interested in defense policy.

443 *America's Security in the 1980s*. Edited by Christoph Bertram. New York: St. Martin's Press, 1982. 117pp. ISBN 0–312–02199–2.

These papers are the product of a 1981 conference on U.S. security in the 1980s held under the sponsorship of the International Institute for Strategic Studies, at Williamsburg, Virginia. Eleven experts on U.S. security contributed papers. There is considerable uncertainty over the future of U.S. security, and the only consensus is on the need to strengthen the alliance system. These essays continue to hold up well even in the mid-1980s.

444 Amundsen, Kersten. *Norway, NATO, and the Forgotten Soviet Challenge*. Berkeley: Institute of International Studies, University of California, 1981. 50pp. ISBN 0–87725–514–8.

Norway and its role in NATO's northern flank is the subject of this book. NATO's northern flank has been relegated to a secondary theater of operations in comparison with the central front, but events in the late 1970s indicate that this region is important to Soviet planning. Norway's military strength needs augmenting by an increase of NATO forces in the region, and the Norwegian government must take action to avoid Soviet intimidation. This study is a welcome addition to the literature on NATO security issues.

445 Anand, V. K. *Insurgency and Counter-Insurgency*. New Delhi: Deep and Deep, 1981. 263pp.

This work identifies the main characteristics of insurgency and the means to counter these movements. By a study of insurgency outbreaks since 1945, the author defines a theory of insurgency and counterinsurgency. He maintains that insurgency is the result of discontent, and counterinsurgency tactics work only in relation to a specific insurgency. While the author's conclusions have value, there is a tendency for him to list problems rather than deal with specific solutions.

446 *Antiballistic Missile Defence in the 1980s*. Edited by Ian Bellany and Coit D. Blacker. London: Frank Cass, 1983. 90pp. ISBN 0–7146–3207–4.

This book is a reprint of a special issue of *Arms Control* (vol. 3, no. 2) under the same title. U.S. and British analysts of strategic studies and arms control contributed essays about antiballistic missile defense programs in the early 1980s. Most attention is directed toward the Reagan administration's policies on antiballistic defense systems, since its approach differs so much from previous positions. This book suffers from the time lags of both a journal and a book, but still has value on perceptions of change in the early 1980s.

447 *Anti-Missile and Anti-Satellite Technologies and Programs: SDI and ASAT*. Park Ridge, NJ: Noyes Publications, 1986. 270pp. ISBN 0–8155–1088–8.

The Department of Defense, the Office of Technology Assessment of the U.S. Congress, and the Heritage Foundation sponsored this book on anti-satellite (ASAT) technologies and the Strategic Defense Initiative (SDI).

While technological and budget realities are examined, special emphasis is given to the extent to which current technological advances will make the SDI system work. The researchers conceive of a multilayered, multitechnological approach to ballistic missile defense that will be able to defend the United States against attack. This book serves as an excellent guide to current SDI and ASAT technology and programs.

448 *Anti-Satellite Weapons and U.S. Military Space Policy.* Lanham, MD: University Press of America, 1986. 42pp. ISBN 0–8191–5477–6.

The Aspen Strategy Group published this report, summarizing the results of its 1985 summer workshop on antisatellite weapons (ASAT) in Aspen, Colorado. At present, neither the Soviet Union nor the United States has a decisive edge in ASAT capability. Continued research on ASAT is in order as there is no indication of the outcome of research on the Strategic Defense Initiative (SDI). This short book is a major statement on ASATs from a bipartisan group.

449 *The Arab-Israeli Conflict: Perspectives.* Edited by Alvin Z. Rubinstein. New York: Praeger, 1984. 221pp. ISBN 0–03–068778–0.

These essays on the Arab-Israeli conflict evaluate the conflict with an emphasis on understanding causes and prospects. The authors are concerned with the nature of the dispute between Israel and the various Arab political entities. One author believes that Israeli settlement policy on the West Bank has made the Palestinians more receptive to negotiations. These essays on the world's longest conflict are a solid attempt to reexamine the conflict as a whole.

450 *Armed Forces and Modern Counter-Insurgency.* Edited by Ian F. W. Beckett and John Pimlott. London: Croom Helm, 1985. 232pp. ISBN 0–7099–3236–7.

Post-1945 counterinsurgency warfare is studied in this book by military specialists on insurgency conflicts. Seven case studies are examined, from the British Dhofar Campaign (1970–1975) to the South African Army's campaign in Namibia since 1966. Except for the U.S. and French involvements in Indochina, most of these conflicts have received little or no previous attention. Information on the different types of counterinsurgency warfare makes this book worth consulting.

451 *Armed Forces and the Welfare Societies: Challenges in the 1980s: Britain, The Netherlands, Germany, Sweden and the United States.* Edited by Gwyn-Harries-Jenkins. London: International Institute for Strategic Studies, 1982. 218pp. ISBN 0–333–33542–2.

The contrasting pressures of defense and social welfare spending on Western society are examined in this book by a variety of scholars. These scholars trace each country's response to the "warfare versus welfare" dilemma. Although each case differs and the quality of the essays varies, the consensus is that the commitment to defense spending in these societies will be lessened by budgetary constraints. This book provides a good look at pressures affecting Western defense budgets in the 1980s.

452 Armed Forces Communications and Electronics Association. *NATO and Western Europe C3: National and International Aspects.* Burke, VA: AFCEA International Press, 1983. 112pp. ISBN 0–916159–00–0.

The Armed Forces Communications and Electronics Association (AFCEA) published this book of its 1983 symposium on command, control, and communications (C3) developments. Twenty-two short technical papers and another dozen statements make up the bulk of this publication. Emphasis is placed on keeping abreast of recent technological developments in C3 research. Despite the brevity of the contributions, this volume is an essential source of the study of developments in the field of C3.

453   Armitage, M. J., and R. A. Mason. *Air Power in the Nuclear Age*, 2d ed. Urbana, IL: University of Illinois, 1985. 318pp. ISBN 0–252–01231–3.

This book focuses on the theories of nuclear and conventional air power, but in a strategic rather than a tactical sense. The authors contend that while air power has the flexibility necessary for rapid deployment, there has been a tendency toward more complex, expensive, and fewer aircraft. Advanced weapons systems will enable air forces to bridge the gap between limited numbers and an expanding role. The value of this book lies in its theoretical treatment of air power.

454   *Arms, Men, and Military Budgets: Issues for Fiscal Year 1981*. By Francis P. Hoeber et al. New Brunswick, NJ: Transaction Books, 1980. 180pp. ISBN 0–87855–804–7.

This book is part of a series of publications by a group of authors lobbying for an increase in the defense budget to counter a Soviet military threat. The authors believe that all U.S. military forces need a massive buildup as a result of fifteen years of neglect. Unless the funds are released for equipment, ships, and weapons systems the United States will be unable to fulfill its worldwide defense responsibilities. This book, along with others of the same genre, were instrumental in the Reagan administration's commitment to a defense buildup campaign in the early 1980s.

455   *Artificial Intelligence and National Security*. Edited by Stephen J. Cimbala. Lexington, MA: Lexington Books, 1987. 223pp. ISBN 0–669–11219–4.

The authors of these papers seek to apply artificial intelligence to national security and foreign policy issues. Failure of foreign policy decisionmakers to take advantage of the microelectronic revolution is hard to imagine but true. Each author analyzes the possible artificial intelligence applications toward a problem or subject in foreign policy. This book explores new territory, and defense and international security researchers will find it invaluable.

456   *Assessing Strategic Defense: Six Roundtable Discussions*. Edited by W. Bruce Weinrod. Washington, DC: Heritage Foundation, 1985. 170pp.

In 1984 the Heritage Foundation hosted a series of discussions on the Strategic Defense Initiative (SDI) and its ramifications for strategic defense. Six panels were held on the subjects in the following order: (1) the technologies of strategic defense; (2) the Soviet response to SDI; (3) the transition from offense to defense; (4) implications for arms reduction; (5) the SDI and the Pacific Basin; and (6) SDI and NATO. While there were differences of opinion among the panelists, most agreed that the SDI system is technically feasible and that partial systems could be deployed within five years. This work by a conservative think tank is one of the more useful publications of the organization.

457 Atkinson, Alexander. *Social Order and the General Theory of Strategy.* London: Routledge and Kegan Paul, 1981. 305pp. ISBN 0–7100–0907–0.

The author advances the thesis that the successes of insurgent warfare in the postwar world have transformed the theory of strategy. These successes mean that insurgents have every advantage to resort to violence. The older professional, state-ordained warfare has been modified to a fight to change the social order. This theoretical study offers new insights into low-intensity warfare, but it is not an easy book to read.

458 *Australian Defence Policy for the 1980s.* Edited by Robert O'Neill and D. M. Horner. St. Lucia, Australia: University of Queensland Press, 1982. 308pp. ISBN 0–7022–1781–6.

Australian defense policy for the 1980s is the subject of this book of essays. Although there is currently no threat to Australia's security, neither the Australian government nor the opposition is complacent about Australia's future defense. Both parties have made a commitment to increased defense spending well into the next decade. These essays give a good picture of Australian defense policy for the immediate future.

459 Averick, Sara M., and Steven J. Rosen. *The Importance of the "West Bank" and Gaza to Israel's Security.* Washington, DC: American Israel Public Affairs Committee, 1985. 68pp.

This short monograph is a defense of current Israeli policy to retain control over the West Bank and Gaza for security reasons. The authors maintain that Israel depends upon defensible borders to offset the numerical superiority of its enemies and to provide depth for military maneuver in case of war. The chances of a negotiated settlement to alter this arrangement are not promising. Lobbying for U.S. support for an Israeli security decision makes this monograph so one-sided as to be of only limited value.

460 Avidar, Yosef. *The Party and the Army in the Soviet Union.* Jerusalem: Magnes Press, 1983. 340pp. ISBN 965–223–495–8.

This book studies the relationship between the Communist party and the armed forces in the Soviet Union from the death of Joseph Stalin until the removal of Nikita Khrushchev in 1964. The author's thesis is that after Stalin's death the Soviet military participated in the struggle for power, gradually assuming a greater role in the party and the state. This change in status meant that since Soviet military chiefs had been unhappy about changes made by Khrushchev in the early 1960s, they made no effort to save him during his removal. This book is by an Israeli scholar and is important in understanding party-military relationships in the Soviet Union.

461 *Avoiding Nuclear War: Common Security as a Strategy for the Defence of the West.* Edited by Stan Windass. London: Brassey's Defence Publishers, 1985. 174pp. ISBN 0–08–031175–X.

These papers from four British and one U.S. defense scholars study the benefits of common security among the NATO states. The authors stress the need to rethink NATO defense strategy in light of recent developments. They are uncomfortable with the present dependence on nuclear weapons, and advocate more conventional forces as well as some type of arms control. These essays are a critical reexamination of ways to avoid nuclear war in Europe, and they provide material for a serious examination of the issue.

462 Baker, David. *The Shape of Wars To Come*. New York: Stein and Day, 1981. 262pp. ISBN 0–8128–2852–6.

This book is a futuristic look at warfare in space. The author wants the United States to direct its scientific and technological resources toward the militarization of space, as this is where the next war will be fought. Soviet energies are directed toward seizing the high ground of space, and the United States under the Reagan administration is taking steps to beat them to it. This book suffers from an excess of zeal, but many of its recommendations are in the process of realization.

463 *Ballistic Missile Defense*. Edited by Ashton B. Carter and David N. Schwartz. Washington, DC: Brookings Institution, 1984. 455pp. ISBN 0–8157–1312–6.

These essays examine the strategic, technological, and political issues raised by ballistic missile defense. The reasons for the increased interest in ballistic missile defense are the publicity surrounding the Strategic Defense Initiative (SDI) and the strategic parity between the Soviet Union and the United States. By combining new technologies and strategic theory, the authors have contributed a valuable work to the field. While most of the essays are intended to present a balanced assessment, there is also a section where other defense specialists offer their opinions on the same topics.

464 Barnaby, Frank. *What on Earth is Star Wars? A Guide to the Strategic Defense Initiative*. London: Fourth Estate, 1986. 192pp. ISBN 0–947795–15–4.

One of the most knowledgeable specialists on arms control and defense issues critiques the Strategic Defense Initiative (SDI). He claims that the huge investment in developing the SDI system will ensure its deployment. The key to the successful operation of such a system will be the development of the computer software to run the weapons system. This book surveys the problems of the SDI in a balanced and systematic way, and it can be recommended for both the specialist and the general reader.

465 Barrett, Archie D. *Reappraising Defense Organization: An Analysis Based on the Defense Organization Study of 1977–1980*. Washington, DC: National Defense University Press, 1983. 325pp.

A former senior officer in the U.S. Air Force assesses the recommendations of the Defense Organization Study of 1977–1980 for improving the overall defense structure. He takes the criticisms of the defense organization and makes a case for limited reorganization. Most of the criticisms are directed toward the Joint Chiefs of Staff and the influence of the four services and the weaknesses of the service secretaries. This book is a comprehensive analysis of the defense organization and is a major contribution to the literature on this subject.

466 Becker, Abraham S. *Sitting on Bayonets: The Soviet Defense Burden and the Slowdown of Soviet Defense Spending*. Santa Barbara, CA: Rand/UCLA Center for the Study of Soviet International Behavior, 1985. 37pp. ISBN 0–8330–0698–3.

The Rand/UCLA Center for the Study of Soviet International Behavior sponsored this study of the Soviet defense budget and its relationship to the Soviet economy. Various studies of the Soviet defense budget were examined, and the consensus is that there has been a considerable slowdown in the growth of defense outlays starting in the mid-1970s. This slowdown matches a weakness in the Soviet economy during this same period, and the state of the economy will prevent an acceleration of defense spending in the 1980s. This short study stands in direct contrast to prevailing opinion on Soviet defense spending.

467 Beckett, Brian. *Weapons of Tomorrow*. New York: Plenum Press, 1982. 160pp. ISBN 0–3664–1383–3.

Future developments in nuclear, chemical, and biological weapons are featured in this publication. The author is particularly concerned with the spillover effect of the use of these weapons on the civilian populations. Each type of weapon, its delivery system, and its potential military impact is analyzed in depth. Good charts, graphs, and illustrations reinforce the author's points.

468 Bellamy, Chris. *Red God of War: Soviet Artillery and Rocket Forces*. London: Brassey's Defence Publishers, 1986. 247pp. ISBN 0–08–031200–4.

This book is a historical and tactical analysis of the Soviet artillery and rocket forces. Past and present Soviet use of artillery are noted along with training, organization, and weapons. Artillery has always been stressed as a weapon of war by the Soviets, and this treatment shows that this preference by the modern Soviet Army has not changed. This book is well documented with maps, diagrams, and photographs, and the analysis is first-rate.

469 Beres, Louis Rene. *Mimicking Sisyphus: America's Countervailing Nuclear Strategy*. Lexington, MA: Lexington Books, 1983. 142pp. ISBN 0–669–06137–9.

A leading critic of U.S. nuclear strategy uses this book as a forum to attack the current direction of U.S. strategy. The futility of seeking peace by depending upon nuclear overkill is apparent. His plan is to implement a strategy of minimum deterrence coupled with a series of negotiated arms control agreements. This book has a series of concrete suggestions that make it a contribution to the literature in the field.

470 Berghahn, Volker R. *Militarism: The History of an International Debate, 1861–1979*. Leamington Spa, England: Berg, 1981. 132pp. ISBN 0–907582–01–X.

The author surveys the scholarly debate on militarism since 1861. He is most interested in the genesis and development of militarism as a concept in the evolution of modern society. In the postwar world two theories of militarism have appeared—the militarism of "new nations" and the "new militarism" of advanced industrial nations. This is a book for anyone interested in learning of the changing ideas about militarism.

471 Berman, Robert P., and John C. Baker. *Soviet Strategic Forces: Requirements and Responses*. Washington, DC: Brookings Institution, 1982. 171pp. ISBN 0–8157–0926–9.

The focus of this book is the evolution of the Soviet Union's strategic forces since 1945. Particular attention is given to Soviet strategic missiles because of the importance of this weapon in the Soviet strategic force structure. More than half of the work is devoted to appendices explaining technical missile matters. This study is a must for anyone interested in the development of the Soviet missile system.

472 Betts, Richard K. *Conventional Strategy, Unconventional Criticism and Conventional Wisdom.* Jerusalem: Magnes Press, 1984. 51pp.

This essay examines U.S. conventional force structure and strategy in an effort to unravel the controversy over military reform. The author, a senior fellow in the Brookings Foreign Policy Studies Program, maintains that major political changes in security planning are a prerequisite for substantial improvement in strategy. Defense funding increases will be wasted unless an emphasis is given more to global mobility and proportional readiness of active forces than force size. This essay is both informative and suggestive, but its prescriptions are not official U.S. government policy.

473 Betts, Richard K. *Cruise Missiles and U.S. Policy.* Washington, DC: Brookings Institution, 1982. 61pp. ISBN 0–8157–0933–1.

This study is an update of the author's larger work *Cruise Missiles: Technology, Strategy, Politics* (Washington, DC: Brookings Institution, 1981). The author is interested in the complexities and interrelationships of the technological, strategic, and political implications of Cruise missile development. Cruise missiles are an inexpensive and versatile weapons system, the development of which was pushed by civilians and the strategic implications of which as a weapon have never been realized. This short book is a stimulating look at a weapons system with limitless potential.

474 Betts, Richard K. *Surprise Attack: Lessons for Defense Planning.* Washington, DC: Brookings Institution, 1982. 318pp. ISBN 0–8157–0930–7.

The theory and application of surprise attacks as a strategic option are the subjects of this book. After a comparative analysis of surprise attacks during the past forty years, the author concentrates on the danger of surprise attacks to the United States and its allies. His conclusion is that the probability of a surprise attack by the Soviets on U.S. forces is improbable, but he lists a number of recommendations to ensure such an attack's failure. His chapters on the comparative aspects of past surprise attacks are the strength of this book.

475 Binkin, Martin. *Military Technology and Defense Manpower.* Washington, DC: Brookings Institution, 1986. 143pp. ISBN 0–8157–0978–1.

The implications of technological innovations on U.S. defense manpower over the last decade are examined in this book by a senior fellow in the Brookings Foreign Policy Studies Program. Complicated weaponry is placing the armed forces in a situation where the need for skilled technicians and specialists is greater than the supply. One solution is to develop less sophisticated weapons systems, which will relieve the shortage of trained personnel. This book is a reasoned argument of a thesis under much discussion in defense circles.

476 Blair, Bruce G. *Strategic Command and Control: Redefining the Nuclear Threat.* Washington, DC: Brookings Institution, 1985. 341pp. ISBN 0–8157–0982–X.

The author is a veteran of the Strategic Air Command (SAC), and utilized his military experience to study the U.S. nuclear control system. His conclusion is that the U.S. strategic command and control network could be severely impaired by a relatively limited nuclear attack by the Soviet Union. There is the need to use new technology to redesign and modernize the U.S. command and control system for assured retaliation against any Soviet first strike. This book is a major contribution to the U.S. defense debate.

477 Bogdanov, Radomir. *The US War Machine and Politics*, rev. ed. Moscow: Progress Publishers, 1986. 283pp.

A Soviet scholar analyzes the U.S. military structure and traces the extent to which the military responds to politics. His attention turns to how the U.S. armed forces, the Department of Defense, the National Security Council, and the think tanks work together to formulate U.S. foreign policy. These policies determine that U.S. military forces are used by the U.S. ruling circles as their instrument in the interest of capitalism. This book gives a Soviet analysis of U.S. military policies in the postwar world, and, despite lapses into Marxist terminology, this work gives insight into Soviet perceptions of U.S. defense.

478 Bova, Ben. *Assured Survival: Putting the Star Wars Defense in Perspective*. Boston: Houghton Mifflin, 1984. 343pp. ISBN 0–395–36405–1.

This book is a defense of the Strategic Defense Initiative (SDI) by a freelance writer. His thesis is that the technology of SDI is in the process of development that, by ensuring survival of the retaliatory missile system, will mitigate against nuclear war. These peacekeeping weapons systems can be the means to promote peace by preventing the use of nuclear weapons. While this popularized version of the SDI is of limited use for research purposes, it is an indication of the possible impact of such a system in the future.

479 Bowman, Robert. *Star Wars: A Defense Insider's Case Against the Strategic Defense Initiative*. Los Angeles: Jeremy P. Tarcher, 1986. 180pp. ISBN 0–0747–7390–3.

The former director of Star Wars programs for the U.S. Air Force has published this book, criticizing the development of the Strategic Defense Initiative (SDI). His criticisms are oriented more toward the political purposes of the development of the SDI rather than technological issues. In its present form, the SDI is designed more as a death star than a defense system. This book shows the author's reservations over the potential use of the SDI rather than its development, and his opposition appears to be more political than scientific.

480 Boyer, Yves. *French National Defence Policy and the New Majority*. Geneva, Switzerland: Programme for Strategic and International Security Studies, 1981. 65pp.

The relationship between French defense policy and domestic politics is the subject of this paper. French defense policy was changed little by François Mitterand's coming to power or under Socialist ministries. Preservation of national sovereignty with close ties to other Western powers remains the cornerstone of French strategic doctrine. While this work has become somewhat dated, it remains a useful source on the background of French defense policy.

481 Bracken, Paul. *The Command and Control of Nuclear Forces*. New Haven, CT: Yale University Press, 1983. 252pp. ISBN 0–300–02946–2.

The management of nuclear forces in peace and war over the last forty years is the subject of this book. Special emphasis is placed upon the extent to which command and control tie together the technical aspects of nuclear decision making. The problem is that the nuclear powers have created a complex technological apparatus without thinking through its purpose or how to control it. The book tends toward the pessimistic, but remains an excellent source to study command and control problems of nuclear forces.

482 Branch, Christopher I. *Fighting a Long Nuclear War*. Washington, DC: National Defense University Press, 1984. 71pp.

The author, a senior officer in the U.S. Air Force, uses his military experience to analyze the adoption of the doctrine of U.S. nuclear forces surviving and functioning in a protracted nuclear war. Presidential Directive 59 directs the employment of nuclear forces 'at range levels lower than all-out retaliation and against selected targets. The means to carry out this doctrine have yet to be developed, and all strategic weapons and their support systems must be enhanced. This book demonstrates that any change of strategic doctrine causes a change in weapons systems at a huge cost and with other military ramifications.

483 Broad, William J. *Star Warriors: A Penetrating Look into the Lives of the Young Scientists behind Our Space Age Weaponry*. New York: Simon and Schuster, 1985. 245pp. ISBN 0–671–54566–3.

A U.S. journalist spent two weeks at the Lawrence Livermore National Laboratory in Livermore, California, talking with a group of young scientists whose job is to design the hardware and software for the Strategic Defense Initiative (SDI). These scientists do not believe that a leakproof shield to stop every Soviet warhead can be developed, but they are certain that a viable defense system can be built. This necessitates an offensive capacity to operate in conjunction with the SDI. This book gives a fascinating glimpse of the young scientists active in developing the SDI system, and it is the personal side of the debate that makes this book worth reading.

484 Brown, Harold. *The Strategic Defense Initiative: Defensive Systems and the Strategic Debate*. Santa Monica, CA: California Seminar on International Security and Foreign Policy, 1985. 34pp.

This monograph was presented as a public lecture at the California Institute of Technology in 1984. The author places the Strategic Defense Initiative (SDI) into the long-ranging U.S. debate over defensive systems. His recommendations include restructuring the SDI for more deterrence and the threat of retaliation rather than population defense and pursuing a comprehensive arms control strategy to include the SDI. This brief lecture and the question and answer session present the views of one of the more authoritative U.S. defense specialists.

485 Brown, Neville. *The Future of Air Power*. London: Croom Helm, 1986. 309pp. ISBN 0–7099–321–X.

This book is an assessment of the future role of air power in warfare. Since the beginning of World War II, aviation has been in the ascendancy in war. While technical innovations in air defense during the last decade have made aircraft more vulnerable in combat, improvements in aircraft and plane defense systems still make air power the most significant military force in the future. This study ponders the realities of air power now and in the future, and it deserves a serious reading.

486 Brown, Neville, and Anthony Farrar-Hockley. *Nuclear First Use*. London: Buchan and Enright, 1985. 108pp. ISBN 0–907675–26–3.

Two leading British authorities on defense issues question the possibility of NATO committing itself to a policy of "no first use" of nuclear weapons. They see no benefits to the adoption of such a policy, and the military risks are too great. NATO needs the flexibility to respond to any type of crisis without restraints. The authors rely on their military expertise to criticize a NATO policy option that they think is dangerous.

487 Bulkeley, Rip, and Graham Spinardi. *Space Weapons: Deterrence or Delusion?* Cambridge, England: Polity Press, 1986. 378pp. ISBN 0–7456–0270–3.

Two British security specialists evaluate past, present, and future space weapons. They believe that now is an appropriate time to consider space weapons because of the confusing debate over the Strategic Defense Initiative (SDI). The SDI has complicated the picture, as it is an effort to expand military systems into space without knowing if the technology can produce an operational system. This book is critical of both Soviet and U.S. efforts to use space as another possible battlefield.

488 Bruns, E. Bradford. *At War in Nicaragua: The Reagan Doctrine and the Politics of Nostalgia.* New York: Harper and Row, 1987. 211pp. ISBN 0–06–055074–0.

The international ramifications of the U.S. sponsorship of the war in Nicaragua is the subject of this book. Concentration of U.S. policy on the use of force to overthrow the Nicaraguan government has been and continues to be a mistake. Obsession rather than reality dominates U.S. policies, and these policies make Third World countries critical of all U.S. policies. The author endorses the Contadora Peace Plan, and his analysis and recommendations make this book an important work on U.S. foreign policy.

489 Bucknell, Howard. *Energy and the National Defense.* Lexington, KY: University of Kentucky, 1981. 235pp. ISBN 0–8131–0402–5.

The subjects of this monograph are the worldwide energy situation and its impact on the national defense of the United States. Dependence on imported oil is a threat to U.S. security, and efforts should be directed toward developing alternative energy sources. This dependence is especially vital in the military sector, because of the excessive dependence on petroleum products for military vehicles. Many of the points in this book are still valid in the mid-1980s, but little government action has taken place to change this energy dependence.

490 Burrows, Bernard, and Geoffrey Edwards. *The Defence of Western Europe.* London: Butterworths Scientific, 1982. 155pp. ISBN 0–408–10702–2.

This book is an assessment of the NATO alliance from the European point of view. The debate revolves around the question of the future direction of the alliance through increasing cooperation between the thirteen European members by means of a European Defense Force. The authors believe that a European Defense Force would be a step toward greater security for Western Europe. Solid research and balanced judgments characterize this book.

491 Buteux, Paul. *The Politics of Nuclear Consultation in NATO, 1965–1980.* Cambridge, England: Cambridge University Press, 1983. 292pp. ISBN 0–521–24798–5.

This book examines the political process within NATO by which a consensus on nuclear policy is achieved or defeated. The most notable institution in NATO for this type of study is the Nuclear Planning Group (NPG). The author concludes that the NPG has been successful as an institution in reconciling political, strategic, and military differences. The author has done a masterful job in outlining the role and importance of the NPG.

492 Buteux, Paul. *Strategy, Doctrine, and the Politics of Alliance: Theatre Nuclear Force Modernisation in NATO.* Boulder, CO: Westview Press, 1983. 158pp. ISBN 0–86531–940–5.

The politics of nuclear force modernization within NATO is the focus of this book. While the author believes that alliance politics, strategic doctrine, and military posture are interrelated, he affirms that a change in political direction modifies all three aspects. A central problem remains the way to maintain an extended deterrent commitment at a time of technological change that is credible to the Soviet Union and also acceptable to the United States. This book is a quality assessment of the impact of the modernization program on the nuclear forces in NATO.

493 Cable, James. *Britain's Naval Future.* Annapolis, MD: Naval Institute Press, 1983. 220pp. ISBN 0–87021–920–0.

The role of the British Royal Navy in the defense of Great Britain is examined in detail and with some pessimism in this work. British naval decline has its roots in Great Britain's weak maritime economy, but more important is Great Britain's land forces commitments to NATO. This book was completed before the lessons of the Falkland War, but the author presents a preface on this war and concludes that it reinforces his thesis of the need for Great Britain to have a strong navy. While much of the material in this book has become dated by the Falkland War, the conclusions are still worth serious consideration.

494 Campbell, Christy. *Weapons of War.* New York: Bedrick Books, 1983. 304pp. ISBN 0–91174–513–0.

This publication is full of data pertaining to strategic and tactical military problems. By use of chronologies, tables, comparisons, maps, and brief analyses of national military forces, the author treats all aspects of the international military environment. The most significant parts of this book are the sections on future weapons systems and the major electronics projects in progress. This book is a work full of data of value to defense and military researchers.

495 Campbell, Duncan. *War Plan UK: The Truth about Civil Defence in Britain.* London: Burnett Books, 1982. 488pp. ISBN 0–09–150670–0.

This book is a critical assessment of the civil defense program in Great Britain. British planning for civil defense places primary emphasis on the control of the civil population and consists of a no-evacuation policy. Primary consideration is given to the preservation of the government and its return to functioning in as brief a time as possible. This detailed critique of current British civil defense procedures deserves to be consulted.

496 Campbell, Edwina S. *Consultation and Consensus in NATO: Implementing the Canadian Article.* Lanham, MD: University Press of America, 1985. 209pp. ISBN 0–8191–4955–1.   .

The history of the Committee on the Challenges of Modern Society (CCMS) is undertaken by a former CCMS officer. This committee originated out of a Canadian proposal to implement nonmilitary cooperation among NATO members. Environmental problems and other nonmilitary issues have been the topics handled by the CCMS. This study shows a side of NATO not otherwise known.

497 *Can America Catch Up?: The U.S.-Soviet Military Balance.* Washington, DC: Committee on the Present Danger, 1984. 59pp.

The Committee on the Present Danger presents this publication as part of its lobbying effort to increase funding for a U.S. military buildup. This group contends that the Soviets have a military superiority over the United States that cannot be countered without a significant increase in the U.S. defense budget. A budget increase will ensure the modernization of all components of U.S. strategic forces, enabling them to form a credible strategic defense. While it is as a lobbying effort that this booklet excels, its lack of balance makes the information in this publication suspect.

498 Canan, James. *War in Space.* New York: Harper and Row, 1982. 186pp. ISBN 0–06–038022–5.

A Washington defense correspondent produced this book to justify his belief that the United States must be able to conduct warfare in space. He surveys the development of satellites and antisatellite (ASAT) weapons in the 1970s and 1980s. Former President Jimmy Carter's efforts to restrain the militarization of space was an incorrect policy, and President Ronald Reagan's revitalization of this effort corrected this folly. This book is packed with information about weapons for space development from sources not otherwise noted in works on this subject.

499 Canby, Steven L. *The Conventional Defense of Europe: The Operational Limits of Emerging Technology.* Washington, DC: International Security Studies Program, the Wilson Center, 1984. 49pp.

This paper is an analysis of the question whether new technologies can offset NATO's inferiority in conventional combat strength in Europe. The author concludes that emerging technologies cannot fill the gap, because the situation is beyond the capability of technology. In particular, he argues that the Deep Attack system is untested and subject to attack and jamming. This paper marshals evidence to question defense assumptions, and this questioning is the contribution of this study.

500 Capitanchik, David, and Richard C. Eichenberg. *Defence and Public Opinion.* London: Routledge and Kegan Paul, 1983. 98pp. ISBN 0–7100–9356–X.

Public opinion about defense issues among key NATO countries is the subject of this book. The attitudes toward defense policies in Denmark, France, the Netherlands, the United Kingdom, the United States, and West Germany are surveyed. Conclusions are that public support for NATO remains high in all the European member states, but the issues of nuclear force modernization, defense budgets, and the decline of the image of the United States have the potential of causing conflict. Besides the use of opinion polls on defense issues to survey attitudes, the best feature of this book is the quality of the analysis.

501 Cartwright, John, and Julian Critchley. *Nuclear Weapons in Europe.* Brussels: North Atlantic Assembly, 1984. 156pp.

The Special Committee on Nuclear Weapons in Europe's report on nuclear weapons stationed in Europe is an outgrowth of a decision by members of the

North Atlantic Assembly to study alliance nuclear weapons issues after
NATO's December 1979 dual-track decision. Differences of objectives
between the Europeans, who regard modernization the price for arms control, and the Americans, who consider arms control the price for modernization, have been the biggest weakness. But despite often bitter opposition
in Europe, NATO's policy has been successful, and it has strengthened
the cohesion of the alliance. This report gives a summary of European military defense as of 1984, and the material should interest most defense
researchers.

502 Carus, W. Seth. *The Military Balance: The Threat to Israel's Air Bases.*
Washington, DC: American Israel Public Affairs Committee, 1985. 75pp.
    The importance of Israeli air base defense to the security of Israel is the
theme of this monograph. Acquisition of advanced aircraft by Arab countries
has made air base survivability a top priority of the Israeli government, and
the cost of air base defense systems has been between 5 and 10 percent of
Israel's total defense spending during the past decade. Western countries
could help Israel by curtailing the supply of advanced weaponry to Israel's
Arab enemies. This monograph points out a serious military problem for
Israel, but the prospect of ending shipments of advanced aircraft to the Arab
countries is unrealistic.

503 Cawthra, Gavin. *Brutal Force: The Apartheid War Machine.* London:
International Defence and Aid Fund for Southern Africa, 1986. 319pp. ISBN
0–904759–71–7.
    The military forces of the Republic of South Africa are analyzed for their
external and internal deployment in this book. Particular emphasis is given
to the strength, deployment, and strategies of the South African Defence
Force (SADF). The author documents the militarization of South Africa and
the extent to which the government depends on military force to survive.
Despite its antiapartheid viewpoint, this book is a solid assessment of the
South African military forces.

504 Chalfont, Alun. *Star Wars: Suicide or Survival?* London: Weidenfeld
and Nicolson, 1985. 169pp. ISBN 0–297–78464–1.
    Cost, technological feasibility, and politico-strategic implications of the
Strategic Defense Initiative (SDI) are examined by Lord Chalfont. The author
believes that the SDI "provides a blueprint for a deterrent based on effective
defences rather than on a suicide pact." He acknowledges that the technology of the system has to be worked out, and that it will be expensive, but the
benefits will be worth it. This British defense of SDI is worth noting because
of the political and strategic arguments advanced by the author.

505 Chalmers, Malcolm. *Paying for Defence: Military Spending and British
Decline.* London: Pluto Press, 1985. 200pp. ISBN 0–7453–0023–5.
    The thesis of this book is that Great Britain's heavy military expenditures
have resulted in British economic decline. This military burden has diverted
resources from the economic sectors of investment and exports to the less
productive military side. The author argues that a 30 percent military budget
reduction could be achieved by restricting national and NATO military commitments. This book is one-dimensional in that only the economic side of
the debate is presented without a serious look at the foreign policy
ramifications of the author's proposals.

506 Chapman, J. W. M., R. Drifte, and I. T. M. Gow. *Japan's Quest for Comprehensive Security: Defence, Diplomacy, Dependence.* London: Frances Pinter, 1983. 259pp. ISBN 0–86187–235–5.

These essays originate from a 1981 seminar on Japanese security policy held by the Department of War Studies at King's College, London. The Japanese have taken awhile to adjust to the U.S. change of policy in the Far East following the Guam Doctrine of 1969. Although there is still a reliance upon the United States, Soviet pressure on China and its relationship with Vietnam have increased Japan's sense of insecurity. This book is an in-depth analysis of Japanese security issues, and the essays are all of high quality.

507 Charlton, Michael. *The Star Wars History: From Deterrence to Defence: The American Strategic Debate.* London: BBC Publications, 1986. 154pp. ISBN 0–563–20505–9.

Interviews of prominent U.S. and European policymakers and politicians by the BBC on the subject of the Strategic Defense Initiative (SDI) are printed in this book. These interviews were recorded in the spring and summer of 1985, and no liberties have been taken with the texts of the remarks. Twenty-six individuals participated in this project, which provides a variety of viewpoints on security and strategic issues.

508 Chichester, Michael, and John Wilkinson. *British Defence: A Blueprint for Reform.* London: Brassey's, 1987. 142pp. ISBN 0–08–034745–2.

A British defense specialist and a conservative MP critique the current British defense effort and propose a realignment of military resources within NATO. The authors charge that there is an overcommitment of military forces in West Germany to the detriment of British maritime strength. West Germany needs to assume defense responsibility on the northern sector of the central front, releasing British resources to concentrate on building up Great Britain's maritime forces. This book is meant to be controversial in order to stimulate debate in Great Britain over defense issues.

509 Chichester, Michael, and John Wilkinson. *The Uncertain Ally: British Defence Policy, 1960–1990.* Aldershot, England: Gower, 1982. 246pp. ISBN 0–566–00534–4.

The authors maintain that the failure of past and present British governments to finance defense expenditures has resulted in British military weakness and difficulty in fulfilling British NATO responsibilities in case of war. There should be some reassignment of responsibilities on NATO's central front, with these forces and funds used to build the British army and navy for other responsibilities. This book argues for a greater defense commitment for Great Britain, but also poses questions about the future of British involvement in NATO.

510 *China and the Bomb.* Edited by Ken Coates. Nottingham, England: Spokesman, 1986. 111pp. ISBN 0–85124–444–0.

This collection of official statements by Chinese government officials on Chinese positions on nuclear weapons since the early 1960s is the result of a 1985 meeting of Chinese, European, Japanese, and South Pacific peace representatives in Beijing, China. Chinese leaders used this occasion to announce new steps for a peace movement in China. This book is an effort to explain Chinese attitudes toward the acquisition and potential uses of nuclear weapons. While official statements are often unreliable, several of the statements, especially one by Nie Rongzehen, are invaluable in studying Chinese nuclear policies since the 1960s.

511 Chizum, David G. *Soviet Radioelectronic Combat*. Boulder, CO: Westview Press, 1985. 125pp. ISBN 0–8133–7134–1.
Soviet radioelectronic combat is the subject of this short book. The author claims that radioelectronic combat differs from electronic warfare by its ideological content. Most of the text concerns Soviet philosophy toward this type of combat, but the strength of the book resides in the annotated bibliography and an excellent glossary. There are only about forty pages of analysis, most of which deals with historical material.

512 *Choices: Nuclear and Non-Nuclear Defence Options*. By Oliver Ranbotham. London: Brassey's, 1987. 473pp. ISBN 0–08–034763–0.
This book provides a forum where the cases both pro and con on continued nuclear weapon deployment in Europe are presented. Each case is argued on the ground of morality and rationality of deployment, and a balanced analysis of points at issue is included. Finally, nineteen prominent spokespersons give their answers to the deployment controversy. This book is the most balanced presentation of the positions on deployment of nuclear weapons on the market.

513 Chubin, Shahram, and Charles Tripp. *Iran and Iraq: War, Society and Politics, 1980–1986*. Geneva, Switzerland: Programme for Strategic and International Security Studies, 1986. 59 leaves.
This paper is the product of a workshop on the impact of the Iran-Iraq War on the respective societies. Both the authors and the participants conclude that the war has strengthened both regimes, but the conclusion of the war may be costly to both since there is the possibility of no victor. The ultimate winner in both countries will be the military. This source has a value much beyond its modest length.

514 Clarfield, Gerard H., and William M. Wiecek. *Nuclear America: Military and Civilian Nuclear Power in the United States, 1940–1980*. New York: Harper and Row, 1984. 518pp. ISBN 0–06–015336–9.
The authors have produced a history of military and civilian nuclear power relationships in the United States since 1940. While tremendous strides have been made in nuclear technology, U.S. defense policymakers have failed to develop constructive approaches to nuclear energy. This book is a solid effort to understand U.S. uses of nuclear energy.

515 Close, Robert. *Time for Action*. Oxford, England: Brassey's, 1983. 233pp. ISBN 0–08–028344–6.
A former general in the Belgian Army and currently a senator in Brussels, the author has been a frequent critic of Western defense policy. This book is a successor to his earlier book, *L'Europe sans defense?* (Brussels: Editions Arts et Voyages, 1976), because he continues to argue that the Western alliance needs to counter Soviet expansionism by expanding its conventional and nuclear forces. He believes that the 1980s will be the key decade to change the direction of NATO. This book is more an article of faith than a work of scholarship.

516 Coates, James, and Michael Kilian. *Heavy Losses: The Dangerous Decline of American Defense.* New York: Viking, 1985. 430pp. ISBN 0–670–80484–3.

The authors, both journalists with the *Chicago Tribune*, have written a book exposing the weakness of the U.S. defense establishment. While the neglect of the military by the Carter administration has hurt U.S. defense, the excesses of the Reagan administration have been just as harmful. The defense drain on the U.S. economy is turning the U.S. into a second-rate industrial power unable to turn out anything but expensive military equipment and weapon systems. This book is a popularized version of many of the critical works on current U.S. defense policies.

517 Cockburn, Andrew. *The Threat: Inside the Soviet Military Machine.* London: Hutchinson, 1983. 338pp. ISBN 0–09–151290–5.

An outgrowth of a documentary file, "The Red Army," for WGBH-TV, Boston, this book is a popular account of the Soviet armed forces and their equipment. Despite its popular flair, the author has produced a credible assessment of the Soviet military machine. His conclusion is that the West has consistently overestimated the size and the quality of the Soviet military machine, and he classifies this as threat inflation. This book is an antidote to other publications extolling the virtues of the Soviet military machine.

518 Cohen, Sam. *The Truth about the Neutron Bomb: The Inventor of the Bomb Speaks Out.* New York: William Morrow, 1983. 226pp. ISBN 0–688–01646–4.

The inventor of the neutron bomb, the author uses this book to correct misconceptions about the development and potential use of neutron bombs, originally designed for use as a tactical weapon on the battlefield. Cohen's treatment of the development of the weapon and the political controversies over its adoption make for fascinating reading. The author pulls few punches about his views, and this book is a classic of its type.

519 Cohen, Sam. *We Can Prevent World War III.* Ottawa, IL: Jameson Books, 1985. 129pp. ISBN 0–915463–10–5.

This book is a critique of U.S. defense and foreign policy by a nuclear arms expert. His conclusions are that the United States conducts an interventionist foreign policy in areas of marginal strategic importance, U.S. nuclear forces are incapable of fighting a nuclear war, and the U.S. public is defenseless in case of a nuclear war. Cohen believes that while there would be survivors in a nuclear war, a better effort would be for the U.S. public to educate itself about the dangers of World War III. More a personal analysis than a serious effort of scholarship, nevertheless this book is a stimulating look at U.S. defense policies.

520 Coker, Christopher. *A Nation in Retreat?* London: Brassey's, 1986. 154pp. ISBN 0–08–031213–6.

A critical look at Great Britain's attitude toward defense and defense spending is made by a British defense specialist with a pro-NATO perspective. Great Britain's postwar economic decline has resulted in a serious decline in British defense spending to .the point of questioning whether British membership in NATO can be maintained. More importantly divisions within the British political party system have weakened Great Britain's commitment to defense. This book is a polemical advocacy of Great Britain's active participation in NATO.

521 Coker, Christopher. *South Africa's Security Dilemmas.* New York: Praeger, 1987. 112pp. ISBN 0–275–92771–7.

A British scholar on international relations assesses the strengths and weaknesses of the South African security forces. The South African Defence Force (SADF) is the most formidable military force in the southern African region, but its weakness is the political turmoil in South Africa. While the military establishment remains a stabilizing influence on the South African political scene, it has limited room to change policies. This book is a balanced and realistic assessment of the role of the South African security forces in South Africa.

522 Coker, Christopher. *US Military Power in the 1980s.* London: Macmillan, 1983. 163pp. ISBN 0–333–35834–1.

The resources of the Royal United Services Institute for Defence Studies (RUSI) were mobilized to study allegations of U.S. military weakness. This book is the result of this effort, and the author is interested in the extent to which the United States can project its military power beyond its frontiers in support of political goals. The author concludes that there has been a decline in U.S. military power since 1969, but in the early 1980s the situation stabilized at parity between the United States and the Soviet Union. This book and the series of short essays by other authors near the end of the work make a solid contribution to the literature of U.S. defense questions.

523 Collins, John M. *Green Berets, SEALS and Spetsnaz: U.S. and Soviet Military Operations.* Washington, DC: Pergamon-Brassey's, 1987. 174pp. ISBN 0–08–035747–4.

The author, a senior specialist in national defense at the Library of Congress, compares special military operations capabilities of the Soviet Union and the United States. Claiming that Soviet efforts in special operations have been supported and appreciated better than those in the United States, the author isolates a series of U.S. problems and includes recommendations for reform. This book is the most complete study of special operations available.

524 Collins, Joseph J. *The Soviet Invasion of Afghanistan: A Study in the Use of Force in Soviet Foreign Policy.* Lexington, MA: Lexington Books, 1986. 195pp. ISBN 0–669–11259–3.

This book is an academic treatment of the military aspects of the Soviet invasion of Afghanistan. An academically trained member of the U.S. Army, the author's thesis is that the Soviets invaded Afghanistan in response to a perceived threat to Soviet security. The invasion was intended to be a temporary army of occupation to establish the Karmal regime, but instead the Soviets found themselves in a lengthy and costly counterinsurgency war. This book is a well researched and balanced treatment of a controversial subject.

525 Condit, D. M. *Modern Revolutionary Warfare: An Analytical Overview.* Kensington, MD: American Institutes for Research, 1983. 134pp.

An update of an earlier work, this report is a review of modern revolutionary warfare from the viewpoint of a government involved in any aspect of revolutionary violence. Special emphasis is given to the extent to which revolutionary warfare is a problem for U.S. security. The author is also interested in the characteristics of successful and failed revolutionary warfare. This monograph poses more questions than it answers, but it is a legitimate effort to study modern revolutionary warfare.

526 Connell, Jon. *The New Maginot Line.* London: Secker and Warburg, 1986. 308pp. ISBN 0–436–10586–1.

A British journalist criticizes the dependence of the Western alliance on high-tech weapons systems. The dependence on a high technology approach to defense has weakened the U.S. capacity to fight a war, and this dependence has resulted in a similar loss in the West's conventional forces. Since neither nuclear weapons nor the Strategic Defense Initiative (SDI) gives the West security, the author maintains that the most realistic policy is a buildup in NATO's conventional forces, less reliance on nuclear weapons, and a greater emphasis on diplomacy. Despite its journalistic flavor, this book is a good source because the author challenges standard assumptions about European defense.

527 *The Conventional Defense of Europe: New Technologies and the New Strategies.* Edited by Andrew J. Pierre. New York: New York University Press, 1986. 185pp. ISBN 0–8147–6599–8.

These essays examine the issue of improving the conventional defense forces of Western Europe. The deteriorating trend in the military balance between NATO and the Warsaw Pact and a growing anxiety among Europeans over dependence on nuclear weaponry have combined to stress the need for a buildup of NATO's conventional forces. These writings reflect this trend as well as the necessity for new technologies and new tactics for conventional warfare. The authors were selected for their contrasting points of view, and it is in these views and the quality of the essays that this book makes a contribution to defense literature.

528 *Conventional Forces and American Defense Policy.* Edited by Steven E. Miller. Princeton, NJ: Princeton University Press, 1986. 341pp. ISBN 0–691–07700–2.

Less fashionable than nuclear weapons, conventional forces have been neglected by military planners and the public alike. This collection of essays intends to remedy this neglect by presenting a comprehensive treatment of conventional forces in U.S. defense policy. While these twelve essays make a major effort in that direction, the subject is so comprehensive that these essays can only begin to deal with the topic.

529 *Conventional Forces and the European Balance.* By Ian Bellany et al. Lancaster, England: Centre for the Study of Arms Control and International Security, 1981. 87pp.

Four British arms control specialists present their views on European defense issues at a 1981 symposium held at the University of Lancaster. These papers deal with military tactics, defense budgeting, and arms control issues. While each paper stands on its own merits, the overall quality of the papers is high. Such papers reflect the British commitment to serious research on arms control and defense issues.

530 Cordesman, Anthony H. *The Arab-Israeli Military Balance and the Art of Operations.* Washington, DC: American Enterprise Institute for Public Policy Research, 1987. 205pp. ISBN 0–8447–1378–3.

The author, a former civilian assistant to the deputy secretary of defense, analyzes the Arab-Israeli conflicts for lessons on the conduct of modern warfare. He studies seven Arab-Israeli wars for information on weapons, tactics, and military organization. His conclusion is that another Arab-Israeli war may be only a few years away, but this time the protagonists will be Syria and Israel. This work has a mass of statistical data on the Arab-Israeli military balance, but the analysis is superficial.

531 Cordesman, Anthony H. *Jordanian Arms and the Middle East Balance.* Washington, DC: Middle East Institute, 1983. 186pp. ISBN 0–916808–20–3.

The role of Jordan in the Middle East, military balance, and the impact of U.S. arms deals with Jordan are analyzed in this book by a U.S. defense specialist. Jordan has become increasingly militarily vulnerable to its potential adversaries, namely, Israel and Syria. Because Jordan can be a convincing guarantor of any peace settlement, Jordan has assumed new importance to U.S. strategic interests, and it needs to be strengthened by U.S. arms deals. This book shows the importance Jordan holds in the peace process in the Middle East.

532 Cordier, Sherwood S. *Calculus of Power: The Current Soviet-American Conventional Military Balance in Central Europe,* 3d ed. Washington, DC: University Press of America, 1980. 140pp. ISBN 0–8191–0883–9.

This essay is an assessment of U.S. and Soviet conventional military power along the central front in Germany. The author has periodically updated his assessment, and this version highlights growing Soviet military capabilities. Special emphasis is given to the introduction of new weapons systems and reorganizations of unit structures. This work is oriented toward the student and the general reader, who will find the book satisfying.

533 Cotter, Donald R., James H. Hansen, and Kirk McConnell. *The Nuclear "Balance" in Europe: Status, Trends, Implications.* Cambridge, MA: United States Strategic Institute, 1983. 48pp.

Three defense specialists review the nuclear balance in Europe between the Western and Soviet blocs. Cotter has been one of the leading exponents of integrating conventional and nuclear strategy into NATO doctrine, and this paper reflects this thesis. The growth of Soviet military strength in Europe requires that NATO engage in a modernization campaign to rebuild conventional forces. Both the viewpoints and material make this paper worth reading.

534 *The Counterfeit Ark: Crisis Relocation for Nuclear War.* Edited by Jennifer Leaning and Langley Keyes. Cambridge, MA: Ballinger, 1984. 337pp. ISBN 0–88410–940–2.

The Reagan administration's crisis relocation planning (CRP) program for civil defense is critiqued in this book of essays. These critics charge that such a program promises survival for 80 percent of the relocated population, but it lacks the wherewithal to approach anywhere near this figure. This type of analysis promotes the belief that the United States could win a nuclear war. These essays prove conclusively that civil defense programs are ineffective in a nuclear war, and, for this reason, this book is educational.

535 Cowen, Regina H. E. *Defense Procurement in the Federal Republic of Germany: Politics and Organization.* Boulder, CO: Westview Press, 1986. 334pp. ISBN 0–8133–7220–8.

West German defense procurement policies and their impact on domestic and alliance politics are the subjects of this book. Successive German governments have adopted military procurement policies designed to consolidate the German position within NATO. But German procurement suffers from organizational inflexibility, which has made changes in orientation difficult and slow. This study reveals much about the West German defense system, and more such studies are necessary before a true picture of NATO emerges.

536 Cox, Andrew, and Stephen Kirby. *Congress, Parliament and Defence: The Impact of Legislative Reform on Defence Accountability in Britain and America.* Houndmills, England: Macmillan, 1986. 315pp. ISBN 0–333–30927–8.

Two British scholars examine the effectiveness of Parliament and Congress in controlling the defense establishment in Great Britain and the United States, respectively. Both Parliament and Congress have tried within the last decade to reform themselves in order to control defense expenditures, but their efforts have failed. In both systems the executive branch has more weapons for launching a defense program than the legislatures have to defeat them. This book is a high-quality assessment that will be a standard work for years to come.

537 *Cruise Missiles: Technology, Strategy, Politics.* Edited by Richard K. Betts. Washington, DC: Brookings Institution, 1981. 612pp. ISBN 0–8157–0932–3.

These essays constitute the most informed opinion and information on all aspects of Cruise missiles available in the early 1980s. The United States has developed the technology of the Cruise missile to such a level that the Soviets will not be able to match U.S. models in the 1980s. But it is in the realm of politics and deployment that most of the problems remain. This book is the best source on Cruise missiles available to scholars and the general public.

538 Curran, Susan L., and Dmitry Ponomareff. *Managing the Ethnic Factor in the Russian and Soviet Armed Forces: An Historical Overview.* Santa Monica, CA: Rand Corporation, 1982. 41pp.

Two Rand analysts examine the problem of ethnic minorities in the Soviet Army. Minorities have long been utilized in the pre-Soviet Russian Army, but on a selective basis. Integration of minority troops into Soviet units took place in the mid-1950s, but there is evidence that Soviet military leadership questions the effectiveness and reliability of non-Russian troops. This paper gives a historical analysis of the ethnic problem in the Soviet military, and this treatment is excellent for background information.

539 Dalgleish, D. Douglas, and Larry Schweikart. *Trident.* Carbondale, IL: Southern Illinois University Press, 1984. 502pp. ISBN 0–8093–1126–7.

The authors undertook this study of the Trident submarine as a policy analysis of a major defense program. Despite major cost overruns, the Trident-class submarines are the most effective weapons any service has ever deployed for strategic deterrence. But the program has revealed serious deficiencies in the U.S. procurement system. This book is a major study of a serious defense procurement problem.

540 Davidson, Basil. *The People's Cause: A History of Guerrillas in Africa.*
Burnt Mill, England: Longman, 1981. 210pp. ISBN 0–582–64680–4.

African insurrections from colonial days to the present are recounted in
this book. Guerrilla activities in the twentieth century are highlighted, with
a section on every struggle from Algeria to Zimbabwe. The author concludes
that any well-directed guerrilla war with a cause has been successful in
Africa during this century. The author provides a good introduction to the
subject of guerrilla warfare in Africa.

541 Davis, William A. *Asymmetries in U.S. and Soviet Strategic Defense
Programs: Implications for Near-Term American Deployment Options.*
Washington, DC: Pergamon-Brassey's, 1986. 76pp. ISBN 0–08–034683–9.

The author critiques U.S. ballistic missile defense (BMD) programs in this
report. His view is that there is a need for a U.S. near-term BMD development
within the Strategic Defense Initiative (SDI) to counter a possible Soviet
breakout from the Anti-Ballistic Missile (ABM) Treaty. The Soviets have
always maintained a balanced program in contrast to the more erratic U.S.
one. This report proposes a near-term as well as a long-range program for
ballistic missile defense, and the author's views are worth consideration.

542 Dean, Jonathan. *Watershed in Europe: Dismantling the East-West Military Confrontation.* Lexington, MA: Lexington Books, 1987. 286pp. ISBN
0–669–11120–1.

The author concludes that the peak of the East-West military confrontation
has probably passed and that there will be a gradual lowering of nuclear and
conventional forces. While Soviet aggression in Europe is no longer an active
threat, there is always the possibility of conflict for other reasons. Serious
consideration needs to be given to the dismantling of confrontation in
Europe and the maintenance of security and stability. The author has produced a controversial but important book.

543 Debastiani, Richard J. *Computers on the Battlefield: Can They Survive?*
Washington, DC: National Defense University Press, 1983. 102pp.

Survivability of military computer systems in combat is the subject of this
study. The author concludes that computers cannot survive nuclear or chemical attack at the present stage of development, and there are still problems
of survivability in conventional warfare. Two recommendations are
advanced: (1) harden the computer or the computer shelters, and (2) stan-
dardize the computer systems. While this book is a solid contribution to the
subject, more analysis of the tactical uses of computers on the battlefield
would strengthen the conclusions.

544 *Defence and Consensus: The Domestic Aspects of Western Security.*
Edited by Christoph Bertram. London: Macmillan, 1983. 136pp. ISBN
0–333–36596–8.

The impact of domestic public opinion on defense policies is the subject
of this book of essays from the 24th Annual Conference of the International
Institute of Strategic Studies in 1982. Participants agreed that there has been
a decline of consensus among the countries of the Western alliance. The
reason for this decline has been the failure of the alliance to sell itself to
the general public. Both the thesis and the solutions make for interesting
reading in this solid book of substantive essays.

545 *The Defence Equation: British Military Systems Policy, Planning and Performance.* Edited by Martin Edmonds. London: Brassey's Defence Publishers, 1986. 238pp. ISBN 0–08–033590–X.

These papers on the management of defense policy planning of the British armed forces since 1945 are the product of British and French defense scholars. They provide insight on the problems facing British defense planners and explanations for a less than impressive record. Several themes become apparent with the need to plan for technology and the problem of coping with the constant reductions in the defense budgets. Several of these papers deal with topics not previously studied, and the sum total is a solid book on British defense planning.

546 *Defending a Free Society.* Edited by Robert W. Poole. Lexington, MA: Lexington Books, 1984. 364pp. ISBN 0–669–07240–0.

The Reason Foundation sponsored an interdisciplinary research team to study the problems of national defense in a free society. Eleven essays were drafted for an assessment of national defense policy from a gathering in Santa Barbara in December 1982. First principles rather than the means of implementation are emphasized in these essays. This book seeks a reappraisal of U.S. defense policy, and the essays are all worth further study because of this approach.

547 *Defending Europe: Options for Security.* Edited by Derek Paul. London: Taylor and Francis, 1985. 351pp. ISBN 0–85066–347–4.

These papers on European security and the Mutual and Balanced Force Reductions (MBFR) in Central Europe are the product of a 1985 conference held at University College, University of Toronto, Canada. This conference included participants from the Soviet Union, Western Europe, the United States, and Canada. While most authors concentrated on conventional defense issues, the range of subjects was broad. Both the papers and discussions make this book an excellent source for viewpoints as well as information.

548 *Defense against Ballistic Missiles: An Assessment of Technologies and Policy Implications.* Washington, DC: U.S. Government Printing Office, 1984. 22pp.

The Department of Defense submitted this report on the assessment of technologies and systems available for a defense against ballistic missiles and the policy implications for such a defense system. This report recommends a vigorous research and development program to develop a ballistic missile defense system along the lines of the Strategic Defense Initiative (SDI). The ramifications of such a system are uncertain because it is impossible to predict Soviet responses. This report is limited in scope to the technology of the SDI, but it does give insight into the original scheme.

549 *Defense Planning for the 1990s.* Edited by William A. Buckingham. Washington, DC: National Defense University Press, 1984. 378pp.

The proceedings of the Tenth National Security Affairs Conference, which was held at Fort McNair, Washington, DC, in 1983, are published in this book. National security experts from government, business, academia, and the media contributed essays on defense planning for the next decade. There were four subjects under discussion: (1) Vietnam and U.S. policy; (2) NATO in the 1990s; (3) low-order violence; and (4) U.S. foreign policy options in

East Asia. These essays are of such high quality that this book should be consulted both now and in the future.

550 *The Defense Policies of Nations: A Comparative Study.* Edited by Douglas J. Murray and Paul R. Viotti. Baltimore: Johns Hopkins University Press, 1982. 525pp. ISBN 0–8018–2636–5.

The defense policies of ten countries are compared in this combination of sourcebook and essays. Each state's defense policy is studied for international environment, national objectives, defense decision making, and defense policy outputs. There are also regional assessments of defense policies and a series of bibliographical essays. This book is a creative approach to an old subject, and has many uses for defense and military specialists.

551 *Defense Policy Formation: Towards Comparative Analysis.* Edited by James M. Roherty. Durham, NC: Carolina Academic Press, 1980. 315pp. ISBN 0–89089–152–4.

These essays were originally prepared for the 1978 biennial conference of the section on military studies of the International Studies Association (ISA) held at Kiawah Island, South Carolina. Fifteen scholars from around the world presented papers on defense policy issues in five countries: Australia, France, India, Japan, and South Africa. They were most interested in defense procurement policies and formulation of defense planning in these defense communities. These essays present a solid comparative overview of defense policy formation from a variety of countries with the U.S. example always in the background.

552 *The Defense Reform Debate: Issues and Analysis.* Edited by Asa A. Clark et al. Baltimore: Johns Hopkins University Press, 1984. 370pp. ISBN 0–8018–3205–5.

These essays originate from a two-day seminar in 1982 on the military reform debate held at the U.S. Military Academy, West Point, NY. While the proposals of the authors differ widely, the goal always remained the same: to reform the U.S. military. Two central points emerge from this debate: (1) shift the emphasis in military doctrine from attrition to maneuver, and (2) place the emphasis in military procurement from a small number of expensive and sophisticated weapons to a large number of simpler less expensive weapons. These papers give a sampling of the defense reform debate, and this book is the place to examine the background of this debate.

553 DeGrasse, Robert W. *Military Expansion, Economic Decline.* New York: Council on Economic Priorities, 1983. 237pp. ISBN 0–87871–021–3.

The findings in this book are the result of a two-year study by the Council on Economic Priorities on the impact of military spending on the U.S. economy. An important finding is that the U.S. higher share of gross domestic product (GDP) spent on the military has contributed to the decline in manufacturing competence. Military spending is also largely responsible for the massive budget deficits. This book shows that a military buildup hurts the U.S. economy, and this conclusion makes it an important source for basic information on this topic.

554 Deitchman, Seymour J. *Military Power and the Advance of Technology: General Purpose Military Forces for the 1980s and Beyond.* Boulder, CO: Westview Press, 1983. 278pp. ISBN 0–86531–573–6.

A revised edition of *New Technology and Military Power* (Boulder, CO: Westview Press, 1979), this book is an assessment of the impact of military technology on military strategy and tactics. Criticism of the cost of technology and frustration over expectations are answered by the author by an in-depth analysis of the problems. The author believes in military technology and the benefits of research and development in weapons systems. This book is an updated and improved version of the earlier work, and should have a large audience of readers.

555 Dellums, Ronald V., R. H. Miller, and H. Lee Halterman. *Defense Sense: The Search for a Rational Military Policy.* Cambridge, MA: Ballinger, 1983. 342pp. ISBN 0–88410–942–9.

This book is intended to be a comprehensive examination of all aspects of U.S. military policy and defense budgeting. Each author proposes a defense issue and places this issue before a defense specialist whose statement is used for further discussion. This potpourri approach culminates in a conclusion that there is a need to reevaluate the amount of defense spending. This book, by a member of Congress and veteran of the Armed Services Committee and his two associates, with its emphasis upon the budgeting processes, makes a solid contribution to knowledge about defense spending.

556 Deschamps, Louis. *The SDI and European Security Interests.* London: Croom Helm, 1987. 61pp. ISBN 0–7099–4549–3.

A French international relations researcher examines European reactions to the Strategic Defense Initiative (SDI). The author acknowledges that the SDI has inspired European opposition, but this debate has taken place during a period of alliance harmony over other issues. Continuation of the SDI debate will cause a more sophisticated discussion of strategic defense among the Western alliance. This short work reexamines the impact of the SDI from a European perspective.

557 Dinter, Elmar, and Paddy Griffith. *Not Over by Christmas: NATO's Central Front in World War III.* Chichester, England: Anthony Bird Publications, 1983. 178pp. ISBN 0–88254–876–X.

Two British defense specialists criticize the excessive dependence of NATO on nuclear weapons. There is a greater likelihood of conventional warfare on Europe's central front than nuclear exchanges. Current NATO military tactical doctrine calls for forward defense in Germany, but the authors believe that it must be a flexible forward defense, free from organizational and tactical rigidity. This book is a mild critique of current NATO tactical strategy, and its conclusions are ground for further debate.

558 Donnelly, C. N. *Heirs of Clausewitz: Change and Continuity in the Soviet War Machine.* London: Institute for European Defence and Strategic Studies, 1985. 40pp. ISBN 0–907967–71–X.

The thesis of this short study is that the Soviet Union's military machine is unique in strategic and tactical philosophy. Only by a total reliance on military force does the Soviet Union retain its status as a world power. But the Red Army is an amalgamation of the Russian military tradition and the revolutionary ideal, with the strengths and weaknesses of both. This study is most useful for the author's viewpoint, since most of the analysis has appeared in other sources.

559 Dorfer, Ingemar. *Arms Deals, When, Why, and How?* Washington, DC: International Security Studies Program, 1980. 15pp.

This paper surveys the intricacies of arms dealing between the advanced nations. The United States continues to be the most important arms dealer in the world, exporting more than 50 percent of the world's arms. Most of the examples come from the selling of aircraft to Norway, Denmark, the Netherlands, and Belgium in 1975. Researchers on arms transfers will find this paper useful but limited.

560 Douglass, Joseph D., and Amoretta M. Hoeber. *Conventional War and Escalation: The Soviet View.* New York: Crane, Russak, 1981. 63pp. ISBN 0–8448–1390–7.

The authors examine the contention that the Soviets have reoriented their military strategy away from nuclear toward conventional warfare. They have surveyed Soviet military literature and found little confirmation for this argument. While Soviet strategy envisages both conventional and nuclear war scenarios, the Soviets expect combat to go nuclear as the conflict progresses. This short monograph studies one issue in depth, and any researcher interested in this issue will find this work useful.

561 Downey, Arthur J. *The Emerging Role of the US Army in Space.* Washington, DC: National Defense University Press, 1985. 92pp.

A senior officer in the U.S. Army argues for the inclusion of the U.S. Army in space projects, claiming that space is a place where many missions can be performed and that the army should play a role in performing these missions. In addition to developing trained personnel for space duty, the army should also involve itself in the Strategic Defense Initiative (SDI) program as well as retain a role in the development of space technology. This study is an overambitious proposal most noteworthy because it reflects interservice rivalry among the military branches.

562 Drell, Sidney D., Philip J. Farley, and David Holloway. *The Reagan Strategic Defense Initiative: A Technical, Political, and Arms Control Assessment.* Cambridge, MA: Ballinger, 1985. 152pp. ISBN 0–88730–064–2.

The viability and purpose of the Strategic Defense Initiative (SDI) is examined in this report, published under the auspices of the Center for International Security and Arms Control at Stanford University. Grave doubts about the feasibility of SDI on both technical and strategic grounds are given. The authors recommend funding for research on a modest scale to prevent destabilization and to use this research as a basis for further arms control negotiations. This report is one of the best assessments of SDI available.

563 Drifte, Reinhard. *Japan's Growing Arms Industry.* Geneva, Switzerland: Programme for Strategic and International Security Studies, 1985. 94pp.

The future of Japanese arms industry is assessed in this paper by a fellow of the International Institute for Strategic Studies, London. Japan's arms industry has been nurtured by the import of U.S. weapons technology, but the use of electronics in modern weapons systems will involve Japan more in the production of arms. There are few barriers for Japanese industry to shift between civilian and military research and development. This paper is another outstanding contribution from this institute.

564 Dupuy, Trevor N. *The Evolution of Weapons and Warfare*. Fairfax, VA: Hero Books, 1984. 350pp. ISBN 0–915979–05–5.

This book is a historical survey of the evolutionary nature of warfare. The author begins his analysis around 2000 B.C. and advances the narrative to the present. His emphasis is on isolating the interaction between technological innovation and warfare. This means considerable detail on weapons systems and the extent to which these weapons determined combat outcomes. The analysis alternates between solid assessment and oversimplification, producing a book of mixed value.

565 Dupuy, Trevor N. *Numbers, Predictions and War: Using History to Evaluate Combat Factors and Predict the Outcome of Battles*. Fairfax, VA: Hero Books, 1985. 256pp. ISBN 0–915979–06–3.

The author has devised an analytical methodology, the Quantified Judgment Method of Analysis of Historical Combat Data (QJMA), to study combat effectiveness. Although QJMA has been used primarily to analyze military campaigns in historical situations, this method has also been utilized to project hypothetical combat situations of the future. Published under the auspices of the Historical Evaluation and Research Organization (HERO), both the book and its methodology are stimulating approaches to combat problems, and scholars of military studies will find this book a worthwhile approach.

566 Dwinger, Carl-Friedrich. *Warning Time and Forward Defence*. Kingston, Canada: Centre for International Relations, Queen's University, 1984. 113pp. ISBN 0–919827–53–5.

Written by an officer in the West German Air Force, this book is a critique of NATO's conventional defense structure. The change of strategy by NATO leadership from massive nuclear retaliation to flexible response has pushed the debate over conventional tactics to the forefront. Efforts must be implemented to absorb the initial Soviet military thrust and strike against second-echelon forces. This assessment is a sound analysis of NATO strategy by a participant in the defense of Western Europe.

567 Dziak, John J. *Soviet Perceptions of Military Power: The Interaction of Theory and Practice*. New York: Crane, Russak, 1981. 72pp. ISBN 0–8448–1389–3.

The author analyzes the Soviet strategic mind-set. His view is that the growth of Soviet military power over the last decade has been accomplished because of Soviet perceptions of the utility of military power. The Soviet Union is a state characterized by a political system dedicated to a near state of war, and the interrelation between the party and the military is an outgrowth of this orientation. This short book is devoted to debunking myths about the Soviets, but is only partially successful.

568 *The Economics of Military Expenditures: Military Expenditures, Economic Growth and Fluctuations*. Edited by Christian Schmidt. Houndmills, England: Macmillan, 1987. 391pp. ISBN 0–333–42238–4.

These papers are the product of a 1986 conference on the economic ramifications of military expenditures held under the auspices of the International Economic Association in Paris. Forty international defense experts presented papers on the economic benefits of military production versus the economic problems of conversion of military industries to civilian production. These participants were most concerned to seek assessments and study better ways to analyze the impact of military expenditures on both the industrialized and developing countries. There is no better source for this subject available.

569 Edwards, John. *Superweapon: The Making of MX.* New York: W. W. Norton, 1982. 287pp. ISBN 0–393–01523–8.

This book is a history of the development of the MX missile system and the basing mode controversy. While it is the convergence of technology and political decision making that produced the MX system, this system has had a destabilizing effect because it has given the United States a true first-strike capability. Because the existence of the MX system has no military purpose, other than as a threat, and because it has not increased U.S. security, the author believes that this missile system should be scrapped. This book is a revealing view of U.S. decision making, and the story does not inspire confidence.

570 Ehrlich, Robert. *Waging Nuclear Peace: The Technology and Politics of Nuclear Weapons.* Albany, NY: State University of New York Press, 1985. 397pp. ISBN 0–87395–919–1.

The author intends to chart a middle course on the nuclear debate in this book. Rather than disarmament, he believes that there are a number of measures that can reduce the risk of nuclear war and retain deterrence. His analysis of the issues reinforces his moderate stance on nuclear weapons. This book is more a textbook on the nuclear debate than a serious work of scholarship, and it is most valuable for undergraduate college coursework.

571 English, John A. *A Perspective on Infantry.* New York: Praeger, 1981. 345pp. ISBN 0–03–059699–8.

A Canadian infantry officer offers his views on the role of the infantry in modern combat. He is most concerned with the fundamentals of infantry operations and training. The author concludes that the infantry is still important in combat, and small-unit actions are often the key to successful engagements. Most of the analysis is based on historical examples, but the book still has its uses for the defense researcher.

572 Epstein, Joshua M. *The Calculus of Conventional War: Dynamic Analysis without Lanchester Theory.* Washington, DC: Brookings Institution, 1985. 31pp. ISBN 0–8157–2451–9.

The author challenges the Lanchester equations and their relevance to modern warfare. He tests these equations on the balance of conventional forces in battle and finds them wanting. Warfare refuses to fit the Lanchester models, because it fails to include feedback for withdrawal or the trading of space for time. The author makes a positive contribution to the Lanchester equations, and his model should be studied as a replacement.

573 Epstein, Joshua M. *Measuring Military Power: The Soviet Air Threat to Europe.* Princeton, NJ: Princeton University Press, 1984. 288pp. ISBN 0–691–07671–5.

The author examines the contention that the Soviet Air Force has air superiority in Europe. This type of study requires U.S.-Soviet air force comparisons, with the U.S. Air Force coming out ahead because of technology and pilot skill. A rigorous mathematical reckoning convinces the author that the Soviets are unable at present to obtain and retain air control in the event of a war in Europe. This book is an outgrowth of the author's dissertation, and it is certain to remain one of the best sources on Soviet air power in existence.

574 Erickson, John, Lynn Hansen, and William Schneider. *Soviet Ground Forces: An Operational Assessment.* Boulder, CO: Westview Press, 1986. 267pp. ISBN 0–89158–796–9.

These authors have made an appraisal of the capabilities of the Soviet Army in the middle 1980s. Emphasis is less on counting units and equipment than on examining Soviet forces in operation and Soviet self-appraisals of performance. The authors conclude that the Soviet Army would function well in a conventional war but less so in a limited nuclear war. This book makes a positive contribution to an assessment of the Soviet Army.

575 Esposito, Lori, and James A. Schear. *The Command and Control of Nuclear Weapons.* Queenstown, MD: Aspen Institute for Humanistic Studies, 1985. 29pp. ISBN 0–89843–067–4.

Major perspectives and ideas of a workshop on the command, control, communications, and intelligence (C3I) systems supporting nuclear forces have been combined in this report. This workshop was sponsored by the Aspen Institute for Humanistic Studies in the summer of 1982. The consensus among the participants is that efforts by the Reagan administration to support C3I research deserve support. This book provides a variety of opinion on the survivability of U.S. nuclear assets in a war, and these viewpoints are worth further study.

576 *Estimating Foreign Military Power.* Edited by Philip Towle. London: Croom Helm, 1982. 276pp. ISBN 0–7099–0434–7.

By studying methods of estimating the military power of foreign countries by drawing on historical examples, this book makes a unique contribution to security problems. Contributors have selected past examples of estimating military power and compared perceptions and actuality. The conclusion is that a good deal of skepticism is necessary before accepting any assessment of military power. While the historical cases are illustrative, it is the post–World War II examples that are the most valuable.

577 Etzold, Thomas H. *Defense or Delusion?: America's Military in the 1980s.* New York: Harper and Row, 1982. 259pp. ISBN 0–06–038011–X.

A veteran of government service and fellow at the U.S. Naval War College, the author critiques the U.S. military in the early 1980s. His thesis is that the U.S. military is in the middle of a malaise and that drastic action will have to take place to restore its capability to carry out its mission of defending the United States. True military renewal will be sustained by a careful attention to manpower and modernization problems, not costly quick fixes. This book is a reasoned and balanced assessment with a prudent plan, but most of the author's recommendations continue to be ignored.

578 *The European Missiles Crisis: Nuclear Weapons and Security Policy.* Edited by Hans-Henrik and Nikolay Petersen. London: Frances Pinter, 1983. 274pp. ISBN 0–86187–355–6.

The political ramifications of the deployment of intermediate-range nuclear missiles in Europe during the early 1980s are considered in this book of essays. Most of the papers have been revised since their presentation at a conference at Ebeltoft, Denmark, in 1983. While the political impact of the NATO double-track decision in December 1979 has been to intensify the debate on the wisdom of introducing these missiles on the European scene, in terms of alliance politics the decision has been a success. This book makes a solid effort to ferret out the decision-making processes in the NATO alliance.

579 Evan, Grant. *The Yellow Rainmakers: Are Chemical Weapons Being Used in Southeast Asia?* London: Verso Editions, 1983. 202pp. ISBN 0–86091–068–7.

The use of chemical warfare in Laos and Kampuchea in the early 1980s is explored in this book by a British journalist. After hearing of incidents of chemical warfare, the author traveled to Southeast Asia in early 1982 for a two-month research expedition into Laos and the refugee camps. He concludes that U.S. charges of chemical warfare in Southeast Asia are without foundation. While the author has not disproved biochemical warfare in this region, he has raised grave doubts about its use.

580 *Evolving European Defense Policies.* Edited by Catherine McArdle Kelleher and Gale A. Mattox. Lexington, MA: Lexington Books, 1987. 340pp. ISBN 0–669–11280–1.

These papers explore the future of the NATO alliance by examining British, French, and German defense options in detail and Scandinavian and Mediterranean cases more summarily. Conclusions are that Europeans will be more involved in the formulation of NATO defense posture in the future, but the withdrawal of U.S. forces might cause Europeans to forsake NATO. The issues of greater public concern about NATO policies and the possible impact of the Strategic Defense Initiative (SDI) both concern the authors. This book is a major contribution toward an understanding of future European defense policies.

581 *The Fallacy of Star Wars: Based on Studies Conducted by the Union of Concerned Scientists.* Edited by John Tirman. New York: Vintage Books, 1984. 293pp. ISBN 0–394–72894–7.

The Union of Concerned Scientists sponsored this book critical of the Strategic Defense Initiative (SDI). President Ronald Reagan's vision of the SDI was for a total missile defense system, but recent interpretations have tended to advocate a modest defense capable of intercepting a high percentage of Soviet missiles. Technology is available for antisatellite (ASAT) weapons, but the technology for the SDI is a long way away. This book is the best source on the market attacking the SDI.

582 Faringdon, Hugh. *Confrontation: The Strategic Geography of NATO and the Warsaw Pact.* London: Routledge and Kegan Paul, 1986. 354pp. ISBN 0–7102–0676–3.

The strategic geographies of the Soviet Union and the United States are examined in this book by a prominent British scholar. He advances the thesis that the modern defense debate ignores geographical and historical perspectives. His analysis depends upon detailed maps of the deployment of NATO and Warsaw Pact forces. This book should be required reading for anyone interested in research on European security subjects.

583 Feld, Werner J., and John K. Wildgen. *Congress and National Defense: The Politics of the Unthinkable.* New York: Praeger, 1985. 126pp. ISBN 0–03–069751–4.

The authors isolate members of Congress who show signs of strategic thinking on defense issues and present their views on strategic issues from the MX missile to a nuclear freeze. Only about a dozen congressmen fall into this category. Views from both sides of the political spectrum are analyzed for their positions on defense issues. While this book had potential to be exciting, the authors produced a work that is fragmented and reflects the authors' viewpoints rather than congressional thinking.

584 Fermoselle, Rafael. *The Evolution of the Cuban Military: 1492–1986.* Miami, FL: Ediciones Universal, 1987. 585pp. ISBN 0–89729–428–9.

The Cuban author presents a history of Cuban military forces from the discovery of Cuba to the current status of its armed forces. He chronicles political involvement of Cuban military leadership in depth before and after the Cuban Revolution of 1958. But it is the material on Cuban military activities after Fidel Castro's revolution that makes this book valuable. While the author's anti-Castro bias is apparent, his treatment of the postrevolution Cuban military establishment is this book's strong point.

585 *Fighting Allies: Tension within the Atlantic Alliance.* Edited by Walter Goldstein. London: Brassey's Defence Publishers, 1986. 235pp. ISBN 0–08–033594–2.

These papers on defense and political tension with the NATO alliance in the mid-1980s are the product of a 1984 conference of the Committee on Atlantic Studies (CAS) held in Italy. Most contributors considered the future of the NATO alliance secure, but the tensions are serious enough to warrant some reorientation of strategy and tactics. Divergence of views between Europeans and Americans over the future of the alliance will continue, but public opinion on both sides of the Atlantic still supports NATO. Younger U.S. and European scholars with new insights contributed to this volume, and their contributions are a welcome addition to the literature in the defense field.

586 *Fighting Armies: Antagonists in the Middle East: A Combat Assessment.* Edited by Richard A. Gabriel. Westport, CT: Greenwood Press, 1983. 176pp. ISBN 0–313–23904–5.

A group of military experts analyze the military forces of the eight countries with sizable armies in the Middle East. Both quantitative and qualitative measurements have been included so that each army can be studied in relation to its potential enemy. This book is an excellent source for any study of Middle East military affairs.

587 *Fighting Armies: Nonaligned, Third World, and Other Ground Armies: A Combat Assessment.* Edited by Richard A. Gabriel. Westport, CT: Greenwood Press, 1983. 276pp. ISBN 0–313–23905–3.

Third World military forces are analyzed in depth in this book of papers by specialists in the military field. Thirty-two ground armies are assessed for combat effectiveness in different military scenarios. The social, cultural, and political backgrounds of each of these nations are integrated into a picture of their military capabilities in case of hostilities. This book is the best source of its type on the market.

588 *Five War Zones: The Views of Local Military Leaders.* By Abdulaziz bin Khalid Alsudairy et al. Washington, DC: Pergamon-Brassey's, 1986. 184pp. ISBN 0–08–034698–7.

Five high-level military officers, a Saudi, an Israeli, a South Korean, an Egyptian, and a Pakistani, look at the strategic situations in their parts of the world. Each contributor provides maps and documents to complement the analysis. The intent of this book is to provide U.S. policymakers and defense strategists the perspectives of foreign military experts. This book combines a new approach and exceptional analysis.

589 Ford, Daniel. *The Button: The Pentagon's Strategic Command and Control System.* New York: Simon and Schuster, 1985. 270pp. ISBN 0–671–50068–6.

A U.S. writer for *The New Yorker* was stimulated by reading that the U.S. capability to retaliate after a Soviet attack was uncertain to research the problem of the U.S. command and control system. His findings are that the U.S. command and control system is indeed vulnerable and works well only in a peacetime environment. Present U.S. strategic policy is based on a preemptive strike on the Soviet Union, and this is the reason for the lack of interest by the Pentagon in developing a better command and control system. While this book suffers from a journalistic flavor, the author has made an important study of deficiencies in the U.S. strategic deterrence system.

590 Fotion, N., and G. Elfstrom. *Military Ethics: Guidelines for Peace and War.* Boston, MA: Routledge and Kegan Paul, 1986. 311pp. ISBN 0–7102–0182–6.

The authors explore the moral issues that arise because of the existence and use of military forces. Because the individual is a small cog in a large organizational machine, military ethics is an ethics of institutions. The debate is between the pacifists who want to do away with the military and the realists who insist on the necessity of the military. This book examines most of the ethical dilemmas facing the military in peace and war, and it makes a solid contribution in this gray area of ethics.

591 *French Security Policy: From Independence to Interdependence.* Edited by Robbin F. Laird. Boulder, CO: Westview Press, 1986. 180pp. ISBN 0–8133–7201–1.

U.S. and French defense experts analyze past and present French security policy in this book. Several problems, i.e., budget, conventional and nuclear modernization, and relations with the Soviet Union and the U.S., are dealt with by the authors. Recent Socialist governments have reaffirmed a commitment to traditional French security issues, and the new conservative government will have to deal with some of the problems of these policies. This book has a number of excellent essays, and no research on French defense issues can ignore this work.

592 *The Future of Air Power.* Edited by John R. Walker. London: Ian Allan, 1986. 99pp. ISBN 0–7110–1670–4.

Six British specialists on air warfare analyze the future of air power for the Royal United Services Institute (RUSI). The experience of air power in the Falkland conflict stands behind every paper and moderates the former British preoccupation with a European war. All the authors recognize the future importance of air power, but they insist on flexibility and range as important factors. This short book gives a good view of current British thought on air power for the next decade.

593 *The Future of British Sea Power.* Edited by Geoffrey Till. London: Macmillan, 1984. 265pp. ISBN 0–333–37976–4.

The future of British sea power in the aftermath of the Defence White of 1981 and the Falkland campaign is the subject of this collection of essays from a 1983 conference in London. A moderately optimistic tone of confidence that there is an active future for British sea power comes out of these proceedings. Budgetary constraints and alliance commitments will play a role, but the Royal Navy can still be a force to reckon with for the rest of the century. This book is a lengthy self-examination of British naval forces, and it provides a source to study the future prospects of the British navy.

594 *The Future of the British Nuclear Deterrent.* Edited by A. F. Allen and Ian Bellany. Lancaster, England: Centre for the Study of Arms Control and International Security, 1980. 158pp.

These papers are the products of a 1980 conference at the University of Lancaster the topic of which was an assessment of British nuclear deterrent strategy. Each paper deals with a specific weapons system and the decision-making processes utilized for the deployment of that system. Particular emphasis is placed upon the replacement costs of each weapons system. Although each paper stands on its own merits, the overall quality of analysis makes this book an excellent source on British nuclear deterrent strategy.

595 *Future War: Armed Conflict in the Next Decade.* Edited by Frank Barnaby. London: Michael Joseph, 1984. 192pp. ISBN 0–7181–2352–2.

British defense specialists muse over the future outlines of armed conflicts in this publication. The technology of warfare has advanced so far that it is hard to envisage future battlefields. Arms control measures have failed to produce nuclear disarmament or even to halt the nuclear arms race. Excellent illustrations and a readable text make this book a good source for the general reader.

596 Gabriel, Richard A. *The Antagonists: A Comparative Combat Assessment of the Soviet and American Soldier.* Westport, CT: Greenwood Press, 1984. 208pp. ISBN 0–313–23127–3.

The author gives a comprehensive overview of the comparative combat capabilities of the U.S. and Soviet armies. This capability is measured in the will to fight and the group cohesion necessary to win in combat. By almost every standard the Soviet Army is better trained for combat than its U.S. counterpart. This book is a pessimistic assessment by a prominent military analyst, and its conclusions are worth pondering.

597 Gabriel, Richard A. *Military Incompetence: Why the American Military Doesn't Win.* New York: Hill and Wang, 1985. 207pp. ISBN 0–809–06928–8.

The author, a former officer in the U.S. Army, uses this book to criticize the U.S. military establishment on its past and present conduct of military operations. He is highly critical of the U.S. officer corps, because he attributes much of the incompetence in the military to faults in the officer system. His solutions are to (1) reform the officer value system; (2) stabilize the assignment structure; (3) adopt a thirty-year service term; (4) tie promotions to age and excellence; (5) abolish the Joint Chiefs of Staff; (6) reform military education; and (7) return the draft. The author proposes an impressive list of reforms, and his analysis of bungled military operations over the last fifteen years makes this book a first-rate addition to any collection.

598　Gabriel, Richard A. *The New Red Legions: A Survey Data Source Book.* Westport, CT: Greenwood Press, 1980. 252pp. ISBN 0–313–21497–2.

The data for this sourcebook on the Soviet Army have been gathered from former members of the Soviet military forces. A total of 113 of the respondents to a questionnaire had served in the Soviet Army since 1971, and constitute the core for this study. The remainder of the book is a statistical breakdown of the questionnaire. This source is unique because it has material on the Soviet Army unavailable elsewhere.

599　Gainsborough, J. R. *The Arab-Israeli Conflict: A Politico-Legal Analysis.* Aldershot, England: Gower, 1986. 345pp. ISBN 0–566–00818–1.

A British scholar presents the legal and political issues involved in the five major wars fought between Israel and the Arab states. The question of rightful claims by Arabs and Jews to the territory of Palestine is posed throughout the book. Until the aspiration for a Palestinian state is fulfilled, there will be no peace in this region and a state of war will continue, with or without fighting. The author intends to be objective, and, despite a lapse or two, succeeds in presenting the legal cases for both sides.

600　Gallacher, Joseph. *Nuclear Stocktaking: A Count of Britain's Warheads.* Lanchester, England: Centre for the Study of Arms Control and International Security, 1982. 29 leaves.

This paper is a survey of Great Britain's nuclear arsenal. Although this study is based on unclassified sources, the author concludes that Great Britain has between 1,557 and 1,947 warheads. This estimate is gathered from defense expenditures and the amount of plutonium and enriched uranium necessary for nuclear weapons. The techniques used to arrive at this figure are almost as important as the conclusions.

601　Garnell, P. *Guided Weapon Control Systems,* 2d ed. London: Brassey's Defence Publishers, 1980. 244pp. ISBN 0–08–025468–3.

The author applies classical control theory for the design of tactical guided weapons systems. This work is based on lecture notes given to the guided weapons systems course at the Royal Military College of Science. Intended for engineers and advanced engineering students, this book presupposes knowledge of linear control theory and other aerospace theorems. Only readers interested in technical details of guided weapons control systems will find this book of interest.

602　*The Genesis of New Weapons: Decision Making for Military R&D.* Edited by Franklin A. Long and Judith Reppy. New York: Pergamon Press, 1980. 210pp. ISBN 0–08–025973–1.

In 1979 the Peace Studies Program of Cornell University sponsored a workshop on research and development topics in New York City. Research and development consumes anywhere from 10 to 12 percent of the total U.S. military budget, and this figure is growing. These papers study the research and development process from planning to implementation of weapons systems, with special emphasis on decision making. This book makes a major contribution to defense literature by dealing with this topic.

603 *The Geography of Defence.* Edited by Michael Bateman and Raymond Riley. London: Croom Helm, 1987. 237pp. ISBN 0–7099–3933–7.

These papers on the geography of defense are an outgrowth of the 1987 Annual Conference of the Institute of British Geographers in Portsmouth, England. The social, economic, and physical consequences of defense are analyzed by these geographers, and historical as well as modern cases are examined for patterns. While this book has a distinct viewpoint, only a few articles are worth more than a passing examination.

604 Gervasi, Tom. *The Myth of Soviet Military Supremacy.* New York: Harper and Row, 1986. 545pp. ISBN 0–06–015574–4.

Nearly half of this book is composed of statistical appendices reinforcing the author's contention that the Reagan administration has distorted the Soviet military capacity for political reasons. These tables alone make the book valuable. The strong anti-Reagan viewpoint of the author, however, is so pervasive that many of the conclusions appear overblown.

605 Glenn, John, Barry E. Carter, and Robert W. Komer. *Rethinking Defense and Conventional Forces.* Washington, DC: Center for National Policy, 1983. 58pp.

The authors trace their positions on increasing defense spending and the buildup of U.S. conventional military forces. Each author presents his argument from a different perspective, but all conclude that Reagan administration policies are failing to meet present military needs. Only conventional forces can fulfill U.S. military commitments, and more glamorous programs have diverted funds from a buildup of conventional forces. This publication is a critique of current defense policies, and the benefit is that each author has enunciated his views in an open forum.

606 Goebel, Hans. *The Wrong Force for the Right Mission.* Kingston, Canada: Centre for International Relations, Queen's University, 1981. 93pp.

A senior officer in the West German Army reports his and other European conclusions that NATO conventional strategy has serious defects. NATO's conventional military situation in Europe is precarious, because its static borderline defense in Central Europe is too easily penetrated, and recourse to nuclear weapons would be the only way to prevent defeat. An adoption of area defense posture, acquisition of a sufficient quantity of good and reliable equipment, and dependence on the infantry will allow NATO forces the ability to counter Soviet combat tactics. The author advances a controversial thesis, but his viewpoint is part of an ongoing reevaluation of NATO's conventional forces.

607 Gold, David, Christopher Paine, and Gail Shields. *Misguided Expenditure: An Analysis of the Proposed MX Missile System.* New York: Council on Economic Priorities, 1981. 179pp. ISBN 0–87871–014–0.

Strategic missile theory and the MX project are critiqued in this study produced by the Council on Economic Priorities. Dissatisfaction with the MX weapon deployment and the cost estimates characterizes the stance of the authors. They conclude that the MX system will not perform as advertised in protecting land-based missiles, and the missile will not serve as a deterrence in the event of either a nuclear or conventional war. This source unites all the arguments against the MX and combines them with lists of MX defense contractors.

608 Golden, James R. *The Dynamics of Change in NATO: A Burden-Sharing Perspective.* New York: Praeger, 1983. 229pp. ISBN 0–03–069562–7.

The problems of the members of the NATO alliance in mobilizing defense resources are analyzed in this book by a career army officer. While the European members of NATO recognize the danger of the Soviet military buildup, economic problems among these states have reduced the capacity to respond by increasing defense spending. Burden-sharing can be achieved by more specialization of combat functions within the alliance. This book is one of the better publications on NATO on the market.

609 Golden, James R. *NATO Burden-Sharing: Risks and Opportunities.* New York: Praeger, 1983. 103pp. ISBN 0–03–062769–9.

The author analyzes the issue of burden-sharing within the NATO alliance. Sharing the burdens of collective defense has in the past meant money and manpower, but now it also means dividing the risks of deterrence. The shift to conventional defense will make burden-sharing more equal among the NATO allies. This book makes a solid contribution and should be read by all who have an interest in NATO.

610 Gordon, Don E. *Electronic Warfare: Element of Strategy and Multiplier of Combat.* New York: Pergamon Press, 1981. 103pp. ISBN 0–08–027189–8.

A senior U.S. Army intelligence officer uses his expertise in electronic warfare to expound the benefits of this type of combat. The author maintains that superb command and control communication systems are necessary to dominate the modern battlefield. There is also a need for electronic resources to be made available to the U.S. Army so that the entire electromagnetic spectrum can be controlled. This book is a sophisticated look at the military uses of electronic technology in combat situations.

611 Gormley, Dennis M. *Soviet Views on Escalation: Implications for Alliance Strategy.* Marina del Rey, CA: European American Institute for Security Research, 1984. 22pp.

Soviet views on the escalation of warfare and the impact of these views on NATO strategy are the subjects of this paper. Soviet strategy has changed from the single threshold war of the 1960s to a flexible strategy envisaging conflict without nuclear weapons. While it remains Soviet policy to recognize the prospects for escalation to nuclear warfare as an option, the Soviets prefer conventional warfighting. The value of this work is that it advances arguments for a more flexible response from NATO to counter Soviet strategy.

612 Gray, Colin S. *American Military Space Policy: Information Systems, Weapon Systems and Arms Control.* Cambridge, MA: Abt Books, 1982. 128pp. ISBN 0–89011–591–5.

Military uses of space are explored in this book. While the author believes that military utilization of space is integral to U.S. national security, he also insists that defense policy should not be driven by what is technologically possible. At present the United States uses space for C3I and surveillance and reconnaissance, but there is potential for wars to be revolutionized by space. This book's value resides in the author's arguments for the United States to establish a coherent military space policy.

613 Gray, Colin S. *Missiles against War: The ICBM Debate Today*. Fairfax, VA: National Institute for Public Policy, 1985. 134pp. ISBN 0–933719–00–0.

This study examines the ICBM modernization program and the MX ICBM deployment in silos project. The author backs ICBMs as a deterrence and as an arms control bargaining chip. Furthermore, the MX ICBM is important both because of the political signals it sends to the Soviet Union and because in its silos it has survivability in the event of war. Despite the author's claims that this study is a balanced assessment, the arguments are all in favor of the Reagan administration's policies on ICBMs.

614 Gray, Colin S. *The MX ICBM and National Security*. New York: Praeger, 1981. 173pp. ISBN 0–03–059442–1.

The MX ICBM system and the strategic implications of its basing system are analyzed in this book. The author is a proponent of horizontal sheltering of the MX, but he is willing to accept the vertical solution. Criticisms of the MX system are answered in depth by the author, and his greatest concern is speedy adoption of the MX in whatever manifestation. This book is a solid, if not objective, view of the MX debate in the late 1970s and early 1980s.

615 Gray, Colin S. *Strategic Studies: A Critical Assessment*. Westport, CT: Greenwood Press, 1982. 213pp. ISBN 0–313–22862–0.

The author, one of the leading civilian defense professionals, uses this book to delve into the subject of U.S. strategic studies. He believes that the United States is incapable of not having a strategic doctrine, because as a superpower strategic studies are forced upon it. But U.S. strategic thinking has been weakened by the lack of strategists able to reflect on changing realities. This book points out many deficiencies of this thinking, but the underlying assumption is that the author and his colleagues are doing a better job now.

616 Green, L. C. *Essays on the Modern Law of War*. Dobbs Ferry, NY: Transnational Publishers, 1985. 281pp. ISBN 0–941320–26–X.

A Canadian lawyer, with experience at the Geneva conventions in 1949 and subsequent international conventions, has produced this series of essays on the law of armed conflict, most of which have appeared previously in various legal journals. The author is most concerned with the fate of civilians in a hostile environment and human rights in general. This book was intended to give students in the field specific practical issues on the laws of war, and the essays fulfill this purpose with distinction.

617 Griffen, Robert B. *US Space System Survivability: Strategic Alternatives for the 1990s*. Washington, DC: National Defense University Press, 1982. 66pp.

Ways to reduce the vulnerability of U.S. space systems are examined by a senior officer in the U.S. Air Force. U.S. space systems are becoming vulnerable to Soviet antisatellite (ASAT) weapons. Steps to protect U.S. satellites include developing an ASAT capability against Soviet satellites, negotiations to limit the use of weapons in space, and hardening and protecting the satellites. While much of this book has. been superseded by the Strategic Defense Initiative (SDI) debate, most of its key points are still valid.

618 Grishchenko, Anatoly, Vladimir Semenov, and Leonid Teplinsky. *Danger: NATO*. Moscow: Progress Publishers, 1985. 175pp.

Three Soviet scholars use documents and other materials to label NATO as a danger to peace. The authors maintain that the United States and other NATO countries are active in brainwashing world public opinion by representing NATO as a deterrence to war. They use information from a variety of Western sources to advance their thesis. This book is an articulate statement of Soviet arguments against NATO.

619 Guertner, Gary L. *The Last Frontier: An Analysis of the Strategic Defense Initiative.* Lexington, MA: Lexington Books, 1986. 158pp. ISBN 0–669–12370–6.

The authors provide an assessment of the feasibility of the Reagan administration's Strategic Defense Initiative (SDI). Many scientific and technological problems have to be overcome before the technical promise of SDI can be determined. The popular appeal of such a weapons system makes research and development on it possible, but such a system has the potential to be a destabilizing factor in Soviet-U.S. relations. This book is a balanced middle-of-the-road assessment of the SDI controversy, and its conclusions deserve serious consideration.

620 Gunston, Bill. *Air Superiority.* London: Ian Allan, 1985. 112pp. ISBN 0–7110–1417–5.

This book is an overview of a potential confrontation between the air forces of the Warsaw Pact and NATO in Europe. All military aircraft, weapons systems, and communications are compared and contrasted for combat efficiency. The author concludes that the Warsaw Pact forces are not only superior in number of aircraft, but their equipment and weapons systems are almost as good. This book is a quality effort by a prolific writer on military aircraft.

621 Gunston, Bill. *Warplanes of the Future: The Most Exciting Combat Aircraft Being Designed Today To Face the Threat of Wars Tomorrow.* Sydney: Hodder and Stoughton, 1985. 208pp. ISBN 0–340–37299–0.

An authority on military aircraft uses his expertise to speculate on future aircraft developments. After a section on upgrade programs in progress on current military aircraft, the author devotes the bulk of this work to analyzing possible new aircraft designs. Stealth design and vertical takeoff and landing (VTOL) are the approaches most favored by the author. Because of the long design time in aircraft development, this book will be a standard source for the next decade.

622 Gurkan, Ihsan. *NATO, Turkey and the Southern Flank: A Mideastern Perspective.* New York: National Strategy Information Center, 1980. 67pp. ISBN 0–87855–825–X.

A Turkish senior officer surveys the military security of NATO's southern flank. Any war in Europe would spread to the Turkish front, which has been weakened by the Greek-Turkish enmity and U.S. actions in response to this dispute. The author believes that NATO's southern flank needs to be reinforced by economic and military assistance from its allies. This book gives attention to a neglected military region in need of more attention.

623 Hackett, John. *The Third World War: The Untold Story.* New York: Macmillan, 1982. 372pp. ISBN 0–02–547110–4.

This book is an elaboration of the author's earlier work, *The Third World War: August 1985* (New York: Macmillan, 1978). Hackett uses fictional personal narrative to reinforce his analysis of the probable course of a war between NATO and the Warsaw Pact. The result is the same, with the NATO forces defeating the Soviet Union and its allies and the Soviet regime replaced by several separate states. This book is an approach that the general reader will appreciate, but its conclusions are pure speculation.

624 Haffa, Robert P. *The Half War: Planning U.S. Rapid Deployment Forces To Meet a Limited Contingency, 1960–1983.* Boulder, CO: Westview Press, 1984. 277pp. ISBN 0–86531–716–X.

The author has interviewed over fifty senior military officers and civilian defense specialists on the strategy, organization, and support of rapid deployment forces (RDF). U.S. conventional forces are not designed or organized for small combat situations, and U.S. policymakers have worked on the idea of rapid deployment forces since the 1960s. Such forces have come into being in the 1980s, but the commitment of resources to carry out these missions has not been forthcoming. This book is a major study on the need for rapid deployment forces for use in Third World military situations.

625 Hagen, Lawrence S. *Twisting Arms: Political, Military, and Economic Aspects of Arms Co-operation in the Atlantic Alliance.* Kingston, Canada: Centre for International Relations, Queen's University, 1980. 188pp.

Cooperative weapons procurement by members of the NATO alliance is studied in this book. The author believes that the political, military, and economic health of NATO is tied to progress in the cooperative production and acquisition of weapons. While the record of past arms cooperation has not been encouraging, NATO standardization requires Atlantic reciprocity in procurement even if the necessary European political and economic restructuring is incomplete. This book has a prescription for success, but the means to carry out the author's recommendations are lacking.

626 Hamm, Manfred. *Chemical Warfare: The Growing Threat to Europe.* London: Alliance Publishers, 1984. 47pp. ISBN 0–9796–7256–1.

The Soviet Union's offensive chemical warfare capability is the subject of this study by the German policy analyst of the Heritage Foundation. Contrasting the superbly equipped Chemical Troops of the Soviet Red Army, the author points out that the depleted and undertrained Chemical Corps of the U.S. Army is no match for its Soviet counterpart. He argues for a NATO policy of chemical rearmament to counter the Soviet threat. While this study has disturbing implications, other works have downplayed the Soviets' training and military capacity in this type of warfare.

627 Handel, Michael I. *Military Deception in Peace and War.* Jerusalem: Magnes Press, 1985. 60pp. ISSN 0334–2786.

Military deception as an operating tactical theory is the subject of this book. *Deception* is defined as any attempt to manipulate the perceptions of an opponent's decisionmakers in order to gain a competitive advantage. The author concludes that historical case studies indicate deception works better for the side that is at a military disadvantage. Israel utilizes military deception as a matter of national survival, and an essay from this source is a welcome addition to security literature.

628 Hanks, Robert J. *The U.S. Military Presence in the Middle East: Problems and Prospects.* Cambridge, MA: Institute for Foreign Policy Analysis, 1982. 80pp. ISBN 0–89549–047–1.

This book is a critique of U.S. military presence in the Middle East by a retired U.S. naval officer. Hanks claims that the Arab-Israeli confrontation and the fall of the Shah of Iran has weakened U.S. military influence in the Indian Ocean–Persian Gulf region, but U.S. interests necessitate a strong presence there. This means that the United States should restructure its relationship with NATO and adopt a maritime national strategy. While this book is full of insight, it advocates political decisions that the U.S. government is reluctant to pursue.

629 Hart, Gary, and William S. Lind. *America Can Win: The Case for Military Reform*. Bethesda, MD: Adler and Adler, 1986. 301pp. ISBN 0–917561–10–4.

Ex-Senator Hart and his military advisor have produced this book on reforming the military to increase combat effectiveness. A long string of military failures means that new defense policies need to be developed. Recommended reforms include (1) increasing competition both in government and in the private sector; (2) reforming military education; and (3) realizing that technology and funding increases are not panaceas. This book uses the advice of many critics of the present U.S. military situation, and it is a useful source for this reason.

630 Hartley, Keith. *NATO Arms Co-operation: A Study in Economics and Politics*. London: Allen and Unwin, 1983. 228pp. ISBN 0–04–341022–7.

Weapons standardization as an indicator of NATO's military efficiency is the focus of this book. The emphasis is on the economics and politics of NATO decision making. The author concludes that market forces and the increasing costs of weapons systems will make NATO countries shop around for better deals. While the author makes a compelling case for competition, his arguments do not counter the defense industry nationalism practiced by most NATO members.

631 *Has America Become Number 2? The U.S.-Soviet Military Balance and American Defense Policies and Programs*. Washington, DC: Committee on the Present Danger, 1982. 42pp.

This publication is another in a series of lobbying efforts by the Committee on the Present Danger, whose thesis is that the United States has fallen behind the Soviet Union in military strength. The United States will continue to be number two unless there is acceleration of the modernization program of U.S. forces and a "quick fix" project to strengthen the U.S. nuclear deterrent. This report backs the Reagan administration's defense program and argues for increased defense funding.

632 Hemsley, John. *Soviet Troop Control: The Role of Command Technology in the Soviet Military System*. Oxford: Brassey's, 1982. 276pp. ISBN 0–08–027008–5.

Soviet concepts of troop command are studied in this book by a senior officer in the British army. Emphasis is upon Soviet perceptions and evaluations of their command, control, and communications (C3) systems in terms of operational doctrine and performance. The author claims that the Soviets are concentrating upon improving command, control, and communications by technological means, including computerization, and any advances in this field will include a change in operational doctrine. This book is an excellent treatment of a technical subject.

633 Herken, Gregg. *Counsels of War*. New York: Knopf, 1985. 409pp. ISBN 0–394–52735–6.

Civilian experts involved in planning U.S. nuclear policy since 1945 have been interviewed by the author, seeking their contributions to the development of U.S. nuclear policy. These civilian experts are scientists, think-tank theorists, and academics. The story is about a group of dedicated people striving to understand the complexities of the nuclear problem and the divisions among them over policy implementation. This book is a fascinating history of the fraternity of experts who have determined U.S. strategic nuclear policies.

634 Hobbs, David. *Alternatives to Trident*. Aberdeen, Scotland: Centre for Defence Studies, 1983. 75pp.

The author questions the decision by the Thatcher government to acquire the U.S. Trident missile system for the next generation of strategic nuclear forces. High cost and excess capability are the major drawbacks to the Trident system. Thirteen alternatives are considered, with specifics and potentialities discussed in depth. This study is full of technical information on various missile systems, and the data will be of interest to both arms control and defense researchers.

635 Hobkirk, Michael D. *The Politics of Defence Budgeting: A Study of Organisation and Resource Allocation in the United Kingdom and the United States*. London: Macmillan, 1984. 177pp. ISBN 0–333–38349–4.

This book is a comparative study of the defense budgeting processes in operation in the United Kingdom and the United States. While each system has its eccentricities, the fundamental problem of allocating and managing defense resources remains the same. The author calls for a strong central planning staff to coordinate defense policies and curtail the waste of interservice rivalries. This book delves into the mire of defense budgeting, and both the analysis and the solutions deserve serious consideration.

636 Hoeber, Amoretta M. *The Chemistry of Defeat: Asymmetries in U.S. and Soviet Chemical Warfare Postures*. Cambridge, MA: Institute for Foreign Policy Analysis, 1981. 94pp. ISBN 0–89549–037–4.

Soviet and U.S. attitudes and capabilities toward chemical warfare are the subjects of this study by a senior researcher in the U.S. Department of Defense. Hoeber claims that the Soviets have a superiority of two or three orders of magnitude in chemical stockpiles and capacities to use chemical weapons. While the U.S. policy since the late 1960s has been to downgrade chemical warfare, this policy needs to be changed, with the U.S. stockpiling chemical weapons for both arms control and military reasons. This defense of chemical warfare remains unconvincing despite the author's insistence that the Soviets have and will use chemical weapons.

637 Hoeber, Francis P. *Military Applications of Modeling: Selected Case Studies*. New York: Gordon and Breach Science Publishers, 1981. 222pp. ISBN 0–677–05840–3.

This book on the military applications of modeling for military operations research is published under the auspices of the Military Operations Research Society. Eight case studies have been modeled for consideration by the Air Force Institute of Technology (AFIT). The author's skepticism over these modeling examples is apparent, but he still believes in the validity of the approach. This book is a sophisticated look at modeling applications for military operations research, but it takes a specialist in the field to handle the methodology.

638   Holland, Lauren H., and Robert A. Hoover. *The MX Decision: A New Direction in U.S. Weapons Procurement Policy?* Boulder, CO: Westview Press, 1985. 289pp. ISBN 0–86531–993–6.

The controversial MX project is dissected from its planning to its latest version in this informative book. At the time of its publication, the Reagan administration's decision on the MX was still under attack for a combination of economic, military, and political reasons. Domestic rather than foreign policy issues are the keys to deciding the fate of the MX, but it is the foreign policy implications that most disturb the authors. This book provides a way to study the politics of U.S. procurement policy in the middle of a controversy.

639   Holloway, David. *The Soviet Union and the Arms Race.* New Haven, CT: Yale University Press, 1983. 211pp. ISBN 0–300–02963–2.

The author looks at the historical experience, the policy objectives, and the institutions that make the Soviet Union a military superpower. Nuclear weapons have long been treated by Soviet leaders as conventional weapons, to be used as instruments of military power and political influence. While arms control is important to the Soviets, the policy of confrontation practiced by the United States may challenge the Soviets to a further expansion of the arms race. This book is disjointed in places, but has information of value for researchers.

640   Holst, Johan J. *Towards a Policy of No First Use of Nuclear Weapons.* Oslo: Norsk Utenrikspolitisk Institutt, 1983. 27pp.

The strategic implications of NATO's adoption of no first use of nuclear weapons are explored in this paper. Current NATO doctrine includes the option of first use of nuclear weapons, but this possibility is only considered at certain stages or in certain situations. The author believes that NATO should adopt the principle of no first use of nuclear weapons for both public relations and strategic reasons. This short paper demonstrates that a high-quality analysis can come in a small package.

641   Howard, Michael. *The Causes of Wars and Other Essays.* London: Temple Smith, 1983. 248pp. ISBN 0–85117–222–9.

Articles, lectures, and essays by the preeminent British military historian make up the contents of this book. Both the scope and depth of this work make it a mine of insight on past events and present policies. Although Howard's viewpoint is conditioned by historical examples, his articles and essays still have a contemporary flavor. Sometimes books of this type become dated rather rapidly, but this work will hold up well for at least another decade.

642   *How Nuclear Weapons Decisions Are Made.* Edited by Scilla McLean. Houndmills, England: Macmillan, 1986. 264pp. ISBN 0–333–40582–X.

Nuclear decision making by the major nuclear powers is the subject of this study by a number of young U.S. and European scholars. U.S., British, Chinese, French, and Soviet nuclear decision-making processes are examined for similarities and differences. The nuclear powers are strikingly similar because of the secrecy and the extent to which those outside the system can influence nuclear policy. Although this work is intended as a basic reference source, the information on nuclear decision making makes it more than just a good introduction into the subject.

643 Hoyt, Edwin P. *The Militarists: The Rise of Japanese Militarism since WWII.* New York: Donald I. Fine, 1985. 256pp. ISBN 0–917657–17–9.

The author advances the thesis that Japan will soon acquire the military strength to match its economic power. Japan is busy rearming, and the military training of its officer corps resembles prewar days. While the United States has been encouraging rearmament, the threat of Japanese militarism may transform the face of Southeast Asia to match the goals of pre–World War II days. The author wants this book to serve as a warning of Japanese militarism, but both his case and presentation are flimsy.

644 Huisken, Ronald. *The Origin of the Strategic Cruise Missile.* New York: Praeger, 1981. 202pp. ISBN 0–03–059378–6.

An Australian defense analyst surveys the history of the development of the strategic Cruise missile. The strategic Cruise missile was explored as a weapon in the 1950s and found wanting, but its resurrection in the 1970s was swift and without the open debate so common with weapons systems. Adoption of this weapons system was pushed by civilian leaders to signal to the Soviet Union that the United States in the mid-1970s would vigorously contest any Soviet bid for strategic superiority. This book poses important questions about U.S. decision-making processes on adopting weapons systems.

645 Huntington, Samuel P. *American Military Strategy.* Berkeley: Institute of International Studies, 1986. 55pp. ISBN 0–87725–528–8.

This book consists of the author's two 1985 Chester W. Nimitz Memorial Lectures on U.S. military strategic policies, including a critique of these lectures by Paul Seabury. Huntington posed the question, How can the United States reconcile an effective long-term security policy in a pluralistic and individualistic U.S. society? His answer is a series of reforms in the U.S. military command structure, which include the adoption of a doctrine of winning future wars. These lectures and the critique by Seabury make this work a stimulating look at a problem still under debate in U.S. civilian and military circles.

646 *Impact of New Military Technology.* Edited by Jonathan Alford. Farnborough, England: Gower, 1981. 132pp. ISBN 0–566–00345–7.

These papers examine the impact of technology on the development of military doctrine and combat performance. Research and development of new weapons systems remain major preoccupations of the superpowers, because the danger of being caught without a countermeasure cannot be calculated. The authors of these papers are aware of the rate of technological change in the military sphere, but they are uncertain about the future with so many advanced weapons systems under development. These papers seek to answer questions about the place of military technology, but in the end the authors pose more questions than answers.

647 Independent Commission on International Humanitarian Issues. *Modern Wars: The Humanitarian Challenge.* London: Zed Books, 1986. 195pp. ISBN 0–86232–694–X.

A group of international experts on the conduct of war issued this report on modern wars under the auspices of the Independent Commission on International Humanitarian Issues (ICIHI). The report called upon 110 governments to adhere to the 1977 Protocols to the Geneva Conventions of 1949. A series of papers examined the extent to which the laws of war are respected in various international scenarios. This book has an excellent premise, but most of the papers are disappointing both in coverage and quality.

648 *Industrial Capacity and Defense Planning: Sustained Conflict and Surge Capacity in the 1980s.* Edited by Lee D. Olvey, Henry A. Leonard, and Bruce E. Arlinghaus. Lexington, MA: Lexington Books, 1983. 169pp. ISBN 0–669–06331–2.

These papers examine the relationship between industrial preparedness for war and defense planning. At present U.S. industrial capacity is at a low ebb because of mineral shortages, a weak vendor base, a lack of engineers, and a lack of surge capability of prime contractors. While the United States has a qualitative advantage over its adversaries, it has a weakness in supplying defense equipment for a short war. The papers document weaknesses in U.S. industrial capacity, and they demonstrate that there is no evidence that there have been any changes since the early 1980s.

649 Indyk, Martin, Charles Kupchan, and Steven J. Rosen. *Israel and the U.S. Air Force.* Washington, DC: American Israel Public Affairs Committee, 1983. 33pp.

These authors pursue the theme of the need for Israeli and U.S. strategic cooperation with regard to the U.S. Air Force. While there has been limited Israeli assistance on comparisons of U.S. and Soviet equipment and intelligence information, close cooperation between air forces has been retarded by U.S. political considerations. The authors recommend closer U.S. military ties with Israel to gain air force bases for staging and support of military missions. This book makes strong arguments for closer military relations with Israel, but the political risks have been incorrectly minimized to almost nothing.

650 Ing, Stanley, and Theodore Olson. *Seeking Common Ground on the Defence of Canada.* Downview, Canada: York University Research Programme in Strategic Studies, 1983. 25pp.

This paper is the result of a 1983 colloquy between strategic analysts and peace activists at the University of York, Canada. The intent is to bridge polemics and establish a dialogue between the two groups. While no consensus emerged, there was a serious exchange of views. The benefit of this short report is in the dialogue between the two sides over philosophical issues.

651 *Insurgency in the Modern World.* Edited by Bard E. O'Neill, William R. Heaton, and Donald J. Alberts. Boulder, CO: Westview Press, 1980. 291pp. ISBN 0–89158–598–2.

These essays combine analytical techniques with a number of case studies in an effort to understand modern insurgency. Six types of insurgency are identified for study: (1) secessionist; (2) revolutionary; (3) restorational; (4) reactionary; (5) conservative; and (6) reformist. Case studies are drawn from Angola, Guatemala, Iraq, Ireland, Oman, Thailand, and Uruguay to illustrate the various insurgency types. This book contains high-quality essays both on theory and on individual cases, of value to any researcher in insurgency studies.

652 *Israeli Society and Its Defense Establishment: The Social and Political Impact of a Protracted Violent Conflict.* Edited by Moshe Lissak. London: Frank Cass, 1984. 152pp. ISBN 0–7146–3235–X.

Israeli scholars use this book to analyze civilian-military relations in Israel since 1948. The emphasis of these essays is on the interplay of civilians and the military during thirty-five years of conflict. Israel's dual civilian-political and military approach is still unproven because it has both strengths and weaknesses. This book provokes more questions than it provides answers, but these essays constitute a good look at Israel's defense establishment.

653 Jasani, Bhupendra, and Christopher Lee. *Countdown to Space War.* London: Taylor and Francis, 1984. 104pp. ISBN 0–85066–261–3.

The authors argue against the introduction of weapons systems into space. They are concerned about the Reagan administration's Strategic Defense Initiative (SDI) and the dangers of antisatellite (ASAT) weapons. Introduction of ASAT weapons will violate several arms control treaties, and the prospects of a space war make a new ASAT treaty imperative. This book is a good introduction to the dangers of SDI.

654 Jastrow, Robert. *How To Make Nuclear Weapons Obsolete.* Boston, MA: Little, Brown and Company, 1985. 175pp. ISBN 0–3164–5828–7.

The author uses this book to argue for the benefits of the Strategic Defense Initiative (SDI) as a means of survival in case of a Soviet-U.S. nuclear war. At present, the Soviet nuclear strike capability is so overwhelming that the U.S. retaliatory capacity is in doubt. An effective SDI system will ensure that the nuclear balance can be maintained, and eventually nuclear arsenals can be reduced. This book is a popularized defense of the SDI, and therefore most useful for general readers and students.

655 Jervis, Robert. *The Illogic of American Nuclear Strategy.* Ithaca, NY: Cornell University Press, 1984. 203pp. ISBN 0–8014–1715–5.

The author critiques past and current U.S. nuclear strategy of dependence on nuclear deterrence. His thesis is that nuclear stalemate increases the chance of nonnuclear conflict rather than guaranteeing peace. He also questions whether there are enough restraints built into the relations between the superpowers to make the adoption of another strategy realistic. While the critique side of this book is much stronger than the proposal side, the work is still a solid effort in an area of controversy.

656 Jockel, Joseph T., and Joel J. Sokolsky. *Canada and Collective Security: Odd Man Out.* New York: Praeger, 1986. 118pp. ISBN 0–275–92217–0.

The Canadian dilemma over its commitments to NATO and the defense of North America are examined by two Canadian security specialists. Canadian contributions to European and North American defense have decreased over the last two decades because of economic and political factors. There is a need for restructuring of Canadian commitments to conform to changing priorities in exchange for greater financial support for defense from Canada. While this book is intended to spur the Mulroney government to carry out its campaign promises, it is a good source to study the Canadian role in NATO and in the North American Air Defense Command (NORAD).

657 Joes, Anthony James. *From the Barrel of a Gun: Armies and Revolutions.* Washington, DC: Pergamon-Brassey's, 1986. 224pp. ISBN 0–08–034238–8.

The role of the military in revolutionary situations is the focus of this study. In most revolutions the military holds the key to success. Case studies from various historical situations are analyzed, and the primacy of the military in revolutionary situations is upheld. While this book is best at historical reconstruction, it also contributes information on more contemporary revolutions.

658 Jones, Ellen. *Red Army and Society: A Sociology of the Soviet Military.* Boston, MA: Allen and Unwin, 1985. 230pp. ISBN 0–04–322011–8.

The author works in the U.S. Department of Defense, and has utilized her position to write this book on the sociology of the Soviet military. Her method is to compare the Soviet military as a social institution with the U.S. military. An interdependence of military and civilian institutions has developed in the Soviet Union, based on shared values, and the use of mass conscription reinforces these shared values. This book is a solid contribution to Soviet military studies, and it also offers insights on the U.S. military.

659 Kahn, Herman. *Thinking about the Unthinkable in the 1980s.* New York: Simon and Schuster, 1984. 250pp. ISBN 0–671–47544–4.

This last effort by one of the Rand group's most knowledgeable defense analysts is a provocative look at the problem of nuclear conflict. Although most of Kahn's analysis is devoted to preventing nuclear war, he is willing to think out the problems of recovery after a nuclear conflict. His emphasis is to prepare for either the success or failure of the deterrence strategy. This book is another major contribution to defense and strategic literature by an outstanding scholar in the field.

660 Kaldor, Mary. *The Baroque Arsenal.* London: Deutsch, 1981. 294pp. ISBN 0–233–97388–5.

This book is a moderate British Marxist view of the arms race. The author views the arms race as "the offspring of the marriage between private enterprise and the state, between the capitalist dynamic of the arms manufacturers and the conservatism that tends to characterise armed forces and defence departments in peacetime." This approach has been so successful in the West that the Soviet Union has also adopted it. The author's solution of cheap, simple, and effective weapons is seductive, but it is a policy not much in favor with either of the superpowers.

661 Kaplan, Fred M. *Dubious Specter: A Skeptical Look at the Soviet Nuclear Threat,* 2d ed. Washington, DC: Institute for Policy Studies, 1980. 93pp. ISBN 0–89758–023–0.

The author examines the standard belief that the Soviet Union's strategic nuclear forces have achieved superiority over U.S. forces. While the Soviet Union has modernized its military capabilities, this buildup does not and will not jeopardize U.S. capacity to deter a nuclear war. Moreover, the Soviet threat has been used to justify several new U.S. weapons systems, most of which are of dubious value. This book is a needed corrective to many of the alarmist treatments of this subject.

662 Kaplan, Fred M. *The Wizards of Armageddon.* New York: Simon and Schuster, 1983. 452pp. ISBN 0–671–42444–0.

This book is a history of the Rand Corporation's role in the development of U.S. nuclear strategy. Beginning as an air force–sponsored think tank, Rand thinkers have produced most of the strategic doctrine adopted as U.S. policy during the last thirty-five years. Part of the fascination of this book is in the matching of strategic doctrine with its most notable proponents. This book combines readability with sólid scholarship, making it must reading for anyone interested in the development of U.S. nuclear policy.

663 Karas, Thomas. *The New High Ground: Systems and Weapons of Space Age War.* New York: Simon and Schuster, 1983. 224pp. ISBN 0–671–47025–6.

The author advocates that the United States start treating space as an arena of military operations rather than an area for research and development. After surveying the state of military space technology, he begins an evaluation of space as the combat arena of the future. While militarization of space has dangers, the United States must develop its capabilities there before the Soviets reach space in force. This book is part of a campaign for the military uses of space.

664 Kaufmann, William W. *Defense in the 1980s.* Washington, DC: Brookings Institution, 1981. 55pp. ISBN 0–8151–4849–3.

In this study the author presents his views on the future direction of the U.S. defense budget. After an analysis of both the Carter and Reagan defense budgets, he maintains that even if there has been underfunding for defense in the past there is no reason to overfund now. His proposals call for a substantial increase, i.e., about $140 billion over a five-year period, in defense funding to increase military readiness and capability. This short study pointed out many of the defense recommendations later adopted by the Reagan administration.

665 Keaney, Thomas A. *Strategic Bombers and Conventional Weapons: Airpower Options.* Washington, DC: National Defense University Press, 1984. 76pp.

An air force officer with extensive combat experience surveys the nonnuclear role of air power since 1945. The conventional role for bombers has been neglected until hostilities commence, and then this role has been hampered by outmoded tactics. The author concludes that a long-range bomber is a necessity and new technologies, tactics, and plans must be developed for these bombers. This short monograph argues a distinct probomber viewpoint, but the author's perspective is worth serious study.

666 Kennedy, Gavin. *Defense Economics.* London: Duckworth, 1983. 248pp. ISBN 0–7156–1687–0.

All aspects of defense expenditures are examined in this balanced treatment by a prominent British defense scholar. Besides an in-depth treatment of defense economics politics, other issues, such as weapon selection, defense management, military alliances, and disarmament economics, are also surveyed from the perspective of cost-benefit for national defense. A pessimistic tone dominates an otherwise excellent book.

667 Kennedy, Thomas J. *NATO Politico-Military Consultation: Shaping Alliance Decisions.* Washington, DC: National Defense University Press, 1984. 86pp.

A senior officer in the U.S. Army critiques current U.S. procedures for consulting with its NATO allies. In the past the United States has been too reluctant to consult with NATO countries on sensitive military matters, and this has resulted in bad feelings on several occasions. Low-key diplomacy in consulting NATO members remains the best key to allied cooperation, and this approach keeps nasty surprises to a minimum. This short monograph is a positive approach to an ongoing problem in NATO.

668 Kerby, William. *The Impact of Space Weapons on Strategic Stability and the Prospects for Disarmament.* Hamburg: Institüt für Friedensforschung und Sicherheitspolitik, 1986. 42pp.

The author examines the Strategic Defense Initiative (SDI) in a quantitative way in order to describe the impact of large defensive forces on strategic stability among the nuclear powers. Unilateral deployment by one super-power would mandate that the other side deploy space weapons. Mutual deployment can promote a nuclear stabilization but only if the systems are operational at the same time. This paper is a major contribution to the SDI debate.

669 Kerr, Thomas J. *Civil Defense in the U.S.: Bandaid for a Holocaust?* Boulder, CO: Westview Press, 1983. 268pp. ISBN 0–86531–586–8.

This book is a history of civil defense activities in the United States since World War II. Apathy has characterized civil defense efforts in the last forty years, except for an occasional episode of government involvement in pro-motion during the Eisenhower and Kennedy years. The Reagan administra-tion has instituted a policy of evacuation as part of its revitalization of the civil defense program, but this effort has also been ineffective. This pes-simistic assessment of past civil defense programs contains a useful counter-balance to other defense subjects.

670 Kitson, Frank. *Warfare as a Whole.* London: Faber and Faber, 1987. 186pp. ISBN 0–571–14693–7.

The author examines British preparations for fighting in various war sce-narios. Despite an increasing interest in conventional forces, he believes that nuclear weapons still dominate the military scene, and that there is little likelihood this will change in the near future. There are a number of reforms proposed by the author as necessary to improve the quality of the British officer corps and to build military efficiency. This book is oriented more toward the author's military experiences rather than research results.

671 Knelman, F. H. *Reagan, God, and the Bomb: From Myth to Policy in the Nuclear Arms Race.* Buffalo, New York: Prometheus Books, 1985. 343pp. ISBN 0–87975–310–2.

The Reagan administration's role in increasing the danger of nuclear war is the focus of this study. This administration's goal is to defeat the Soviet Union, and this strategy includes the possibility of both winning and surviv-ing a nuclear war. Such a policy has meant that the Reagan administration has introduced a quantitative and qualitative change for the worse in the arms race. The author is a longtime activist in peace and nuclear disarma-ment activities, and this book is an articulate reflection of this viewpoint.

672 Komer, Robert W. *Maritime Strategy or Coalition Defense?* Cambridge, MA: Abt Books, 1984. 116pp. ISBN 0–89011–594–X.

This book is an assessment of U.S. conventional strategic options in the mid-1980s. Nuclear stalemate has made conventional warfare more viable, but this means making difficult economic, military, and political decisions on the nature of conventional forces. The central issue is that the United States must decide on a maritime strategy or continue a continental commitment to collective defense, since the country lacks the resources for both strategies. While the author opts for the latter strategy, this book remains a welcome addition to the literature of strategic thinking.

673 Krauss, Melvyn. *How NATO Weakens the West.* New York: Simon and Schuster, 1986. 271pp. ISBN 0–671–54455–1.

After a U.S. economist surveys the NATO alliance, he charges that the United States is too dominant in strategic decision making and the Europeans are free-riding on defense expenditures. The lack of political will on the part of Western Europe is the reason for the military imbalance today in Europe. By a gradual U.S. withdrawal of military forces from NATO, the Europeans will have to make a commitment to defend themselves. This book advocates a position that may make sense on paper, but the nature of alliance politics renders it almost unworkable.

674 Kross, Walter. *Military Reform: The High-Tech Debate in Tactical Air Forces.* Washington, DC: National Defense University Press, 1985. 241pp.

A senior officer of the U.S. Air Force has written a book on the pros and cons of military reform. The controversy over military reform revolves around the high-tech weapons debate, and the belief of reformers in the need for less costly and simpler weapons systems. While the author acknowledges the merits of some of the reformers' arguments, he believes that the defense establishment's views are the more sound. This book starts out as an objective look at both sides of the military reform debate, but ends solidly on the side of the author's military service.

675 *Laser Weapons in Space: Policy and Doctrine.* Edited by Keith B. Payne. Boulder, CO: Westview Press, 1983. 227pp. ISBN 0–86531–937–5.

The development of space-based laser weapons and the impact of these weapons on U.S. strategic defense are examined in these papers. All of the authors recommend the development of space-based laser weapons as a way to protect against Soviet missiles. Deployment of such a system means that the United States must revise or withdraw from the Anti-Ballistic Missile (ABM) Treaty. Most of the arguments encountered in this book have reappeared in the later debate on the Strategic Defense Initiative (SDI).

676 *The Latin American Military Institution.* Edited by Robert Wesson. New York: Praeger, 1986. 234pp. ISBN 0–275–92084–4.

Nine armed forces in Latin American states have been selected for study in this work because of their size and the political role of their military establishments. They are Argentina, Brazil, Chile, Colombia, Guatemala, Mexico, Panama, Peru, and Venezuela. A subject approach has been adopted, with specialists on each country contributing insight into these armed forces. Both the approach and contents make this book an ideal source for a comparative analysis of Latin American military forces.

677 *Leadership on the Future Battlefield.* Edited by James G. Hunt and John D. Blair. Washington, DC: Pergamon-Brassey's, 1985. 349pp. ISBN 0–080316–21–2.

This book is a product of a May 1983 symposium on military leadership conducted at Texas Tech University. Particular emphasis was placed on examining leadership management and organizational implications of the new U.S. military concepts of AirLand Battle 2000 and ARMY21. A combination of civilian and military personnel presented papers and acted out the problems. The book appears to reflect only a portion of the activities of the symposium, but the results are still useful.

678 Lebow, Richard Ned. *Nuclear Crisis Management: A Dangerous Illusion*. Ithaca, NY: Cornell University Press, 1987. 226pp. ISBN 0–8014–1989–1.

U.S. understanding of the place of crisis management in superpower strategic relations is questioned in this book by a former scholar-in-residence of the National War College and the CIA. Lebow uses past examples of crisis mismanagement, particularly World War I, to point out stages of management danger zones. Arms control is a realistic goal, but improvement of command and control is the one means to ensure survivability in a nuclear crisis. This book is disjointed, mixing historical examples and modern analysis, but the author's conclusions are worth further study.

679 Lee, Christopher. *War in Space*. London: Hamish Hamilton, 1986. 242pp. ISBN 0–241–11591–4.

Almost every area of superpower military strategic and tactical planning, communications, and execution relies heavily on space-based systems. This book outlines the technology of military space programs and proposes future directions for this technology. An arms control agreement for weapons in space is too difficult to negotiate, but an antisatellite (ASAT) treaty is in the realm of possibility. Because this book is such an excellent introduction to space weapon technology, it is recommended for both the general reader and the specialist.

680 Lee, R. G. *Introduction to Battlefield Weapons Systems*, 2d ed. London: Brassey's Defence, 1985. 259pp. ISBN 0–08031–199–7.

This publication is a primer on the tactical and technical aspects of battlefield weapons systems. It provides an analysis of the most up-to-date weapons system information available from both Soviet and Western sources. A combination of illustrations and technical data makes this book an excellent reference source for any researcher on advanced weapons systems.

681 Legge, J. Michael. *Theater Nuclear Weapons and the NATO Strategy of Flexible Response*. Santa Monica, CA: Rand Corporation, 1983. 93pp. ISBN 0–8330–0475–1.

This report examines the NATO strategy of flexible response from its adoption in 1967 to the early 1980s. The author concludes that this is the only strategy capable of replacing flexible response, and that this strategy will continue to be adhered to by NATO well into the next decade. Although acknowledging the limitations of flexible response, the author believes that NATO has made the correct decision. This report is a solid contribution to the literature on NATO nuclear strategy.

682 Leites, Nathan. *Soviet Style in War*. New York: Crane, Russak, 1982. 398pp. ISBN 0–8448–1415–6.

The author seeks to ascertain the Soviet style of combat through an examination of modern Soviet writings and Soviet and German sources from

World War II. Soviet commanders are always trained to attack, because inaction is feared above setbacks. Speed and exploitation of any successes are maxims preached to and relied upon by Soviet commanders. This book makes strange reading, because the author deals with Soviet perceptions of combat, which are so different from Western military experience.

683 *The Lessons of Recent Wars in the Third World*. Volume I: *Approaches and Case Studies*. Edited by Robert E. Harkavy and Stephanie G. Neuman. Lexington, MA: Lexington Books, 1985. 304pp. ISBN 0–669–06765–2.

This volume is the first of two projected volumes devoted to the study of recent wars. Emphasis in this volume is on methodological approaches to the study of wars and eight case studies of recent wars. The eight case studies are (1) Ethiopia-Somalia (1977–1978); (2)Western Sahara (1975–present); (3) China-Vietnam (1979); (4) Central America's revolutionary wars (1972–1984); (5) Soviet-Afghan war (1977–present); (6) Iran-Iraq (1980–present); (7) Falklands (1982); and (8) Israel-Syria (1982). Both the analysis of war methodologies and the case studies make a solid contribution, resulting in one of the best sources on recent warfare on the market.

684 Lider, Julian. *Military Force: An Analysis of Marxist-Leninist Concepts*. Westmead, England: Gower, 1981. 345pp. ISBN 0–566–00296–5.

This book is an interpretive study of Marxist-Leninist theories on the origin and use of armed forces. The author outlines the sociopolitical theory of Marxist-Leninist thought and the application of these concepts to the international scene. Western military strategists have difficulty in understanding the Soviet military mind because of its Marxist-Leninist framework. This work serves a useful function by presenting the Marxist military viewpoint, but the writing style makes for difficult reading.

685 Lider, Julian. *Military Thought of a Medium Power: 1960s and Afterwards*. Stockholm: Swedish Institute of International Affairs, 1983. 439pp.

British military thought from the 1960s to the present is the subject of this theoretical study. The author notes the shift of the British military position away from independence in the nuclear arms field and the continuation of the retreat from an empire toward greater military participation in Western Europe and NATO. But this shift has resulted in the transition of Great Britain from a world power to a medium power. British military thought has failed to conform and adjust to this change in status. This book reinforces the difficulty of medium-power states adjusting to changes in the international scene.

686 Lider, Julian. *Problems of the Classification of Wars*. Stockholm: Swedish Institute of International Affairs, 1980. 185pp. ISBN 91–7182–376–X.

The methodology of classifying wars and the establishment of standards of classification constitute the subjects of this study. The work's terminology is often confusing, but the author classifies wars by causes, opposing parties, issues, historical role, or the way the wars are fought. This book serves as a good introduction to the methodological problem, but it is apparent that more research is needed before such classification systems become meaningful.

687 Littleton, James. *Target Nation: Canada and the Western Intelligence Network*. Toronto: Lester and Orpren Dennys Limited, 1986. 228pp. ISBN 0–88619–118–1.

Canada's role in the intelligence battle between the superpowers is the subject of this book by a television journalist. Much of his information was gathered in the research for a CBC television series "On Guard for Thee" in 1980–1981. He questions the uncritical acceptance of cold-war assumptions about international relations. Despite the disjointed structure and often incomplete analyses, the author uses this book to ask controversial but necessary questions.

688 Lockwood, Jonathan Samuel. *The Soviet View of U.S. Strategic Doctrine: Implications for Decision Making.* New Brunswick, NJ: Transaction Books, 1983. 202pp. ISBN 0–87855–467–X.

Soviet perceptions of U.S. strategic concepts and capabilities and the impact of these views on Soviet strategic thinking are the subjects of this book. The author comes to two conclusions: (1) Soviet analysts project their strategic views onto U.S. strategic planners and interpret the results accordingly, and (2) the ideology of Marxism-Leninism still has an influence on Soviet analysts interpreting U.S. strategic planning. U.S. planners must realize that the Soviets have a different strategic mind-set and that Soviet leadership conducts Soviet strategic policy from this mind-set. This study makes a significant contribution to an understanding of Soviet strategic planning.

689 London, Herbert I. *Military Doctrine and the American Character: Reflections on AirLand Battle.* New York: National Strategy Information Center, 1984. 67pp. ISBN 0–88738–614–8.

Recent modifications in training and doctrine by the U.S. Army is the subject of this short monograph. Responding to criticism made outside and inside the army, the military has undertaken steps to reconcile military doctrine with modern combat conditions. The resulting concept is the "AirLand Battle," which coordinates various types of forces into a maneuver warfare scenario. Both the commentary and the analysis of the new army battle tactics make this book the official statement of this doctrine.

690 Luttwak, Edward N. *The Pentagon and the Art of War: The Question of Military Reform.* New York: Simon and Schuster, 1984. 333pp. ISBN 0–671–52432–1.

A major critic of the U.S. defense establishment uses this book to recommend military reform for the U.S. armed forces. The military mistakes made during Vietnam and subsequent operations have shown the defects in the U.S. military conduct of war. There is need of a central military staff— the National Defense Staff—to replace the Joint Chiefs of Staff and plan a national defense strategy. This book is an important study, and many of its recommendations make sense.

691 Mackenzie, Kenneth. *Greece and Turkey: Disarray on NATO's Southern Flank.* London: Institute for the Study of Conflict, 1983. 27pp.

The traditional rivalry between Greece and Turkey is analyzed for its impact on the security of NATO's southern flank. Little progress toward solving any of the long-standing disputes has been made in recent years, and the Greek-Turkish enmity presents difficulties for any stability on the southern front. Turkey is more important for geopolitical reasons than Greece, but Turkey has internal political problems that may weaken its commitment to NATO. This paper makes a good case for questioning the political-military stability of NATO's southern front.

692 Macksey, Kenneth. *First Clash: Combat Close-up in World War Three.* London: Arms and Armour Press, 1985. 248pp. ISBN 0–85368–736–6.

This book is a reprint of the handbook of the Canadian Army (B-GL-309-006/FT-001), in which an armored battle group engages a Soviet tank division during the first stages of World War III. Intended as a training aid, this book also serves as a model for armored engagements by Canadian forces. The author is a prominent military historian and former officer of the Royal Tank Regiment. This battlefield scenario is unique in that it is based on projections of fighting efficiency gathered from recent intelligence on Soviet armored forces.

693 Mako, William P. *U.S. Ground Forces and the Defense of Central Europe.* Washington, DC: Brookings Institution, 1983. 137pp. ISBN 0–8157–5444–7.

The questions whether Western Europe can be defended by conventional ground forces in Central Europe and whether the United States has the ground forces necessary for such a defense are studied by a member of the Brookings Foreign Policy Studies Program. There now exists a relative balance of forces between NATO and the Warsaw Pact, and Western Europe's central front has been stabilized. This means present U.S. ground forces are adequate to fulfill defense requirements, but some redirection of these ground forces may be appropriate for greater flexibility. While this book is more optimistic about necessary conventional force levels than most recent studies, the author's assessment adds more material to a lively debate.

694 Malone, Peter. *The British Nuclear Deterrent.* London: Croom Helm, 1984. 200pp. ISBN 0–7099–1790–2.

The British nuclear deterrent posture in the aftermath of the Thatcher government's decision on Trident missiles is the subject of this book. The author believes that the British decision on the Trident II missiles was necessary. Moreover, British nuclear policies have been remarkably successful during the last few decades in keeping a creditable deterrence at a low cost. This book is full of the type of analysis that most researchers will find stimulating.

695 Manno, Jack. *Arming the Heavens: The Hidden Military Agenda for Space, 1945–1995.* New York: Dodd, Mead, 1984. 245pp. ISBN 0–396–08211–4.

The author critiques the U.S. space program and argues that it has served as a cover for the militarization of space. Military uses for space were a consideration from the beginning, and only the technology needs to be developed. Now space weapons technology is advanced enough that space weapons systems can be designed, and only an arms control agreement can stop the militarization of space. This book is a journalistic treatment of an advanced subject and suffers from too much rhetoric and insufficient information.

696 Marcy, Sam. *Generals over the White House: The Impact of the Military-Industrial Complex.* New York: World View Publishers, 1980. 59pp. ISBN 0–89567–042–9.

This book is a radical assessment of the new militarism existing in the United States in the early 1980s. New militarism was oriented toward convincing the U.S. elite and the public that the U.S. geopolitical position had become weak in comparison to the growing strength and aggressiveness of the Soviet Union. The author charges that the Carter administration surrendered to the new militarism in the late 1970s, and the Reagan administration adopted it entirely. Despite the Marxist terminology, this essay presents a counterweight to traditional thinking on U.S. foreign policy initiatives.

697 Martel, William C., and Paul L. Savage. *Strategic Nuclear War: What the Superpowers Target and Why.* Westport, CT: Greenwood Press, 1986. 249pp. ISBN 0–313–24192–9.
   This book is based on a simulated model of nuclear war between the Soviet Union and the United States. Through the use of computer simulation, the nuclear arsenals of the Soviet Union and the United States are deployed against six hundred cities, which constitute the majority of the population and economic resources of both nations. The resulting model has been utilized in computer war games on college campuses with startling results. This book is a stimulating look at strategic nuclear war from the viewpoint of war gaming.

698 Martin, Laurence. *Before the Day After: Can NATO Defend Europe?* Feltham, England: Newnes Books, 1985. 159pp. ISBN 0–600–33282–9.
   The author maintains that Europe is the leading theater for a potential war, because of the large number of military forces facing each other. Answers to the questions "Does NATO have sufficient forces to deter Soviet aggression?" is a "probable," and "If deterrence did fail, could the conflict be contained short of nuclear war?" is a "perhaps." NATO is now at a disadvantage both quantitatively and qualitatively to the Warsaw Pact forces, and this disadvantage means NATO cannot defend Europe. This book combines illustrations and text for a readable analysis of NATO defense capabilities.

699 May, Simon. *The Problems and Prerequisites of Public Support for the Defence of Western Europe.* Brussels: Centre for European Policy Studies, 1986. 32pp.
   This paper addresses ways to increase European public support for NATO policies. Three factors promote European antinuclear protest: (1) lack of trust in the U.S. use of its political-military power; (2) tensions between the Soviet Union and the United States; and (3) the presence of U.S. nuclear missiles on Western European soil. Removal of ballistic missiles by transferring some to sea, closer cooperation between U.S. and European members on conventional force issues, and progress in lowering tensions between the superpowers are all ways to increase acceptance of defense burdens by the Europeans. This paper makes a series of solid policy recommendations all of which are worth studying.

700 McIntosh, Malcolm. *Japan Re-armed.* London: Frances Pinter, 1986. 169pp. ISBN 0–86187–545–1.
   A British author examines the rearmament of Japan and its impact on Japanese foreign policy. The question is the extent to which Japan's new economic prominence will be translated into a more active Japanese foreign policy. In contrast to the U.S. goal of a militarized Pacific, the author advocates a nuclear-free Pacific, with Japan playing the role of peacemaker between the superpowers. This book is a curious mix of pragmatism and naiveté that both stimulates and disappoints.

701 McLaurin, John C. *Accelerated Production: The Air-to-Air Missile Case*. Washington, DC: National Defense University Press, 1981. 68pp.

A U.S. naval captain questions the success of the Industrial Preparedness Planning Program (1969) in strengthening industrial capacity to meet military mobilization needs. He evaluates the air-to-air missile production as a case study and concludes that the current stockpile of these missiles is inadequate. Contracts with defense contractors should incorporate provisions for mobilization scenarios. This monograph shows deficiencies in U.S. industrial capacity to sustain a rapid mobilization.

702 McNaught, L. W. *Nuclear Weapons and Their Effects*. Oxford: Brassey's Defence Publishers, 1984. 136pp. ISBN 0–08–028328–4.

Military applications of nuclear weapons and the factors affecting their use are the subjects of this publication. The author educates by use of numerous diagrams and charts, showing the effectiveness of nuclear weaponry on the battlefield. Nuclear weapons have a place in combat, but their destructive powers must be used with caution. This data and the interpretations of nuclear weapons make this book invaluable for researchers of both military and peace subjects.

703 *The Mechanized Battlefield: A Tactical Analysis*. Edited by J. A. English, J. Addicott, and P. J. Kramers. Washington, DC: Pergamon-Brassey's, 1985. 188pp. ISBN 0–08–025405–5.

These papers on the impact of technology on low-level combat are the product of an American-Commonwealth gathering at the Canadian Forces Base Gagetown in 1983 where the authors presented their version of the mechanized battlefield of the 1990s. The importance of combined forces operations is the one point stressed by all authors. This book gives a variety of opinions on small unit tactics and combat and is the best source of its type on the market.

704 Miall, Hugh. *Nuclear Weapons: Who's in Charge?* Houndmills, England: Macmillan, 1987. 167pp. ISBN 0–333–44676–3.

This book is a companion volume to an earlier book, *How Nuclear Weapons Decisions Are Made* (Houndmills, England: Macmillan, 1986), by the Oxford Research Group. The emphasis is on weapons development and the identification of the organizations involved in this process in China, France, Great Britain, the Soviet Union, and the United States. These decisionmakers are subject to little accountability because they have become isolated from the outside world. The author paints a pessimistic picture of chances for disarmament unless fundamental changes are made in the international political order.

705 Midgley, John J. *Deadly Illusions: Army Policy for the Nuclear Battlefield*. Boulder, CO: Westview Press, 1986. 220pp. ISBN 0–8133–7282–8.

The author challenges the use of battlefield nuclear weapons by the U.S. Army. Development of the tactical doctrine of battlefield nuclear weapons is traced in military thought since 1945. Despite numerous analyses of the unworkability of field nuclear weapons, the army has continued to search for more advanced short-range nuclear systems. This book chronicles a failed policy from its inception to the present.

706 *The Militarization of High Technology.* Edited by John Tirman. Cambridge, MA: Ballinger, 1984. 247pp. ISBN 0–88410–947–X.

The relationship between U.S. military and high-tech industries is studied in this book of essays. While emphasis is given the military technology's effects on the U.S. economy, the analysis is also informative on the procurement and development of high technology for military defense. The authors agree that defense procurement has weakened commercial technology, and the dependence of the military on high technology has not enhanced U.S. security. These high-quality essays give another side of the Department of Defense's procurement policies.

707 *Military and Society: The European Experience.* Edited by Jurgen Kuhlmann. Munich: Sozialwissenschaftliches Institüt der Bundeswehr, 1984. 446pp.

These papers were presented at the 1983 Inter-University Seminar on Armed Forces and Society held in Chicago, where a variety of U.S. and European scholars gathered together to study the sociology of military institutions of Western Europe. Most papers deal with civil-military relations or militarism in NATO countries. This volume provides a variety of perspectives on the military and European society, and its papers are good background material.

708 *Military Strategy in Transition: Defense and Deterrence in the 1980s.* Edited by Keith A. Dunn and William O. Staudenmaier. Boulder, CO: Westview Press, 1984. 225pp. ISBN 0–86531–789–5.

These papers are the result of a 1983 conference on NATO strategy held at the U.S. Army War College. Thirteen specialists on U.S. strategic and military doctrine analyze whether NATO should adopt a conventional retaliatory offensive military strategy. The Huntington thesis on the need of conventional retaliatory strategy is critiqued, with most of the authors disagreeing on aspects of his analysis. This book gives arguments pro and con on increasing NATO conventional forces, a debate still underway years after the publication of this book.

709 Miller, Steven E. *Arms and the Third World: Indigenous Weapons Production.* Geneva: Programme for Strategic and International Security Studies, 1980. 62 leaves.

Domestic weapons production by Third World countries is the subject of this paper. Most Third World arms producers have specialized in making less sophisticated small arms weapons, but India, Israel, and Brazil have managed to establish substantial arms industries that produce high-grade weapons systems. The author is also interested in arms transfers to Third World countries. While the analysis is of high quality, the value of the book resides in the statistical data contained in the charts and tables.

710 *The Mind of the Soviet Fighting Man: A Quantitative Survey of Soviet Soldiers, Sailors, and Airmen.* Compiled by Richard A. Gabriel. Westport, CT: Greenwood Press, 1984. 156pp. ISBN 0–313–24187–2.

This book is in many respects a follow-up to the author's earlier work, the *New Red Legions* (Westport, CT: Greenwood Press, 1980), but this time there is no analysis, merely raw data from the questionnaire. The data was accumulated from 207 respondents to a questionnaire sent to veterans of the Soviet armed forces. The author breaks down the data to reflect attitudes from the three services—army, air force, and navy. There has been no update to reflect Soviet activities in Afghanistan, and this is the most disappointing side to the book.

711 *Missiles for the Nineties: ICBMs and Strategic Policy.* Edited by Barry R. Schneider, Colin S. Gray, and Keith B. Payne. Boulder, CO: Westview Press, 1984. 169pp. ISBN 0–8133–7001–9.

These essays explore the problems of Intercontinental Ballistic Missiles (ICBMs) in modern U.S. strategic thought. The authors are most concerned about the survival rate of ICBMs in silos and targeting problems. They believe that ICBM modernization is necessary, but they are uncertain about the form of the modernization. This book in an in-depth analysis of ICBMs in U.S. strategic policy.

712 Moineville, Hubert. *Naval Warfare Today and Tomorrow*. London: Blackwell, 1983. 141pp. ISBN 0–631–13253–8.

An English translation of *La guerre navale* (Paris: Presses Universitaires de France, 1982), this book is an assessment of the state of naval warfare in the 1980s by a former French naval officer. His conclusions reflect three themes: (1) the range of political purposes for naval forces has widened; (2) the possibility of naval confrontations has increased; and (3) the race for naval superiority revolves around naval technology. Consequently, naval policy must be integrated into current military and political policies. The benefit of this book resides in its theoretical approach to naval policy and the emphasis upon naval technology.

713 Moore, J. E., and R. Compton-Hall. *Submarine Warfare: Today and Tomorrow*. London: Michael Joseph, 1986. 308pp. ISBN 0–7181–2743–9.

Two British submarine officers survey current submarine operations for insights into underwater warfare. The authors are less concerned with submarine technology than the ways that the technology is translated into combat effectiveness. They conclude that the West needs to build up its submarine fleet to threaten Soviet surface and submarine fleets. The authors intended this work to stimulate debate on submarine warfare, and they more than accomplished this intent.

714 Mottale, Morris Mehrdad. *The Arms Buildup in the Persian Gulf*. Lanham, MD: University Press of America, 1986. 235pp. ISBN 0–8191–5202–1.

Arms buildups in the Persian Gulf region by Iran, Iraq, and Saudi Arabia since 1973 constitute the subject matter of this monograph. These buildups have been fueled by societies predisposed to accept military authoritarianism, and these military regimes are well endowed with capital from oil revenues to pay for such buildups. The willingness of the Soviet Union and the United States to supply arms has also played a factor, but the primary significance of these arms buildups lies in the political sphere, where the leaders gain prestige and power from the acquisition of modern sophisticated weapons systems. This book is a major contribution to the study of the defense policies of the major regional powers in the Persian Gulf.

715 *National Interests and the Military Use of Space.* Edited by William J. Durch. Cambridge, MA: Ballinger, 1984. 286pp. ISBN 0–88410–974–7.

This book on the military use of space by the United States and the Soviet Union is the result of the collaboration of young defense scholars of the

Space Working Group, which is affiliated with Harvard's Center for Science and International Affairs (CSIA). These scholars are concerned with the past, current, and prospective military uses of space, space law, and space arms control. While a variety of opinions are included, the consensus is that there is no escaping the future use of space for military purposes. This book contains solid analyses of the future military role of space, and the conclusions of the authors are solid contributions to this literature.

716 *National Security Crisis Forecasting and Management.* Edited by Gerald W. Hopple, Stephen J. Andriole, and Amos Freedy. Boulder, CO: Westview Press, 1984. 208pp. ISBN 0–86531–913–8.

Crisis analysis as a means to study international crises is questioned in this book of essays. The editors believe that both the volume and quality of crisis forecasting and crisis management literature have declined in the last decade. With few exceptions, most of the essays reflect the ideas of the editors. This book offers little except warnings about the methodology and use of the results of crisis research.

717 *National Security Policy: The Decision-making Process.* Edited by Robert L. Pfaltzgraff and Uri Ra'anan. Hamden, CT: Archon Books, 1984. 311pp. ISBN 0–208–02003–9.

These papers are the product of a 1983 conference on national security policy decision making at the Fletcher School of Law and Diplomacy, Tufts University, Medford, MA. Most of the papers deal with the development of organizations to handle decision making in the executive branch of government. The key institution in this process is the National Security Council and its staff. The number of high-quality articles on national security planning and implementation makes this book a good source for defense researchers.

718 *NATO and the Mediterranean.* Edited by Lawrence S. Kaplan, Robert W. Clawson, and Raimondo Luraghi. Wilmington, DE: Scholarly Resources, 1985. 263pp. ISBN 0–8420–2221–X.

Two centers—the Lyman L. Lemnitzer Center and Centro Studi sulla Difesa of the University of Genoa—produced this book of essays from a conference on NATO and the Mediterranean. Nationals from six NATO countries were represented as speakers and another two as commentators. Despite the importance of the Mediterranean region, the disarray of NATO in this area makes the southern flank of NATO open to Soviet adventurism. This book is a sampling of opinion on the weakness of NATO's southern flank and should be read in this sense.

719 *NATO's Northern Allies: The National Security Policies of Belgium, Denmark, the Netherlands and Norway.* Edited by Gregory Flynn. Totowa, NJ: Rowman and Allanheld, 1985. 294pp. ISBN 0–7099–1051–7.

Changes in public opinion on security issues among the northern members of NATO are traced in this book of essays. The decision to modernize the NATO nuclear arsenal has caused political difficulties in Belgium, Denmark, the Netherlands, and Norway. By studying the political situations in each of these countries, the authors conclude that the conflicting needs of security in NATO and the political fallout over alliance decisions have produced strains in the political systems of the northern members of NATO. This book is strong on both security and decision-making issues, making it an excellent source for both subjects.

720 *NATO's Strategic Options: Arms Control and Defense.* Edited by David Yost. New York: Pergamon Press, 1981. 258pp. ISBN 0–08–027184–7.

NATO's strategic options between an increasing defense commitment or relying on arms control negotiations are considered in this book of essays. At the same time, the authors review the current state of NATO as a functioning alliance. Most of the authors agrée that recent U.S.–Western European disagreements over policy decisions have hurt the alliance, and there remains a need for greater unanimity among NATO governments. While these essays are above average in quality, they are beginning to show the influence of changing events.

721 *Naval Forces and Western Security.* By Francis J. West et al. Washington, DC: Pergamon-Brassey's, 1986. 63pp. ISBN 0–08–035543–9.

The role of naval forces in NATO military strategy is surveyed in this report published under the auspices of the Institute for Foreign Policy Analysis, Cambridge, Massachusetts. Excessive concern by NATO over the central front has resulted in the deterioration of maritime forces necessary to support operations on the northern and Mediterranean fronts. A need exists to rebuild the naval forces to carry out maritime missions and to rethink the use of naval power in the alliance. This short monograph is intended to stimulate debate on naval affairs, and it is effective in that role.

722 Nelson, Daniel N. *Alliance Behavior in the Warsaw Pact.* Boulder, CO: Westview Press, 1986. 134pp. ISBN 0–8133–7224–0.

The subject of this book is alliance behavior in the Warsaw Pact with regard to cohesion, reliability, and defense burden. Evidence in this study indicates that the Warsaw Pact is not an alliance prepared for aggressive military action, as differences among member states have surfaced to reduce cohesion, weaken reliability, and make uneven the defense burden. Only the German Democratic Republic (GDR) and Bulgaria are assets to the alliance in all spheres, and neither is an ideal partner. This book is a behavioral assessment of an alliance system, and the techniques utilized by the author make it a significant contribution to defense literature.

723 Nincic, Miroslav. *The Arms Race: The Political Economy of Military Growth.* New York: Praeger, 1982. 207pp. ISBN 0–03–060332–3.

The author studies military growth in both the Soviet Union and the United States as an indication of the expansion of the arms race. Disputing the contention that the arms race has increased security for either superpower, Nincic claims that the arms race promotes fear and distrust on both sides and prevents meaningful arms control agreements. This pessimistic assessment of the arms race hides a solid piece of scholarship on the subject.

724 *Nonnuclear Conflicts in the Nuclear Age.* Edited by Sam C. Sarkesian. New York: Praeger, 1980. 404pp. ISBN 0–03–056138–8.

These papers are the products of several conferences held in 1979, and they address the problem of building a balanced U.S. military force capable of fighting both nuclear and nonnuclear wars. While there is little doubt about the U.S. capability of conducting a nuclear war, most of the authors direct their attention to building up nonnuclear forces. Perceived military strength and political resolve are the key elements of the U.S. ability to achieve political-military goals without resorting to military force. This book seeks to resolve the "Vietnam Syndrome" and is only partially successful.

725 *The Northern Flank in a Central European War.* Edited by Lars B. Wallin. Stockholm: Swedish National Defence Research Institute, 1982. 174pp. ISBN 91–7056–062–5.

The papers in this book are the proceedings of a 1980 symposium on the impact of a Central European war on the Scandinavian countries held in Stockholm, Sweden, under the sponsorship of the Swedish National Defence Research Institute (FOA). A number of foreign experts were invited to present papers and exchange views. Most participants were doubtful of the prospects of a Central European war but believed that, in the case of hostilities, the fighting would spread to the northern flank as a matter of course. NATO strategy and Swedish neutrality were other topics covered in this valuable study of the northern front.

726 *Nuclear Weapons: Report of the Secretary General of the United Nations.* Brookline, MA: Autumn Press, 1981. 223pp. ISBN 0–914398–45–8.

A group of international experts on nuclear weapons compiled a report to be presented to the secretary-general of the United Nations on present nuclear arsenals, nuclear technology, and the potential of nuclear war. The report concludes that the development of nuclear weapon technology has a momentum of its own; so much so that new weapons systems are developed beyond military or security requirements. Nuclear deterrence as a security doctrine is too dangerous for humankind for such a system to continue. While the report ends with a plea for disarmament, the material within the book gives several reasons mitigating against disarmament.

727 *Nuclear Weapons in Europe.* Edited by William G. Hyland. New York: Council on Foreign Relations, 1984. 118pp. ISBN 0–87609–000–5.

This book presents contrasting views by U.S. and European security specialists on the role of U.S. nuclear weapons in the defense of Western Europe. They agree upon the need to consider carefully the role of nuclear weapons in Europe vis-à-vis the Soviet bloc. But they disagree on the need for nuclear weapons and their political recommendations for settling the controversy. The range of views expressed by the two Americans and the two Europeans makes this book valuable for perspectives on the presence of nuclear weapons in Europe.

728 *Nuclear Weapons in Europe: Modernization and Limitation.* Edited by Marsha McGraw Olive and Jeffrey D. Porro. Lexington, MA: Lexington Books, 1983. 167pp. ISBN 0–669–05655–3.

These papers are a product of a 1981 conference on the modernization and limitation of nuclear weapons in Europe held in Brussels, Belgium. The intent of this conference was to study missile modernization by both NATO and the Warsaw Pact and the extent to which modernization might lead to intermediate nuclear force (INF) negotiations. Papers on both the pros and cons of nuclear weapon modernization were presented by an international cast of defense specialists. Despite the change of emphasis on defense topics, this book remains a solid source on the 1979 NATO dual-track decision.

729 Nunn, Jack H. *The Soviet First Strike Threat: The U.S. Perspective.* New York: Praeger, 1982. 292pp. ISBN 0–03–060607–1.

The U.S. assessment of Soviet first-strike capabilities and the impact of this appraisal on U.S. security strategy are the subjects of this book. Technical developments in nuclear weapons and delivery systems combined with

Soviet intentions have concerned U.S. strategists over a disarming nuclear first strike. This preoccupation with a bolt-from-the-blue first strike has resulted in the United States pursuing policies that have little relevance to the strategic picture. This critical but suggestive book is a solid contribution to the literature of U.S. strategic thinking.

730 Okazaki, Hisahiko. *A Grand Strategy for Japanese Defense.* Lanham, MD: Abt Books, 1986. 155pp. ISBN 0–8191–5325–7.

The realities of Japanese defense posture are examined in this critical study by a Japanese defense specialist. Korea serves as a buffer for Japan, and, if Korea falls, then the Japanese defense posture will have to be reconfigured. Japan's geostrategic situation does not give her any other option than an alliance with the United States. The author argues for an increased Japanese defense commitment, and this recommendation and his supporting analysis make this book an important source of ideas in Japanese defense circles.

731 Oldag, Andreas. *Allianzpolitische Konflikte in der NATO.* Baden-Baden, West Germany: Nomos Verlagsgesellschaft, 1985. 185pp. ISBN 3–7890–1100–2.

Divisions within NATO between the United States and its Western European allies are analyzed in this book by a West German author. Since its origins, NATO has been under the domination of the United States. In the 1980s, however, this has been changing because of growing economic and political strength of Western Europe. Unless there are fundamental reforms in NATO's decision-making process, the alliance may disintegrate. This book makes a persuasive case for a more active role for European states in NATO.

732 Openshaw, Stan, Philip Steadman, and Owen Greene. *Doomsday: Britain after Nuclear Attack.* Oxford, England: Basil Blackwell, 1983. 296pp. ISBN 0–631–12292–3.

The probable environmental, political, and social effects of a nuclear attack on Great Britain are surveyed in this book. Methods of calculation of casualties and damages have been gathered from a variety of scientific publications. One conclusion is that civil defense would be inadequate to handle the casualties of a nuclear attack, and this would mean the breakdown of civil order in Great Britain. Various scenarios and detailed projections make this book one of the better sources of its type.

733 Orr, George E. *Combat Operation C3I: Fundamentals and Interactions.* Washington, DC: Air University Press, 1983. 99pp.

This book is a theoretical analysis of combat operations, military theory, and command, control, communications, and intelligence (C3I) by an active duty officer in the U.S. Air Force. His dissatisfaction with the treatment of strategy and C3I in engagement modeling made him rethink basic principles. By redefining the nature of modern technology-intensive war, the author presents a view of modern warfare that incorporates the changing nature of modern combat. This is a technical treatise intended for military decision-makers, but it also offers a fresh look at modern warfare.

734 O'Sullivan, Patrick, and Jesse W. Miller. *The Geography of Warfare.* London: Croom Helm, 1983. 172pp. ISBN 0–7099–1918–2.

Geopolitical realities of modern warfare are the subject of this book. The authors maintain that global strategies are geopolitical in nature, and failure to recognize this invites disaster in warfare. A variety of geopolitical situations are examined in the light of this thesis. This book is filled with historical instances highlighting the authors' thesis, but the best sections are on guerrilla and urban warfare.

735 Parfit, Michael. *The Boys behind the Bombs*. Boston: Little, Brown, 1983. 298pp. ISBN 0–316–69057–0.
The journalist author of this book takes the reader behind the scenes of the debate over the MX missile system. He uses personal interviews with a variety of military men, politicians, and scientists to make his story. Most of the interviews defend the MX system, because they were involved in the designing of it. There is a decided journalistic flavor to this book, and the use of interviews makes it a source more valuable for the study of attitudes than general information.

736 Park, William. *Defending the West: A History of NATO*. Brighton, England: Wheatsheaf Books, 1986. 242pp. ISBN 0–7450–0199–8.
The author has produced a standard history of NATO. His emphasis is on the totality of NATO's force posture in the eventuality of a confrontation with the Soviet bloc rather than concentration on a single or combination of military factors. NATO has been a successful alliance, withstanding criticism and protest without damage, but it is European societal changes that most threaten its unity. *Balanced* and *objective* are the best terms to describe this book, but it lacks a thesis to hold it together.

737 Parrott, Bruce. *The Soviet Union and Ballistic Missile Defense*. Boulder, CO: Westview Press, 1987. 121pp. ISBN 0–8133–7429–4.
The author considers the impact of the Strategic Defense Initiative (SDI) on Soviet ballistic missile defense planning. U.S. officials have been negligent in assuming that Soviet missile defense policy is permanently fixed. The Soviets have been reluctant to build an SDI-type system because of cost, technical feasibility, and U.S. technological superiority, but the SDI will stimulate the Soviets into construction of a ballistic missile defense system. This book is a solid assessment of the SDI from the Soviet perspective, and it is a welcome addition to defense literature.

738 Payne, Keith B. *Strategic Defense: "Star Wars" in Perspective*. Lanham, MD: Hamilton Press, 1986. 250pp. ISBN 0–8191–5109–2.
The benefits of the Strategic Defense Initiative (SDI) for U.S. national security are highlighted in this book. While acknowledging the possibility that the technology for the SDI may never be developed, the potential for this system to permit a new course in U.S. strategic thinking makes it imperative to try to develop such a system. Most of the criticisms of the effort to build the SDI system are questionable. Despite the author's claim that this book is for educational purposes, this book is a classic defense of the SDI by one of its strongest supporters.

739 Peebles, Curtis. *Battle for Space*. New York: Beaufort Books, 1983. 192pp. ISBN 0–8253–0160–2.
The weapons and tactics for warfare in space are examined in this book. Both the technology and the weapons systems are in various stages of development for such a space war. Most of this war will be between the surveillance satellites and the antisatellite (ASAT) weapons, and the victory will go

to the side that develops the most advanced weapons systems for space warfare—the Soviet Union or the United States. This book is a solid introduction to the technology of future space warfare.

740 Perkins, Stuart L. *Global Demands: Limited Forces: US Army Deployment.* Washington, DC: National Defense University Press, 1984. 123pp.

The author, a senior officer in the U.S. Army, questions current deployment strategy given the size of present U.S. conventional forces. Adoption of programs enabling the United States to meet worldwide threats simultaneously without a buildup of the necessary military forces has been the result of current policy. The U.S. Army has been assigned tasks far beyond its present capabilities, and reallocation of resources is necessary before commitment of military forces. This book is a plea for a bigger cut in the military budget for the U.S. Army, and, despite reservations over his conclusions, the author does make several effective points.

741 Petersen, Philip A. *Soviet Air Power and the Pursuit of New Military Options.* Washington, DC: U.S. Government Printing Office, 1981. 71pp.

The expansion of Soviet military aviation as an instrument in power projection is the subject of this book. Soviet aviation has expanded to the point that the Soviets can fight a nonnuclear conflict in Europe with a reasonable chance for success. NATO has to ensure the survivability of its aviation and nuclear resources to withstand this threat. This short book is a solid appraisal of the Soviet Air Force in the early 1980s based on recent intelligence information.

742 *Planning U.S. Security.* Edited by Philip S. Kronenberg. Washington, DC: National Defense University Press, 1981. 214pp.

These papers are the result of a series of seminars in 1980 and 1981 on national security planning processes sponsored by the U.S. Department of Defense. The participants were prominent defense and security specialists from the government, military, and academia. Most of the authors were concerned about the fragmentation in strategic thought and planning, and this deficiency continues to plague U.S. security planning. These papers broach long-standing problems, and their conclusions are worth pondering.

743 *The Political Dilemmas of Military Regimes.* Edited by Christopher Clapham and George Philip. London: Croom Helm, 1985. 282pp. ISBN 0–7099–3416–5.

These essays address the problems that military regimes face after the seizure of power. Most of the case studies involve Third World military regimes. The major problem these regimes come up against is the political limitations imposed by their own values and structures. This book presents a variety of case studies on modern civilian-military relations unavailable elsewhere.

744 Polmar, Norman. *Strategic Weapons: An Introduction,* rev. ed. New York: Crane, Russak, 1982. 126pp. ISBN 0–8448–1399–0.

Revised from an earlier work, this book inventories the U.S. and Soviet strategic weapons arsenals. The author maintains that the United States produces more sophisticated weapons systems than the Soviet Union, but that the Soviets have narrowed the technology gap and deploy more weapons. A number of excellent illustrations help the author make his points on weapon developments. This book provides an excellent introduction to the history and progress of U.S. and Soviet weapons systems.

745 Prados, John. *Pentagon Games: Wargames and the American Military.* New York: Harper and Row, 1987. 81pp. ISBN 0–06–096130–9.

This book presents three board games based on wargame methods used by Pentagon strategists to plan military action. The three games are: (1) the last days of Saigon; (2) Pentagon defense budget; and (3) the research and development game. These games resemble those used by military planners, and the scenarios are quite realistic. This book can be recommended for introductory and advanced college coursework on defense subjects.

746 Prados, John. *Presidents' Secret Wars: CIA and Pentagon Covert Operations since World War II.* New York: Morrow, 1986. 480pp. ISBN 0–688–05384–X.

Covert operations—in particular, paramilitary actions—of the U.S. government are analyzed in this book by a critic of these types of operations. CIA activities are recounted in detail since its organization in 1947. Present covert activities are only a continuation of previous CIA operations, and most paramilitary operations have not been successful. Both the activities and presidential oversight of covert operations have been defective, and it is in the accounting of these deficiencies that this book makes it contribution.

747 Prados, John. *The Soviet Estimate: U.S. Intelligence Analysis and Russian Military Strength.* New York: Dial Press, 1982. 367pp. ISBN 0–385–27211–1.

The effectiveness of U.S. intelligence in estimating Soviet strategic nuclear forces is the subject of this book. Efforts have been made to create independent intelligence authorities to analyze intelligence data, but there have been numerous cases of underestimates and overestimates of Soviet nuclear forces. Estimates from the U.S. intelligence community will always have a degree of uncertainty no matter what the precautions. This book gives a clear picture of the limitations of U.S. intelligence capability, and this accomplishment alone makes the work a solid addition to defense literature.

748 Pressler, Larry. *Star Wars: The Strategic Defense Initiative Debates in Congress.* New York: Praeger, 1986. 179pp. ISBN 0–275–92052–6.

Senator Larry Pressler's (R-SD) services as the chairman of the Senate Foreign Relations Subcommittee on Arms Control (1981–1985) and other committee assignments give him insight into the debate in Congress over the Strategic Defense Initiative (SDI). His intent here is to present an objective picture of the principal issues of the SDI debate with emphasis on the political positions in Congress. The author concludes that this debate shows how difficult it is for Congress to assess and initiate a new strategic proposal. This book makes an important contribution in demonstrating difficulties Congress has in dealing with the executive branch's defense initiatives.

749 Pringle, Peter, and William Arkin. *SIOP: The Secret U.S. Plan for Nuclear War.* New York: W. W. Norton, 1983. 287pp. ISBN 0–393–01798–2.

This book is a critique of the U.S. military's contingency plan for waging a nuclear war with the Soviet Union. SIOP stands for Single Integrated Operational Plan, and it integrates the contingency plans of all military theaters into a single comprehensive plan. The authors fear this plan, because in certain military scenarios it commits the United States to nuclear war. Although this book makes effective points against SIOP, this plan is another example of the military always designing contingency plans.

750 *Promise or Peril: The Strategic Defense Initiative.* Edited by Zbigniew Brzezinski. Washington, DC: Ethics and Public Policy Center, 1986. 479pp. ISBN 0–89633–103–2.

Writings from thirty-five politicians, scholars, and strategic analysts are gathered together here for a comprehensive look at the Strategic Defense Initiative (SDI). The editor intends this book to give the reader a well-rounded picture of the key issues surrounding the SDI debate. All aspects of the issue are explored, but the most interesting sections are Soviet responses to SDI and the political and technical dimensions of SDI. The variety of opinion expressed in this book makes it an excellent source for the general reader, student, and scholar.

751 Pry, Peter. *Israel's Nuclear Arsenal.* Boulder, CO: Westview Press, 1984. 150pp. ISBN 0–86531–739–9.

Israel's atomic weapon capabilities are analyzed in this monograph by a graduate student in international relations at UCLA. While Israel's intentionally ambiguous position about its nuclear status makes any accurate assessment of Israel's nuclear capabilities difficult, educated guesswork places its nuclear arsenal at thirty-one plutonium A-bombs and ten uranium A-bombs. These nuclear weapons have a delivery system based on the F-15 Eagle. The author emphasizes the destabilizing influence of nuclear weapons in this solid introduction to the subject.

752 *The Public and Atlantic Defense.* Edited by Gregory Flynn and Hans Rattinger. Totowa, NJ: Rowman and Allanheld, 1985. 398pp. ISBN 0–8476–7365–0.

This study of European public opinion and the defense policies of NATO stems from an international research effort of the Atlantic Institute for International Affairs and the Atlantic Treaty Association. Public opinion data were gathered from France, Great Britain, Italy, Norway, the Netherlands, and West Germany, and the data have been interpreted by public opinion specialists from host countries. Conclusions are that Europeans have become more security conscious, the Soviets are still distrusted, the United States has lost much of its good reputation, and NATO is still supported as a defensive alliance. Both the methodology and the conclusions make this book a valuable source.

753 Quigley, Carroll. *Weapon Systems and Political Stability: A History.* Washington, DC: University Press of America, 1983. 1,043pp. ISBN 0–8191–2947–X.

This book is an unfinished work on the impact over time of weapons systems on political structures. The author's thesis is that weapons systems have been decisive in shaping human social, economic, and political decisions. The most recent development is that, since 1935, the army of specialists has brought forth the politics of managerial bureaucracy. While this work is incomplete and the treatment ends in the fifteenth century, the approach is nevertheless stimulating and worthy of consideration.

754 Quinlan, David A. *The Role of the Marine Corps in Rapid Deployment Forces.* Washington, DC: National Defense University Press, 1983. 47pp.

The author, a senior officer in the U.S. Marine Corps, examines the rapid deployment forces (RDF) concept from the Marine Corps perspective. His thesis is that the Marine Corps has all of the military characteristics of an intervention force with the capability of sustained operations. The Marine Corps has always been trained for rapid deployment, and the buildup of a separate force is unnecessary. The case for the Marine Corps in the RDF is presented effectively in this short book.

755 Rabinovich, Itamar. *The War for Lebanon, 1970–1985*, rev. ed. Ithaca, NY: Cornell University Press, 1985. 262pp. ISBN 0–8014–1879–4.
The interplay between Lebanon's domestic politics and military and political interventions from outsiders is the subject of this book. Special emphasis is placed on the 1982 war because of the subsequent international complications. Civil war and outside interventions have dismantled the Lebanese state, and the process continued into the mid-1980s. The story of the collapse of a prosperous ministate into civil war and invasions is told here in detail and with sympathy.

756 Raj, Christopher. *American Military in Europe: Controversy over NATO Burden Sharing*. New Delhi: ABC Publishing, 1983. 380pp.
An Indian defense specialist presents a history of the politics of U.S. military forces in Europe since 1945. This commitment of U.S. troops has had the support of Europeans, but it has led to debate between the executive and the legislative branches of U.S. government over possible troop reductions. The Soviet threat and European pressure have made reduction efforts fail, and the debate over burden sharing continues without much chance of resolution. More a history than an analysis, the book's most useful feature is providing general information on past NATO crises.

757 Ranft, Bryan, and Geoffrey Till. *The Sea in Soviet Strategy*. London: Macmillan, 1983. 240pp. ISBN 0–333–26226–3.
The authors concentrate on finding the Soviet rationale for the construction of a strong navy in the postwar era. Soviet emphasis on naval power is a reflection of the Soviet leadership's belief that great powers need large navies. While there exists relative parity in the number of ships between the Soviet and U.S. navies, NATO naval forces remain superior, with the European navies making the difference. This book is a major source for any study of Soviet naval policy.

758 Rasor, Dina. *The Pentagon Underground*. New York: Time Books, 1985. 310pp. ISBN 0–8129–1249–7.
A U.S. journalist uses her expertise as a critic of the M-1 tank to investigate the U.S. weapons procurement system. She has been active with the Project on Military Procurement, an organization founded to expose Pentagon fraud and waste. Her contacts in the Pentagon have allowed her to present a picture of a procurement system that performs poorly. Despite the journalistic flavor of this book, the information contained in it makes it a good source for understanding U.S. defense procurement policies.

759 *The Reagan Defense Program: An Interim Assessment*. Edited by Stephen J. Cimbala. Wilmington, DE: Scholarly Resources, 1986. 215pp. ISBN 0–8420–2243–0.
A study of the direction and scope of the Reagan defense program has been undertaken by an impressive list of commentators. Each component has

been examined, with the assessment that the new defense program has been a mixed blessing. While President Ronald Reagan's program has been strong on manpower and defense budget growth, it has been less successful on the other issues. Arms control has been a nonstarter. This assessment provides a balanced picture of the Reagan defense program in the mid-1980s.

760 *Reduction of Military Budgets: Construction of Military Price Indexes and Purchasing-Power Parities for Comparison of Military Expenditures.* New York: United Nations, 1986. 75pp. ISBN 91–1–142117–9.

In 1982 the United Nations General Assembly requested a body of experts to prepare construction price indices and purchasing-power parities for military expenditures of selected states. Australia, Austria, Finland, Italy, Norway, Sweden, the United Kingdom, and the United States participated in this study. The result is a mass of statistical data on military expenditures of these eight states. No study on military budgets can ignore either the data or the methodology of this work.

761 *The Regionalization of Warfare: The Falkland/Malvinas Islands, Lebanon, and the Iran-Iraq Conflict.* Edited by James Brown and William P. Snyder. New Brunswick, NJ: Transaction Books, 1985. 291pp. ISBN 0–88738–022–0.

Military warfare in 1982 has been studied for strategic and tactical lessons in these essays. The wars in the Falklands, Lebanon, and Iran-Iraq were analyzed for problems in manpower procurement, training and readiness, weapons, research and development, tactics, and combat leadership. While military technology had its impact in these wars, effectiveness was determined by the training and the quality of the military forces. Despite references to all the wars, the bulk of the analysis concentrates on the lessons of the Falkland War.

762 *The Reluctant Supplier: U.S. Decisionmaking for Arms Sales.* By Paul Y. H. Hammond et al. Cambridge, MA: Oelgeschlager, Gunn and Hain, 1983. 310pp. ISBN 0–691–06921–2.

Four authors examine arms transfers as an instrument of U.S. foreign policy. They maintain that an arms transfer policy promotes U.S. foreign policy goals and has economic benefits as well. Efforts to restrain global arms transfers under former President Jimmy Carter's administration were shortsighted and doomed to fail, and President Ronald Reagan's administration corrected this policy. This book advances a controversial thesis, but the analysis is solid, and the conclusions are worth considering.

763 *Reorganizing America's Defense: Leadership in War and Peace.* Edited by Robert J. Art, Vincent Davis, and Samuel P. Huntington. Washington, DC: Pergamon-Brassey's, 1985. 433pp. ISBN 0–08–031973–4.

These papers were presented in 1983 at two conferences on civilian-military management. The defense policy-making organizations in the Soviet Union, Israel, Canada, Great Britain, and West Germany are studied to contrast with those in the United States. Consensus among the authors is that the U.S. system needs drastic overhauling to correct an imbalance that weakens U.S. capability to respond to military crises. This book holds an impressive number of high-quality articles on civilian-military relations.

764 Ricci, Fred J., and Daniel Schutzer. *U.S. Military Communications: A C3I Force Multiplier.* Rockville, MD: Computer Science Press, 1986. 263pp. ISBN 0–88175–016–6.

This book is an assessment of the state-of-the-art U.S. military communications. The latest advances in communication technology are explained, and the steps taken to incorporate this technology into military systems are outlined. The position is advanced that combat operational requirements determine the design, development, and implementation of military communication systems. This book is a technical assessment of military communication systems and the best source of its type available.

765 Rice, Condoleezza. *The Soviet Union and the Czechoslovak Army, 1948–1983: Uncertain Allegiance.* Princeton, NJ: Princeton University Press, 1984. 303pp. ISBN 0–691–06921–2.

The relationship between civilian and military leaders in Czechoslovakia in the period from 1948 to 1983 and the role of the Czech military with their Soviet counterparts are the subject of this study. Because Eastern European armed forces are both national forces and members of a socialist world order, this combination makes Czechoslovakian civilian-military affairs unique. In 1968 Czechoslovakia was a test case, and it proved that the military lacked cohesion and loyalty to the Czechoslovakian state. This book is a case study of a member of the Warsaw Pact, and its conclusions are worth pondering.

766 Richelson, Jeffrey. *Sword and Shield: The Soviet Intelligence and Security Apparatus.* Cambridge, MA: Ballinger, 1986. 279pp. ISBN 0–88730–035–9.

Soviet intelligence operations and organizations are examined in this book. Attention is focused on two Soviet intelligence organizations: the KGB and the GRU. Much of the attention of these organizations is devoted to acquiring foreign policy, defense, intelligence, and economic information from foreign sources, infiltrating Western political groups and conducting counterintelligence operations. This book is a scholarly assessment of Soviet intelligence organizations, and its analysis is of a high quality.

767 Richey, George. *Britain's Strategic Role in NATO.* London: Macmillan, 1986. 172pp. ISBN 0–333–42292–9.

The author seeks to find Great Britain's strategic role in NATO. Present British policy is to negotiate a realignment of resources toward emphasizing its role as the major European maritime power within NATO. This means reduction of land forces in Germany and building a rapid deployment force to protect North Sea oil. This book is a cogent defense of British plans for a redeployment of forces within NATO.

768 Ritchie, David. *Spacewar.* New York: Atheneum, 1982. 224pp. ISBN 0–689–11264–5.

A professional science writer utilizes this book to envisage a future war in space. This book began as an article for a 1980 issue of *Inquiry* magazine, but because of interest in the subject expressed by the U.S. public it has expanded into a book-length publication. The author analyzes all the available scientific data in the early 1980s for his projections on war in space. This book is a readable popularized version of a topic under much debate in the mid-1980s, and the general reader will still find it fascinating.

769 Roberts, Adam. *Nations in Arms: The Theory and Practice of Territorial Defence,* 2d ed. Houndmills, England: Macmillan, 1986. 310pp. ISBN 0–333–39306–6.

The original 1976 version has been reprinted with a new introduction and a lengthy postscript on territorial defense in the 1980s. Territorial defense is a national defense policy combining the army and the civil population in combat, using various forms of fighting including guerrilla warfare. Events in the 1980s confirm the author's contentions that this type of national defense is still difficult to defeat. This book remains a classic of its type.

770 Romm, Joe, and Kosta Tsipis. *Analysis of Dense Pack Vulnerabilities.* Cambridge, MA: Program in Science and Technology for International Security, 1982. 49pp.

This report studies the Dense Pack Theory, or the closely spaced basing concept, for survivability of ICBMs in reinforced concrete silos. The Dense Pack depends upon the theory of *fratricide,* which is a term describing the effects caused by the detonation of an incoming nuclear warhead that are capable of destroying other nearby nuclear warheads by spontaneous blast effects. The authors conclude that the fratricide effects can be bypassed by enemy timing mechanisms, and only a small number of warheads could eradicate Dense Pack. By testing a theory and proving ways of neutralization, this report makes a significant contribution to defense studies.

771 Rose, François de, and Yves Boyer. *Nouvelles technologies et défense et l'Europe.* Paris: Institut Française des Relations Internationales, 1985. 118pp. ISBN 2–86592–019–4.

Two French defense specialists analyze the impact of new military technologies on the defense of Europe. These new technologies are transforming the field of battle, and they provide an alternative to nuclear warfare. The authors, however, are cautious about the new systems, because they too have vulnerabilities. This book by two respected French military analysts is a valuable contribution to European defense literature.

772 Rosefielde, Steven. *False Science: Underestimating the Soviet Arms Buildup: An Appraisal of the CIA's Direct Costing Effort, 1960–80.* New Brunswick, NJ: Transaction Books, 1982. 321pp. ISBN 0–87855–868–3.

The author challenges the accuracy of the CIA's direct-cost estimates of the Soviet arms expenditures from 1960 onwards. These estimates are much too low and fail to reflect the rapid quantitative and qualitative improvements in Soviet weapons development. He proves this contention by testing CIA figures with new data acquired from other sources. This book examines a complex subject, but one of fundamental importance to U.S. defense planning.

773 Rotblat, Joseph. *Nuclear Radiation in Warfare.* London: Taylor and Francis, 1981. 149pp. ISBN 0–89946–104–2.

The radiation effects of nuclear weapons are examined in this book published under the sponsorship of the Stockholm International Peace Research Institute (SIPRI). Blast, heat, and ionizing radiations are all studied for casualty ratios. Global fallout from a nuclear war would result in long-term damage in all countries. The scientific data presented in this volume are impressive, and the book should be required reading for defense and security specialists.

774 Rumble, Greville. *The Politics of Nuclear Defence: A Comprehensive Introduction.* Cambridge, England: Polity Press, 1985. 285pp. ISBN 0-7456-0194-4.

Although this book deals with the politics of nuclear defense, the intent of the author is to challenge the British government's present defense policy. He uses the nuclear defense issue to argue against the NATO alliance and U.S. nuclear policies, denying that nuclear deterrence has served as a beneficial strategy for Great Britain. This book is another in a series of publications challenging British defense policy by British writers, and it is a good example of this genre.

775 Schmidt, Peter. *Europeanization of Defense: Prospects of Consensus?* Santa Monica, CA: Rand Corporation, 1984. 40pp.

This short monograph is a study of the prospects of consensus developing among the Western European countries on a "Europeanization" of defense policy. There remain widespread disagreements about Europe's role in defense, since many of the countries still have difficulty trusting West Germany, and they are uncertain over the problem of nuclear decision making. Consequently, most countries want to strengthen European influence over military affairs within the Atlantic alliance. This monograph details the political disputes among the European allies, which constitutes the strength of this study.

776 Schroeer, Dietrich. *Science, Technology, and the Nuclear Arms Race.* New York: Wiley, 1984. 414pp. ISBN 0-471-88141-4.

A physicist explains scientific-technological developments and their impact both on military strategy and the arms race. Although the author's goal is to obtain technical literacy and not technical expertise, the book is full of technical explanations and information that would please any researcher in the field. Excellent illustrations complement the text. This book is an excellent sourcebook for undergraduate and graduate courses on arms control issues.

777 Schwartz, David N. *NATO's Nuclear Dilemmas.* Washington, DC: Brookings Institution, 1983. 270pp. ISBN 0-8157-7772-8.

The author, a research associate at the Brookings Foreign Policy Studies Program, studies the history of NATO decision making over nuclear weapons since the mid-1950s to the 1979 dual-track decision. Reliability of the U.S. strategic guarantee on nuclear weapons has long been a source of controversy within the NATO alliance. The 1979 decision was the culmination of three decades of similar debates, but it may be only a temporary stage in this long-term controversy. This book makes its contribution in developing a better understanding of the politics of the NATO alliance.

778 Schwarz, Jürgen. *Structural Development of the North Atlantic Treaty Organization.* Munich: Hochschule der Bundeswehr, 1982. 94pp.

The development of NATO's organizational structure is the subject of this paper. Several times in recent history there have been subtle structural shifts within NATO, most of which have come from the interplay between U.S. and Western European perceptions over relations with the Soviet bloc. The NATO alliance system has always worked out its problems, but there will have to be growing coordination between the United States and the

European allies for it to continue successfully. Besides the analysis, there are documents and statistical data on NATO that will make this paper useful for researchers.

779 Schwok, René. *Elements de la pensée stratégique israelienne*. Geneva: Programme for Strategic and International Security Studies, 1984. 58pp.

The author examines the Israeli concept of strategy from the Israeli perspective. Israeli conception of security is to forge a military force able to defeat a larger and strategically better positioned enemy whose intent it is to destroy the state of Israel. Special emphasis is given by Israeli strategic planners to territorial defense because of the Israeli lack of strategic depth. This short monograph is a solid introduction to Israeli strategic thought.

780 Scott, Harriet Fast, and William F. Scott. *The Armed Forces of the USSR*, 3d ed. Boulder, CO: Westview Press, 1984. 455pp. ISBN 0–85368–680–7.

Since the original version in 1979, the authors have been busy revising and updating their assessments of the Soviet military establishment in relationship to the Soviet state. After a section on the historical development of the Soviet military since 1917, the remainder of the book deals with Soviet military doctrine and strategy, military organization, and the military-industrial complex. Little attention is devoted to weapons systems because they are a product rather than the end of the Soviet military establishment. This book serves as an excellent reference source for further studies on the Soviet military.

781 Scott, Harriet Fast, and William F. Scott. *The Soviet Control Structure: Capabilities for Wartime Survival*. New York: Crane, Russak, 1983. 146pp. ISBN 0–8448–1452–0.

The authors have produced a critique of the Soviet state's war-making capability. Soviet centralized control makes Soviet society adjust easily to war, but a nuclear war introduces different dangers into the system. The lack of dependable allies and the need to control dissidents and minority groups are possible subjects of concern to the Soviet leadership. This book contributes factual information on the organization of the Soviet state, but the analysis is often at an elementary level.

782 Scoville, Herbert. *MX: Prescription for Disaster*. Cambridge, MA: MIT Press, 1981. 231pp. ISBN 0–262–19199–7.

The author, who is active in the Arms Control Association and a former senior official in the CIA, argues against the deployment of the MX missile system. Both unnecessary and expensive, this system is also destabilizing since it will lead to an acceleration of the arms race. Although many of the author's criticisms refer to the Carter administration's original project, most of the points also apply to the Ronald Reagan administration's final program. This book is the most complete critique of the MX missile system in its original and derivative forms available.

783 Seagrave, Sterling. *Yellow Rain: A Journey through the Terror of Chemical Warfare*. New York: M. Evans, 1981. 316pp. ISBN 0–87131–349–9.

A U.S. freelance writer surveys the development and use of chemical weapons. While Seagrave examines the history of chemical warfare, most of his interest lies in its possible use in present-day warfare. Trips to Yemen,

Laos, and Afghanistan to study reported incidents of chemical use have convinced the author that chemical weapons have been used in these countries. This book is worth examining for the author's proof of chemical usage, but the treatment suffers from his eagerness to prove the charges.

784 Sedacca, Sandra, and Robert DeGrasse. *Star Wars: Questions and Answers on the Space Weapons Debate.* Washington, DC: Common Cause, 1985. 36pp.

Common Cause published this short publication as part of its lobbying campaign against the Strategic Defense Initiative (SDI). The authors utilize a question-and-answer format to make substantive points against the SDI. Together the authors present the most cogent arguments of the critics of SDI, and this booklet is a good introduction to the views of those opposing its development.

785 Segal, Gerald. *Defending China.* Oxford, England: Oxford University Press, 1985. 264pp. ISBN 0–19–827470–X.

This book is a comprehensive analysis of the strategic and military defense policy of the People's Republic of China since 1949. Geographical, historical, ideological, and institutional characteristics are examined before case studies of Chinese military involvements are surveyed. The author concludes that there is a new pragmatism and flexibility in Chinese foreign and domestic policy, traits that extend into the defense policy. This book is a well-balanced assessment of Chinese defense policy that should prove useful for researchers in this field.

786 Seiler, George J. *Strategic Nuclear Force Requirements and Issues,* rev. ed. Maxwell Air Force Base, AL: Air University Press, 1983. 182pp.

The author, a career Air Force officer with a Ph.D. in atomic physics, examines U.S. strategic nuclear forces to assess their strengths and weaknesses. All aspects of strategic nuclear forces from missile systems to bombers are surveyed, with the question of how much is enough behind the analysis. His answer is not absolute, but the increase in Soviet strike capacity means that more is necessary unless there are balanced reductions on both sides. This book is an ambitious undertaking, and both the analysis and the conclusions make solid contributions to strategic studies.

787 Shackley, Theodore. *The Third Option: An American View of Counterinsurgency Operations.* New York: Reader's Digest Press, 1981. 185pp. ISBN 0–07–056382–9.

A former CIA officer argues for the use of covert military assistance to foster or to defeat so-called "revolutionary wars." Soviet-backed insurgencies make it necessary for the United States to conduct and maintain competence in covert action and counterinsurgency. At present, the CIA is incapable of running such a program after the series of cuts in personnel under former President Jimmy Carter's administration. The author uses this book to argue for an increased role of the CIA in U.S. foreign policy, and, at the same time, vent his dislike for Carter's policies.

788 Shaffer, Stephen M. *West European Public Opinion on Key Security Issues, 1981–82.* Washington, DC: Office of Research (European Branch), U.S. International Communication Agency, 1982. 82 leaves.

This paper summarizes Western European public opinion in 1981–82 on security issues gathered from U.S. International Communication Agency surveys. Large-scale, antinuclear demonstrations and protests took place in Europe during this period, but the survey results show that Western Europeans want superpower arms control negotiations and do perceive a clear threat to their security from the Soviet Union. While there remains a residue of good will toward the United States, Western Europeans have less confidence in U.S. foreign policy. This study presents a variety of valuable Western European public opinion data from three different public opinion polling services.

789 Sharp, Gene. *Making Europe Unconquerable: The Potential of Civilian-Based Deterrence and Defence.* London: Taylor and Francis, 1985. 250pp. ISBN 0–85066–336–9.

Civilian-based defense as a means to deter Soviet aggression by making Western Europe unrulable is the subject of this book. Adoption of this strategy would end Western Europe's dependence upon a nuclear strategy, and the Soviets would be unable to launch a successful invasion or internal takeover. Noncooperation and defiance are the twin principles upon which civilian-based defense rests. This book is an articulate argument for a departure away from a nuclear deterrence strategy toward an experiment with an untried system, and, because it advances cogent reasons for such a change, should be read.

790 *Shattering Europe's Defense Consensus: the Antinuclear Protest Movement and the Future of NATO.* Edited by James E. Dougherty and Robert L. Pfaltzgraff. Washington, DC: Pergamon-Brassey's, 1985. 226pp. ISBN 0–08–032770–2.

This book is a collection of essays about the impact of the European antinuclear movement on the future of NATO. Each of the major protest movements—France, Great Britain, Holland, Italy, and West Germany—are studied in detail. Although there is a distinct tone of anti-Americanism in each of the movements, national historical circumstances mark each nation's antinuclear movement, and the end result has been a weakening of NATO. Despite the general dissatisfaction by the authors with these antinuclear movements, the essays are of a uniform high quality and deserve reading.

791 Shazly, Saad El. *The Arab Military Option.* San Francisco: American Mideast Publishing, 1986. 329pp. ISBN 0–9604562–1–X.

An Egyptian general outlines the military strategy behind the Arab campaign to dismantle the Israeli state. After analyzing the respective military and political strengths, the author concludes that time is on the side of the Arabs. Israel can be defeated only by a combination of Syria reaching a balance of forces with Israel and Egypt abrogating the Camp David Treaty, allying with the Syrians and Iraqi forces in a common war against Israel. The author marshals an impressive amount of data to support his thesis, and this book should be studied by scholars interested in Middle East military affairs.

792 Sherr, Alan B. *The Case Against the MX Missile.* Boston: Lawyers Alliance for Nuclear Arms Control, 1983. 38pp.

This short study is a critique of President Ronald Reagan's administration's proposal to build the MX missile system. The author is president of the Lawyers Alliance for Nuclear Arms Control, Boston. He argues that the MX undercuts the prospects for reaching verifiable nuclear arms agreements by heating up the arms race, and that the MX is too costly and ineffective for its intended purpose. While this study lacks a balanced presentation, it does represent a current of thought in the United States on arms control.

793 *Sicherheit—zu welchem Preis? Die Zukunft der westlichen Allianz.* Edited by Wolf Dieter Eberwein and Catherine M. Kelleher. Munich: Günter Olzog Verlag, 1983. 338pp. ISBN 3–7892–9894–8.

U.S. and European defense specialists examine the financial ramifications of present and future defense budgets for the members of the NATO alliance. Five countries—France, Great Britain, the Netherlands, the United States, and West Germany—have been targeted for close scrutiny. There is some doubt among the contributors whether NATO member states will be able or willing to increase the financial burden for NATO. These essays are all high-quality efforts, making this book a valuable addition to NATO literature.

794 Sigal, Leon V. *Nuclear Forces in Europe: Enduring Dilemmas, Present Prospects.* Washington, DC: Brookings Institution, 1984. 181pp. ISBN 0–8157–7904–6.

The author examines the dilemmas created by NATO's nuclear doctrines and the ambivalence of Western Europeans about the role of nuclear weapons. Deployment of U.S. missiles has provoked a Soviet response of implementation of a long-delayed Soviet weapons program. This response and the belief of many Europeans that the United States is equally responsible for endangering Europe have weakened NATO's bonds of solidarity. This book and its argument on the need for arms control is a solid contribution to defense literature.

795 Simon, Jeffrey. *Warsaw Pact Forces: Problems of Command and Control.* Boulder, CO: Westview Press, 1985. 246pp. ISBN 0–8133–7017–5.

Soviet problems in maintaining command and control of non-Soviet Warsaw Pact forces is the subject of this book. Efforts to upgrade the military value of non-Soviet Warsaw Pact forces have been successful, and these forces constitute an important part of the Soviet attack scenario in Central Europe. Most of this emphasis has been on building up the Warsaw Pact's conventional warfare capability. This book is a balanced assessment of the command and control problems of the Soviets with Warsaw Pact forces.

796 Simpkin, Richard E. *Antitank: An Airmechanized Response to Armored Threats in the 90s.* Oxford, England: Brassey's Publishers, 1982. 320pp. ISBN 0–08–027036–0.

The author of this book examines various ways to neutralize armor in combat situations. He stresses that antitank warfare is part of a balance between offensive and defensive forces. The efficiency of antitank weapons systems, especially helicopter gunships, has endangered the main battle tank (MBT) so much that smaller, more mobile tanks need to be developed by the West. Although this book is disjointed and not easy to read, the author's insights make it a valuable source on tank warfare.

797 Simpkin, Richard E. *Human Factors in Mechanized Warfare.* Oxford, England: Brassey's Publishers, 1983. 173pp. ISBN 0–08–028340–3.

The leading British expert on armored warfare uses this book to discuss the human factors in mechanized warfare. He is especially concerned with the effect of tank types on crew morale and survivability. Soviet designs are superior to Western models because they select crews to fit their tanks rather than building tanks around crews. This book is a companion volume to the author's other books on tank warfare, and no author produces more authoritative works on armored warfare than Simpkin.

798 Sloan, C. E. E. *Mine Warfare on Land*. London: Brassey's, 1986. 153pp. ISBN 0–08–031196–2.

The role of mines in modern warfare is analyzed by a senior officer in the British army. The author directs particular attention to antitank mines and the importance of this weapon on tank warfare. Recent combat experience in Vietnam and the Falkland Islands indicates that mines are still a formidable military weapon, and new technologies are making this weapon more difficult to detect and disarm. This book is the best source available on the function and deployment of mines in modern warfare.

799 Smith, Theresa C. *Trojan Peace: Some Deterrence Propositions Tested*. Denver, CO: Graduate School of International Studies, 1982. 137pp. ISBN 0–87940–069–2.

The author tests various deterrence theories by use of discriminant analysis in studying arms races from 1860 to 1977. While the results are not conclusive, the materials show that conducting arms races as a deterrent does not prevent war. Moreover, a marked military superiority is not a reliable safeguard for peace between arms-race rivals. This monograph is disappointing in its lack of solid conclusions, but it is still noteworthy for its application of advanced methodology.

800 Snow, Donald M. *National Security: Enduring Problems of U.S. Defense Policy*. New York: St. Martin's Press, 1987. 272pp. ISBN 0–312–55955–0.

U.S. defense policy is analyzed in depth in this book by a U.S. defense scholar. His concern is the extent to which U.S. interests need to be protected by military force. Another issue is the building of a political economy to support U.S. national security interests. This book is a speculative essay filled with insight, posing more questions than answers.

801 Snyder, Jed C. *Defending the Fringe: NATO, the Mediterranean and the Persian Gulf*. Boulder, CO: Westview Press, 1987. 149pp. ISBN 0–8133–0417–2.

The growing strategic importance of NATO's southern flank is addressed by a security analyst at the Hudson Institute, Indianapolis, IN. Most military attention has been directed to the central front in Central Europe, but NATO's deteriorating position along the Mediterranean coast makes the southern front a target for Soviet adventurism. More attention and more resources need to be allocated to the southern front, and there is need of mediation efforts between Greece and Turkey. This book is a much-needed reassessment of the strategic importance of the Mediterranean region.

802 Sollinger, Jerry M. *Improving U.S. Theater Nuclear Doctrine: A Critical Analysis*. Washington, DC: National Defense University Press, 1983. 68pp.

A senior officer in the U.S. Army questions the present capability of the U.S. armed forces to fight and win a tactical nuclear war. His thesis is that the current doctrine, equipment, and training of U.S. military forces are unable to meet the demands of fighting a theater nuclear war. There is a need for increased flexibility and decentralized execution, and this necessitates better equipment and improved training at both the individual and unit levels. This short monograph points out deficiencies and recommends reforms.

803 *The Soviet Air Forces.* Edited by Paul J. Murphy. Jefferson, NC: McFarland, 1984. 375pp. ISBN 0–89950–078–1.

All aspects of the operation of the Soviet Air Force are covered in this book of essays by leading authorities on this organization. Particularly useful is the treatment of the Soviet Air Force leadership and organization. Another valuable feature is an excellent glossary of Soviet aviation terms. This book is indispensable reading for anyone interested in research on the Soviet Air Force.

804 *Soviet Allies: The Warsaw Pact and the Issue of Reliability.* Edited by Daniel N. Nelson. Boulder, CO: Westview Press, 1984. 273pp. ISBN 0–86531–359–8.

The issue of the military reliability of the non-Soviet Warsaw Pact forces in case of war is the subject of these essays. By analyzing both the concept of military reliability and the six Soviet allies, the consensus among the authors is that all the allies would experience reliability problems during the early stages of hostilities. Only East Germany (GDR) and Bulgaria appear to have the socioeconomic and political conditions to be reliable Soviet allies in case of war. This analysis and its conclusions make this book an important source of defense studies.

805 *The Soviet Far East Military Buildup: Nuclear Dilemmas and Asian Security.* Edited by Richard H. Solomon and Masataka Kosaka. Dover, MA: Auburn House, 1986. 301pp. ISBN 0–86569–140–1.

These essays are the result of a 1984 workshop sponsored by the Security Conference on Asia and the Pacific (SeCAP) held in San Diego, California. Far East security specialists from the United States and Asia convened to pose questions and find answers to the Soviet Far East military buildup. Soviet military capacity has grown in the Far East to such an extent that the United States can counter it only by coalition building and an increase in conventional and nuclear forces. This book has fourteen excellent essays, all of which should be of interest to specialists in the field.

806 *The Soviet Navy: Strengths and Liabilities.* Edited by Bruce W. Watson and Susan M. Watson. Boulder, CO: Westview Press, 1986. 333pp. ISBN 0–86531–767–4.

This book of essays assesses the strengths and weaknesses of the Soviet Navy. Acknowledging that the Soviet Navy has become the most important branch of the Soviet armed forces with respect to foreign policy, the authors class naval tradition, poor morale, and a rigid command and control system as weaknesses. The most important strength of the Soviet Navy lies in its leaders' singleness of purpose. This book is one of the best available sources on the Soviet Navy.

807 *Soviet Perceptions of War and Peace.* Edited by Graham D. Vernon. Washington, DC: National Defense University Press, 1981. 185pp.

These essays from scholars from a variety of government research institutes and universities deal with Soviet perceptions of their strategic realities and U.S. military postures. The Soviet strategic and military doctrine is the product of its interaction with the Soviet Communist party, and the Red Army carries out party policies faithfully. Although war is the least desirable of policy options, the Soviets intend to win any such war. Despite the government and military backgrounds of most of the authors, this book presents a good look at Soviet perceptions of their strategic position.

808 *Soviet Propaganda Campaign against NATO.* Washington, DC: U.S. Arms Control Agency, 1983. 53pp.

The U.S. Arms Control and Disarmament Agency published this report on the Soviet propaganda campaign against NATO's December 1979 decision on modernization of its ballistic missile systems. All the Soviet propaganda themes are dissected for tactics and subject content. While this campaign failed in the long run, Soviet propaganda had initial successes with certain themes among European disarmament and peace groups. This report is important because it reveals both the intensity and effectiveness of Soviet propaganda in the early 1980s.

809 *Soviet Strategic Deception.* Edited by Brian D. Dailey and Patrick J. Parker. Lexington, MA: Lexington Books, 1987. 538pp. ISBN 0–669–13208–X.

The use of strategic deception by the Soviet Union is detailed in this book of essays taken from a 1985 conference held at the Naval Postgraduate School. Soviet policy is to use deception and misinformation to achieve strategic goals. This strategy is intended to drive wedges between the United States and its allies and to weaken the United States at every opportunity. These essays are of a high quality, but viewpoints are limited by an open anti-Soviet bias.

810 *Soviet Strategic Defense Programs.* Washington, DC: U.S. Government Printing Office, 1985. 27pp.

The U.S. Department of Defense produced this booklet to reinforce its lobbying campaign for the Strategic Defense Initiative (SDI). It shows that Soviet strategic defense programs have neutralized much of the U.S. deterrence potential. Unless the United States responds with the SDI, the strategic balance will shift to the Soviet Union in the foreseeable future. This glossy propaganda piece has some interesting illustrations and charts, but the analysis is too self-serving.

811 Sowell, Lewis C. *Base Development and the Rapid Deployment Force: A Window to the Future.* Washington, DC: National Defense University Press, 1982. 39pp.

The importance of base development to the successful functioning of a rapid deployment force (RDF) is the subject of this short monograph by a senior officer of the U.S. Army. Any ability to deploy and sustain military forces in remote areas will depend on the development of supply bases. This requires a base-development planning staff able to foresee basing requirements. While this monograph is directed toward a narrow audience, it is still a good source for those interested in RDF studies.

812 *Space Weapons and International Security.* Edited by Bhupendra Jasani. Oxford, England: Oxford University Press, 1987. 366pp. ISBN 0–19–829102–7.

International experts examined the technical and political issues related to space weapons at a 1985 conference held in Stockholm, Sweden. Most of the papers dealt with aspects of the Strategic Defense Initiative (SDI), both pro and con. The majority of the participants, however, believe that the SDI system is destabilizing and possibly not workable. This volume is one of the best sources on the SDI on the market.

813   *Spain: Studies in Political Security.* Edited by Joyce Lasky Shub and Raymond Carr. New York: Praeger, 1985. 134pp. ISBN 0–03–007148–8.

Spain's contributions to Western defense are examined in this book of papers, mostly by Spanish authors. These authors emphasize Spanish autonomy within NATO and avoidance of "satellization." The Soviet threat is ignored, as defense issues are seen through the prism of domestic politics by a nation lacking interest in and ignorant of international affairs. This book provides a good picture of Spain's defense posture in the mid-1980s.

814   *Special Operation in US Strategy.* Edited by Frank R. Barnett, B. Hugh Tovar, and Richard Shultz. Washington, DC: National Defense University Press, 1984. 326pp.

The role of special operations in U.S. national defense planning is the subject of these papers from a two-day symposium in 1983, produced under the sponsorship of the National Strategy Information Center, Georgetown University's National Security Studies Program, and the National Defense University. While threats of low-intensity warfare are a more real concern than the possibility of an outbreak of nuclear war, the United States is unprepared to fight unconventional wars. Almost all of the participants agreed on the need for a U.S. capability to fight and win low-intensity conflicts. The book reflects a shared consensus on the nature of the problem by the conference participants that is not agreed upon by all defense specialists.

815   Sperling, Goetz. *German Perspectives on the Defence of Europe: An Analysis of Alternative Approaches to NATO Strategy.* Kingston, Canada: Centre for International Relations, Queen's University, 1985. 167pp.

A senior officer in the West German Army undertakes a presentation of the collective views of West German defense experts on European security concerns. Present NATO military strategy of flexible response is under debate in many European countries, but nowhere is the debate as intense as in West Germany. While West German defense specialists accept the strategy of flexible response as workable, they insist that NATO must upgrade its conventional forces. This book reaffirms current NATO strategy as acceptable with modifications of defense strategy.

816   Spiers, Edward M. *Chemical Warfare.* Urbana, IL: University of Illinois Press, 1986. 277pp. ISBN 0–252–01273–9.

In this work a prominent British historian traces the planning and use of chemical weapons in the twentieth century. Lethal, incapacitating, and irritating chemicals are studied for their employment in battlefield situations. The author maintains that the Soviets have made a considerable investment in chemical weapons, and NATO and the United States need to build a credible chemical deterrence. This book is a balanced treatment of the development and use of chemical weapons and can be recommended to any researcher in the field.

817   Spinney, Franklin C. *Defense Facts of Life: The Plans/Reality Mismatch.* Boulder, CO: Westview Press, 1985. 260pp. ISBN 0–86531–718–6.

A defense analyst examines the difference between the plans for U.S. defense budgets and the actual expenditures. Currently, procurement planning lacks the overall perspective necessary for good planning with huge cost overruns and reduction of weapóns programs. Among the author's recommendations are repricing the procurement budget, establishing macrolevel planning, changing the Planning, Programming, Budgeting System (PPBS), and reorganizing the Office of the Secretary of Defense. The author attacks the U.S. procurement system with a vengeance, and makes a series of recommendations worth serious consideration by defense specialists.

818   Stares, Paul B. *Space and National Security.* Washington, DC: Brookings Institute, 1987. 219pp. ISBN 0–8157–8110–5.

The author evaluates official U.S. government rationales for the deployment of antisatellite (ASAT) weapons systems. Current U.S. commitment to the Strategic Defense Initiative (SDI) threatens the possibility of any ASAT limitation agreements. The author maintains that the best policy would be a negotiated agreement on these weapons with the Soviet Union, but that the United States should also develop an antisatellite system as a policy option. This book by one of the Brookings Institute's foremost security analysts is a welcome addition to defense literature.

819   *Star Wars.* Edited by E. P. Thompson. Harmondsworth, England: Penguin Books, 1985. 165pp. ISBN 0–14–052371–5.

Several British and U.S. writers came together to produce this attack on the Reagan administration's Star Wars project. They condemn this project as too expensive, technically infeasible, and in violation of the Anti-Ballistic Missile (ABM) Treaty. Although this popular account is sometimes marred by polemics, it serves as an example of the type of attacks on the Star Wars project current among European and U.S. intellectuals.

820   Stefanick, Tom. *Strategic Antisubmarine Warfare and Naval Strategy.* Lexington, MA: Lexington Books, 1987. 390pp. ISBN 0–669–14015–5.

The author compares and contrasts U.S. and Soviet antisubmarine warfare for impact on naval strategy. U.S. submarines have the advantage of survivability because they are quieter than Soviet submarines. This advantage allows the United States to depend more heavily on strategic submarines (SSBNs) and endangers the operations life of the Soviet submarine fleet. This book is a complex technical analysis of antisubmarine warfare that many naval and strategic researchers will welcome.

821   Stein, Jonathan B. *From H-Bomb to Star Wars: The Politics of Strategic Decision Making.* Lexington, MA: Lexington Books, 1984. 118pp. ISBN 0–669–08968–0.

The relationship between political forces and technological innovations are examined in the case studies of the hydrogen bomb decision of 1950 and the Strategic Defense Initiative (SDI) in 1983. In both cases, the author maintains that political forces dictated the outcome. The technology of building both types of weapons systems was to be developed after the political decision was made by the president. This book adds new dimensions to the literature on political decision making and technological innovation.

822 Stine, G. Harry. *Confrontation in Space.* Englewood Cliffs, NJ: Prentice-Hall, 1981. 209pp. ISBN 0–13–167437–4.

The theory and possible practice of warfare in space are analyzed by a seminal U.S. thinker on modern strategy. The author maintains that space war must be recognized as a reality, and the United States has no option except to prepare for its possible eventuality. Space warfare will have to be modified to the space environment, and new types of weapons will have to be developed that can be deployed in this environment. Although some of the data are superseded by developments in the mid-1980s, this book is still one of the best sources on future space warfare on the market.

823 *Strategic Defences and the Future of the Arms Race: A Pugwash Symposium.* Edited by John P. Holdren and Joseph Rotblat. Houndmills, England: Macmillan, 1987. 266pp. ISBN 0–333–44873–1.

These papers are the product of a 1985 Pugwash symposium on strategic defense issues held in London. Most of the papers deal with the strategic implications of the U.S. Strategic Defense Initiative (SDI), with most contributors skeptical about it as either a defense system or a deterrent. They are also concerned about the SDI's impact on future arms control talks. This book is filled with quality essays on strategic defense issues from a variety of U.S., European, and Soviet perspectives.

824 *Strategic Defense and the Western Alliance.* Edited by Sanford Lakoff and Randy Willoughby. Lexington, MA: Lexington Books, 1987. 218pp. ISBN 0–669–15839–9.

The majority of the papers in this book are the outgrowth of a 1986 conference on the Strategic Defense Initiative (SDI) held in San Diego, California. A variety of opinions are expressed by the contributors on the technology, deployment, military and political ramifications, and role in superpower relations. The contributors maintain that while the SDI may be a U.S. initiative, its deployment remains a concern of the entire Western alliance. This book is another in a series of excellent works on the ramifications of the SDI program.

825 *The Strategic Defense Debate: Can "Star Wars" Make Us Safe?* Edited by Craig Snyder. Philadelphia, PA: University of Pennsylvania Press, 1986. 247pp. ISBN 0–8122–8040–7.

These papers are a product of a 1985 conference in Philadelphia on the Strategic Defense Initiative (SDI), sponsored by the World Affairs Council of Philadelphia. Experts on both sides of the SDI debate used this conference to express their viewpoints. Most of the arguments about the SDI rest on conclusions about technology that have yet to be determined. This book is intended to promote debate on the SDI, and succeeds in its purpose.

826 *Strategic Defense in the 21st Century.* Edited by Hans Binnendijk. Washington, DC: Foreign Service Institute, 1986. 151pp.

These papers are the result of a 1985 conference on the Strategic Defense Initiative (SDI) hosted by the Foreign Service Institute's Center for the Study of Foreign Affairs. Fourteen defense specialists express their views on the merits and demerits of the SDI. Considerable disagreement over the effectiveness and reliability of the SDI system is expressed, but a majority of the participants are in favor of further development of the system. The center designed this volume to serve as a primer on strategic defense issues, and effective use of illustrations, a glossary, and official government statements make this book a good introduction to the Reagan administration's view of the SDI.

827 *The Strategic Defense Initiative: Costs, Contractors and Consequences.* By William D. Hartung et al. New York: Council on Economic Priorities, 1985. 215pp. ISBN 0–87871–024–8.

The Council on Economic Priorities commissioned this report on the economic implications of the Strategic Defense Initiative (SDI). Cost of the SDI will range between $400 to $800 billion, and it will crowd out funds for other defense research and development projects. Recommendations are that the government institute a smaller targeted research effort geared to developing the technology for the SDI before trying to build a total system. This report is the best source on the financial ramifications of the SDI on the market.

828 *Strategic Defense Initiative: Folly or Future?* Edited by P. Edward Haley and Jack Merritt. Boulder, CO: Westview Press, 1986. 193pp. ISBN 0–8133–0414–8.

Representative opinions for and against the Strategic Defense Initiative (SDI) have been gathered in this book for information enabling a public debate. Several key aspects, such as strategic and technical feasibility and the impact of SDI on U.S.-Soviet and U.S.-allied relations, have contributions from experts in the field. Short bibliographies on each section are also of value. This book of readings is a good introductory source for college-level students.

829 *The Strategic Defense Initiative: New Perspectives on Deterrence.* Edited by Dorinda G. Dallmeyer. Boulder, CO: Westview Press, 1986. 112pp. ISBN 0–8133–7238–0.

These essays come out of a conference at the University of Georgia where scholars presented papers on the strategic, technological, and economic aspects of the Reagan administration's Strategic Defense Initiative (SDI). Arguments vary between the need of SDI for deterrence and the technological obstacles to building the system. There is also concern that the SDI will damage relations with our NATO allies. The benefit of this book is that it presents arguments on both sides of the question.

830 *Strategic Nuclear Targeting.* Edited by Desmond Ball and Jeffrey Richelson. Ithaca, NY: Cornell University Press, 1986. 367pp. ISBN 0–8014–1898–4.

Strategic nuclear targeting in the target planning process is studied in these critical essays on past and present targeting. Although there is interest in the targeting theories of France, Great Britain, and the Soviet Union, attention is primarily devoted to U.S. planning. Most of the authors are concerned with the rationale of targeting plans and the selection of targets. This book surveys a controversial topic, and the quality and depth of analysis of the essays make it a significant work.

831 *Strategic Requirements for the Army to the Year 2000.* Edited by Robert H. Kupperman and William J. Taylor. Lexington, MA: Lexington Books, 1984. 539pp. ISBN 0–669–07343–1.

These essays on the future strategic requirements of the U.S. Army have been prepared under the auspices of the Center for Strategic and International Studies (CSIS) and the U.S. Department of the Army. Both civilian and army planners directed their energies toward long-range planning by studying political-military scenarios for five regions of the world where the army might face deployment in the next fifteen years. The authors were less concerned with the possibility of a European land war than low-intensity, unconventional, and proxy conflicts in the Third World. This book is a futuristic analysis of the army's role over the next fifteen years, and the essays are both suggestive and fruitful for further research on these topics.

832 *Strategy and Defence: Australian Essays.* Edited by Desmond Ball. Sydney: Allen and Unwin, 1982. 402pp. ISBN 0–86861–316–9.

These short essays on international strategic and defense issues are by Australian authors for Australian students and military officers interested in academic writings on national security. Most of the essays have been written with an Australian viewpoint. Despite the eclectic nature of the writings, the essays provide a considerable amount of material of interest to researchers concerned about South Pacific defense and military issues.

833 *The Strategy of Electromagnetic Conflict.* Edited by Richard E. Fitts. Los Altos, CA: Peninsula Publishing, 1980. 283pp. ISBN 0–932146–02–3.

The faculty members of the Department of Electrical Engineering of the U.S. Air Force Academy produced this book on the strategy of electromagnetic warfare. They were concerned that the concept of electronic warfare is not well understood throughout the military. The result is a work that covers all aspects of electromagnetic technology, especially as it relates to air combat. This book is must reading for anybody interested in military weapons systems.

834 *Strengthening Conventional Deterrence in Europe: A Program for the 1980s.* Report of the European Security Study. Boulder, CO: Westview Press, 1985. 150pp. ISBN 0–8133–7078–7.

This report is a follow-up to the 1983 policy recommendations of the European Security Study (ESECS), which focus on additional detail and analysis for improving NATO conventional forces. Specific recommendations on the development of communications, weapons systems, and tactics are made. This report needs to be read in conjunction with the earlier report, both of which constitute major contributions to European defense literature.

835 *Strengthening Conventional Deterrence in Europe: Proposals for the 1980s.* Report of the European Security Study. London: Macmillan, 1983. 260pp. ISBN 0–333–36023–0.

The European Security Study (ESECS) produced this book on ways for NATO to improve its conventional deterrence posture. Twenty-six U.S. and European defense specialists worked together to formulate proposals to improve NATO's conventional deterrence. While these specialists make no criticism of current NATO military strategy, they insist on an upgrading of NATO forces to create a credible deterrence to Soviet military actions in Europe. This report is long on recommendations but short on the political avenues to carry out their proposals.

836 *The Structure of the Defense Industry: An International Survey.* Edited by Nicole Ball and Milton Leitenberg. New York: St. Martin's Press, 1983. 372pp. ISBN 0–312–76757–9.

The economic parameters of the industrial-military complex in ten different states are the subjects of this book. It has been the lack of information on the economic impact of the closing of defense industries that has often been cited as a limitation whenever there is a debate on arms control issues. This comparative study indicates that only minor economic dislocation would occur in nearly all cases of disarmament scenarios. This work should be required reading for both economists and politicians.

837 *Submarine: Design and Development.* Annapolis, MD: Naval Institute Press, 1984. 192pp. ISBN 0–87021–954–5.

The author traces the story of submarine design and development from pre–World War I to the present. His interest is directed toward submarine technology and its impact on submarine warfare. The present emphasis in submarine design is on fast and silent submarines, but the debate is still in progress on the merits of diesel versus nuclear power plants. This work is a solid introduction to the design and development of modern submarines.

838 Suddaby, Adam. *The Nuclear War Game.* London: Longman, 1983. 239pp. ISBN 0–582–38483–4.

This book provides an overview of the debate over nuclear weapons and weapons systems from the British perspective. The coverage is broad, including data on the effects and types of nuclear weapons from Hiroshima (1945) to the present. Rival arguments are presented on all aspects of the nuclear arms race. Both the technical information and the illustrations make this book a good reference source for both the general public and novice researchers.

839 Suter, Keith. *An International Law of Guerrilla Warfare: The Global Politics of Law-Making.* New York: St. Martin's Press, 1984. 192pp. ISBN 0–312–42290–3.

The author, an Australian, surveys the status of guerrilla warfare in international law. Recent attempts by international organizations to devise rules for guerrilla warfare are examined and found wanting. There was the lack of political will among most governments to create a satisfactory international law of guerrilla warfare. This book is an excellent source for outlining political difficulties inherent in any examination of international law.

840 Suvorov, Viktor. *Inside Soviet Military Intelligence.* New York: Macmillan, 1984. 193pp. ISBN 0–02–615510–9.

A former high official in the Soviet military intelligence (GRU) describes the history, organization, and operation of Soviet military intelligence gathering. He combines personal insight with operational analysis of the GRU. Listings of past and present GRU leadership and tactics are of particular interest. This book is the best source on Soviet military intelligence in print.

841 *Swords and Shields: NATO, the USSR, and New Choices for Long-Range Offense and Defense.* Edited by Fred S. Hoffman, Albert Wohlstetter, and David S. Yost. Lexington, MA: Lexington Books, 1987. 369pp. ISBN 0–669–14249–2.

These papers examine the impact of new technologies on offensive and defensive strategy of both NATO and the Soviet Union. Defense specialists from the military and think tanks provided these essays. The result is various analyses on the short- and long-range effect of the Strategic Defense Initiative

(SDI) on the military strategy of the Soviet Union, the United States, and Western Europe. These essays are a major contribution to defense literature.

842 *Systems Analysis and Modeling in Defense: Development, Trends, and Issues.* Edited by Reiner K. Huber. New York: Plenum Press, 1984. 913pp. ISBN 0–306–41609–3.

This book contains the proceedings of a 1982 international symposium on modeling and analysis of defense processes in modern warfare held at NATO's Defense Research Group (DRG) in Brussels, Belgium. Papers were organized around three panels: modeling methodology, methodology of analysis, and analysis issues. A total of fifty-three papers are included on a variety of issues on modeling and systems analysis. This huge book has a number of significant papers for anyone interested in modeling and systems analysis.

843 Tayacan. *Psychological Operations in Guerrilla Warfare.* Washington, DC: Library of Congress, 1984. 40pp.

This publication is a translation by the Congressional Research Service of a manual on psychological operations for Latin American guerrillas. Since guerrilla warfare is political, it must operate effectively in the political environment. The guerrillas' target is the minds of the population, and all tactics must be directed toward this end. This manual is the guidebook for psychological operations for the Contras in the war in Nicaragua.

844 Taylor, Trevor. *European Defence Cooperation.* London: Routledge and Kegan Paul, 1984. 97pp. ISBN 0–7102–0299–7.

The feasibility of increased European defense cooperation with NATO is here examined by a British defense specialist. European members of the Atlantic alliance need to reassure their publics that NATO does not exist only for U.S. policy, and that there is a need for European countries to match U.S. military resources. The author recommends that the European defense community move ahead incrementally to improve European defenses. This study provides persuasive recommendations, but the European members of NATO are still pursuing the old policy of dependence on the United States.

845 *The Technology, Strategy and Politics of SDI.* Boulder, CO: Westview Press, 1987. 252pp. ISBN 0–8133–7116–3.

The decision, technology, and implementation of the Strategic Defense Initiative (SDI) are examined in these essays by prominent U.S. defense specialists. Debate among supporters of the SDI concerns the defense versus offense dilemma, but critics attack the technology and strategy of SDI. These papers cover all aspects of the SDI debate, but most authors fall into the pro-SDI camp. This book makes a major contribution to the literature on the SDI.

846 Thakur, Ramesh. *In Defence of New Zealand: Foreign Policy Choices in the Nuclear Age.* Boulder, CO: Westview Press, 1986. 247pp. ISBN 0–8133–0361–3.

The foreign and defense policy options of New Zealand are examined in this study by a New Zealand academic scholar. New Zealand has no security concerns except for the danger of nuclear war, and its foreign policy has revolved around the ANZUS alliance. Both the author and public opinion in New Zealand desire a nuclear-free zone for the South Pacific. Because of recent decisions by the New Zealand government, this paper is invaluable in understanding the background of the controversy between New Zealand and the United States.

847 Thee, Marek. *Military Technology, Military Strategy and the Arms Race.* London: Croom Helm, 1986. 139pp. ISBN 0–7099–4312–1.

This book is a study of the extent to which military technology has become the deciding factor in determining military strategy. Military research and development has gained so much momentum that there is no way to curtail armaments and reverse the arms race unless this momentum is halted. Arms control negotiations have been protracted by both sides to gain time for development of new weapons systems. While this book contributes a novel thesis and evidence to support it, the author's treatment lacks balance.

848 Thies, Wallace J. *The Atlantic Alliance, Nuclear Weapons and European Attitudes: Reexamining the Conventional Wisdom.* Berkeley, CA: Institute of International Studies, 1983. 59pp. ISBN 0–87725–519–9.

The author challenges the contention that NATO is in disarray and the cause is the modernization of the alliance's long-range theater nuclear forces (LRTNF) in Europe. Questions of military preparedness and deterrence are always sensitive and controversial among democratic societies. The crisis over modernization is no more than a typical disagreement among allies, and evidence shows that European public opinion still supports NATO. This essay argues persuasively against misjudging the state of the crisis within the Atlantic alliance, and it is this thesis and the supporting arguments that make this paper a good source.

849 Thomas, Andy. *Effects of Chemical Warfare: A Selective Review and Bibliography of British State Papers.* London: Taylor and Francis, 1985. 125pp. ISBN 0–85066–307–5.

The author has explored the state papers of the United Kingdom in an effort to locate all information about the past use of chemical warfare by British forces. Most of the information refers to incidents or policies during World War I and World War II, but there is some data about postwar chemical weapons development. The intent of this analysis is to document long-range effects of chemical warfare on Europe. An excellent bibliography makes this monograph a useful reference source.

850 *Threats, Weapons, and Foreign Policy.* Edited by Pat McGowan and Charles W. Kegley. Beverly Hills, CA: Sage, 1980. 324pp. ISBN 0–8039–1154–8.

Essays on the interaction between national security and foreign policy behavior constitute the bulk of this book. The focus is on applying new concepts and methodologies to the subjects of threats, weapons, and the arms race. While no consensus develops among the authors, the nine studies combine solid research and analytical skills, making this book a major contribution to both defense and foreign policy studies.

851 Till, Geoffrey. *Modern Sea Power: An Introduction.* London: Brassey's, 1987. 179pp. ISBN 0–08–033623–X.

A British authority on naval affairs investigates the impact of naval technology on modern naval warfare. The author is most concerned with correlating new development in naval technology with current naval tactics. He concludes that modern technology has not reduced the value of sea power, but it has increased the economic costs for maritime countries. This work is an indispensable introduction for researchers on sea power.

852 *Toward a More Effective Defense: Report of the Defense Organization Project.* Edited by Barry M. Blechman and William J. Lynn. Cambridge, MA: Ballinger, 1985. 247pp. ISBN 0–88730–026–X.

These papers are an outgrowth of the Defense Organization Project of Georgetown University's Center for Strategic and International Studies. This project intended to survey the organizational and procedural problems of the U.S. defense establishment and propose a number of reforms. Because most of the contributors have spent a portion of their careers in the defense industry or Congress, they suggest a series of moderate changes to improve the U.S. defense infrastructure. This book is an authoritative look at U.S. defense problems, and its recommendations should be considered.

853. Tritten, James J. *Soviet Naval Forces and Nuclear Warfare: Weapons Employment and Policy.* Boulder, CO: Westview Press, 1986. 282pp. ISBN 0–8133–7206–2.

In this book the author advances the thesis that the primary role of the Soviet Navy is to prepare for fighting a nuclear war with the United States. He uses content analysis from Soviet writings and speeches to support his thesis. The Soviet Navy is envisaged by its leaders to be an offensive weapon, and it has been steadily expanding to be able to hold its own in combat with the U.S. Navy. While the author attempts to produce more than he can deliver, his book is still a useful approach to the study of Soviet naval strategy.

854 Tritten, James J. *Soviet Navy Data Base: 1982–83.* Santa Monica: Rand Corporation, 1983. 80pp.

This database of the Soviet Navy's war-making capabilities was developed by the author for his Ph.D. at the University of Southern California's Defense and Strategic Studies Program. The author takes five issues—navy composition, fleet assignments, fleet organization, ship availability, and fleet mobilization potential—and identifies likely Soviet naval postures in various ocean areas under wartime conditions. He uses unclassified naval data from the major naval research institutes. This database has uses for anyone interested in Soviet naval deployment in peace or war.

855 Tsipis, Kosta. *Arsenal: Understanding Weapons in the Nuclear Age.* New York: Simon and Schuster, 1983. 342pp. ISBN 0–671–44073–X.

The author advances the thesis that the U.S. public has been excluded from policy decisions on nuclear weapons by the self-proclaimed nuclear experts. This book is an effort to rectify this situation by explaining the basics of nuclear weapons and nuclear strategy. The author has kept the text free from scientific and mathematical jargon, and the technical details are relegated to the appendices. This book can serve as an excellent textbook for introductory courses on nuclear weaponry.

856 *UK Military R and D: Report of a Working Party Council for Science and Society.* Oxford, England: Oxford University Press, 1986. 65pp. ISBN 0–19–859930–7.

A committee of members of the Council for Science and Society produced this report on British military research and development. Since half of

British government spending on science and technology is for the development of military weapons, this committee decided to investigate British research and development. The recommendations are reduction and concentration of resources, closer relations with other scientific and technological activity, more attention to arms-race curbs, and more public accountability. This report is more important for its conclusions than its data.

857 *The Uncertain Course: Strategies and Mind-sets.* Edited by Carl G. Jacobsen. Oxford, England: Oxford University Press, 1987. 349pp. ISBN 0–19–829115–9.

A mix of U.S., British, Canadian, and Swedish scholars examine the interactions among new military technology, military operations, and strategic planning. They note a growing incompatibility between new military technology and ways to control these weapons, which hurts arms control efforts. Almost as important for arms control is how the political leaders of both power blocs view new weapons systems. This book contains a series of high-quality articles of interest to everyone in the defense and security fields.

858 *Understanding U.S. Strategy: A Reader.* Edited by Terry L. Heyns. Washington, DC: National Defense University Press, 1983. 408pp.

In 1982 the Ninth National Security Affairs Conference was the occasion of the presentation of these papers on U.S. national security problems. A variety of subjects and perspectives is included, but two notable points are made: (1) the United States is overcommitted in its relationship to its economic and military strength; and (2) outer space is where the next strategic move by the United States will take place. This book has something for everyone interested in defense and security issues.

859 Union of Concerned Scientists. *Space-Based Missile Defense: A Report by the Union of Concerned Scientists.* Cambridge, MA: Union of Concerned Scientists, 1984. 106pp.

This report examines the space-based missile defense system of the Strategic Defense Initiative (SDI) for technological and performance characteristics. The system must destroy at the boost phase, otherwise it is impossible to wipe out all the multiple warheads, but the chemical laser "battle stations" in low orbit and excimer lasers on the ground will cost upwards of $110 billion. Any technological breakthroughs by the Soviets will magnify the problems and make the SDI less effective. This study group concludes that the SDI is too costly and ineffective to constitute a creditable missile defense system.

860 *Unity and Conflict in the Warsaw Pact.* Edited by Ingmar Oldberg. Stockholm: Swedish National Defence Research Institute, 1984. 158pp. ISBN 91–7056–068–4.

This book contains the proceedings of a symposium on the Warsaw Pact arranged by the Division for International Security Studies of the Swedish National Defence Research Institute (FOA). Four specialists from Austria, Great Britain, the United States, and West Germany presented papers on cultural, economic, military, and political aspects of the Warsaw Pact, and they responded to questions from Swedish participants. The diversity of approach makes these papers differ, but the authors agree that there are significant unity problems among the Warsaw Pact countries. This book is a mixed bag of good-to-fair papers and sometimes revealing commentary.

861   Urban, Mark L. *Soviet Land Power*. New York: Hippocrene Books, 1985. 120pp. ISBN 0–87052–027–X.

A British military specialist uses this book to provide an objective analysis of Soviet ground capabilities by examining Soviet military organization, deployment, command, and efficiency. The result is a publication that combines analysis with copious use of statistical data and illustrations to advance the author's thesis that the Soviet military machine is not designed for surprise attacks, and the deficiencies in manpower and training hurt its military capabilities. This book is a perceptive look at all aspects of Soviet fighting abilities.

862   *The U.S. Defense Mobilization Infrastructure: Problems and Priorities*. Cambridge, MA: Institute for Foreign Policy Analysis, 1981. 25pp. ISBN 0–89549–034–X.

This report is the result of the Tenth Annual Conference of the International Security Studies Program of the Fletcher School of Law and Diplomacy in Cambridge, Massachusetts, on the problems of U.S. defense mobilization in time of war. U.S. mobilization potential has eroded because of economic decline, raw material shortages, and shortages in quality personnel. A series of recommendations is made, including economic incentives to U.S. defense industries, exploring an emergency national draft, maintaining survivable command, control, and communications systems, and upgrading strategic minerals stockpiles. This report is a major reevaluation of the U.S. defense mobilization infrastructure.

863   U.S. Department of Defense. *The Strategic Defense Initiative: Defensive Technologies Study*. Washington, DC: U.S. Government Printing Office, 1984. 27pp.

The Department of Defense published this booklet in April 1984 on the technological feasibility of the Strategic Defense Initiative (SDI). A Defensive Technologies Study Team recommended a continuation of the development of SDI technologies. It also focused on the need for research on some of the new technologies. This optimistic study of the SDI by a government task force gives a picture of the Reagan administration's version of the SDI.

864   *The U.S. Navy: The View from the Mid-1980s*. Edited by James L. George. Boulder, CO: Westview Press, 1985. 385pp. ISBN 0–8133–7052–3.

A combination of active duty naval officers and naval specialists has written papers on the state of the U.S. Navy in the mid-1980s. The general consensus is that the U.S. Navy is in the best shape it has been in over a decade. Better budgeting and ship-building policies have made the six hundred-ship navy a realistic goal. This optimistic assessment of the condition of the U.S. Navy now and for the remainder of the century is a good look at planning and morale in the naval establishment.

865   Vigor, P. H. *Soviet Blitzkrieg Theory*. London: Macmillan, 1983. 218pp. ISBN 0–333–27077–0.

A British defense specialist analyzes Soviet military strategy for winning a war with NATO. Any war with the West will have to be short, because Soviet military thinkers believe that the Soviet Union would lose a long war. Consequently, Soviet strategy is based on rapid exploitation of a military situation, and this tactic means the use of surprise with at most sixty-two divisions. The analysis and conclusion are not reassuring for NATO, but every NATO officer and politician should be familiar with this book.

866 Volgyes, Ivan. *The Political Reliability of the Warsaw Pact Armies: The Southern Tier.* Durham, NC: Duke Press Policy Studies, 1982. 115pp. ISBN 0–8223–0509–7.

The reliability of the military establishments of Bulgaria, Hungary, and Romania to the Warsaw Treaty Organization (WTO) in the event of hostilities is the subject of this book. Only Bulgaria has indicated that the Soviet Union can depend upon it in any type of emergency. But the implications for U.S. foreign policy toward Eastern European countries is to work for long-term evolutionary change and a moderate policy of the advancement of human rights. This book is a serious and realistic assessment of the political reliability of the southern tier of the Warsaw Pact.

867 Walker, J. R. *Air-to-Ground Operations.* London: Brassey's, 1987. 152pp. ISBN 0–08–033612–4.

A British air vice marshal examines the tactical use of the fighter-bomber on the conduct of air-to-ground operations. This work is in keeping with the Royal Air Force's current offensive air capability. Modern technology is changing the nature of air combat with the development of smart weapons and change in the balance between manned and unmanned vehicles. While this book may be too elementary for the military professional, it is a state-of-the-art treatise for the rest of us.

868 Walker, Richard Lee. *Strategic Target Planning: Bridging the Gap between Theory and Practice.* Washington, DC: National Defense University, 1983. 46pp.

The author is a senior officer in the U.S. Air Force, and he examines strategic targeting and practice from the vantage point of his military expertise. His thesis is that in the change of nuclear strategy from massive retaliation to flexible response there has developed a severe targeting problem. Technical limitations are such that flexible targeting depends too heavily on nuclear forces and communications, command, control, and intelligence (C3I) resources capable of surviving in a protracted nuclear war. These warnings by an officer engaged in strategic targeting make this short book a welcome source.

869 *War in Europe.* Edited by Lars B. Wallin. Stockholm: Swedish National Defence Research Institute, 1982. 130pp. ISBN 91–7056–061–7.

These papers are the proceedings of a 1977 symposium on war in Europe held in Stockholm under the auspices of the Swedish National Defence Research Institute. Both the papers and the discussions were mostly concerned with the impact of weapons technology on the conduct of any future European war. Much of the debate revolved around the role of the neutron bomb in combat. Despite the time lag between the symposium and the publication of its proceedings, many of the same topics appeared in the late 1970s as are reappearing in the mid-1980s.

870 *War in the Third Dimension: Essays in Contemporary Air Power.* Edited by R. A. Mason. London: Brassey's, 1986. 228pp. ISBN 0–08–031187–3.

These essays on air power in the mid-1980s are by senior officers in the Royal Air Force and the U.S. Air Force, and distinguished academics. The authors survey the current state of air power in relation to past, present, and future military operations. They give special emphasis to the differences in doctrine and tactics between NATO and Soviet air forces. This work's major contribution is to provide a forum for Western thinking on air power.

871 *War, State and Society.* Edited by Martin Shaw. London: Macmillan, 1984. 266pp. ISBN 0–333–33992–4.

This book on the impact or threat of war on the modern industrialized state is the product of a conference held at the University of Hull in 1981. Most of the contributors are British academics with ties to the European nuclear disarmament movement, but all are concerned with the role of war in society and the state. Two intellectual traditions appear and clash in this book—academic sociology and Marxism. This work contains strong essays on the subject of warfare and society and should be a good source for ideas for the future.

872 *The Warsaw Pact: Political Purpose and Military Means.* Edited by Robert W. Clawson and Lawrence S. Kaplan. Wilmington, DE: Scholarly Resources, 1982. 297pp. ISBN 0–8420–2198–1.

These papers on the Warsaw Pact are an outgrowth of a conference at Kent State University in 1981. Recent military reorganization among Warsaw Pact military forces has made analysis difficult, but the analysts are impressed with the military potential of its forces. There are problems with the political reliability of the non-Soviet states, but these problems are minor in comparison with military readiness. Most of the papers are of a high quality, and this book can be recommended for defense studies.

873 Wasserman, Sherri L. *The Neutron Bomb Controversy: A Study in Alliance Politics.* New York: Praeger, 1983. 151pp. ISBN 0–03–064154–3.

The controversy in Western Europe and the United States over the neutron bomb is the subject of this book. Thanks to differing policies by the Carter and Reagan administrations and the lack of consultation within NATO, the neutron bomb has come to symbolize nuclear malaise in the Atlantic alliance. The NATO countries will need to have consultation for future modernization of nuclear weapons, and there is the possibility of further political crises over modernization. This book is a major contribution to the literature on defense issues in the NATO alliance.

874 Watson, Bruce W. *Red Navy at Sea: Soviet Naval Operations on the High Seas, 1956–1980.* Boulder, CO: Westview Press, 1982. 245pp. ISBN 0–86531–204–4.

This book is a history of Soviet naval operations on the high seas since the appointment of Admiral Gorshkov in 1956. The Soviets have built a strong navy since 1956, making it a major sea power able to challenge the U.S. Navy in the next decade. Soviet strategy is to use their navy both for defense and foreign policy objectives. Both the analysis and the tables in the appendix make this book the most authoritative source on the operations of the Soviet Navy available in the West.

875 Watts, Barry D. *The Foundations of U.S. Air Doctrine: The Problem of Friction in War.* Maxwell Air Force Base, AL: Air University Press, 1984. 166pp.

The author is a career air force officer whose intent is to study the difference between idealized warfare and actual combat. His thesis is that the U.S. Air Force doctrine is too dependent upon the idealized view of warfare instead of the uncertainties and difficulties of real warfare. This theory is named *friction*, and it is one of the fundamentals of war. This book is an effective presentation of the author's rejection of mechanistic warfare.

876 Webber, Philip, Graeme Wilkinson, and Barry Rubin. *Crisis over Cruise.* Harmondsworth, England: Penguin Books, 1983. 110pp. ISBN 0-14052-354-5.

Three British scientists wrote this book to provide technical information on the functioning and capabilities of cruise missiles. These authors want the crisis over the deployment of cruise missiles to serve as a catalyst for arms control and disarmament. This book provides a useful treatise on the characteristics of cruise missiles, but the authors' anticruise viewpoint limits their objectivity.

877 Weida, William J., and Frank L. Gertcher. *The Political Economy of National Defense.* Boulder, CO: Westview Press, 1987. 230pp. ISBN 0-8133-0432-6.

The authors combine defense economics and the political aspects of defense spending for an overview of the political economy of U.S. national defense. They conclude that the United States lacks a cohesive national strategy to direct the allocation of scarce resources to defense uses, and that this problem is a cause of economic woes in the defense establishment. Without meaningful national objectives, wasteful inefficiencies in the defense field will continue to plague the United States. This book is both an assessment and a warning about the economic burdens of defense.

878 *West-European Navies and the Future.* Edited by Jan H. Veldman and Frits Th. Olivier. Den Helder, the Netherlands: Royal Netherlands Naval College, 1980. 251pp. ISBN 90-9000-1042.

In 1979 experts on naval affairs from various NATO countries gathered at the Royal Netherlands Naval College to discuss the future role of Western European navies. Both the papers and the discussions were concerned with the growing Soviet threat to NATO's naval forces. There is the need for Western European naval expansion, but budgetary constraints make this unlikely. The discussions rather than the papers make this book a useful source for views on European maritime issues.

879 Wettig, Gerhard. *Umstrittene Sicherheit: Friedenswahrung und Rustungsbegrunzung in Europa.* Berlin: Berlin Verlag, 1982. 192pp. ISBN 3-87061-236-3.

In this work, one of West Germany's foremost specialists on strategic studies undertakes an analysis of European defense options. After surveying both NATO and Soviet military strategy, the author covers European public opinion on defense issues. His thesis is that there is a growing body of opinion challenging the European defense status quo, which has the potential to change policies on both sides. This book is a major study of changing opinions on defense policies in Europe.

880 *Whence the Threat to Peace,* 3d ed. Moscow: Military Publishing House, 1984. 96pp.

This publication is the official Soviet source on U.S. military forces. It serves the same propaganda function as the U.S. government's publications on Soviet military forces and appears approximately every two years.

Illustrations, maps, and graphs are used to supplement the analysis. This booklet suffers in comparison to similar types of publications produced by the U.S. Department of Defense.

881 Wilkinson, David. *Deadly Quarrels: Lewis F. Richardson and the Statistical Study of War.* Berkeĺey: University of California Press, 1980. 206pp. ISBN 0–520–03829–0.

The author has approached the model of Lewis Fry Richardson on theories of war based on statistical data. He critiques Richardson's methodology and concludes that the code symbols need overhauling so that more cases can be included. His overall assessment, however, is that Richardson's work is methodologically and theoretically fruitful and suggestive. This book indicates that Richardson's model is a worthy one to build on for future statistical research on wars.

882 Willcox, A. M., M. G. Slade, and P. A. Ramsdale. *Command, Control, and Communications (C3).* Oxford, England: Brassey's Defence Publishers, 1983. 150pp. ISBN 0–08–028332–2.

The outlines of current and future communications technology are examined in this technical study. Electronic warfare is the wave of the future in warfare, and only with an understanding of military command, control, and communications (C3) will the reader comprehend this type of warfare. By providing information on communication developments in the 1980s, this publication fills a void in defense literature.

883 Williams, E. S. *The Soviet Military: Political Education, Training and Morale.* Houndmills, England: Macmillan, 1987. 203pp. ISBN 0–333–38561–6.

The author and two collaborators seek to assess the nature of the Soviet military. They start with political education and training and move toward a composite picture of the Soviet soldier, airman, and sailor. Particular emphasis is placed upon gauging the collective morale of the Soviet forces, and the conclusion is that the Soviet serviceman's morale is variable. While this book deals with a complex and evasive problem, the result is a suggestive work that will be of interest to most defense scholars.

884 Williams, Geoffrey. *Global Defence: Motivation and Policy in a Nuclear Age.* New Delhi: Vikas, 1984. 366pp. ISBN 0–7069–2478–9.

This book is a comparative study of the defense policies of the ten major military states—Australia, France, Great Britain, India, Japan, South Africa, the Soviet Union, Sweden, the United States, and West Germany. Each state has its defense policy determined by its strategic environment, and this means constant reassessment of its position vis-à-vis potential enemies. This book contains a variety of insights on differing attitudes toward defense in its sample of ten countries, and this is its contribution to defense literature.

885 Williams, Geoffrey Lee, and Alan Lee Williams. *The European Defence Initiative: Europe's Bid for Equality.* London: Macmillan, 1986. 242pp. ISBN 0–333–38730–9.

The theme of this book is that Europe and the United States must be equal partners in the NATO alliance. This "Europeanization" of NATO's defense posture would strengthen European participation in decision making and public opinion. Such an approach to restructuring NATO has its appeal, but the assuming of an increasing financial burden by the European countries makes this restructuring less certain.

886 Williams, Phil. *US Troops in Europe.* London: Routledge and Kegan Paul, 1984. 87pp. ISBN 0–7102–0422–1.

The debate both in Europe and the United States over U.S. military forces in Europe is surveyed and assessed by a British scholar. Demands by U.S. politicians for a reduction in U.S. troop strength in Europe have been decried by most European governments. But such forces have resulted in excessive dependence of Western Europe on U.S. policies, and many European observers have come to question this dependence. The author concludes that some cuts in U.S. troop strength might be permissible, but the continued deployment of U.S. forces in Europe for the foreseeable future is a necessity. This book is a balanced assessment of a controversial topic both in Europe and the United States.

887 Wong-Fraser, Agatha S. Y. *Symmetry and Selectivity in U.S. Defense Policy: A Grand Design or a Major Mistake?* Lanham, MD: University Press of America, 1980. 164pp. ISBN 0–8191–1182–1.

The author uses this book to explore the background and conduct of the "Schlesinger Doctrine" on U.S. nuclear strategy. Selectivity and symmetry of response were the twin features of Schlesinger's contribution to nuclear strategy. Schlesinger attempted to achieve flexibility on political and social demands from within and without. This book is a solid assessment of the Schlesinger Doctrine on nuclear policy, and it deserves consideration for its treatment of this doctrine.

888 Woods, Stan. *Weapons Acquisition in the Soviet Union.* Aberdeen, Scotland: Centre for Defence Studies, 1982. 68pp.

The author examines the Soviet weapons acquisition system's performance record. While conservatism of design is a key factor in Soviet weapons systems, the Soviet procurement system has produced a number of successful weapons. Western efforts to claim superiority over the Soviet procurement apparatus are mistaken, because the Soviets are highly successful in the production of effective hardware. This paper is a corrective to many Western critics of the Soviet procurement system.

889 Wyllie, James H. *The Influence of British Arms: An Analysis of British Intervention since 1956.* London: Allen and Unwin, 1984. 125pp. ISBN 0–04–320161–X.

British military intervention since the Suez crisis of 1956 is the subject of this book. Case studies of specific instances of British interventions are studied for strengths and weaknesses. The conclusion is that British intervention can only succeed if there is a sound moral and legal basis, adequate military capabilities, policy consensus with the United States, and a clear political purpose for the use of military force. This book is less than enthusiastic over the prospects of British military intervention, and this viewpoint along with the case studies makes it worthwhile.

890 Yost, David S. *France and Conventional Defense in Central Europe.* Boulder, CO: Westview Press, 1985. 132pp. ISBN 0–8133–7054–X.

France's role in conventional defense in central Europe has assumed more importance since NATO adopted the "flexible response" strategy. But the

French response has been less than enthusiastic, because its planners still depend upon a nuclear response. This book is an articulate study of French reluctance to expand its conventional forces for the defense in central Europe, and its analysis should have an impact on NATO strategists.

891 Zuckerman, Solly. *Nuclear'Illusion and Reality*. London: Collins, 1982. 154pp. ISBN 0–00–216555–4.

The fallacy of the nuclear retaliation doctrine is advanced by this prominent British authority on strategic affairs. Reliance on nuclear weapons in the event of conflict would only expand the war and invite mass destruction. The companion argument is that NATO's conventional forces must be built up to match the Soviet threat. This book is a restatement of a thesis that the author has been advancing for over twenty years, but his viewpoint is still worthy of notice.

892 Zuckerman, Solly. *Star Wars in a Nuclear World*. London: William Kimber, 1986. 226pp. ISBN 0–7183–0615–5.

These lectures were delivered between 1983 and 1985 and deal with the nuclear arms race and the Strategic Defense Initiative (SDI). The emphasis of these lectures and a number of reprinted articles is on the relationship among politicians, the military, and scientists and the development of technology for the SDI and related weapons systems. Debate over the SDI is part of an ongoing problem between the products of scientific and technologic research and military and political design for these products. This book is a major source on the incapacity of the two sides to reach an understanding.

CHAPTER THREE:
International Security

International security is an umbrella term for a variety of subjects. In contrast to defense issues, international security is a more general subject category that includes any topic that involves relations between two states, or any area of actual or potential crisis. A total of 481 entries constitute this category.

Annuals and Yearbooks

893 *Annual of Power and Conflict.* London: Institute for the Study of Conflict, 1972– . ISSN 0307–031X. $100.

Sources of political instability—especially revolutionary, subversive, and terrorist movements—in more than 120 countries are covered in this annual. It is the product of the Institute for the Study of Conflict (ISC), which is a nonprofit organization studying world political instability. Particularly useful for researchers is the feature tracing each country's incidences of violence during the current year. While this publication remains the top annual in its field, it has a slow publishing cycle.

894 *Arès: Défense et sécurité.* Grenoble, France: Société pour le Developpement des Études de Défense et de Sécurité Internationale, 1978– . ISSN 0181–009X. $18.

The influential French institute, Société pour le Developpement des Études de Défense et de Sécurité Internationale, publishes this annual on defense and security issues. Lengthy articles on defense and military subjects of concern to French researchers are produced each year. Additional features are sections on chronology of international security events and a lengthy bibliography. This publication is the most influential French annual in the field of security studies.

895 *Asian Security.* London: Brassey's Defence, 1979– . ISBN 0–08–033610–8. $29.95.

This publication is the annual report of the Research Institute for Peace and Security, Tokyo. It chronicles events in Asia and on the international scene that have an impact on Asian security. Special features are tables that compare various countries in the region, and political, security, and economic chronologies of events. This annual is the best publication on Asian security on the market.

896   *The Canadian Strategic Review.* Toronto: Canadian Institute of Strategic Studies, 1983– . ISSN 0824–2216. $25.
This annual deals with all aspects of Canadian national security issues. In this review *strategy* is defined in such broad terms as to include economic as well as national defense issues. It is a product of a Canadian think tank, the Institute of Strategic Studies, Toronto. While the quality of analysis is high, the narrow scope of the subject matter makes this annual useful only as a gauge of strategic thought in Canada.

897   *International Security Yearbook.* Edited by Barry M. Blechman and Edward N. Luttwak. New York: St. Martin's Press, 1984– . ISSN 0740–4867. $52.
The intent of this yearbook is to present an empirical and objective analysis of the events of the past year that influence Western security. Although the emphasis is upon the balance of U.S. and Soviet military power, security questions involving the four subregions—Latin America, southern Africa, the Persian Gulf, and the Middle East—are also covered. This yearbook is published under the auspices of the Georgetown University Center for Strategic and International Studies in Washington, DC.

898   *The Middle East and North Africa.* London: Europa Publications, 1948– . $140.
Statistical information on all of the countries in the Middle East and North Africa is provided in this yearbook. Each issue highlights several key events during the year. This publication is a good source of basic reference material for Middle East and North African countries.

899   *The Middle East Annual.* Boston: G. K. Hall, 1980– . ISSN 0733–5350. $92.
Each annual in this series presents an analysis of contemporary affairs in the Middle East. Besides a lengthy chronicle of the events of that year, there are articles by Middle East specialists on selected topics. Finally, there is an excellent bibliography of the year's publications in Middle Eastern studies. This annual is an informative source for Middle East political developments and their impact on the international scene.

900   *Middle East Contemporary Survey.* Edited by Colin Legum. New York: Holmes and Meier, 1976– . ISSN 0163–5476. $198.
This annual survey of political, economic, military, and international developments in the Middle East is produced by the Shiloah Center for Middle Eastern and African Studies of Tel Aviv University. It provides researchers with up-to-date material about contemporary affairs in the Middle East. Half of this publication consists of essays on Middle East subjects, and the other half comprises a country-by-country survey of each of the Middle Eastern states.

901   *Southeast Asian Affairs.* Singapore: Institute of Southeast Asian Studies, 1974– . ISSN 0377–5437. $25.

Economic, political, and security trends in Southeast Asia are surveyed in this annual. After a series of articles on regional issues, there is a country-by-country analysis of the internal political situation. A consistent theme in this annual is a concern for regional stability in Southeast Asia. This publication is always a good source for background information on Southeast Asia.

902 *Strategic Survey.* London: International Institute for Strategic Studies, 1966– . ISSN 0459–7230. $9.

An in-depth analysis of the international strategic situation is presented in this annual publication produced by the International Institute for Strategic Studies in London. Each region is covered, with key subjects receiving special treatment. Another feature is the regional chronologies of strategic events. There is no other source that provides as good an analysis as this publication.

Bibliographies

903 American Security Council Foundation. *Quarterly Strategic Bibliography.* Boston: American Security Council Foundation, 1975– . $84.

This quarterly bibliography from the American Security Council Foundation lists articles on strategic issues from 175 periodicals, congressional documents, dissertations, monographs, and reports. It contains an excellent glossary of terms and author and subject indexes. Since it appears at regular intervals and carries an array of diverse materials, this publication is the most comprehensive bibliography on strategic issues in the field.

904 *ASEAN: A Bibliography.* Edited by Patricia Lim. Singapore: Institute of Southeast Asian Studies, 1984. 487pp. ISBN 9971–902–74–5.

The Association of Southeast Asian Nations (ASEAN) represents a group of Southeast Asian countries in the midst of rapid economic development and expanding international influence. This bibliography is an attempt to provide information on ASEAN for decisionmakers in government and business, and for scholarship in the academic community. The six countries covered by ASEAN studies are Brunei, Indonesia, Malaysia, Philippines, Thailand, and Singapore. Only a portion of this bibliography has citations on international security topics, but these citations refer to sources unavailable elsewhere.

905 Purhadi, Ibrahim V. *Iran and the United States, 1979–1981: Three Years of Confrontation.* Washington, DC: Mideast Directions, 1982. 37pp.

Articles and reports on relations between Iran and the United States have been compiled in this bibliography by a librarian at the Library of Congress, African and Middle East Division, Near East Section. Whenever possible the compiler has added short annotations. The absence of an index of any type makes this bibliography somewhat difficult to use. This bibliography is of marginal value for security specialists.

906 Schwarz, Gunter. *Sicherheit und Zusammenarbeit: Eine Bibliographie zu MBFR, SALT und KSZE.* Baden-Baden: Nomos Verlagsgesellschaft, 1980. 150pp. ISBN 3–7890–0540–1.

Material on arms control negotiations involving Western Europe is highlighted in this short bibliography. It lists books and articles dealing with arms control and security issues published in the years between 1970 and 1979. The author received editorial support from the Institute for Peace Research and Defense Politics at Hamburg University, Hamburg, West Germany. This publication lists sources from Western Europe unavailable elsewhere.

907 Underdown, Michael. *Threat Perception: A Bibliography and Introductory Essay.* Parkville, Victoria: Program in Public Policy Studies, the University of Melbourne, 1982. 131pp.

Journal articles and government papers dealing with the analysis of threat perception are provided in this bibliography from the University of Melbourne's Program in Public Policy Studies. *Threat perception* is defined here as a complicated element of the early warning and crisis management processes. Most of the material was gathered by computer searches from various databases. The topic is of considerable research interest in the defense community, and this bibliography is a good place to begin research on this subject.

908 *The United States in East Asia: A Historical Bibliography.* Edited by Jessica S. Brown and Susan K. Kinnell. Santa Barbara, CA: ABC-Clio, 1985. ISBN 0–87436–452–3.

This bibliography provides access to journal articles on U.S. involvement in East Asia published from 1973 to 1984. There are 1,176 article abstracts in this work, which have been culled from the ABC-Clio history database. Subject and author indexes make this bibliography easy to use. This bibliography is only of marginal interest to security specialists because of its historical rather than international politics orientation.

Databooks, Handbooks, and Sourcebooks

909 *L'Année strategique: Forces armées dans le monde, analyses geopolitiques, les nouvelles donnes stratégiques.* Edited by Pascal Boniface. Paris: Editions Maritimes et d'Outre-mer, 1985. 378pp.

Worldwide geopolitical and strategic realities in the mid-1980s are examined in this sourcebook. Beginning with Europe, but extending to every political entity, population size and military forces are examined for characteristics. This sourcebook also includes a series of strategic maps and statistical tables on military forces and weapons systems. Sources such as this provide a mass of useful data, but this book is not as easy to use or as authoritative as other publications in the field.

910 *Arms Production in the Third World.* Edited by Michael Brzoska and Thomas Ohlson. London: Taylor and Francis, 1986. 391pp. ISBN 0–85066–341–5.

Indigenous arms production in the Third World is the subject of this sourcebook. After an overview of arms production among the developing countries, each country's arms industry is analyzed for current and future production trends. This publication has gathered most of its data from SIPRI's computerized databases on the production and trade in major conventional weapons. Both this source and the database from which it derives are special resources available to researchers in the field of international security.

911 Ball, Nicole. *Third-World Security Expenditure: A Statistical Compendium.* Stockholm: Swedish National Defence Research Institute, 1983.

The Swedish Agency for Research Cooperation with Developing Countries (SAREC) sponsored this statistical analysis of Third World security expenditures. It covers the military expenditures of forty-eight countries using the UN reporting matrix. Despite a few gaps caused by lack of available information, this publication contains statistical data from the years between 1950 and 1980. This sourcebook is a major contribution to the field.

912 Bellany, Ian. *Nuclear Vulnerability Handbook: Ready Reckoner.* Lancaster, England: University of Lancaster, 1981. 174pp.

This handbook consists of log tables on the statistical probability of silo survival in the event of a nuclear attack. After a brief introduction explaining the tables, the book is divided into sections on attacking warhead reliability compared to point target hardness. It is published under the auspices of the Centre for the Study of Arms Control and International Security at the University of Lancaster, England. This handbook is an invaluable source for anyone interested in silo survival.

913 *Border and Territorial Disputes,* 2d ed. Edited by Alan J. Day. London: Longman, 1987. 462pp. ISBN 0–8103–2543–8.

The aim of this publication is to trace current unresolved border and territorial issues between states around the world. A total of eighty present or potential situations have been studied after a determination that each had territorial and/or political significance. It is particularly helpful for historical antecedents of current disputes. This publication is the best sourcebook of its type on the market.

914 *Documents on the Israeli-Palestinian Conflict, 1967–1983.* Edited by Yehuda Lukacs. Cambridge, England: Cambridge University Press, 1984. 247pp. ISBN 0–521–26795–1.

The International Center for Peace in the Middle East published this sourcebook in response to requests from the Israeli Knesset for a documentary history of the Israeli-Palestinian conflict. The book consists of key documents and statements of the respective parties to the conflict from 1967 to 1983. Emphasis is placed on presenting those documents most frequently cited by both antagonists and scholars. This sourcebook has documents and statements difficult to find in other sources.

915 Levie, Howard S. *The Code of International Armed Conflict.* 2 vols. London: Oceana Publications, 1986. ISBN 0–379–20803–2.

This two-volume set brings together the rules and regulations for the conduct of war. All of the items contained in these volumes are laws of war, which may be considered to have a valid international basis. Each citation provides the rule, the source, and a commentary. This source is easy to use and the most recent update of the code for the conduct of war.

916 *The North Atlantic Treaty Organisation: Facts and Figures,* 10th ed. Brussels: NATO Information Service, 1981. 380pp.

Now in its tenth edition, this publication is the official handbook of NATO activities. While it is filled with facts on the organization and the workings of NATO, the handbook's most useful function is in providing background material for studies on NATO. This is only a marginal source for advanced researchers but is acceptable for the beginner.

917 Schmid, Alex P. *Soviet Military Interventions since 1945*. New Brunswick, NJ: Transaction Books, 1985. 223pp. ISBN 0–88738–063–8.

This sourcebook surveys about fifty cases of alleged Soviet interventions in the post–World War II era. Ten cases have been isolated for a more in-depth treatment. These interventions have been divided into intrabloc, interbloc, and extrabloc conflicts. It is in the epilogue, where the author uses charts on the various types of interventions, that this publication makes its contribution.

918 *Treaties and Related Documents*. Vol. 6 of *Benedict on Admiralty*. New York: Matthew Bender, 1985.

This six-volume set contains all international agreements and treaties regarding maritime affairs. It has the text of each agreement and the date that this agreement entered into force. The information in this publication is invaluable for any study on maritime affairs or incidents on the high seas. Researchers will find this source contains information on maritime affairs difficult to find in other sources.

Dictionaries

919 *The Encyclopaedic Dictionary of International Law*. Edited by Clive Parry and John P. Grant. New York: Oceana, 1986. 564pp. ISBN 0–379–20828–8.

This dictionary provides legal definitions of the key terms and concepts in international law. Each term is given the legal definition, followed by court cases that have determined the usage. This dictionary is excellent for background information on international security subjects.

920 Plano, Jack C., and Roy Olton. *The International Relations Dictionary*, 4th ed. Santa Barbara, CA: ABC-Clio, 1988. 446pp. ISBN 0–87436–477–9.

Now in its fourth edition, this dictionary has been updated to include new material. Entries are grouped into subject-matter chapters to facilitate usage with international relations textbooks. The authors have selected only those terms that they consider most pertinent to an understanding of international relations. Entries are cross-referenced, and the work also contains a comprehensive index. This dictionary provides basic terms on international relations usage and is recommended for high school and undergraduate levels.

Digests

921 *Foreign Broadcast Information Service Daily Reports: Asia and Pacific, Eastern Europe, Middle East and Africa, South Asia and Western Europe*. Springfield, VA: National Technical Information Service, 1977– .

The Foreign Broadcast Information Service (FBIS) monitors foreign radio and television broadcasts, news agency transmissions, newspapers, and periodicals and publishes the highlights in these daily reports. It is an invaluable source in understanding informed public opinion from around the world. Paper copy is so expensive that most libraries acquire it on microfiche. No other source covers the information that this digest contains.

922 *IRCCS Bulletin: The Contemporary World through the Prism of the Soviet Press.* Jerusalem: International Research Center on Contemporary Society, 1985– .

This digest is a monthly survey of selected topics of current interest in the Soviet press. Each issue traces a trend or highlights a feature of Soviet domestic and/or foreign policy. A team of Soviet experts compiles this survey under the supervision of the International Research Center on Contemporary Society, Jerusalem. While this source has a distinct orientation, once this viewpoint is understood it can be used profitably.

923 *Joint Publication Research Service.* Washington, DC: National Technical Information Service, 1957– .

The National Technical Information Service publishes this series of political, economic, and technical translations from foreign sources for the research needs of the government and the U.S. scholar. While most of the translations are made from the communist media, Western Europe, Latin America, and Asia are also covered. Of particular interest to scholars working on international security topics are Worldwide Reports' Nuclear Development Proliferation; China Serials; Political, Sociological and Military Affairs; and the USSR Serials' Military Affairs. While there is about a four-month lag time between the date of original publication and the arrival of these translations, the end result is worth the wait.

924 *The Middle East Clipboard.* Washington, DC: American Educational Trust, 1984– . $395.

Produced by the American Educational Trust, this publication is the most comprehensive newspaper clipboard service on the Middle East. Each weekly issue has from 125 to 150 clippings selected from U.S., British, and Middle Eastern publications. It also has a brief executive report on the top issues of the week. This clipboard service is expensive, but Middle East scholars and students will appreciate this publication.

925 *The Soviet Union and the Middle East: A Monthly Summary and Analysis of the Soviet Press.* Jerusalem: Soviet and East European Research Centre of the Hebrew University, 1975– . ISSN 0334–4142. $15.

Seven Soviet newspapers are reviewed for contents dealing with Soviet–Middle East policy—*Pravda, Izvestiia, Komsonol'skaia pravda, Kransnaia avezda, Trud, Sovetskaia Rossiia,* and *Literaturnaia gazeta.* Specific references to a position taken by a newspaper make this press summary service an invaluable resource in determining the outlines of official Soviet policy in the Middle East.

926 *Update: Mideast.* Monthly Press and Documents Review. New York: Claremont Research and Publications Institute, 1984– . ISSN 0742–7840. $75.

This monthly review of Middle East and North African issues is a product of the Claremont Research and Publications Institute. It provides a collection of information from newspapers, magazines, and journals from U.S. and British sources. Special features are a chronology of the month's happenings and a limited number of translations of announcements and/or press conferences. While this source has its uses, the coverage is superficial.

Directories

927 *Directory Guide of European Security and Defense Research.* Edited by Luc Reychler and Robert Rudney. Leuven, Belgium: Leuven University Press, 1985. 376pp. ISBN 90–6186–164–0.

This research directory contains information about and reference material on over two hundred research centers in nineteen European countries. The authors believe that increased communication and cooperation among European research centers will stimulate research on defense, disarmament, and security subjects. This directory was published under the auspices of the Division of International Relations at the Catholic University of Leuven, Belgium. This directory gives the addresses and specialties of these institutes, allowing scholars to contact research centers of interest to them.

928 Wilson, Rodney. *The Arab World: An International Statistical Directory.* Boulder, CO: Westview Press, 1984. 176pp. ISBN 0–81330–095–9.

Seventeen Arab states are profiled in this statistical directory. There are over one hundred tables derived from national statistical sources along with another thirty-five tables based on international sources. This directory serves as a good introductory guide for comparing the economic and financial structures of the Arab world.

Guidebooks

929 Arkin, William M. *Research Guide to Current Military and Strategic Affairs.* Washington, DC: Institute for Policy Studies, 1981. 232pp. ISBN 0–89758–025–7.

The author, a former army intelligence analyst and a senior staff analyst at the Center for Defense Information, presents an impressive guide through the tangle of military and strategic affairs. Although most attention is devoted to U.S. government and military affairs, there is also material on worldwide military and strategic issues. Another useful feature is a listing of reference tools and treatment of current issues and events. Every collection has room for a research guide of this caliber.

930 Campbell, Christy. *Nuclear Facts: A Guide to Nuclear Weapon Systems and Strategy.* London: Hamlyn, 1984. 192pp. ISBN 0–6003–8522–1.

Each of the nuclear powers has been analyzed and projections have been made on each country's future strategic and technological developments in this guidebook. This book is an update of the author's *War Facts Now* (London: Fontana Paperbacks, 1982). Although the author maintains that this is a book of information and not of opinion, his selection of data involves editorial discretion. Nevertheless, researchers and the general public will find this guidebook worth examining.

931 Kuniholm, Bruce R. *The Palestinian Problem and United States Policy: A Guide to Issues and References.* Claremont, CA: Regina Books, 1986. 157pp. ISBN 0–941690–18–0.

This guidebook combines an essay on the Palestinian question and a bibliography of sources on the Palestinian problem. The author of the essay characterizes the problem as a clash between Israel's search for security and the Palestinian quest for self-determination. U.S. policy has been that a mutually beneficial compromise is possible, but only if the United States can persuade Israel that the West Bank territories should comprise a Palestinian state. Both the essay and the bibliography form a solid contribution to the field of Middle East security.

932 Kuniholm, Bruce R. *The Persian Gulf and United States Policy: A Guide to Issues and References.* Claremont, CA: Regina Books, 1984. 220pp. ISBN 0–941690–12–1.

This book is a combination of an analysis of U.S. policy toward the Persian Gulf region and a bibliography of sources on the strategic issues of this region. The analysis centers around the slowness of U.S. strategic thinkers to consider the strategic importance of the Persian Gulf and the lack of agreement on a strategic policy. English language sources on U.S. policy toward the Persian Gulf region up to January 1984 are emphasized. Both the analysis and the bibliography are contributions to the literature on the subject, but both appear incomplete.

933 Ornstein, Norman. *Who Decides: A Citizen's Guide to Government Decision-Making on Nuclear War.* Washington, DC: Common Cause, 1984. 36pp.

Common Cause issued this short guidebook for the general public to understand the political decision-making process for starting a nuclear war. The author explains that the U.S. system is complicated by conflicting political agendas, but that there are avenues through which U.S. citizens can become part of the decision-making process. Each institution from Congress to the presidency is examined for ways to influence decision making. This short guidebook is a direct-action source that the general reader will find instructive.

934 Sedacca, Sandra. *Up in Arms: A Common Cause Guide to Understanding Nuclear Arms Policy.* Washington, DC: Common Cause, 1984. 130pp. ISBN 0–91438–901–7.

A senior research associate at Common Cause produced this guidebook on nuclear arms policy. It seeks to give the average U.S. citizen information about the terminology, strategies and tactics, and arguments of the nuclear arms debate. The format is to present material on all aspects of the problem to encourage the reader to become more active in the politics of the nuclear question. This guidebook is one of the more informative sources on this subject available to the general reader.

Hearings

935 House Committee on Foreign Affairs. U.S. Congress. *The Soviet Role in Asia.* Washington, DC: U.S. Government Printing Office, 1983. 576pp.

Seven hearings on the Soviet role in Asia were held between July and October 1983. Statements and documents from witnesses surveyed current and future Soviet ambitions in the various Asian regions. The consensus of the Soviet security experts was that the Soviet Union will continue to play an active role in Asian politics. These hearings constitute an important source of viewpoints for researchers on this subject.

Journals

936 *AEI Foreign Policy and Defense Review*. Washington, DC: American Enterprise Institute for Public Policy Research, 1979– . ISSN 0264–0643. $12.

Formerly the *AEI Defense Revjew*, this bimonthly journal provides a forum for an examination of U.S. foreign policy. Although the original review was devoted mostly to articles on defense policy concerns, the scope has changed recently to more writings on foreign policy subjects. Each issue has a theme and includes one or more articles written by distinguished authorities in the foreign policy field.

937 *Australian Outlook: The Australian Journal of International Affairs*. Canberra: Australian Institute of International Affairs, 1946– . ISSN 0004–9913. $20.

The Australian Institute of International Affairs sponsors this monthly journal as its official forum for encouraging scholarship on Australia's role in international affairs. It also provides a place where Australian government officials can test proposals and where scholars can criticize these proposals. By combining scholarship with policy making, this journal serves a useful function in determining the outlines of past and future Australian foreign policy.

938 *Comparative Strategy: An International Journal*. New York: Crane, Russak, 1978– . ISSN 0149–5933. $48.

The primary objective of this quarterly journal is to articulate significant foreign policy issues and to disseminate these issues to the academic, research, government, and business communities. It is published by the Strategic Studies Center and is intended to examine international strategic issues from a range of political, military, and economic perspectives. The articles are of a high quality, and the authors examine important questions of international strategy. Both the quality and the scope of the articles make this journal the best of its type on the market.

939 *Conflict: All Warfare Short of War: An International Journal*. New York: Crane, Russak, 1979– . ISSN 0149–5941. $60.

This quarterly journal is an effort to bridge the gap between information provided by the press and the specialized literature of research institutions on the subject of international hostilities. Despite limiting itself to covering conflicts without the formal declaration of war, there is enough scholarly interest on quasi-wars for two or three quality articles a quarter. This journal fills a narrow subject niche but fulfills its function well.

940 *Conflict Quarterly*. Fredericton, Canada: Centre for Conflict Studies, 1981– . ISSN 0227–1311. $15.

This Canadian journal is published quarterly under the auspices of the Centre for Conflict Studies, University of New Brunswick. It features medium-length scholarly articles on international and internal conflict subjects. Each issue contains selected book reviews and a list of books recently received. This publication is another solid journal in the field but offers little to distinguish it from its contemporaries.

941 *Contemporary Southeast Asia*. Singapore: Institute of Southeast Asian Studies, 1979– . ISSN 0129–797X. $16.

Problems of economic, political, and social development in Southeast Asia are addressed in this quarterly journal. International security topics appear in every issue, but more important than these timely articles for researchers in Southeast Asian security is the publication of this region's international agreements. This journal is the best publication of its type on Southeast Asian affairs.

942 *Foreign Affairs.* New York: Council of Foreign Relations, 1922– . ISSN 0015–7120. $22.

This journal is the leading establishment forum for writings on U.S. and international foreign policy. Periodically it provides short reviews of books on international relations topics, lists of source materials for further research, and chronologies of events in different subject areas. This journal appears five times a year and is a must for any serious arms control and/or international security collection.

943 *FPI International Report.* New York: Free Press International, 1981– . $80.

Features of international significance are the subjects of this newsletter produced by the Free Press International. It gives background briefings on events of strategic significance in a concise eight- to ten-page format. There are several feature articles followed by summaries of events on the international scene. This publication has a variety of useful information but a hefty price tag.

944 *International Security.* Cambridge, MA: MIT Press, 1976– . ISSN 0162–2889. $48.

The Center for Science and International Affairs, Harvard University, sponsors this quarterly journal, which publishes high-grade articles on international security problems. Each issue has substantive articles of interest both to arms control and international security researchers. A special feature is the section on policy focus, where short statements from a variety of commentators outline the parameters of a controversy. It serves as the leading journal for research in the international security field.

945 *International Security Review.* Boston, VA: Center for International Security Studies of the American Security Council Foundation, 1975– . ISSN 0191–8028. $14.

This quarterly journal contains articles in the field of international security. It is a product of the conservative Center for International Security Studies of the American Security Council Foundation, and the writings reflect this conservative political orientation. The articles are worth reading both for their ideas and research perspective.

946 *ISSUP Strategic Review: Strategiese Oorsig.* Pretoria, South Africa: Institute for Strategic Studies, 1977– . ISSN 0250–1961. $22.

Published by the Institute for Strategic Studies at the University of Pretoria, South Africa, this review serves as a sounding board for articles on strategic issues dealing with South African security. Each issue has three or four short articles on strategic issues concerning South Africa, Africa, and the surrounding ocean areas. Although most articles are written from a pro–South African strategic viewpoint, the majority of the authors are American.

947   *The Jerusalem Journal of International Relations.* Jerusalem: Magnes Press, 1975– . ISSN 0363–2865. $25.

All aspects of international politics are featured in this Israeli journal. This quarterly specializes in the politics of small- and medium-sized states and theoretical model application to the Middle East conflict. Occasionally, special issues on selected international problems also appear. This journal is a product of the Leonard Davis Institute for International Relations at the Hebrew University of Jerusalem and is the best journal of its type from the Middle East.

948   *Journal of Asian-Pacific and World Perspectives.* Honolulu: Asian-Pacific Services Institute, 1977– . $25.

Each semiannual issue of this journal on Asian-Pacific affairs has a theme that is used to solicit articles. The end product is a journal with four or five quality articles organized around the theme. Published under the sponsorship of the Asian-Pacific Services Institute, Honolulu, Hawaii, this journal is a good place to locate current research on Asian-Pacific affairs.

949   *Millennium: Journal of International Studies.* Oxford, England: Martin Robertson, 1971– . ISSN 0305–8298. $47.50.

Historical and theoretical articles on international affairs characterize this scholarly journal, which appears three times a year. Besides excellent articles, each issue contains excellent full-length book reviews on the most significant works in the field. Published under the auspices of the London School of Economics, this journal contains articles of lasting value for most researchers.

950   *Orbis: A Journal of World Affairs.* Philadelphia: Foreign Policy Research Institute, 1957– . ISSN 0030–4387. $35.

Quality scholarly articles on arms control, disarmament, and international affairs are published in this quarterly journal. It also has excellent review essays and brief reviews of publications. Sponsored by the Foreign Policy Research Institute in Philadelphia, this publication is another solid journal in the international security field.

951   *Strategic Review.* Cambridge, MA: United States Strategic Institute, 1973– . ISSN 0091–6846. $15.

This quarterly journal was established by the U.S. Strategic Institute to contribute to the understanding of U.S. foreign policy and national defense. It provides a forum for an exchange of ideas on U.S. foreign policy objectives. The publication's editorial policy and its contributors tend to reflect the strategic views of the U.S. government.

952   *Stratégique: revue trimestrielle de recherches et d'études stratégiques.* Paris: Fondation pour les Études de Défense Nationale, 1979– .

This journal's purpose is to study different international strategic realities. Although writings on French strategic concerns predominate, the journal aims to specialize in international strategic questions. It is a publication of the Foundation for National Defense Studies, Paris. Most of the quality French research on international security appears in this journal.

953   *The Washington Quarterly: a Review of Strategic and International Issues.* Washington, DC: Center for Strategic and International Studies of Georgetown University, 1977– . ISSN 0163–660X. $35.

Few journals have a more impressive array of contributors than this quarterly review of strategic and international issues. Its strength lies in its articulation of U.S. strategic and defense postures by U.S. government spokespersons and independent scholars. Publication of an occasional White Paper on a foreign policy issue is another speciality of this journal.

954 *World Politics: A Quarterly Journal of International Relations.* Princeton, NJ: Princeton University Press, 1948– . ISSN 0043–8871. $25.

Each issue of this publication contains scholarly articles on different aspects of international relations and comparative politics. Articles are published from a variety of sources, and each topic is covered in depth. Particularly useful are the review essays on selected books. This publication is one of the top journals in the international relations field.

Newsletters

955 *IDAF News Notes.* Cambridge, MA: United States Committee of the International Defense and Aid Fund for Southern Africa, n.d.

The International Defense and Aid for Southern Africa (IDAF) publishes this newsletter to publicize events in South Africa. Its antiapartheid position is defended in numerous short articles. A bimonthly chronology of South African politics is printed in each issue. Both the current data on South Africa and the viewpoints represented in the articles make this newsletter a useful source.

956 *Strategic and Defence Studies Centre Newsletter.* Canberra: Australian National University, ca. 1980– .

The Strategic and Defence Studies Centre, Canberra, produces this newsletter which chronicles the research activities and the personnel changes of the centre. Although most of the research of this think tank concerns Southeastern Pacific strategic and defense issues, its articles cover international issues from all areas of the world. This newsletter is a good source for researchers interested in Australian and Oceania security concerns.

Papers

957 Jaffee Center for Strategic Studies. *Papers.* Tel Aviv: Tel Aviv University, 1977– .

These papers come at regular intervals from the Israeli think tank, the Jaffee Center for Strategic Studies, Tel Aviv. The objective of the center is to contribute to the knowledge on strategic subjects and to promote public understanding of matters of Israeli and international security. Each publication represents the findings and the assessments of the center's research staff.

958 *PSIS Occasional Papers.* Geneva: Programme for Strategic and International Security Studies, 1980– .

The Programme for Strategic and International Security Studies, Geneva, Switzerland, is active in publishing a series of occasional papers on strategic and international security issues. Between three and four papers appear a year at irregular intervals. These studies are lengthy and cover a variety of international subjects in depth.

Strategic Atlases

959 Chaliand, Gerard, and Jean-Pierre Rageau. *A Strategic Atlas: Comparative Geopolitics of the World's Powers*, 2d ed. New York: Harper and Row, 1985. 224pp. ISBN 0–06015–387–3.

This work was originally published in France under the title *Atlas strategique* in 1983. It has been updated, and its purpose is to delineate the geopolitical forces at play on the international scene. Visual representation of geographical hotspots and statistical information make this source unique. This book is most valuable as an introduction for college-level coursework.

960 Freedman, Lawrence. *Atlas of Global Strategy*. London: Macmillan, 1985. 192pp. ISBN 0–333–8416–1.

This atlas presents an analysis of contemporary conflict and military strategy through the use of graphs, maps, and pictures. Although the author claims that this publication is not a straightforward reference work, the information contained in it makes it a first-class reference source. This atlas should reside in every research collection on international security.

Textbooks

961 *The Arms Race and Nuclear War*. Edited by William M. Evan and Stephen Hilgartner. Englewood Cliffs, NJ: Prentice-Hall, 1987. 342pp. ISBN 0–13–046301–9.

The risks of nuclear war are traced in detail in this textbook of readings. Both classic works and more recent writings have been included for a well-rounded collection. Different perspectives have also been selected to provide the reader with a variety of viewpoints. This textbook can be recommended for college coursework at both the undergraduate and graduate levels.

962 Brown, Seyom. *The Causes and Prevention of War*. New York: St. Martin's Press, 1987. 274pp. ISBN 0–312–00473–7.

A foreign policy analyst addresses the problem of the causes and prevention of war. Only an integrated strategy for peace by means of morality, social structure, diplomacy, military capability, and military strategy can prevent war. By decreasing the likelihood of war, peace can be maintained. The most beneficial use of this book is as a text for introductory-level college coursework.

963 *Choices: A Unit on Conflict and Nuclear War*. Washington, DC: National Education Association, 1983. 144pp. ISBN 0–8106–1425–1.

In cooperation with the Massachusetts Teachers Association and the National Education Association, the Union of Concerned Scientists has produced this textbook for junior and senior high students. Fundamental questions about conflict, war, and nuclear weapons are posed for the benefit of the students. Excellent illustrations and good appendices full of data make this textbook a recommended source for this age student. Teachers will find this textbook most useful for social science units.

964 Schloming, Gordon C. *American Foreign Policy and the Nuclear Dilemma*. Englewood Cliffs, NJ: Prentice-Hall, 1987. 284pp. ISBN 0–13–026725–2.

The author envisaged this book on U.S. foreign policy and nuclear arms as a way to present complex issues to the general public. His thesis is that the United States has failed to solve the basic problems of our national security by pursuing mistaken foreign policy options. The United States has to reorder its priorities and stand for self-determination, human rights, and arms control. This book's best function is for textbook use in introductory courses in college, or honors-level coursework in high school.

965 Smoke, Richard. *National Security and the Nuclear Dilemma: An Introduction to the American Experience.* Reading, MA: Addison-Wesley, 1984. 271pp. ISBN 0–201–16420–5.

This textbook on national security and the nuclear question is an outgrowth of an earlier monograph entitled "National Security Affairs" in *Handbook of Political Science* (Reading, MA: Addison-Wesley, 1975). It has been revised and updated for the 1980s, but the material still retains the handbook format. This book is most useful for introductory courses dealing with national security problems.

966 Stover, William James. *International Conflict Simulation: Playing Statesmen's Games,* 3d ed. Bristol, IN: Wyndham Hall Press, 1985. 57pp. ISBN 0–932269–27–3.

This book is an instructional text on the simulation of international conflict designed for international relations courses. Computers and/or separate classrooms are not required. All the rules and background data are provided, but with a few changes different scenarios can be used. While the test is simple, it allows the students to learn by simulating a variety of international conflicts with a number of possible outcomes.

967 *Thinking about Nuclear Weapons: Analyses and Prescriptions.* Edited by Fred Holroyd. London: Croom Helm, 1985. 409pp. ISBN 0–7099–3775–X.

This book is an anthology of writings by some of the leading authorities on the nuclear weapons debate. It has been compiled for a course on nuclear weapons at the Open University, London. It has a diverse offering of articles on all aspects of the nuclear weapons debate. While this book of readings is more oriented toward the antinuclear side, it has its educational uses.

968 Yoder, Amos. *World Politics and the Causes of War since 1914.* Lanham, MD: University Press of America, 1986. 241pp. ISBN 0–8191–5045–2.

The major wars in the twentieth century have been analyzed in this textbook for the purpose of establishing a theory of the causes of wars. More than half of the wars studied here have taken place after 1945. Extreme nationalism as a cause and totalitarian regimes as a system are the prime causes for the starting of wars in this century. This book is too elementary for most purposes except for possible use in undergraduate courses.

969 Ziegler, David W. *War, Peace and International Politics,* 3d ed. Boston: Little, Brown, 1984. 458pp. ISBN 0–316–98772–7.

War as a central problem in international politics is the subject of this textbook. Other aspects such as peace and methods to control wars are considered, but war remains the central topic. This textbook is directed toward undergraduate courses, but the treatment has its uses for more advanced students. Both up-to-date material and a readable format make this textbook ideal for basic college coursework.

Monographs

970 Abt, Clark C. *A Strategy for Terminating a Nuclear War.* Boulder, CO: Westview Press, 1985. 253pp. ISBN 0–8133–7050–7.

Termination of nuclear war as a strategy for the prevention of nuclear conflicts is the subject of this book. Political acceptability, military feasibility, and psychological credibility are the tests for a successful nuclear war termination strategy. The author contends that determining war termination strategies may be the best method to deter nuclear wars. By examining different termination scenarios, this study makes a unique contribution both in its approach and in its conclusions.

971 *African Crisis Areas and U.S. Foreign Policy.* Edited by Gerald J. Bender, James S. Coleman, and Richard L. Sklar. Berkeley: University of California Press, 1985. 373pp. ISBN 0–520–05548–9.

American foreign policy toward Africa is the subject of these essays, most of which were prepared for a conference at UCLA. The habit of U.S. policymakers to subordinate U.S. African policies within the dictates of an anti-communist and anti-Soviet strategy is critiqued in most of these essays. Primary emphasis, however, is devoted to analyzing past and present crisis spots in Africa. Solid scholarship characterizes the articles in this book.

972 Ahsan, Syed Akhtar. *Strategic Concepts of the Indian Ocean.* Maidstone, England: George Mann Books, 1981. 184pp. ISBN 0–7041–0204–8.

That the Indian Ocean has assumed a greater strategic role because of its location near oil-producing states is the thesis of this book by a Pakistani author. Both Soviet and U.S. naval strategists have become aware of the strategic importance of the Indian Ocean. Any direct intervention by a great power would entail the danger of starting a third world war. The author presents a case for the strategic importance of the Indian Ocean that goes counter to many Western strategists, who have difficulty deciding its role.

973 Albinski, Henry S. *The Australian-American Security Relationship: A Regional and International Perspective.* New York: St. Martin's Press, 1981. 257pp. ISBN 0–312–06119–6.

The special security relationship between Australia and the United States is analyzed in this book. Most of the material covers the period of the Carter administration in the United States and the Fraser government in Australia. Relations between the two powers on security matters have been close except for several incidents during the Whitlam government, and current policy on both sides will continue this relationship. This book will be of interest only to those concerned with Pacific security issues.

974 Allen, Philip M. *Security and Nationalism in the Indian Ocean: Lessons from the Latin Quarter Islands.* Boulder, CO: Westview Press, 1987. 260pp. ISBN 0–8133–7171–6.

A former foreign service officer turned academic examines the strategic position of the Indian Ocean's Latin Quarter Islands. These islands are Madagascar, Mauritius, the Seychelles, the Comoros, and the French Overseas Department of Reunion. The author concludes that domestic, national, and international rivalries combine to make this a volatile region. This book covers a strategically important but neglected part of the world.

975 *Alliance Security: NATO and the No-First-Use Question.* Edited by John D. Steinbruner and Leon V. Sigal. Washington, DC: Brookings Institution, 1983. 222pp. ISBN 0–8157–8117–2.

U.S. and European scholars critique the possible adoption by NATO of the no-first-use of nuclear weapons policy. This issue calls into question NATO's past and current nuclear deterrence doctrine. These contributors propose a modest modification of NATO's nuclear policy, but they are reluctant to recommend adoption of the no-first-use doctrine. This book reveals the depth of feeling produced by the proposal of a no-first-use recommendation.

976 Allison, Graham T., Albert Carnesale, and Joseph S. Nye. *Hawks, Doves and Owls: An Agenda for Avoiding Nuclear War.* New York: Norton, 1985. 282pp. ISBN 0–393–01995–0.

The authors of these papers concentrate on the problem of avoiding a nuclear war between the United States and the Soviet Union. Various scenarios leading to hostilities are examined in depth, and the authors conclude with a series of recommendations that, in their view, will lessen the possibility of any crisis developing into a nuclear war. The authors have made a serious effort to understand the causes of warmaking, and their conclusions should be studied with respect.

977 Alves, Dora. *The ANZUS Partners.* Washington, DC: Center for Strategic and International Studies, 1984. 80pp. ISBN 0–89206–056–5.

The political and strategic relationships among Australia, New Zealand, and the United States are the subjects of this book. Most attention is devoted to the ANZUS Treaty of 1951 and the subsequent changes of interpretation by members of the alliance. While there has been a recent shift of geopolitical focus to the Indian Ocean–Persian Gulf area, the ANZUS alliance still has validity and continues to be both useful and necessary. Recent changes of relations between the ANZUS partners make this book appear dated, but the underlying realities of the alliance remain the same.

978 Amin, S. H. *Political and Strategic Issues in the Persian-Arabian Gulf.* Glasgow: Royston, 1984. 327pp. ISBN 0–946706–07–7.

The eight Gulf states are analyzed for political, strategic, and economic issues by the author. This area is considered as one of the regional hotspots upon which the world's economic and political stability depend. Rather than relying upon the United States or any other superpower, Gulf security and survival rests upon regional cooperation. This book serves as an excellent background source for further studies on strategic issues in the Persian-Arabian Gulf region.

979 *Analysing Conflict and Its Resolution: Some Mathematical Contributions.* Edited by P. G. Bennett. Oxford, England: Clarendon Press, 1987. 349pp. ISBN 0–19–853611–9.

These papers on the use of mathematics in analyzing conflicts and in the resolution of conflicts are a product of a 1984 conference held at Churchill College, Cambridge University. Papers on modeling, Lewis Fry Richardson's theories on arms races, and F. W. Lanchester's theories on battle are included. This book is intended to give insight into the extent to which mathematics can be used to study conflict. This work has limited appeal, but those interested in mathematical applications will find it fascinating.

980 Andren, Nils. *Essays on Swedish Security in the Nordic Environment.*
Stockholm: Swedish Defence Research Institute, 1982. 102pp.

Previously published in Swedish journals, the author presents this English
version of essays to inform others of Swedish security concerns. Despite
Sweden's neutral position, it is a part of the Nordic security bloc, if only by
geographical proximity. Sweden has a strong defense program and needs
such a program to retain its nonaligned status. These essays will help
researchers interested in Swedish foreign policy to understand its role in
Nordic security affairs.

981 Andriole, Stephen J., and Gerald W. Hopple. *Revolution and Political
Instability: Applied Research Methods.* London: Frances Pinter, 1984.
198pp. ISBN 0–86187–471–4.

The research literature on revolutions and political instability since 1960
is surveyed in this book. Special emphasis is given to basic and applied
quantitative and qualitative research, and the authors' assessment is
grounded upon a combination of accuracy, verifiability, and implementation
requirements. The conclusion is that political research methodologies favor
the use of qualitative methods over purely quantitative ones. This book is
most useful for international security researchers concerned with research
methods.

982 *The ANZAC Connection.* Edited by Desmond Ball. Sydney: Allen and
Unwin, 1985. 169pp. ISBN 0–86861–503–X.

The strategic situation of Australia and New Zealand in the 1980s is the
subject of this book of essays. While there have been differences over strategic and defense matters between these regional powers, the common cultural
heritage and geostrategic position facilitates cooperation. Listing of ANZAC
agreements and the Australian and New Zealand orders of battle are additional features of this book. Although the essays were written before New
Zealand's antinuclear stance, this book is an informative treatment of strategic situations of Australia and New Zealand in the 1980s.

983 *The Arab Gulf and the West.* Edited by B. R. Pridham. London: Croom
Helm, 1985. 251pp. ISBN 0–7099–4011–4.

These essays are the product of a 1984 symposium on the relations
between Arab Gulf states and the Western states, which was held at Exeter
University's Centre for Arab Gulf Studies. The purpose of this meeting was
to provide a forum for both Gulf and Western approaches to the economic
and security problems of the relationship. This exchange highlights the
differences between the two viewpoints. Differences of opinion over security
issues in this region by the participants make this volume a useful source for
security researchers.

984 Arbatov, Georgi A., and Willem Oltmans. *The Soviet Viewpoint.* New
York: Dodd, Mead, 1983. 219pp. ISBN 0–306–08058–8.

A Dutch security scholar interviews the director of the Institute of United
States and Canadian Studies, Moscow, and a member of the Central Committee, on the Soviet view of security affairs. His views are that the Soviet
policies in favor of détente, disarmament, and international cooperation are
the correct approaches, and he is critical of the U.S. return to Cold War
politics. The author is an articulate spokesperson for the Soviet position, and
his viewpoint should be noted.

985 *Armed Separatism in Southeast Asia.* Edited by Lim Joo-Jock and Vani S. Singapore: Institute of Southeast Asian Studies, 1984. 270pp. ISBN 9971–902–51–6.

Armed separatist movements in Southeast Asia as a cause of regional instability is the subject of this book of essays. Separatist struggles in Burma, Indonesia, the Philippines, and Thailand are studied in some depth. The conclusion is that the only serious armed separatist movements are located in frontier areas, and, considering the recent origins of these nation-states, the strength of these states against separatist movements is surprising. This book is a solid effort, mostly by Asian scholars, to provide a conceptual basis for understanding armed separatist movements in Southeast Asia.

986 Armellini, Antonio. *The Nature of the Soviet Regime and Its Fundamental Policy Objectives.* Brussels: Centre for European Policy Studies, 1983. 26pp.

This paper is an analysis of the Soviet power structure in the Soviet Union. The author, an Italian civil servant, maintains that the elevation of Yuri Andropov to Soviet leadership gives the West a political advantage in foreign policy dealings with the Soviets. Western policy needs to be coordinated to take advantage of this opportunity. This work could easily have been published several years later and the same thesis advanced with only name changes.

987 *Arms and the African: Military Influences on Africa's International Relations.* Edited by William J. Foltz and Henry S. Bienen. New Haven, CT: Yale University Press, 1985. 221pp. ISBN 0–300–03347–8.

The increased militarization of Africa's international relations is the subject of this book of essays. Arming of African countries from outside states has produced a volatile mixture of conflicting ideologies and territorial claims, culminating in obscure quarrels over territory that escalate into interstate conflicts. These essays detail these developments and the extent to which these conflicts attract superpower attention. The seven essays in this book make a major contribution to an understanding of security issues in Africa.

988 Aronson, Ronald. *Technological Madness: Towards a Theory of the Impending Nuclear Holocaust.* London: Menard Press, 1983. 24pp. ISBN 0–903400–86–3.

A psychological interpretation of the superpowers' reliance on nuclear weapons is the subject of this paper. The author insists that military and civilian reliance upon nuclear weapons reflects a kind of technological madness, revealed in the fantasy world of those in charge of this technology. This essay is a personal statement by the author expressing his fears of the political structure that is allowing this system to lead the world toward nuclear war.

989 Ashley, Richard K. *The Political Economy of War and Peace: The Sino-Soviet-American Triangle and the Modern Security Problematique.* London: Frances Pinter, 1980. 384pp. ISBN 0–903804–69–7.

The author analyzes the military rivalry and the balance of power between the People's Republic of China, the Soviet Union, and the United States by studying the political economy of each. Sophisticated modeling techniques of econometrics are utilized for long-term security trends. He concludes that these three powers have an interdependence, because of the dynamics of growth and lateral pressure. This book is an ambitious work, and it needs to be read despite some of its excesses of enthusiasm for the benefits of methodology.

990 *Asian Security in the 1980s: Problems and Policies for a Time of Transition.* Edited by Richard H. Solomon. Cambridge, MA: Oelgeschlager, Gunn and Hain, 1980. 324pp. ISBN 0–89946–037–2.

The Rand Corporation held a conference on East Asian security in 1979, and these papers are the result of this conference. Security specialists from Rand and from a variety of East Asian countries presented papers on Asian security issues for the 1980s. Special emphasis was given to rethinking U.S. policies in the Pacific theater. These twelve papers present a reassessment of East Asian security concerns at the beginning of the 1980s.

991 *The Atlantic Alliance: Perspectives from the Successor Generation.* Edited by Alan Platt. Santa Monica, CA: Rand Corporation, 1983. 189pp.

This book consists of eleven papers from a 1983 Rand Corporation–sponsored conference held in Santa Monica, California, on the future of the Atlantic alliance from the perspective of the postwar generation. Two issues dominated discussions at this conference: (1) the different U.S. and European perceptions of the Soviet Union; and (2) the growing role of domestic and economic forces in NATO countries. None of the differences of opinion, however, were serious enough for any of the participants to assume an anti-NATO stance. These essays and the discussion indicate the variety of opinions among NATO supporters.

992 Ausland, John C. *Nordic Security and the Great Powers.* Boulder, CO: Westview Press, 1986. 202pp. ISBN 0–8133–7189–9.

A U.S. specialist on Scandinavian affairs studies the interaction of the Nordic states with neighbors, allies, and potential foes. It has been the combination of a Soviet military and a belated NATO response that has disturbed the tranquility of the Scandinavian scene. Despite the popularity of the concept of a Nordic nuclear-free zone, the Nordic countries have no alternatives except to continue their current security policies. This book is a survey of the security concerns of the Nordic states, and it is a good source to begin study of this region.

993 *Avoiding Inadvertent War: Crisis Management.* Edited by Hilliard Roderick with Ulla Magnusson. Austin, TX: Lyndon B. Johnson School of Public Affairs, 1983. 184pp. ISBN 0–89940–005–1.

Crisis management and its application in avoiding an inadvertent war is the subject of this book of papers and discussions from a 1983 conference held at the University of Texas in Austin, Texas. The participants conclude that crisis management has been a neglected tool of U.S. national security policy, and there is a strong possibility that crisis control will be necessary in future U.S.-Soviet relations. Only by planning for future crises can the probability of inadvertent war be lessened. These papers and discussions present a solid case for the inclusion of crisis management in U.S. national security planning.

994 *Avoiding War in the Nuclear Age: Confidence-Building Measures for Crisis Stability.* Edited by John Borawski. Boulder, CO: Westview Press, 1986. 234pp. ISBN 0–8133–7141–4.

These essays are a serious effort to develop confidence-building measures (CBM) into stabilizing factors to prevent international crises and conflicts. CBM consists of a series of techniques designed to promote mutual trust in negotiating difficult issues. Only by CBMs is there a possibility of arms control. While this indirect approach toward arms control is obtuse, these essays present a novel way to envisage arms control in operation.

995 Ayoob, Mohammed. *Southwest Asia: Beginnings of a New Cold War.* Canberra: Strategic and Defence Studies Centre, 1981. 19pp. ISBN 0–86784–034–X.

This paper chronicles the shift of the revived Cold War between the Soviet Union and the United States from Europe to the northwestern quadrant of the Indian Ocean. The Iranian Revolution and Soviet intervention in Afghanistan have weakened the formerly strong position of the United States in Southwest Asia, which is caught in the middle of a superpower competition that threatens the stability of the region. This essay is a constructive look at the changing power structure in a vital region.

996 Babbage, Ross. *Rethinking Australia's Defence.* St. Lucia, Australia: University of Queensland Press, 1980. 312pp. ISBN 0–7022–1486–8.

The outgrowth of an Australian National University dissertation, this book reexamines many of the fundamentals of Australia's security policy. The author maintains that Australia can no longer depend upon the United States or Great Britain for assistance in case of future Australian commitments. This means that the forward defense concept is no longer a viable strategy for Australian defense. Such arguments for a new Australian defense policy are suggestive of the problem that medium-sized states have in international affairs.

997 *The Balance of Power in East Asia.* Edited by Michael Leifer. Houndmills, England: Macmillan, 1986. 157pp. ISBN 0–333–37992–6.

In this book of essays British scholars analyze the balance of power in East Asia in terms of contending and convergent interests of the superpowers and the regional states. East Asia remains a geographic junction of contending interests because no one state, even with client support, can exercise a dominating influence. There exists a balance of power in this region because actual and potential conflicts have been kept within a framework of constraint by the major powers. This book contains high-quality essays researchers in the field should consult.

998 Ball, George W., Edward J. Derwinski, and Philip L. Geyelin. *United States Policy in the Middle East.* Washington, DC: Center for Contemporary Arab Studies, 1984. 23pp.

This publication is an outgrowth of a panel discussion on the topic of U.S. policy options in the Middle East. Ball is extremely critical of U.S. support for the Israeli invasion of Lebanon and is not convinced that Lebanon has any political or strategic importance. Both Derwinski and Geyelin are less hostile toward U.S. policy in the Middle East. This booklet is important because it shows the variety of opinions on the Middle East by former and current U.S. government policymakers.

999 Barber, James, Jesmond Blumenfeld, and Christopher R. Hill. *The West and South Africa.* London: Routledge and Kegan Paul, 1982. 106pp. ISBN 0–7100–9232–6.

The dilemma facing Western governments in dealing with South Africa is the subject of this study. Dependence upon South African strategic materials by Great Britain, France, and the United States, and the geographical location of South Africa makes the Republic of South Africa vital to the West for strategic reasons. The authors propose that the Western powers ensure against disruptions in strategic minerals by stockpiling and conservation, and by applying pressure against the South African government to modify its regime away from apartheid. While none of the proposals in this book has much of a chance of altering the situation in South Africa, they reveal the poverty of ideas on this subject in the West.

1000 Barclay, Glen St. J. *Friends in High Places: Australian-American Diplomatic Relations since 1945.* Melbourne: Oxford University Press, 1985. 245pp. ISBN 0–19–554608–3.
The close diplomatic relationship between Australia and the United States since 1945 is chronicled in this book. Emphasis is placed more on the Australian side in its efforts to form a security alliance in the Pacific with the United States. This theme runs throughout the history of the ups and downs of diplomatic relations between the two Pacific powers. This book is a well-written standard diplomatic history by an Australian historian.

1001 Barnet, Richard J. *Real Security: Restoring American Power in a Dangerous Decade.* New York: Simon and Schuster, 1981. 127pp. ISBN 0–671–43172–2.
The author presents his views on the decline of U.S. power in the preceding decade and the ways to restore U.S. influence in the world. U.S. dominance lasted only twenty-six years, a period wasted by the United States in its failure to create greater world stability. Less use of military strategies and more attention to political and economic realities will restore much U.S. preeminence. This book is a thoughtful analysis of the ramifications of great-power status that most readers will find suggestive.

1002 Barnett, A. Doak. *The Making of Foreign Policy in China: Structure and Process.* Boulder, CO: Westview Press, 1985. 160pp. ISBN 0–8133–0232–3.
The author utilized recent contacts with China to arrange interviews with Chinese officials and party leaders to analyze the structure and process of foreign policy making in China. Since 1981–1982, China has adopted a middle-of-the-road position between the Soviet Union and the United States because Chinese leaders believe that this policy best serves China's interests. While this policy shift has been sponsored by current party leadership, it has also been supported by most Chinese foreign affairs professionals. This book is an excellent glimpse of foreign policy decision making in China.

1003 Barnett, A. Doak. *U.S. Arms Sales: The China-Taiwan Tangle.* Washington, DC: Brookings Institution, 1982. 70pp. ISBN 0–8157–0829–7.
The dispute between the United States and China over arms sales to Taiwan in the early 1980s is the subject of this monograph. Efforts were underway in 1980–1981 for the U.S. government to sponsor military hardware sales to China, but the issue of U.S. arms sales to Taiwan ended this initiative. The author believes that the United States should exercise restraint on arms sales both to China and to Taiwan, and, instead, concentrate on economic aid to China. This solid analysis of a touchy issue in

U.S.-China and U.S.-Taiwan relationships reveals the difficulty of any state reconciling its foreign policy objectives.

1004 Baugh, William H. *The Politics of Nuclear Balance: Ambiguity and Continuity in Strategic Policies.* New York: Longman, 1984. 276pp. ISBN 0–582–28423–6.

The author surveys the problems of the management of nuclear strategic balance in the 1980s and beyond. While management of strategic policy has become important in U.S. foreign and domestic politics, the lack of agreement on the parameters of the problem makes management difficult. Fear of Soviet nuclear supremacy seems to be the only constant in the debate. This book is both insightful and sobering, and it deserves a reading on both counts.

1005 Beilenson, Laurence W. *Survival and Peace in the Nuclear Age.* Chicago: Regnery/Gateway, 1980. 169pp. ISBN 0–89526–672–5.

This book is an eclectic essay on the strategy for the U.S. to survive in the nuclear age. The author maintains that the United States is a unique country whose adversaries are busy undermining its interests. While the United States has made foreign policy and military mistakes, dependence upon U.S. self-interest is the best policy. The arguments in this book are so disjointed that the points are hard to follow, and only the most dedicated readers will find the work of any but passing interest.

1006 Ben-Zvi, Abraham. *Alliance Politics and the Limits of Influence: the Case of the US and Israel, 1975–1983.* Jerusalem: Jaffee Center for Strategic Studies, 1984. 79pp. ISSN 0334–3642.

Diplomatic and security ties between Israel and the United States between 1975 and 1983 are examined in this book by an Israeli scholar. The author's conclusions are that U.S. administrations since 1975 have been unable to bring enough pressure on Israel to change Israeli policies. Superpower rivalry in the Middle East and Arab intransigence on peacemaking has made it difficult for U.S. administrations to mobilize domestic public opinion to pursue coercive policies against Israel. This study is an excellent example of objective scholarship on a delicate subject.

1007 Bergesen, Helge, Arild Moe, and Willy Ostreng. *Soviet Oil and Security Interests in the Barents Sea.* London: Frances Pinter, 1987. 144pp. ISBN 0–86187–689–X.

Three authors examine Arctic security issues and Soviet energy policy. The Soviets have conflicting oil and security needs in the Barents Sea region and will have to reconcile these needs before exploring for oil. Economic and political benefits of exporting oil will probably cause the Soviets to develop the energy resources of the Barents Sea area. This book treats a tricky subject with first-rate analysis.

1008 Best, Edward. *US Policy and Regional Security in Central America.* Aldershot, England: Gower, 1987. 182pp. ISBN 0–566–05383–7.

The regional security interests of the United States in Central America are examined in this monograph. U.S. policy calls for a stable isthmus ruled by centrist and democratic regimes free of Cuban and Soviet influence, but the Reagan administration remains reluctant to intervene in this region. Among the policy options available to the United States, only a political and military settlement offers any hope of success. This book is a realistic look at U.S. policy options, and both the text and conclusions will stimulate reader response.

1009 Betts, Richard K. *Nuclear Blackmail and Nuclear Balance.* Washington, DC: Brookings Institution, 1987. 240pp. ISBN 0–8157–0936–6.

A prominent security analyst in the Brookings Foreign Policy Studies Program examines case studies of U.S. and Soviet use of nuclear pressure in international confrontations. He asks the question, To what extent has nuclear blackmail ensured a nuclear balance and stable international relations? U.S. policy has been to use nuclear blackmail in crises more than the Soviets, but this policy has its foreign policy dangers. This book is an exceptional analysis of a complex subject.

1010 *Beyond Containment: Alternative American Policies toward the Soviet Union.* Edited by Aaron Wildavsky. San Francisco: ICS Press, 1983. 264pp. ISBN 0–917616–61–8.

Six leading foreign policy experts present their critiques of the U.S. policy of containment toward the Soviet Union, concluding that the policy of minimum containment has not worked in curtailing the aggressiveness of Soviet policies. Most of the authors recommend a U.S. policy beyond minimum containment, but only the editor argues for a strategy of maximal containment to stop Soviet aggressive tendencies at its borders. These essays give the reader a variety of options, all of which are directed toward containment of Soviet adventurism.

1011 Bonosky, Phillip. *Washington's Secret War against Afghanistan.* New York: International Publishers, 1985. 263pp. ISBN 0–7178–0618–9.

The charge that the United States is prolonging the war in Afghanistan as a way to weaken the Soviet Union is the thesis of this book. By marshalling all the evidence that he can locate in the Western press, the author argues that U.S. aid is the only reason the war in Afghanistan continues. Both the Carter and the Reagan administrations share the blame for this policy. While the author's treatment suffers from a distinct anti-U.S. viewpoint, the book is interesting for material on U.S. aid to Afghanistan.

1012 Brams, Steven J. *Superpower Games: Applying Game Theory to Superpower Conflict.* New Haven, CT: Yale University Press, 1985. 176pp. ISBN 0–33–03323–0.

The author uses game theory as a basis for understanding superpower rivalry. Three different sets of games are considered: (1) deterrence games; (2) arms-race games; and (3) verification games. His conclusion is that game theory captures a substantial part of the superpower rivalry processes and can serve as a framework for its analysis. This book is the best games-theory study on international security on the market.

1013 Brenchley, Frank. *Norway and her Soviet Neighbour: NATO's Arctic Frontier.* London: Institute for the Study of Conflict, 1982. 20pp.

The strategic geography of the Norway-USSR frontier near the Arctic Circle is examined in this short monograph. This border is the only NATO–Soviet Union frontier in Europe. Norway has to continue its firmness in dealing with the Soviet Union to discourage Soviet pressure and possible blackmail. This short monograph is a succinct analysis of the Norwegian-Soviet military balance in this region.

1014 *Buffer States in World Politics.* Edited by John Chay and Thomas E. Ross. Boulder, CO: Westview Press, 1986. 245pp. ISBN 0–8133–7264–X.

These essays on the buffer-state concept and its effect upon world political affairs are the results of papers presented at the 25th Annual Meeting of the International Studies Association, held in Atlanta, Georgia, in 1984. Buffer states refer to countries geographically and/or politically situated between larger powers whose role is to prevent war between the larger states. The authors conclude that buffer states still function in modern international relations, but that the concept needs to be broadened to reflect political situations. This book combines historical and contemporary examples to construct a theory, and it succeeds in serving as a model for such studies.

1015 Burton, John W. *Global Conflict: The Domestic Sources of International Crisis.* Brighton, England: Wheatsheaf Books, 1984. 194pp. ISBN 0–7108–0737–6.

The failure of power politics as a method of international behavior and the influence of domestic political problems on the world system are the twin themes of this book. Problem solving and conflict resolution as means to solve international crises are emphasized. Human needs are the starting point in the consideration of any theory of behavior. The author attempts to reorient thinking on global conflict, but there is difficulty in following many of his points.

1016 Buszynski, Leszek. *SEATO: The Failure of an Alliance Strategy.* Singapore: Singapore University Press, 1983. 262pp. ISBN 9971–69–060–8.

The author chronicles the rise and collapse of the Southeast Asia Treaty Organization (SEATO) as an example of an alliance system in trouble. SEATO was formed as a counterpoint to NATO, but from the beginning the alliance masked differences over strategic interests among its member states. It was the U.S. disengagement from Indochina that brought about the eventual dismantling of SEATO. This study is an excellent example of a failure in alliance politics.

1017 Buszynski, Leszek. *Soviet Foreign Policy and Southeast Asia.* London: Croom Helm, 1986. 303pp. ISBN 0–7099–3221–9.

Soviet foreign policy objectives in Southeast Asia since 1969 are studied in this book. The Soviet-Vietnamese Treaty of 1978 has intensified Soviet strategic interests in Southeast Asia. This Soviet presence has caused the Reagan administration to work for a balance-of-power arrangement with the People's Republic of China and the Association of Southeast Asian Nations (ASEAN) countries. "Balanced" and "solid" are the characteristics that best describe this book.

1018 Butts, Kent Hughes, and Paul R. Thomas. *The Geopolitics of Southern Africa: South Africa as Regional Superpower.* Boulder, CO: Westview Press, 1986. 193pp. ISBN 0–8133–7261–5.

South Africa's role as the dominant force in Southern Africa and this region's increasing strategic importance to the West are studied in this book by a political scientist and an international minerals economist. The political instability of Southern Africa threatens the national security of the West and opens the way for Soviet expansion. Apartheid must be abolished, and all ethnic groups have to participate in the governance of South

Africa before South Africa can assume its rightful position as regional super-power. This book is a solid contribution to the study of Southern African security concerns.

1019 Buzan, Barry. *People, States, and Fear: the National Security Problem in International Relations.* Brighton, England: Wheatsheaf Books, 1983. 262pp. ISBN 0–7108–0101–7.

This book is an analysis of the concept of security and the role of this term in strategic studies. Three variants are studied—individual security, national security, and international security—because the concept of security demands a holistic perspective. This means that a systematic security policy needs a more stable base than it has at present. This book operates at a high level of abstraction, and only the most sophisticated readers will profit from reading it.

1020 Buzan, Barry, and Gowher Rizwi. *South Asian Insecurity and the Great Powers.* Houndmills, England: Macmillan, 1986. 257pp. ISBN 0–333–39012–1.

The international security problems of South Asia are viewed through the framework of regional security analysis. This system envisions an examination of the security situation of a single state and goes on to "build up a picture of the successive layers from internal to global that define both its security context and its security problem." The results of this analysis indicate that India and Pakistan will continue to balance out each other in this region, and that the great powers will reinforce this balance-of-power tendency by their policies. This book is an important contribution to the understanding of South Asian security issues.

1021 Calder, Nigel. *Nuclear Nightmares: An Investigation into Possible Wars.* New York: Viking Press, 1980. 168pp. ISBN 0–670–51820–4.

The author surveys the current knowledge on the possible outbreak and consequences of a nuclear war. Negotiated disarmament remains the chief hope of avoiding a nuclear war, but progress is continually sabotaged because of conflicting interests. His view is that it takes only one madman, one impatient politician or soldier, or one fool who misinterprets a crisis to start a nuclear war. This book is a personal look at prospects for a nuclear war, and both the analysis and the interpretation are at the level of the general reader.

1022 Calvert, Peter. *Revolution and International Politics.* London: Frances Pinter, 1984. 222pp. ISBN 0–86187–299–1.

Revolution and its role in international politics is the subject of this book. Revolution is the forcible overthrow of a government or regime, and this concept is studied here to learn ways to cope with revolutionary movements before and after the revolution. The major conclusion is that intervention by an outside state does not stop revolutions but strengthens the political control of the revolutionaries. This book is a major effort to understand revolutions on the international scene.

1023 Catudal, Honore M. *Nuclear Deterrence: Does it Deter?* London: Mansell, 1985. 528pp. ISBN 0–7201–1759–3.

This book is a study of the concept of nuclear deterrence and the evolution of various U.S. deterrence theories since World War II. Sixteen varieties of nuclear strategies have been considered by U.S. strategists over the years. The author concludes that there is a growing body of evidence that suggests that nuclear deterrence does not deter by altering the behavior of the intended adversary. This book is a significant addition to the literature of international security, providing a different approach to the study of deterrence.

1024 *Central America and the Western Alliance.* Edited by Joseph Cirincione. New York: Holmes and Meier, 1985. 238pp. ISBN 0–8419–1003–0.

These papers are the result of a 1984 conference on the role of Central America in the Western alliance held in Washington, DC, under the auspices of the Carnegie Endowment for International Peace and the International Institute for Strategic Studies, London. Participants from Central America joined those from NATO to present papers on Central American security issues. While differences of opinion on the strategic importance of Central America raged among the American authors, the European papers reflected the disenchantment and puzzlement over U.S. policies. Together these papers offer a strategic overview of the Central American situation with a range of options for future policymakers.

1025 Chadda, Maya. *Paradox of Power: The United States in Southwest Asia, 1973–1984.* Santa Barbara, CA: ABC-CLIO, 1986. 278pp. ISBN 0–87436–454–X.

The author examines U.S. policies toward Southwest Asia during the past three administrations. Chadda counters the arguments of conservative critics that the decline of U.S. military power has weakened its influence in Southwest Asia, claiming that this is a misconception. U.S. policies have worked in this region despite several minor political setbacks. This book is one of the more objective works on the Middle East and the Persian Gulf on the market.

1026 *Challenges to the Western Alliance: an International Symposium on the Changing Political, Economic and Military Setting.* Edited by Joseph Godson. London: Times Books Ltd., 1984. 208pp. ISBN 0–7230–0264–9.

This book is a collection of essays from the London *Times* and from a 1984 conference in Brussels, Belgium, sponsored by Georgetown University's Center for Strategic and International Studies (CSIS) on the topic of the survival of NATO as a viable alliance. Most of the essays were written by government leaders and security specialists. The contributions are short statements on the threats to NATO from the Soviet Union and about the threat of internal disunity. There is little new information contained in these essays, making this book of marginal interest to security specialists.

1027 Chester, Edward W. *The United States and Six Atlantic Outposts: The Military and Economic Considerations.* Port Washington, NY: Kennikat Press, 1980. 260pp. ISBN 0–8046–9236–X.

The military and economic relationship between six Atlantic island states and the United States is studied in this book. Each of the states—the Azores, the Bahamas, Bermuda, Iceland, Greenland, and Jamaica—is examined for the impact of U.S. bases. This book shows the marginal economic and political impacts that U.S. bases have on host countries.

1028 Child, Jack. *Geopolitics and Conflict in South America: Quarrels among Neighbors.* New York: Praeger, 1985. 196pp. ISBN 0–03–001453–0.

The impact of geopolitical thinking in South America is the subject of this book. Geopolitical thinking became popular among the larger military establishments of South America in the 1960s and 1970s, but in the middle 1980s the Falkland War cooled expansionist plans. Latin American states in the Southern Cone—Argentina, Bolivia, Brazil, Chile, Paraguay, and Uruguay—have been more susceptible to geopolitical schemes than their northern neighbors. This study's suggestion that conflicts could occur among the Southern Cone states makes this book's conclusions worth considering.

1029   Child, James W. *Nuclear War: The Moral Dimension.* New Brunswick, NJ: Transaction Books, 1986. 197pp. ISBN 0–912051–09–4.

In this book the author argues that strategic nuclear weapons have a moral purpose to preserve U.S. security, and that a creditable argument can be made to justify waging a defensive nuclear war. While every step should be taken to avoid nuclear war, the United States has a moral right to fight if attacked with nuclear weapons. This book gives the moral dimensions of the current U.S. position on nuclear war.

1030   *The China Question: Essays on Current Relations between Mainland China and Taiwan.* Edited by Yu San Wang. New York: Praeger, 1985. 164pp. ISBN 0–03–055379–X.

These essays are products of a 1983 conference of the International Studies Association (ISA) held in Mexico City, Mexico, and they deal with the competition between the People's Republic of China and Taiwan in the international arena. The key issue between the two governments remains reunification, but the inability of either state to compromise on its political system makes reunification unlikely. Taiwan will, therefore, continue its existence as a separate state with an independent foreign policy. This book presents solid articles on the interactions between the two states and serves as a useful source for the next crisis in this region.

1031   *China, the Soviet Union, and the West: Strategic and Political Dimensions in the 1980s.* Edited by Douglas T. Stuart and William T. Tow. Boulder, CO: Westview Press, 1982. 309pp. ISBN 0–86531–091–2.

The ramifications of the Sino-Soviet rift for the Western alliance are examined in this book of essays from the West's most respected Sinologists and Sovietologists. Most of the contributors concentrated on interpreting the events from 1978 to 1981 when Sino-Soviet relations were at their worst. The authors stress that the relations between China and the Soviet Union are in a state of flux but disagree on the long-term impact of this rivalry. This book is a major contribution to the security literature on the Sino-Soviet rivalry.

1032   Chubin, Shahram. *The Nature of Security Problems of Developing Countries: Intra-Regional Relations.* Geneva: Programme for Strategic and International Security Studies, 1984. 33 leaves.

This paper is a study of regional security arrangements among Third World countries. These security arrangements have the potential to prevent interstate conflicts, but in practice regional pacts have had serious weaknesses. Third World countries have flocked to regional pacts, but these security arrangements have been conservative in their approach to international security. This short paper is only an introduction to regional security pacts, but it is a solid start.

1033 Clark, Ian. *Limited Nuclear War: Political Theory and War Conventions.* Princeton, NJ: Princeton University Press, 1982. 266pp. ISBN 0–691–07644–8.

Limited nuclear war as an option in strategic doctrine is the subject of this book. The doctrine of limited nuclear warfare has been adopted by the United States since 1980, and the Soviet Union has made contingency plans based on this scenario. While the author outlines the restraints on this type of warfare, he points out that the weakness of present theory is the lack of a convincing theory of limitation. Dependence upon past political theorists and the complexity of the subject make this book stimulating but at times contradictory.

1034 Clark, Ian. *Nuclear Past, Nuclear Present: Hiroshima, Nagasaki and Contemporary Strategy.* Boulder, CO: Westview Press, 1985. 146pp. ISBN 0–8133–7049–3.

The relationship between modern nuclear strategy and the atomic bombings of Hiroshima and Nagasaki is the subject of this book. A set of false assumptions have come out of the use of nuclear weapons in 1945, assumptions that currently influence modern nuclear strategy. Nonrational political decision making was the true situation of the use of nuclear weapons in 1945, and this false picture is still with us in the deployment of nuclear weapons in the 1980s. This book is an excellent example of the use of a historical case study to delineate modern strategic thought.

1035 Cline, Ray S. *World Power Trends and U.S. Foreign Policy for the 1980s.* Boulder, CO: Westview Press, 1980. 228pp. ISBN 0–89158–917–1.

This book is the third comprehensive survey of the economic and military variables in the balance of world power by a former deputy director of the CIA. Major power elements are identified and measured on an overall scale, showing both strengths and weaknesses. The final assessment of perceived power of the top ten powers as of 1978 was as follows: the Soviet Union, the United States, Brazil, West Germany, Japan, Australia, China, France, the United Kingdom, and Canada. This book is a stimulating approach to understanding the world's balance of power.

1036 Clough, Ralph N. *Embattled Korea: the Rivalry for International Support.* Boulder, CO: Westview Press, 1987. 401pp. ISBN 0–8133–7324–7.

This book is a study of the national and international rivalry between North and South Korea. After a brief history of the division of Korea in the late 1940s, the author gives a solid treatment of the political and economic changes in the two Koreas from the mid-1950s to the 1980s. It is in the sections on the place of Korea in the superpower rivalry that this work makes its contribution to security literature. Its insight on the international status of Korea makes this work a good source on Far East politics.

1037 *The Common Security Interests of Japan, the United States and NATO.* By the Joint Working Group of the Atlantic Council of the United States and the Research Institute for Peace and Security, Tokyo. Cambridge, MA: Ballinger, 1981. 232pp. ISBN 0–88410–698–5.

The common security interests of Japan, the United States, and Western Europe are analyzed in this book of essays, sponsored by two research institutes. Although the theme is the interdependence of the security concerns of Japan, the United States, and NATO, most attention is devoted to Japanese security. The increasing threat of the Soviet Union in the Far East as well as elsewhere is the unifying thread of the essays. Anyone studying Far Eastern security issues will find this volume of value.

1038 *Concepts of Security*. Edited by Anders Ferm. New York: United Nations, 1986. 53pp. ISBN 92–1–142115–2.

Responding to a United Nations General Assembly call for a comprehensive study of concepts of security, a panel of experts present their views on security. Experts from Algeria, the People's Republic of China, the German Democratic Republic (GDR), Sweden, and Venezuela collaborated on this task. They agreed on certain principles: (1) the right to security; (2) the right of self-defense, disarmament, and arms limitations; and (3) the maintenance of the rule of law in international relations. While there are no breakthroughs in this report, it does reaffirm certain principles of security.

1039 *The Conduct of East-West Relations in the 1980s*. Edited by Robert O'Neill. Houndmills, England: Macmillan, 1985. 182pp. ISBN 0–333–38422–9.

These papers are the product of a 1983 annual conference of the International Institute for Strategic Studies (IISS) on East-West relations. The growth in tensions between the Warsaw Pact and NATO is examined by U.S. and European scholars. Since the twelve essays represent a broad spectrum of thought about East-West relations, no consensus of viewpoint is reached, except that the West needs to counter the expansionism of the Eastern bloc. Many of the top experts on security affairs have contributed to this book, making it a prime source of ideas.

1040 *Confidence-Building Measures*. Edited by Karl Kaiser. Bonn: Europa Union Verlag, 1983. 237pp. ISBN 3–7713–0211–0.

Confidence-building measures as a method to promote stability and peace in international relations constitute the subject of this book of papers from a conference sponsored by the Research Institute of the German Society for Foreign Affairs, Bonn, West Germany. This approach is a way to use political rather than military means to solve international crises. While the papers reflect the differences between the industrialized states and the Third World, confidence-building techniques work in all regions. This approach is full of promise, but the papers are weak when addressing the means to implement the proposals.

1041 *Conflict in the Persian Gulf*. Edited by Murray Gordon. New York: Facts on File, 1981. 173pp. ISBN 0–87196–158–X.

The strategic importance of the Persian Gulf is analyzed in this book of essays. Oil makes this region of vital importance to the West and Japan, but the collapse of the Shah of Iran in 1979 has left the United States in a weakened condition to promote regional stability. Current U.S. policy is to protect the Persian Gulf through its own resources, one that could bring the United States into direct confrontation with the Soviet Union. This book is a good introduction to the strategic realities of the Persian Gulf.

1042 *Conflict in World Society: A New Perspective on International Relations*. Edited by Michael Banks. Brighton, England: Wheatsheaf Books, 1984. 234pp. ISBN 0–7108–0735–X.

These essays on applied conflict resolution originate from the British research group, the Centre for the Analysis of Conflict. The group commissioned this study of the behavioral theories on conflict resolution of John Burton by a cross-section of Burton's colleagues, former students, and friends. The result is a potpourri of analysis on the validity of Burton's theories. This book gives a picture of the impact of a theorist on the study of conflict resolution.

1043 *Conflict Management in the Middle East.* Edited by David B. Dewitt. Lexington, MA: Lexington Books, 1987. 323pp. ISBN 0–669–14173–9.

These essays on conflict management in the Middle East are the result of a 1985 workshop and conference held under the joint sponsorship of the Centre for International and Strategic Studies at York University, and the Dayan Center for Middle Eastern and African Studies in Tel Aviv, Israel. The authors are most concerned with the difficulty of solving the Arab-Israeli conflict. They conclude that the best approach for termination of hostilities is the adoption of the notion of the "ripe moment" for reorientation of the respective political positions of the belligerents. This book is a major contribution to the study of conflict management in the Middle East.

1044 *Conflict Processes and the Breakdown of International Systems: Merriam Seminar Series on Research Frontiers.* Edited by Dina A. Zinnes. Denver, CO: University of Denver, 1983. 160pp. ISBN 0–87940–073–0.

The problem of system breakdowns is the focus of these papers by scholars interested in quantitative international politics. Each article examines different models to explain system collapse, but all are based upon a rigid application of analytical techniques. No single theme emerges from this book, since each author devotes attention to a specific topic. These types of studies challenge the reader because of their mathematic approach and because of the exploratory nature of the topics.

1045 *Confronting Moscow: An Agenda for the Post-Detente Era.* Edited by W. Bruce Weinrod. Washington, DC: Heritage Foundation, 1985. 75pp. ISBN 0–89195–217–9.

These essays constitute a hardline attack on Soviet economic and military policies by conservative critics of the Soviet Union. The authors advocate an aggressive U.S. foreign policy to limit Soviet expansionism. This approach will necessitate a long-range strategic plan, including a massive buildup of U.S. military forces and the reform of the present Soviet system. These essays by representatives from a conservative think tank, the Heritage Foundation, present an agenda that ensures increased conflict with the Soviet Union for at least the next decade.

1046 *Continuity of Discord: Crises and Responses in the Atlantic Community.* Edited by Robert J. Jackson. New York: Praeger, 1985. 276pp. ISBN 0–03–000048–3.

These papers originate from the annual 1983 conference of the Committee on Atlantic Studies, held in Racine, Wisconsin. The papers focus on whether present discord in the Atlantic alliance differs from the normal periodic crisis, or whether the alliance is in a state of dissolution. Despite some disagreements over the nature of the present crisis, the consensus is that the Atlantic alliance will continue but in a somewhat modified form. Excellent articles by solid scholars characterize this work.

1047 *Contribution of Technology to International Conflict Resolution.* Edited by H. Chestnut. Oxford, England: Pergamon Press, 1987. 157pp. ISBN 0–08–034915–3.

The International Federation of Automatic Control (IFAC) convened a 1986 workshop in Cleveland, Ohio, to study ways in which nations can settle international disputes before the need to go to war. Authors looked to various technologies to monitor disputes and to provide ways to promote conflict resolution. For technology to be effective in conflict solving there must be more financial support from private and public sources. This book is a pioneering effort but is only partially successful as a guide for further research in this field.

1048 *Controlling Latin American Conflicts: Ten Approaches.* Edited by Michael A. Morris and Victor Millan. Boulder, CO: Westview Press, 1983. 272pp. ISBN 0–86531–938–3.

This book contains essays on the subject of Latin American conflicts and ways in which to control the escalation of such crises. More than thirty conflict situations are identified and analyzed for patterns, and ten approaches are considered for controlling these situations. All the contributors recognize that Latin America has become a more conflict-prone region, but they are also optimistic about chances for conflict control. This book is an excellent treatment of the subject of Latin American conflicts, and its proposals deserve consideration.

1049 Cordesman, Anthony H. *The Gulf and the Search for Strategic Stability: Saudi Arabia, the Military Balance in the Gulf, and Trends in the Arab-Israeli Military Balance.* Boulder, CO: Westview Press, 1984. 1,041pp. ISBN 0–86531–619–8.

This book surveys the international security situation in the Persian Gulf and the military balance in the Middle East. Saudi Arabia and the conservative Gulf states are the only countries in this region receptive to overtures from the United States and the U.S. has to establish a strategic relationship with them in order to provide stability in the Persian Gulf. The key to this region remains an Arab-Israeli peace settlement, as without peace there can be no stability in this region. The combination of quality analysis and effective use of statistical data makes this book an indispensable source on the political and military scene in the Middle East.

1050 Cottrell, Alvin J., and Michael L. Moodie. *The United States and the Persian Gulf: Past Mistakes, Present Needs.* New York: National Strategy Information Center, 1984. 50pp. ISBN 0–87855–909–4.

This book is a study of the strategic importance of the Persian Gulf region. The authors assert that this region is of such importance that the United States needs an enhanced naval presence in the Indian Ocean–Persian Gulf area. Since regional destabilization favors the Soviet Union, the United States must help stabilize this region by its naval presence and the rapid deployment force (RDF). This paper is limited in scope, but it does advocate policies that reflect those adopted by the Reagan administration.

1051 Cox, Arthur Macy. *Russian Roulette: The Superpower Game.* New York: Times Books, 1982. 248pp. ISBN 0–8129–1011–7.

In this work the author examines the possibility of an accidental or unintentional nuclear war between the superpowers, claiming that Soviet adventurism and U.S. intransigence combine to make for a dangerous scenario for the start of an accidental war. More realistic than the United States in realizing the stakes of a nuclear war, Europeans are more receptive to arms control initiatives. This book is a balanced assessment of the dangers of the arms race, which every security specialist should read.

1052 *The Credibility of the NATO Deterrent: Bringing the NATO Deterrent Up to Date.* By the Atlantic Council's Working Group. Washington, DC: Atlantic Council of the United States, 1981. 54pp.

The Atlantic Council of the United States is an organization whose purpose is to study problems of international security. This booklet is an analysis of the functioning of NATO's deterrence in response to growing Soviet military power. The organization concludes that NATO's deterrent capacity needs to be augmented, both in conventional and nuclear forces, and that NATO should expand its military scope beyond Europe. The group has produced this analysis to lobby for more U.S. and European defense and security commitments.

1053 *Crisis Management and the Super-Powers in the Middle East.* Edited by Gregory Treverton. Farnborough, England: Gower, 1981. 183pp. ISBN 0–916672–73–5.

These essays explore the major issues in the Middle East region along with efforts to prevent these issues from sparking further conflicts. Three events have transformed Middle East politics: (1) the 1973 Yom Kippur War; (2) the 1978 Camp David Accords; and (3) the 1979 Iranian Revolution. These and other subjects are covered in essays by Middle East specialists. All of the essays are of a high quality, and they serve as good sources for further study of security problems in the Middle East.

1054 Cyr, Arthur. *U.S. Foreign Policy and European Security.* Houndmills, England: Macmillan, 1987. 156pp. ISBN 0–333–32859–0.

The author scrutinizes the problems facing the Western alliance in the last quarter of the century. NATO has witnessed a number of internal strains in the past, but European economic and political developments have introduced the most recent and most lasting stress on the alliance. NATO will survive, however, because it has served the combined interests of the alliance effectively. This book is a reexamination of the Western alliance and NATO, but it offers little new insight.

1055 *The Dangers of New Weapon Systems.* Edited by William Gutteridge and Trevor Taylor. New York: St. Martin's Press, 1983. 241pp. ISBN 0–321–18217–1.

These papers were given at a 1980 Pugwash symposium at the Ciba Foundation in London. Scholars from both superpower blocs and the Third World presented papers on the dangers of the new technology on the development of weapons systems. Again and again the authors returned to the theme of methods to control these new systems. Technological advances and many of the systems discussed in this book are now in the process of being replaced, but the authors' concern over the destabilizing influence of new weapons systems remains.

1056 David, Steven R. *Third World Coup d'Etat and International Security.* Baltimore, MD: Johns Hopkins University Press, 1987. 191pp. ISBN 0–8018–3307–8.

The international dimensions of political overthrows of Third World regimes are examined in this book. While there has been a decline in the number of coups d'etat since 1970, an increase in foreign attention and intervention has occurred during the same period. U.S. policy has been cautious, but U.S. security leaders have the option of intervening in certain political situations. This book is a major assessment of the impact of coups d'etat in the international arena, and it deserves a serious reading.

1057 Davidson, Scott. *Grenada: A Study in Politics and the Limits of International Law.* Aldershot, England: Avebury, 1987. 196pp. ISBN 0–566–05052–8.

The military intervention in Grenada during 1983 by the United States and the Organisation of Eastern Caribbean States, and the resulting condemnation of this intervention by the world community are studied by a British scholar. While the intervention is recognized as a violation of international law, the political benefits to the interveners have been positive. This case shows the limits of international law in restraining such interventions. The author has produced a balanced assessment of a case study of military intervention.

1058 Dean, Jonathan. *Watershed in Europe: Dismantling the East-West Military Confrontation.* Lexington, MA: Lexington Books, 1987. 286pp. ISBN 0–669–11120–1.

The author tries to forecast the future of the NATO–Warsaw Pact confrontation in the coming decades. He envisions the possibility of a gradual decline in the rivalry between the two superpower blocs. While NATO has regained military parity with the Warsaw Pact's military forces—making the chances of war slim—the chances of arms control and/or disarmament also remain slight. This book is a solid assessment of European security for the next twenty years.

1059 *The Defense of the West: Strategic and European Security Issues Reappraised.* Edited by Robert Kennedy and John M. Weinstein. Boulder, CO: Westview Press, 1984. 451pp. ISBN 0–865316–12–0.

The authors, all former or current analysts of the U.S. Army War College's Strategic Studies Institute, have combined to produce a book on U.S. and European security issues. Certain points emerge in NATO strategic circles: (1) the ongoing difficulty in separating strategic and theater defense issues; (2) the impossibility of calculating the military balance between the United States and the Soviet Union; and (3) the overstatement of Soviet capabilities causing public relations problems for the commitment of U.S. military forces. This book is one of the better works on strategic questions on the market.

1060 DeLeon, Peter. *The Altered Strategic Environment: Toward the Year 2000.* Lexington, MA: Lexington Books, 1987. 113pp. ISBN 0–669–14576–9.

A former strategic affairs analyst for the Rand Corporation, now an academic, surveys the altered strategic environment caused by recent strategic trends. These trends are the possibility of nuclear winter, the proposal of the Strategic Defense Initiative (SDI), the new technology of conventional weapons, and the inclination of the general public to become involved in these issues. These developments have not yet merged to produce a strategic world view, as the ramifications of each are only beginning to be understood.

This book is only partially successful in its efforts to break new ground in strategic studies by synthesizing current developments.

1061 DePorte, A. W. *Europe between the Superpowers: The Enduring Balance*, 2d ed. New Haven, CT: Yale University Press, 1986. 256pp. ISBN 0-300-03758-9.

This edition is an update of a book published in 1978. The author feels that since the late 1970s events have tested the relationship between Europe and the United States and justify a reassessment. Despite this testing of the Atlantic alliance, the author remains optimistic that the alliance will remain viable until the end of the century. This reassessment by a former State Department official is another of a series of examinations of Europe's future role in NATO.

1062 *Deterrence in the 1980s: Crisis and Dilemma*. Edited by R. B. Byers. London: Croom Helm, 1985. 235pp. ISBN 0-7099-3288-X.

These papers originate from a 1984 conference on the state of deterrence in the 1980s held at York University by its Research Programme in Strategic Studies. Considerable dissatisfaction over deterrence as a strategic theory was expressed by the participants. While deterrence has flaws as a strategic policy, most of the authors maintain that it still plays a role as part of an integrated defense policy. Researchers will find most of these papers extremely suggestive and informative.

1063 Dhanapala, Jayantha. *China and the Third World*. New Delhi: Vikas, 1985. 133pp. ISBN 0-7069-2517-3.

This book is a collection of essays by a security scholar from India on China and its contacts and policies with Third World countries. Because each essay was written to stand alone, there is little continuity between them. This weakness and the author's preoccupation with historical analyses of China's postwar policies toward nonaligned countries make this book of marginal interest.

1064 Dibb, Paul. *Soviet Capabilities, Interests and Strategies in East Asia in the 1980s*. Canberra: Strategic and Defence Studies Centre, 1982. 22 leaves. ISBN 0-86784-067-6.

Soviet ambitions and policies in East Asia during the 1980s are the subjects of this paper. The possibility of an anti-Soviet coalition of the People's Republic of China, Japan, and the United States raises the spectre of strategic encirclement by the middle of the 1980s. Soviet policy has been a spectacular failure in East Asia, but its political rigidity has earned the Soviets the enmity of all of the East Asian countries. Despite the fact that the anti-Soviet coalition has failed to materialize, this paper's assessment of future directions of Soviet policy in this region is still of interest for the author's views.

1065 Dibb, Paul. *The Soviet Union: The Incomplete Superpower*. Houndmills, England: Macmillan, 1986. 293pp. ISBN 0-333-36281-0.

The author uses his experience both as an intelligence analyst and as a scholar to examine the limits of Soviet military power. He tries to estimate Soviet military power projections from the viewpoint of Moscow, and from this perspective, Soviet power has its limits. Economic problems, uncertain allies, and an unstable international scene contribute to these limits, as does the Soviet record on the use of military power. This book serves as a corrective to other works extolling Soviet military strength.

1066 Dillon, G. M. *Dependence and Deterrence: Success and Civility in the Anglo-American Special Nuclear Relationship, 1962–1982.* Aldershot, England: Gower, 1983. 206pp. ISBN 0–56600–588–3.

British strategic nuclear weapons policy and Great Britain's relationship with the United States are the subjects of this book. Since World War II, Great Britain has obtained nuclear deterrence at the cost of its strategic dependence upon the United States. Security has been achieved through an alliance system at a time when Great Britain conducted its imperial withdrawal. But this dependence has become accelerated because British industry is lagging in military technology. This book is an excellent treatment of the problems of a junior member of a security alliance.

1067 *The Dissolving Alliance: The United States and the Future of Europe.* Edited by Richard L. Rubenstein. New York: Paragon House Publishers, 1987. 190pp. ISBN 0–88702–216–2.

These papers are the product of a 1986 conference held in Washington, DC, on the status of the Atlantic alliance, sponsored by the Washington Institute for Values in Public Policy. An international cast of security experts presented papers, and a consensus emerged that the United States has no creditable deterrence against a Soviet attack on Western Europe. The inability of the United States to sustain the certainty of a nuclear response in the event of Soviet aggressiveness is the reason the NATO alliance is dissolving. Such a variety of papers on problem areas of relations between the United States and its European allies makes this book an asset for researchers on security issues.

1068 *Dominant Powers and Subordinate States: The United States in Latin America and the Soviet Union in Eastern Europe.* Edited by Jan F. Triska. Durham, NC: Duke University Press, 1986. 504pp. ISBN 0–8223–0686–7.

These papers are the products of a 1986 conference at Stanford University on the comparison of the United States and the USSR as regional powers. Despite the difference in ideologies and political systems, as global superpowers both the Soviet Union and the United States have spheres of influence over subordinate states. The collective evidence of this book indicates that domination of the United States over Latin America and the Soviet Union over Eastern Europe are no longer in the national interest of either superpower. While this book contains a number of suggestive points, its general conclusions are most worthwhile.

1069 Douglass, Joseph D. *Soviet Military Strategy in Europe.* New York: Pergamon Press, 1980. 238pp. ISBN 0–08–023702–9.

Soviet strategic thinking toward Europe is the focus of this book by a military analyst in the U.S. Department of Defense. The author concentrates on Soviet military literature to study Soviet objectives rather than current Soviet capabilities. He concludes that at the time the United States and NATO were downgrading their military capacities in the 1970s the Soviets were busy expanding their forces. His arguments reflect the viewpoint of the Department of Defense, and most of his views have been adopted by the Reagan administration.

1070 Dror, Yehezkel. *Crazy States: A Counterconvention Strategic Problem,* rev. ed. Millwood, NY: Kraus Reprints, 1980. 118pp. ISBN 0–527–25140–2.

This edition is an update of a book published in 1970, which advanced the thesis that there are states that display erratic behavior in security and international affairs. The author claims that the decade of the 1970s has only further proved his crazy-states thesis. These states have aggressive goals, an acceptance of high risks, a willingness to act immorally and illegally in the interest of these goals, and a belief in the need to export their goals. Despite the age of this thesis, this book has withstood the test of events and provides insight on a number of maverick states.

1071 Duner, Bertil. *Military Intervention in Civil Wars: The 1970s.* Aldershot, England: Gower, 1985. 197pp. ISBN 0–566–00793–2.

Characteristics of military intervention in civil wars during the 1970s are examined in this theoretical work by a fellow at the Department of Peace and Conflict Research at the University of Uppsala, Sweden. Each instance of outside intervention is studied for tendencies. The author concludes that there is a strong tendency for intervention by outsiders in a civil war, and, in most cases, multiple interveners. This study is an effort to find patterns of military intervention, and, despite some methodological problems, the author succeeds.

1072 Duner, Bertil. *Military Involvement: the Escalation of Internal Conflicts.* Stockholm: Swedish Institute of International Affairs, 1980. 68pp. ISBN 91–7182–406–5.

Military intervention as the cause of an escalation of hostilities in an interstate conflict or a civil war is the subject of this study. The author posits a number of hypotheses on the nature of military intervention. One common denominator is that there is always some foreign military involvement in every internal conflict, but this involvement tends to be at a low level of intensity. While this study suggests more than it is able to produce, it is still worth notice.

1073 *East-West Rivalry in the Third World: Security Issues and Regional Perspectives.* Edited by Robert W. Clawson. 348pp. Wilmington, DE: Scholarly Resources, 1986. ISBN 0–8420–2236–8.

These papers are the product of a 1984 conference sponsored by the Lyman L. Lemnitzer Center for NATO Studies held at Kent State University in Kent, Ohio. The theme of the conference was the extent to which the continuing East-West rivalry affects the security and security policies of Third World states. General conclusions are that neither superpower bloc is winning in its competition for influence in Third World countries because of the intensity of nationalism and the complexity of problems in dealing with these states. These essays are high-quality efforts, and international security researchers will find them suggestive.

1074 Al-Ebraheem, Hassan Ali. *Kuwait and the Gulf: Small States and the International System.* Washington, DC: Center for Contemporary Arab Studies, 1984. 117pp. ISBN 0–932568–08–4.

The author, a political scientist from Kuwait, is interested in the problems of small states in the international system, and he isolates Kuwait as a case study of how the system works. While the existence of small states is generally precarious, the small Gulf states with their wealth and oil are even more tempting targets. The Gulf Cooperation Council is the first step toward integration of the Gulf states for security and defense purposes. This short book provides a balanced assessment of the security problems of Kuwait and the Gulf states.

1075 *Economics and Pacific Security: The 1986 Pacific Symposium.* Washington, DC: National Defense University Press, 1987. 260pp.

The interrelations of economic and political development with security issues are analyzed in these papers from the 1986 Pacific Symposium sponsored by the National Defense University, Washington, DC. Special attention is given to the growing roles of Japan and the People's Republic of China in Pacific economic development. The Pacific region is a growth area, and regional security is a high priority for the countries in this region. These essays from a variety of scholars from Asia and the United States highlight the future strategic importance of this region.

1076 Edwards, A. J. C. *Nuclear Weapons, the Balance of Terror, the Quest for Peace.* Houndmills, England: Macmillan, 1986. 275pp. ISBN 0–333–39564–6.

This book is a synthesis of what the author considers the fundamental issue of the 1980s—the balance of terror. By balance of terror the author includes deterrence and defense, nuclear arms, and peace and war. He admits to guarded optimism that the present policies will continue to work, but the West needs to increase its military capabilities to retain its balance of terror. While this book is strong on analysis, it lacks any distinguishing characteristics to make it better than a number of other books on the same subject.

1077 *Die Einhegung sowjetischer Macht: Kontrolliertes militarisches Gleichgewicht als Bedingung europäischer Sicherheit.* Edited by Uwe Nerlich. Baden-Baden: Nomos Verlagsgesellschaft, 1982. 500pp. ISBN 3–7890–0810–9.

Various representatives from NATO countries contributed papers to this book on Soviet military power projections. The increase in Soviet military power and its impact on Soviet foreign policy is of concern to these writers, because this imbalance threatens the security of Europe. These authors stress the need to modernize NATO forces and discuss ways to neutralize Soviet military advantages through arms control negotiations. Sixteen high-quality essays exploring different aspects of the problem are the product of this study.

1078 *Elements of World Instability: Armaments, Communication, Food, International Division of Labour: Proceedings of the International Peace Research Association.* Edited by Egbert Jahn and Yoshikazu Sakamoto. Frankfurt: Campus Verlag, 1981. 389pp. ISBN 3–593–32851–8.

European experts on détente, disarmament, and military and peace education came together at the Eighth International Peace Research Association (IPRA) in Frankfurt, West Germany, in 1981. While these essays are only part of the contributions from the conference, they constitute another approach to these issues. The sections on world military affairs and détente are especially worthwhile.

1079 Elliot, David C. *Decision at Brussels: The Politics of Nuclear Forces.* Santa Monica, CA: California Seminar on International Security and Foreign Policy, 1981. 57pp.

This study is an analysis of the 1979 decision by NATO foreign and defense ministers to revise NATO's nuclear defense posture. Rearmament and arms control negotiations were part of a dual approach decided upon by the ministers. This strategy of arming to parley is a reflection of an increased European influence within NATO. Short studies such as this delineation of a change in alliance policy make a contribution by narrowing in on a single topic for an in-depth view.

1080 Epstein, Joshua M. *Strategy and Force Planning: The Case of the Persian Gulf.* Washington, DC: Brookings Institution, 1987. 169pp. ISBN 0–8157–2454–3.

The author seeks to solve the problem of deterring Soviet adventurism in the Persian Gulf region. In particular, a projected Soviet invasion of the oil field of Khuzestan is studied for ways to counter an invasion. The speedy intervention of a five-division rapid deployment force (RDF) would prevent Soviet seizure of these oil fields. The statistical data in the numerous appendices are the most intriguing part of this book.

1081 *Escalation and Intervention: Multilateral Security and Its Alternatives.* Edited by Arthur R. Day and Michael W. Doyle. Boulder, CO: Westview Press, 1986. 181pp. ISBN 0–7201–1847–6.

The Multilateral Project of the United Nations Association of the USA sponsored this book of essays on multilateral means to control and resolve local conflicts. By studying recent examples of conflicts, the authors have confronted the problems of escalation of hostilities and outside military intervention. The UN has had a mixed record on dealing with conflicts, but no multilateral approach has proven much more successful. This book is an original look at handling local conflicts, and its conclusions are worth noting.

1082 *Ethics and International Relations.* Edited by Anthony Ellis. Manchester, England: Manchester University Press, 1986. 232pp. ISBN 0–7190–1974–5.

These papers record the proceedings of the second Fulbright colloquium on ethics and international relations held at the University of St. Andrews in 1984. U.S., British, and Canadian scholars contributed papers on ethical questions of deterrence, intervention, and other international problems. The central problem covered by all participants is the extent to which the conduct of any state is subject to compliance to moral norms. This question and the debate over the morality of deterrence make this book another type of contribution to security literature.

1083 *Europe and the Superpowers: Political, Economic, and Military Policies in the 1980s.* Edited by Steven Bethlen and Ivan Volgyes. Boulder, CO: Westview Press, 1985. 164pp. ISBN 0–86531–887–5.

These essays on Europe's changing relationship with the Soviet Union and the United States are the result of a 1984 conference of U.S. and German scholars held at Wildbad Kreuth, West Germany. At the heart of these contributions is the belief that both Eastern and Western Europe have progressed far enough in economic and political matters to constitute independent entities from the superpowers. The extent of this independence provided most of the divergence of views among conference participants. This book constitutes a major contribution to the study of alliance politics.

1084 *European Security: Nuclear or Conventional Defence?* Edited by Michel de Perrot. Oxford, England: Pergamon Press, 1984. 352pp. ISBN 0–08–031–3221.

These papers are the result of a 1983 international colloquium on European security, which was held in Geneva, Switzerland, under the auspices of the Groupe de Bellerive. An international cast of U.S. and European security specialists contributed papers. Most of the authors conclude that there are sufficient conventional forces to deter a Soviet aggressor, and that the problem resides in nuclear defense. Over twenty contributions from divergent points of view make this book a valuable source on European security issues.

1085 *European Security and the Atlantic Alliance.* Edited by Hans Sjoberg. Stockholm: Swedish National Defence Research Institute, 1984. 78pp. ISBN 91–7056–066–8.

European views on European security and the future of the Atlantic alliance were presented at a 1982 symposium at the Division for International Security Studies of the Swedish National Defence Research Institute (FOA), Stockholm. Three scholars made presentations on British, French, and German views of European security. While there is considerable debate in all three countries over NATO and security, the Atlantic alliance remains functioning, although subjected to growing scrutiny. Both the papers and the discussions indicate considerable unease among Europeans over European security.

1086 *European Security in the Global Context.* Brussels: Editions de l'Université de Bruxelles, 1983. 72pp. ISBN 2–8004–0815–4.

These lectures are a product of a 1983 conference at Wepion, Belgium, where participants discussed European security issues. Each lecture covered a different topic, but all speakers stressed the need for Europe to be able to defend itself from the threat of Soviet aggression. Strengthening cooperation among members of the Atlantic alliance is the best approach to countering a Soviet threat. This book has a series of statements on European security by U.S. and West European participants, and the value of the volume lies in this sampling of viewpoints.

1087 *European Security, Nuclear Weapons and Public Confidence.* Edited by William Gutteridge. London: Macmillan, 1982. 236pp. ISBN 0–333–30959–6.

This book is a collection of papers presented at various Pugwash symposiums held in Europe from 1977 to 1979. Twenty-one essays from a variety of European security specialists from both NATO and the Warsaw bloc are included, most of which have been rewritten or translated for this publication. These essays are short position papers that are most useful for reflecting different viewpoints rather than substantive issues.

1088 *Evolving Strategic Realities: Implications for US Policymakers.* Edited by Franklin D. Margiotta. Washington, DC: National Defense University Press, 1980. 222pp.

The papers in this book are an outgrowth of a series of seminars held in 1979–1980 at the National Security Affairs Institute of the National Defense University. New issues were included as events dictated, but attention was focused primarily on the Soviet-U.S. relationship. Behind these sessions was the thought of the capability of the United States to have the means or the will to deal with international crises. The consensus was a "perhaps." These essays are little more than expert reaction to current events with the notable exception of the Petrov contribution.

1089 *Exterminism and Cold War.* Edited by the *New Left Review.* London: NLB, 1982. 358pp. ISBN 0–86091–051–2.

Sixteen socialists from the United States, Europe, and the Soviet Union contributed papers on the threat of nuclear war to this book published by the *New Left Review.* These papers are critical of the arms race and growing world militarization. While most'of the contributors are Marxists, the problems of exterminism and responsibility for the Cold War are addressed from a variety of perspectives. The issues contained in this book needed expounding, and the authors do a good job in accomplishing this task.

1090 Feldman, Shai. *Israeli Nuclear Deterrence: A Strategy for the 1980s.* New York: Columbia University Press, 1982. 310pp. ISBN 0–231–05546–3.

This book is a study of the risks and benefits of a shift of Israeli military strategy from conventional warfare to nuclear deterrence. The author, an Israeli scholar, does not advocate nuclear deterrence but believes that such a strategy should be considered. Any nuclear-deterrence benefits will come only through Israel's open introduction of this strategy and a possible pullback to the 1967 boundaries. This book is a stimulating look at the possible adoption of a new Israeli strategy.

1091 Ferencz, Benjamin B. *Enforcing International Law—A Way to World Peace: A Documentary History and Analysis.* 2 vols. London: Oceana Publications, 1983. ISBN 0–379–12147–6.

The author of this two-volume set is concerned with the evolution of the idea of enforcing international law on transgressing states. Beginning with sixteenth-century theorists and continuing to the present, he studies the means for ensuring state compliance with the rules of international law. Documents are provided to show advances and obstacles to enforcement. This work has a variety of information useful for any researcher on international security.

1092 Flynn, Gregory. *The Internal Fabric of Western Security.* Totowa, NJ: Allanheld, Osmun, 1981. 249pp. ISBN 0–86598–039–X.

An analysis of the impact of domestic considerations on the security policies of the Western alliance is the subject of this book of essays, published under the sponsorship of the Atlantic Institute for International Affairs. Four countries—France, Great Britain, Italy, and West Germany—are selected for case studies, but other essays draw on examples from all NATO countries. Domestic considerations have become so significant that there is a danger of damage to the Western alliance. While many of the points in this book changed by the middle 1980s, the basic thesis of the influence of domestic politics on security decisions remains viable.

1093 Freedman, Lawrence. *The Evolution of Nuclear Strategy.* New York: St. Martin's Press, 1981. 473pp. ISBN 0–312–27269–3.

An eminent British scholar on strategic issues produced this history of the development of nuclear strategy. His intent is to present a detailed and critical history of the official and unofficial attempts by both power blocs to construct a plausible nuclear strategy. Both the lack of credibility of deterrence and the enormity of the uncertainties of implementation mitigate against a successful nuclear strategy, but somehow the system works. This book is a major undertaking by one of the authorities in the field.

1094 Freedman, Lawrence. *The Price of Peace: Living with the Nuclear Dilemma.* London: Firethorn Press, 1986. 288pp. ISBN 0–947752–95–1.

This book is a collection of essays by a prominent British scholar on strategic policies. The author is concerned about reaping the benefits from the fear of nuclear war in moderating international behavior, while at the same time reducing the risks of nuclear confrontation. Most of these essays have appeared in other publications, but the author has brought them together to form a corpus of his works. The essays are all high quality; a lengthy introduction places them in context.

1095 Frei, Daniel, and Christian Catrina. *Risks of Unintentional Nuclear War.* Geneva: Palais des Nations, 1982. 255pp. ISBN 92–9045–003–7.

This study on the threat of nuclear war based on false assumptions by the superpowers was commissioned by the United Nations Institute for Disarmament Research (UNIDIR). Nuclear war based on false assumptions means substandard performance by decisionmakers in crisis situations, which results in the use of nuclear weapons. This possibility is enhanced by the mismatch of strategic doctrine between the United States and the Soviet Union. This book broaches several useful concepts and ideas that are worth future study.

1096 Fukuyama, Francis. *The Soviet Threat to the Persian Gulf.* Santa Monica, CA: Rand Corporation, 1981. 30pp.

The parameters of the Soviet threat to the Persian Gulf are examined in this study prepared for the Security Conference on Asia and the Pacific, held in Tokyo in 1980. Soviet ability to exploit internal political events in the Middle East means that the United States and its Western allies must increase their capabilities to project power into the Persian Gulf. Moreover, the United States must communicate clearly to the Soviets its intention to use its military resources to protect Western interests in the Gulf. This short paper has many recommendations, several of which have been adopted by the Reagan administration and, for this reason alone, is worth studying.

1097 *The Future for European Energy Security.* Edited by Curt Gasteyger. London: Frances Pinter, 1985. 177pp. ISBN 0–86187–573–7.

An international workshop on European energy security was organized in 1983, and these papers are the product of this gathering. Despite sufficient energy supplies in the mid-1980s, Europe remains and will continue to remain dependent on oil from the Middle East well into the next century. Further exploration in the North Sea and conservation are necessary, but the best solution for energy dependency is consultation, coordination, and cooperation among the European countries. This book presents more problems than solutions but is still a solid source on the subject of European energy security.

1098 *The Future of Conflict in the 1980s.* Edited by William J. Taylor and Steven A. Maranen. Lexington, MA: Lexington Books, 1982. 504pp. ISBN 0–669–06145–X.

These essays explore the dangers to the United States on the international scene in the 1980s. The authors conclude that U.S. national interests in this era will be most threatened by low-intensity conflict in a Third World region. Since the number of these conflicts will be high, the probability of U.S. involvement is almost a certainty. This book is a stimulating look at possible international conflicts by a variety of security specialists.

1099 Galtung, Johan. *Environment, Development and Military Activity: Towards Alternative Security Doctrines.* Oslo: Universitetsforlaget, 1982. 142pp. ISBN 82–00–06360–7.

The author explores alternative security theories toward the goals of increasing security and placing less pressure on scarce resources. Nuclear war and its impact on the environment are so severe that alternative approaches to the waste of war need to be considered. Disarmament is a goal, but a more meaningful approach is to strengthen defense measures and build invulnerability. This book is a speculative treatment of security, but many of the author's ideas are worth serious consideration.

1100 Garden, Timothy. *Can Deterrence Last? Peace through a Nuclear Strategy.* London: Buchan and Enright, 1984. 128pp. ISBN 0–907675–32–8.

A Royal Air Force officer poses the question whether nuclear deterrence can last as a strategic policy. After studying both the theory of deterrence and individual national policies, he concludes that the best chance of continued stability depends on nuclear weapons systems impervious to preemptive strike. He has little confidence that arms control agreements will be successful in replacing deterrence. This book is a succinct defense of the deterrence strategy.

1101 Garner, William V. *Soviet Threat Perceptions of NATO's Eurostrategic Missiles.* Paris: Atlantic Institute for International Affairs, 1983. 113pp.

This book is a study on further NATO deployment of medium-range nuclear missiles and the impact of this decision on arms control negotiations. The author concludes that the Soviets have used this deployment for propaganda purposes to influence the course of negotiations. A compromise is in the works with a limited U.S. missile deployment and an interim agreement ending further deployment. This book is a technical treatise with excellent charts on missile systems that make it valuable for scholars interested in the status of negotiations as of mid-1983.

1102 Garthoff, Raymond L. *Détente and Confrontation: American-Soviet Relations from Nixon to Reagan.* Washington, DC: Brookings Institution, 1985. 1,147pp. ISBN 0–8157–3044–6.

Foreign relations between the Soviet Union and the United States in the period between 1969 and 1984 are featured in this study. The author was involved in the U.S. diplomatic service during most of this period and more recently a member of the Brookings Institution. Détente failed as a policy because the superpowers interpreted it differently, but direct confrontation as practiced by the Reagan administration also has its dangers. This huge book is full of rigorous and thoughtful analysis that makes it a standard work on the subject.

1103 Garthoff, Raymond L. *Perspectives on the Strategic Balance.* Washington, DC: Brookings Institution, 1983. 34pp. ISBN 0–8157–3047–0.

The author, a senior fellow in the Brookings Foreign Policy Studies Program, examines the problem of evaluating the strategic balance between the United States and the Soviet Union. At present, there is strategic parity between the two sides because of comparable nuclear retaliatory capacity. But the debate has broadened to include numbers of weapons and weapons systems. The Soviets made great strides in reaching a strategic balance in the early 1980s, but these efforts have been perceived by U.S. analysts as a drive for strategic superiority. This paper is a balanced assessment of a controversial subject.

1104 Gelber, H. G. *Australia, the U.S., and the Strategic Balance: Some Comments on the Joint Facilities.* 'Canberra: Strategic and Defence Studies Centre, 1982. 39 leaves. ISBN 0–86784–126–5.

Australia's involvement with the strategic and intelligence systems of the major Western powers since 1945 is the subject of this paper. At first most of the ties were with Great Britain, but since the Korean War the United States has become the main partner. By the 1980s U.S.-Australian cooperation is close, with sharing of information of common interest and with cooperative facilities on Australian soil. However, there remains a need to assess Australian security needs outside this relationship. This paper is excellent on addressing the ties between the United States and Australia on defense issues, but weaker when examining strategic problems.

1105 George, Timothy, Robert Litwak, and Shahram Chubin. *India and the Great Powers.* Aldershot, England: Gower, 1984. 242pp. ISBN 0–566–00652–9.

India's role as the dominant military and political power in South Asia is assessed in this book. This strategic position makes India's relationship with the People's Republic of China, the Soviet Union and the United States of great importance. Moreover, India has the option to use great-power rivalries to augment her strategic position in South Asia. This assessment of India's role in South Asia is balanced and full of insight.

1106 Gerner, Kristian. *The Soviet Union and Central Europe in the Post-War Era: A Study in Precarious Security.* Stockholm: Utrikespotiska Institutet, 1984. 238pp.

The question of Central Europe's political stability within the Soviet bloc since 1968 is examined in this book by a Swedish security specialist. For the purpose of this study Central Europe is interpreted to include Czechoslovakia, Hungary, and Poland. Political instability of these countries has meant that the Soviet Union has been more concerned with military than other factors. This study indicates that the Soviets have experienced and continue to experience security problems with the Central European states.

1107 Glasser, Robert D. *Nuclear Pre-emption and Crisis Stability, 1985–1990.* Canberra: Strategic and Defence Studies Centre, 1986. 102pp. ISBN 0–86784–791–3.

The author studies the possibility of nuclear crisis instability among the superpowers in the period from 1985 to 1990. His conclusion is that this period will be marked by crisis instability caused by increasing vulnerability to both superpowers from improvements in missile accuracies and weaknesses in command and control systems. Incentives for a first strike in such an unstable environment are weighed by the author, but he concludes that preemptive strikes are not viable as a winning strategy. This book studies a serious problem with a combination of first-rate analysis and common sense.

1108 *Global Collective Security in the 1980s.* Edited by Geoffrey Stewart-Smith. Richmond, England: Foreign Affairs Publishing, 1982. 142pp. ISBN 0–0900380–30–6.

This book is an outgrowth of the First Annual World Balance of Power Conference held at Leeds Castle in Kent in 1981, where representatives from twenty-six countries participated in a discussion of balance-of-power and collective security issues. Sixteen papers are published here to reflect the arguments and positions of the participants. The overwhelming focus of this conference was on the need of the Atlantic alliance to regain strategic parity with the Soviet Union. These papers are more position statements than serious pieces of scholarship.

1109 *Global Militarization.* Edited by Peter Wallensteen, Johan Galtung, and Carlos Portales. Boulder, CO: Westview Press, 1985. 240pp. ISBN 0–86531–699–6.

These essays examine the worldwide trend toward growing militarization and ways to reverse this trend. *Militarization* is defined as both a social formation and a structure between states, and this definition includes behavior resulting in violent courses of action. The product of a conference on militarization held in Oslo in 1981, this book provides a variety of fascinating and important articles from a number of different sources.

1110 *Global Resources and International Conflict: Environmental Factors in Strategic Policy and Action.* Edited by Arthur H. Westing. Oxford, England: Oxford University Press, 1986. 280pp. ISBN 0–19–829104–3.

The impact of global natural resources on international security issues is the subject of these papers, published under the auspices of the Stockholm International Peace Research Institute (SIPRI). A common theme is that shortages, irregular distribution, and degradation of natural resources are threats to world security. Efforts must be undertaken for an equitable utilization of shared natural resources by international agreements. This book looks at international security from a different but much-needed perspective.

1111 Gordon, Lincoln. *Eroding Empire: Western Relations with Eastern Europe.* Washington, DC: Brookings Institution, 1987. 359pp. ISBN 0–8157–3214–7.

Four foreign policy specialists analyze Western attitudes and policies toward Eastern Europe since 1945. There is considerable dissatisfaction among the Eastern European bloc over its relationship with the Soviet Union. Western Europeans, especially West Germans, have an interest in Eastern Europe, but this interest only increases during crises in this region. This book is an excellent introduction to the politics of Western and Eastern Europe.

1112 Gray, Colin S. *Nuclear Strategy and National Style.* Lanham, MD: Hamilton Press, 1986. 363pp. ISBN 0–8191–5333–8.

The author compares U.S. and Soviet national styles in nuclear strategy. His thesis is that the United States has allowed misconceptions about the Soviets to influence its strategic strategy. Because the Soviet Union remains a permanent adversary due to its ideological commitments, U.S. policy must be attuned to this orientation in developing its nuclear strategic policies. This is a provocative book by a prolific author on defense and security issues.

1113 Gray, Colin S. *Nuclear Strategy and Strategic Planning.* Philadelphia: Foreign Policy Research Institute, 1984. 130pp. ISBN 0–910191–07–7.

Strategic planning for the use of nuclear weapons is the subject of this book by an authority on strategic issues. The author presents five options for nuclear strategic policy: (1) mutual assured vulnerability; (2) mutual assured vulnerability with targeting flexibility; (3) counterforce and countercontrol preeminence with recovery denial; (4) damage limitation for deterrence and coercion; and (5) damage limitation with defense dominance. While the author favors the fourth and, in theory, the fifth option, he recognizes that the United States has never established a clear strategic policy because it suffers from a lack of authority. Both stimulating and suggestive, this book is a major contribution to the study of strategic planning.

1114 *The Great-Power Triangle and Asian Security.* Edited by Raju G. C. Thomas. Lexington, MA: Lexington Books, 1983. 200pp. ISBN 0–669–06405–X.

Problems of regional security and superpower rivalries in Asia are explored in these essays by U.S. scholars. Most of the contributions are concerned with strategic linkages and the political and military interdependencies between the great powers (the People's Republic of China, the Soviet Union, and the United States) and Asian regional powers. Case studies of nine Asian states are compared for linkages and interdependencies. Most of these essays are of a high quality, and they provide a good source for answering the questions posed in this book.

1115 *Greece and Turkey: Adversity in Alliance.* Edited by Jonathan Alford. Aldershot, England: Gower, 1984. 151pp. ISBN 0–566–00676–6.

Two Greeks, two Turks, and one American contribute essays on the rivalry between two NATO allies—Greece and Turkey. While this dispute over territory on the European mainland and the Aegean Sea has existed for centuries, Cyprus provides the arena in which Greek and Turkish interests clash today. Greece considers Turkey its main adversary, but Turkey regards the Soviet Union as almost as important a security threat as Greece. These essays from both sides of the question make it easier to understand the enmity between the two sides.

1116 Gregor, A. James, and Maria Hsia Chang. *The Iron Triangle: A U.S. Security Policy for Northeast Asia.* Stanford, CA: Hoover Institution Press, 1984. 160pp. ISBN 0–8179–7921–2.

Security issues of Northeast Asia are detailed in this book by two U.S. scholars. The Iron Triangle countries of Japan, South Korea, and Taiwan all owe their prosperity to U.S. presence in this region. It is in the best interests of the United States to support the economic and political independence of these states against both the Soviet Union and China. The authors argue against closer ties with China, and it is this viewpoint and the accompanying analysis that make this book worth consulting.

1117 Greilsammer, Ilan, and Joseph Weiler. *Europe's Middle East Dilemma: The Quest for a Unified Stance.* Boulder, CO: Westview Press, 1987. 156pp. ISBN 0–8133–7359–X.

The authors trace the decision by the member states of the European Economic Community (EEC) for a common and balanced foreign policy toward the Arab-Israeli antagonists and the foreign policy ramifications of this policy. This balanced policy has had little impact on the course of the Arab-Israeli rivalry, because all the demands have been made on Israel. European initiatives suffer from the needs for internal unity and a better perspective on the antagonists. This book is a solid effort to understand European options in the ongoing Arab-Israeli conflict.

1118 Griffith, William E. *The Superpowers and Regional Tensions: The USSR, the United States, and Europe.* Lexington, MA: Lexington Books, 1982. 135pp. ISBN 0–669–04702–3.

The interaction between Soviet-U.S. bilateral relations and European problems is the focus of this book. Divisions between Western Europe, favoring détente, the United States, advocating a defense buildup, and the Soviet Union's military superiority produced an international situation in flux during the mid-1980s. The solution is to make NATO a real alliance by strengthening European decision making and for the West European states to negotiate with the United States as a unit. This book treats a variety of problems, but its solutions are much weaker than its information.

1119 Grosser, Alfred. *The Western Alliance: European-American Relations since 1945.* New York: Continuum, 1980. 375pp. ISBN 0–8264–0004–3.

The author of this assessment of the development of the Western alliance is a prominent French scholar and France's leading analyst of postwar Germany. His viewpoint is Western European in orientation, which his assessment of the Atlantic alliance reflects. Despite differences of perspective between the United States and the Europeans, the Western alliance is built upon three common factors: (1) defense; (2) economics; and (3) similarity of regimes. This book is a work of synthesis by one of Europe's outstanding scholars and, as such, deserves serious consideration.

1120 *Gulf Security and the Iran-Iraq War.* Edited by Thomas Naff. Washington, DC: National Defense University Press, 1985. 193pp.

These papers are a product of a series of seminars on the impact of the Iran-Iraq War on defense policies in the Persian Gulf states held under the joint auspices of the National Defense University and the Middle East Research Institute. The United States has made commitments for military action in the Persian Gulf region first by President Jimmy Carter followed by President Ronald Reagan without the military means to carry out this policy. But the Iran-Iraq War remains the source of instability in this region, and until this conflict is settled this region will be a crisis zone. These contributions from eight Middle East specialists make this book a solid source for further study on Persian Gulf region security issues.

1121 Gupta, R. C. *American Arms in West Asia.* New Delhi: Puneet Publications, 1985. 256pp.

The thesis of this book by an Indian specialist on international affairs is that the United States has used large-scale arms sales as an instrument to promote U.S. foreign policy objectives in the Middle East. Three countries— Iran, Saudi Arabia, and Israel—have been chosen as case studies. U.S. support was not able to save the Shah's regime in Iran, and the stability of the Saudi regime depends on domestic political support, not arms from abroad. This book is a good introduction to the subject of the consequences of arms sales in the Middle East.

1122 Hackel, Erwin, Karl Kaiser, and Pierre Lellouche. *Nuclear Policy in Europe: France, Germany and the International Debate.* Bonn: Europa Union Verlag, 1980. 133pp. ISBN 3–7713–0137–8.

Three European scholars present articles on French and West German nuclear policy. Policy decisions on nuclear energy and nonproliferation of nuclear facilities are dealt with in depth. The authors believe that the national policies of both France and West Germany are in tune with national priorities, and proliferation issues are viewed from this national perspective. These articles are narrow treatments of specific policy decisions, and, for this reason, the book promises more than the articles produce.

1123 Halle, Louis J. *The Elements of International Strategy: A Primer for the Nuclear Age.* Lanham, MD: University Press of America, 1984. 121pp. ISBN 0–8191–3700–6.

These essays by a respected commentator on international affairs look at the philosophical basis of international strategy. The author's thesis is that since strategic studies have lost their military orientation, they now have almost an exclusively political nature. The author then examines the political side of international strategy by use of historical analysis. This short book is full of insight and a solid contribution to international security literature.

1124 Hameed, Mazher A. *Saudi Arabia, the West and the Security of the Gulf.* London: Croom Helm, 1986. 189pp. ISBN 0–7099–4663–5.

The author believes that the Persian Gulf region remains the strategic vortex of international politics and that current U.S. policy does not reflect this emphasis. Because U.S. policy is so tied to the oil question, the United States must conduct a policy of support for the Gulf Cooperation Council (GCC) states. This policy means upgrading the defense capacities of these countries by providing advanced air defense systems and armored equipment. This book makes a compelling defense for increased military aid for Persian Gulf states, but most of these arguments have appeared earlier to justify aid for prerevolutionary Iran.

1125 Hammarstrom, Mats. *Securing Resources by Force: The Need for Raw Materials and Military Intervention by Major Powers in Less Developed Countries.* Uppsala, Sweden: Department of Peace and Conflict Research, 1986. 183pp. ISBN 91–506–0496–1.

The correlation between military intervention by major powers in less-developed countries since 1945 and the need of the industrialized countries for raw materials is examined in this book. Third World conflicts are studied with regard to France, the United Kingdom, and the United States in light of this thesis. The conclusion is that intervention by a major capitalist power is not related to the importance of a less-developed country as a supplier of essential minerals. This is an important book that contradicts the Marxist theory of economic imperialism.

1126 Hanks, Robert J. *American Sea Power and Global Strategy.* Washington, DC: Pergamon-Brassey's, 1985. 97pp. ISBN 0–08–033171–8.

The past use and future promise of modern sea power is the subject of this study by a retired rear admiral in the U.S. Navy. The author claims that the expansion of Soviet naval forces has increased the necessity for a strong U.S. Navy. While U.S. naval expansion since 1980 has reversed a former downward trend, a deficiency in smaller vessels still needs to be corrected before the United States can counter the Soviet naval threat. The arguments presented in this study resemble those adopted by the Reagan administration.

1127 Harkabi, Yehoshafat. *The Bar Kokhba Syndrome: Risk and Realism in International Politics.* Chappaqua, NY: Rossel Books, 1983. 206pp. ISBN 0–940646–01–3.

An Israeli author utilizes the Bar Kokhba Rebellion (132–135 B.C.) to furnish an example of an unrealistic assessment of historical and political circumstances. Present-day Israel faces a similar risk-taking dilemma when it pursues policies that risk the existence of Israel as a state. There is a need for realism in the international policies of every country, especially Israel. This book is a good example of advancing a creditable thesis from a theory constructed out of a historical context.

1128 Harkavy, Robert E. *Great Power Competition for Overseas Bases: The Geopolitics of Access Diplomacy.* New York: Pergamon Press, 1982. 361pp. ISBN 0–08–025089–0.

The requirements of the superpowers for overseas bases are examined in this critical study. The race for overseas bases has been restricted to the Soviet Union and the United States, but the stakes for gaining access to bases have become high. Military aid, including arms transfers, and strategic access have become interrelated as the superpowers jockey for strategic position. The strength of this book lies in the author's assessment of the theories of the acquisition of overseas bases and the role of the superpowers in this rivalry.

1129 Held, Karl, and Theo Ebel. *Krieg und Frieden: Politische Ökonomie des Weltfriedens.* Frankfurt: Suhrkamp Verlag, 1983. 324pp. ISBN 3–518–11149–3.

Two West German authors critique the state of international politics in the early 1980s. Both authors are especially concerned about the cost benefits of the superpower arms race. They believe that there are dynamics within capitalism that fuel this rivalry. This book is a creative approach to the study of international politics, but its viewpoint rather than its information makes this work most fascinating.

1130 Hill, J. R. *Maritime Strategy for Medium Powers.* London: Croom Helm, 1986. 247pp. ISBN 0–7099–3719–9.

A retired British admiral utilizes his naval experience to study the naval problems of medium-sized powers. Seven countries fit the medium power classification—Australia, Brazil, France, Great Britain, India, Israel, and Japan. These states need a maritime strategy, because whether or not they belong to an alliance sea power is a necessity for independence. This book is a major contribution to maritime security studies.

1131 Hoffmann, Erik P., and Robbin F. Laird. *"The Scientific-Technological Revolution" and Soviet Foreign Policy.* New York: Pergamon Press, 1982. 242pp. ISBN 0–08–028065–X.

The impact of thinking by Soviet leaders and international affairs specialists on the "scientific-technological revolution" and the influence of this theory on Soviet foreign policy are analyzed in this book. These leaders find that science and technology form the basis of almost all modern international relations, but that Soviet conservatives and modernizers disagree about foreign policy priorities. This debate was most noticeable during the Leonid Brezhnev years, but many of these views have carried over into the 1980s. Speculations about mind-sets of the Soviet political elite are always dangerous, but the authors have provided a stimulating and thought-provoking analysis.

1132 Holbraad, Carsten. *Middle Powers in International Politics.* London: Macmillan, 1984. 234pp. ISBN 0–333–35443–5.

The typical role of middle-sized powers in contemporary international politics is the focus of this study. Recent changes in international politics have made these states more important as the influence of superpowers decreases. But the international conduct of the middle powers has not been wiser or more just than the great or small states. This book is a good look at middle-sized countries on the international scene, and it is a solid contribution to the literature of international security.

1133 Holst, Johan J. *Norway and NATO in the 1980's.* Oslo: Norsk Utenrikspolitisk Institutt, 1984. 20pp.

The role of Norway in the NATO alliance is analyzed in this work. NATO remains the cornerstone of Norwegian security policy, but it has been more a marriage of strategic convenience than ideological passion. Although nuclear weapons are neither deployed nor stored in the country, Norway's strategic location means that in case of hostilities it will be defended by its NATO allies. This short paper is invaluable in understanding Norway's future role in NATO.

1134 Houweling, Hank W., and Jan G. Siccama. *Time-Space Interaction in Warfare: Some Theoretical and Empirical Aspects of the Epidemiology of Collective Violence, 1816–1980.* Amsterdam: University of Amsterdam, 1983. 44pp.

Two Dutch authors presented this paper at a 1983 workshop in Freiburg, West Germany, and the subject was to study time-space interaction in warfare. Wars from 1816 to 1980 are examined in a time-space continuum for warfare patterns and trends. The results show that space and time interact, and that warfare is epidemiological in character. This paper contains an impressive variety of statistical analyses, but weak conclusions mar an otherwise promising approach.

1135 *Improving the Means for Intergovernmental Communications in Crisis.* By Dale M. Lani et al. Santa Monica, CA: Rand Corporation, 1984. 29pp.

This report is an assessment of various communication measures for use by the superpowers in the middle of a nuclear crisis. The focus is on controlling a crisis rather than arms limitations. Hot-line enhancement, a military communications link, and high-data-rate embassy communications are all measures necessary to improve intergovernmental communications between the Soviet Union and the United States. This appraisal of bilateral arrangements between the Soviet Union and the United States is a practical but useful approach to the problem.

1136 *India and the Nuclear Challenge.* Edited by K. Subrahmanyam. New Delhi: Lancer International, 1986. 321pp.

Indian scholars have produced these essays in an effort to fix the relationship of India and the nuclear arms race. India and Pakistan have a rivalry that make the Non-Proliferation Treaty (NPT) and nuclear-free zones ineffective in the South Asian region, but both at present have not rushed into developing nuclear weapons. India should play a leading role in ending this arms race. These essays escape much of the parochialism of many Indian writings.

1137 *The Indian Ocean: Perspectives on a Strategic Arena.* Edited by William L. Dowdy and Russell B. Trood. Durham, NC: Duke University Press, 1985. 613pp. ISBN 0–8223–0649–2.

These papers are revised versions of papers presented at a 1982 conference on the strategic importance of the Indian Ocean region held in Halifax, Nova Scotia, Canada. The result is thirty papers on Indian Ocean security issues, many of which indicate that this region's strategic importance has attracted enough superpower intervention to cause regional instability. This instability and rivalries among states in this region may make the Indian Ocean region even more volatile in the future. Both the coverage and quality of the papers make this book an invaluable source on this topic.

1138 *Intelligence Policy and National Security.* Edited by Robert L. Pfaltzgraff, Uri Ra'anan, and Warren Milberg. London: Macmillan, 1981. 318pp. ISBN 0–333–30728–3.

Numerous authorities on intelligence operations attended a 1979 conference at the Fletcher School of Law and Diplomacy in Cambridge, Massachusetts. This book is a product of this conference, and the papers deal with the problems of accurate intelligence gathering. Past failures and successes of U.S. intelligence agencies are analyzed for lessons for the future. Because organizational and policy-making problems are treated in depth, this book provides considerable material for researchers interested in the security aspects of intelligence operations.

1139 *Intelligence Requirements for the 1980's: Covert Action.* Edited by Roy Godson. New Brunswick, NJ: Transaction Books, 1981. 243pp. ISBN 0–87855–830–6.

Over sixty academics and intelligence specialists were part of a 1980 colloquium, sponsored by the Consortium for the Study of Intelligence (CSI), National Strategy Information Center, Washington, DC, to study covert intelligence activities, and the essays in this book are a product of this meeting. Covert activities are attempts by a government to influence events in another state or territory without revealing its involvement. Three main points emerge from the papers and discussions: (1) covert action has been in such disfavor in the United States since the late 1970s that such operations have almost ceased; (2) the Soviet Union's use of covert action has been steady and successful; and (3) there is a need for covert intelligence operations by U.S. agencies in the 1980s. Both the papers and the discussions provide valuable insights into past covert action policies, and the participants at this colloquium predict the readoption of covert action by the Reagan administration.

1140 *Internal and External Security Issues in Asia.* Edited by Robert A. Scalapino, Seizaburo Sato, and Jusuf Wanandi. Berkeley: Institute of East Asian Studies, University of California, 1986. 273pp. ISBN 0–912966–83–1.

The problems of internal and external security among the states of Asia are analyzed by a body of Asian specialists. While no Asian state can isolate itself today from global strategic considerations of the rivalry between the Soviet Union and the U. S., there is also a threat of insurgency because of the inability of Asian governments to administer to the needs or desires of the governed. This means that these states will have to emphasize continued growth in economic and social affairs as well as increasing military expenditures. These essays cover most of the states in the Pacific-Asian region, and they are a major contribution to the study of Asian security.

1141　*International and Regional Conflict: Analytic Approaches.* Edited by Walter Isard and Yoshimi Nagao. New York: Ballinger, 1983. 236pp. ISBN 0–88410–030–8.

Analytical tools of conflict analysis and conflict management at the international level are utilized by these papers from a 1981 international symposium at Kyoto, Japan, sponsored by the World University of the World Academy of Arts and Science, the Kansai Branch of Japan Association for Planning Administration, and the Japan Section of the Peace Science Society, International. The authors concentrate on highly technical and mathematical problems, seeking to isolate sources of conflict. No combination of themes emerges, because the emphasis is on creative approaches and ideas rather than in-depth analysis of particular situations. This book has a number of stimulating but highly mathematical papers, all of which are worth further study.

1142　*International Conflict Resolution: Theory and Practice.* Edited by Edward E. Azar and John W. Burton. Brighton, England: Wheatsheaf Books, 1986. 159pp. ISBN 0–931477–71–9.

U.S. and English authors have written a series of essays on the theory and practice of international conflict resolution. These authors challenge the power politics thesis of the nation-state and replace it with a theory of ways to settle conflicts. All the papers are favorable toward conflict resolution theory, but the writers differ on ways of application. This book contains a number of stimulating ideas, making it a good introduction to conflict resolution theory.

1143　*International Security and the Arms Race.* Edited by Curt Gasteyger. Geneva, Switzerland: Programme for Strategic and International Security Studies, 1986. 64pp.

Four eminent personalities—Carl Friedrich von Weizsacker, Helmut Schmidt, Richard Perle, and Denis Healey—presented lectures on the arms race for the Programme for Strategic and International Security Studies, Geneva, Switzerland, in 1985. While the U.S. contributor lauds the benefits of military technology, the three Europeans warn about the dangers of its use. The Europeans are also much more disposed toward arms control agreements than their U.S. counterpart. These lectures show the diversity of opinion within the Western alliance, and the depth of feeling these issues can generate.

1144　*International Security and the Brezhnev Doctrine.* New York: CAUSA Publications, 1985. 125pp.

The International Security Council sponsored a 1985 conference on the Brezhnev Doctrine and international security in Brussels, Belgium, where international security experts presented short papers on the international security implications of the Brezhnev Doctrine. These papers dispute the Brezhnev Doctrine that once a socialist country accepts membership in the "community of socialist states" its submission to Soviet hegemony is irreversible. The participants challenge this doctrine, but concrete recommendations to fight it are lacking.

1145　International Security Council. *Crisis and Response: A Roundtable on Mexico.* New York: CAUSA, 1986. 98pp. ISSN 0882–4878.

These papers are the result of a 1986 conference sponsored by the International Security Council (ISC) and held in San Diego, California. Mexico's internal problems and the impact of these problems on Mexican-American relations are the subjects of this book. Mexico's political instability poses a threat to U.S. strategic interests, and the United States should take positive steps to promote economic growth in Mexico to relieve potential discontent. Although most of the essays contained in this work are short, there are enough substantive issues presented to make the book informative.

1146 International Security Council. *The United States, China and the Soviet Union: Strategic Dilemmas and Options.* New York: CAUSA, 1986. 22pp. ISSN 0882–4878.

The strategic importance of Asia and the Pacific Basin, and the interplay of China, the Soviet Union, and the United States in this region are the subjects of this short monograph. China provides a valuable buffer zone separating the Soviet Union and the United States, but the Taiwan question hampers the possibility of a full-scale alliance with the United States. Taiwan is strategically located for a new "containment line" reaching from South Korea and Japan to the Philippines. This essay is full of suggestive ideas, but its brevity prevents a complete analysis.

1147 *International Security Dimensions of Space.* Edited by Uri Ra'anan and Robert L. Pfaltzgraff. Hamden, CT: Archon Books, 1984. 324pp. ISBN 0–208–02023–3.

These papers are the result of the International Security Studies Program of the Fletcher School of Law and Diplomacy's Eleventh Annual Conference, Tufts University, Medford, MA. Participants were most concerned with the need for the United States to adopt a coherent national space policy with both civilian and military components. This position is part of a shared belief that the United States should take the lead in introducing military weapons into space. Many of the proposals and recommendations made by these authors have subsequently been adopted as parts of the Reagan administration's space policy.

1148 *International Security in Southwest Asia.* Edited by Hafeez Malik. New York: Praeger, 1984. 232pp. ISBN 0–03–071011–1.

Security issues in South Asia, the Persian/Arabian Gulf, and the Middle East have been brought together as the result of a 1983 seminar held at Villanova University, Philadelphia. While the essays highlight troublespots in these volatile regions, the overview of seminar discussions contributes the most information and viewpoints. The give and take of opinions by participants and the high quality of the essays make this book a good introductory source.

1149 *International Security in the Southeast Asian and Southwest Pacific Region.* Edited by T. B. Millar. St. Lucia, Australia: University of Queensland Press, 1983. 317pp. ISBN 0–7022–1973–8.

Scholars from Australia and South Asia attended a 1982 conference on Asian security issues hosted by the Strategic and Defence Studies Centre at the Australian National University, and this organization published these papers. Most of the contributors found the changing international scene in Southeast Asia unsettling because of its long-range implications. There are three threats to this region—global disorder, regional disputes, and internal instability—but none of these threats is imminent. This book is a balanced assessment of the changing international scene in a vital region of the world.

1150 *Intervention in World Politics.* Edited by Hedley Bull. Oxford, England: Clarendon Press, 1984. 198pp. ISBN 0–19827–467–1.

These papers on the issue of military intervention in world politics are a product of a course of lectures at Oxford University in 1982. The consensus of opinion among the authors is that military and political intervention is a built-in feature of the international order. But beyond this point, the authors disagree on the legal and moral justifications for interventionism. Each paper is of a high quality, and this book is worth consulting on the theory and practice of interventionism.

1151 *Ireland and the Threat of Nuclear War.* Edited by Bill McSweeney. Dublin: Dominican Publications, 1985. 203pp. ISBN 0–907271–52–9.

Under the auspices of the Department of Peace Studies, Irish School of Ecumenics, Dublin, European security specialists undertook a study of the effectiveness of Irish neutrality in a world threatened by nuclear war. After the authors debated the merits and demerits of Irish neutrality, the consensus developed that Irish policy on neutrality is the best course for Ireland to pursue. But this neutrality has to be active, not isolationist, and Irish foreign policy should continue to be directed toward establishing nuclear-free zones and promoting nonproliferation of nuclear weapons. These writings present the best case scenario for neutrality, and many of the arguments are also valid for other small states.

1152 *Israeli Security Planning in the 1980s: Its Politics and Economics.* Edited by Zavi Lanir. New York: Praeger, 1984. 271pp. ISBN 0–03–063802–X.

The structural aspect of the Israeli national defense establishment is the topic of this study by Israeli scholars under the sponsorship of the Jaffee Center for Strategic Studies, Tel Aviv. Much attention is devoted to an examination of Israeli defense needs and the capacity of the economy to respond to these requirements. The conclusion is that national defense requirements have weakened the Israeli economy almost to a danger point. This book is an important addition to the ongoing debate on the interaction between defense spending and economic growth, and it also contributes to an understanding of Israeli security problems.

1153 Jacobsen, Carl G. *The Nuclear Era: Its History, Its Implications.* Cambridge, MA: Oelgeschlager, Gunn and Hain, 1982. 142pp. ISBN 0–89946–158–1.

This essay by a Soviet area specialist and strategic defense analyst draws together a variety of perspectives on the present international scene. It grew out of a five-part University of the Air series for Canadian Television (CTV). The result is a balanced assessment of the current nuclear balance of power and the dangers of nuclear proliferation. Ideas rather than information make this book a good source for the general reader.

1154 Jain, B. M. *South Asian Security: Problems and Prospects.* New Delhi: Radiant Publishers, 1985. 201pp. ISBN 81–7027–085–5.

South Asian security problems are surveyed in this book by a prominent Indian scholar. The author concludes that great-power intervention in the South Asian region and the resulting military competition have hurt the political and economic development of this region, and that South Asian states should eschew outside aid and work to build and strengthen economic, social, and food security in order to ensure stability and order in the region.

While both the anti-U.S. and anti-Pakistan biases lessen the objectivity of this book, the author does express a significant viewpoint current in India.

1155　Johnson, Maxwell Orme. *The Military as an Instrument of U.S. Policy in Southwest Asia: The Rapid Deployment Joint Task Force, 1979–1982.* Boulder, CO: Westview Press, 1983. 134pp. ISBN 0–86531–952–9.

The development of the Rapid Deployment Joint Task Force (RDJTF) from the Carter to the Reagan administrations and its role in U.S. policy in Southwest Asia are the subjects of this book. This force was established by President Jimmy Carter's commitment of the United States to the defense of the Persian Gulf. President Ronald Reagan has continued this policy, and the RDJTF is a valuable instrument of U.S. foreign policy. Both the history and the evaluation of the RDJTF make this book a valuable source.

1156　Johnstone, Diana. *The Politics of Euromissiles: Europe's Role in America's World.* London: Verso, 1984. 218pp. ISBN 0–86091–082–2.

The European correspondent for the U.S. weekly *In These Times* analyzes the controversy in Europe over the deployment of nuclear missiles in Europe. She charges that Western European governments have been drawn into closer military involvement with the United States as a result of the Euromissiles crisis, and her views are hostile toward the nuclear deterrence strategy of the Reagan administration. This book is a vehicle for the author's opinions rather than a scholarly treatment, and the analysis suffers.

1157　Jones, Rodney W. *Modern Weapons and Third World Powers.* Boulder, CO: Westview Press, 1984. 125pp. ISBN 0–86531–871–9.

This book is a broad overview of the papers presented at a 1983 conference sponsored by the Center for Strategic and International Studies, Georgetown University, Washington, DC. The findings are that regional Third World powers are weaker militarily than is commonly supposed, and that threats to these regimes are more domestic than external. Nevertheless, the author concludes that conflicts are far more likely in the Third World than among the industrialized states, and that demand for modern weapons will remain high in the Third World. Current U.S. policy is to participate in arms transfers to the Third World with the justification that otherwise other countries will supply the weapons.

1158　Karsh, Ephraim. *The Cautious Bear: Soviet Military Engagement in Middle East Wars in the Post-1967 Era.* Boulder, CO: Westview Press, 1985. 97pp. ISBN 0–8133–0325–7.

This study analyzes characteristics of Soviet military engagement in the Middle East since 1967. The author recognizes two types of Soviet military policy—military involvement and military intervention. Soviet actions in the Middle East have included military involvement, supplying equipment and advisors, but otherwise Soviet behavior has been and remains conservative. This book shows the Soviet distaste for military interventionism.

1159　Karsten, Peter, Peter O. Howell, and Artis Frances Allen. *Military Threats: A Systematic Historical Analysis of the Determinants of Success.* Westport, CT: Greenwood Press, 1984. 166pp. ISBN 0–313–23825–1.

Direct military threat as a strategic concept is the subject of this book. A study of eighty-three historical cases provides the data, but the interpretations are intended to apply to present and future situations. Important conclusions of this study are that the standard interpretations of the benefits of threatening are less apparent than supposed and that a threatening power must allow for the possibility of having its bluff called. This book is an important work, not because of its thesis, but because several of the standard hypotheses proved weak under scrutiny.

1160   Katz, Mark N. *The Third World in Soviet Military Thought*. Baltimore, MD: Johns Hopkins University Press, 1982. 188pp. ISBN 0–8018–2875–9.
Military thought on Third World conflicts during the Leonid Brezhnev era (1964–1981) is the subject of this book. The military had a strong role in formulating Soviet ideas about conflict in the Third World. After an initial period of optimism about Soviet gains through low-level, low-cost involvement in Third World conflicts, the Soviet military became more pessimistic about achieving foreign policy gains without large-scale, long-term commitments. This book marks the changes in Soviet attitudes toward Third World conflicts, and its value resides in identifying this trend.

1161   Kaushik, Brij Mohan, and O. N. Mehrotra. *Pakistan's Nuclear Bomb*. New Delhi: Sopan Publishing House, 1980. 228pp.
Two Indian security specialists examine Pakistan's nuclear policy and assess its nuclear capability. They recognize that Pakistan's drive for nuclear weapons is in response to its rivalry with India, and that part of this is the fault of the Indian government and its policy of not explaining its nuclear position, but maintain that Pakistan's acquisition of nuclear weapons endangers peace in South Asia. This book is more balanced on this subject than most Indian writings, but the gravity of the problem to India is apparent.

1162   Kaushik, Devendra. *The Indian Ocean: A Strategic Dimension*. New Delhi: Vikas Publishing House, 1983. 107pp. ISBN 0–7069–2335–9.
The author uses this book to attack the U.S. presence in the Indian Ocean. U.S. strategy has been aimed at the Indian Ocean for advancing neocolonial domination of this region. India has been active and should continue to be in favor of an Indian Ocean Peace Zone free of outside maritime powers. This author argues for a situation in which India assumes the role of the dominant naval power in the Indian Ocean, and his anti-U.S. tone is part of this campaign.

1163   Khalilzad, Zalmay. *Security of Southwest Asia*. London: Gower, 1984. 191pp. ISBN 0–566–00651–0.
Security issues in Southwest Asia are analyzed by a scholar at the International Institute for Strategic Studies, London. Afghanistan, India, Iran, and Pakistan's security problems are outlined, and each state's major external or internal crises are highlighted. Because of these problems, there is no stability in this region at this time and little likelihood of stability in the near future. This book provides a good introduction to the security problems of Southwest Asia.

1164   El-Khawas, Mohamed, and Samir Abed-Rabbo. *American Aid to Israel: Nature and Impact*. Brattleboro, VT: Amana Books, 1984. 191pp. ISBN 0–915597–03–9.
Critics of U.S. military aid to Israel produced this book to marshal evidence against further financial assistance to Israel. They use a draft report

from the General Accounting Office (GAO) to reinforce their contentions. Their arguments are that U.S. aid buttresses the aggressive policies of the Israeli state. This book argues a case, but it is with the publication of the GAO report that the authors make their contribution.

1165 Klare, Michael T. *Beyond the "Vietnam Syndrome": U.S. Interventionism in the 1980s.* Washington, DC: Institute for Policy Studies, 1981. 137pp. ISBN 0–89758–027–3.

U.S. interventionist policy in the early years of the Reagan administration is the subject of this study by the director of the Militarism and Disarmament Project of the Institute for Policy Studies. His thesis is that official attitudes in the U.S. government have shifted away from the nonintervention policy of the immediate post-Vietnam era toward armed intervention. Moreover, the United States has a far more formidable capacity for long-distance interventionary operations than the Soviet Union. While several of the potential battlefields have changed, the main thesis of the study is still worth notice and further study.

1166 Klieman, Aaron S. *Israel's Global Reach: Arms Sales as Diplomacy.* Washington, DC: Pergamon-Brassey's, 1985. 240pp. ISBN 0–08–031924–6.

The role of Israel as an arms exporter to the Third World and the relationship of this trade to diplomatic goals are examined in detail in this book by an Israeli author. Israel gains political, security, and economic benefits from this trade, but it remains sensitive to publicity about arms deals. Most of this trade has been on the lower level of arms technology, but there are trends for entry into top-of-the-line, technologically sophisticated systems. This book is both a scholarly treatment of a complex subject and a warning for the Israeli government to go slow on its arms trade.

1167 Kolodziej, Edward A. *French Arms Transfers and the Military-Industrial Complex.* Chicago: Chicago Council on Foreign Relations, 1980. 32pp.

The author examines the influence of arms exports on the arms industry of the world's third largest arms dealer. French political leaders support arms exports from a variety of national security, foreign policy, and domestic economic and political objectives. This support and the economic benefits to the French economy ensure that France will continue to be a major arms supplier. This short monograph shows the importance of arms sales to a national economy, and the difficulty of any attempt to curtail this trade.

1168 Kratochwil, Friedrich, Paul Rohrlick, and Harpreet Mahajan. *Peace and Disputed Sovereignty: Reflections on Conflict over Territory.* Lanham, MD: University Press of America, 1985. 159pp. ISBN 0–8191–4953–5.

This book is an analysis of unresolved cases of disputed sovereignty and border disputes worldwide. Using a series of case studies, the authors examine current and potential areas of conflict and trace patterns of conflict in every region of the world. They conclude that there are unit-environment, interunit, and center-periphery relations considerations in any recurring border and territorial disputes. The intent of this book is to furnish a conceptual basis for resolving conflicts, and it is both stimulating and a significant work of scholarship.

1169 Krickus, Richard J. *The Superpowers in Crisis: Implications of Domestic Discord.* Washington, DC: Pergamon-Brassey's, 1987. 236pp. ISBN 0–08–034705–3.

The author advances the thesis that both the Soviet Union and the United States are in the throes of a societal crisis that will increase East-West tensions to the danger point. While Soviet economic, political, and military problems are worse than those of the United States, neither side is immune to its type of crisis. It is in the realm of economics that the greatest dangers to both systems reside. This book is a mixture of solid analysis and conjecture, making it a stimulating but uneven work.

1170   Laird, Robbin F. *France, the Soviet Union, and the Nuclear Weapons Issue*. Boulder, CO: Westview Press, 1985. 142pp. ISBN 0–8133–7018–3.
The conflict between the Soviet Union and France over the role of nuclear weapons in European defense is examined in this book. France has a key role in determining the cohesion of the Western alliance, because of its nuclear assets. The continued independent stance of France works to the advantage of the Soviets and to the detriment of NATO. This monograph gives a balanced assessment of the importance of France to the Western alliance, and it is a work worth reading.

1171   Laird, Robbin F., and Dale R. Herspring. *The Soviet Union and Strategic Arms*. Boulder, CO: Westview Press, 1984. 160pp. ISBN 0–8133–0054–1.
This book is an assessment of Soviet foreign and military policy since 1970. The authors fear that an endless and unregulated arms race may be the result of Soviet perceptions of U.S. efforts to regain military superiority. A weakness of this book is that it bases its treatment of Soviet perceptions upon incomplete or polemical materials. Despite this limitation, it is a stimulating book on a difficult subject.

1172   Larson, Deborah Welch. *Origins of Containment: A Psychological Explanation*. Princeton, NJ: Princeton University Press, 1985. 380pp. ISBN 0–691–07691–X.
The author seeks to analyze the historical origins of the containment policy by the use of cognitive social psychology. Four key figures—W. Averell Harriman, Harry S Truman, James F. Byrnes, and Dean Acheson—are studied for their influence in shaping containment doctrine. It was the international distribution of power and domestic politics that combined to cause these leaders to turn to a containment policy. While this study deals with historical situations, it contributes more than history, and its value is its examination of the development of the Cold War mentality.

1173   Lasater, Martin L. *Taiwan: Facing Mounting Threats*, rev. ed. Washington, DC: Heritage Foundation, 1987. 82pp. ISBN 0–89195–220–9.
The author gauges the strength of the threat to the Republic of China (ROC) on Taiwan from the People's Republic of China (PRC). By use of the threat assessment format, the author concludes that the PRC does not pose an imminent threat of invasion against Taiwan, but it has the capability of causing trouble for Taiwan. Moreover, the probability of a PRC use of force against Taiwan over the next few years is small. This short book from a conservative think tank is a realistic assessment of a problem long troublesome to U.S. conservatives.

1174   Lasater, Martin L. *The Taiwan Issue in Sino-American Strategic Relations*. Boulder, CO: Westview Press, 1984. 283pp. ISBN 0–86531–842–5.
The role of Taiwan in determining relations between the People's Republic of China (PRC) and the United States is examined in this book. While Taiwan

provides an irritant in Sino-U.S. relations, the PRC is more concerned with friendly relations with the United States. Chinese leaders desire the security and the freedom to modernize, and U.S. leaders like the counterbalance of the PRC against the Soviet Union. This book is a solid assessment of Taiwan's position in the context of Sino-U.S. relations.

1175 Lawrence, Robert G. *US Policy in Southwest Asia: A Failure in Perspective.* Washington, DC: National Defense University Press, 1984. 65pp.
  The author, a senior officer in the U.S. Air Force, advances the thesis that overreliance on military action has hurt U.S. foreign policy in Southwest Asia. This is because of the failure of U.S. policymakers to understand the historical, political, and religious dynamics of Southwest Asian states. Interviews with over fifty Arab political leaders, scholars, and businessmen reinforce this point. Both the information from these interviews and the author's recommendations make this short book a welcome addition to security literature.

1176 Lebow, Richard Ned. *Between Peace and War: The Nature of International Crisis.* Baltimore, MD: Johns Hopkins University Press, 1981. 350pp. ISBN 0−8018−2311−0.
  The relationship between crisis and war is examined by the author to determine the extent to which a crisis influences the course of a conflict. Twenty-six historical cases are utilized for data, and Lebow concludes that the immediate cause of war can exercise an important and even decisive influence on the course of a conflict and that a narrow research focus on techniques of crisis management is not likely to lead to improved crisis performance. This book is both stimulating and suggestive, and its combination of historical analysis and crisis theory make it worth reading.

1177 Levite, Ariel, and Athanassios Platias. *Evaluating Small States' Dependence on Arms Imports: An Alternative Perspective.* Ithaca, NY: Peace Studies Program, 1983. 73pp.
  Issues of power, influence, and leverage between small states and their arms suppliers are the subjects of this monograph. The suppliers of arms have the goal of gaining influence and leverage over the recipients of this aid. A conclusion is that small states have been able to withstand pressure from their arms suppliers. This work looks at a narrow topic, but it provides useful insight into a problem of long standing.

1178 Link, Werner. *The East-West Conflict: The Organization of International Relations in the Twentieth Century.* Leamington Spa, England: Berg, 1986. 198pp. ISBN 0−907582−05−2.
  This book is a revised version of an earlier work, *Der Ost-West-Konflikt* (Stuttgart, West Germany, Kohlhammer, 1980), by an eminent West German scholar on international affairs. While the East-West conflict is not the only conflict configuration in international politics, it still dominates world politics because the protagonists are the Soviet Union and the United States. The central factor of this relationship has been the new emphasis on balance-of-power politics. This book is a high-quality effort to study the East-West conflict by a recognized authority on the subject.

1179 Lowenthal, Abraham F. *Partners in Conflict: The United States and Latin America.* Baltimore, MD: Johns Hopkins University Press, 1987. 240pp. ISBN 0−8018−3397−3.

The author surveys past and current relations between the United States and Latin America and concludes that traditional concepts and concerns of the United States toward this region are outmoded. Current obsession with Central America is part of this dated approach, because exclusive concentration on U.S. security interests fails to note economic and political changes in the Caribbean and Latin American world. Cooperation rather than confrontation is the best policy for the United States to adopt in its relations with this region. This book argues a persuasive case, but present political trends in the United States make most of the author's recommendations impractical.

1180 Luard, Evan. *War in International Society: A Study in International Sociology.* London: I. B. Tauris, 1986. 468pp. ISBN 1-85043-0128.
The author undertakes the study of war and its impact on international relations. Using sociological theories and historical examples, he concludes that war has no social functions, but it has been tolerated as a normal undertaking. Most wars today have their origins as civil wars, and the decline in the number of these wars will depend on the means of securing changes in states without the need to resort to conflict. While this book is difficult to read, it contains thoughtful analysis that should stimulate further research on the nature of war.

1181 Luttwak, Edward N. *The Grand Strategy of the Soviet Union.* London: Weidenfeld and Nicolson, 1983. 242pp. ISBN 0-297-78217-7.
This book is an assessment of the Soviet Union and its strategy toward the world. The author maintains that the Soviets handle the Soviet Union much as the czars did Russia, and this drive for empire is the source of most of the international problems of the postwar world. Continued growth of Soviet military power will be able to neutralize the Western alliance by frightening some members into neutrality. The evil empire thesis is outlined at its best, or worst, in this book.

1182 Lutz, Dieter S. *The Unintended World War III: On the Danger of War, the Various Scenarios, the Chance of Damage Limiting and the Bonus of the First Strike.* Hamburg, West Germany: Institüt für Friedensforschung und Sicherheitspolitik, 1983. 31 leaves.
The author examines the probability of war breaking out in the 1980s and the outcome of any such a war. Various scenarios of warfare are examined—conventional offensive, conventional blitzkrieg, and nuclear offensive—with nuclear weapons becoming important in each scenario. The probability of war is slight, but it will come because of mutual mistrust rather than Soviet adventurism. This paper has calculated the probability and form of war in this decade, and this projection is of considerable interest.

1183 Luzin, Nikolai. *Nuclear Strategy and Common Sense.* Moscow: Progress Publishers, 1981. 350pp.
This book is a historical treatise on the development of NATO's nuclear strategy from the Soviet viewpoint. Not surprising is that the Soviet author is critical of NATO military strategy and favorable to Soviet foreign policy goals. He favors détente, and most of his hostility is directed toward the critics of this policy. There is little useful information in this book that cannot be found elsewhere.

1184 MacFarlane, Neil. *Soviet Intervention in Third World Conflict.* Geneva, Switzerland: Programme for Strategic and International Security Studies, 1983. 58 leaves.

This paper is an examination of recent Soviet interventions in Afghanistan, Angola, and Ethiopia and an assessment of gains and losses in these types of military interventions. Sóviet interventionist behavior in the 1970s has been reactive and opportunistic, but growing internal problems may force the Soviets to pursue a more moderate foreign policy. However, it is in the best interests of the United States to adopt a firmer posture toward Soviet interventions. This paper presents an array of information that most security specialists will welcome.

1185 *The Making of America's Soviet Policy.* Edited by Joseph S. Nye. New Haven, CT: Yale University Press, 1984. 369pp. ISBN 0–300–03140–8.

These papers originate out of a collective enterprise of the Council for International Relations and two Harvard University research centers—the Center for International Affairs and the Center for Science and International Affairs. The authors focus on U.S. institutions and capabilities for dealing with the Soviet Union. U.S. policy has been successful in avoiding nuclear war, but less so in containing the spread of Soviet power and ideology and in changing the nature and behavior of the Soviet Union. This book contains a number of high-quality papers, and it is the caliber of the scholarship that makes the work important.

1186 Mandebaum, Michael. *The Nuclear Future.* Ithaca, NY: Cornell University Press, 1983. 131pp. ISBN 0–8014–1619–1.

This essay describes the world nuclear state so that the general reader can better understand the debate about nuclear weapons. The author's conclusion is that the nuclear future will follow the middle path between nuclear war and nuclear disarmament. Both the superpowers will continue to deter each other, but the rivalry will endure with an arms race and proxy wars. Despite the author's limited intent, this book is a balanced assessment that international security specialists will find stimulating.

1187 Mansfield, Sue. *The Gestalts of War: An Inquiry into Its Origins and Meanings as a Social Institution.* New York: Dial Press, 1982. 274pp. ISBN 0–86979–572–4.

The author integrates theories of gestalt psychology to approach an understanding of the sociology of war. By studying the theory of aggression and its place in war, she deals with the problem of the modification of human behavior from the individual to the state. She concludes that attempts for immediate nuclear disarmament are counterproductive because decision-makers are too deeply frightened by the consequences. This book is stimulating, but it will remain controversial because of its psychological approach and its conclusions.

1188 Marais, N. *Deterrence and Deterrence Interaction.* Pretoria, South Africa: Institute for Strategic Studies, 1984. 74pp. ISBN 086979–572–4.

The concepts of strategic deterrence and deterrence interaction are analyzed by a South African scholar. By analyzing nuclear, conventional, and Cold War deterrence levels the author attempts to isolate the best type of deterrence with the Republic of South Africa as the test case. Every possible situation of deterrence interaction is considered, but the author concludes that the decisive factor remains the opponent's perception of deterrence. While this monograph lacks clarity of presentation, scholars of deterrence theory should still find it stimulating.

1189 *The Maritime Strategy.* Edited by James A. Barber. Annapolis, MD: U.S. Naval Institute, 1986. 47pp.

This publication is the closest thing to an official U.S. government statement of policy on maritime strategy. It contains three articles by leaders of maritime strategic policy—Admiral James D. Watkins, General P. X. Kelley, and John F. Lehman, Jr. There is also an excellent bibliography of contemporary U.S. naval strategy, 1979–1985. Together the articles give a good indication of the thinking of the current administration on maritime affairs.

1190 Martin, Laurence. *The Two-Edged Sword: Armed Force in the Modern World.* New York: W. W. Norton, 1982. 108pp. ISBN 0–393–01655–2.

The author has published his six lectures from the Reith Lectures in 1981 on security issues facing the international community. While he treats various issues from deterrence to arms control, Martin is most emphatic that the present strategic system is dangerous and that nuclear deterrence is a faulty doctrine. However, he is less enthusiastic about any of the other theories to retain the strategic balance between the superpowers. These essays suffer from their brevity as lectures, but the author has produced a series of remarkable think-pieces of value to scholars in the field.

1191 Martin, Lenore G. *The Unstable Gulf: Threats from Within.* Lexington, MA: Lexington Books, 1984. 232pp. ISBN 0–669–05558–1.

The author devotes this book to an examination of U.S. policy options for achieving security in the Persian Gulf region in the remaining decades of this century. Both the Carter Doctrine and the Reagan corollary commit the United States to the defense of the region from external and internal threats. While territorial disputes, internal cleavages, and religious divisions promote instability in this region, this instability presents no clear present dangers to the achievement of U.S. goals. This is a solid work by a competent scholar, and her analysis is worth the price of the book.

1192 Al-Mashat, Aldul-Monem. *National Security in the Third World.* Boulder, CO: Westview Press, 1985. 153pp. ISBN 0–86531–834–4.

The interaction between domestic politics and national security concerns in Third World countries is the subject of this book. At first Third World countries concentrated on building up political freedom and territorial sovereignty, but this emphasis has now changed in the same countries to supporting the economy and improving social services. This change has meant that security and development have become interchangeable components of Third World national security. The author uses various methodological tools to rank developing countries, and these rankings make this work an important source.

1193 MccGwire, Michael. *Military Objectives in Soviet Foreign Policy.* Washington, DC: Brookings Institution, 1987. 530pp. ISBN 0–8157–5552–X.

The author is a senior fellow at the Brookings Institution, and his area of concentration is on strategic objectives in Soviet military thinking as it applies to foreign policy. Beginning with a decision in 1966, the Soviets changed strategic objectives to avoid nuclear conflict and improve their chances in a conventional war. Arms control becomes a part of this strategy, but the introduction of the Strategic Defense Initiative (SDI) endangers this Soviet strategy and contributes to international instability. The author has produced a stimulating book of value to any researcher in the security field.

1194 McKinlay, R. D., and A. Mughan. *Aid and Arms to the Third World: An Analysis of the Distribution and Impact of US Official Transfers*. London: Frances Pinter, 1984. 282pp. ISBN 0–903804–87–5.

U.S. official transfers of economic aid, military assistance, and arms sales to the Third World between 1950 and 1979 are surveyed in this book. Both the volume and objectives of these transfers were studied for trends. The authors conclude that power politics and competition with the Soviet Union influence U.S. transfers of aid more than economic or other political motives. This study is an important contribution to the study of U.S. aid transfers because it eschews polemics for an analytical approach.

1195 McNaugher, Thomas L. *Arms and Oil: U.S. Military Strategy and the Persian Gulf*. Washington, DC: Brookings Institution, 1985. 226pp. ISBN 0–8157–5624–0.

In this book the role of the United States in the oil-rich Persian Gulf is examined by a research associate in the Brookings Foreign Policy Studies Program. The author contends that U.S. military planning needs to be integrated into regional diplomacy, and military equipment acquired to improve air- and sealift capability. Gulf security cannot be handled by the United States unilaterally, and informal diplomatic arrangements can be used to acquire support for military operations. This book is a critical study of Persian Gulf security issues, and events have reinforced many of the author's contentions.

1196 Mendl, Wolf. *Western Europe and Japan between the Superpowers*. London: Croom Helm, 1984. 181pp. ISBN 0–7099–1722–8.

A British security scholar examines the relationship of Western Europe and Japan with the superpowers. Both powers identify with the direction provided by the United States, but there are political and economic reasons for changing the nature of this relationship. Rather than a global alliance dominated by the United States or nonalignment, the author suggests a third course—a basic security agreement with the United States and a promotion of internationalism outside of the two superpower blocs. This book is an assessment of a reorientation of the Western alliance without the prospect of a corresponding change in the Soviet bloc.

1197 Menon, Rajan. *Soviet Power and the Third World*. New Haven, CT: Yale University Press, 1986. 261pp. ISBN 0–300–03500–4.

The role of the Soviet Union in the affairs of the Third World is the subject of this book. Since around 1970, the Soviets have engaged more in overt and covert military intervention in the Third World because of an increase of confidence in Soviet power by it leadership. However, recent setbacks in the 1980s made the Soviets more conservative in aid and military commitments to socialist-oriented states in the Third World. This book is an objective assessment of Soviet objectives in the Third World, and its analysis makes it an important addition to security literature.

1198 *The Middle East in the 1980s: Problems and Prospects.* Edited by Philip H. Stoddard. Washington, DC: Middle East Institute, 1983. 189pp. ISBN 0–916808–25–4.

These papers are the products of a two-day conference in 1983 at the National Defense University, Washington, DC. Middle East specialists from the government and academia presented papers on economic, international security, and political trends in the Middle East. While no consensus developed among the participants, the strategic importance of the Middle East was acknowledged by all, as was the difficulty of solving the political problems of the region. These papers are not major contributions to the security field, but they are solid attempts to understand the issues at stake in the Middle East.

1199 *Militarization in the Non-Hispanic Caribbean.* Edited by Alma H. Young and Dion E. Phillips. Boulder, CO: Lynne Rienner, 1986. 178pp. ISBN 0–931477–78–6.

These papers are products of a panel on military policies in the non-Hispanic Caribbean presented at the Ninth Annual Meeting of the Caribbean Studies Association in St. Kitts, 1984. The Caribbean has been an area of frenzied preoccupation with security affairs since the overthrow of Somoza in Nicaragua and Grenada in 1979. U.S. policies have dictated this militarization because of the perceived need to protect its economic and security interests. This book is a solid addition to the literature on security issues of this region.

1200 *The Military Balance in Europe.* Stockholm: Swedish Institute of International Affairs, 1982. 152pp. ISBN 91–7182–4561.

The theme of this series of essays is that there is a relative military balance in Europe between NATO and the Warsaw Pact forces. Statistical data is presented to back this assertion, and the authors emphasize the place of Sweden in this military balance. It is by its balanced pro-Swedish viewpoint that this book makes its contribution.

1201 *The Military Intelligence Community.* Edited by Gerald W. Hopple and Bruce W. Watson. Boulder, CO: Westview Press, 1986. 298pp. ISBN 0–8133–7009–4.

By outlining the organization and the processes of intelligence gathering by the U.S. military intelligence community, this book of essays attempts to dispel myths about these agencies and to point out the positive aspects of U.S. military intelligence. The increase in size of intelligence activities and the development of intelligence-gathering technology are the two most notable trends during the recent past. This book is an upbeat analysis of U.S. military intelligence operations, and it makes a positive contribution to understanding the aspirations of the intelligence community.

1202 *Military Intervention in the Third World: Threats, Constraints, and Options.* Edited by John H. Maurer and Richard H. Porth. New York: Praeger, 1984. 237pp. ISBN 0–03–071174–6.

The essays in this book deal with both the theoretical and practical aspects of military intervention in Third World countries with special reference to U.S. policies. U.S. policy has had the problem of balancing its strategic interests in Third World states with the dangers of military intervention. Any intervention is predicated on the organization of the right type of military forces to carry out the mission, and the United States has yet to develop this type of military organization. These essays reinforce the contention that military intervention in the Third World is a dangerous policy for either of the superpowers.

1203 *Military Power and Policy in Asian States: China, India, Japan.* Edited by Onkar Marwah and Jonathan D. Pollack. Boulder, CO: Westview Press, 1980. 180pp. ISBN 0–89158–407–2.

These papers examine the security and military policies in three Asian states—China, India, and Japan—to trace their development away from dependence on major powers. These states have become challenger-states because their policies challenge the status quo. These papers delineate the ways these Asian states have deviated from the two superpower blocs to pursue independent policies. This book has solid articles useful for any student of international security.

1204 Millar, T. B. *The East-West Strategic Balance.* London: Allen and Unwin, 1981. 199pp. ISBN 0–04–355015–0.

This book surveys the strategic military balance between the United States and the Soviet Union, and their allies and associates, from the viewpoint of an Australian security expert. The author treats the alliance systems, areas of potential danger, and areas of strategic competition in a comparative fashion and concludes that recent shifts in foreign policy during the 1970s have strengthened the Soviet bloc and weakened the Western bloc. This book is meant more as an introduction to the problem than a summation, but the author's treatment of the subject is solid.

1205 Morgan, Patrick M. *Deterrence: A Conceptual Analysis,* 2d ed. Beverly Hills, CA: Sage Publications, 1983. 240pp. ISBN 8–8039–1977–8.

The conceptual basis of the strategic theory of deterrence is the topic of this book. While deterrence has been the cornerstone of U.S. national security policy since 1946, deterrence is not sufficiently capable of preventing war. The thesis is that deterrence works by reinforcing the normal unwillingness of governments to do risky and dangerous things, but it fails when a variety of factors and conditions makes governments take risks. This updating of an earlier work still makes a solid contribution to security literature.

1206 Mushkat, Marion. *The Third World and Peace: Some Aspects of the Interrelationship of Underdevelopment and International Security.* New York: St. Martin's Press, 1982. 260pp. ISBN 0–312–80039–8.

In this book an Israeli scholar examines the impact of militarization on economic development in Third World countries. Economic development in the Third World has been hurt by the superpower rivalry and the arms race. Foreign intervention and failures of Third World governing elites are other factors hindering development in the underdeveloped countries. The author places most of the blame on the Soviet Union, but his book still remains a useful attempt to understand Third World development problems.

1207 Muttam, John. *Arms and Insecurity in the Persian Gulf.* New Delhi: Radiant Publishers, 1984. 227pp.

The arms race and its impact on the security of the Persian Gulf states is the subject of this book. Competitive arms procurement from the developed countries by states in the Persian Gulf region has served as a destabilizing factor in this area. The author maintains that regional arms races are by-products of intervention by the great powers in the politics of developing countries, and that only by arms control can these states regain their independence. This plea for arms control in the Persian Gulf outlines the problems with little difficulty, but the author's solutions lack practical application.

1208 Mutz, Reinhard. *Common Security: Elements of an Alternative to Deterrence Peace.* Hamburg, West Germany: Institut für Friedensforschung und Sicherheitspolitik, 1986. 84pp.
Common security as a way out of the problem of security against war and aggression is the subject of this book. Two criteria must be confronted before the concept of common security can work: efficacy and practicability. There is nothing to prevent the workability of common security, but critics on the sides of pessimism and optimism fail to note that recognition of the mutual interest of survival is the key to making common security work. This book is a theoretical analysis of the concept of common security, and the ideas in it are worth further consideration.

1209 Nacht, Michael. *The Age of Vulnerability: Threats to the Nuclear Stalemate.* Washington, DC: Brookings Institution, 1985. 209pp. ISBN 0–8157–5964–9.
The author investigates the role played by nuclear weapons in the national security policies of the Soviet Union and the United States. A nuclear stalemate has developed between the two superpowers, and this stalemate should be preserved rather than undermined. Because of Soviet insecurity, the Soviet government must be treated with firmness but without belligerence. Although the author selected a difficult subject, his treatment is a solid contribution to the literature on international security.

1210 Nashif, Taysir N. *Nuclear Warfare in the Middle East: Dimensions and Responsibilities.* Princeton, NJ: Kinston Press, 1984. 142pp. ISBN 0–940670–20–8.
This work examines the political, military and psychological impacts of the introduction of nuclear weapons into the Middle East. Israel has a nuclear arsenal, and it has come to rely on the threat of nuclear weapons to counter the Arab threat. Arab response has been and will continue to be to match Israel both in conventional and nuclear weaponry. This book is a sobering analysis of nuclear proliferation in one of the danger regions of the world.

1211 *National Interests and the Military Use of Space.* Edited by William J. Durch. Cambridge, MA: Ballinger, 1984. 281pp. ISBN 0–88410–974–7.
These papers on the military use of space by the Soviet Union and the United States are a product of the Space Working Group, a body of individuals knowledgeable about the politics and technologies of the military uses of outer space. An assumption common in all the papers is that there is no alternative to the use of space for military purposes. It will be the limits of technology that will limit Soviet and U.S. deployment of space weapons systems. While this book remains an invaluable source for the technology of military uses of outer space, many of its assumptions and conclusions could be questioned.

1212 *National Security and International Stability.* Edited by Bernard Brodie, Michael D. Intriligator, and Roman Kolkowicz. Cambridge, MA: Oelgeschlager, Gunn and Hain, 1983. 441pp. ISBN 0–89946–172–7.

The essays in this book are reassessments of the validity of earlier writings on the problems of national security, strategy, and arms control. A reexamination of these theories on deterrénce and national security from the golden age of strategic thought tests them for applicability in the 1980s. Over twenty scholars presented essays on these assessments in their areas of specialty. This book is a critical look at past U.S. strategic thought, and it reflects high intellectual standards of scholarship.

1213 *National Security Interests in the Pacific Basin.* Edited by Claude A. Buss. Stanford, CA: Hoover Institution Press, 1985. 317pp. ISBN 0–8179–8191–8.

These papers are from a 1984 conference on security issues of the Pacific Basin held under the auspices of the Hoover Institution, Palo Alto, CA. The goal of the conference was a critical examination of security threats to the Pacific Basin region. While the primary threat to this region remains the Soviet Union, the diversity of security concerns complicates a single-theme analysis. Both the papers and the discussions make this book a valuable source for Pacific Basin security issues.

1214 *NATO—the Next Generation.* Edited by Robert E. Hunter. Boulder, CO: Westview Press, 1984. 272pp. ISBN 0–8133–0119–X.

These papers on the future of NATO are the product of a 1984 conference at the Palais d'Egmont in Brussels, sponsored by the Center for Strategic and International Studies (CSIS) of Georgetown University. The consensus is that NATO has problems among its members over defense and economic issues, but the alliance is working now and for the next generation. Problem areas remain the Soviet threat, economic imbalances, and the geographical scope of NATO, but none of these problems is insurmountable. This book can be recommended because of its high-quality papers by authorities in the field of NATO studies.

1215 *NATO in the 1980s: Challenges and Responses.* Edited by Linda P. Brady and Joyce P. Kaufman. New York: Praeger, 1985. 274pp. ISBN 0–03–001772–6.

NATO's military, economic, and political challenges in the 1980s are the focus of this book of essays from the 22nd Annual Meeting of the International Studies Association, Philadelphia, in 1981. NATO has become more than a military alliance because politics, economics, and military matters have become intertwined. The consensus of these essays is that the NATO alliance is experiencing a period of crisis, but the allies have the resources and will respond to this period of uncertainty. These essays break little new ground, but they restate the case for NATO in the 1980s.

1216 *The Naval Arms Race.* Edited by A. Alatas. New York: United Nations, 1986. 100pp. ISBN 92–1–142116–0.

The impact of the naval arms race on international security and the freedom of the high seas is the focus of this United Nations report. A panel of naval experts concludes that rapid technological innovation and development and nuclear weapons have changed the nature of naval warfare. Nuclear weapon limitation and disarmament are the two proposals from this panel, but the members are less than sure of means of implementation. This report gives a solid overview of the naval arms race, but its conclusions are less noteworthy.

1217 *New Directions in Strategic Thinking*. Edited by Robert O'Neill and D. M. Horner. London: Allen and Unwin, 1981. 318pp. ISBN 0–04–355013–4.

Strategic thinking during the 1970s and its possible impact on the 1980s are the subjects of this book of essays by an international cast of authors. These writers combine international strategic relations and developments along national lines to present a broad picture of recent strategic concepts. Two realities emerge from these essays: (1) the international situation is turning harsher in the 1980s, and (2) there is a tendency toward disintegration of alliances. These essays present a good picture of changing strategic thinking, and this book is worth consulting.

1218 Nincic, Miroslav. *How War Might Spread to Europe*. London: Taylor and Francis, 1985. 109pp. ISBN 0–85066–302–4.

The author examines the risks that conflicts in other parts of the world will spread to Europe and cause a war. Four areas of potential conflict—Persian Gulf/Western Indian Ocean, eastern Mediterranean, East Asia and the Pacific, and the Caribbean Basin—are surveyed, and the first two areas are considered most volatile. The possibility of an outside crisis triggering a European war is real enough for steps to be considered to reduce the risks. This book is another major effort published under the sponsorship of the Stockholm International Peace Research Institute (SIPRI).

1219 Nishihara, Masashi. *East Asian Security and the Trilateral Countries*. New York: New York University Press, 1985. 111pp. ISBN 0–81475–58–8.

This report was prepared for the Trilateral Commission by a professor at the National Defense Academy. The relationship of the trilateral countries of North America, Western Europe, and Japan with the East Asian region is the subject of this report. Almost as significant as the analysis is the statistical appendix of trilateral transactions with East Asia. This study is a different approach to the interaction between states, and this approach has its uses.

1220 *No-First-Use*. Edited by Frank Blackaby, Jozef Goldblat, and Sverre Lodgaard. London: Taylor and Francis, 1984. 151pp. ISBN 0–85066–274–5.

More a sourcebook of commentary and readings than a work of scholarship, this book presents arguments pro and con on the first use of nuclear weapons. The original part of this book is the commentary by nine scholars on the articles representing the two points of view. This contribution is another quality product sponsored by the Stockholm International Peace Research Institute (SIPRI).

1221 *Nonproliferation and U.S. Foreign Policy*. By Richard K. Betts et al. Washington, DC: Brookings Institution, 1980. 438pp. ISBN 0–8157–9674–9.

This book of essays traces the rate of proliferation of nuclear weapons in a nation-by-nation survey. Each region and country with the potential of developing a nuclear capability is analyzed. Behind each analysis is consideration of the extent to which the emergence of another nuclear power will affect U.S. foreign policy. This book gives a solid picture of U.S. foreign policy and its role in the rate of nuclear proliferation as of 1980.

1222 *Northeast Asia Security after Vietnam.* Edited by Martin E. Winstein. Urbana, IL: University of Illinois Press, 1982. 182pp. ISBN 0–252–00966–5.

This book consists of essays on the state of political and military affairs of Northeast Asia by scholars of Northeast Asian security problems. These authors believe that this region—China, Japan, and Korea—forms one of the most sensitive and crucial areas in contemporary affairs. Moreover, they believe that the regional military balance has shifted in favor of the Soviet Union. This book serves as a good introduction to security problems in the Northeast Asia region.

1223 *Northern Europe: Security Issues for the 1990s.* Edited by Paul M. Cole and Dougals M. Hart. Boulder, CO: Westview Press, 1986. 160pp. ISBN 0–8133–7245–3.

In this book U.S. and European security specialists appraise the role of northern Europe in future East-West conflict. Although northern Europe stands little chance of escaping involvement in a conflict between NATO and the Soviet bloc, the Nordic nations have kept an aloof and neutral stance. An increasing Soviet presence in this area, however, is threatening to erode Scandinavian regional stability, and the Nordic states will each have to reexamine their security status. These essays are major efforts by prominent security specialists to understand Nordic security issues.

1224 *Northern Waters: Security and Resource Issues.* Edited by Clive Archer and David Scrivener. London: Croom Helm, 1986. 240pp. ISBN 0–7099–0570–X.

The sea area from Canada's eastern seaboard to Norway's northern coast and the Barents Sea is the subject of this book of papers from the Northern Waters Study Group. Economic and strategic interests make this area of major importance to both the Soviet Union and the United States. These papers point out that there is significant interaction between resource and security issues in this region. These papers by scholars from NATO member countries are brief, but they are important contributions to understanding the strategic issues of the northern waters.

1225 *Norway's Security and European Foreign Policy in the 1980's:* Report by the European Movement in Norway. Oslo: Universitetsforlaget, 1981. 80pp. ISBN 82–00–05710–0.

The European Movement in Norway study group considers the role of Norway in European cooperation on security and foreign policy affairs in this book. Western European cooperation on foreign policy developed rapidly in the early 1980s, and Norway has been outside of this cooperation. This study group recommends that Norway involve itself in the decision-making organs of Western Europe to have a say in NATO policies. Norway's quasi-independent status in NATO would be changed to a more active role if these recommendations were carried out.

1226 *The Nuclear Arms Race—Control or Catastrophe?* Edited by Frank Barnaby and Geoffrey Thomas. London: Frances Pinter, 1982. 250pp. ISBN 0–86187–229–0.

These papers were presented to the General Section of the British Association for the Advancement of Science in 1981 at York, England. This meeting was an occasion where scientists and others could discuss the problems associated with the arms race. Participants explored ways to control the arms race, from deterrence theory to disarmament, without forming a consensus. This book shows increasing involvement of scientists in the vital problems of the arms race.

1227 *The Nuclear Confrontation in Europe*. Edited by Jeffrey D. Boutwell, Paul Doty, and Gregory F. Treverton. London: Croom Helm, 1985. 247pp. ISBN 0–86569–128–2.

This book of essays studies the nuclear rivalry between NATO and the Soviet Union in Europe. This rivalry will continue for the remainder of this century because of the superpower arms race between the Soviet Union and the United States, but this nuclear arms race will also spark the European peace movement to renewed activity. While these essays are optimistic that the confrontation between the superpowers in Europe will not trigger a war, there is considerable concern over any escalation of the nuclear arms race.

1228 *The Nuclear Crisis Reader*. Edited by Gwyn Prins. New York: Vintage Books, 1984. 251pp. ISBN 0–394–72768–1.

These essays on defense and security issues of the nuclear debate are a product of a 1983 seminar at Emmanuel College, Cambridge University. This seminar brought together international security experts to examine the breakdown of the consensus over current nuclear policy. The majority of the participants believe that possession of nuclear weapons does not constitute a cogent security guarantee. The book presents a series of powerful essays on security issues of value to both the specialist and the general reader.

1229 *Nuclear Deterrence: Ethics and Strategy*. Edited by Russell Hardin et al. Chicago: University of Chicago Press, 1985. 395pp. ISBN 0–22631–702–1.

The papers in this volume were all originally published in various issues of *Ethics: An International Journal of Social, Political and Legal Philosophy*. Philosophers and strategists articulate their views on the ethics of nuclear weapons policies, and there is considerable difference in viewpoints because the strategists view deterrence as necessary for survival with the Soviet Union as the adversary, while the philosophers are concerned with deterrence as a moral system. This juxtaposition of two contrasting viewpoints makes this book valuable for understanding different mind-sets.

1230 *Nuclear War in Europe*. Edited by H. W. Tromp and G. R. La Rocque. Groningen, the Netherlands: Groningen University Press, 1982. 302pp. ISBN 90–70595–01–X.

Western European and U.S. military experts gathered at a 1981 conference at Groningen, Holland, to present papers on the causes, combat, consequences, and avoidance of nuclear war in Europe. Their conclusion is that nuclear war in Europe is possible and becoming more probable, but they also believe that the consequence of a nuclear war would be a devastated Europe and severe damage to the rest of the world. These papers deal with the realistic possibility of a nuclear war in Europe, and their conclusions are worth reading.

1231 Olivier, B. J. *The Strategic Significance of Angola*. Pretoria, South Africa: Institute for Strategic Studies, 1984. 107pp. ISBN 0–86979–560–0.

A South African author studies Angola for its strategic significance in the Southern Africa region. Despite a colonial heritage and civil war, its mineral wealth, agricultural potential, and geographical position enhance Angola's strategic significance. Angola's connection with international socialism and its support of liberation movements in Southern Africa, however, make it a threat to other countries in this region. While the author's attempt to place

Angola into a conceptual strategic framework is awkward, the factual material makes this paper worth consulting.

1232 Olsen, Edward A. *U.S.-Japan Strategic Reciprocity: A Neo-Internationalist View.* Stanford, CA: Hoover Institution Press, 1985. 194pp. ISBN 0–8179–8071–7.

In this book the author analyzes U.S.-Japan security relations for past policies and future trends. He believes that reciprocal strategic cooperation is necessary for both Japan and the United States, but he is skeptical of continued progress along these lines. He notes that there is considerable feeling against increasing Japanese military force among Asian countries, but that this feeling is not strong enough to restrict U.S.-Japanese options. Although this book is a cautious assessment of U.S.-Japan security relations, it is still a first-rate treatment of this subject.

1233 O'Neill, Robert. *Strategic Concepts in the 1980's: Problems of the Central Balance and East-Asian Security.* Geneva, Switzerland: Programme for Strategic and International Security Studies, 1984. 45 leaves.

In this essay the author considers the need for strategic planners to understand the political climate in formulating future policies in the East Asian region. The failure of the United States to comprehend this lesson in Vietnam helped cost the United States the war. Western countries need to become more aware of economic, political, and strategic affairs of East Asia and the South Pacific because this region is becoming more important strategically. Papers with a narrow research focus can be important as think pieces, and this essay is above average for this purpose.

1234 *On Geopolitics: Classical and Nuclear.* Edited by Ciro E. Zoppo and Charles Zorgbibe. Dordrecht, the Netherlands: Martinus Nijhoff, 1985. 310pp. ISBN 90–247–3119–4.

The impact of nuclear weapons on the world's geopolitical situation is the subject of this book of essays. While geography remains one of the most fundamental factors in foreign policy, the invention of nuclear weapons transformed relations between states. The essays analyze this change by studying the relations between the superpowers and their client states. This book contains both informative and suggestive material, and its conclusions are worth further study.

1235 Organski, A. F. K., and Jacek Kugler. *The War Ledger.* Chicago: University of Chicago Press, 1980. 292pp. ISBN 0–226–63279–2.

The authors use this book to study the beginnings, outcomes, and consequences of hostilities in relation to national growth and international war. National growth as the key determinant in the military power of a state is the theme of most interest to the authors. The most startling conclusion is that nuclear weapons do not deter and that they are built because of internal rather than external political pressures. This book poses several points worth further study, and it is recommended for its general conclusions on the nature of war.

1236 Osgood, Robert E. *Containment, Soviet Behavior, and Grand Strategy.* Berkeley: Institute of International Studies, University of California, 1981. 86pp. ISBN 0–87725–516–4.

In this book the author uses his study of U.S. strategic policy toward the Soviet Union as a source of commentary for leading scholars in international relations and Soviet studies. Both the paper and the commentaries were presented at a 1980 conference sponsored by the Institute of International Studies and the Los Alamos Scientific Laboratories. The combination of Osgood's paper and the scholars' assessment of his ideas makes this book both stimulating and a source for new research directions.

1237 *Overcoming Threats to Europe: A New Deal for Confidence and Security.* Edited by Sverre Lodgaard and Karl Birnbaum. Oxford, England: Oxford University Press, 1987. 235pp. ISBN 0–19–829112–4.

This book includes papers by eight representatives from Western Europe on European security threats. These authors are most concerned with the interrelationship between military and political determinants of threats to Western and Eastern European security. They examine six countries—France, Hungary, Poland, Sweden, West Germany, and Yugoslavia—for the interaction between threat perceptions and national security policies. This book is a major contribution to international security literature.

1238 *The Pacific Rim and the Western World: Strategic, Economic and Cultural Perspectives.* Edited by Philip West and Frans A. M. Alting von Geusau. Boulder, CO: Westview Press, 1987. 330pp. ISBN 0–8133–7338–7.

These papers are a product of a 1985 colloquium on the Far East held at Eindhoven, the Netherlands. The participants devoted considerable attention to exchanges about differences between Asian and Western perspectives on security questions involving Western Pacific rim countries. The result is a series of papers emphasizing that economic development problems are as serious a concern in East Asia as security issues. Any researcher interested in the interrelations of economic and security affairs will find this work of value.

1239 Paul, T. V. *Reaching for the Bomb: The Indo-Pak Nuclear Scenario.* New Delhi: Dialogue Publications, 1984. 199pp.

An Indian scholar examines the nuclear rivalry between India and Pakistan and prospects for a continuing nuclear arms race. By the end of the 1980s both Pakistan and India will have the capability for small nuclear weapons forces. The author feels that this development of a nuclear strike force would be a mistake for either India or Pakistan, and that India needs to take a leading role in reducing this threat. This book is a balanced assessment of a controversial subject.

1240 Payne, Keith B. *Nuclear Deterrence in U.S.-Soviet Relations.* Boulder, CO: Westview Press, 1982. 239pp. ISBN 0–86531–903–0.

The author examines the theories of deterrence and stability advanced during the 1970s and finds them based upon wrong assumptions. Soviet strategic nuclear superiority gained in the late 1970s and early 1980s has made previous U.S. strategy suspect. Payne finds that both sides of the mutual vulnerability doctrine—assured vulnerability and flexible targeting—have fatal flaws, and he believes all such doctrines should be replaced by a deterrence doctrine based on denying victory and damage limitation. This book is heavy on criticism and much weaker on the economic and political ramifications of its proposals.

1241 Peck, Juliana S. *The Reagan Administration and the Palestinian Question: The First Thousand Days.* Washington, DC: Institute for Palestine Studies, 1984. 138pp.

This book is an analysis of the Reagan administration's Palestinian policy in the early 1980s. The author notes the shifts of policy away from President

Jimmy Carter's initiatives, and she concludes that the only constant has been President Ronald Reagan's determination to counter the Soviet threat in the Middle East. Reagan and his administration have shown little understanding of the Palestinian question and its significance in Middle East politics. Solid studies such as this provide useful insights into the decision-making processes of the U.S. government.

1242 Peterson, J. E. *Defending Arabia.* London: Croom Helm, 1986. 275pp. ISBN 0–7099–2044–X.

Gulf security as it impacts on the states of the Arabian peninsula is the subject of this book. The author believes that security in the Gulf region cannot be understood without a knowledge of the historical background of the region's security problems. He maintains that the United States and Saudi Arabia, and to a lesser extent the five other Gulf states, will remain mutually dependent far into the next century because of oil and security concerns. This book is an excellent look at strategic realities in a key region.

1243 Pigasse, Jean-Paul. *Le bouclier d'Europe: vers une autonomie militaire de la Communauté Européenne.* Paris: Editions Seghers, 1982. 285pp. ISBN 2–221–01043–4.

The author claims that the military equilibrium between the superpowers has maintained peace in Europe for the last forty years, but that to ensure a continuation of peace the Europeans will have to band together for a common defense. This will mean a less active role for the United States and an increased military burden for the European states. France will play one of the leading roles in this revamping of Europe's defense structure. This book suffers from the illusion that France can assume leadership in any reorganization of European defense.

1244 Pike, Douglas. *Vietnam and the Soviet Union: Anatomy of an Alliance.* Boulder, CO: Westview Press, 1987. 271pp. ISBN 0–8133–0470–9.

The Vietnamese perspective on its political, economic, and diplomatic relationship with the Soviet Union is presented in this book by one of the foremost U.S. authorities on Vietnam. His conclusion is that for the foreseeable future Vietnam and the Soviet Union will be bound together by self-interest, but the Sino-Soviet dispute will determine the future direction of this relationship. There is little in common between the two states except self-interest, and ideological incongruence will limit further intimate contact. This book provides valuable insights on an important aspect of Far East security, and security specialists will benefit from its quality analysis.

1245 Pipes, Richard. *U.S.-Soviet Relations in the Era of Detente.* Boulder, CO: Westview Press, 1981. 227pp. ISBN 0–86531–154–4.

These essays by a U.S. hardliner on U.S.-Soviet relations constitute an attack on the diplomacy of détente. The author has been a critic of détente from the beginning because he believed that the leaders of U.S. foreign policy were ignorant of the expansionist nature of the Soviet regime. Increasing Soviet military strength in the late 1970s reinforced the author's opposition. The essays in this book helped turn public opinion against détente and worsen relations between the Soviet Union and the United States.

1246 *Polarity and War: The Changing Structure of International Conflict.* Edited by Alan Ned Sabrosky. Boulder, CO: Westview Press, 1985. 231pp. ISBN 0–8133–7000–0.

These papers combine historical, theoretical, and policy approaches to explore the subject of polarity and war. Most of the examples fall into the core period from 1815 to 1975. Few general conclusions emerge from these papers, but there is a recurrent theme that the moderation of a bipolar international structure to a multipolar system has not lessened the chance of war and instead may increase the possibilities. Because these papers are a scientific approach to international relations, their methodology is as important as their conclusions.

1247 *Policies for Common Security.* By the Stockholm International Peace Research Institute. London: Taylor and Francis, 1985. 250pp. ISBN 0–85066–301–6.

These papers on common security result from a SIPRI-sponsored 1983 conference on this topic in Stockholm, Sweden. The idea of common security is an outgrowth of the Palme Commission's (the Independent Commission on Disarmament and Security Issues) report suggesting such a policy. Most of the papers deal with the relationship between common security (stressing disarmament) and deterrence strategy (oriented toward warfighting). These essays attempt with varying degrees of success to consider the concept of common security, and the effort needs further refinement.

1248 Pollack, Jonathan D. *Security, Strategy, and the Logic of Chinese Foreign Policy.* Berkeley, CA: Institute of East Asian Studies, 1981. 66pp. ISBN 0–912966–34–3.

Chinese perceptions of foreign policy options since the mid-1960s are the subject of this short monograph. The author maintains that Chinese policies have been highly responsive to changes in the international situation, and that this is because Chinese analyses of strategy and security have been more oriented toward global assessments than regional concerns. This essay is a perceptive study of past and present Chinese foreign and strategic policies.

1249 Pollack, Jonathan D. *The Sino-Soviet Rivalry and Chinese Security Debate.* Santa Monica, CA: Rand Corporation, 1982. 112pp. ISBN 0–8330–0419–0.

This Rand Corporation report describes and analyzes Chinese security and foreign policy issues vis-à-vis the Soviet Union since the mid-1960s. While Chinese leadership since the 1960s has changed, Sino-Soviet relations are still cool because the Chinese distrust the Soviets. Deng Xiaoping has opted for closer relations with the United States to counter Soviet aspirations in Asia, but current difficulties between the United States and China have weakened this policy. This report is a good example of a detailed analysis of specific foreign policy issues.

1250 Porter, Bruce D. *The USSR in Third World Conflicts: Soviet Arms and Diplomacy in Local Wars, 1945–1980.* Cambridge, England: Cambridge University Press, 1984. 248pp. ISBN 0–521–26308–5.

This revised dissertation considers Soviet military and diplomatic involvement in Third World conflicts from 1945 to 1980. The author presents five case studies of instances of Soviet military intervention. The Soviets have been careful to restrict their military and economic activities to conflicts with a good chance for military success, but on the diplomatic side they have been less successful. These case studies reveal Soviet interventions in action, and this makes this book a solid contribution to the study of international security.

1251 Powaski, Ronald E. *March to Armageddon: The United States and the Nuclear Arms Race, 1939 to the Present.* New York: Oxford University Press, 1987. 300pp. ISBN 0–19–503878–9.

This book is a history of the role of the United States in the nuclear arms race from 1939 to the present. Despite the vows of numerous presidents to end the nuclear arms race, the United States has been a leader in designing and acquiring nuclear weapons in the name of power politics. Efforts at nuclear arms control have been blocked by the U.S. political system, especially by Pentagon opposition. This book provides perspective for any study of the role of the United States in the nuclear arms race.

1252 *Power, Strategy and Security.* Edited by Klaus Knorr. Princeton, NJ: Princeton University Press, 1983. 279pp. ISBN 0–691–05665–X.

This volume contains reprints of the best articles on international security issues from *World Politics.* These articles by some of the top names in the security field address the role of national power in interstate relations. The international scene in the late 1970s and early 1980s caused a return to the theory of the importance of military power in determining great power influence. These articles represent the best-quality research on national power and security from 1977 to 1982.

1253 Powers, Thomas. *Thinking about the Next War.* New York: Knopf, 1982. 153pp. ISBN 0–394–52831–X.

These essays on the nature of the next world war originally appeared in various issues of *Commonweal.* The author is a freelance writer who specializes in analysis of current affairs. His thesis is that momentum is driving the superpowers toward a nuclear war, and that there is nothing visible on the horizon to change this drive to destruction. The essays in this book are well written and suggestive, and many specialists will agree with Powers's thesis.

1254 Prescott, J. R. V. *The Maritime Political Boundaries of the World.* London: Methuen, 1985. 377pp. ISBN 0–416–41750–7.

This book traces the maritime political boundaries of the world's maritime regions. The author is a political geographer whose interest is in practical applications rather than theory making. After five chapters detailing maritime claims and boundaries, the remainder of the book provides a regional treatment of the problems of maritime boundaries. This publication is the best source available for this type of information.

1255 *Projection of Power: Perspectives, Perceptions and Problems.* Edited by Uri Ra'anan, Robert L. Pfaltzgraff and Geoffrey Kemp. Hamden, CT: Archon Books, 1982. 351pp. ISBN 0–208–01954–5.

These papers are the result of the Ninth Annual Conference of the Fletcher School's International Security Studies Program, held in Cambridge, Massachusetts, in 1980. Participants examine both the historical and contemporary uses of military power projection for theoretical and practical purposes, and they agree that the power projection of the Soviet Union is growing in contrast to the shrinking power projection of the United States. Despite the problems of exploring new concepts and theories, these papers make a positive contribution to the understanding of power and its benefits.

1256 *Prospects of Soviet Power in the 1980s.* Edited by Christoph Bertram. Hamden, CT: Archon Books, 1980. 126pp. ISBN 0–208–01885–9.

This book of essays by Soviet specialists from Europe and the United States examines the nature of Soviet power and the prospects of its use in the 1980s. While all the contributors noted constraints on Soviet power, problems in the Soviet economy and with control over Eastern Europe are unlikely to produce any major changes in Soviet policy. Military power is the chief instrument of Soviet policy, and it is this fact that is of most concern to the U.S. policymakers. Each of these essays looks at a component of Soviet power, and together they make this book a solid addition to international security literature.

1257 Quester, George H. *The Future of Nuclear Deterrence.* Lexington, MA: Lexington Books, 1986. 333pp. ISBN 0–669–11565–7.

The author defends the strategic doctrine of nuclear deterrence and forecasts that deterrence doctrine has a future in preventing nuclear war. He notes some improvements in the process of arms negotiation but believes progress in military technology will promote more instability. Despite setbacks, there is little likelihood that U.S.-Soviet relations will revert back to the low points of the 1940s and 1950s. While the author alternates between optimism and pessimism, his conclusions tend toward the probability of peace.

1258 Rais, Rasul B. *The Indian Ocean and the Superpowers: Economic, Political and Strategic Perspectives.* London: Croom Helm, 1986. 215pp. ISBN 0–7099–4241–9.

This book examines the role of superpower rivalry in the Indian Ocean region. Political events in this region since 1979 have resulted in an increased presence of the superpowers in the Indian Ocean region. This continues to produce instability in this area, but the superpower presence has not been directed toward developing a capacity to wage war but rather toward influencing the policies of local powers. This book is a realistic assessment of the superpower rivalry in the Indian Ocean.

1259 Rallo, Joseph C. *Defending Europe in the 1990s: The New Divide of High Technology.* London: Frances Pinter, 1986. 136pp. ISBN 0–86187–615–6.

This work considers the feasibility of establishing a security relationship in the European Community (EC). The author thinks EC successes in the economic sphere could be duplicated in the security field, but this would mean that the dominant U.S. security role would be exchanged for European dominance. Any such development depends on citizen, member, and regional inputs before such a change of policy can be successfully implemented. This book calls for a Europeanization of the Atlantic alliance, and the author's plans depend too heavily on a break between Western Europe and the United States for such a policy to succeed.

1260 Rasiulis, Andrew P. *On the Utility of War in the Nuclear Age.* Toronto: Canadian Institute of International Affairs, 1981. 95pp. ISBN 0–919084–38–9.

The author is a strategic analyst with the Canadian Department of National Defence, and this monograph is his effort to present a conceptual understanding of the utility of war in the nuclear age. Most of his attention is devoted to the middle range of wars because these wars can be justified by rational political objectives. War continues to be an instrument of national policy, and the maximum rational level of conflict is the limited conventional border war of attrition. This monograph is a serious effort to rationalize war, but the analysis is on the simplistic side.

1261 *The Reagan Administration's Foreign Policy: Facts and Judgement of the International Tribunal.* Edited by Hans Kochler. Vienna: International Progress Organization, 1986. 470pp. ISBN 0–86199–0222–6.

The International Progress Organization (IPO) organized a 1984 international conference and tribunal on the Reagan administration's foreign policy in Brussels, Belgium. Representatives came from all over the world to condemn U.S. foreign policy, especially in Central America. A mock tribunal was formed for a trial of Reagan's foreign policy, and the verdict was against U.S. policies. This book is an indictment of current and past U.S. policies, and, despite the merits of the arguments, the case is too one-sided.

1262 Rearden, Steven L. *The Evolution of the American Strategic Doctrine: Paul H. Nitze and the Soviet Challenge.* Boulder, CO: Westview Press, 1984. 131pp. ISBN 0–86531–898–0.

This book is an assessment of the influence of Paul H. Nitze on the development of U.S. strategic doctrine since 1945. The author contends that Nitze has been the architect of most of the major ideas in postwar U.S. strategic doctrine. Nitze's belief that the Soviet Union is the enemy was embodied in his National Security Council report in 1950 (NSC 68), and he has continued to embrace this theme even to the negotiations on arms control issues in the 1980s. This survey of the influence of Nitze's ideas on U.S. strategic doctrine is a major contribution on security issues.

1263 *Reassessing the Soviet Challenge in Africa.* Edited by Michael Clough. Berkeley: Institute of International Studies, University of California, 1986. 105pp. ISBN 0–87725–525–3.

These five essays narrow in on Soviet policy options in Africa. Soviet successes in Angola, Ethiopia, and Mozambique in the 1970s have turned sub-Saharan Africa into a region where the superpowers are maneuvering for political influence. But in the mid-1980s, when the United States is turning its attention toward confronting Soviet interests in Africa, the Soviets have found success fleeting in this region. The authors seek a pragmatic approach to dealing with the Soviets in Africa, and this approach makes this short book a jewel.

1264 *Regionalism and Global Security.* Edited by Gavin Boyd. Lexington, MA: Lexington Books, 1984. 194pp. ISBN 0–669–06153–0.

This collection of essays studies the problems of global security and economic development together with attempts to build regional support to solve these problems. Each of the major regions—Atlantic countries, Africa, the Pacific, Latin America, and the Middle East—is examined in light of cooperation on security and economic development. The United States has to assume a leadership role in regional cooperation, or else give way to rivals. This book looks at regionalism as a positive step toward the future, and these essays are a quality effort to stimulate further research on this topic.

1265 *Regional Security in the Third World: Case Studies from Southeast Asia and the Middle East.* Edited by Mohammed Ayoob. London: Croom Helm, 1986. 284pp. ISBN 0–7099–0579–3.

These essays are the product of a 1984 workshop on the problems of regional security in the Middle East and Southeast Asia held in Singapore. Scholars from Southeast Asia, the Middle East, India, and the United Kingdom gathered together to discuss comparative assessments of regional security issues. While each paper stands on its own merits, the comment section on each paper by another specialist in the field is especially valuable. This book is one of the better contributions in the field of Third World regional security problems on the market.

1266 *Rethinking the U.S. Strategic Posture: A Report from the Aspen Consortium on Arms Control and Security Issues.* Edited by Barry M. Blechman. Cambridge, MA: Ballinger, 1982. 308pp. ISBN 0–88410–910–0.

This report from the Aspen Consortium on arms control and security issues is the product of a series of meetings between 1980 and 1982. A group of arms control specialists, defense analysts, and scientists gathered together to reevaluate U.S. strategic options. The conclusions of this report are numerous, but the report emphasizes that the future of arms control depends on Soviet foreign policy behavior and the extent to which the United States fits arms control into its relationship with the Soviet Union. Both the conclusions and the diversity of opinions make this volume useful for studying U.S. defense and military policies.

1267 Ries, Tomas. *The Nordic Dilemma in the 80's: Maintaining Regional Stability under New Strategic Conditions.* Geneva, Switzerland: Programme for Strategic and International Security Studies, 1982. 60pp.

This paper assesses the strategic position of the Nordic states relative to the Soviet Union. In the past the five Nordic states have had to maintain a credible deterrence to avoid Soviet pressure and at the same time to reassure the Soviet Union that its vital regional interests were not threatened. This balancing act has become more difficult as the Soviets have increased their military forces in adjacent areas and as Nordic public opinion challenges the old policy. This paper has solid material to back its thesis, and it constitutes an excellent source for further research.

1268 Rona, Thomas P. *Our Changing Geopolitical Premises.* New Brunswick, NJ: Transaction Books, 1982. 352pp. ISBN 0–87855–897–7.

The author, an engineer at The Boeing Company, looks at changes on the international scene for their impact on U.S. national security. He finds that economic and political changes have altered the U.S. strategic position for the worse, and that many of these geopolitical shifts have also influenced the strategic position of the Soviet Union. This book seeks to isolate international realities, and, despite some inconsistencies, the author is successful in finding many of these geopolitical realities.

1269 Ronfeldt, David. *Geopolitics, Security and U.S. Strategy in the Caribbean Basin.* Santa Monica, CA: Rand Corporation, 1983. 93pp. ISBN 0–8330–0531–6.

This report examines the strategic options for U.S. policy in the Caribbean basin. The author believes that this area may be kept secure for U.S. interests by pursuing preventive and anticipatory policies, but that this will mean that the United States will have to expand its role in the Caribbean basin's political, economic, and military affairs and preempt further expansion by the Soviet-Cuban bloc. This study is a realistic assessment of the need for a strong U.S. presence in the Caribbean basin, and the author's arguments are suggestive.

1270 Rood, Harold W. *Kingdoms of the Blind: How the Great Democracies Have Resumed the Follies That So Nearly Cost Them Their Life.* Durham, NC: Carolina Academic Press, 1980. 294pp. ISBN 0–089089–121–4.

The author uses this book as a warning of the dangers of defense unpreparedness to U.S. security. Soviet military preparations endanger the Western alliance because the West has allowed its defense effort to slacken. If the Soviet Union attacks Western Europe, the United States will have to make a decision to fight or wait its turn to be invaded. This book is of limited appeal because of the polemical tone of the writing.

1271 Rose, Francois de. *European Security and France.* Urbana, IL: University of Illinois Press, 1983. ISBN 0–252–01176–7.

An English translation of *Contre la strategie des Curiaces* (Paris: Julliard, 1983), this book is a treatise on the need for European states to play a more active role in the defense of Europe. The author believes that France should rejoin the Western alliance by taking a more active role in NATO affairs. Europeans have to replace the United States in providing leadership for the defense of Europe. This argument for reintegration of France into NATO reflects a changing mood in France.

1272 Rosen, Steven J. *The Strategic Value of Israel.* Washington, DC: American Israel Public Affairs Committee, 1982. 20pp.

This paper by the director of research and information at the American Israel Public Affairs Committee (AIPAC) details the strategic value of a close relationship between the United States and Israel. Rosen's thesis is that Israel's strategic value derives from its geostrategic position in the Middle East and from other factors such as political stability, political reliability, and advanced society. He considers the refusal to consider Israel as a staging area for a rapid deployment force (RDF) a mistaken policy of appeasement to Arab opinion. This short position paper makes a persuasive case for increased U.S.-Israeli cooperation.

1273 Ruloff, Dieter. *Wie Kriege beginnen.* Munich: Verlag C. H. Beck, 1985. 158pp. ISBN 3–406–30487–7.

The author has produced a theoretical analysis of military and political conditions that culminate in an outbreak of war. His treatment concerns only European wars, and his analysis deals only with wars since 1789. The result is a classic study of the comparative origins of war. This study is useful because the author has successfully integrated other scholarship into his analysis.

1274 Sarkesian, Sam. *The New Battlefield: The United States and Unconventional Conflicts.* Westport, CT: Greenwood Press, 1986. 344pp. ISBN 0–313–24890–7.

The inability of the United States to respond to unconventional conflicts is the theme of this book. Unconventional conflicts are problems developing out of the internal instability of Third World states, and they include terrorism, revolution, and counterrevolution. U.S. policy needs to be designed to cope with these unconventional warfare scenarios, which may include military intervention, but this may mean a change of the U.S. political-psychological posture toward interventionism. The author argues for a more interventionist U.S. foreign policy, and it is more his viewpoint than the analysis that makes this book of interest.

1275 Savigear, Peter. *Cold War or Detente: the International Politics of American-Soviet Relations.* Brighton, England: Wheatsheaf Books, 1987. 196pp. ISBN 0–7450–0123–8.

This work examines the relationship between the Soviet Union and the United States in the 1980s for its impact on international relations. Both powers have been involved in the affairs of other states during the 1980s, and they are widely regarded as imperial states. But the collapse of détente and changing international realities have loosened the hold of the superpowers over international politics. Any attempt to isolate an era suffers the danger of becoming dated, but this book should hold up well because of its balanced treatment of the subject.

1276 Scheer, Robert. *With Enough Shovels: Reagan, Bush and Nuclear War.* New York: Random House, 1982. 285pp. ISBN 0–394–41482–9.

The author is a journalist with the *Los Angeles Times,* and he decided to write this book after interviewing officials of the Reagan administration. This book is about the Reagan administration's plans for waging and winning a nuclear war with the Soviet Union. His thesis is that nuclear war is less frightening to these officials than the idea of appeasing the Soviet Union. While the author's analysis is significant, the value of this book is in the texts of a series of interviews in the appendices.

1277 Schrodt, Philip A. *Preserving Arms Distributions in a Multi-Polar World: A Mathematical Study.* Denver, CO: Graduate School of International Studies, University of Denver, 1981. 119pp. ISBN 0–87940–067–6.

This study focuses on classical balance-of-power theory and the theory of arms race models. Three conceptual theories are examined: (1) categories of arms distribution; (2) the Richardson model; and (3) the concept of "preservation." The results show that each of these theories offers insights into the stability of international relations in a multipolar world. This book is a sophisticated mathematical study, but the results are disappointing considering the effort expended.

1278 Scientific Research Council on Peace and Disarmament. *Latin America: Arms Build-up and Disarmament.* Moscow: Nauka Publishers, 1983. 130pp.

This booklet is a group effort of the Latin American Institute of the USSR Academy of Science. Much attention is devoted to U.S. arms buildups in Latin America and to militarist regimes in the region, and nuclear proliferation in Latin America is another subject explored. While most of the analysis is standard Marxist-Leninist interpretation of imperialism in action, the section on nuclear proliferation in Latin America is the most useful.

1279 Scott, Andrew M. *The Revolution in Statecraft: Intervention in an Age of Interdependence,* rev. ed. Durham, NC: Duke Press Policy Studies, 1982. 214pp. ISBN 0–8223–0494–5.

An introduction and two new chapters have been added to this book, originally published in 1965. The original thesis, that techniques have emerged since 1945 providing a government with direct access to another society, has been expanded. New governments can reach inside other societies and shape events without direct intervention. This classic study has been updated to the early 1980s, and the thesis has withstood the test of time.

1280 *SDI and U.S. Foreign Policy.* Edited by Robert W. Tucker et al. Boulder, CO: Westview Press, 1987. 126pp. ISBN 0–8133–0468–7.

Four members of the School of Advanced International Studies (SAIS), Washington, DC, ponder the impact of space technology on the foreign policy of the United States. These authors are especially concerned about the ramifications of the adoption of the Strategic Defense Initiative (SDI) on relations between the NATO allies. The U.S. defense posture may be improved by SDI, but the European allies are committed to a different defense strategy. These essays are all solid contributions to the continuing security debate within the Atlantic alliance.

1281 *The Second Cold War.* Edited by K. Subrahmanyam. New Delhi: ABC Publishing House, 1983. 215pp.

Members of the staff of the Institute for Defence Studies and Analyses, New Delhi, India, contributed these essays on the renewal of great-power tensions in the early 1980s. These authors were most concerned about the impact on Third World countries of the rise of competition between the superpower blocs. They place most of the blame for restarting Cold War tensions on U.S. policies starting in 1978 and intensifying during the Reagan presidency. This book gives a different perspective on the superpower rivalry in the 1980s.

1282 *Securing Europe's Future.* Edited by Stephen J. Flanagan and Fen Osler Hampson. London: Croom Helm, 1986. 334pp. ISBN 0–7099–1086–X.

Twelve scholars, fellows and affiliates of the Center for Science and International Affairs at Harvard University, present their views on European security issues. These authors are concerned about the divergence of views on the Atlantic alliance now held by many Europeans—views that are on a collision course with policies advanced by the United States. That the Europeans will form a distinctive European defense identity is almost a certainty. Most of these papers are from young scholars who provide refreshing viewpoints on the future of the Atlantic alliance.

1283 *Security Commitments and Capabilities: Elements of an American Global Strategy.* Edited by Uri Ra'anan and Robert L. Pfaltzgraff. Hamden, CT: Archon, 1985. 204pp. ISBN 0–208–02095–0.

This book of papers from the thirteenth annual conference at the Fletcher School's International Security Studies Program, Tufts University, Medford, MA, in 1984 examines elements of the U.S. global strategy. Most of the eminent contributors concentrate on the growing gap between U.S. resources and military and political commitments, but they also agree that the security interests of the United States depend upon the independence of an arc of states including Western Europe and extending through the Mediterranean littoral to the Asian Pacific area. This book is an excellent assessment of the difficulty of distinguishing between perceptions of commitments and resources.

1284 *The Security Gamble: Deterrence Dilemmas in the Nuclear Age.* Edited by Douglas MacLean. Totowa, NJ: Rowman and Allanheld, 1984. 170pp. ISBN 0–8476–7329–4.

These papers are the result of a 1983 conference on nuclear deterrence held at the University of Maryland. Most of the authors are concerned with the philosophical issues of deterrence, because the theory of deterrence is so difficult to comprehend without the moral element. Deterrence appears to work, but no one can specify the reasons why it works or when it could fail. This book deals with the ethics of deterrence, and the essays contribute to this debate.

1285 *Security Implications of Nationalism in Eastern Europe.* Edited by Jeffrey Simon and Trond Gilberg. Boulder, CO: Westview Press, 1986. 327pp. ISBN 0–8133–7047–7.

These essays on security implications of nationalism in Eastern Europe are an outgrowth of a 1984 conference sponsored by the Strategic Studies Institute and held at the U.S. Army War College, Carlisle, PA. The economic and military performance of Eastern European states has turned these states into a liability for the Soviet Union. It is in the best interests of U.S. strategic policy to encourage Eastern European autonomy and nationalism. This book has a number of high-quality papers of interest to security researchers.

1286 *Security in East Asia.* Edited by Robert O'Neill. Aldershot, England: Gower, 1984. 195pp. ISBN 0–566–00674–X.

These essays on security issues in East Asia detail its shifting security realities. There are four levels of security in this region: (1) superpowers (the Soviet Union and the United States); (2) regional great powers (China and Japan); (3) subregional powers of Northeast and Southeast Asia (North and South Korea, Vietnam, and the Association of Southeast Asian Nations [ASEAN] states); and (4) domestic instability. The contributors note this clash of competing interests and influence and calculate prospects for conflict. These essays seek to clarify security issues in East Asia, but rather they show the complexity of security affairs in this part of the world.

1287 *Security in the Persian Gulf.* Edited by Shahram Chubin et al. Montclair, NJ: Allanheld, Osmun, 1981. 4 vols. ISBN 0–86598–044–6 (vol. 1); ISBN 0–86598–045–4 (vol. 2); ISBN 0–06598–046–2 (vol. 3); ISBN 0–06598–047–0 (vol. 4).

These volumes are the product of several international conferences sponsored by the International Institute for Strategic Studies, London, during the period 1979–1981 on Persian Gulf security issues. Most of the contributors emphasize the domestic political instability of the states in the Persian Gulf and the extent to which this instability impacts on regional security. They also direct attention toward future economic and political problems in Saudi Arabia, Kuwait, Bahrain, and the United Arab Emirates. These essays are an excellent introduction to the realities and complexities of security problems in the Persian Gulf states.

1288 *The Security of Korea: U.S. and Japanese Perspectives on the 1980s.* Edited by Franklin B. Weinstein and Fujii Kamiya. Boulder, CO: Westview Press, 1980. 276pp. ISBN 0–89158–668–7.

Korean security is of vital concern to both Japan and the United States and this book is a reflection of that concern. U.S. and Japanese scholars met in a series of meetings in the late 1970s under the auspices of Stanford University's Project on United States–Japan Relations to discuss the importance of Korean security. Presented in a question-and-answer format, Japanese views are less extreme than those of the U.S. scholars, but both believe that U.S. troop withdrawal proposals are wrong. Little new data is contained in this book, but the views of the Japanese participants make it a good source on Japanese academic opinions.

1289 *Security or Armageddon: Israel's Nuclear Strategy.* Edited by Louis Rene Beres. Lexington, MA: Lexington Books, 1986. 242pp. ISBN 0–669–11131–7.

These papers study the complex problem that Israel faces in deciding whether to base its defense policy on nuclear deterrence. The problem with this strategy is whether the threat of use of nuclear weapons can serve as a deterrent to Israel's Arab enemies. Most contributors believe that a better solution for Israeli security is a negotiated settlement of the Palestinian question. This book is a major contribution to the study of Middle East security.

1290 *Security Policies of Developing Countries.* Edited by Edward A. Kolodziej. Lexington, MA: Lexington Books, 1982. 393pp. ISBN 0–669–02897–5.

This book surveys security policies of fourteen key Third World states in relation to global security. These states—Argentina, Brazil, Cuba, Egypt, India, Indonesia, Iran, Iraq, Israel, Nigeria, Pakistan, South Africa, Syria, and Vietnam—are the leading military powers in the Third World, and each is examined in detail. All of these states find themselves involved in regional and global security regimes, and they have the military wherewithal to influence changing regional balances of power. This book consists of a series of outstanding essays culminating in a solid conclusion.

1291 *Security within the Pacific Rim.* Edited by Douglas T. Stuart. Aldershot, England: Gower, 1987. 166pp. ISBN 0–566–05246–6.

These papers are the products of a 1984 conference on Pacific security issues held at Seoul, South Korea. An international cast of scholars contributed papers, and they were most interested in the new roles developing for China and Japan in the Pacific Rim region. While superpower rivalry is still the dominant theme in this region, new realities may change the pattern of this rivalry. These essays are a fresh look at a region of increasing importance on the international scene.

1292 Segal, Gerald. *The Great Power Triangle.* New York: St. Martin's Press, 1982. 195pp. ISBN 0–312–34653–0.

The concept of a great-power triangle between the Soviet Union, the People's Republic of China, and the United States in the 1960s is the subject of this book. Changes of attitude among these powers are monitored, from the crisis over Laos in 1961 to the beginning of Sino-U.S. détente in 1968. The tripolar great-power configuration has continued into the 1980s because the conditions that caused the original split have progressed further. Despite its period limitations, this book still has meaning for scholars interested in tripolar relationships of China, the Soviet Union, and the United States.

1293 Segal, Gerald. *The Soviet "Threat" at China's Gates*. London: Institute for the Study of Conflict, 1983. 22pp.

The nature of the Soviet military threat to the People's Republic of China (PRC) is analyzed in this short study. While there has been a gradual lessening of tension between the Soviet Union and PRC in the 1980s, the Chinese strategy has become based upon pragmatism rather than ideology. Despite some steps toward détente, the PRC will negotiate with the Soviet Union only from a position of military strength. While the treatment of this subject is brief, it is based on sound scholarship.

1294 *Semialignment and Western Security*. Edited by Nils Orvik. London: Croom Helm, 1986. 286pp. ISBN 0–7099–1951–4.

Canadian and Dutch authors present a series of papers on the theory of semialignment in which a state has alliance obligations but also retains independence of action. Case studies of states practicing semialignment—Canada, Denmark, Greece, Norway, and the Netherlands—are treated in depth. While all of these states participate in alliance systems, they are on the fringe of decision making because of their lack of commitment. This book treats an issue ignored in most security literature.

1295 Sepulveda, Francisco L. de. *Crisis y amenaza nuclear*. Barcelona: Editorial Planeta, 1982. 236pp. ISBN 84–320–7311–3.

A Spanish author examines the international scene for evidence of rationality in the nuclear arms race. The author contends that in a world with so many disparities of wealth among nations, the presence of an arms race depleting resources is obscene. He believes Spain can serve as a moderating force by entering NATO and working for ways to restrain the arms race. This book is a reflective work by an author seeking to find answers, and it is this process that most readers will find profitable.

1296 Shaffer, Stephen M., and Lisa Robock Shaffer. *The Politics of International Cooperation: A Comparison of U.S. Experience in Space and in Security*. Denver, CO: Graduate School of International Studies, University of Denver, 1980. 73pp. ISBN 0–87940–063–3.

In this short monograph the authors examine cooperative efforts on scientific and technical matters by the National Aeronautics and Space Administration (NASA) and on political and military security with NATO members. The authors conclude that such cooperation furthers U.S. foreign policy objectives by U.S. dominance over other nations in scientific, technological, and military capabilities. Such predominance changes as other nations catch up in these fields, but time delays and economic costs become problems for these late entrants. This book is an introductory study on this topic, but it paves the way for more research on the benefits and costs of international cooperation.

1297 Shenfield, Stephen. *The Nuclear Predicament: Explorations in Soviet Ideology*. London: Routledge and Kegan Paul, 1987. 126pp. ISBN 0–7102–1228–3.

The author explores the development of Soviet ideology toward nuclear war in the post-Stalin Soviet Union. Recent changes in Soviet arms control bargaining positions are partly the result of the growing realization of the dangers of nuclear war to the Soviet homeland. This shift to peace from a military orientation has its risks for the West because it can easily be reversed back to military adventurism. This book is a major effort to understand the recent change of Soviet policies, but it suffers from the standard problem of Americans dealing with the Soviet mind-set.

1298 Shoemaker, Christopher C., and John Spanier. *Patron-Client State Relationships: Multilateral Crises in the Nuclear Age.* New York: Praeger, 1984. 211pp. ISBN 0–03–063881–X.

Crisis management in international relations is the subject of this book, but the emphasis is on the way political and military conflicts among regional states involve the superpowers in hostilities. The authors describe this type of crisis management as "bipolycentric crises," and they study the patron–client state relationship for the implications of this theory. By using the Soviet-Egyptian model, the authors conclude that such relationships are both dynamic and unstable, but that because of the current international realities, patron–client state relationships will continue to develop. This book is an excellent example of theory and case studies working together to produce a major contribution to security literature.

1299 Simpson, John. *The Independent Nuclear State: The United States, Britain and the Military Atom,* 2d ed. London: Macmillan, 1986. 341pp. ISBN 0–333–38661–2.

This book is a revised edition of an earlier work (1983) on the history of the British military atomic energy program. While it deals with British research, development, and production activities, the major emphasis is on the linkage between British and U.S. nuclear weapons development. Although Anglo-U.S. cooperation on nuclear weapons has been sporadic, the common theme has been to provide Great Britain with a technically effective strategic deterrent at minimum cost. Secrecy by both the U.S. and British governments has prevented much research in this field, and this book breaks new ground on an important subject.

1300 Singh, Bhupinder. *Indian Ocean and Regional Security.* Patiala, India: B. C. Publishers, 1983. 140pp.

The geopolitical and military significance of the Indian Ocean is the subject of this study by a former Indian military officer. Superpower rivalry has turned the Indian Ocean into a crisis hotspot since the establishment of the U.S. base at Diego Garcia. Only by cooperation among the Indian Ocean states can the security of the region be maintained by excluding the superpowers. This treatise is a plea for neutralization of the Indian Ocean region, but behind this plan is the fact that such a neutralization would leave India the dominant power in the region.

1301 Singham, A. W., and Shirley Hune. *Non-alignment in an Age of Alignments.* Westport, CT: Lawrence Hill, 1986. 420pp. ISBN 0–88208–214–0.

This book studies the role of the nonaligned Third World countries in international politics from the perspective of the Non-aligned Movement. The authors give special attention to the Non-aligned Movement as an agent of social change in the international community from 1961 to 1985. Studies of documents and interviews with Third World policymakers show that political and economic crises need a third force between the two superpower blocs to counteract the effects of the rivalry. This book represents the viewpoints past and present of the Non-aligned Movement, and it deserves serious study by security specialists to understand its viewpoints.

1302   Siracusa, Joseph M. *Rearming for the Cold War: Paul H. Nitze, the H-Bomb and the Origins of a Soviet First Strike.* Los Angeles, CA: Center for the Study of Armament and Disarmament, 1983. 42pp.

A U.S. foreign policy specialist studies the impact of Paul H. Nitze on the development of U.S. strategic policy. He gives special attention to an analysis of National Security Council Policy Paper Number 68 (NSC 68). This document and its subsequent interpretations have made it the most important policy statement in the postwar era. While this short paper is devoted to a single theme, the importance of NSC 68 in U.S. security history makes this contribution invaluable for researchers of U.S. strategic doctrine.

1303   Sloan, Stanley R. *NATO's Future: Toward a New Transatlantic Bargain.* Washington, DC: National Defense University Press, 1985. 241pp.

The author, a former CIA analyst and now a specialist on NATO for the Congressional Research Service, undertakes an examination of the future of NATO. His analysis foresees a dramatic change in the nature of NATO, with a readjustment of burdens and responsibilities. It is possible for the European states to agree upon a European security arrangement outside of and including NATO. The author seeks insight into the evolutionary processes of NATO, and his ideas are most suggestive.

1304   *Small is Dangerous: Micro States in a Macro World.* Edited by Sheila Harden. London: Frances Pinter, 1985. 212pp. ISBN 0–86187–539–7.

This book is the report of a Study Group of the David Davies Memorial Institute of International Studies on the security problems of small states. The breakup of the colonial empires has left numerous very small states, and they are always vulnerable to international power politics. Because these states lack economic and physical means to resist attacks, they should cooperate in forming regional security understandings and use the United Nations as a forum for disputes. This report contributes to a better understanding of the problems of small states in international relations.

1305   *Small Nuclear Forces and U.S. Security Policy: Threats and Potential Conflicts in the Middle East and South Asia.* Edited by Rodney W. Jones. Lexington, MA: Lexington Books, 1984. 289pp. ISBN 0–669–06736–9.

This book of essays sponsored by the Center for Strategic and International Studies (CSIS), Georgetown University, considers the proliferation of nuclear weapons to the Middle East and South Asia and its implications for U.S. security policy. Proliferation to these states will only cause further destabilization and possibly nuclear war. The U.S. must keep its options open, including protection of vital interests, but crisis management techniques must also be developed. This book provides a strong base for further research on the impact of nuclear proliferation.

1306   Snow, Donald M. *The Necessary Peace: Nuclear Weapons and Superpower Relations.* Lexington, MA: Lexington Books, 1987. 147pp. ISBN 0–6691–5332–X.

The author presents a thesis that nuclear weapons have had a stabilizing and tranquilizing effect on U.S.-Soviet relations. Any changes to the existing deterrence system must be examined, and proponents of change bear the burden of demonstrating that it will improve matters. Any arms control agreement has to fulfill this requirement, and the likelihood of this happening is slim. This book is a hardline defense of current nuclear deterrence theory.

1307 Snow, Donald M. *The Nuclear Future: Toward a Strategy of Uncertainty.* University, AL: University of Alabama Press, 1983. 189pp. ISBN 0–8173–0117–8.

The author has revised previously published articles on the strategic doctrine of deterrence for publication in this book. His thesis is that the development of new technology on warheads and missile defenses brings into question many of the tenets and assumptions underlying the strategy of deterrence. The solution is to adopt an uncertainty-based nuclear strategy incorporating unpredictability as the key principle. This strategy is suggestive, as is the rest of the book, but there remains a credibility gap for the author's conclusions.

1308 Soppelsa, Jacques. *Des tensions et des armes.* Paris: Publications de la Sorbonne, 1984. 156pp. ISBN 2–85–944–082–8.

The author uses the geopolitical theory of Sir Halford MacKinder to analyze the breakdown of the bipolar security system in the mid-1980s. Economic, military, and political crises worldwide have weakened the political controls of the two superpowers, the Soviet Union and the United States. The growth of international terrorism is a manifestation of this breakdown of the postwar situation. Because this book is a think piece and the author draws on such a variety of disciplines and theories for his thesis, it is worth reading for his analysis.

1309 Soppelsa, Jacques. *Geographie des armements.* Paris: Masson, 1980. 277pp. ISBN 2–225–67177–X.

The geographical foundations of strategic relations are the focus of this book. An impressive number of illustrations and statistical tables enables the author to establish the affinity between geography and strategic considerations. The sections on arms transfers and the economics of defense are of special interest. Although this work is becoming dated, its perspective and data still make it a useful source.

1310 *South Africa's Plan and Capability in the Nuclear Field.* New York: United Nations Centre for Disarmament, 1981. 40pp.

This report was commissioned by the United Nations to study the nuclear capabilities of the Republic of South Africa. The conclusion is that because of its uranium mining industry South Africa has the technical capability to make nuclear weapons and the means of delivery. A test in the Kalahari Desert in September 1979 makes it probable that South Africa has a nuclear arsenal, and the determination of the South African government to retain its political system makes this an ominous development. Although much of the information in this report is based on hearsay evidence, it is still useful for background purposes.

1311 *Southern Africa: Regional Security Problems and Prospects.* Edited by Robert Jaster. Aldershot, England: Gower, 1985. 170pp. ISBN 0–566–00866–1.

These essays analyze the sources of conflict in Southern Africa and the implications for Western security interests. South Africa plays the central role in this region, and its policies have shown an aggressive and belligerent attitude toward its neighboring states. U.S. policy in this region has been restricted to "preventive diplomacy," but its Angola policy has been a political disaster. Southern Africa continues to be a source of international conflict, and this book of essays promotes a better understanding of this region's problems.

1312 *The Soviet Calculus of Nuclear War.* Edited by Roman Kolkowicz and Ellen Propper Mickiewicz. Lexington, MA: Lexington Books, 1986. 276pp. ISBN 0–669115–66–5.

This book considers the posture, doctrine, missions, and capabilities of the Soviet Union with respect to strategic nuclear questions. While the book is a compendium of writings from several symposia, the author's goals are to examine Soviet military policy and strategic planning from a variety of perspectives. The result combines all available information on Soviet security doctrine. This book shows the differences between Soviet and U.S. approaches to strategic problems, and this contrast is the contribution of these essays.

1313 *Soviet Interests in the Third World.* Edited by Robert Cassen. London: Sage, 1985. 329pp. ISBN 0–8039–9720–3.

A Study Group of the Royal Institute of International Affairs met during 1983–1984 to study Soviet economic interests in Third World countries, and the·papers in this book are the result of this activity. Most of the authors share the view that the Soviet Union is a beleaguered major power rather than an aggressive, expansionist empire. While the Soviets accrue economic benefits from their trade with the Third World, they also accumulate political and military advantages from these policies. These papers are all high-quality works of scholarship, and this book is a good addition for any researcher interested in Soviet policies.

1314 *Soviet International Behavior and U.S. Policy Options.* Edited by Dan Caldwell. Lexington, MA: Lexington Books, 1985. 291pp. ISBN 0–669–09125–1.

Most of these papers on U.S. policy options toward Soviet international behavior were presented at seminars at the Center for Foreign Policy Development during 1983. Soviet affairs experts from academia and government analyze Soviet international behavior to ascertain behavioral characteristics, and they conclude that there are three Soviet priorities: (1) protection of the homeland; (2) security of the Soviet empire; and (3) recognition as a superpower. The United States remains the only adversary that can threaten any of these priorities. This book presents a series of quality papers that help the reader understand Soviet behavior on the international scene.

1315 *Soviet–Latin American Relations in the 1980s.* Edited by Augusto Varas. Boulder, CO: Westview Press, 1987. 290pp. ISBN 0–8133–7123–6.

These essays trace the political and economic linkage between the Soviet Union and Latin American countries, and the ramifications of this contact on U.S. policies toward Latin America. Latin American countries have become more independent from the United States, and many are willing to use the Soviet Union against the United States for domestic support. The result is regional instability and growing U.S. impatience with Soviet policies in Latin America. These essays by prominent Latin American scholars show the depth of feeling among Latin American intellectuals toward past and present U.S. policies.

1316 *Soviet Strategy.* Edited by John Baylis and Gerald Segal. London: Croom Helm, 1981. 263pp. ISBN 0–86598–0505–0.

This book is an analysis of Soviet strategy in international relations by a number of U.S. and European scholars on strategic studies. The editors selected articles with a balanced viewpoint to ensure that both hardline and softline viewpoints were represented. This balance makes this book a good introduction for further research on Soviet strategy on foreign relations and military topics. Such a volume also has its uses for graduate and undergraduate college courses.

1317 *The Soviet Union: Security Policies and Constraints.* Edited by Jonathan Alford. Aldershot, England: Gower, 1985. 180pp. ISBN 0–566–00865–3.

Seven U.S. and European security specialists present essays on Soviet security policies and constraints on its military power in this volume. The theme behind Soviet policy is a drive toward absolute security, and this drive is expressed by the use of military force to expand Soviet power. These essays on Soviet security themes are all of a uniform high quality and by top scholars in the field.

1318 *The Soviet Union and the Middle East in the 1980s: Opportunities, Constraints and Dilemmas.* Edited by Mark V. Kauppi and C. Craig Nation. Lexington, MA: Lexington Books, 1983. 292pp. ISBN 0–669–05966–8.

These papers are the product of a 1981 USC–U.S. Army Russian Institute (USARI) symposium on the Soviet Union and the Middle East. At the beginning of 1983 the Soviet Union's influence in the Middle East was at its lowest ebb since 1955, and Arab regimes turned to the Soviets only because of the lack of alternative sources of external support. This lack of influence has benefitted the United States, but it is the result of events in the Middle East rather than of U.S. policies. These essays are all of a high quality, and this book is an important source for an understanding of the politics of the Middle East.

1319 *The Soviet Union and the Third World: The Last Three Decades.* Edited by Andrzej Korbonki and Francis Fukuyama. Ithaca, NY: Cornell University Press, 1987. 317pp. ISBN 0–8014–2032–6.

These papers analyze Soviet politics toward Third World countries from the 1960s through the 1980s, and they are a product of a 1985 conference sponsored by the UCLA Center for the Study of Soviet International Behavior (CSSIB) in Bellagio, Italy. During the last three decades, the Soviets have had their ups and downs in their relations with the Third World. Present Soviet leadership is reluctant to push Soviet initiatives in the Third World, but they will intervene in certain scenarios to exploit U.S. mistakes. This book has a number of solid essays of interest to researchers on security issues.

1320 *The "Special Relationship": Anglo-American Relations since 1945.* Edited by Wm. Roger Louis and Hedley Bull. Oxford, England: Clarendon Press, 1986. 408pp. ISBN 0–19–822925–9.

These papers are the results of several conferences held in 1984 and 1985 attempting to define the relationship between Great Britain and the United States. U.S. and British authors debate the closeness of ties between the two countries. Consensus of opinion is that the special relationship has never been as close as advertised, and that even a similarity of outlook is less important now than in the past. These essays are all excellent, and no study of U.S.-British relations can ignore this book.

1321 Sreedhar. *Arms Flow into the Gulf: Process of Buying Security.* Canberra: Strategic and Defence Studies Centre, 1982. 21pp.

This study by an Indian security specialist examines the threat perceptions of the Persian Gulf states and their arms procurement policies. The author maintains that there is no correlation between the perceived threats and the type of arms being acquired by these countries. Except for Iran, no state envisages a threat from either of the superpowers, and domestic insurgency is the only perceived threat. While this short study of arms transfers into the Persian Gulf region is not the last word, it, nevertheless, makes a solid contribution to study of the issue.

1322   Stares, Paul B. *Space Weapons and US Strategy: Origins and Development.* London: Croom Helm, 1985. 334pp. ISBN 0–7099–2369–4.

Although this book is an outgrowth of a British dissertation, it has been expanded by enough additional research to constitute a solid contribution to the study of the military uses of outer space. Only during the last decade has the technology developed for the military uses of outer space. The author maintains that the significance of space weapons systems is as a destabilizing factor, and that development of space weapon systems will trigger a space arms race.

1323   Steele, Jonathan. *Soviet Power: The Kremlin's Foreign Policy—Brezhnev to Chernenko*, rev. ed. New York: Simon and Schuster, 1984. 289pp. ISBN 0–671–52813–0.

The author of this critique of Soviet foreign policy in the early 1980s is the correspondent on East-West relations for the *Guardian*. His contention is that Soviet policy has been less threatening than Western commentators have been willing to admit. At the same time as Soviet military power has increased in the 1960s and 1970s, its political influence in almost every region of the world has declined. This analysis is a corrective for some of the worst-case scenarios by U.S. critics of Soviet policy, but it has become dated by the elevation of Gorbachev to Soviet leadership.

1324   Stevenson, Richard W. *The Rise and Fall of Detente: Relaxations of Tension in US-Soviet Relations, 1953–84.* Urbana, IL: University of Illinois Press, 1985. 238pp. ISBN 0–252–01215–1.

The author examines the phenomenon of superpower detente in the era from 1953 to 1984. There have been four periods of detente—Geneva in 1955, Camp David in 1959, post–missile crisis detente in 1963–1964, and the Moscow detente in 1972–1975. While the accomplishments of 1960s and 1970s detente have been enduring, there has been no linear pattern of progress. This book is an important work of scholarship on a controversial subject.

1325   *Strategic Deterrence in a Changing Environment.* Edited by Christoph Bertram. Farnborough, England: Gower, 1981. 194pp. ISBN 0–566–00346–5.

These papers survey the international debate on strategic deterrence during the 1970s. The loss of unquestioned U.S. nuclear superiority has sharpened the debate. Now questions arise over the protection of nuclear missiles against a first strike and the ability of the United States to continue to link the threat of its nuclear arsenal to the security of allies. These papers discuss these issues and others, making this book a good source for studying strategic deterrence doctrine.

1326   *The Strategic Imperative: New Policies for American Security.* Edited by Samuel P. Huntington. Cambridge, MA: Ballinger, 1982. 360pp. ISBN 0–88410–895–3.

This collection of essays includes various views on U.S. strategic interests. Most of the authors are present or former associates of the Program in National Security Studies at the Harvard Center for International Affairs. Each author looks at a segment of past and present strategic thinking and comments on the validity of that concept for the future. This book has a number of significant essays of lasting value.

1327 *Strategic Minerals: A Resource Crisis.* Washington, DC: Council on Economics and National Security, 1981. 105pp.

Scarcity of strategic minerals as a national security problem is the subject of this series of lectures from a 1981 conference in New York City. Manganese, chromium, platinum, and cobalt are the most important of the sixty-two strategic minerals the United States must import from abroad. But 75 percent of strategic minerals are imported from Southern Africa, making stability in this region of vital concern to U.S. national security. These papers provide a wealth of information vital for researchers in international security.

1328 *Strategy and Nuclear Deterrence.* Edited by Steven E. Miller. Princeton, NJ: Princeton University Press, 1984. 297pp. ISBN 0–691–04712–X.

The essays in this volume address the problems that statesmen and strategists face in determining what configuration of nuclear forces best minimizes the possibility of nuclear war. But this problem is also part of a debate that the authors have among themselves on whether there is a winner possible in a nuclear war. Most of the authors are hardliners on nuclear weapons strategy, and they lean toward the strategic benefits of nuclear deterrence. While the essays are of a uniform high quality, the authors never answer the key question of the consequences of the failure of nuclear deterrence.

1329 *Studies of War and Peace.* Edited by Oyvind Osterud. Oslo: Norwegian University Press, 1986. 281pp. ISBN 82–00–07749–7.

These papers are the product of the Nobel Symposium on war and peace, held in Noresund, Norway, in 1985. Distinguished scholars contributed papers on the present knowledge and research on war and peace. Three types of studies appear: (1) causes of war; (2) arms control measures; and (3) the functioning of the international system. Each of the contributors to this volume produced a solid piece of research, making this book one of the better available sources on war and peace.

1330 Subramanian, Ram Rajan. *Nuclear Proliferation in South Asia: Security in the 1980s.* Canberra: Strategic and Defence Studies Centre, 1982. 47pp. ISBN 0–86784–091–9.

Pakistan's effort to attain or develop a nuclear capability is the subject of this study by an Indian scholar. Proliferation of nuclear technology to India's primary rival in South Asia concerns the Indian government and defense community. Two factors are the most disturbing—Pakistan as a military theocratic state and the short range between military targets in India. This paper expresses a legitimate concern over the destabilizing effects of the acquisition of nuclear weapons in a specific region, but India started the process by introducing nuclear technology into this region in the 1970s.

1331 *The Successor Generation: International Perspectives of Postwar Europeans.* Edited by Stephen F. Szabo. London: Butterworths, 1983. 183pp. ISBN 0–408–10817–7.

These papers study the impact on NATO of a new generation of leaders unfamiliar with the origins of the Atlantic alliance. The authors consult public opinion surveys in Great Britain, France, Italy, Spain, and West Germany for shifts of attitude on security and defense issues. While postwar Europeans have little attraction toward the Soviet Union as a society or its international position, there is also a tendency to distance themselves from the United States in favor of European solutions. Any study of future NATO policies will have to take into account the material in this book.

1332 *Superpower Involvement in the Middle East: Dynamics of Foreign Policy.* Edited by Paul Marantz and Blema S. Steinberg. Boulder, CO: Westview Press, 1985. 301pp. ISBN 0–8133–7100–7.

These articles on the role of the superpowers in the Middle East are a product of a 1984 conference of the Canadian Professors for Peace in the Middle East, held at the University of Toronto, Toronto, Canada. A group of U.S. and Canadian scholars examine U.S. and Soviet options in the Middle East. The consensus is that neither superpower has conducted a successful policy in the Middle East, and that an uncertain demand for oil and Islamic fundamentalism are constraints to both superpowers. This book brings together diverse views of superpower involvement in the Middle East in an important contribution to security literature.

1333 Talbott, Strobe. *The Russians and Reagan.* New York: Vintage Books, 1984. 140pp. ISBN 0–394–72635–9.

The relationship between the U.S. and Soviet governments in 1984 is the subject of this book by the diplomatic correspondent of *Time*. Soviet perceptions of the Reagan administration's hardline policy toward the Soviet Union have strengthened the hawks in the Kremlin, and Andropov's death has only temporarily moderated the hostility on both sides. This book deals with perceptions about the leadership of the two superpowers, and, despite changes within Soviet leadership, it offers valuable insights into Soviet leadership circles.

1334 *Ten Years after Helsinki: The Making of the European Security Regime.* Edited by Kari Mottola. Boulder, CO: Westview Press, 1986. 184pp. ISBN 0–8133–7192–9.

These papers come from an international roundtable seminar organized by the Finnish Institute of International Affairs (FIIA), Helsinki, in 1985. The emphasis of the seminar was to discuss European security issues and the role of the Conference on Security and Cooperation in Europe (CSCE) in promoting security cooperation. Most of the authors recognize that there are elements in the European scene to promote European cooperation, but political changes will have to take place before further progress. All the authors are Europeans, nearly half are Finnish, and these viewpoints differ from other European sources.

1335 *Termination of Wars: Processes, Procedures and Aftermaths.* Edited by Nissan Oren. Jerusalem: Magnes Press, 1982. 277pp. ISBN 965–223–442–7.

This volume of essays undertakes to study the termination of wars rather than the causes. Most of the examples are derived from the Israeli experience of settlements after wars, but there are several essays using examples from other wars. Each essay stands on its own merits; the only common theme is the difficulty of successfully terminating wars. War termination theory is relatively new as a field of study but full of promise, and these essays fall into the same category.

1336 *Third-World Conflict and International Security.* Edited by Christoph Bertram. London: Macmillan, 1982. 121pp. ISBN 0–333–32955–4.

These papers were presented at the International Institute for Strategic Studies 1980 Annual Conference in Stresa on conflict and security in the Third World. Internal instability of Third World states and external fluidity on the international scene combined for a nasty scenario in the early 1980s. Regional cooperation is the one development that brightens the picture and may prevent further Third World conflicts. These papers are high-quality assessments of an ongoing problem among Third World states.

1337 *Third-World Marxist-Leninist Regimes: Strengths, Vulnerabilities and U.S. Policy.* By Uri Ra'anan et al. Washington, DC: Pergamon-Brassey's, 1985. 130pp. ISBN 0–08–033160–2.

This book of essays deals with the strengths and vulnerabilities of Third World Marxist-Leninist states. Nine states—Afghanistan, Angola, Cuba, Ethiopia, Mozambique, Nicaragua, North Korea, the People's Democratic Republic of Yemen, and Vietnam—are analyzed for their relationship with the Soviet Union and for their internal differences and similarities. Finally, the threat that this type of state poses for U.S. security, particularly in Latin America, is detailed. While the analysis in these essays provides valuable information about these regimes, the conservative viewpoint of the authors weakens the conclusions.

1338 *Third World Militarization: A Challenge to Third World Diplomacy.* Edited by Jagat S. Mehta. Austin, TX: Lyndon B. Johnson School of Public Affairs, 1985. 279pp. ISBN 0–89940–006–X.

These essays from the Seventh Tom Slick Conference for World Peace at Austin, TX, in 1984, deal with the ongoing problem of Third World militarization. While Cold War politics stimulated this militarization, it has continued because of prestige and nationalism. All the essays have their virtues, but the appendix of data on military and social trends is the most valuable part of this book. It is another in a series of works on Third World militarization, but it is not of the caliber of the other books on the topic.

1339 Thomas, Raju G. C. *Indian Security Policy.* Princeton, NJ: Princeton University Press, 1986. 312pp. ISBN 0–691–07724–X.

The theme of this book is that only by understanding Indian security policies can South Asia and Indian Ocean regional stability be comprehended. India views security threats from Pakistan and to a lesser extent from China as more significant than threats from beyond the subcontinent. Both external and internal threats have advanced the importance of the military in India, but for the present India is successfully dealing with its security problems. This book is a high-quality assessment of Indian security policy, and it can be recommended for anyone interested in South Asia and Indian Ocean security issues.

1340 *Threats to Security in East Asia-Pacific: National and Regional Perspectives.* Edited by Charles E. Morrison. Lexington, MA: Lexington Books, 1983. 221pp. ISBN 0–669–06369–X.

The Pacific Forum has been active in studying different national perceptions of threats to security among the countries of East Asia and the Pacific.

These fifteen essays are an outcome of a 1982 symposium in Waikoloa, Hawaii, on threat perceptions in this region. There are considerable differences in perceptions of threat among the various countries and among leadership segments. This book is an effort to study a single problem from a variety of viewpoints, and that is both its strength and its weakness.

1341 *Threats, Weapons, and Foreign Policy.* Edited by Pat McGowan and Charles W. Kegley. Beverly Hills, CA: Sage Publications, 1980. 324pp. ISBN 0–8039–1154–8.

The editors intended this book to be a place where defense analysts and foreign policy experts could study the interaction between national security and foreign policy behavior. This emphasis on concepts and methodologies is directed to three types of subjects: (1) threats, (2) weapons, and (3) arms races. The result is nine articles by eighteen authors exploring aspects of these subjects. This book presents a series of unique articles of value to both defense and security specialists.

1342 *Toward a New Security: Lessons of the Forty Years since Trinity.* Cambridge, MA: Union of Concerned Scientists, 1985. 73pp.

The Union of Concerned Scientists produced this commemorative report on the origins of the atomic era and its lessons for today and tomorrow. Despite technical enhancements in the last forty years, the world has gained nothing in increased security. A series of short articles by specialists in the field makes proposals for arms control and reduced defense research. This report is too brief for a complete analysis of the problem, but the quality of the articles and the viewpoints make it still worth reading.

1343 *Trilateralism in Asia: Problems and Prospects in U.S.-Japan-ASEAN Relations.* Edited by K. S. Nathan and M. Pathmanathan. Kuala Lumpur, Malaysia: Antara, 1986. 205pp.

These papers are the product of a 1985 Regional Seminar on Trilateralism in Asia cosponsored by the University of Malaysia and the Malaysian International Affairs Forum (MIAF). The authors are a mixture of Asian and Western scholars concerned with the international economic and political relations between the Association of Southeast Asian Nations (ASEAN), Japan, and the United States. Trilateralism depends upon a common perception of external threats and shared economic interests, and trilateralism in Asia among ASEAN, Japan, and the United States does not exist at the present time. These essays present a divergence of views on Asian perspectives that security scholars will appreciate.

1344 Trofimenko, Henry. *Changing Attitudes toward Deterrence.* Los Angeles, CA: Center for International and Strategic Affairs, 1980. 60pp.

This study of the evolution of the theory of deterrence in the postwar world is by a prominent Soviet scholar. His treatment of the subject emphasizes U.S. contributions to the doctrine of deterrence. The author's thesis is that the deterrence theories promulgated by the United States have made the Soviet Union react, building its deterrence posture to the point of mutual deterrence. Despite a mild Soviet bias, this essay is a major contribution to the study of deterrence theory, and it is a unique example of sound scholarship from the Soviet side.

1345   *The Troubled Alliance: Atlantic Relations in the 1980s.* Edited by Lawrence Freedman. London: Heinemann, 1983. 170pp. ISBN 0–435–83326–X.

These papers were presented at a 1983 conference on U.S.-European relations held at Chatham House, London. Most of the papers deal with the changing strategic environment' of the Soviet Union's achievement of nuclear parity, or the impact of Western Europe's economic recovery, which places the European allies on a par with the United States. Despite the importance of the Soviet threat to the alliance, most of the participants felt economic policy coordination within the alliance was its most important problem. This work takes a solid look at many of the problems facing NATO countries in the near future, and it is therefore worth reading.

1346   Tsurutani, Taketsugu. *Japanese Policy and East Asian Security.* New York: Praeger, 1981. 208pp. ISBN 0–03–059806–0.

The increasing Japanese role in East Asian security during the 1980s is the subject of this book by a Japanese security specialist. This active role by Japan will mean a reappraisal of Japanese-U.S. security arrangements, leading to Japan assuming a greater military role in East Asia. But this adoption of a positive and activist defense and foreign policy does not mean the acquisition of strategic weapons. This reappraisal of Japanese defense and foreign policy is a welcome addition to international security literature.

1347   Tucker, Anthony, and John Gleisner. *Crucible of Despair: The Effects of Nuclear War.* London: Menard Press, 1982. 62pp. ISBN 0–903400–72–3.

This book is in response to the British government's assertion that there would be survivors in a nuclear war. The authors maintain that civil defense will have only a marginal effect on the chances of survival of a significant portion of the British population and none at all on the quality of society left after a nuclear attack. A medical plan for nuclear war envisaged by the British government is not supported by scientific and medical evidence. This study points out the medical hazards of nuclear war in a clear and convincing fashion.

1348   Tucker, Robert W. *The Nuclear Debate: Deterrence and the Lapse of Faith.* New York: Holmes and Meier, 1985. 132pp. ISBN 0–8419–1039–1.

A U.S. scholar on international security examines the lapse of faith in the doctrine of nuclear deterrence. This fall from grace of deterrence is manifested in the growth of the peace movement and in the advocacy of the Strategic Defense Initiative (SDI) by the Reagan administration. The old deterrence structure may be gone, and in its place some sort of crisis management structure needs to be resurrected. This book is a thoughtful analysis of changing thought patterns on international security.

1349   Turner, John, and SIPRI. *Arms in the '80s: New Developments in Global Arms Race.* London: Taylor and Francis, 1985. 118pp. ISBN 0–85–662–98–2.

This publication is a more popular account of the SIPRI Yearbook 1985. While it updates information on armaments and disarmament issues, the advantage of this publication is that it narrows the focus of attention to specific issues. It also has excellent charts and graphs. This type of update is a valuable tool for security specialists.

1350 Ulam, Adam B. *Dangerous Relations: the Soviet Union in World Politics, 1970–1982.* New York: Oxford University Press, 1983. 325pp. ISBN 0–19–503237–3.

This critical study by a leading U.S. Soviet specialist examines Soviet foreign policy and Soviet-U.S. relations during the age of détente. Soviet leaders believe that internal security is inextricably tied to advances of Soviet external power and authority, and this results in a worldwide Soviet-U.S. rivalry. But the Soviets also believe in the benefits of some cooperation, and they have held to détente much longer than expected because of this. This book is a chronological treatment of the subject, and any researcher will find something of value in it.

1351 Ury, William Langer, and Richard Smoke. *Beyond the Hotline: Controlling a Nuclear Crisis.* Cambridge, MA: Nuclear Negotiation Project, Harvard Law School, 1984. 87pp.

The Nuclear Negotiation Project (NNP) is affiliated with the Harvard Law School, and this group studies the theory and the practice of U.S.-Soviet negotiating processes. The authors suggest a number of proposals to mitigate against the escalation of a crisis to nuclear war. These proposals are (1) agreed-upon crisis procedures; (2) a nuclear crisis control center; (3) a crisis consultation period; (4) nuclear risk reduction talks; (5) a presidential crisis control seminar; and (6) enhanced third-party roles in defusing regional conflicts. This book is a practical treatment of ways to defuse international crisis situations, and it should be required reading.

1352 *The Use of Force: International Politics and Foreign Policy,* 2d ed. Edited by Robert J. Art and Kenneth N. Waltz. Lanham, MD: University Press of America, 1983. 664pp. ISBN 0–8191–3425–2.

The use of military power as an instrument of foreign policy in twentieth-century international politics is the subject of this book of essays. An earlier edition appeared in 1971, and this version has been updated with many new selections. The section on issues for the 1980s is brand new, and it is most valuable as a research source for security specialists. This book can be recommended for both the student at an introductory level and the scholar at an advanced level.

1353 *U.S. Policy and Low-Intensity Conflict: Potentials for Military Struggles in the 1980s.* Edited by Sam C. Sarkesian and William L. Scully. New Brunswick, NJ: Transaction Books, 1981. 221pp. ISBN 0–87855–851–9.

These papers were presented at a 1979 workshop on low-intensity nonnuclear conflict at Loyola University of Chicago in 1979. While participants had difficulty in agreeing on a definition of terms, a consensus developed that the United States needs to prepare for a more unconventional type of warfare. It was also recognized by all that military capability, national will, and political-military policy needed integration before any type of U.S. interventionist policy could succeed. These essays reveal the lack of consensus among U.S. policymakers in dealing with low-intensity conflicts.

1354 *US Strategic Interests in the Gulf Region.* Edited by Wm. J. Olson. Boulder, CO: Westview Press, 1987. 234pp. ISBN 0–8133–7119–8.

These papers result from a two-day conference in 1985 at the Strategic Studies Institute, U.S. Army War College, on U.S. strategic interests in the Persian Gulf. Most of the essays are concerned with the effect of U.S. policies in the region rather than with U.S.-Soviet rivalry. The papers are divided between studies of sources and types of instability in the region and studies of U.S. political-military responses to this instability. Each of the papers is a high-quality assessment of a theme or response to a problem, and the cumulative effect is a strong book useful for the advanced researcher in the field.

1355 *The Utility of International Economic Sanctions.* Edited by David Leyton-Brown. New York: St. Martin's Press, 1987. 320pp. ISBN 0–312–00369–2.

These papers are the product of a 1983 conference on international economic sanctions held at York University, Toronto, Canada. The authors are interested in the use of economic sanctions as tools in specific peacetime conflict situations. They conclude that economic sanctions can be effective, but only if due attention is given to objectives and termination. This book is a solid source on the use and effectiveness of international economic sanctions as a foreign policy option.

1356 Van Slyck, Philip. *Strategies for the 1980s: Lessons of Cuba, Vietnam and Afghanistan.* Westport, CT: Greenwood Press, 1981. 108pp. ISBN 0–313–22975–9.

This book is a theoretical analysis of U.S. strategic thought at the beginning of the 1980s. The author uses Cuba, Vietnam, and Afghanistan as case studies for U.S. strategic options, but the author believes that the 1979 Soviet invasion of Afghanistan constitutes a watershed, ending détente and inaugurating an era of increased defense spending in the United States. Negotiating from strength to restore a stable balance of power between the Soviet Union and the United States is the goal of the author. Although this book has become dated by passing events, the author's viewpoint is important in understanding Reagan administration policies in the early 1980s.

1357 Vigeveno, Guido. *The Bomb and European Security.* Bloomington, IN: Indiana University Press, 1983. 131pp. ISBN 0–253–31208–6.

The theory of deterrence and the importance of nuclear deterrence today are the subjects of this book. Deterrence works only so long as the Soviet leaders believe that U.S. weapons might be used in a crisis situation. This means that U.S. and NATO forces must have a nuclear arsenal large enough to constitute a creditable threat to the Soviet Union. This book concentrates on the military aspects of deterrence theory, and this emphasis is its contribution to security literature.

1358 Walters, Ronald W. *South Africa and the Bomb: Responsibility and Deterrence.* Lexington, MA: Lexington Books, 1987. 176pp. ISBN 0–669–14197–6.

The dangers of South African nuclear capability are highlighted in this book. International nuclear proliferation policies have failed to prevent the technology and raw materials for building nuclear weapons from reaching the Republic of South Africa. South Africa's regional security problems give it a rationale for the acquisition of nuclear weapons. This book examines the extent to which a maverick state can acquire nuclear weapons and threaten to use them to buttress a regime's political power.

1359 Walton, John. *Reluctant Rebels: Comparative Studies of Revolution and Underdevelopment.* New York: Columbia University Press, 1984. 230pp. ISBN 0–231–05728–8.

The themes of this book are the nature of violent political upheavals in the Third World and the future of these events. A series of national revolts—the Huk Rebellion in the Philippines, La Violencia in Colombia, and the Mau Mau Revolt in Kenya—are analyzed for comparative patterns. The author concludes that national revolts occur in the context of modernization crises, and that these modernization crises are common in the developing world. Despite the depth of analysis, this book is only partially successful in finding the roots of revolution in the developing world.

1360 Ward, Michael Don. *Research Gaps in Alliance Dynamics*. Denver, CO: Graduate School of International Studies, 1982. 107pp. ISBN 0–87940–068–4.

This book is a review of the literature on alliances, alignments, and coalitions. The emphasis is on the role these entanglements have on interstate behavior. Material for the literature review was gathered from the most prominent journals in international relations, and the articles date from 1960 to 1980. This type of review is a useful gauge of the research in the field, and this review is one of the better examples of the type.

1361 *The War System: An Interdisciplinary Approach*. Edited by Richard A. Falk and Samuel S. Kim. Boulder, CO: Westview Press, 1980. 659pp. ISBN 0–89158–569–9.

War as a social system is the focus of this book of interdisciplinary writings. Twenty-seven essays explore different topics on the nature of war. Besides understanding the social system of war, most of the contributors are interested in ways to control war, or modify its popularity. This anthology of writings constitutes a good introduction to this subject, and this book can be recommended for college-level coursework.

1362 *Western Europe and the Crisis in U.S.-Soviet Relations*. Edited by Richard H. Ullman and Mario Zucconi. New York: Praeger, 1987. 123pp. ISBN 0–275–92584–6.

These papers, presented at a 1985 conference at the Istituto Universitario Orientale, Naples, Italy, examine tensions between Western European countries created by a downturn in U.S.-Soviet relations in the early 1980s. Both the papers and the commentaries reveal that the crisis between the superpowers has produced unease among the populations of the Western European countries. The most divisive element is now and will continue to be the Strategic Defense Initiative (SDI). This book presents a series of views on problem areas in the Western alliance, and both the viewpoints and the comments are of a quality that makes them of value to researchers on security topics.

1363 Wettig, Gerhard. *Konflikt und Kooperation zwischen Ost und West: Entspannung in Theorie und Praxis Aussen- und sicherheitspolitische Analyse*. Bonn, West Germany: Osang, 1981. 217pp. ISBN 3–7894–0082–3.

This book is an analysis of the relationship between the two superpower blocs. The author is a West German security specialist, and he attempts to find the motivating factor behind the ebb and flow of relations between the Eastern and Western blocs. This understanding is important because the relations between the two blocs is in a crucial phase, because of changes of leadership and increasing tensions. This book is a balanced treatment of relations between the two blocs.

1364 *What about the Russians—and Nuclear War?* New York: Pocket Books, 1983. 236pp. ISBN 0–671–47209–7.

Ground Zero sponsored this book on the policies of the Soviet Union and the impact of these policies on U.S. security. The Soviet Union is a closed society, and it is difficult for Americans to understand its politics and foreign policy, but no international settlément on ending the arms race can ignore the Soviet Union. Despite economic problems and a general malaise, the Soviet Union is a rival to the United States in power and prestige, and only slow progress toward reconciling interests between the two superpowers is possible. This book is directed toward the general reader, and it provides basic information on the Soviet Union.

1365 White, Ralph K. *Fearful Warriors: A Psychological Profile of U.S.-Soviet Relations.* New York: Free Press, 1984. 374pp. ISBN 0–02–933760–7.

This book is a psychological study of policymakers in both the Soviet Union and the United States in an effort to understand the causes of war and to prevent future outbreaks of hostilities. The problem is that leaders in each bloc misperceive the intentions of their adversary, and, consequently, both have been busy building huge military arsenals. There is grounds for hope, and the author lists ten developments supporting this belief. This book was intended for the general reader, but the author has expanded its scope into a plea for arms control and peace.

1366 Wiarda, Howard J. *Ethnocentrism in Foreign Policy: Can We Understand the Third World?* Washington, DC: American Enterprise Institute for Public Policy Research, 1985. 67pp. ISBN 0–8447–3569–8.

This paper deals with the inability of U.S. policymakers to understand Third World problems. The author maintains that U.S. ethnocentrism is the reason U.S. policies toward the Third World are so misguided, and that this Western orientation will have to change because the Third World rejects Western values. "Suggestive" is the best description of this essay, and the author's thesis also extends to Third World security issues.

1367 Windass, Stan. *The Rite of War.* London: Brassey's Defence Publishers, 1986. 132pp. ISBN 0–08–033605–1.

The author uses mock drama to illustrate the dangers of the arms race. He attempts to be impartial by presenting charges of imperialism against both the Soviet Union and the United States. While both sides are guilty of contributing to the arms race, steps need to be taken to reduce dependence on nuclear weapons by turning to a more conventional defense posture. This book is a creative approach to the problem of international security, and the author's conclusions are worth attention.

1368 Wolfe, Alan. *The Rise and Fall of the Soviet Threat: Domestic Sources of the Cold War Consensus.* Boston: South End Press, 1984. 145pp. ISBN 0–89608–206–7.

The interaction between U.S. politics and the perceived Soviet threat is the subject of this worthwhile study. The author's thesis is that U.S. domestic politics produces anti-Soviet feeling in cycles because the Soviet threat justifies the United States acting as a global superpower. He charges that "U.S. perceptions of hostile Soviet intentions had increased, not when the Russians have become more aggressive or militaristic, but when certain constellations of political forces have come together within the U.S. to force the question of the Soviet threat onto the American political agenda." This is a thought-provoking and provocative book.

1369 *World Energy Supply and International Security.* By Herman Franssen et al. Cambridge, MA: Institute for Foreign Policy Analysis, 1983. 96pp. ISBN 0–89549–048–X.

The authors present three essays on the political, economic, and military problems of a stable world energy supply. An energy crisis can erupt at any time, because Western and Japanese oil supply continues to depend on OPEC sources, mostly from the Persian Gulf. The authors recommend oil stockpiling, cooperative energy sharing, exploration of alternative energy supplies, and promotion of advanced nuclear energy technologies. These papers are realistic assessments of an ongoing problem that Western leaders seem to ignore.

1370 Yaniv, Avner. *Deterrence without the Bomb: The Politics of Israeli Strategy.* Lexington, MA: Lexington Books, 1987. 324pp. ISBN 0–669–11104–X.

The author, a former staff officer in the Israeli Army, analyzes Israeli national security from the perspective of deterrence theory. Deterrence is a theory based on a rough symmetry in power between disputing parties, and it either completely succeeds or completely fails. Israeli dependence on conventional deterrence has worked in the past with a varying degree of success, but it is a foregone conclusion that Israel will have to depend on a nuclear deterrent in the future. This book is an exploratory effort to understand Israel's position in deterrence theory, and the author has produced an interesting but incomplete picture.

1371 Yaniv, Avner. *Dilemmas of Security: Politics, Strategy, and the Israeli Experience in Lebanon.* New York: Oxford University Press, 1987. 355pp. ISBN 0–19–504122–4.

An Israeli political scientist examines the security questions involved in the Israeli intervention into Lebanon in 1982. Israel has never escaped its security problem of danger from the Arab states, and the invasion of Lebanon was part of the military and political response to this dilemma. The invasion plan was to neutralize the Palestine Liberation Organization (PLO), but the consequences of the invasion produced a public reaction in Israel that caused a domestic political crisis. This book is a perceptive look at Israel's security problems and its options.

1372 Yodfat, Aryeh Y. *The Soviet Union and Revolutionary Iran.* London: Croom Helm, 1984. 168pp. ISBN 0–312–74910–4.

This book highlights the Soviet Union's relationship with Iran from the mid-1950s to 1982. Soviet interest in Iran has been steady, and the fall of the Shah of Iran in 1979 was welcomed because of the chance to expand Soviet influence in Iran. But the Khomeini regime has rejected Soviet overtures, and relations have worsened since the early 1980s. This book presents a chronological history of Soviet-Iranian relations, and it serves as a good introduction for further study on this topic.

1373 Yodfat, Aryeh Y. *The Soviet Union and the Arabian Peninsula: Soviet Policy towards the Persian Gulf and Arabia.* London: Croom Helm, 1983. 191pp. ISBN 0–312–74907–4.

An Israeli scholar reviews and analyzes relations between the Soviet Union and the countries in the Persian Gulf and the Arabian peninsula from the 1960s to 1982. The Soviet Union has had an interest in the Gulf region because of its strategic location and huge oil resources. Soviet policy is to keep an ongoing presence in this region because of the current instability among the region's regimes. This book is a solid treatment of Soviet policies in the Persian Gulf region.

CHAPTER FOUR:
Peace

Peace subjects are normally self-explanatory, but for purposes of this bibliography peace includes any topic that deals with peace movements, ethics of war, or consequences of war, and any work with an intent to promote peace. This category has 223 entries.

Annuals and Yearbooks

1374 *UNESCO Yearbook on Peace and Conflict Studies.* Westport, CT: Greenwood Press, 1980– . ISBN 0–313–22922–8. $30.

This yearbook is published under the auspices of UNESCO and contains articles from a wide variety of contributors dealing with the issues of peace and conflict. The emphasis is on providing teachers and researchers of peace and conflict studies with information to use in teaching situations. An ongoing weakness of this publication is the three-year delay in publishing. It is the standard annual in the field of peace studies.

Bibliographies

1375 Carroll, Berenice A., Clinton R. Fink, and Jane E. Mohraz. *Peace and War: A Guide to Bibliographies.* Santa Barbara, CA: ABC-Clio, 1983. 580pp. ISBN 0–87436–322–5.

This publication is a bibliography of bibliographies and as such it is a serious attempt to achieve bibliographical control over the literature on peace and war. It is an annotated guide to bibliographies published from 1785 through 1980. The bibliographies are arranged into thirty-four subject categories with a subject index to assist the reader. This work was published under the auspices of the Center for the Study of Armament and Disarmament at California State University, Los Angeles, and it remains the indispensable bibliography in the field.

1376 Woito, Robert S. *To End War: A New Approach to International Conflict.* New York: Pilgrim Press, 1982. 755pp. ISBN 0–8298–0464–1.

Underlying the bibliographical data in this publication is the philosophy that war should be defined as a problem and that efforts should be directed toward its elimination. Its viewpoint makes this book more a direct-action guide than a bibliography, but peace researchers will still find the bibliographical entries on U.S. sources useful. An added feature is the considerable space devoted to listing peace-oriented organizations. This book is another top bibliography in the peace studies field.

Databooks, Handbooks, and Sourcebooks

1377 *Approaching Disarmament Education.* Edited by Magnus Haavelsrud. Guildford, England: Westburg House, 1981. 280pp. ISBN 0–86103–043–5.

Seventeen essays by leading international workers in peace research and disarmament education are presented in this direct-action handbook. The essays give a survey of international efforts for peace education. Advocacy of disarmament and social justice are recurring themes throughout the book. It is a good source for presenting various educational perspectives on peace education.

1378 *Basic Documents on United Nations and Related Peace-Keeping Forces.* By Robert C. R. Siekmann. Dordrecht, Holland: Martinus Nijhoff Publishers, 1985. 273pp. ISBN 90–347–3163–1.

The essential documents relating to peace-keeping efforts of the United Nations are compiled in this sourcebook. The United Nations has undertaken some thirteen peace-keeping operations since the creation of the first mission in 1956. Besides providing documents for each of the peace-keeping operations, the author treats the objectives of each of the missions. Here is the place to find basic information on UN peace-keeping activities.

1379 Brayton, Abbott A., and Stepahan J. Lanwehr. *The Politics of War and Peace: A Survey of Thought.* Washington, DC: University Press of America, 1981. 294pp. ISBN 0–8191–1726–9.

Nearly 3,500 years of judgments and observations on war and peace comprise this book of readings. The selections are divided by type of subject irrespective of chronological sequence. Most of the writings come from pre–twentieth-century commentators. This book has its value as a sourcebook for course readings, but most of the selections are too short for more than a statement of the writer's thesis.

1380 *First and Final War: A Basic Information Manual on the Effects of Nuclear War Applied to Australasia.* Edited by David Blair. Oxford, England: Oxford University Press, 1986. 80pp. ISBN 0–19–554645–8.

This sourcebook presents basic information on the construction and operation of nuclear weapons and the effects of such weapons on the Australasian region. Current information on the environmental impact of nuclear war is included, but the viewpoint is openly antiwar. The section on the theory of nuclear weapon construction is the best part of the book. This publication provides a vast amount of material on the effects of nuclear war, and its best use is as an introductory source.

1381 Green, N. A. Maryan. *International Law: Law of Peace*, 2d ed. Estover, England: Macdonald and Evans, 1982. 254pp. ISBN 0–7121–0956–0.

This book is an outline of the main rules of the contemporary law of peace. Multilateral conventions on peace are listed along with international law cases. While the author acknowledges a pro-European bias, the effectiveness of the treatment is by no means altered. This book is an outstanding sourcebook on legal issues involving peace.

1382 *Keeping the Peace: A Women's Peace Handbook.* Edited by Lynne Jones. London: Women's Press, 1983. 161pp. ISBN 0–7043–3901–3.

This handbook is a direct-action guide for women interested in working for peace. Representatives from various women's peace groups have contributed essays on women's role in keeping the peace. By combining feminism and peace, the authors hope to end the arms race. These personal statements by European feminists are valuable for the insights they give on the European peace movement.

1383 *Nuclear War: Opposing Viewpoints.* Edited by Bonnie Szumski. St. Paul, MN: Greenhaven Press, 1985. 249pp. ISBN 0–899083–78–1.

The Opposing Viewpoints Series presents opposing views by scholars on a single topic. This publication is devoted to sampling viewpoints on nuclear war. Besides the arguments pro and con, there are a number of short bibliographies and a listing of organizations to contact for more information on the subject of nuclear war. This source is of limited value except for introductory courses at the undergraduate level.

1384 *Peacekeeper's Handbook.* New York: Pergamon Press, 1984. 439pp. ISBN 0–08–031921–1.

This handbook is a ready reference source for the planning and conducting of peace-keeping operations. It is a product of the International Peace Academy (IPA), which is an educational institute designed for dispute settlement and conflict management. Although most of the IPA's activities have been devoted to conducting international training seminars on peace-keeping, negotiation, and mediation, it did produce this worthwhile informative handbook.

1385 *Peace-Making in the Middle East.* Edited by Lester A. Sobel. New York: Facts on File, 1980. 286pp. ISBN 0–87196–267–5.

This book chronicles the peacemaking processes in the Middle East from 1973 to the Egyptian-Israeli Peace Treaty. The material was compiled from the Facts on File weekly reports on world affairs. The editor makes a conscientious effort to avoid bias by reporting statements from both sides of the peace issue. This book serves as an excellent reference source because of its balanced treatment of the subject.

1386 Popkess, Barry. *The Nuclear Survival Handbook: Living through and after a Nuclear Attack.* New York: Collier Books, 1980. 345pp. ISBN 0–02–081170–5.

A British author has compiled a survival handbook in both U.S. and British versions to educate the general public on surviving a nuclear attack. All the postattack hazards are treated—nuclear, biological, environmental, and social consequences. Numerous appendices give insights on survival.

This handbook gives a mass of invaluable information from planting certain types of trees to the hunting value of ferrets.

1387 Seeley, Robert A. *Handbook for Conscientious Objectors*, 13th ed. Philadelphia: Central Committee for Conscientious Objectors, 1981. 218pp. ISBN 0–93336–803–8.

Now in its thirteenth edition, this handbook is still the most reliable guide on conscientious objection for Americans in existence. This version was published when draft registration was reestablished in the early 1980s. Besides legal advice for conscientious objectors, it has an excellent bibliography on conscientious objection, war, and nonviolence. This source is most useful as a reference for basic information on conscientious objectors.

1388 *Waging Peace: A Handbook for the Struggle To Abolish Nuclear Weapons*. Edited by Jim Wallis. San Francisco, CA: Harper and Row, 1982. 304pp. ISBN 0–06–069240–5.

An updated and expanded version of *A Matter of Faith*, this handbook is an educational and informational vehicle for those who are concerned about preventing nuclear war. It is divided into twelve sections, each designed to elucidate a concept or a principle promoting peace. This source is only of marginal interest to peace researchers.

1389 *Working for Peace: A Handbook of Practical Psychology and Other Tools*. Edited by Neil Wollman. San Luis Obispo, CA: Impact Publishers, 1985. 270pp. ISBN 0–915166–37–2.

Personal and interpersonal psychological principles are the subject of this peace workers handbook. Specialists from a variety of disciplines have come together to provide the material, and this handbook is a unique source with a perspective not available elsewhere.

Dictionaries

1390 *Biographical Dictionary of Internationalists*. Edited by Warren Kuehl. Westport, CT: Greenwood Press, 1985. 934pp. ISBN 0–31322–129–4.

For the purposes of this biographical dictionary the editor defines an *internationalist* as one who promotes world organization or international cooperation. He concentrates only on individuals active in the nineteenth and twentieth centuries. There are cross-references between this dictionary and its companion volume, the *Biographical Dictionary of Modern Peace Leaders* (see next entry). This work is most useful for studies of career patterns of leaders of international organizations.

1391 *Biographical Dictionary of Modern Peace Leaders*. Edited by Harold Josephson. Westport, CT: Greenwood Press, 1985. 1,133pp. ISBN 0–31322–565–6.

The Conference on Peace Research in History initiated this biographical dictionary of peace leaders past and present. Only individuals alive after 1800 and deceased before 1985 are included in this publication. Each entry follows a set format for biographical details, including aspects of the subject's work, thought, and activities as a peace leader. These entries and a valuable chronology of peace movements between 1815 and 1983 make this publication a good introduction to peace research.

Directories

1392 *Peace Research and Activists Groups: A North American Directory.* Chicago: Task Force on Peace Information Exchange, 1981– .

The Task Force on Peace Information Exchange, Social Responsibilities Round Table of the American Library Association published this directory as a way of fostering attention on the need for disarmament and peace. It is based on several earlier directories and updated by means of a questionnaire distributed in the spring of 1981. This directory needs more frequent updating to be reliable.

1393 *World Directory of Peace Research Institutions,* 4th ed. Paris: UNESCO, 1981. 213pp. ISBN 92–3–101902–3.

This directory updates earlier editions, which appeared in 1966, 1973, and 1979. The peace research organizations are divided into international and regional organizations and national organizations. A total of 313 organizations are included, with the address, type of organization, specialities, type of publications, number of researchers, and annual budget. This directory is the best source of its type available, but more frequent updating would increase its value for peace researchers.

Guidebooks

1394 *Guide to the Swarthmore College Peace Collection,* 2d ed. Swarthmore, PA: Swarthmore College, 1981. 158pp.

The Swarthmore College Peace Collection is an archival and research library collection of materials on peace, disarmament, pacifism, conscientious objection and nonviolent social change. The collection contains 122 major document groups and another 1,500 smaller collections. This guidebook has annotations and status information on all the major collections. Any scholar interested in U.S. peace activities during the period 1900 to 1980 will find this guidebook invaluable.

1395 Larson, Joyce E., and William C. Brodie. *The Intelligent Layperson's Guide to the Nuclear Freeze and Peace Debate.* New York: National Strategy Information Center, 1983. 65pp.

The authors pose twenty questions and provide twenty possible answers for those interested in more information about a nuclear freeze and peace debates. They gathered material from a variety of sources to make this short guide valuable both for the general public and students. This short publication is a good introduction to the ongoing debate over a nuclear freeze.

1396 Mack, Andrew. *Peace Research in the 1980s.* Canberra: Strategic and Defence Studies Centre, 1985. 139pp.

This book is a combination directory and guidebook to peace research activities and organizations in the early 1980s. While this publication claims not to be definitive, it provides a good look at peace research activities worldwide. Besides an excellent bibliography and a list of peace organizations, there are sections on peace research in Western Europe, the United States, and the Third World. This book fulfills a useful function in monitoring peace research wherever it exists.

1397 *Nucleography: An Annotated Resource Guide for Parents and Educators on Nuclear Energy, War, and Peace.* Edited by Jacqueline Barber, Gigi Bridges, and Cary Sneider. Berkeley, CA: Nucleography, 1982. 110pp.

This publication is an annotated resource guide dealing with nuclear technology and its impact on society. The editors consider each entry a valuable resource for teaching or learning about nuclear energy, war, and/or peace. The editors present this book as an interactive document and invite the reader to contribute to the next edition. There is no other resource guide that compares with this publication in type of coverage.

1398 *Peace and World Order Studies: A Curriculum Guide,* 4th ed. Edited by Barbara J. Wien. New York: World Policy Institute, 1984. 741pp. ISBN 0–9164–620–2.

Now in its fourth edition, this curriculum guide was prepared for U.S. college-level instruction. Its variety of both course offerings and sources also makes it useful for secondary school teachers and community groups concerned about the issues of peace and world order. This publication is a good place for the beginner to start learning more about research on peace studies.

1399 *Peace Resource Book: A Comprehensive Guide to Issues, Groups, and Literature 1986.* By Elizabeth Berstein et al. Cambridge, MA: Ballinger, 1986. 416pp.

As the much-expanded successor to the *American Peace Directory 1984*, this publication by the Institute for Defense and Disarmament Studies, Cambridge, Massachusetts, is intended as a handy guide for activists, organizations, journalists, teachers, and students interested in learning more about peace. It has listings of peace organizations by states with addresses, telephone numbers, and specialties. An excellent annotated bibliography of peace-related literature is also useful. The authors envisage this publication as an annual, and whatever its appearance frequency this source will always be a useful tool for peace researchers.

1400 Phillips, Crispin, and Ian R. F. Ross. *The Nuclear Casebook: An Illustrated Guide.* Edinburgh, Scotland: Polygon Books, 1983. 47pp. ISBN 0–904919–71–4.

Two British medical doctors, who are affiliated with the Medical Campaign Against Nuclear Weapons, produced this illustrated guide to the medical effects of the use of nuclear weapons. The result is an effective treatise on the horrors of nuclear war. Much of the data come from the work of Stan Openshaw and Philip Steadman and their critique of the Home Office's estimates on British nuclear war casualties. This guidebook is an effective use of illustrations and statistics to argue a peace cause.

Hearings

1401 U.S. Congress. Commission on Security and Cooperation in Europe. *Implementation of the Helsinki Accords.* Washington, DC: U.S. Government Printing Office, 1984. 87pp.

This hearing by a combined House and Senate commission was called to survey the status of the human rights provisions of the Helsinki Accords in the Soviet Union. The commission considered the position of private peace groups in the Soviet Union, and, in particular, Andrei Sakharov and Elena

Bonner. Witnesses and statements attest that the Soviet Union has not upheld the human rights provisions of the Helsinki Accords. This publication is important because of the documents it contains.

1402 U.S. Congress. House. Committee on Foreign Affairs. *Perspectives on the Middle East Peace Process, December 1981.* Washington, DC: U.S. Government Printing Office, 1982. 145pp.

This hearing was called to examine the report *The Path to Peace,* which dealt with the Middle East peace processes. The authors of this report testified on their report and discussed their findings on fhe future of the peace process in this region. Both the report and the comments were pessimistic about the peace process because participants see no alternative to prolonged hostilities between Israel and the Arab world. This hearing provides valuable insight into the origins of the original report.

1403 U.S. Congress. House. Joint Hearings. *Nuclear Winter.* Washington, DC: U.S. Government Printing Office, 1985. 313pp.

Scientists and defense officials presented testimony and supporting documents before the Committee on Science and Technology and the Committee on Interior and Insular Affairs in 1985 on the atmospheric effects of a nuclear war. Various views on the nature of nuclear winter are advanced, and Reagan administration officials countered assertions of nuclear winter with the claim that more scientific research on the issue is needed. The testimony of witnesses occupies much less space than the supporting documents. This publication is a good place to start research on nuclear winter.

1404 U.S. Congress. Joint Economic Committee. *The Consequences of Nuclear War.* Washington, DC: U.S. Government Printing Office, 1986. 297pp.

Two joint hearings of Congress were held in July 1984 to study the nuclear winter thesis. The committee solicited scientific testimony from both inside and outside government circles. Both the testimony and the supporting documents indicate that the economic, environmental, and social consequences of nuclear war would be severe and lasting, with nuclear winter as a possibility. These hearings provided a forum where proponents of the nuclear winter thesis were questioned on their scientific conclusions.

Journals

1405 *Bulletin of Peace Proposals.* Oslo: Universitetsforlaget, 1970– . ISSN 0007–5035. $44.

This quarterly journal's purpose is to motivate research on peace issues. An international cast of authors makes the articles published in this journal invaluable for peace researchers. This journal is produced by the internationally renowned International Peace Research Institute, Oslo, and is one of the best places for researchers to start their peace studies.

1406 *Bulletin of the Atomic Scientists* Chicago: Educational Foundation for Nuclear Science, 1945– . ISSN 0096–3402. $25.

Eminent scientists and scholars in the peace field use this monthly publication to inform opinion makers and the general public about nuclear energy and the danger of nuclear war. The journal is most famous for its nuclear clock estimating the status of nuclear war. Besides peace issues, there are also a number of articles dealing with arms control, international security, and nuclear policy. This journal is the most prestigious publication in the field of peace studies.

1407 *International Journal on World Peace.* New York: Professors World Peace Academy, 1984– . ISSN 0742–3640. $20.

Among the newer journals appearing on peace issues is this scholarly, multidisciplinary, and cross-cultural publication. Each issue of this quarterly journal contains three or four substantive articles and a lengthy book review section. Its coverage includes all aspects of peace research. Both the peace specialist and the informed general public are targeted as the audience for this publication.

1408 *Journal of Peace Research.* Oslo: Universitetsforlaget, 1964– . ISSN 0022–3433. $33.

This quarterly journal is an interdisciplinary and international publication dealing with scientific reports in the field of peace research. Its main focus is on studies concerning direct and structural violence, conflict theory, and theoretical debates. Editorial support comes from the International Peace Research Institute, Oslo, Norway. This journal serves as a forum for European views on peace issues.

1409 *Peace and Change: A Journal of Peace Research.* Kent, OH: Center for Peaceful Change, 1972– . ISSN 0149–0508. $21.

Topics relating to peace and war, social change, and justice are the specialities of this journal, which appears between three and four times a year. It attempts to provide an arena where peace research, education, and direct action can be brought together. On occasion, this journal publishes special issues on peace subjects. The Conference on Peace Research in History and the Consortium on Peace Research, Education and Development (COPRED) cosponsor this publication.

1410 *Peace Research Abstracts Journal.* Dundas, Canada: Peace Research Institute–Dundas, 1964– . ISSN 0031–3599. $140.

Published under the auspices of both UNESCO and the International Peace Research Association, this journal publishes abstracts of books, journal articles, and conference proceedings dealing with arms control, disarmament, international security, military affairs, and peace issues. Besides subject access it also has an author index. This abstract service provides access to material otherwise unavailable. No other source contains as much material on peace subjects as does this journal.

Newsletters

1411 *The Anti-Draft.* Washington, DC: Committee Against Registration and the Draft, 1983– .

Short articles on draft issues and military affairs characterize this monthly newsletter. It is a product of the Committee Against Registration and the Draft, founded in 1979. Many of the articles deal with military and social issues. Most are skimpy and only of marginal interest except to peace researchers interested in antidraft activities.

1412   *Boston Mobilizer: Newsletter of the Boston Mobilization for Survival.*
Cambridge, MA: Survival Education Fund, 1977– .

The Boston Mobilization for Survival publishes this monthly direct-action
newsletter with feature articles on antiwar topics, short news briefs, and a
calendar of antiwar events in the Boston area. Since the Boston area has long
been active in peace activities, the activities in this area are of interest to
peace researchers nationwide. This newsletter is especially valuable for
gauging trends in the eastern U.S. peace movement.

1413   *Breakthrough: A Publication of Global Education Associates.* East
Orange, NJ: Global Education Associates, 1979– .

The Global Education Associates publishes this quarterly newsletter as
part of its mission to publish educational materials promoting social and
economic justice, peace, ecological balance, and participation in decision
making. Each issue has four or five short articles on these subjects. There are
also sections with short bibliographies and book reviews. Most of the articles
are of limited interest to any but peace education researchers.

1414   *CCCO News Notes Covering War, Peace and Conscience.* Philadelphia: Central Committee for Conscientious Objectors, 1948– .

This newsletter is the official publication of the Central Committee for
Conscientious Objectors (CCCO). Newsletters appear four times a year, and
articles and commentaries deal with developments in military and draft
laws that have an impact on GIs and draft registrants. Each issue features
articles on war, conscience, and/or militarism. This newsletter is a valuable
source for these topics.

1415   *COPRED Peace Chronicle.* Urbana, IL: Consortium on Peace
Research, Education and Development, 1976– . $25.

The Consortium on Peace Research, Education and Development
(COPRED) publishes this monthly newsletter to provide information about
the peace movement in the United States and abroad. Its strength is in the
information concerning conferences, networks, and peace organizations. A
listing of recent publications in the peace field is also a useful feature.
Because of the nature of the consortium, this publication has information
gathered from a variety of sources unavailable in any other publication.

1416   *Dovetail.* Edited by Peggy Huppert. Des Moines, IA: Iowa Peace Network, 1976– . $10.

The Iowa Peace Network (IPN), Des Moines, Iowa, publishes *Dovetail* to
provide a forum for sharing views on peace. Although there is financial
support for the IPN from religious organizations, this publication's orientation is exclusively on the promotion of peace activities in Iowa. This publication is of marginal interest except in studying grassroots peace activities.

1417   *East-West Outlook.* Washington, DC: American Committee on East-
West Accord, 1977– . $12.

The American Committee on East-West Accord, Washington, DC, produces this monthly newsletter as a way to promote studies on international
relations between the Western and Soviet blocs. It has a format of commentaries on informal remarks by government officials from both sides and an
occasional short article. This publication is of marginal value because it
promotes rather than explains Soviet-U.S. relations.

1418 *Fellowship.* Nyack, NY: Fellowship of Reconciliation, 1935– . ISSN 0014–9810. $10.

The Fellowship of Reconciliation, an organization devoted to resolving human conflict, publishes this newsletter. It appears eight times a year with four double issues. Articles on peace and nonviolence surface regularly along with news of the organization. This publication serves as a newsletter/magazine for the peacemaking activities of the parent organization.

1419 *Friedensforschung Aktuell.* Frankfurt, West Germany: Hessische Stiftung Friedens- und Konfliktforschung, 1975– . $20.

The Hessische Stiftung Friedens- und Konfliktforschung (Peace Research Institute Frankfurt) is an organization devoted to sponsoring research on peace issues. This newsletter appears four times a year and includes articles, short features, and news about the institute's activities and peace research. Most peace researchers will find this publication useful for European sources.

1420 *Global Report: Progress toward a World of Peace with Justice.* Edited by Richard Hudson. New York: Center for War/Peace Studies, n.d. $10.

This propeace newsletter is published by the Center for War/Peace Studies (CW/PS) on an occasional basis depending on events and on the production of CW/PS Special Studies. Each issue features a topic of special concern determined by the editor. It has an added purpose as a sounding board for new research topics by the Center for War/Peace Studies. This latter feature and the general information make this publication valuable for learning about peace research trends.

1421 *Heartland: Deep West Peace Press.* Jackson, WY: OpenSpace, 1982– . $8.

This publication is a quarterly direct-action newsletter that chronicles peace activities in the intermountain area of the United States. This newsletter promulgates the philosophy of nonviolence as a way of life. A special feature is its publication of a directory of peace organizations in the intermountain region. This newsletter is important for showing grassroots peace activities in the intermountain area.

1422 *The Human Rights Internet Reporter.* Washington, DC: Human Rights Internet, 1976– . $10.

Human Rights Internet (HRI) is a reporting service on human rights conditions worldwide. This publication appears five times a year, and it covers instances of human rights violations regardless of the country. HRI is currently establishing a computer database on international human rights. This newsletter is the best source available for learning about human rights violations.

1423 *Information.* Berlin, East Germany: Peace Council of the German Democratic Republic, n.d. Free.

This newsletter represents the official East German position on peace issues. News about East German meetings and personalities is highlighted in each issue. This publication appears monthly in German, English, French, Spanish, and Italian. While most of the information is propaganda, the listing of peace activities in the GDR does provide an index of official support for the peace movement.

1424 *International Mobilisation: Against Apartheid and for the Liberation of Southern Africa.* Helsinki: World Peace Council, 1979– . $12.

This newsletter is published monthly by the World Peace Council in cooperation with the United Nations Centre Against Apartheid. Each issue features short articles and news briefs in opposition to apartheid and the South African government. This newsletter is influential in mobilizing European public opinion against the South African government's policies.

1425 *International Peace Research Newsletter.* Hanover, NH: International Peace Research Association, 1962– .

The International Peace Research Association (IPRA) publishes this newsletter four times a year chronicling international peace research activities. Each issue has reports from peace organizations detailing their activities and listing their publications in progress. This newsletter provides access to a variety of peace groups because it gives names and addresses of contact persons in these international organizations. These contacts make this source valuable for learning about peace research in progress.

1426 *International Peace Studies Newsletter.* Akron, OH: Center for Peace Studies, 1970– .

Educational activities related to peace are the speciality of this monthly newsletter. It is published by the Center for Peace Studies, University of Akron. News about peace programs on university campuses is highlighted along with international peace news. This newsletter is useful for researchers interested in peace education.

1427 *IPJ Newsletter.* St. Louis, MO: Institute for Peace and Justice, 1979– .

This newsletter appears three times a year to inform the membership of the Institute for Peace and Justice (IPJ), St. Louis, Missouri, of its activities. While each issue features short articles on peace or a political topic, most attention is paid to midwestern peace activities. This newsletter is only of regional interest to researchers.

1428 *Jane Addams Peace Association/Women's International League for Peace and Freedom Committee on Education Newsletter.* Edmonds, WA: JAPA/WILPF Committee on Education, 1984– . $10.

This monthly newsletter combines feminist and peace issues. It provides an educational forum in which the editors collect diverse materials on international feminist and peace subjects. News notes, short bibliographies and questionnaires characterize this six-page newsletter, which is interesting because it combines two different perspectives.

1429 *Militarism Resource Project News.* Philadelphia, PA: Militarism Resource Project, 1985– . $10.

The impact of militarism on the U.S. armed forces is the focus of this quarterly newsletter. News on legal and social problems of persons serving in the military is highlighted. It specializes in how military policies affect low-income youth. This newsletter serves more as an outlet for the authors' frustration than a forum of news on militarism.

1430 *The Mobilizer.* New York: Mobilization for Survival, 1981– . $10.

Mobilization for Survival is a national coalition of grassroots groups working for disarmament, environmental concerns, human needs, and peace. It publishes this quarterly newsletter as part of its campaign against nuclear weapons and for social justice. Issues are filled with short articles, news briefs, and short bibliographies. This newsletter is an excellent source for gauging grassroots peace activities in the United States.

1431 *Newsletter of the Peace Science Society (International).* Ithaca, NY: Peace Science Society, n.d.
This monthly newsletter serves as a means for communication between the leadership and the membership on the educational and scholarly activities of the Peace Science Society. Meetings, papers, and sessions are announced in each issue for the benefit of the society's membership. This newsletter is only of marginal interest for researchers in peace studies.

1432 *The Nonviolent Activist: The Magazine of the War Resisters League.* New York, NY: War Resisters League, 1984– .
The War Resisters League publishes this combination journal-magazine-newsletter ten times a year in an effort to further its views on peace and social justice. Each issue has several medium-length articles on current topics. There is also a section on resources and events. This source presents a variety of useful information for the benefit of peace researchers.

1433 *The Nuclear Free Press.* Peterborough, Canada: Nuclear Free Press, 1980– . $25.
Formerly *The Birch Bark Alliance,* this combination newsletter-newspaper from Canada appears quarterly and is filled with information and news on nuclear affairs. It consists of newspaper-length articles on Canadian, international, and U.S. nuclear news. While the orientation is the promotion of antinuclear policies, the information contained in this publication is still useful.

1434 *Nuclear Times.* New York: Nuclear Times, 1982– . ISSN 0734–5836. $35.
This publication appears ten times a year as a combination magazine-newsletter on nuclear issues. It features short but informative articles on nuclear weapons, nuclear energy, and political topics. Peace activities around the United States are also noted in a grassroots section. This publication serves a variety of functions, and it deserves a place in any peace collection.

1435 *Nukewatch: A Public Education Project of the Progressive Foundation.* Madison, WI: Nukewatch, n.d. $5.
This infrequent newsletter is the product of an activist group involved in monitoring the movement of nuclear materials and weapons. This group has branches all over the United States, and this newsletter coordinates its activities. Short antinuclear articles also appear in this publication, which is filled with a variety of information on nuclear affairs unavailable elsewhere.

1436 *Our Planet: YMCA International Institute for Peace.* Hiroshima: YMCA International Institute for Peace, 1984– . $8.
This publication is published twice a year by the YMCA International Institute for Peace, Hiroshima, Japan, in its campaign for a world without war. Each issue has medium-length articles on peace and disarmament subjects from the Japanese viewpoint. The concentration on international news makes this newsletter of considerable interest to peace scholars.

1437 *Peace and Freedom.* Philadelphia: Women's International League for Peace and Freedom, 1940– . ISSN 0015–9093. $10.

This newsletter is the official publication of the U.S. Section of the Women's International League for Peace and Freedom (WILPF), Philadelphia. Appearing monthly, this publication contains articles, information, and news of· WILPF activities. By combining feminist and peace concerns, this newsletter makes a solid contribution in an area not fully explored before.

1438 *Peace Developments.* Amherst, MA: Peace Development Fund, n.d. $10.

The Peace Development Fund and its affiliate, the Pacific Peace Fund, produce this newsletter. Organizational activities and news are featured in each issue. It is also the place where Peace Development Fund Grants are listed. Coverage of grassroots peace activities in the U.S. makes this newsletter a worthwhile source for peace researchers.

1439 *Peace Ed News.* Miami Beach, FL: Grace Contrino Abrams Peace Education Foundation, 1981– . $4.

This biannual newsletter provides information on peace education activities in the Miami, Florida, area. Besides announcements and news about peace education, there are also a few short articles on peace issues. The Grace Contrino Abrams Peace Education Foundation, Miami Beach, Florida, sponsors this publication. Regional efforts at peace education can be studied in this grassroots newsletter.

1440 *Peace Magazine.* Toronto: Canadian Disarmament Information Service, 1985– . $20.

The Canadian Disarmament Information Service (CANDIS) publishes this cross between a magazine and newsletter monthly to further its efforts for multilateral nuclear disarmament. This publication features excellent disarmament and peace articles by respected authors. There are also useful sections on peace news and a calendar of Canadian events. Despite its Canadian origin, this newsletter is a valuable source for information on international peace issues.

1441 *Sane World: Newsletter of the Committee for a Sane Nuclear Policy.* Washington, DC: Sane, 1962– . ISSN 0036–4304. $20.

The Committee for a Sane Nuclear Policy publishes this bimonthly newsletter as a way to disseminate its anti–nuclear war message. Each issue has three or four short articles on nuclear policy either in the United States or abroad. Other features are the grassroots and resources sections, where organizational activities are described and works listed for further study. This newsletter is one of the better sources of its type available.

Kits

1442 *Nuclear War Prevention Kit.* Washington, DC: Center for Defense Information, 1985. $12.

This kit is produced by the Center for Defense Information and is intended to serve as a guide for mobilizing public opinion against nuclear war. It also has a list of publications and audiovisual resources for citizen action. The Center for Defense Information is an organization of former military personnel, educators, and public officials interested in U.S. defense policies.

Textbooks

1443 Beer, Francis A. *Peace against War: The Ecology of International Violence.* San Francisco: Freeman, 1981. 447pp. ISBN 0–7167–1250–4.

This textbook gathers together contemporary knowledge about peace and war and presents this information in a readable format. The author has compiled statistical information on peace and war from a variety of sources, and the statistical tables are numerous and informative. An extensive bibliography makes this book even more valuable. This book is filled with useful data for researchers in any of the arms control, disarmament, and peace fields.

1444 Craig, Paul P., and John A. Jungerman. *Nuclear Arms Race: Technology and Society.* New York: McGraw-Hill, 1986. 461pp. ISBN 0–07–013345–X.

This textbook covers the technical and social aspects of the nuclear arms race. Current information on nuclear technology is summarized in a readable format. While there are a number of technical chapters on problems of nuclear physics, this book is an excellent source for teaching an introductory course on the nuclear arms race.

1445 Glosson, Ronald J. *Confronting War: An Examination of Humanity's Most Pressing Problem.* Jefferson, NC: McFarland, 1983. 290pp. ISBN 0–89950–073–0.

This textbook intends to educate the reader with some of the facts, ideas, and arguments related to the war problem and its solution. The author emphasizes the causes of war and proposals for solving the problem of war. The intended audience is high school and college students in a classroom environment. This book is a good example of an elementary textbook on war.

Monographs

1446 *The Aftermath: The Human and Ecological Consequences of Nuclear War.* Edited by Jeannie Person. New York: Pantheon Books, 1983. 196pp. ISBN 0–394–72042–3.

This book on the consequences of a nuclear war is based on a special issue of the international journal *Ambio*, which is published by the Royal Swedish Academy of Sciences. An international cast of contributors present papers on the human and ecological costs of a medium-sized nuclear war. There would be survivors in a nuclear war, but the environment would be so transformed that their fate is extremely uncertain. This source is an excellent introduction to the most up-to-date calculations on the ecological damage of a nuclear war.

1447 *Aktive Friedenspolitik.* Edited by Friedrich Wilhelm Rothenpieler, Klaus Wagener, and Theo Waigel. Munich: Günter Olzog Verlag, 1982. 309pp. ISBN 3–7892–9884–0.

This series of essays from two seminars on peace issues, held in West Germany during 1981, analyzes the Christian peace movement. Most of the essays concern European peace movements, with special emphasis on their religious ties. Discussion sections with statements from other seminar participants are also included. This book is a solid source on the religious aspects of the European peace movements.

1448 Allsebrook, Mary. *Prototypes of Peacemaking: The First Forty Years of the United Nations.* New York: United Nations, 1986. 160pp. ISBN 0–582–98701–6.

This book surveys the peacemaking role of the United Nations since its origins in 1945. All the cases that have gone to the United Nations over the forty years are listed, along with the results of the mediation. Another section covers all the past and present International Court of Justice cases. This book shows the accomplishments of the United Nations in its peacemaking mission.

1449 Alternative Defence Commission. *Without the Bomb: Non-Nuclear Defence Policies for Britain.* London: Granada, 1985. 92pp. ISBN 0–586–08527–0.

This book is a revised and shorter version of a report published by the Alternative Defence Commission in 1983. The thesis of both the report and this book is that Great Britain should reject nuclear weapons and refuse to have them based on its territory. Britain should remain in NATO only if NATO ends its reliance on nuclear weapons and emphasizes conventional warfare. Both the report and this book are part of an ongoing reassessment by British thinkers on Britain's defense role, and, for this reason, this book is worth studying.

1450 Alves, Dora. *Anti-Nuclear Attitudes in New Zealand and Australia.* Washington, DC: National Defense University Press, 1985. 89pp.

The author is a specialist in the South Pacific area, and she uses her expertise to analyze the antinuclear movements in New Zealand and Australia. Sentiment is strong in New Zealand for a Pacific nuclear-free zone, and this is the origin of the Lange government's refusal to accept nuclear ships at New Zealand's ports. The Australia, New Zealand, and the United States (ANZUS) alliance is still in operation, but New Zealand is the odd man out. This book is an assessment of public opinion on nuclear weapons in Australia and New Zealand, and the author concludes that the evidence indicates the Lange government's policies are mistaken.

1451 *The Apocalyptic Premise: Nuclear Arms Debated.* Edited by Ernest W. Lefever and E. Stephen Hunt. Washington, DC: Ethics and Public Policy Center, 1982. 417pp. ISBN 0–89633–062–1.

Thirty-one statesmen, scholars, religious leaders, and journalists produced these essays on aspects of the nuclear arms debate. Most of these essays have appeared in other publications, but together these writings give the major arguments pro and con on arms control, the peace movement, and nuclear morality. In the last part of the book official views on arms control are given by leaders of Great Britain, the Soviet Union, and the United States. This book is a good place for the general reader to find viewpoints by prominent authorities in the field.

1452 *Argumente für Frieden und Freiheit.* By Franz Böckle et al. Melle, West Germany: Verlag Ernst Knoth, 1983. 192pp. ISBN 3–88368–069–9.

Prominent West German politicians and scholars contributed papers on ethical questions about peace and defense policies to this volume. While there is a strong religious component in many of these papers, defense and military questions also receive a hearing. A broad spectrum of opinion appears in this book, from a desire for peace in Europe to the need to counter

Soviet military pressure. This book is worth reading to understand the variety of opinions on peace and defense in West Germany.

1453 *Assessing the Nuclear Age: Selections from the Bulletin of the Atomic Scientists.* Edited by Len Ackland and Steven McGuire. Chicago: Educational Foundation for Nuclear Science, 1986. 382pp. ISBN 0–941682–07–2.

Most of the articles in this book were previously published in the August 1985 anniversary issue of the *Bulletin of Atomic Scientists*, but some articles were deleted and others added from other issues. The result is a broad assessment of nuclear developments from the perspective of the past, present, and future. This book features a range of subjects from nuclear technology to arms control and proliferation. It is a mine of information and should be a standard reference source for the next decade or so.

1454 Au, William A. *The Cross, the Flag, and the Bomb: American Catholics Debate War and Peace, 1960–1983.* Westport, CT: Greenwood Press, 1985. 278pp. ISBN 0–313–24754–4.

This book is an analysis of Roman Catholic contributions to the nuclear arms debate since 1960. From a position of reluctance to enter the debate on peace or war before 1960, Catholics have become active in the antinuclear and disarmament movements. The issue of war has made U.S. Catholics reassess their place in the modern world. The author is an associate pastor in the Archdiocese of Baltimore, and he reflects the concerns of U.S. Catholics on the issue of peace and war.

1455 *Australia and Nuclear War.* Edited by Michael Denborough. Sydney: Croom Helm, 1983. 270pp. ISBN 0–949614–09–2.

These papers are the result of a 1983 symposium on nuclear war in Australia held at the Australian National University, Canberra, Australia. An international cast of security scholars and peace activists joined together to study the consequences of nuclear war for Australia. The consensus was that the consequences for Australia would be disastrous and that every step should be taken to apply political pressure to end the arms race. This book is a potpourri of papers, some of which are substantive and others more like position papers.

1456 Barnaby, Frank. *Prospects for Peace.* Oxford, England: Pergamon Press, 1980. 88pp. ISBN 0–08–027399–8.

The author believes that the probability of a nuclear war is increasing because of the growth of nuclear arsenals. The shortage of energy supplies and uncontrolled military technology endanger world peace. While there is no evil group plotting nuclear war, the nuclear states and others lack the intelligence required to set up the political and social institutions to stop the process. Despite the pessimism of the author, this book offers a variety of approaches to improve the prospects for peace.

1457 Bastian, Gert. *Atomtod oder europäische Sicherheitsgemeinschaft: Abrüstung statt Abschreckung.* Köln: Pahl-Rugenstein, 1982. 136pp. ISBN 3–7609–0618–8.

This book is a collection of talks and writings by a West German critic of NATO's defense policies. The author is a former senior officer in the Bundeswehr and a prominent spokesman against current NATO strategic doctrine. His arguments against NATO's modernization policies and his commitment to the peace movement make his position unique among former West German military men. This book is a good example of the growing strength of the European peace movement.

1458 Bauer, Alfred W. *"Dear Mr. President": An Open Letter to Ronald Reagan about War and Peace and Our Chances for Survival in a World Gone Nuclear-Mad.* Kirkland, WA: A. W. Bauer, 1984. 170pp.

A medical doctor from Washington published this book at his expense to pose questions about the arms race and U.S. defense policies. He uses historical examples to buttress his opposition to the Reagan administration's position, and illustrations to make political points are also effective. This is one of the better U.S. peace books on the market.

1459 Beres, Louis Rene. *Apocalypse: Nuclear Catastrophe in World Politics.* Chicago: University of Chicago Press, 1980. 315pp. ISBN 0–226–04360–6.

The author assesses the prospect of nuclear war, its implications for human life, and strategies that might avert nuclear war. He emphasizes informing the public on the nuclear threat and detailing plans for averting nuclear war. There are three major scenarios of nuclear war: (1) nuclear war between the superpowers; (2) nuclear war through proliferation; and (3) nuclear terrorism. Despite some sensationalism, this book is a welcome addition to peace literature.

1460 Best, Keith, et al. *Playing at Peace: A Study of the Peace Movement in Great Britain and the Federal Republic of Germany.* London: Bow Publications, 1983. 120pp.

This essay is an attack on the peace movements in Great Britain and West Germany by British and West German conservatives affiliated with the Bow Group and the Konrad-Adenauer-Stiftung. These authors maintain that the leaders of these peace movements are left-wingers, often Marxist, and that the majority of the backers are misguided idealists. The essays assert that mistaken beliefs in pacificism and unilateral disarmament make these movements dangerous because they play into the hands of the Soviets. This critique of the peace movements by British and German conservatives reflects the official position of the Conservative party in Great Britain and the CDU in West Germany, but the authors' polemics and lack of balanced treatment weaken this book.

1461 Bradley, C. Paul. *The Camp David Peace Process: A Study of Carter Administration Policies (1977–1980).* Grantham, NH: Thompson and Rutter, 1981. 79pp. ISBN 0–93698–803–7.

This book is a study of the policies pursued by the Carter administration from 1977 to 1980 to conclude a peace treaty between Egypt and Israel. Despite the accomplishments of the Camp David peace process, the author concludes that there is no possibility of an imminent breakthrough at the end of 1980. Further progress was unlikely because of the new Reagan administration and the lack of participation by Palestinians. This treatment is more interpretative than substantial, and it is intended to serve as complementary material for undergraduate courses on Middle East politics.

1462 Brauch, Hans Günter. *Perspektiven einer Europäischen Friedensordnung.* Berlin, West Germany: Berlin Verlag, 1983. 94pp. ISBN 3–8706–1267–3.

This book by a West German scholar surveys the prospects of the European Parliament playing a role in the creation of a European peace order. The author believes that the European Parliament should play a role in European peace and security problems, and that such a role can be a start for more integration of European states into a united Europe. This book is an essay on the possibility of the European Parliament becoming more active in European affairs, and it should be read for the author's perspective rather than as serious research.

1463 Brock-Utne, Birgit. *Educating for Peace.* New York: Pergamon Press, 1985. 174pp. ISBN 0–08–032370–7.

A Norwegian social scientist gives a feminist perspective on the education of youth for peace. Her argument is that the oppression of women makes them victims of the structural violence of male-dominated society. Women should have a leading role in educating the populace for peace, because they are not captives of the militarization process that subjugates men. This book is a stimulating but offbeat look at peace from a feminist perspective.

1464 Brown, Robert McAfee. *Making Peace in the Global Village.* Philadelphia: Westminister Press, 1981. 118pp. ISBN 0–664–24343–6.

Peacemaking as a world view is the subject of this study. The author examines ways to look at the world and the steps necessary to bring about world peace. His vision is based on a religious view of peace, the arms race, and nuclear war. Because this book is strictly a personal look at peacemaking, it presents little new information for the benefit of peace researchers.

1465 Bukovsky, Vladimir. *The Peace Movement and the Soviet Union.* London: The Coalition for Peace Through Security, 1982. 57pp. ISBN 0–9508267–0–7.

The author was the leader of the Soviet Human Rights Movement until he left the Soviet Union in 1976. His thesis is that the Soviets have used the peace movement as both a weapon of Communist propaganda and an instrument of Soviet policy since 1917. Détente was just another tactic used by the Soviets to achieve economic and political ends. This booklet is a savage critique of the Soviet peace movement, and it should be read more for the author's viewpoint than the substance of the charges.

1466 Burton, John. *Dear Survivors: Planning after Nuclear Holocaust.* London: Frances Pinter, 1982. 137pp. ISBN 0–86531–455–1.

The author uses an epistle method to address the problem of war avoidance by studying possible post–nuclear war scenarios. He first defines possible reasons for the outbreak of nuclear war and follows with an enumeration of war avoidance policies. Behind this analysis is the author's belief that comprehension of the problem will produce a willingness to avoid nuclear war. This book is a clever way of broaching an old problem, but the reasoning is at a much higher level than the average reader can comprehend.

1467 Caldicott, Helen. *Missile Envy: The Arms Race and Nuclear War,* rev. ed. Toronto: Bantam Books, 1986. 346pp. ISBN 0–553–19384–8.

This book is a personal look at the nuclear arms race by an Australian pediatrician who was formerly at Harvard Medical School. While she argues passionately against the prospect for nuclear war on moral grounds, she is also convinced that the United States has the capability and the design for a nuclear first strike against the Soviet Union. Her advice for Americans is to enter the political arena and change U.S. policies. While this book is strong on moral indignation, it offers little evidence for the author's contentions.

1468 Calvocaressi, Peter. *A Time for Peace: Pacifism, Internationalism and Protest Forces in the Reduction of War.* London: Hutchinson, 1987. 195pp. ISBN 0–09–167550–2.

The moral arguments against war are presented in this book. Prevention of war lies in the hands of statesmen, but they are influenced by the prevailing moral attitudes of their times. This leaves an important role to the general public in determining the current moral environment for peace. The author seeks to prevent wars, not to abolish them, because this is the most effective approach.

1469 Castelli, Jim. *The Bishops and the Bomb: Waging Peace in a Nuclear Age.* New York: Image Books, 1983. 283pp. ISBN 0–385–18760–2.

This book by a U.S. journalist traces the process leading up to the passage of the Catholic bishops' pastoral letter, "The Challenge of Peace: God's Promise and Our Response" (1983). It includes several drafts of the letter and a summary and complete text of the final letter. The emphasis is on the personal side, on the process of drafting of the pastoral letter. This book is an invaluable source for researchers concerned with the religious side of the peace movement.

1470 *Catholics and Nuclear War: A Commentary on "The Challenge of Peace," the U.S. Catholic Bishops' Pastoral Life Center.* Edited by Philip J. Murnion. New York: Crossroad, 1983. 346pp. ISBN 0–8245–0600–6.

Commentaries on "The Challenge of Peace" pastoral letter (1983) are brought together here as a critique of the letter. Commentaries by experts on each aspect of the letter follow the order of the letter. These essays continue the debate and provide further background on the issues. Anyone interested in the religious side of the peace question will find this book illuminating.

1471 *The Church and the Bomb: Nuclear Weapons and Christian Conscience.* Edited by John Austin Baker, Bishop of Salisbury. London: Hodder and Stoughton, 1982. 190pp. ISBN 0–340–32371–X.

This report is the result of a 1979 resolution of the General Synod of the Church of England to study the church's role in the acceptance of nuclear weapons as a legitimate weapon of war. The conclusions of the report are that the "just war" theory rules out the use of nuclear weapons and that moral duty makes the survival of humankind imperative. The members conclude that nuclear weapons are a direct denial of the Christian concept of peace. Many of the conclusions of this report were adopted in the Catholic church's 1983 pastoral letter, and these publications should be considered together.

1472 *Citizen Summitry: Keeping the Peace When It Matters Too Much To Be Left to Politicians.* Edited by Don Carlson and Craig Comstock. Lafayette, CA: Ark Communications Institute, 1986. 396pp. ISBN 0–87477–406–3.

The editors have brought together in this book a series of writings on the relationship of the individual to the peace process. Efforts are made to look at different sides of a question and see similarities rather than differences. Grassroots opinions rather than government policies are emphasized, with the peace theme always there. This book contains the most positive affirmation of the ways to peace of any peace source on the market.

1473 Clarke, Magnus. *The Nuclear Destruction of Britain*. London: Croom Helm, 1982. 291pp. ISBN 0–7099–0458–4.

The effect of a nuclear war on the United Kingdom is the subject of this book by a British security analyst. By examining both the physical and human destruction of a nuclear attack and the environmental and social damage after the attack, the author concludes that the collapse of the United Kingdom seems not merely possible but probable. A reconstituted Britain would reappear but in a different form, whether under Soviet occupation or another type of civil government. This book deals only with the political and social side of nuclear war, and other books should be consulted on the possible environmental damage.

1474 Claude, Henri. *La troisième course aux armements: une nouvelle guerre mondiale est-elle fatale?* Paris: Editions Sociales, 1982. 203pp. ISBN 2–209–05472–9.

A French economist examines the influence of the third wave of new weapons technology on the international scene. It is the combination of new weapons technology and increasing worldwide militarization that most threatens peace. Only a vigorous international peace movement can reverse the current trend toward world war. The author compares the present arms race with that of the years preceding 1914, and his arguments are persuasive.

1475 Coates, Ken. *The Most Dangerous Decade: World Militarism and the New Non-Aligned Peace Movement*. Nottingham, England: Spokesman, 1984. 211pp. ISBN 0–85124–405–X.

This book presents various articles, documents, letters, speeches, and statements on antinuclear and peace issues. It contains polemical descriptions of the arms race and chronicles the activities of the European peace movements. While this potpourri of peace literature alternates between substantive articles and ephemeral types of peace literature, the author has made the selection of subjects a personal statement on the need for peace. For this reason, it is more an anthology than a work of scholarship.

1476 Comerford, Patrick. *Do You Want to Die for NATO?* Dublin: Mercer Press, 1984. 104pp. ISBN 0–8534–723–2.

The author, a journalist for *The Irish Times*, presents the case for the continuation of the Irish policy of neutrality. Irish neutrality has been an asset, and any commitment to NATO would only drag Ireland into the political malaise of the arms race. He proposes positive steps to ensure a permanent guarantee of this neutrality, from consideration of a constitutional referendum to advocacy of direct action. This book shows the intensity of feeling among the Irish for neutrality.

1477 *Consensus and Peace*. Edited by Beseat Kifle Selassie. Paris: UNESCO, 1980. 231pp. ISBN 92–3–101851–5.

These papers are from a 1980 symposium on the need for consensus on peace issues held at Oslo, Norway. Seven authors from around the world contributed papers on the consensus and peace theme. The result is a collection of ideas on the need for a worldwide agreement on the benefits of peace.

This book was published under the sponsorship of UNESCO, and it suffers from the failings of other UN publications, desiring a goal without working out the means to implement that goal.

1478 Cox, Gray. *The Ways of Peace: A Philosophy of Peace as Action.* New York: Paulist Press, 1986. 211pp. ISBN 0–8091–2797–0.

This book is a study on the philosophy of peace. The author is more concerned with a discussion of the wide variety of problems associated with peace than with concrete solutions. Consequently, he offers a menu of choices of steps toward peace, with the logic to be supplied by the reader. This book is a different approach toward peace seeking, and it should be read for its perspective rather than for information.

1479 Crozier, Brian. *The Price of Peace,* rev. ed. Washington, DC: National Center for Public Policy Research, 1983. 45pp.

This tract is a critique of the peace movements in Western Europe and the United States. The author asserts that the peace movement is manipulated from the Soviet Union through the World Peace Council (WPC). By bringing pressure against current defense and strategic policies, the peace movement plays into the hands of the Soviets and threatens world peace. Polemics and stock phrases characterize this treatise, and, except for its viewpoint, this work offers little.

1480 *Dangers of Deterrence: Philosophers on Nuclear Strategy.* Edited by Nigel Blake and Kay Pole. London: Routledge and Kegan Paul, 1983. 184pp. ISBN 0–7100–9885–5.

These essays are a critical assessment of the theory of nuclear deterrence by British academic scholars. They argue that nuclear deterrence provides only an illusion of security and that instead it provokes nuclear proliferation and international instability. The arguments presented here are effective against prevailing attitudes by state leaders and the general public, but these writers have difficulty proposing an alternative solution. These philosophical assessments of deterrence theory have little substance, but they are suggestive.

1481 Daubert, Victoria, and Sue Ellen Moran. *Origins, Goals, and Tactics of the U.S. Anti-Nuclear Protest Movement.* Santa Monica, CA: Rand Corporation, 1985. 117pp.

This study was designed to assess the threat of the anti–nuclear weapons and anti–nuclear energy protest movements in the United States to U.S. nuclear energy and nuclear weapons installations. Meticulous planning and nonviolence characterize U.S. antinuclear protest activities. The peak year of activity was 1978 for anti–nuclear energy protests and 1983 for anti–nuclear weapons protests. Both the analysis and a lengthy chronology of antinuclear protests from 1977 to 1983 make this a major source for further study of the U.S. antinuclear protest movement.

1482 *The Deadly Connection: Nuclear War and U.S. Intervention.* Edited by Joseph Gerson. Philadelphia: New Society Publishers, 1986. 253pp. ISBN 0–86571–068–6.

This book is a study of the relationship between U.S. nuclear war policy and U.S. military and political interventions. Published under the sponsorship of the New England Regional Office of the American Friends Service

Committee, the articles and speeches of twenty-three authors are included in this anthology of writings by prominent members of the U.S. peace movement. The theme is that Soviet and/or U.S. interventions in the affairs of other states may trigger a nuclear war. While these essays fluctuate in quality, the overall value of this publication resides in the viewpoints of the authors.

1483   Doob, Leonard W. *The Pursuit of Peace.* Westport, CT: Greenwood Press, 1981. 335pp. ISBN 0–313–22630–X.

This book is a philosophical and psychological analysis of the peace-war continuum. Beginning with individual behavior and ending with international politics, the author explores different approaches to the peace-war problem. His solutions are the rearing of less aggressive adults and improving economic and political structures. Since this approach differs from the traditional way of looking at peace and war, this book's contribution is in its unique orientation.

1484   Dyson, Freeman. *Weapons and Hope.* New York: Harper and Row, 1984. 340pp. ISBN 0–06–039031–X.

The author has written a book exploring the historical and cultural context in which nuclear weapons have developed, and, at the same time, he looks for practical ways of dealing with the problem of nuclear weapons in the future. His viewpoint is that of a scientist since he is a member of Jason, a group of scientists who work on technical problems for the Department of Defense and other U.S. agencies. Although his outlook is one of hope for the future, his analysis is more pessimistic. This book is a popular treatment of the nuclear arms race by a scientist who understands the complexities of the issues.

1485   Easlea, Brian. *Fathering the Unthinkable: Masculinity, Scientists and the Nuclear Arms Race.* London: Pluto Press, 1983. 230pp. ISBN 0–86104–391–X.

The author, formerly a nuclear physicist and now teaching science studies at Sussex University, advances the thesis that the nuclear arms race is in large part the result of masculine behavior in the pursuit of science. Such masculine behavior led to the development of the atomic bomb and then to its successor weapons. The reverse side of this argument is that by moderating this masculine element the arms race can be slowed. This book has little merit except for the offbeat viewpoint of the author.

1486   *Education and the Threat of Nuclear War.* Edited by Belle Zars, Beth Wilson, and Ariel Phillips. Cambridge, MA: Harvard Educational Review, 1985. 166pp. ISBN 0–916690–20–2.

This book is an expanded and revised version of the *Harvard Educational Review*'s August 1984 special issue. Experts from a variety of interdisciplinary perspectives present their views on the threat of nuclear war and educational efforts to end the threat. Other contributors highlight their classroom experience in teaching about the dangers of nuclear war. These essays give a good indication of educational initiatives taken on U.S. campuses on teaching about nuclear war.

1487   *Education for Peace and Disarmament: Toward a Living World.* Edited by Douglas Sloan. New York: Teachers College Press, 1983. 288pp. ISBN 0–8077–2747–4.

This is a collection of articles by educators interested in stimulating educational efforts toward ending the arms race and obtaining peace. The writers assert that education is meant to marshal resources and forces to end the threat of war, and that it should begin the long-range task of bringing about conditions for peace. The editor describes this book as a combination of an antiwar effort and a propeace vision. This book is hard to categorize, but the articles are of a consistently high quality.

1488 *Essays in Peace Studies.* Edited by Vilho Harle. Aldershot, England: Avebury, 1987. 207pp. ISBN 0–566–05375–6.

This book of essays on the peace tradition was published under the auspices of the Tampere Peace Research Institute, Tampere, Finland. The editors were more interested in finding theoretical essays than empirical studies. While most of the Finnish authors concentrated on peace trends in history, the intent of the book was to provide stimulus for peace studies in the future. This book has several impressive essays, but most of the material is too specialized for the peace activist.

1489 *Ethics, Deterrence and National Security.* By James E. Dougherty et al. Washington, DC: Pergamon-Brassey's, 1985. 95pp. ISBN 0–08–032767–2.

This book presents six papers from a 1983 conference in Bonn, West Germany, on the antinuclear movements in Western Europe and their security implications. These authors argue that the antinuclear movements are a clear threat to Western security because the activists espouse anti-Western values. While the Soviets do not direct Western peace activities, the goals advocated by these groups play into the hands of the Soviets. Little understanding of the motivation of European peace movements is shown by the authors in this book.

1490 *European Peace Movements and the Future of the Western Alliance.* Edited by Walter Laquerer and Robert Hunter. New Brunswick, NJ: Transaction Books, 1985. 450pp. ISBN 0–88738–035–2.

European peace movements and the future of NATO are the subjects of this book of essays by leading scholars in the field of security studies. These authors contend that an emphasis on unilateral disarmament makes peace movements in Western Europe a threat to European security. The result of these peace movements has been an erosion of consensus on European defense that has long-term implications. These essays consider the dual problems of the peace movement and European security by approaching the subjects from a variety of vantage points, and this diversity of approach makes this book worth reading.

1491 *Evangelicals and the Bishops' Pastoral Letter.* Edited by Dean C. Curry. Grand Rapids, MI: William B. Eerdmans Publishing, 1984. 254pp. ISBN 0–8028–1985–0.

These papers by U.S. scholars with Evangelical ties critique the stance against the use of nuclear weapons taken by the Catholic bishops in their famous pastoral letter of 1983. This letter has made Protestant denominations reexamine their positions on peace and war. The papers here reflect the divisions within the Evangelical movement on the issues of nuclear weapons and deterrence doctrine. This book is another in a series of publications responding to the debate among Christians over the ethics of nuclear war.

1492   Fahmy, Ismail. *Negotiating for Peace in the Middle East*. Baltimore, MD: Johns Hopkins University Press, 1983. 331pp. ISBN 0–80180–301–6.

Fahmy was deputy prime minister and foreign minister of Egypt during the early stages of peace negotiations between Egypt and Israel in 1977. These memoirs are the justification for the author's resignation before Sadat's trip to Jerusalem. He charges that Sadat's decision to negotiate with Israel hurt the cause of peace in the Middle East. This is a curious book in that the author purports to want peace in the Middle East, but his criticism of Sadat and his initiative indicates reluctance to negotiate with Israel.

1493   *Faslane: Diary of a Peace Camp*. Edinburgh, Scotland: Polygon Books, 1984. 86pp. ISBN 0–904919–87–0.

Members of the Faslane Peace Camp produced this short book on the creation and functioning of their peace camp. Faslane is located in Scotland near several defense establishments, and the members of the camp use this location to protest against defense policies. Most of this book consists of personal statements on the philosophy of the camp and on the nature of the protests. This book gives a picture of some of the more radical British peace protesters and a unique approach to direct-action politics.

1494   Feher, Ferenc, and Agnes Heller. *Doomsday or Deterrence? On the Antinuclear Issue*. Armonk, NY: M. E. Sharpe, 1986. 153pp. ISBN 0–87332–368–8.

The authors are Hungarian refugees who have written a critique of the antinuclear movement. Both authors are Socialists who are unhappy with the identification of the antinuclear movement with the European left. They are staunchly anti-Soviet, and their critique is based upon the need for socialism, not unilateral disarmament. This book has a unique viewpoint, and it is a vehicle of opinion rather than scholarship.

1495   Ferencz, Benjamin B. *A Common Sense Guide to World Peace*. London: Oceana Publications, 1985. 112pp. ISBN 0–379–20797–4.

A specialist in international law uses his expertise to show the extent to which international law has developed procedures and institutions to settle disputes. After a historical section on the development of international laws to the present, the author gives his prescription for world peace. His thesis is that peace resides in three major interlocking components—law, courts, and enforcement. This book is the author's affirmation of his belief in the rule of law and its benefits.

1496   *The Final Epidemic: Physicians and Scientists on Nuclear War.* Edited by Ruth Adams and Susan Cullen. Chicago: Educational Foundation for Nuclear Science, 1981. 172pp. ISBN 0–14080–444–7.

This book of essays, published under the auspices of the Educational Foundation for Nuclear Science in cooperation with the Physicians for Social Responsibility and the Council for a Livable World Education Fund, analyzes the medical consequences of a nuclear war. While physicians, scientists, and politicians are concerned about the immediate aftermath of a nuclear attack, most of the authors' attention was devoted to understanding the long-term health epidemics facing the survivors. The conclusion is that the long-term health effects of a nuclear exchange may be more devastating for the human race than the war itself. This book presents the state of scientific knowledge on nuclear war health problems in the early 1980s.

1497 Foot, Peter. *The Protesters: Doubt, Dissent and British Nuclear Weapons.* Aberdeen, Scotland: Centre for Defence Studies, 1983. 51pp.

This paper examines the British protest movement for its impact on British defense policy. Recent acquisition of new weapons systems by Great Britain has revitalized the peace groups' attacks on the direction of British defense. But moral arguments from the protest groups and hardline realism from the British government has left decision making to those in the middle, who at present are uncertain over the issues. This paper shows the variety of thought on defense issues current in British political circles.

1498 *For Peace and Life: Some Indian Impressions of Prague Assembly.* Edited by R. Sadananda. New Delhi: New Literature, 1983. 111pp.

The Indian participants in the World Assembly for Peace and Life, Against Nuclear War, which was held in Prague, Czechoslovakia, in June 1983, give their views on the assembly and the Communist peace movement. They subscribe to the thesis that the policies of the U.S. government and NATO have caused the arms race and brought the world to the brink of nuclear war. There were also strong feelings on the need for disarmament. This book reflects the growing peace and disarmament movement in India and around the world.

1499 Freeman, Harold. *If You Give a Damn about Life.* New York: Dodd, Mead, 1985. 88pp. ISBN 0–396–08615–2.

The case for peace is advanced in this short book on the consequences of a nuclear attack on a single area, Europe. These consequences are so severe that, after a full-scale nuclear exchange, life as we know it would end. Step-by-step disarmament is necessary, but unless political leaders allow themselves to be convinced, the solution is massive public anti–nuclear war demonstrations. This book is a direct-action guide to ending the nuclear arms race, and the presentation of material is succinct but appealing.

1500 Freund, Ronald. *What One Person Can Do To Help Prevent Nuclear War.* Mystic, CT: Twenty-Third Publications, 1982. 185pp. ISBN 0–89622–192–X.

This book is the author's approach to a theology and a politics of responsibility that has as its goal international peace. He has long been active in the peace movement, beginning with opposition to the Vietnam War. His approach is to describe personal commitments to peace from individuals of different faiths and occupations. This book chronicles individual efforts toward peace, and its contribution is showing these personal perspectives.

1501 *Friedensbewegungen: Beingungen und Wirkungen.* Edited by Gernot Heiss and Heinrich Lutz. Munichen: Oldenbourg Verlag, 1984. 207pp. ISBN 3–486–52421–6.

This book of essays is a historical look at the development of European peace movements. Beginning with sixteenth-century peace movements, the story ends with contemporary antinuclear movements. Because of its treatment of modern peace activities, the last third of the book is the most valuable for peace studies researchers. This book is a solid overview of the origins and development of European peace movements.

1502 Galtung, Johan. *Peace Problems: Some Case Studies: Essays in Peace Research.* Copenhagen: Christian Eilers, 1980. 498pp. ISBN 87–7241–372–7.

The author, the former director of the International Peace Research Institute (PRIO) in Oslo, Norway, has brought together a number of articles on

contemporary peace problems. Two types of peace problems are analyzed—
geographical aspects of major world conflicts and general peace problems.
Most of these essays have been previously published, but several are internal
PRIO documents. While this book of essays deals mostly with peace problems of the 1970s, the originality of the author still makes the book an
important source.

1503 Galtung, Johan. *There Are Alternatives! Four Roads to Peace
and Security.* Nottingham, England: Spokesman, 1984. 221pp. ISBN
0–85124–393–2.
The author is a British peace researcher who has written this book to
explore alternatives to nuclear war. His thesis is that there are four
approaches to peace and security: (1) conflict resolution; (2) balance of
power; (3) disarmament; and (4) alternative security policies. Each of these
approaches is studied for ways to end the arms race and the threat of nuclear
war. This book is one of the better works on peace studies on the market.

1504 Gazit, Mordechai. *The Peace Process, 1969–1973: Efforts and Contacts.* Jerusalem: Magnes Press, 1983. 155pp.
Peace initiatives proposed by the Israeli government between 1969 and
1973 and the responses are the subjects of this book. A question behind this
analysis is whether or not a peace settlement between Israel and the Arab
states was possible in this era. The answer is that no real opportunities
developed to encourage the Israeli government to initiate peace overtures
between 1969 and 1973. This study serves as a solid background for research
into the peace negotiations between Egypt and Israel after 1973.

1505 Gorbachev, Mikhail S. *A Time for Peace.* New York: Richardson and
Steirman, 1985. 298pp. ISBN 0–931922–08–0.
This book is a collection of lectures, speeches, and statements by the
general secretary of the Communist Party Central Committee of the Soviet
Union since his elevation to that post in the spring of 1985. Although these
are official statements at government and state affairs, the theme is the need
to develop good relations between the superpowers in order to promote
peace. This book has its uses because the statements reveal much about the
present holder of power in the Soviet Union.

1506 *Greenham Common: Women at the Wire.* Edited by Barbara Harford and
Sarah Hopkins. London: Women's Press, 1984. 171pp. ISBN 0–7043–3926–9.
This book presents the story of the Women's Peace Camp at Greenham
Common near the USAF base at Greenham, Great Britain. Beginning as a
protest against the introduction of U.S. cruise missiles into Britain in 1979,
this movement has become a long-lasting commitment to fighting nuclear
terror, male domination, and imperialist exploitation. Diaries, journals, letters, and personal narratives have been brought together to tell this story.
This book is another useful source for the feminist left of the British peace
movement in the mid-1980s.

1507 Gress, David. *Peace and Survival: West Germany, the Peace Movement and European Security.* Stanford, CA: Hoover Institution Press, 1985.
266pp. ISBN 0–8179–8091–1.
The subjects of this book are the transformation of German public opinion
toward accommodation with a divided Europe and the emergence of the
German peace movement. Most Germans believed up until the 1970s that

Soviet policies toward Germany were the main source of tension and threat to peace, but now many Germans regard provocative U.S. and NATO policies as an equal problem. The Sozialdemokratische Partei Deutschlands (SPD), the Greens, the peace movement, and influential leftist-liberal media have combined to oppose NATO policies and constitute a threat to European security. This change of attitude in West Germany is opposed by the author, but his points are worth considering.

1508 *Grosse Schrittewagen: Über die Zukunft oder Friedensbewegung.* Edited by Klaus Gerosa. Munichen: Paul List Verlag, 1984. 192pp. ISBN 3–471–77637–0.

This collection of essays studies the future of the West German peace movements. Besides high-quality essays on current and future peace issues of concern to West Germans, there are listings of various West German peace organizations. In a different arrangement these organizations are listed by profession. This book serves as a reference source for West German peace activities.

1509 Harwell, Mark A. *Nuclear Winter: The Human and Environmental Consequences of Nuclear War.* New York: Springer-Verlag, 1984. 179pp. ISBN 0–387–96093–7.

This book surveys the atmospheric and climatic consequences of nuclear war and the impact of these changes on the human population. By using scenario and consequence analyses, the author enhances his picture of the results of a large-scale nuclear exchange. Conditions would deteriorate to the point that human society would cease to exist, and there is the possibility of mankind's extinction. This book is an accumulation of the most recent scientific data on the consequences of nuclear war, and it should be required reading.

1510 Heater, Derek. *Peace through Education: The Contribution of the Council for Education in World Citizenship.* London: Falmer Press, 1984. 228pp. ISBN 0–85000–001–8.

The accomplishments of the Council for Education in World Citizenship (CEWC) are documented in this history of the organization. Since its beginning in 1939, this organization has been in the forefront of educational efforts for peace. This book is a standard organizational history with the merits and demerits of this genre. Only peace researchers interested in peace education will find this book of much value.

1511 Houghton, Robert B., and Frank G. Trinka. *Multinational Peacekeeping in the Middle East.* Washington, DC: Foreign Service Institute, U.S. Department of State, 1984. 108pp.

Two U.S. Foreign Service veterans analyze UN and non-UN peace-keeping activities in this assessment of the nature and the dynamics of multinational peace-keeping undertakings. Most of the data are gathered from four peace-keeping missions: (1) the 1973 ceasefire in the Arab-Israeli War; (2) the use of UN forces in Lebanon in 1978; (3) the Sinai operation in 1980; and (4) the Beirut operation in 1982. The authors conclude that there is little to choose between UN and non-UN multinational peace-keeping operations. This book is an excellent study of these peace-keeping operations, and it should prove a useful source for a number of years.

1512 *How Peace Came to the World.* Edited by Earl W. Foell and Richard A. Nenneman. Cambridge, MA: MIT Press, 1986. 257pp. ISBN 0–262–06100–7.

These essays are contributions from a peace essay contest conducted in 1985 by the *Christian Science Monitor.* More than 1,300 people submitted essays based on the rules of thinking ahead to the year 2010 and looking back to explain how the world had achieved peace in the intervening twenty-five years. A variety of opinions were expressed by the contributors, and this book analyzes these viewpoints as well as printing the winning essays. This book is a creative approach to studying the issues of peace.

1513 *The Hundred Percent Challenge: Building a National Institute of Peace.* Edited by Charles Duryea Smith. Cabin John, MD: Seven Locks Press, 1985. 256pp. ISBN 0–93020–30–5.

These essays commemorate the founding of the United States Institute of Peace in 1984. Besides essays on the purpose of the institute, several authors present substantial pieces on the need for peacemaking. An added feature is the excerpts from the Matsunaga Commission Report. This book is a unique source for understanding the political story behind the establishment of the Institute of Peace.

1514 *In letzter Stunde: Aufruf zum Frieden.* Edited by Walter Jens. Munichen: Kindler Verlag, 1982. 167pp. ISBN 3–463–00840–8.

Seven West German authors from a variety of professions explore peace issues in this book. They survey ideas on peace from their respective professional perspectives. Their concern is that the superpower rivalry has fueled the arms race to the point that there is the possibility of a war in Europe. This book is more a summation of views than a work of scholarship.

1515 Institute of International Peace Studies. *Peace Studies.* Seoul: Kyung Hee University Press, 1983. 686pp.

This book is a collection of viewpoints from educators from around the world on the role of higher education in promoting world peace. This cast of prominent educators also considers the need for economic development and technology transfer, but most attention is devoted to the prospect of higher education playing a major role in promoting peaceful change. This book has a variety of essays, most of which are substantial enough for serious consideration.

1516 Johnson, James Turner. *Can Modern War Be Just?* New Haven, CT: Yale University Press, 1984. 215pp. ISBN 0–300–03165–3.

This book presents the debate over morality and war in the context of the "just war" tradition. Modern international law has reduced the just war doctrine to one of self-defense as the only just cause. The author accepts the morality of defense as the key factor in answering the question whether modern war can be just. This book deals with a variety of ideas about the morality of modern war that may be of interest to peace students.

1517 *Juristen Gegen Kriegsgefahr im Europa: Protokoll einer Internationalen Konferenz.* Edited by Norman Paech and Gerhard Stuby. Köln, West Germany: Presseverlag Ralf Theurer, 1983. 181pp. ISBN 3–8161–0104–6.

These papers are the product of an 1982 international conference on the legal profession's position on the threat of a European war held at Frankfurt am Main, West Germany. Four papers were presented, two from the Soviet bloc and two from NATO. The rest of the proceedings consisted of a series of statements from other participants in the conference on the issue of war prevention. This book gives various viewpoints on the ethical and legal aspects of the European situation.

1518 Katz, Arthur M. *Life after Nuclear War: The Economic and Social Impacts of Nuclear Attacks on the United States.* Cambridge, MA: Ballinger, 1982. 422pp. ISBN 0–88410–907–0.

This book details the scenario of life in the United States after a nuclear war. It is an updated and expanded version of a report prepared for the U.S. Congress Joint Committee on Defense Production in 1979. Emphasis is given to the economic and social consequences of both limited and total nuclear war, but in either case the consequences would be catastrophic. This book is one of the best sources on this aspect of nuclear war on the market.

1519 Katz, Shmuel. *The Hollow Peace.* Jerusalem: Dvir, 1981. 342pp. ISBN 965–01–0060–1.

The former Israeli minister of information abroad to the U.S. under the Begin government critiques the Egyptian-Israeli peace process in this book. His view is that the treaty settled nothing and that the settlement has only set the stage for another Egyptian-Israeli War. Israel's policy is dependent on keeping secure borders; therefore no further territorial concessions favoring the Palestinians are possible. This book by an intransigent Israeli politician is an indication of the difficulties the peace process must face even in Israel.

1520 *Key Issues of Peace Research.* Edited by Yoshikazu Sakamoto and Ruth Klaassen. Dundas, Canada: International Peace Research Association, 1983. 333pp.

These papers on peace research issues are a product of the ninth conference of the International Peace Research Association, Orillia, Ontario, Canada, in 1981. The authors devote most of their attention to growing global militarization and ways to prevent further militarization. They believe efforts should be directed toward economic development and peace education. This book has a variety of stimulating papers on peace research worth consultation by peace researchers.

1521 Kortunov, Vadim. *The Policy of Nuclear Adventurism: A Threat to World Peace.* New Delhi: Sterling, 1985. 96pp.

The author accuses the Reagan administration of nuclear adventurism because of the policies adopted by the United States in the 1980s. By renouncing détente and pursuing aggressive policies, the United States has heightened international tensions. The Soviet Union, in contrast, has proposed a series of peace initiatives that will end the threat of nuclear war. While this book is a pedestrian attack on U.S. policy, it is obvious that the Soviet author is addressing his arguments toward an Indian market.

1522 Koszegi, Ferenc, and E. P. Thompson. *The New Hungarian Peace Movement.* London: Black Rose, 1984. 53pp. ISBN 0–85036–294–6.

Two authors examine the Hungarian peace movement in the 1980s in this booklet. Most Communist countries have a state-sponsored peace movement, but in Hungary this movement is more autonomous and flexible. Although there are similarities between the Hungarian and Western European peace movements, it is misleading to apply Western European standards because the Hungarian movement consists of small cell groups in universities and secondary schools. The contribution of this book is in showing that the appeal of peace in Hungary has reached behind state sponsorship to the grassroots.

1523 Kovel, Joel. *Against the State of Nuclear Terror*. Boston: South End Press, 1983. 250pp. ISBN 0–89608–220–2.

This book is a critique of the nuclear state as it is represented by its nuclear policies. The author advocates a radical transformation of society to overturn the power structure of the nuclear state. A plague on both East and West nuclear states is the attitude of the author. This book is an articulate statement of the position of the Western unilateral disarmament movement.

1524 Lawler, Philip F. *The Ultimate Weapon*. Chicago: Regnery Gateway, 1984. 126pp. ISBN 0–89526–826–4.

This book is a commentary to the Catholic church's pastoral letter "The Challenge of Peace: God's Promise and Our Response" (1983). The author intends to define and interpret the Catholic church's approach to nuclear strategy. But this interpretation is critical of the pastoral letter both in its approach and in many of its conclusions. Only those interested in the moral side of nuclear strategy will find this book worthwhile.

1525 Lens, Sidney. *The Bomb*. New York: Dutton, 1982. 139pp. ISBN 0–525–66752–0.

A noted freelance writer and labor leader expresses his concern over the arms race in this book. In this short history of nuclear weapons he presents his view that any policy designed to win a nuclear war risks a catastrophe beyond conception, and that present Reagan administration policies are unrealistic and endanger world peace. The author has long been active in the peace movement, and this book reflects his preoccupations.

1526 Levi, Werner. *The Coming End of War*. Beverly Hills, CA: Sage Publications, 1981. 182pp. ISBN 0–8039–1523–3.

The author advances the thesis that nuclear war is so counterproductive for both military and economic reasons that no such war will be fought. States are developing nonviolent means for handling conflicts because they shrink from engaging in modern wars. This analysis fits only those states with the capacity for nuclear warfare. This essay is suggestive and informative, but the thesis remains unproven and dubious.

1527 Lewis, William H. *The Prevention of Nuclear War: A United States Approach*. Boston: Oelgeschlager, Gunn and Hain, 1986. 101pp. ISBN 0–89946–206–5.

This book focuses on the prevention of nuclear war from the U.S. perspective. It is one of three studies from the United Nations Institute for Training and Research (UNITAR) designed to promote coverage of the problem of preventing nuclear war. The emphasis is restricted to U.S. proposals for arms control since the late 1950s. This book is only of marginal interest because its analysis lacks depth.

1528 *Living with Nuclear Weapons*. By the Harvard Nuclear Study Group. Cambridge, MA: Harvard University Press, 1983. 268pp. ISBN 0–674–53665–7.

The Harvard Nuclear Study Group is an informal body of six Harvard scholars who were entrusted by the president of Harvard, Derek Bok, to present a collective view of the nuclear problems facing the United States. Their philosophy consists of a moderate approach to coexistence with nuclear weapons by reducing the probability of nuclear war and gradually improving international relations. They believe in building a long-term solution to the nuclear problem, and in avoiding atomic escapism. This book is a solid, balanced work more suited to the general reader than the research scholar.

1529 Loeb, Paul Rogat. *Hope in Hard Times: America's Peace Movement and the Reagan Era.* Lexington, MA: Lexington Books, 1987. 322pp. ISBN 0–669–13022–2.

The author is a freelance writer and lecturer who wrote this book to describe low-level U.S. peace activities in the early 1980s. He has selected peace activities in a variety of out-of-the-way places as an indication that the U.S. peace movement is alive, and this is in keeping with his thesis that individuals rather than mass movements are the key to peace. This book is a unique look at U.S. grassroots peace activities.

1530 *London after the Bomb: What a Nuclear Attack Really Means.* By Owen Greene et al. Oxford, England: Oxford University Press, 1982. 142pp. ISBN 0–19–285123–3.

Five British research scientists present the latest information on the consequences of a nuclear attack on a major city. This book was written to counter the optimistic assurances of the British Home Office on population survivability during a nuclear attack. London would be devastated in a nuclear attack, with 76 percent of the Greater London population dead within twelve weeks after the attack and the rest suffering from radiation sickness. This book is another in a series showing scientific evidence on the effects of a nuclear war.

1531 *The Long Darkness: Psychological and Moral Perspectives on Nuclear Winter.* Edited by Lester Grinspoon. New Haven, CT: Yale University Press, 1986. 213pp. ISBN 0–300–03663–9.

The destructive power of nuclear weapons is examined in this book of essays from participants at a 1983 symposium at the annual meeting of the American Psychiatric Association in Los Angeles. Several articles deal with the environmental aspects of nuclear winter, and others cover the psychological aspect of the aftermath of nuclear war. Together these essays provide a graphic view of the consequences of a nuclear war. The viewpoints of a distinguished group of specialists make this an important book.

1532 Meltzer, Milton. *Ain't Gonna Study War No More: The Story of America's Peace Seekers.* New York: Harper and Row, 1985. 282pp. ISBN 0–06–024199–3.

The author has produced a history of pacifism and conscientious objection in the United States since colonial times. Almost every individual and/or movement advocating resistance to war in U.S. history is cited. The propeace theme of the book is reinforced by the use of illustrations of key leaders of the various pacifist movements. This book can be recommended for high school students.

1533 *Middle East Peace Plans.* Edited by Willard A. Beling. London: Croom Helm, 1986. 240pp. ISBN 0–7099–3967–1.

This book of essays treats the peace proposals of the main protagonists in the Middle East. Each plan is studied for its contents and the prospects of its being implemented. While no peace plan has been accepted by the principals, the fact that every state and the Palestine Liberation Organization (PLO) have considered such plans is a positive step. This book shows the diversity of thought surrounding a Middle East peace plan, and, for this reason alone, this source has value for peace scholars.

1534 Mitchell, C. R. *Peacemaking and the Consultant's Role.* Westmead, England: Gower, 1981. 169pp. ISBN 0–566–00389–9.

Third-party mediation in the peacemaking process is the subject of this book. The author believes that earlier types of mediation of conflicts have been unsuccessful because of the bargaining approach, and that problem solving rather than bargaining is the best method, because of its nondirective approach. The author argues his case for third-party consultancy persuasively, but, as in any single-solution argument, the position is too one-sided.

1535 Moulton, Phillips P. *Ammunition for Peace-Makers: Answers for Activists.* New York: Pilgrim Press, 1986. 137pp. ISBN 0–8298–0732–2.

The author attempts in this book to provide peace activists with the information to counter the arguments of the hardline "peace through strength" advocates. He focuses most of his attention on the major points where the two sides differ. His solution is the development of nonviolent national defense, which would increase national security and enhance the quality of life. This book is most effective in dealing with substantive policy questions and least effective on philosophical issues.

1536 Mroz, John Edwin. *Beyond Security: Private Perceptions among Arabs and Israelis.* New York: Pergamon Press, 1980. 214pp. ISBN 0–08–027517–6.

The author as a member of the Middle East Task Force of the International Peace Academy has produced this book of private interviews with Arab and Israeli leaders. In the late 1970s more than 175 government leaders and nongovernment officials discussed the issues of peace and war. The conclusion is that political and psychological problems hinder peace in this region as much as national security considerations. This type of study with interviews of leaders on both sides is invaluable, and this book is one of the better examples of this type.

1537 *New Social Movements and the Perception of Threat in Western Democracies.* Munich: Sozialwissenschaftliches Institut der Bundeswehr, 1983. 205pp.

These essays are a product of a 1982 conference on the political psychology of European peace movements in Washington, DC. The shift in security policy of NATO in 1979 caused a series of new social movements with propeace and antimilitary orientations. Most of the emphasis in this book is on examining the peace positions of the Italian and West German peace movements. This book is another solid work from U.S. and European scholars on an issue of continuing interest.

1538 Nixon, Richard. *Real Peace.* Boston, MA: Little, Brown, 1984. 107pp. ISBN 0–316–61149–2.

This essay contains the personal observations of former President of the United States Richard Nixon on the conditions necessary for world peace. For him, the key to real peace is a new relationship between the Soviet Union and the United States, but this relationship must be based on verifiable negotiated arms control agreements between equals. He recommends a hard-headed détente that promotes peaceful competition. This essay should be judged on its merits as the personal statement of a person interested in international relations problems.

1539 Novak, Michael. *Moral Clarity in the Nuclear Age.* Nashville, TN: Thomas Nelson, 1983. 144pp. ISBN 0–8407–5879–0.
This book is a response to the Catholic bishops' Pastoral Letter by the religious editor of the *National Review*. His essays on this subject have been gathered together into this book of readings. The author supports deterrence by the threat of nuclear weapons as an effective policy to preserve peace. He defends present policies from the moral and religious perspective, and this book should be read to contrast with the arguments of the Pastoral Letter.

1540 *The Nuclear Almanac: Confronting the Atom in War and Peace.* Edited by Faculty Members at the Massachusetts Institute of Technology. Reading, MA: Addison-Wesley, 1982. 546pp. ISBN 0–201–05331–4.
This book is a factual account of the development and use of nuclear energy for civilian and military uses. Twenty-six articles survey nuclear weapons, nuclear weapons effects, nuclear warfare, radiation problems, nuclear arms control, and technical aspects of nuclear energy. Each author makes a substantive contribution to the book by presenting a scholarly analysis of one of these topics. This book is the best introduction to all aspects of nuclear affairs in existence.

1541 *The Nuclear Dilemma and the Just War Tradition.* Edited by William V. O'Brien and John Langan. Lexington, MA: Lexington Books, 1986. 260pp. ISBN 0–669–12599–7.
These papers are the product of a 1984 conference on justice and war held at Georgetown University, Washington, DC. The occasion was the debates over Cruise missiles in Europe and the U.S. Catholic bishops' 1983 pastoral letter, but the significance of nuclear weapons in the just war tradition became the main theme of the conference. The question of whether deterrence or nuclear war fall into the just war doctrine are argued, and the outcome is a matter of interpretation. This book is one of the better studies on the ethical dilemma of nuclear war.

1542 *Nuclear-Free Defence.* Edited by Louis Mackay and David Fernbach. London: Heretic Books, 1983. 223pp. ISBN 0–946097–04–6.
These contributions face the question of British defense after the dismantling of the nuclear weapons system. Most of the contributors have their roots in the British peace movement. The intent of the book is to collect a range of views on alternative methods of national defense. By use of the question-and-answer format these views are combined to give the British Peace movement's collective position on defense issues.

1543 *Nuclear War: What's in It For You?* By Ground Zero. New York: Pocket Books, 1982. 272pp. ISBN 0–671–45096–4.
Ground Zero is a nonpartisan educational program whose purpose is to provide information and balance on the nuclear issue. This book is a primary educational resource to inform the general public about the facts of a nuclear war. Despite the claims of balance, the bulk of the information is directed

toward proving the dangers of nuclear war. This book is an effective presentation of the dangers of nuclear war as it might affect the average U.S. resident.

1544 *Nuclear Weapons and Law.* Edited by Arthur Selwyn Miller and Martin Feinrider. Westport, CT: Greenwood Press, 1984. 415pp. ISBN 0–313–24206–2.

These papers are a mixture of contributions from a 1983 conference at Nova Law Center and reprints from law journals. Twenty-seven papers are presented covering a variety of perspectives on legal questions about nuclear weapons, but the central problem remains that the lack of an institutionalized enforcement mechanism hinders the development of international law. This book serves a useful function as a textbook for introductory and advanced college-level courses.

1545 *Nuclear Weapons, the Peace Movement and the Law.* Edited by John Dewar et al. Houndmills, England: Macmillan, 1986. 255pp. ISBN 0–0333–41410–1.

This book is about law and its relationship to the peace movement. It is a product of a series of public lectures at the School of Law, University of Warwick, in 1983–1984. The articles range from such topics as principles of international law to the legality of various protest tactics. This book is in response to demand from peace protesters for information about their legal rights in anti–nuclear weapon protests.

1546 Nye, Joseph S. *Nuclear Ethics.* New York: Free Press, 1986. 162pp. ISBN 0–02–922460–8.

The author examines the moral dilemmas of the possession and use of nuclear weapons. He argues that the morality of nuclear deterrence is conditional upon the justification of use. By drawing on the just war doctrine, the author believes that the use of nuclear weapons can be justified in a "just defense doctrine." This book is a serious look at the possible use of nuclear weapons in a variety of moral situations, and its conclusions will interest a variety of readers.

1547 O'Connell, James, and Adam Curle. *Peace with Work to Do: The Academic Study of Peace.* Leamington Spa, England: Berg, 1985. 50pp. ISBN 0–90758–277–X.

The study of peace as an academic discipline is the subject of these essays. Peace has been left out of the academic curriculum because this type of study has been left to those outside the main institutions of society, or to those with different values from the establishment. Only recently has peace become an acceptable arena for serious scholarly research in universities and colleges. Both essays advocate aggressive research on peace as a way to preserve peace.

1548 *On the Endings of Wars.* Edited by Stuart Albert and Edward C. Luck. Port Washington, NY: Kennikat Press, 1980. 174pp. ISBN 0–8046–9240–8.

These essays present an interdisciplinary analysis of the attitudes and values associated with the transition from war to peace. While most of the examples of war endings utilized originate from historical case studies, the aim of the authors is to understand the process. The theme in all the essays is that a better comprehension of the ending of wars is a way to understand the causes of war. Since both the essays and the arguments are high-quality efforts, this book would be a good addition to any collection.

1549 *Out of Justice, Peace: Winning the Peace.* Edited by James V. Schall. San Francisco, CA: Ignatius Press, 1984. 124pp. ISBN 0–89870–043–4.

These pastoral letters from West German bishops and French bishops respectively represent the Catholic church's response to Christian reasoning on questions of peace and war in the nuclear age. Both documents stress that it is better to confront the wills behind political power than the weapons issue. Positive recommendations rather than fear characterize both letters. These letters stand as historical documents on the Catholic church's stance on peace in the 1980s.

1550 *Pacifism and War.* Leicester, England: Inter-Varsity Press, 1984. 256pp. ISBN 0–85110–727–3.

This book provides a forum for authors of differing perspectives to write defenses of their viewpoints. The subject is pacifism versus nonpacifism. *Pacifism* in this context is a strict adherence to Christian theology and ethics against defense or war, and the narrowness of the definition restricts the appeal of this book, but it does outline the position of Christian pacifism in some detail.

1551 *Pacifisme et dissuasion: la contestation pacifiste et l'avenir de la sécurité de l'Europe.* Edited by Pierre Lellouche and Nicole Gnesotto. Paris: Institut Français de Relations Internationales, 1983. 329pp. ISBN 2–86592–009–7.

The impact of pacifism on peace movements in the NATO and Warsaw Pact blocs is the subject of this book of essays. Each of the European countries, the Soviet Union, and the United States has its peace movements analyzed by scholars specializing in the politics of these countries. Peace movements have had a significant impact on the military policies of these countries because of the effectiveness of the protests in political circles. While most of the emphasis is upon Europe, the book makes a positive contribution to the understanding of the relationship between domestic politics and security worldwide.

1552 *The Path to Peace: Arab-Israeli Peace and the United States: Report of a Study Mission to the Middle East.* By Joseph N. Greene et al. Mount Kisco, NY: Seven Springs Center, 1981. 50pp.

This book is a report by a four-member private study group that traveled to the Middle East in the summer of 1981 to study the prospects for an Arab-Israeli peace. The report's conclusions are that hopes for a negotiated peace between Israel and its neighbors are fading since there appears to be no alternative to confrontation as long as the Palestinian question is unresolved. Only the United States can resolve the impasse, but trust in the United States is at a low ebb in the Middle East. This report is based on interviews with Arabs, Palestinians, and Israelis, and it serves as a good introduction to the state of relations in the Middle East during the early 1980s.

1553 *Peace and War: Cross-Cultural Perspectives.* Edited by Mary LeCron Foster and Robert A. Rubinstein. New Brunswick, NJ: Transaction Books, 1986. 369pp. ISBN 0–88738–069–7.

These papers are the outgrowth of sessions of a symposium sponsored by the American Anthropological Association. The authors concentrated on how diverse societies approach the problems of peace and war. Emphasis is given to the cultural factors that support war and a cultural approach to finding ways to prevent conflicts. While the papers are of uneven quality, the book has a novel approach and should encourage further research along these lines.

1554 *Peace in a Nuclear Age: The Bishops' Pastoral Letter in Perspective.* Edited by Charles J. Reid. Washington, DC: Catholic University of America Press, 1986. 426pp. ISBN 0–8132–0624–3.

These essays come out of several workshops during the academic year 1983–1984 at the Catholic University of America in response to the pastoral letter, "The Challenge of Peace: God's Promise and Our Response" (1983). A variety of opinions on the ways to peace are presented in this volume, but all opinions hinge on ways to implement the goals of the pastoral letter. Ongoing education and continuing dialogue are the keys to success. This book gives pros and cons of the pastoral letter, and it is a good companion volume to the letter.

1555 *Peacekeeping: Appraisals and Proposals.* New York: Pergamon Press, 1983. 461pp. ISBN 0–08–027554–0.

These essays study peace-keeping as a feature of the international system. Most of the essays use UN peace-keeping activities as a model, but several authors consider peace-keeping beyond the UN experience. They believe that peace-keeping, both in theory and practice, has the potential to solve international crises. While this book is better on the historical side of past peace-keeping activities, it has coverage of future trends.

1556 *Peacemakers: Christian Voices from the New Abolitionist Movement.* Edited by Jim Wallis. San Francisco, CA: Harper and Row, 1983. 156pp. ISBN 0–06069–244–8.

This book consists of short essays by members of the U.S. peace movement the purpose of which is to campaign for the abolishment of nuclear weapons. The emphasis is religious because the majority of authors believe that only efforts by the Christian community can halt the arms race. Most of the essays are short personal statements of opposition to war and nuclear weapons. These personal statements reveal the depth of commitment by the U.S. peace movement.

1557 *The Peacemaking Struggle: Militarism and Resistance.* Edited by Ronald H. Stone and Dana W. Wilbanks. Lanham, MD: University Press of America, 1985. 294pp. ISBN 0–8191–4772–9.

These essays reflect the concern of the Presbyterian Church (U.S.A.) on the relationship of the Christian faith to the issue of resistance to militarism. *Militarism* is defined to include the nuclear arms race, proliferation of nuclear and conventional weapons, and repression of internal opposition. The authors of these essays believe militarism is an issue that needs to be fought. This book is another Christian approach to peace.

1558 *The Peace Movements in Europe and the United States.* Edited by Werner Kaltefleiter and Robert L. Pfaltzgraff. New York: St. Martin's Press, 1985. 211pp. ISBN 0–312–59932–3.

These papers on peace movements in Europe and the United States are the product of a 1984 conference held at the Christian-Albrechts-University,

Kiel, West Germany. An international cast of peace scholars presented papers on the status of national peace movements. Particular emphasis was placed by these writers on putting the peace movement into the context of its society. This book is especially valuable because it studies each peace movement both in its national context and for comparative purposes.

1559 *Peace Research in Finnish and Soviet Scientific Literature.* Edited by Jakob Berger and Unta Vesa. Tampere, Finland: Tampere Peace Research Institute, 1983. 190pp. ISBN 951–706–060–2.

These papers are a joint publication of the Tampere Peace Research Institute (TAPRI) and the Soviet Union's Institute of Scientific Information on Social Sciences (INION). Finnish and Soviet research on the problems of war and peace is surveyed for progress on peace issues. The result is a book that looks at peace research projects undertaken in the 1970s and 1980s. While more information is made available on Finnish research, this work is still a useful glimpse of peace research activities from two important research institutes.

1560 *Die Philosophie des Friedens im Kampf gegen die Ideologie des Krieges.* Edited by the Militarakademie "Friedrich Engels." Berlin, East Germany: Dietz Verlag, 1984. 282pp.

Six East German scholars give their analysis of present-day peace and war issues. Their viewpoints are conditioned by Marxist-Leninist interpretation of capitalism and imperialism. They charge that imperialist confrontation politics makes peaceful coexistence almost impossible. This book is an example of East German scholarship, and its viewpoint is more interesting than illuminating.

1561 Pillar, Paul R. *Negotiating Peace: War Termination as a Bargaining Process.* Princeton, NJ: Princeton University Press, 1983. 282pp. ISBN 0–691–07656–1.

War termination as part of the bargaining process in peace negotiations is the subject of this monograph. The author maintains that war termination is susceptible to theorizing because there are discernible patterns in past conflicts. He concludes that decision making during wartime bargaining is determined by the perceptions of the participants, and these statesmen have the obligation to foresee possible futures and recognize the viewpoints of the enemy. This book is suggestive and presents a different vantage point, both of which make it worth reading.

1562 *Positionen der Friedensbewegung: die Auseinandersetzung um den US-Mittelstreckenrakelenbeschluss: Dokumente, Appelle, Beträge.* Edited by Lutz Plumer. Frankfurt, West Germany: Sendler Verlag, 1981. 155pp. ISBN 3–88048–053–2.

This book contains documents, reports, statements, and newspaper articles on West German peace activities. Most of the material falls into the period 1979 to 1981. Particularly valuable are the official statements by West German political parties. This book is a good primary source on West German peace activities in the early 1980s.

1563 Preddy, George. *Nuclear Disaster: A New Way of Thinking Down Under.* Wellington, New Zealand: Asia Pacific Books, 1985. 175pp. ISBN 0–908583–11–7.

The author is a former member of the New Zealand Commission for the Future and presently in the New Zealand Ministry of Civil Defence. He uses his experiences in those bodies to provide material for this book, which surveys nuclear war from a New Zealand perspective. His version has New Zealand as the last refugee from a nuclear war if it pursues a neutralist policy now. This book is eclectic, but it argues a positive case for nonalignment for New Zealand.

1564 Price, Jerome. *The Antinuclear Movement.* Boston, MA: Twayne Publishers, 1982. 207pp. ISBN 0–8057–9705–X.

The author studies the antinuclear movement from the perspective of an antinuclear activist. He explores the values, organizations, and ideologies of diverse antinuclear groups in the United States. Although much of the opposition to nuclear power is environmental, there is a strong anti–nuclear weapons theme in most of these groups. This book is a sociological interpretation of the antinuclear movement by a U.S. sociologist, and his treatment is a unique study of this movement.

1565 *Psychosocial Aspects of Nuclear Developments.* Washington, DC: American Psychiatric Association, 1982. 96pp. ISBN 0–89042–220–6.

Six U.S. psychiatrists present papers from the Task Force on Psychosocial Aspects of Nuclear Development from the American Psychiatrist Association (APA) on the psychological dilemmas posed by the nuclear arms race and nuclear technology. They trace the fears most Americans have about nuclear war and nuclear accidents. The report recommends that these findings be communicated to political decisionmakers. This report by the APA is not a major piece of scholarship, but it shows another group of professionals interested in finding ways to end the arms race.

1566 Quandt, William B. *Camp David: Peacemaking and Politics.* Washington, DC: Brookings Institution, 1986. 426pp. ISBN 0–8157–7290–4.

This book uses the Camp David Accords as a case study in U.S. foreign policy making. The author is a former staff member of the National Security Council, and he was a participant in the negotiations of the accords. His conclusions are that there is little left of the Camp David Accords to build upon for another peace initiative in the Middle East, and that the U.S. political system makes it difficult to conduct peace initiatives since it takes presidential commitment. This book is the most significant monograph to appear on this subject, and it should be required reading for specialists in the field.

1567 Reule, Fred J. *Nuclear Winter: Asymmetrical Problems and Unilateral Solutions.* Maxwell Air Force Base, AL: Air University Press, 1986. 42pp.

The impact of the nuclear winter thesis on military and civilian policymakers is the subject of this short monograph by a senior officer in the U.S. Air Force. Creditable use of nuclear weapons has been hurt by the nuclear winter thesis, because tactical use of nuclear weapons appears to policymakers to be too great a gamble. While research is in progress to test the validity of this thesis, a search is also under way for a substitute deterrence doctrine. The author proposes his solution, but the analysis on the impact of the nuclear winter thesis is the important part of this monograph.

1568 Richter, Horst-Eberhard. *Zur Psychologie des Friedens.* Hamburg, West Germany: Rowohlt Verlag, 1982. 312pp. ISBN 3–498–056–964.

This book is an analysis of the psychology of peace. The author concentrates on the desire for peace among individuals and social groups, and the psychological barriers against obtaining this goal. Most organizations subscribe to a belief in the benefits of peace, but the realities of the arms race make peace seem remote. This book is a major contribution to the understanding of the psychology of peace.

1569 Rikhye, Indar Jit. *The Theory and Practice of Peacekeeping.* London: Hurst, 1984. 255pp. ISBN 0–905838–82–3.

By combining the functions of a historical survey of UN peace-keeping activities with an analysis of the theoretical application of the international system of peace-keeping, this publication covers all aspects of UN peace-keeping operations. It is based on the author's observations of UN peace-keeping activities in Cyprus and the Middle East. The author believes that the success of international peace-keeping is too dependent upon the superpowers, but he still maintains that experience in peace-keeping will enhance the possibilities of limiting the spread of conflicts. This book continues a series of publications on UN peace-keeping, and its contribution is to extend the study into the middle 1980s.

1570 Roche, Douglas. *Politicians for Peace: A New Global Network of Legislators Working for Human Survival.* Toronto: NC Press Limited, 1983. 175pp. ISBN 0–919601–83–9.

This book is a laudatory treatment of a new global network of legislators belonging to the peace organization Parliamentarians for World Order (PWO). The author is a member of PWO from its origins in the early 1980s. A list of legislators and their commitment to this organization are the strengths of this publication. Although this work is organized haphazardly, it still provides a useful picture of this new peace organization and its leaders.

1571 *Rumors of War: A Moral and Theological Perspective on the Arms Race.* Edited by C. A. Cesaretti and Joseph T. Vitale. New York: Seabury Press, 1982. 138pp. ISBN 0–8164–2365–2.

This book is a resource book for adults striving to understand the nature of peace. It has four sessions devised to promote thought and discussion with Bible readings and articles about war and peace. Each session revolves around two positions: a crusade for peace and the just war doctrine. This book is a resource book most useful for those interested in the moral dimensions of war and peace.

1572 Ruston, Roger. *Nuclear Deterrence—Right or Wrong?* Abbots Langley, England: Catholic Information Services, 1981. 80pp. ISBN 0–905241–09–6.

This book is a study of the morality of nuclear deterrence. The author prepared this book under the sponsorship of the Commission for International Justice and Peace of England and Wales as a way to open up discussion on the reversal of the nuclear arms race and the elimination of nuclear weapons. His conclusion is that the doctrine of nuclear deterrence is morally indefensible, because of the illogic of threatening the use of nuclear weapons. This book is another statement on the morality of nuclear deterrence, but this time from the perspective of a British Catholic.

1573   Saunders, Harold H. *The Other Walls: The Politics of the Arab-Israeli Peace Process.* Washington, DC: American Enterprise Institute for Public Policy Research, 1985. 179pp. ISBN 0–8447–3590–6.

This treatment of the Arab-Israeli peace process is from the point of view of a former career officer in the U.S. State Department. The author was involved in the U.S. side of the negotiations in five Arab-Israeli agreements between 1973 and 1979. Both the Israelis and the Palestinians need to accept each other on human grounds before any settlement is possible. In this book another participant of the Arab-Israeli peace negotiations illuminates the problems of a Middle East peace.

1574   *The Sociology of War and Peace.* Edited by Colin Creighton and Martin Shaw. Houndmills, England: Macmillan, 1987. 245pp. ISBN 0–333–41838–7.

These papers are the results of a 1985 conference of the British Sociological Association on war, violence, and social change, held at the University of Hull, Great Britain. The *sociology of war and peace* is defined as the theoretical, historical, and empirical study of war, war preparation, the social effects of war, and the social processes that prevent war. These papers present a variety of approaches to the sociology of war and peace, and at least half of the papers should be of interest to peace researchers.

1575   Soelle, Dorothee. *The Arms Race Kills Even without War.* Philadelphia: Fortress Press, 1983. 111pp. ISBN 0–8006–1701–0.

This book is an English translation of radio broadcasts, speeches, and articles from a German theologian. Her thesis is that the arms race is destructive because it deprives Third World countries of development funds. The military focus also results in scientists becoming preoccupied with military research rather than with research to solve world problems. This book is a reflective look at the arms race by a person active in the peace movement.

1576   Somer, Mark. *Beyond the Bomb: Living without Nuclear Weapons.* Boston: Expo Press, 1985. 180pp. ISBN 0–936391–00–6.

The author envisages the world after the removal of nuclear weapons. He describes this book as a field guide to alternative strategies for building a stable peace. While nuclear weapons are the symbol, it is the ending of war that is the ultimate goal. This book rambles along as the author deals with the problems of nuclear arms, war, and peace.

1577   Spaeth, Robert L. *No Easy Answers: Christians Debate Nuclear Arms.* Minneapolis, MN: Winston Press, 1983. 128pp. ISBN 0–86683–802–3.

This book examines the morality of nuclear weapons and the response of U.S. religious leaders to this problem. The author presents information, review of issues, and discussions on moral perspectives rather than conclusions. He attempts to present a balanced picture of the issues at stake in the nuclear arms race and any type of arms reduction. This book is a solid introduction to the religious side of the nuclear arms debate for the general reader.

1578   *Strategies for Peace and Security in a Nuclear Age.* Guelph, Canada: Division of Continuing Education, University of Guelph, 1983. 47pp.

These proceedings from a 1983 conference at the University of Guelph, Canada, address the problems of arms control, disarmament, and peace. An international cast of participants made statements on the need to seek peaceful solutions to world problems. There were other activities, involving talks and discussion groups, at the conference that this publication only makes oblique references to here. This book gives only a glimpse of the positions of the speakers and the discussions, and, for this reason, it is of limited value.

1579 Thompson, E. P. *Beyond the Cold War: A New Approach to the Arms Race and Nuclear Annihilation.* New York: Pantheon Books, 1982. 198pp. ISBN 0–394–52796–8.

The author, who is a former journalist and active in the British disarmament and peace movements, presents this series of essays advocating a nuclear-free Europe. NATO's decision to modernize its nuclear weaponry was the catalyst for European peace movements to protest against the arms race. European peace movements are busy coordinating efforts across national lines to combat the arms race in Europe. This book is part of a personal crusade by the author for peace and disarmament, and it is a valuable source for those interested in the British peace movement.

1580 Totten, Sam, and Martha Wescoat Totten. *Facing the Danger: Interviews with 20 Anti-Nuclear Activists.* Trumansburg, NY: Crossing Press, 1984. 154pp. ISBN 0–89594–124–4.

Two anti–nuclear war activists give their views on the arms race and the threat of nuclear war in a series of interviews conducted by two U.S. interviewers. A common theme is the issue of personal responsibility for changing present policies fueling the arms race. Most of these interviews took place in 1980, and the twenty selected for this book were from over 150 social activists interviewed. This book presents the views and goals of the leaders of antinuclear activities in the United States.

1581 *Towards a Just World Peace: Perspectives from Social Movements.* Edited by Saul H. Mendlovitz and R. B. J. Walker. London: Butterworths, 1987. 403pp. ISBN 0–408–24400–3.

These papers on contemporary peace movements were published under the auspices of the Committee for a Just World Peace. An international cast of researchers on peace studies contributed papers on peace subjects. These authors find the current militarization of world resources unacceptable, and they trace social movements dedicated to changing the waste of the arms race. This book has a number of solid essays on peace subjects.

1582 Vanderhaar, Gerard A. *Christians and Nonviolence in the Nuclear Age: Scripture, the Arms Race, and You.* Mystic, CT: Twenty-Third Publications, 1982. 128pp. ISBN 0–89622–162–8.

The author advocates active nonviolence as a personal response to the arms race and the threat of nuclear war. His conviction is that if people face the implications of nuclear weapons then they will seek alternatives. Peace can be achieved by steadily working toward it one step at a time. This book reflects the personal concerns of a peace activist.

1583 Verrier, Anthony. *International Peacekeeping: United Nations Forces in a Troubled World.* Harmondsworth, England: Penguin Books, 1981. 172pp. ISBN 0–14–08–0444–7.

This book is a history of UN peace-keeping operations since 1947. From the beginning there has been a gap between a mandate and the means to execute that mandate, and this problem has hurt the effectiveness of UN peace-keeping activities. Politics among UN members has been the other factor limiting its peace-keeping record. This book gives a complete summary of UN peace-keeping operations, and it is a good source to start with for further research on this subject.

1584 *Violence and Peace-Building in the Middle East.* Edited by Marion Mushkat. Munichen: K. G. Saur, 1981. 192pp. ISBN 3–598–10355–7.

These papers are the proceedings of a 1980 symposium sponsored by the Israeli Institute for the Study of International Affairs (IISIA). Twenty-five scholars contributed papers on the peace process in the Middle East. Most contributors were pessimistic about present chances for a lasting peace in the Middle East, but they were more optimistic for the future. Most of the papers are too brief to be much more than statements, but this book does give a variety of opinions on the peace process in the Middle East.

1585 *War, Peace and the News Media.* Edited by David M. Rubin and Ann Marie Cunningham. New York: Department of Journalism and Mass Communication, New York University, 1983. 285pp.

These proceedings are the product of a 1983 conference on the role of the news media in reporting international affairs held at New York University. Scholars and journalists from Canada, Mexico, and the United States participated in an exchange of views on news media and peace issues. Two speeches and three position papers stimulated the debate. This book provides a variety of viewpoints and shows the diversity of opinion on news media coverage of events.

1586 *Weapons of Peace: How New Technology Can Revitalize Peacekeeping. A Report of the International Peace Academy.* New York: International Peace Academy, 1980. 59pp.

This report consists of a number of papers outlining ways new technology has made peace-keeping easier. Particular emphasis is placed on electronic systems for detection, identification, assessment, and communication. Examples of these systems were gathered from UN peace-keeping operations. The technical assessments are on the vague side, and a more technical treatise will be necessary for better understanding of peace-keeping technology.

1587 *We Are Ordinary Women: A Chronicle of the Puget Sound Women's Peace Camp.* Seattle, WA: Seal Press, 1985. 115pp. ISBN 0–931188–27–X.

The story of the Puget Sound Women's Peace Camp is told from journals, statements, poems, and songs. This camp opened in September 1982, and the book covers the period from the beginning to 18 June 1983. U.S. veterans of the Greenham Common Camp used their experience to launch a campaign for peace in Puget Sound. This short book gives a good picture of U.S. feminist peace activists in the Pacific Northwest region.

1588 Weizman, Ezer. *The Battle for Peace.* Toronto: Bantam Books, 1981. 395pp. ISBN 0–553–05002–8.

This book presents the Israeli side of the Egyptian-Israeli peace treaty in 1977. The author was the Israeli minister of defense, and he was actively involved in the negotiations. While he approved the peace process, he resigned over the Begin government's retreat from the peace treaty. This book is a personal account of his role in the peace negotiations and his attitudes toward the final product.

1589 *Western European Pacifism and the Strategy for Peace.* Edited by Peter van den Bungen. London: Macmillan, 1985. 218pp. ISBN 0–333–36555–0.

These papers are a product of a 1982 colloquium of the Professors World Peace Academy (PWPA) in Paris, France. Twenty European specialists on communism, peace, and disarmament gathered together to present their views. Pacifism and its impact on European security was the dominant theme. The quality of the essays is uneven, but the book has the redeeming virtue of representing a different point of view.

1590 *What Hope in an Armed World?* Edited by Richard Harries. London: Pickering and Inglis, 1982. 144pp. ISBN 0–7208–0526–0.

These essays on Christian ethics and the defense of Great Britain are by present and former members of King's College, London. Each specialist takes a different approach, but all share the conviction that ethical considerations must relate to the real world. Both pessimism and hope emerge from these essays. While this book is a mixed bag of conflicting viewpoints, it does reveal the complexity of dealing with ethical issues in an uncertain environment.

1591 Willems, Harold. *The Trimtab Factor: How Business Executives Can Help Solve the Nuclear Weapons Crisis.* New York: William Morrow, 1984. 144pp. ISBN 0–688–02661–3.

The author is a businessman who has adapted business techniques to the problem of the nuclear arms race. His theory is that the pragmatism and political experience of businessmen can provide the leverage necessary to change the direction of the arms race. This theory is called the Trimtab Factor, which is taken from a tiny rudder on large oceangoing ships. This book is highly suggestive work, the thesis of which is worth further examination.

1592 Wittner, Lawrence S. *Rebels against War: The American Peace Movement, 1933–1983,* rev. ed. Philadelphia: Temple University Press, 1984. 364pp. ISBN 0–87722–346–7.

An updated version of an earlier edition, this book is a historical assessment of the U.S. peace movement from 1933 to 1983. Certain conclusions emerge, such as the contention that the peace movement has achieved its greatest popularity in the United States in times of progressive ferment, and that it has usually suffered its strongest setbacks during periods of right-wing resurgence. Moreover, the peace movement has often developed politically astute analyses of world events. This book is a solid addition to the literature in the peace field.

1593 *World Parliament of the Peoples for Peace.* Edited by Georgi Dimitrov-Goshkin. Sofia, Bulgaria: Sofia Press Publishing House, 1982. 312pp.

The proceedings of a 1980 international peace conference held in Sofia, Bulgaria, are published in this book. This conference attracted representatives from most of the major peace organizations in the world. Most of the resolutions were directed toward NATO and U.S. policies. This book shows the sponsorship of peace movements by Communist countries.

1594 *World Peace and the Developing Countries: Annals of Pugwash 1985.* Edited by Joseph Rotblat and Ubiratan D'Ambrosio. Houndmills, England: Macmillan, 1986. 272pp. ISBN 0–333–43636–9.

Each year since 1983 material from several Pugwash meetings is combined into a book of essays on a specific topic. The topic for 1985 is world peace and the developing countries. Contributors from a variety of academic specialties study the security problems of Third World countries. This book has twenty-two quality essays to recommend it.

1595 Young, Ronald J. *Missed Opportunities for Peace: U.S. Middle East Policy, 1981–1986.* Philadelphia: American Friends Service Committee, 1987. 192pp. ISBN 0–910082–11–1.

The author, the former Middle East representative for the American Friends Service Committee, utilizes his contacts among Arabs and Israelis to analyze prospects for a Middle East peace in the early and middle 1980s. He and his wife conducted several hundred interviews from all sides of the Arab-Israeli debate. The United States has overestimated the influence of military power, and it has underestimated the power of popular movements, resulting in a series of missed opportunities for the United States to become a peacemaker in this region. This work is a personal interpretation of Middle East events, but the author's objective analysis makes it a balanced assessment of the problems of peacemaking in this region.

1596 Zagladin, Vadim. *The Soviet Peace Philosophy: Peace Programme in Action, 1981.* Moscow: Novosti Press Agency Publishing House, 1981. 167pp.

This book is a statement of the official Soviet position on foreign policy and peace. The view comes from the Twenty-sixth Congress of the Soviet Communist Party (1981), translated by a Soviet historian. The statement concludes that Soviet foreign policy has been successful in the 1970s and that its chances are better for the future. This book is mostly propaganda, but it is still useful as a measure of how the Soviets view their foreign policy.

Publishers

ABC-Clio, Inc.
Riviera Campus
2040 Alameda Padre Serra,
Box 4397
Santa Barbara, CA 93140-4397

ABC Publishing House
72-A, Shanker Market
Connaught Circus
New Delhi
India

Abt Books
55 Wheeler Street
Cambridge, MA 02138

Academic International Press
Box 1111
Gulf Breeze, FL 32561

Addison-Wesley
1 Jacob Way
Reading, MA 01867

Adler and Adler, Publishers, Inc.
4550 Montgomery Avenue
Bethesda, MD 20814

Aero Pubs. Inc.
329 W. Aviation Rd.
Fallbrook, CA 92028

AFCEA International Press
Armed Forces Communications
  and Electronics Association
  (AFCEA)
4400 Fair Lakes Ct.
Fairfax, VA 22033

Afrique defence
11, rue de Teheran
75008 Paris
France

Air University Press
Superintendent of Documents
Washington, DC 20402

Allan (Ian) Ltd.
Coombelands House, Addlestone
Weybridge, Surrey, KT15 1HY
England

Allanheld, Osmun and Co.
6 South Fullerton Avenue
Montclair, NJ 07042

Allen (George) and Unwin Ltd.
40 Museum St.
London WC1A 1LU
England

Alliance Publishers
P.O. Box 25004
Ft. Lauderdale, FL 33320

Amana Books
58 Elliot Street
Brattleboro, VT 05301

American Association for the Advancement of Science
1515 Massachusetts Avenue NW
Washington, DC 20005

American Committee on East-West Accord
109 11th St. SE
Washington, DC 20003

The American Defense
   Preparedness Association
Suite 900
1700 N. Moore St.
Arlington, VA 22209

American Educational Trust
P.O. Box 53062
Washington, DC 20009

American Enterprise Institute for
   Public Policy Research
1150 17th St. NW
Washington, DC 20036

American Institutes for Research
P.O. Box 1113
Palo Alto, CA 94302

American Israel Public Affairs
   Committee
1100 17th St. NW
Washington, DC 20036

American Mideast Publishing
3315 Sacramento Street, Suite 511
San Francisco, CA 94118

American Psychiatric Association
1400 K St. NW
Washington, DC 20005

American Security Council Press
1336 Kingston Avenue
Alexandria, VA 22302

Andre Deutsch
See Deutsch (Andre) Ltd.

Antara Book Company
399A Jalan Tuanku Abdul Rahman
50100 Kuala Lumpur
Malaysia

Anthony Bird Publications Ltd.
Strettington House, Strettington
Chichester, Sussex PO18 1LA
England

Archon Books
P.O. Box 4327
995 Sherman Ave.
Hamden, CT 06514

Arco Publishing, Inc.
215 Park Ave. S.
New York, NY 10003

Ark Communications Institute
250 Lafayette Circle
Lafayette, CA 94549

Armament and Disarmament
   Information Unit
University of Sussex
Mantell Building
Falmer
Brighton, East Sussex BN1 9RF
England

Arms and Armour Press
2–6 Hampstead High St.
London NW3 1QQ
England

The Arms Control Association
11 Dupont Circle NW
Washington, DC 20036

Ashi Evening News
P.O. Box 555
Tokyo Central
Japan

Asian-Pacific Services Institute
2115 Oahu Ave.
Honolulu, HI 96822

Asia Pacific Books
5 Maurice Terrace, P.O. Box 3979
Wellington
New Zealand

Aspen Institute for Humanistic
   Studies
Wye Plantation, P.O. Box 222
Queenstown, MD 21658

Associated University Presses,
   Inc.
4 Cornwall Drive
East Brunswick, NJ 08816

Associated University Presses,
   Ltd.
27 Chancery Lane
London WC2A 1NF
England

The Association for
   Transarmament Studies
3636 Lafayette Ave.
Omaha, NE 68131

Association Française pour les Études de Défense et de Desarmement
Institut National Superieur d'Études de Défense et de Desarmement (INSED)
Université de Paris-I
9, rue Malher
75004 Paris
France

Atheneum Publishers
115 Fifth Ave.
New York, NY 10003

Atlantic Council of the United States
1616 H St. NW
Washington, DC 20006

The Atlantic Institute for International Affairs
120, rue de Longchamp
75116 Paris
France

Auburn House
14 Dedham
Dover, MA 02030

Australian Government Publishing Service
Canberra, ACT 2600
Australia

Australian Institute of International Affairs
Coombs Building
Australian National University
Canberra City, ACT 2601
Australia

Australian National University Press
P.O. Box 4
Canberra, ACT 2600
Australia
U.S. office:
Australian National University Press
15601 SW 83rd Ave.
Miami, FL 33157

Autumn Press
1318 Beacon Street
Brookline, MA 02146

Avebury
Gower Publishing Company Ltd.
Gower House, Croft Rd.
Aldershot, Hants GU11 3HR
England

Avery Publishing Group
142 Fulton Ave.
Garden City Park, NY 11040

Ballinger Publishing Company
54 Church St., Harvard Square
Cambridge, MA 02138

Bantam Books
666 Fifth Ave.
New York, NY 10103

Basil Blackwell
See **Blackwell (Basil) Publishers Ltd.**

Batsford (B. T.) Ltd.
4 Fitzhardinge St.
London W1H 0AH
England

BBC Publications
35 Marylebone High St.
London W1M 4AA
England

B. C. Publishers
9C Ajitnagan
Opposite Fatima Convent
Patiala - 147001
India

Beacon Press
25 Beacon St.
Boston, MA 02108

Beaufort Books, Inc.
9 E. 40th St.
New York, NY 10016

Beck (C. H.) Verlag
Postfach 400340
D-8000 Munich 40
West Germany

Bender (Matthew) and Co., Inc.
235 E. 45th St.
New York, NY 10017

Berg Publishers
24, Binswood Ave.
Leamington Spa
Warwickshire CV32 5SQ
England

Berlin Verlag
Pacellialee 5 u. Ehrenbergstrasse
D-1000 Berlin 33
West Germany

Bernard Grasset
61, rue des Saints-Perès
75006 Paris
France

Billner and Rouse, Inc.
260 W. 35th St.
New York, NY 10001

Black Rose Books
3981 boul. St. Laurent
Montreal, Quebec H2W 1Y5
Canada

Blackwell (Basil) Publishers Ltd.
108 Cowley Road
Oxford OX4 1JF
England

Bow Publications
240 High Holborn
London WC1V 7DT
England

Brassey's Defence Publishers Ltd.
Maxwell House
74 Worship St.
London EC2A 2EN
England

Brick House Publishing Company, Inc.
34 Main St.
Andover, MA 01810

The Brookings Institution
1775 Massachusetts Ave. NW
Washington, DC 20036

Buchan and Enright, Publishers Ltd.
53 Fleet St.
London EC4Y 1BE
England

Bundesinstituts für Ostwissenschaftliche und Internationale Studien
Lindenbornstrasse 22
5000 Koln 30
West Germany

Butterworths and Co. (Publishers) Ltd.
80 Montvale Ave.
Stoneham, MA 02180

Butterworths Scientific
80 Montvale Ave.
Stoneham, MA 02180

California Seminar on International Security and Foreign Policy
California Institute of Technology
P.O. Box 925
Santa Monica, CA 90406

Cambridge University Press
The Edinburgh Building
Shaftesbury Rd.
Cambridge CB2 2RU
England

Campus Verlag
Myliusstrasse 15
6000 Frankfurt 1
West Germany

Canadian Disarmament Information Service
10 Trinity Square
Toronto, Ontario M5G 1B1
Canada

Canadian Institute of International Affairs
15 King's College Circle
Toronto, Ontario M5S 2V9
Canada

Canadian Institute of Strategic Studies
Suite 202, 1 St. Clair Ave. West
Toronto, Ontario M4V 1K6
Canada

Carolina Academic Press
P.O. Box 8795, Forest Hills Station
Durham, NC 27707

Cass (Frank) and Co. Ltd.
Gainsborough House
11 Gainsborough Rd., Leytonstone
London E11 1RS
England

Catholic Information Services
Abbots Langley
England

The Catholic University of America Press
620 Michigan Ave. NE
Washington, DC 20064

CAUSA International
401 Fifth Ave.
New York, NY 10010

CCCO
See **Central Committee for Conscientious Objectors (CCCO)**

Center for Contemporary Arab Studies
Georgetown University
Washington, DC 20057

Center for Defense Information
303 Capitol Gallery W.
600 Maryland Ave. SW
Washington, DC 20024

The Center for Foreign Policy Development
Box 1948
Brown University
Providence, RI 02912

Center for International and Strategic Affairs
11383 Bunche Hall, UCLA
405 Hilgard Avenue
Los Angeles, CA 90024

Center for International Security Studies
See **American Security Council Press**

Center for National Policy
236 Massachusetts Ave. NE
Washington, DC 20002

Center for Naval Analyses
2000 North Beauregard St.
Alexandria, VA 22311

Center for Peaceful Change
Kent State University
Kent, OH 44242

Center for Peace Studies
University of Akron
Akron, OH 44325

Center for Strategic and International Studies
Georgetown University
1800 K St. NW
Washington, DC 20006

Center for the Study of Armament and Disarmament
California State University, Los Angeles
5151 State University Dr.
Los Angeles, CA 90032

Center for War/Peace Studies
218 E. 18th St.
New York, NY 10003

Central Committee for Conscientious Objectors (CCCO)
2208 South St.
Philadelphia, PA 19146

Centre d'Études de Défense Nationale
1, place Joffre
75700 Paris
France

Centre for Conflict Studies
University of New Brunswick
Fredericton, New Brunswick E3B 5A3
Canada

Centre for Defence Studies
University of Aberdeen
Edward Wright Building
Dunbar Street
Aberdeen AB9 2TY
Scotland

Centre for European Policy Studies
Rue Ducale 33
1000 Brussels
Belgium

Centre for International Relations
Queen's University
Kingston, Ontario K7L 3N6
Canada

Centre for the Study of Arms Control and International Security
University of Lancaster
Fylde College, Bailrigg
Lancaster LA1 4YF
England

Charles Scribner's Sons
See **Scribner's (Charles) Sons**

The Chicago Council on Foreign Relations
116 South Michigan Ave.
Chicago, IL 60603

Christian Ejlers' Forlag A/S
Brolaeggestraede 4
DK-1211 Kobehavn K
Denmark

Claremont Research and Publications
160 Claremont Ave.
New York, NY 10027

Clarendon Press
Oxford Unity Press
Walton St.
Oxford OX2 6DP
England

Coalition for Peace Through Security
2d Floor
35 Westminister Bridge Rd.
London SE1 7JB
England

College of Combat
Mhow
India

Collier Books
866 Third Ave.
New York, NY 10022

Collins (William) Sons and Co. Ltd.
8 Grafton St.
London W1X 3LA
England

Columbia University Press
562 W. 114th St.
New York, NY 10027

Committee Against Registration and the Draft
Room 111
201 Massachusetts Ave. NE
Washington, DC 20002

Committee for a Sane Nuclear Policy
514 C St. NE
Washington, DC 20002

Committee on the Present Danger
905 16th St. NW
Washington, DC 20006

Common Cause
2030 M St. NW
Washington, DC 20036

Computer Science Press
11 Taft Court
Rockville, MD 20850

Congressional Budget Office
U.S. Government Printing Office
710 N. Capital St. NW
Washington, DC 20402

Consortium on Peace Research, Education and Development (COPRED)
Center for Conflict Resolution
George Mason University
4400 University Dr.
Fairfax, VA 22030

Continuum Publishing Company
370 Lexington Ave.
New York, NY 10017

Cornell University Press
124 Roberts Place
P.O. Box 250
Ithaca, NY 14851

The Council for Arms Control
Faraday House
B-10 Charing Cross Rd.
London WC2H 0HG
England

Council of Europe
Avenue de l'Europe, BP 431 R6
F-67006 Strasbourg CEDEX
France

Council on Economic Priorities
30 Irving Place
New York, NY 10003

Council on Economics and National Security
1730 Rhode Island Ave. NW,
Suite 601
Washington, DC 20036

Council on Foreign Relations
58 E. 44th St.
New York, NY 10021

Crane, Russak and Company
3 E. 44th St.
New York, NY 10017

Crisis and Conflict Analysis Team
The Institute of Strategic Studies
8, Khyaban-E-Iqbal F/6/3
Islamabad
Pakistan

Croom Helm
Provident House, Burrell Row
Beckenham, Kent BR3 1AT
England

The Crossing Press
Trumansburg, NY 14886

Crossroad Publishing Company
370 Lexington Ave.
New York, NY 10017

Deep and Deep Publications
D-1/24, Rajouri
New Delhi-110027
India

**Defence Scientific Information
and Documentation Centre**
Metcalfe House
New Delhi-110054
India

Defense and Foreign Affairs
1777 T St. NW
Washington, DC 20009

Defense Marketing Services
See **DMS Inc.**

Défense Nationale
See **Fondation pour les Études de
Défense Nationale**

**Department for Disarmament
Affairs**
See **UN Department for
Disarmament Affairs**

Department of Defense
See **U.S. Department of Defense**

**Department of Peace and Conflict
Research**
Uppsala University
Oestra Agatan 53
P.O. Box 278
75103 Uppsala
Sweden

Deutsch (Andre) Ltd.
105 Great Russell St.
London WC1B 3LJ
England

The Devin-Adair Company
143 Sound Beach Ave.
Old Greenwich, CT 06870

Dialogue Publications
5 Pearl Rd.
Calcutta-700017
India

The Dial Press
1 Dag Hammarskjold Plaza
New York, NY 10017

Dietz Verlag
Hauser Strasse 33
D-8493 Kötzling
East Germany

**Disarmament Program,
Fellowship of Reconciliation**
Box 271
Nyack, NY 10960

Division of Continuing Education
University of Guelph
Guelph, Ontario N1G 2W1
Canada

DMS Inc.
100 Northfield St.
Greenwich, CT 06830

DMS Market Intelligence Reports
See **DMS Inc.**

Dodd, Mead & Co.
79 Madison Ave.
New York, NY 10016

Dominican Publications
St. Saviour's
Dublin 1
Ireland

Donald I. Fine
See **Fine (Donald I.)**

Duckworth (Gerald) and Co. Ltd.
The Old Piano Factory
43 Gloucester Crescent
London NW1 7DY
England

Duke Press Policy Studies
6697 College Station
Durham, NC 27708

Duke University Press
6697 College Station
Durham, NC 27708

Dutton (E. P.)
2 Park Ave.
New York, NY 10016

Dvir Publishing Ltd.
58 Mazeh St., P.O. Box 149
Tel Aviv 61001
Israel

Ebury Press
National Magazine House
72 Broadwick St.
London W1V 2BP
England

Economica
49, rue Hericart
75015 Paris
France

Ediciones Universal
3090 SW Eighth St.
Miami, FL 33135

**Editions de l'Université de
  Bruxelles**
Avenue Paul Heger 26
1050 Brussels
Belgium

Editions Larivière
15–17, Quai de l'Oise
75019 Paris
France

Editions Maritimes et d'Outre-mer
17, rue Jacob
75006 Paris
France

Editions Mazarine
75, rue des Saints-Peres
Paris VIe
France

Editions Seghers
6, place Saint-Sulpice
75006 Paris
France

Editions Sociales
146, rue du Faubourg Poissonière
75010 Paris
France

Editorial Planeta, S.A.
Corcegg, 273–277
Barcelona-8
Spain

Editorial Research Service
P.O. Box 1832
Kansas City, MO 64141

**Educational Foundation for
  Nuclear Science**
1020 East 58th St.
Chicago, IL 60637

**Eerdmans (William B.) Publishing
  Company**
255 Jefferson Ave., S.E.
Grand Rapids, MI 49503

E. P. Dutton
See **Dutton (E. P.)**

Ethics and Public Policy Center
1030 15th St. NW
Washington, DC 20005

Europa Publications
18 Bedford Square
London WC1B 3JN
England

Europa Union Verlag GmbH.
Bachstrasse 32, Postfach 1529
D-5300 Bonn 1
West Germany

European Nuclear Disarmament
11 Goodwin St.
London N4
England

EW Communications, Inc.
1170 East Meadow Dr.
Palo Alto, CA 94303

Expo Press
Distributed by The Talman
  Company
150 Fifth Ave.
New York, NY 10011

Faber and Faber Ltd.
3 Queen Square
London WC1N 3AU
England

Facts on File
119 W. 57th St.
New York, NY 10019

Falmer Press
4 John St.
London WC1N 2ET
England

Fellowship of Reconciliation
P.O. Box 271
Nyack, NY 10960

Fine (Donald I.)
128 E. 36th St.
New York, NY 10016

Firethorn Press
49 Hays Mews
London W1X 7RT
England

Fondation pour les Études de Défense Nationale
Hotel National des Invalides
75007 Paris
France

Fontana Paperbacks
See **Collins (William) Sons and Co. Ltd.**

Foreign Affairs Publishing Co. Ltd.
139 Petersham Rd.
Richmond, Surrey TW10 7AA
England

Foreign Policy Association
205 Lexington Ave.
New York, NY 10016

Foreign Policy Research Institute
3508 Market St., Suite 350
Philadelphia, PA 19104

Foreign Service Institute
U.S. Department of State
Washington, DC

Fortress Press
2900 Queen Lane
Philadelphia, PA 19129

Fourth Estate Ltd.
Classic House
113 Westbourne Grove
London W2 4UP
England

Frances Pinter (Publishers) Ltd.
5 Dryden St.
London WC2E 9NW
England

Frank Cass
See **Cass (Frank) and Co. Ltd.**

Franklin Watts Inc.
387 Park Ave. S.
New York, NY 10016

Freeman (W. H.) and Company
41 Madison Ave., 37th Floor
New York, NY 10010

The Free Press International
866 Third Ave.
New York, NY 10022

Gale Research Company
Book Tower
Detroit, MI 48226

Garland Publishing, Inc.
136 Madison Ave.
New York, NY 10016

George Allen and Unwin Ltd.
See **Allen (George) and Unwin Ltd.**

George Mann Books
See **Mann (George) Books**

Georgetown University Press
Intercultural Center, Room 111
Washington, DC 20057

G. K. Hall
See **Hall (G. K.)**

Global Education Associates
552 Park Ave.
East Orange, NJ 07017

GMP Publishers Ltd.
P.O. Box 247
London N15 6RW
England

Gordon and Breach Science Publishers Ltd.
1 Park Ave.
New York, NY 10016

Government Business Worldwide Reports
P.O. Box 39178
Washington, DC 20016

Gower Publishing Company
Old Post Road
Brookfield, VT 05036

Gower Publishing Company Ltd.
Gower House, Croft Rd.
Aldershot, Hants GU11 3HR
England

Grace Contrino Abrams Peace Education Foundation
P.O. Box 19-1153
Miami Beach, FL 33118

Graduate School of International Studies
University of Denver
Denver, CO 80208

Grafton Books
8 Grafton St.
London X1X 3LA
England

Granada Ltd.
See **Grafton Books**

Grant McIntyre Ltd.
Ceased publication; list acquired by
Blackwell (Basil) Publisher Ltd.

Greenhaven Press
577 Shoreview Park Rd.
St. Paul, MN 55126

Greenwood Press
88 Post Rd. West
Westport, CT 06881

Groningen University Press
Broerstraat 5, P.O. Box 72
9700 AB Groningen
The Netherlands

Guide Publications
60/20 Prabhat Road, Karol Bagh
New Delhi-110005
India

Günter Olzog Verlag
See **Olzog (Günter) Verlag**

Hall (G. K.)
70 Lincoln St.
Boston, MA 02111

Hamilton Press
4720 Boston Way
Lanham, MD 20706

Hamish Hamilton Ltd.
Garden House
57–59 Long Acre
London WC2E 9JZ
England

Hamlyn Publishing Group
Bridge House
69 London Rd.
Twichenham TW1 3SB
England

Harper and Row Publishers
10 E. 53rd St.
New York, NY 10022

Harrap Ltd.
19–23 Ludgate Hill
London EC4M 7PD
England

Harvard Educational Review
Longfellow Hall, 13 Appian Way
Cambridge, MA 02138

Harvard University Press
79 Garden St.
Cambridge, MA 02138

Heinemann (William) Ltd.
10 Upper Grosvenor St.
London W1X 9PA
England

Heretic Books
P.O. Box 247
London N15 6RW
England

The Heritage Foundation
214 Massachusetts Ave. NE
Washington, DC 20002

Hero Publishing
P.O. Box 157
Dunn Loring, VA 22027

Hessische Stiftung Friedens- und Konfliktforschung
Leimenrode 29
6000 Frankfurt 1
West Germany

Hill and Wang
19 Union Square W.
New York, NY 10003

Hippocrene Books, Inc.
171 Madison Ave.
New York, NY 10016

Hochschule des Bundeswehr
Winzererstrasse 52
8000 Munich 40
West Germany

Hodder and Stoughton Limited
P.O. Box 6
Mill Rd., Dunton Green
Sevenoaks, Kent TN13 2XX
England

Holmes and Meier
30 Irving Place
IUB Bldg.
New York, NY 10003

Holt, Rinehart and Winston
383 Madison Ave.
New York, NY 10017

Hoover Institution Press
Stanford University
Stanford, CA 94305

Houghton Mifflin
2 Park St.
Boston, MA 02108

Hudson Institute
Quaker Ridge Rd.
Croton-on-Hudson, NY 10520

Human Rights Internet
1502 Ogden St. NW
Washington, DC 20010

Hurst (C.) and Co. (Publishers) Ltd.
38 King St.
London WC2E 8JT
England

Hutchinson and Company Ltd.
17–21 Conway St.
London W1P 6JD
England

Ian Allan
See **Allan (Ian) Ltd.**

I. B. Tauris and Co., Ltd.
3 Henrietta Street
Covent Garden
London WC2E 8PW
England

ICS Press
Institute for Contemporary Studies
785 Market St., Suite 750
San Francisco, CA 94103

Ignatius Press
P.O. Box 18990
San Francisco, CA 94118

Image Books
501 Franklin Ave.
Garden City, NY 11530

Impact Publishers, Inc.
P.O. Box 1094
San Luis Obispo, CA 93406

Indiana University Press
Tenth and Morton Streets
Bloomington, IN 47405

**Institute for Defense and
  Disarmament Studies**
2001 Beacon St.
Brookline, MA 02146

**The Institute for European
  Defence and Strategic Studies**
13/14 Golden Square
London W1R 3AG
England

**Institute for Foreign Policy
  Analysis**
Central Plaza Building, 10th Floor
675 Massachusetts Ave.
Cambridge, MA 02139

Institute for Palestine Studies
P.O. Box 19449
Washington, DC 20036

Institute for Peace and Justice
4144 Lindell Blvd., Suite 400
St. Louis, MO 63108

Institute for Policy Studies
1901 Q St. NW
Washington, DC 20009

Institute for Strategic Studies
University of Pretoria
Pretoria 0002
South Africa

Institute for the Study of Conflict
12/12a Golden Square
London W1R 3AF
England

Institute of East Asian Studies
University of California, Berkeley
2223 Fulton St., 6th Floor
Berkeley, CA 94720

Institute of Education
University of London
57 Gordon Square
London WC1
England

Institute of International Studies (IIS)
215 Moses Hall
University of California, Berkeley
Berkeley, CA 94720

Institute of Southeast Asian Studies
Heng Mui Keng Terrace
Pasir Panjang
Singapore 0511

Institut Français de Relations Internationales
6, rue Ferrus
75683 Paris Cedex 14
France

Institüt für Friedensforschung und Sicherheitspolitik
Universität Hamburg
2000 Hamburg 55
West Germany

Institüt für Strategische Grundlagenforschung
Zentraldokumentation
Stiftgasse 2a
1070 Vienna
Austria

Instituto de Cuestiones Internacionales
Almirante 1
Madrid 4
Spain

Interavia S.A.
86, Avenue Louis Casai
1216 Cointrin
Geneva
Switzerland

International Defence and Aid Fund for Southern Africa
Canon Collins House
64 Essex Road
London N1 8LR
England

International Institute for Comparative Social Research
Steinplatz 2
1000 Berlin 12
West Germany

International Institute for Strategic Studies
23 Tavistock St.
London WC2E 7NQ
England

International Peace Academy
777 United Nations Plaza
New York, NY 10017

International Peace Research Association
Rua Paulino Fernandes 32
CEP 22270 Rio de Janeiro
RJ Brasil

International Press Center
Box 61
1, Blvd. Charlemagne
B-1040 Brussels
Belgium

International Progress Organization
Reindorfgrasse 5
Vienna
Austria

International Publishers
381 Park Ave. S., Suite 1301
New York, NY 10016

International Research Center on Contemporary Society (IRCCS)
687 Jerusalem 91006
Israel

International Security Council
393 Fifth Ave.
New York, NY 10016

International Security Studies Program
Wilson International Center for Scholars
Smithsonian Institution Building
Washington, DC 20560

Inter-Varsity Press
38 De Montfort St.
Leicester LE1 7SP
England

Investor Responsibility Research Center
1319 F St. NW, Suite 900
Washington, DC 20004

Iowa Peace Network
Des Moines, IA 50317

Israel Defense Forces
Military Post 01025
Israel

Jaffee Center for Strategic Studies
Tel Aviv University
Tel Aviv
Israel

Jameson Books
P.O. Box 738
Ottawa, IL 61350

Jane Adams Peace Association (JAPA)
777 United Nations Plaza
New York, NY 10017

Jane's Publishing Co. Ltd.
238 City Rd.
London EC1
England

JAPA/WILPF Committee on Education
1010 Brookmere Drive
Edmonds, WA 98020
See also **Jane Adams Peace Association (JAPA); Women's International League for Peace and Freedom (WILPF)**

Jeremy P. Tarcher
See **Tarcher (Jeremy P.) Inc.**

The Johns Hopkins University Press
Baltimore, MD 21218

John Wiley and Sons, Inc.
See **Wiley (John) and Sons, Inc.**

The Joint Chiefs of Staff
Pentagon
Washington, DC 20301

Joseph (Michael) Ltd.
27 Occupation Lane
London SE18
England

Journal of Political and Military Sociology
Dept. of Sociology
Northern Illinois University
DeKalb, IL 60115

Jules Perel's Publishing
P.O. Box 913
35 Matterhorn
NL-1186 ED Amstelveen
The Netherlands

Julian Messmer
Simon and Schuster Building
1230 Ave. of the Americas
New York, NY 10020

Kennikat Press
Rt. 100
Millwood, NY 10546

K. G. Saur
See **Saur (K. G.) Verlag**

Kimber (William) and Co. Ltd.
100 Jermyn St.
London SW1Y 6EE
England

Kindler Verlag
Rauchstrasse 9–11
Postfach 800480
D-8000 Munich 80
West Germany

King Publishing Group
627 National Press Building
Washington, DC 20045

The Kingston Press
P.O. Box 1456
Princeton, NJ 08542

Knopf (Alfred A.) Inc.
201 E. 50th St.
New York, NY 10022

Krasnaya Zwezda
Moscow
Soviet Union

Kraus Reprints and Periodicals
Rt. 100
Millwood, NY 10546

Kyung Hee University Press
53, 3-ka Myungrun-dong
Chongro-gu, Seoul 110
South Korea

Lancer International
Post Box No. 3802
New Delhi-110049
India

Lawrence Hill and Co.
520 Riverside Ave.
Westport, CT 06880

**Lawyers Alliance for Nuclear
   Arms Control**
43 Charles St., Suite 3
Boston, MA 02114

Lester and Arpen Denny Limited
78 Sullivan St.
Toronto M5T 1C1
Canada

Leuven University Press V.Z.W.
Krakenstraate
B-3000 Leuven/Louvain
Belgium

Lexington Books
125 Spring St.
Lexington, MA 02173

Librairie Artheme Fayard
75, rue des Saints-Peres
Paris VIe
France

Library of Congress
Washington, DC 20540

Little, Brown and Company
34 Beacon St.
Boston, MA 02106

Llewellyn King Publishers
See **King Publishing Group**

Longman Group Ltd.
Longman House, Burnt Mill
Harlow, Essex CM20 2JE
England

**Lyndon B. Johnson School of
   Public Affairs**
Policy Research Institute (PRI)
University of Texas at Austin
Drawer Y, University Station
Austin, TX 78713

Lynne Rienner
See **Rienner (Lynne) Pubs., Inc.**

M. E. Sharpe
See **Sharpe (M. E.) Inc.**

M. Evans and Company, Inc.
216 E. 49th St.
New York, NY 10017

Macdonald and Evans
Estover, Plymouth PL6 7PZ
England

Macmillan Publishers Ltd.
4 Little Essex St.
London WC2R 3LF
England

Magnes Press
Hebrew University
P.O. Box 7695
Jerusalem 91076
Israel

Manchester University Press
Oxford Rd.
Manchester M13 9PL
England

Mann (George) Books
P.O. Box 22
Maidstone, Kent ME14 1AH
England

Mansell Publishing Ltd.
6 All Saints St.
London N1 9RL
England

Martin Robertson
108 Cowley Rd.
Oxford OX4 3BQ
England

Martinus Nijhoff Publishers
P.O. Box 163
330 AD Dordrecht
The Netherlands

Masson S.A.
120 BD. Saint-Germain
75280 Paris Cedex 06
France

Matthew Bender
See **Bender (Matthew) and Co., Inc.**

McFarland and Company
P.O. Box 611
Jefferson, NC 28640

McGill-Queen's University Press
849 Sherbrooke St. West
Montreal, Quebec H3A 2T5
Canada

McGraw-Hill
1221 Ave. of the Americas
New York, NY 10020

The Menard Press
8 The Oaks
Woodside Avenue
London N12 8AR
England

Mercier Press Limited
4 Bridge Street, Cork
24 Lower Abbey St.
Dublin 1
Ireland

Merlin Press
3 Manchester Rd.
London E14 9BD
England

Methuen and Co. Ltd.
11 New Fetter Lane
London EC4P 4EE
England

Michael Joseph
See **Joseph (Michael) Ltd.**

The Middle East Institute
1761 N St. NW
Washington, DC 20036

Mideast Directions
Near East Section
African and Middle Eastern
   Division
Library of Congress
Washington, DC 20540

Militarism Resource Project
P.O. Box 13416
Philadelphia, PA 19101-3416

The Military Press Ltd.
92a Church Way, Iffley
Oxford OX4 4EF
England

Military Publishing House
Moscow
USSR

MIT Press
28 Carleton St.
Cambridge, MA 02142

Mobilization for Survival
3610 Locust Walk
Philadelphia, PA 19104

Monch Publishing Group
See **Verlag Wehr und Wissen**

Morrow (William) and Company
105 Madison Ave.
New York, NY 10016

National Academy Press
2101 Constitution Ave.
Washington, DC 20418

**National Campaign to Save the
   ABM Treaty**
1601 Connecticut Ave. NW
Washington, DC 20009

**The National Center for Public
   Policy Research**
300 I St. NE, Suite 3
Washington, DC 20002

National Defense
See **American Defense
   Preparedness Association**

National Defense University Press
The Superintendent of Documents
U.S. Government Printing Office
Washington, DC 20402

National Education Association
1201 16th St. NW
Washington, DC 20036

National Institute for Public Policy
8408 Arlington Blvd.
Fairfax, VA 22031

**National Strategy Information
   Center**
150 E. 58th St.
New York, NY 10155

**National Technical Information
, Service**
U.S. Department of Commerce
14th and Constitution Ave.,
      Room 1067
Washington, DC 20230

NATO Information Service
B1110 Brussels
Belgium

Nauka Publishers
Profsajuznaja ul. 90, 117485
Moscow
USSR

Nautical and Aviation Press
8 Randall St.
Annapolis, MD 21401

Naval Institute Press
U.S. Naval Institute
Annapolis, MD 21402

NC Press Ltd.
260 Richmond St. West,
   Suite 40
Toronto, Ontario M5V 1W5
Canada

Nelson (Thomas) Pubs.
P.O. Box 141000
Nelson Place at Elm Hill Pike
Nashville, TN 37214

**New Literature Publishing
   Company**
181, Dr. Dadabhoy Naoroji Rd.
Fort Bombay-400001
India

Newnes Book
The Hamlyn Publishing Group Ltd.
84-88, the Centre
Feltham, Middlesex
England

New Society Publishers
4722 Baltimore Ave.
Philadelphia, PA 19143

New York University Press
562 W. 113th St.
New York, NY 10025

**NGO (Non-Governmental
   Organizations) Disarmament
   Committee**
777 United Nations Plaza,
   Room 7B
New York, NY 10017

NLB
See **Verso/NLB**

Nomos Verlagsgesellschaft
Waldseestrasse 3-5
Postfach 610
D-7570 Baden-Baden
West Germany

Norsk Utenrikspolitisk Institutt
See **Norwegian Institute of
   International Affairs**

North Atlantic Assembly
B-1110 Brussels
Belgium

**North-Holland Publishing
   Company**
Postbus 211
NL-1000
AE Amsterdam
The Netherlands

Northwest Nuclear Xchange
Good Shepherd Center
4649 Sunnyside Ave. N.
Seattle, WA 98103

Norton (W. W.) and Co., Inc.
500 Fifth Ave.
New York, NY 10110

**Norwegian Institute of
   International Affairs**
P.O. Box 8159
DEP Oslo
Norway

**Norwegian University Press
   (Universitetsforlaget AS)**
P.O. Box 2959, Toyen
N-0608 Oslo 6
Norway
U.S. Office:
   Publications Expediting, Inc.
   200 Meacham Ave.
   Elmont, NY 11003

**Novosti Press Agency Publishing
   House**
B. Poscovaja ul. 7
Moscow
USSR

Noyes Publications
Mill Road
Park Ridge, NJ 07656

The Nuclear Free Press
Trent University
Peterborough, Ontario K9J.7B8
Canada

Nuclear Negotiation Project
Harvard Law School
Cambridge, MA 02138

Nuclear Times, Inc.
298 Fifth Ave., Room 512
New York, NY 10001

Nuclear War Graphics Project
100 Nevada St.
Northfield, MN 55057

Nucleography
2847 Fulton St.
Berkeley, CA 94705

Nukewatch
315 W. Gorham St.
Madison, WI 53703

Oceana Publications
34 Buckingham Palace Rd.
London SW1W
England

Oelgeschlager, Gunn and Hain
131 Clarendon St.
Boston, MA 02116

**Office of Arms Control, Disarmament
and International Security**
330 Davenport Hall
Urbana, IL 61801

Office of Public Affairs (ACDA)
See **U.S. Arms Control and
Disarmament Agency**

**Office of Research (European
Branch)**
U.S. International Communication
Agency
1919 M St. NW
Washington, DC 20554

Office of Social Science Research
Dept. of Sociology
Northern Illinois University
DeKalb, IL 60115-2854

**Office of the Chief of Naval
Operations**
Pentagon
Washington, DC 20350

Ohio University Press
Scott Quadrangle, Room 144
Athens, OH 45701

Oldenbourg Verlag
Rosenheimer Strasse 145
Postfach 801360
D-8000 Munich 80
West Germany

Olzog (Günter) Verlag
Thierschstrasse 11
D-8000 Munich 22
West Germany

OpenSpace
Jackson, WY 83001

**Operational Research and
Analysis Establishment**
Department of National Defence
Ottawa K1A 0K2
Canada

Osang
Am Romerlager 2
D-5300 Bonn 1
West Germany

Osprey Publishing Ltd.
27A Floral St.
London WC2E 9DP
England

Oxford University Press
Walton St.
Oxford OX2 6DP
England

Pahl-Rugenstein Verlag
Gottesweg 54
D-5000 Koln 51
West Germany

Palais des Nations
CH-1211 Geneva 20
Switzerland

Pantheon Books
201 E. 50th St.
New York, NY 10022

Paragon House Publishers
2 Hammarskjold Plaza
New York, NY 10017

Paulist Press
997 MacArthur Blvd.
Mahwah, NJ 07430

Paul List Verlag
Goethestrasse 43
D-8000 Munich 2
West Germany

Peace Council of the German Democratic Republic
Clara-Zetkin Strasse 103
1080 Berlin
East Germany

Peace Development Fund
44 N. Prospect St.
P.O. Box 270
Amherst, MA 01004

Peace Research Institute–Dundas
25 Dundana Ave.
Dundas, Ontario L9H 4E5
Canada

Peace Science Society (International)
Field of Peace Studies and Peace Science
Cornell University
Ithaca, NY 14850

Peace Studies Program
Cornell University
180 Uris Hall
Ithaca, NY 14850

Penguin Books Ltd.
Bath Rd., Harmondsworth
West Drayton, Middlesex UB7 0DA
England

Peninsula Publishing
P.O. Box 867
Los Altos, CA 94022

Pergamon-Brassey's International Defense Publishers
1340 Old Chain Bridge Rd.
McLean, VA 22101

Pergamon Press Ltd.
Headington Hill Hall
Oxford OX3 0BW
England

The Perth Corporation
1777 T Street NW
Washington, DC 20009

Pickering and Inglis, Ltd.
3, Beggarwood Lane
Basingstoke RG23 7LP
England

Pilgrim Press
30–01 43rd Ave.
Long Island City, NY 11101

Plenum Press
233 Spring St.
New York, NY 10013

Pluto Press Ltd.
The Works
105A Torriano Ave.
London NW5 2RX
England

Pocket Books
1230 Ave. of the Americas
New York, NY 10020

Polity Press
Dales Brewery
Gwydir Street
Cambridge CB1 2IJ
England

Polygon Books
48 Pleasance
Edinburgh EH8 9TJ
Scotland

Praeger Publishers
521 Fifth Ave.
New York, NY 10175

Predicasts
11001 Cedar Ave.
Cleveland, OH 44106

Prentice-Hall
Rt. 9 W.
Englewood Cliffs, NJ 07632

Presidio Press
31 Pamaron Way
Novato, CA 94947

Presseverlag Ralf Theurer
Aachener Strasse 261
D-5000 Köln 41
West Germany

Princeton University Press
41 Williams St.
Princeton, NJ 08540

Professors World Peace Academy
G.P.O. Box 1311
New York, NY 10116

Program in Public Policy Studies
University of Melbourne
Parkville, Victoria
Australia

**Program in Science and
Technology for International
Security (PSTIS)**
Massachusetts Institute of
Technology
77 Massachusetts Ave.
Cambridge, MA 02139

**Programme for Strategic and
International Security Studies**
132, rue de Lausanne
1211 Geneva 21
Switzerland

Progress Publishers
17 Zubovsky Boulevard
Moscow
USSR

Prometheus Books
700 E. Amherst St.
Buffalo, NY 14215

Publications de la Sorbonne
14, rue Cujas
75230 Paris Cedex 05
France

Puneet Publications
18/38, Shakti Nagar
New Delhi-110007
India

Quarterly Strategic Bibliography
1336 Kingston Ave.
Alexandria, VA 22302

Quartet Books
27/29 Goodge St.
London W1P 1FD
England

Radiant Publishers
E-155 Kalkaji
New Delhi-110019
India

Rand Corporation
1700 Main St.
Santa Monica, CA 90406

Random House
201 E. 50th St.
New York, NY 10022

Reader's Digest Press
200 Park Ave.
New York, NY 10166

Regina Books
P.O. Box 280
Claremont, CA 91711

Regnery Gateway
360 W. Superior St.
Chicago, IL 60610

Richardson and Steirman
246 Fifth Ave.
New York, NY 10001

Rienner (Lynne) Pubs., Inc.
948 North St., No. 8
Boulder, CO 80302

Rossel Books
44 Dunbow Dr.
Chappaqua, NY 10514

Routledge and Kegan Paul
39 Store St.
London WC1E 7DD
England

Rowman and Allanheld
81 Adams Dr.
Totowa, NJ 07512

Rowohlt
Hamburger Strasse 17
Postfach 1349
D-2057 Reinbek
West Germany

**The Royal Institute of
International Affairs**
Chatham House
10 St. James' Square
London SW1Y 4LE
England

Royal Netherlands Naval College
Het Nieuwe Diep 8
Den Helder
The Netherlands

Royston Ltd.
Crown Road North
Glasgow GI2 9H
Scotland

Rush Franklin Publishing
300 Orchard City Dr.
Campbell, CA 95008

Sage Publications Inc.
275 S. Beverly Dr.
Beverly Hills, CA 90212

Salamander Books Ltd.
Salamander House
27 Old Gloucester St.
London WC1N 3AF
England

SANE
711 G St. SE
Washington, DC 20003

Satvahan Publications
119 Masijd Moth
New Delhi-110049
India

Saur (K. G.) Verlag
Heilmannstrasse 17, Postfach
  711009
D-8000 Munich 71
West Germany

Scarecrow Press
52 Liberty St., Box 656
Metuchen, NJ 08840

Scherer, John L., Jr.
4900 18th Ave. S.
Minneapolis, MN 55417

Scholarly Resources
104 Greenhill Ave.
Wilmington, DE 19805

The School of Peace Studies
University of Bradford
Richmand Rd.
Bradford BD7 1DP
England

**Scientific Research Council on
  Peace and Disarmament**
Moscow
USSR

Scribner's (Charles) Sons
597 Fifth Ave.
New York, NY 10017

The Seabury Press
815 Second Ave.
New York, NY 10017

Seal Press-Feminist
312 S. Washington
Seattle, WA 98104

Secker (Martin) and Warburg Ltd.
54 Poland St.
London W1V 3DF
England

Sendler Verlag
Postfach 111162
Mainzer Landstrasse 147
D-6000 Frankfurt 1
West Germany

Seven Locks Press
7425 MacArthur Blvd.
P.O. Box 72
Cabin John, MD 20818

Seven Springs Center
RD3, Oregon Rd.
Mount Kisco, NY 10549

Sharpe (M. E.) Inc.
80 Business Park Dr.
Armonk, NY 60091

Sidgwick and Jackson Ltd.
1 Tavistock Chambers
Bloomsbury Way
London WC1A 2SG
England

Sijthoff and Noordhoff
Alphen aan den Rijn
The Netherlands
Subsidiary of **Kluwer Academic
  Publishers**
P.O. Box 358
Accord Station
Hingham, MA 02018

Simon and Schuster
Rockefeller Center
1230 Ave. of the Americas
New York, NY 10020

Singapore University Press
National University of Singapore
Ground Floor, Yusof Ishak House
Kent Ridge
Singapore 0511

**Société pour le Developpement
  des Études de Défense et de
  Sécurité Internationale**
Faculté de Droit de Grenoble
Domaine Universitaire de
  Saint-Martin-d'Heres, 47X
38040 Grenoble Cedex
France

Sofia Press Publishing House
1 Levski St.
1040 Sofia
Bulgaria

Sopan Publishing House
R-13 Main Market
Inder Puri
New Delhi-110012
India

South End Press
302 Columbus Ave.
Boston, MA 02116

Southern Illinois University Press
P.O. Box 3697
Carbondale, IL 62901

The Soviet and East European Research Centre
The Hebrew University of Jerusalem
Mount Scopus
Jerusalem 91905
Israel

Sozialwissenschaftliches Institut der Bundeswehr
Winzerstrasse 52
8000 Munich 40
West Germany

Spokesman
Bertrand Russell House
Gamble Street
Nottingham NG7 4ET
England

Springer-Verlag New York, Inc.
175 Fifth Ave.
New York, NY 10010

Stackpole Books
P.O. Box 1832
Cameron and Kelker Streets
Harrisburg, PA 17105

Stanford University Press
Stanford, CA 94305

Stanley Foundation
420 E. Third St.
Muscatine, IA 52761

State University of New York Press
State University Plaza
Albany, NY 12246

Stein and Day
Scarborough House
Briarcliff Manor
New York, NY 10510

Sterling Publishers Private Ltd.
New Delhi-110016
India

St. Martin's Press, Inc.
175 Fifth Ave.
New York, NY 10010

Stockton Press
15 E. 26th St., Suite 1712
New York, NY 10010

The Strategic and Defence Studies Centre
Research School of Pacific Studies
The Australian National University
Box 4, P.O.
Canberra, ACT 2600
Australia

Suhrkamp Verlag
Postfach 101945
Landenstrasse 29–35
D-6000 Frankfurt 1
West Germany

Survival Education Fund
11 Garden
Cambridge, MA 02138

Swarthmore College Peace Collection
McCable Library
Swarthmore, PA 19081

The Swedish Institute of International Affairs
Lilla Nygatan 23
11128 Stockholm
Sweden

The Swedish National Defence Research Institute
Box 27322
10254 Stockholm
Sweden

Syracuse University Press
1600 Jamesville Ave.
Syracuse, NY 13210

Tarcher (Jeremy P.) Inc.
9110 Sunset Blvd., Suite 250
Los Angeles, CA 90069

Task Force on Peace Information Exchange
American Library Association
50 East Huron St.
Chicago, IL 60611

Taylor and Francis
4 John St.
London WC1N 2ET
England

Teachers College Press
Columbia University
1234 Amsterdam Ave.
New York, NY 10027

Temple Smith (Maurice) Ltd.
Gower House, Croft Rd.
Aldershot, Hants GU11 3HR
England

Temple University Press
Philadelphia, PA 19122

Thomas, Charles C., Pub.
2600 S. First St.
Springfield, IL 62717

Thomas Nelson
See **Nelson (Thomas) Pubs.**

Thompson and Rutter, Inc.
P.O. Box 297
Grantham, NH 03753

Times Books
201 E. 50th St.
New York, NY 10022

Transaction Books
Bldg. 4051
Rutgers—the State University
New Brunswick, NJ 08903

Transnational Publishers
P.O. Box 7282
Ardsley-on-Hudson, NY 10503

Twayne Publishers
70 Lincoln St.
Boston, MA 02111

Twenty-Third Publications
P.O. Box 180
Mystic, CT 06355

UDH Publishers Distributors
4070 1st Floor
Nai Sarak
New Delhi-110006
India

Umschau Verlag Breidenstein
Postfach 11 02 62
6000 Frankfurt a. M. 1
West Germany

UN Department for Disarmament Affairs
Sales Section, Publishing Division
New York, NY 10017

UNESCO
See **United Nations Educational, Scientific and Cultural Organization (UNESCO)**

Union of Concerned Scientists
1384 Massachusetts Ave.
Cambridge, MA 02238

United Nations
Sales Section, Publishing Division
New York, NY 10017

United Nations Association of the United States of America
300 E. 42d St.
New York, NY 10017

United Nations Centre for Disarmament
See **UN Department for Disarmament Affairs**

United Nations Educational, Scientific and Cultural Organization (UNESCO)
7, place de Fontenoy
75700 Paris
France

The United Nations University
29th Floor
Toho Seimei Bldg. 2–15–1
Shibuya, Shibuya-ku
Tokyo 150
Japan

United States Air Force
See **U.S. Air Force**

United States Arms Control and Disarmament Agency
See **U.S. Arms Control and Disarmament Agency**

United States Strategic Institute
20 Memorial Dr.
Cambridge, MA 02142

Universe Books
381 Park Ave. S.
New York, NY 94720

Universitetsforlaget AS
See **Norwegian University Press**

University of Alabama Press
P.O. Box 2877
University, AL 35486

University of Amsterdam
Spui 21
1012 WX Amsterdam
The Netherlands

University of California Press
2120 Berkeley Way
Berkeley, CA 94720

University of Chicago Press
5801 Ellis Ave., 4th Floor South
Chicago, IL 60637

University of Denver
Graduate School of International Relations
Denver, CO 80208

University of Illinois Press
54 E. Gregory Dr.
Champaign, IL 61820

University of Kentucky Press
Lexington, KY 40506

University of Massachusetts Press
P.O. Box 429
Amherst, MA 01004

University of Pennsylvania Press
Blockley Hall
418 Service Dr.
Philadelphia, PA 19104

University of Queensland Press
St. Lucia
Queensland 4067
Australia

University of Sussex
Armament and Disarmament Information Unit
Mantell Building
Falmer
Brighton, East Sussex BN1 9RF
England

University of Washington Press
P.O. Box 85569
Seattle, WA 98145

University of Wisconsin Press
114 N. Murray St.
Madison, WI 53715

University Press of America
4720 Boston Way
Lanham, MD 20706

University Publications of America
44 N. Market St.
Frederick, MD 21701

U.S. Air Force
U.S. Government Printing Office
710 N. Capital St. NW
Washington, DC 20402

U.S. Arms Control and Disarmament Agency
Dept. of State Building
Washington, DC 20451

U.S. Department of Defense
Pentagon
Washington, DC 20301

U.S. Department of State
Dept. of State Building
Washington, DC 20451

U.S. Government Printing Office
710 N. Capital St. NW
Washington, DC 20402

U.S. Naval Institute
See **Naval Institute Press**

Utrikespotiska Institet
S-106 91 Stockholm
Sweden

Verein für Friedenspadgaogik Tubingen e. V.
Backgasse 22
7400 Tubingen
West Germany

Verlag Ernst Knoth
Gesmolder Strasse 19
Postfach 226
D-4520 Melle 1
West Germany

Verlag Soldat und Technik im Umschau Verlag
See **Umschau Verlag Breidenstein**

Verlag Wehr und Wissen
HRA
1061 Koblenz
West Germany
U.S. Office:
  Monch Media, Inc.
  1350 Beverly Road
  Suite 221
  McLean, VA 22101

Verso/NLB
15 Greek Street
London W1V 5LF
England

Vikas Publishing House Private Ltd.
5 Ansari Road
New Delhi-110002
India

Viking-Penguin
40 W. 23rd St.
New York, NY 10010

Vintage Trade Books
201 E. 50th St.
New York, NY 10022

Walter de Gruyter
Genthiner Strasse 13
Postfach 110240
D-1000 Berlin 30
West Germany

War Resisters League
339 Lafayette St.
New York, NY 10012

Weidenfeld and Nicolson, Ltd.
91 Clapham High St.
London SW4 7TA
England

Westbury House
See **Butterworths and Co. (Publishers) Ltd.**

Westminister Press
925 Chestnut St.
Philadelphia, PA 19107

Westview Press
5500 Central Ave.
Boulder, CO 80301

Wheatsheaf Books Ltd.
16 Ship St.
Brighton BN1 1AD
England

Whitten Press Ltd.
Queensway House
2 Queensway, Redhill
Surrey RH1 1QS
England

Wiley (John) and Sons, Inc.
605 Third Ave.
New York, NY 10158

William B. Eerdmans Publishing Company
See **Eerdmans (William B.) Publishing Company**

William Kimber
See **Kimber (William) and Co. Ltd.**

William Morrow
See **Morrow (William) and Company**

Winston Press
430 Oak Grove
Minneapolis, MN 55403

Women's International League for Peace and Freedom (WILPF)
1213 Race St.
Philadelphia, PA 19107

The Women's Press Ltd.
34 Great Sutton St.
London EC1V 0DX
England

World Health Organization
CH-1211
Geneva 27
Switzerland

World Peace Council
Lonnrotinkatu 25 A 6 Krs.
00180 Helsinki 18
Finland

World Policy Institute
777 United Nations Plaza
New York, NY 10017

World Priorities
P.O. Box 25140
Washington, DC 20007

World View Publishers
46 W. 21st St.
New York, NY 10010

Wyndham Hall Press
P.O. Box 877
The Farm Rectory C.R. 21
Bristol, IN 46507

Yale University Press
302 Temple St.
New Haven, CT 06520

YMCA International Institute for Peace
Hiroshima
Japan

York University Research Programme in Strategic Studies
4700 Keele St.
North York
Ontario M3J 1P3
Canada

Zed Books
57 Caledonian Rd.
London N1 9BU
England

Author/Title Index

All references are to entry numbers, not page numbers.

Subject Index

All references are to entry numbers, not page numbers.